PORTFOLIO

ANDY GROVE

Richard S. Tedlow is the Class of 1949 Professor of Business Administration at Harvard Business School. His previous books include *Giants of Enterprise* (one of *BusinessWeek*'s ten best books of 2001) and *The Watson Dynasty*, and he has written articles for the *Harvard Business Review*, *Fortune*, and many other publications. He lives in Newton, Massachusetts.

Andy Grove

THE LIFE AND TIMES
OF AN AMERICAN BUSINESS ICON

RICHARD S. TEDLOW

PORTFOLIO

PORTFOLIO
Published by the Penguin Group
Penguin Group (USA) Inc., 375 Hudson Street, New York, New York 10014, U.S.A. • Penguin Group (Canada),
90 Eglinton Avenue East, Suite 700, Toronto, Ontario, Canada M4P 2Y3 (a division of Pearson Penguin Canada Inc.)
• Penguin Books Ltd, 80 Strand, London WC2R 0RL, England • Penguin Ireland, 25 St Stephen's Green, Dublin 2,
Ireland (a division of Penguin Books Ltd) • Penguin Group (Australia), 250 Camberwell Road, Camberwell,
Victoria 3124, Australia (a division of Pearson Australia Group Pty Ltd) • Penguin Books India Pvt Ltd, 11
Community Centre, Panchsheel Park, New Delhi – 110 017, India • Penguin Group (NZ), 67 Apollo Drive,
Rosedale, North Shore 0632, New Zealand (a division of Pearson New Zealand Ltd) • Penguin Books (South Africa)
(Pty) Ltd, 24 Sturdee Avenue, Rosebank, Johannesburg 2196, South Africa

Penguin Books Ltd, Registered Offices:
80 Strand, London WC2R 0RL, England

First published in the United States of America by Portfolio, a member of Penguin Group (USA) Inc. 2006
This paperback edition published 2007

1 3 5 7 9 10 8 6 4 2

Copyright © Richard S. Tedlow, 2006
All rights reserved
Photographs on insert pages 5, 6, 7, 8, 13, and 14 courtesy of Intel. All other photographs courtesy of Andy Grove.

THE LIBRARY OF CONGRESS HAS CATALOGUED THE HARDCOVER EDITION AS FOLLOWS:
Tedlow, Richard S.
Andy Grove : the life and times of an American / Richard S. Tedlow.
p. cm.
Includes index.
ISBN 1-59184-139-9 (hc.)
ISBN 978-1-59184-182-1 (pbk.)
1. Grove, Andrew S.   2. Chief executive officers—United States.   3. Intel Corporation.
4. United States—Biography.   I. Grove, Andy, 1936–   II. Title.
HD9696.S44T588   2006
338.7'621395092—dc22
[B]   2006049829

Printed in the United States of America
Set in Minion
Designed by Helene Berinsky

*This book is dedicated to
my late, beloved wife*

Joyce R. Tedlow, MD

"You are always in danger. You are in danger of competitors, you are in danger of new ways of doing things, but most importantly, you have a danger that the way you have conducted your business is going to lose relevance."

ANDREW S. GROVE

CONTENTS

PREFACE: The Trip You Are About to Take   xi

INTRODUCTION   xiii

1. Andy Grove Returns to Hungary   1

2. The Grove Family, Hungary, and the Early Years of World War II   12

3. Coming of Age in Stalinist Hungary   31

4. Andy Grove in America   61

5. "A Hotheaded 30-Year-Old Running Around Like a Drunken Rat," or Andy Grove Comes to the Valley of the Heart's Delight   101

6. "Off and Limping"   117

7. "Orchestrated Brilliance"   145

8. The Long and Winding Road   155

9. Andy Grove in 1986: At Work and at Home   188

10. "The Valley of Death"   198

11. "The PC Is It"   211

12. "Awesome Intel"   230

13. Intel Inside 248

14. "We Almost Killed the Company" 261

15. Cultivating the Creosote Bush 273

16. That Championship Season 281

17. The Buck Stopped There: Bill Gates and Andy Grove 294

18. Wintel 306

19. The Pentium Launch: Intel Meets the Internet 318

20. Life Is What Happens While You're Making Other Plans 340

21. The Darwinian Device 357

22. "What Are You Paranoid About These Days?" 368

23. The Year of Decision 385

24. "Frozen in Silicon" 394

25. Andy Grove—Ex-CEO 410

26. "I Think That Experiment Has Been Run" 416

27. Andy and the Board 427

28. The Bubble Bursts 434

29. Outside Intel 452

30. Still Swimming 459

ACKNOWLEDGMENTS 463

NOTES 467

BIBLIOGRAPHY 533

INDEX 555

PREFACE

The Trip You Are About to Take

This is the story of a man who made history. But "made" really is the wrong word. He is still making history. Andy Grove is a vital man who is demanding of others and more demanding of himself. His primary interest at this time is health care; and few who know him doubt that the health care system will be different because of what he is doing today and what he will do tomorrow, next week, and next year.

Andy is a moving target. Now seventy years of age, he has lived a half dozen lives. We can play historian with his youth because we have some perspective. In covering his more recent years, we move into a more journalistic mode. As has often been said, journalism is the first draft of history. Our reportage carries us through 2006.

The first fifteen chapters of this book average about nineteen pages in length. The child is the father of the man, especially so in Andy's case as you will see. Chapters sixteen through thirty average about twelve pages in length. Form follows function. As we migrate from historian to journalist, the pace quickens.

What are the lessons of Andy Grove's life? There are many, and it would cheapen them to try to list them here. They are in the book. His life is his lesson.

One trait does stand out: joie de vivre. He has an insatiable appetite for life's challenges. The old saying—he lives the life he loves and loves the life he lives—applies to Andy Grove more than to most of us.

This is a book about Andy Grove. You cannot write about him without writing about Intel and about Silicon Valley.

What is Intel? It is one of the anchor tenants of the Valley. Intel brought discipline to its industry. It is a global company but has an American identity.

Intel was "born again." First it was a memory company. Then it was a microprocessor company. Twice born. The issue it faces today is: Are there third acts in American life?

What is Silicon Valley? It is a geographic location but also a state of mind. It is a place where the intensity of the desire to make money can hardly be overstated. However, neither can one overstate the intensity of the desire to "make a dent in the world."

The balance between these two impulses, the mercenary and the marine, is different in each company. It is different in each person. Where else but in Silicon Valley could an email security company backed by venture capitalists fly flags in front of its headquarters proclaiming: "Fixing Email: it's not just a career, it's a cause."

There have been other "Silicon Valleys"—in Lancashire for textiles in 1900, for example, or in Akron for tires in 1920. Those valleys were eroded. Will the same happen between San Francisco and San Jose?

This is a history book. We leave such questions to the future.

INTRODUCTION

"I want to know how he thinks."

"I want to know how all these decisions really did get made."

"I want to know all the stuff that he won't tell you about."

In writing this book, I interviewed dozens of people about the life and times of Andy Grove. During the course of these interviews, I often asked, "What would make this book a page-turner for you? What would this book need in order to keep you up at night because you simply could not stop reading it?" The three quotations above are among the answers I received. These comments, not atypical, were each offered by a wealthy and powerful person.

The curiosity expressed is understandable. In 2003 and 2004, when these questions were being asked, Andy Grove was arguably the most admired and influential businessperson in the United States.[1] He had lived the American dream. A penniless refugee from Hungary at the age of twenty, he attended City College of New York, from which he graduated first in his engineering class in 1960.[2] He fell in love with the United States and also with Eva Kastan, an Austrian refugee who came to the United States by way of Bolivia. They met when they had summer jobs (she was a waitress and he a busboy) in a New Hampshire resort.[3] They were married on June 8, 1958. Grove did not like New York City, so he and his bride drove across the continent to San Francisco. They spent the summer there in 1959 and moved out permanently the following year. Grove enrolled in the University of California at Berkeley, from which he earned a PhD in chemical engineering in three years under the sponsorship of Professor Andreas Acrivos.[4]

In 1963, Grove was hired by Gordon Moore to join a high-risk, high-reward high flier in what was to become known as Silicon Valley called Fairchild Semiconductor. This career choice was out of the ordinary. Most chemical engineers in the early 1960s were going into either the chemical industry or the oil and gas industry,[5] but Grove had had summer jobs at a Chevron laboratory and at the Stauffer Chemical Company and was not enthusiastic about either one.[6] He also considered Lockheed, a major defense contractor that had a plant in Silicon Valley, but was similarly uninspired. With a systematic approach to his work life that was to become his hallmark, he investigated twenty-two companies. He divided them into jobs for which he was qualified but in which he was uninterested and those in which he was interested but for which he was perhaps not qualified. The search eventually narrowed to two firms. One was Bell Labs, the prestigious home of great inventions, including, for example, the transistor in 1947.[7] The other was Fairchild. Grove chose the latter. He immediately felt a special bond with Gordon Moore, head of research and development there, who had made him the offer.

Moore and Robert Noyce left Fairchild to create their own firm in 1968. When Grove learned that Moore was founding a company, he asked to join him. When Moore said the firm was being founded in partnership with Bob Noyce, Grove was disappointed. Grove was one of the few top executives in Silicon Valley who was immune to Noyce's famed charisma. It was the brilliant but quiet and mild-mannered Moore by whom he was impressed.

Grove became the third employee of Intel (short for Integrated Electronics), which today is a global company with about 100,000 employees. Over the past four decades, Intel has been one of the most profitable firms in the world. And more than anyone else—more than Noyce or Moore or anyone who has come since—Intel has been Andy Grove's company.

The semiconductor industry is strewn with bankruptcies. Intel itself had a brush with disaster in the mid-1980s. As late as 1986, it ranked only tenth among the world's semiconductor manufacturers and lost money.[8] This is a highly capital-intensive industry with scale economies, and Intel either had to move up or face possible extinction.

Grove's tenure as Intel's CEO lasted from the spring of 1987 to the spring of 1998. During this period, measured from the end of the respective calendar years, the company's sales and profits increased from $1.9 billion and $246 million to $26.3 billion and $6.1 billion respectively. Market capitalization increased from $4.3 billion to $197.6 billion, a compound annual growth rate of 42 percent and a total increase of almost 4,500 percent.[9] This performance compares favorably with that of any other corporate chief executive officer anywhere in the world at any time in history.

When the "dot-com" bubble burst and the technology world fell into a deep depression between 2000 and 2003, Intel suffered along with the rest of the industry. During these years, Grove had relinquished formal, day-to-day operating responsibility to his successor, Craig R. Barrett, but he continued to serve as chairman of the board of directors, a position from which he stepped down on May 18, 2005. He maintained his relationship to Intel thereafter as "senior advisor."[10] The company got a lot of bad press during the downturn as it marched through the proverbial "valley of death." Barrett and the rest of the executive team were attacked for their billions of dollars of venture investments—made in an effort to develop an ecology in which Intel Architecture would flourish not only within the personal computer business but in a host of environments including health care, telecommunications, and home entertainment—investments that had generated almost no returns. (Terms such as "Intel Architecture" will be explained in due course. Please bear with me for now.)

Intel's top management was also sharply attacked for continuing to invest in manufacturing facilities in the face of soft demand. Analysts and business journalists accused Barrett of incomprehensibly bad judgment. *BusinessWeek* featured a picture of him on its cover, looking bloodied and bowed.[11]

What Barrett and Intel's leadership knew that the critics did not fully appreciate was that the semiconductor industry was cyclical. They knew that Intel's core product, the microprocessor, was essential for modern life and that it would continue to be so well into the twenty-first century. They knew that the time to build capacity was when demand was weak because prices for building the fantastically expensive manufacturing plants ("fabs," as they are known, which is short for semiconductor fabrication facilities) are lower than when demand for product is great. They knew that when the industry bounced back from its depression, demand for their product would increase very quickly, far more quickly than they could build capacity to meet it. It requires courage and daring to invest capital in such facilities in anticipation of demand rather than waiting until there is a backlog of orders on hand. However, if you believe in your product and you want your company to lead the world, this is what is required, no matter the doubt that might greet such investments among the "chattering classes" who do not share your point of view.

The Intel strategy emerged in 2003 as spectacularly successful. Demand soared. Intel had the capacity to meet it and made a fortune that year—$2.2 billion in the fourth quarter alone, the most profitable quarter in the company's history. Craig Barrett had a luscious "I told you so" moment. At the annual convention of Intel's sales and marketing group on February 3, 2004, he had the unflattering *BusinessWeek* cover of him reproduced on a gigantic screen as he stood alone on the stage in front of forty-five hundred employees. The cover was blown up (digitally) before everyone's eyes.

In the months following that meeting, however, Intel had more than its share of problems. Barrett wrote a letter to the whole company that, for bluntness, is hard to equal. Intel has a history of looking bad news in the face, and Barrett's letter falls squarely in that tradition. At this writing, Intel's earnings remain strong. However, the price of its stock has not performed well, especially in comparison to such Silicon Valley firms as Google, Yahoo!, eBay, and Apple. Despite its undeniable strengths, Intel has been beset by doubts about its future, doubts shared by investors.[12] The brokerage house Sanford C. Bernstein issued a report critical of the company and of Barrett specifically in March 2006.[13]

Andy Grove was at the same convention at which Barrett made his presentation. He was in semiretirement from Intel at the age of sixty-seven. But to the attendees and to the outside world, it was still Andy's company. It is surely an exaggeration to label a global business the size of Intel the lengthened shadow of a single man.[14] But it is perhaps not an outrageous exaggeration. Intel and Andy were one—to employees, customers, shareholders, analysts, the general public, and to Andy.

Given that fact and given further that Intel was among the most valuable companies in the world, it is perhaps not surprising that people wanted to know how Andy thinks. From another point of view, however, the comments with which this chapter begins and so many similar ones I heard give one pause. This is true for a number of reasons.

First, Andy Grove has hardly sneaked through life quietly. He has written more than forty technical articles and a widely used textbook, *Physics and*

Technology of Semiconductor Devices.[15] As his career developed, he turned his attention steadily more toward management. It was about that subject that he began to write in the 1980s, and his books and articles achieved a remarkably wide readership among businesspeople and within universities. In 1983, he published *High Output Management,*[16] which remains, more than two decades after its publication, an astute guide to its subject. In 1987 came *One-on-One with Andy Grove: How to Manage Your Boss, Yourself and Your Coworkers.*[17] This is a delightful compendium of columns Grove published in the *San Jose Mercury News.* Readers wrote him describing various problems they encountered on the job, and he offered his advice on how best to deal with them. He was said to have adopted the role of corporate "Dear Abby."

In 1996 Grove published his most famous book, *Only the Paranoid Survive: How to Exploit the Crisis Points That Challenge Every Company.*[18] This bestseller introduced phrases such as "strategic inflection point" and "the '10X' Change," which have gained wide currency in the business world. When considered together with *High Output Management,* it is fair to say that no other American businessperson of Grove's stature has ever written with such acuity about the art and science of management.[19]

In addition to his technical and managerial writings, Grove has also written about himself. His *Fortune* magazine article on how he dealt with prostate cancer became famous.[20] Most remarkable is his autobiography, *Swimming Across: A Memoir.* This book tells the story of the first twenty tumultuous years of Grove's life and is the only book ever written by a major American business executive that can be regarded as a genuine literary achievement.

All of this is to say that if you want to find out about Andy Grove, there is an extensive published record for you to consult. Yet when you have read it all, questions remain. The more Grove explains his views and the more he explains himself, the more explanation we crave. Supply creates its own demand. There seems to be an irreducible element of mystery about Andy Grove—a code that, if we could crack it, might enable us to achieve some of the success that he has enjoyed.

What is the cause of this mystery? It has, I think, a number of roots.

One is simply the magnitude of Grove's success and the distance he traveled in his life. He was born into a family that was solidly middle class. Grove's father was a "partner in a medium-sized dairy business that he owned jointly with several friends." His mother "was cultured without being snobbish."[21] They were married on June 16, 1933.[22] Andy was born on September 2, 1936.

Sounds good so far. But all was not well. Andy was born András István Gróf. He was known by the diminutive "Andris" and never used his middle name. The city in which he was born was Budapest, Hungary. His parents were Jewish. They were not observant and appeared thoroughly assimilated. They did not belong to a Jewish community. But Adolf Hitler had his own ideas about the assimilation of Jews into the general population. So did the Arrow Cross, Hungary's homegrown anti-Semitic fascist organization. George and Maria Gróf, Andy's parents, were identified in official documents as Jews.[23]

In Grove's own account of his earliest years, Jewishness has a shadowy presence. On the one hand, his family felt no identification with the observant Jews who followed their religion's beliefs and dressed in accord with traditional Eastern European Jewish culture. "There was a Jewish quarter in Budapest," Grove has written. "It was located about a mile or so from where we lived. It was a strange, foreign area, where the men wore black hats and dark coats and long side curls and smelled odd. . . . [T]hey were part of a different world."[24]

On the other hand, there was that special radar that Jews have been said to possess about the religious affiliations of others. Thus, when he was only about three years old, Grove noted of one of his father's closest friends that he "was different. . . . He wasn't Jewish."[25] Grove felt Hungarians had the same special radar with regard to Jews. "Hungarians almost always knew who was or wasn't Jewish, kids or adults."[26]

As Hungarian Jews, Grove's family would go through hell before they would eventually be reunited in America. They may have begun as middle class, but soon they would become victims of history. First came the Nazis. They were followed by the Russians, who brought with them their own portion of anxiety and horror. When Andy reached America, he depended upon the kindness of relatives he had never met—a sister of his cousin Manci, whom he referred to as his aunt because she was considerably older than he. Manci's sister Lenke and brother-in-law Lajos had immigrated to New York City in the 1930s. In 1956, when Grove was planning his escape from Hungary, his parents worried that Lenke and Lajos were weak reeds to lean on. But Andy and his family did not have much choice at the time.[27]

When he was four, Grove was stricken with scarlet fever, and his life was at risk. For weeks that turned into months, he battled the illness and its side effects. He underwent surgery to save his hearing. His eyesight and his heart were affected by the disease, but the longest-lasting impact was on his hearing. "[His] eardrums were perforated like a colander, the result of a middle-ear infection." Five operations on his ears were required over the next four decades.[28] For years he wore prominent, odd-looking hearing aids. He had to sit in the front row of classes so he could hear the instructors. He had to guard against getting his ears wet when bathing or swimming. The illness caused permanent damage. To this day, Grove's hearing is better in his left than his right ear.

One element of the touch of mystery that adheres to Grove is how he managed to clear the hurdle after hurdle in his path before he could achieve success on a magnitude equaled by few. Then there is the fact that he is Hungarian, as is, by chance, Intel's fourth employee, Les Vadasz.

Hungary, though nestled in Central Europe, has a distinctive history, and it is not a happy one. The area of present-day Hungary was occupied by the Magyars, originally an Asian tribe, at the end of the ninth century. "Hungary" in the Hungarian language is "Magyarország." In 1000 or 1001 (accounts vary) King Stephen, later canonized, adopted Christianity for his nation and was accepted into the fold by Pope Sylvester II.[29] In 1241 Hungary was conquered by the Mongolian Tatars. "Their presence," it has been said, lasted only a year but "halted development for at least a century."[30] The return to Christian rule lasted until 1526, when the Turks annihilated the Hungarian army at Mohács.[31]

Not until 1686 was Budapest[32] retaken by a Christian army, and Hungary became part of the Austrian Empire. To say that the Austrian Empire was a polyglot affair understates matters. The profusion of nationalities became the bane of the Habsburgs, the ruling dynasty. During the course of the nineteenth century, forces of nationalism began to undermine dynastic loyalties. Eventually those forces would lead to the assassination of Archduke Franz Ferdinand, son of the emperor of Austria-Hungary, Franz Josef, on June 28, 1914, by a Serbian living under Austrian rule in the city of Sarajevo in the province of Bosnia.

Nationalism had grown strong enough in Hungary by the second half of the nineteenth century that the Habsburg emperor agreed to the creation of the dual monarchy in 1867. Now Hungary was the junior partner in the Austro-Hungarian Empire and would remain so until it declared itself an independent nation on October 31, 1918. A Communist revolution followed soon upon the heels of that declaration but, amid general chaos, was put down at least in part because of an invasion from neighboring Romania. Much diminished in size, Hungary was thus launched into the post–World War I environment.

Hungary's national anthem describes Hungarians as people "torn by . . . fate."[33] One cannot imagine a similar phrase in "The Star-Spangled Banner." Indeed, fate was not kind to Hungary, which served as a battleground often during its history and has the melancholy distinction of being on the losing side of both of the twentieth century's world wars. The nation's greatest novelist, Imre Kertész, won the Nobel Prize in 2002 "[f]or writing that upholds the fragile experience of the individual against the barbaric arbitrariness of history."[34] The title of Kertész's most important book is *Fatelessness*.[35] A critical part of Andy Grove's life struggle was to take his fate into his own hands, not to be the victim of "fatelessness."

Among the oddities of Hungary is its language. Hungarian is not related to the languages spoken in the surrounding countries, and its distinctiveness has often been commented upon. An Austrian theoretical physicist named Fritz Houtermans, referring to the galaxy of famous Hungarian physicists, advanced the idea that "these people were really visitors from Mars. . . . [For them] it was difficult to speak without an accent that would give them away and therefore they chose to pretend to be Hungarians whose inability to speak any language without accent is well known."[36] This was, of course, a joke, but it achieved its own jocular currency.[37]

Somehow it seems appropriate that the Hungarian chief of state for a quarter of a century, from 1920 to 1944, was an admiral named Miklos Horthy de Nagybánya. Officially, he was the regent for a country that had no monarch. Horthy professed undying loyalty to the Habsburg monarchy, yet he helped to prevent a Habsburg from being crowned.[38] He wore his admiral's uniform on state occasions. Hungary is landlocked.[39]

Even in his later years, Andy Grove had an accent that could be described as more than merely noticeable. What his English, which he had studied while still in Hungary, must have sounded like at the City College of New York (CCNY), or Berkeley, or Fairchild, we can only imagine. His wife, Eva, said that when they met in the late 1950s, "He had a bad accent, even though he doesn't think so!"[40] Sometimes people with special talent can master a second language better than native speakers. Such was the case with Conrad and Nabokov, and with Grove as well.[41] Coupled with this accent is the fact that

Grove is superb at expressing himself. He is widely read, liberally educated, and seems to know something about everything. He can be witty, courtly, or caustic. Those who worked with him knew that if he were in high dudgeon about something, they could expect to hear a lot of expletives soon.

Grove is quite capable of using words as weapons. He is so smart that he can win arguments even if he is wrong.[42] So one has to listen very carefully when he speaks. His fluency in English is enviable, but sometimes his accent causes his auditors to replay his words so that they could be certain of what he had said. When you hear "archipelago" pronounced with the heavy accent on the fourth syllable rather than the third, you do a double take.[43]

Grove has used his fluency in public often. He spoke innumerable times before industry gatherings and, as the 1980s gave way to the 1990s, before businesspeople all over the world, as well as students. He has taught at both Berkeley and Stanford. There is more than a little of the "ham" in him. His public appearances were carefully and often cleverly managed for maximum impact.

As much as any other important businessperson, Grove kept his fingers on the pulse of the public. While he was running Intel, public relations played an important role. The cubicles of Intel's public relations executives were located nearby his at Intel's home in the RNB (Robert Noyce Building) at the company's headquarters in Santa Clara, California, which is in Silicon Valley. They were often the first people to whom he spoke as his day began.[44]

Part of the mystery of Andy Grove derives from the fact that he is two people—the person and the persona. The persona was managed for the advancement of Intel. The person, until 2001, was very private. When *Time* chose him as its "Man of the Year" in 1997, he asked that the names of his daughters not be used in the article.[45] Through the 1990s, he was reticent about his family, his religion, and other aspects of his personal life. Here, for example, is the report of an interview Grove had with Terry Gross of National Public Radio's program *Fresh Air* in 1996. The occasion was the publication of *Only the Paranoid Survive*. But Gross also wanted to ask Grove about his youth in Hungary. Midway through the interview, this exchange took place:

GROSS: You grew up in World War II, and I'm wondering how your
    family was affected.
(Pause.)
GROSS: [again] Are you Jewish?

GROVE: Umm-hmmm. Yes.

GROSS: Did you have to hide during the war?

GROVE: Umm-hmmm. Yes.

GROSS: Was your whole family successful in hiding, or did you have
family that was unsuccessful?

GROVE: Well, I don't want to get into the details of it. But some of my
family survived and others didn't.[46]

Gross sprung her questions upon Grove in the midst of another subject.
He knows how to defend himself, even when taken unawares, which is why he
shut this line of questioning off as quickly as he did. This public man was still
keeping part of himself very private. There is nothing about this exchange between him and Gross that was likely to dispel the mystery about him.

Who is Andrew S. Grove really? Where did he come from? What did he
go through?

Quite by surprise to most people who had followed his career, Grove
published *Swimming Across: A Memoir* in 2001. As he became progressively
less engaged with the day-to-day operations of Intel, he began to feel freer to
tell the story of his early life. In *Swimming Across* he recounts in intimate detail the years from his birth in 1936 to his escape to America two decades
later. It is the story of how András István Gróf, Hungarian, became Andrew
Stephen Grove, American.[47]

Swimming Across is a great work about that most American of characters,
the self-made man. The quintessential self-made American, Benjamin Franklin, wrote to his son that "I have raised myself." Franklin became the new
nation's tutor on how to create a "persona" separate from the real person.
Grove's life followed in part a well-trodden, distinctively American path.[48]

Perhaps not surprisingly, *Swimming Across* raises questions as well as
answers them. One thing, at least, it did make clear. Andy Grove had not returned to Hungary after his escape in 1956. He would never return.

I'm not entirely sure why. Maybe I don't want to remind myself of the
events I wrote about. Maybe I want to let memories stay memories. Or
maybe the reason is something simpler than that: My life started over in
the United States. I have set roots here. Whatever roots I had in Hungary were cut off when I left and have since withered and died.[49]

Andy Grove

1

Andy Grove Returns to Hungary

On September 28, 2003, Andy Grove appeared before a large audience in Chicago gathered to raise money for America's Holocaust Museum. His participation in a Hebrew blessing over bread that began the evening was mildly surprising. His whole life he had been religiously nonobservant. During a question-and-answer session, one woman asked, "I understand that you have never returned to Budapest. Could you discuss your feelings about your homeland?"

"I will," Grove answered:

I will, but I don't think I will succeed in conveying them to you. I have a hard time explaining what it is. My life in Hungary was—to understate it—a negative experience.

The obvious parts are, excuse me, obvious. The war part was obviously negative. Being shot at was negative. Living under a Communist regime and being told what to think and what to see and what to read and what not to think and on and on and on was pretty bad. Having my relatives imprisoned randomly was bad. But that's not . . . those things . . . Some are changed.

What didn't change in my gut and in my heart is being told at age six that Jews like you killed Jesus Christ, and we're going to push all of you into the Danube. To have a good friend of mine at age eight, when I told him who I was—his father took all the particulars down just in case the Germans came back to make sure this one doesn't get away either.

And people on the ship coming across the Atlantic after the Revolution being upset by being told by their Hungarian minister that you have to leave your anti-Semitism behind. They were very upset about that.

My life was marred with personal experiences like that. I don't have any emotional energy to devote to that. There is nothing for me that justifies picking on those scabs.[1]

It is true that Andy Grove has never returned to Hungary. The title of this chapter, however, is not a mistake. He has certainly returned by proxy. Intel microprocessors power computers in Hungary just as they do throughout the world. Commercially, through Intel, Grove has returned to Hungary.

On the literary level, Grove has returned through *Swimming Across*. Not merely because it has been translated into Hungarian—some of his other writings have as well—but because he re-creates his childhood, boyhood, and youth in such a vivid yet restrained fashion that he has to have expended considerable energy in making his memory speak. He has to have put himself back there.

Prior to World War I, Hungary, and specifically the Magyars, had reached their apogee in the old Austro-Hungarian Empire and indeed in Europe. Hungary stretched from deep into present-day Romania, past the Carpathian Mountains in the east, all the way through Slovenia and Croatia to the shores of the Adriatic Sea in the west. So defined, the Magyars actually constituted a minority (48 percent) of Hungary's population of about twenty million.

If you were an ethnic Magyar in 1914, you could make a credible claim to being a pretty big fish in a pretty big pond. Eastern Europe was dominated by Germany, Russia, and Austria-Hungary.[2] The Treaty of Trianon posed a grave affront to Magyar self-regard. By one estimate, Hungary, which signed the treaty on June 4, 1920, thus formally ending its participation in World War I, lost almost three-quarters of its territory and two-thirds of its population, including 28 percent of its Magyar speakers.[3] The Treaty of Trianon was as popular in Hungary as the Treaty of Versailles was in Germany. To this day, Hungarians object to it.[4]

The Hungarians signed the treaty because they had little choice. Hungary was in a state of chaos after the war. The Social Democrats allied themselves with the Communists in 1919. A Communist revolution, spearheaded by Béla Kun, seized control of the government in Budapest.

Kun was born into an assimilated Jewish family (the Anglicized form of "Kun" is "Kohn") in a small Hungarian village on February 20, 1886.[5] During World War I, he served in the Hungarian army and was captured by the Russians in the summer of 1916.[6] By 1917, there were two million prisoners of war in Russian hands, and when Lenin and the Communists seized power in late 1917, they realized that these POWs could be a powerful asset both in securing "Red" rule in Russia in the war against "White" counterrevolutionaries and also by spreading the revolution abroad.

Kun attracted Lenin's attention, and he himself was attracted to communism. By November 17, 1918, he was back in Budapest at the head of the Hungarian Communist Party.[7] When the Hungarian Social Democrats and Communists took control of the government, Kun was their leader and suddenly found himself the most important man in Hungary.

The "Hungarian Soviet Republic" was proclaimed on March 21, 1919. It was, after the Soviet Union, the world's second Communist regime.[8] The government lasted 133 days.[9] Kun did what old-fashioned Communists did. He nationalized everything he could, and in the process he made a lot of enemies both within Hungary and outside it. The Czechs occupied the Hungarian highlands in the north, which became Slovakia. The Romanians marched all the way to Budapest and sacked the city on July 30.

On August 1, 1919, Kun was out.[10] His short-lived Hungarian Soviet Republic is forgotten today but was "widely resonant in its time."[11] It was known as a period of "Red Terror" in Hungary and not completely without reason. The memory of the executions, the confiscations, and the bread lines was kept alive for decades by the counterrevolutionary "White Terrorists" who took power following the overthrow of the Kun regime. Because of the large number of Jews among Hungarian Communists, this episode led to increased anti-Semitism.

Anti-Semitism has a long, horrifying history in Europe, climaxing with the annihilation of the Jews in the period from Adolf Hitler's ascent to power on January 30, 1933, to his suicide on April 30, 1945. (I am not implying that anti-Semitism disappeared from Europe after these years.) The mass slaughter of the Jews has come to be known as the Holocaust, an appropriate name for an apocalyptic event.

Periodically, Europe had been seized with paroxysms of hatred of the

Jews for over fifteen hundred years, ever since Christianity became the continent's dominant religion, and there was plenty of anti-Semitism there prior to World War I.[12] In the capital of Austria-Hungary, we encounter the demagogue Karl Lueger. Elected mayor of Vienna five times from 1897 to 1910, he used anti-Semitism as one of the pillars of his political career. Lueger was no favorite of the revered emperor, Franz Josef, who once declared that "there will be no Jew-baiting in my land."[13] The political party that Lueger helped to found, the Christian Socialists, was allied to the Roman Catholic Church and "was anti-liberal, anti-Jewish, anti-Marxist, anti-capitalist."[14] "I regard this man," Hitler wrote in Mein Kampf, "as the greatest German mayor of all times."[15]

The use of the word "German" is not a mistake, even though Lueger was the mayor of Vienna. What Hitler meant was that Lueger was of the German "race." He wrote that Christian Socialism failed in pre–World War I Austria because it regarded Judaism as a religion not as a race.

In fact, not only the Christian Socialist Party but Lueger himself practiced a traditional anti-Semitism, which was fundamentally opportunistic. The vitriol of Mein Kampf would have been quite foreign to him.[16] He had Jewish friends and once announced that "I decide who is a Jew." One of his successors, Ignaz Seipel, said of the anti-Semitism of the Christian Socialist Party that "it was for the gutter."[17]

Like other European countries, Hungary had its share of anti-Semitism, and, as we have noted, Kun and his Hungarian Soviet Republic did not help matters. Thirty-one of the Kun government's forty-nine commissars were of Jewish origin.[18] The chairman of the revolutionary governing council was a gentile, selected, Mátyás Rákosi later quipped, "to have someone who could sign the death sentences on Saturday."[19]

When the social and human costs, economic dislocation, and narcissistic injury caused by the loss of territory are combined with a radical leftist government that was heavily Jewish in composition, we have a recipe for increased anti-Semitism. Someone, after all, had to be blamed for Hungary's low estate. Jews had historically served such purposes in Europe.

When the Communists were expelled in August 1919, the country saw a resurgence of "White" conservatism. Admiral Horthy entered Budapest on November 16. He officially became regent on March 1, 1920. Soon thereafter, a law was enacted that prohibited universities and law schools from admitting a larger proportion of Jewish students than there were Jews in the population as a whole. Jews accounted for 12.5 percent of the students in these institutions but only about 5 percent of the general population. It is possible that this is the first anti-Semitic legislation passed by any European nation following World War I. According to one expert, there was, in 1920, "a blaze of pogroms [that] raged in Hungary, particularly in the provinces."[20] The combination of legislation and extralegal violence boded ill.

During the 1920s, however, anti-Jewish agitation abated in Hungary and in most of Europe. To be sure, anti-Semitism was always there, always simmering not far below the surface of daily life. There was, at the center of Europe, always Germany, and in Germany there was, following World War I, always Hitler. However, we must remember the cautionary observation of the English historian Frederick W. Maitland to the effect that events now in the past were once in the future.[21] Despite everything, Jews made remarkable progress toward emancipation in Europe during the nineteenth century. It was not unreasonable to hope that such advances might continue.

Most important, it was difficult for a sane person to take Hitler and what he advocated seriously in the 1920s. His was a splinter group of a splinter group, with no significant support until the Great Depression. The anti-Semitism that was at the heart of the "new order" he preached was hard for a civilized human being to understand. He mocked the "sham anti-Semitism" of Austria's prewar Christian Socialist Party: "In a short time the Jew had become so accustomed to this type of anti-Semitism that he would have missed its disappearance more than its presence inconvenienced him."[22]

For Hitler, Jews were an omnipresent race. "Race" is a word with no scientific meaning, but it carries a great deal of polemical freight. Neither conversion—that "splash of baptismal water"—nor forced emigration nor confiscation of property nor strict segregation could solve what in Hitler's perverted mind was a dilemma of such insidious enormity.[23] The realization of Hitler's ideology demanded nothing less than the elimination from the planet Earth of a pool of genes. "Genocide" is a commonly used word today. In fact, it is a new addition to the English language. It was invented in 1944 by a Polish Jew named Raphael Lemkin who lost almost his entire family in the Holocaust. "By 'genocide,'" he wrote, "we mean the destruction of a nation or of an ethnic group. . . . [Modern] techniques of genocide represent an elaborate, almost scientific system" unprecedented in history.[24]

In many ways, Adolf Hitler and Nazi Germany were something new under the sun. Not in all ways. There had been innumerable horrors prior to the Holocaust, and there have been many since, but Hitler did somehow succeed in establishing himself and his regime as distinctly sinister entries in the human calendar.

The magnitude of the disaster to come made it difficult to conceive and to combat. Certainly a Jew living in Hungary in, say, 1930 had no particular reason to cringe at the future.[25] If you were a Jew, assimilated and cosmopolitan or not, you knew it and the government knew it. You were identifiably different from your countrymen. Riots aimed at your coreligionists had taken place before. Who was to say they would not break out again?

On the other hand, the situation in 1930 was in most ways not particularly menacing. There were 445,000 Jews living in Hungary, giving it one of the largest Jewish populations of any country in the world.

Half of Hungary's Jews lived in Budapest, comprising slightly more than 20 percent of the city's population. "In a country with a landed aristocracy and a large peasantry," Lucy Dawidowicz has written, "the Jews were distinctively middle class." Almost 40 percent of the gainfully employed Jews were self-employed businessmen.[26] Despite the anti-Semitism that existed, it would have been difficult indeed to imagine that over two-thirds of Hungary's Jews would, within fifteen years, be murdered.

One of Hungary's Jewish businessmen was George Gróf. Born in 1905, Gróf was a partner in a dairy that bought milk from surrounding farmers and processed it into various products. As his son recalled, the dairy was especially "proud of the quality of their butter." Their slogan was, "This butter is a delicacy."[27]

The dairy was located in the country town of Bacsalmas, about ninety-five miles south of Budapest. George Gróf, or Gyurka, the nickname by which he was known, regularly traveled to Budapest to sell its products to retailers in the city. One of the shops to which he sold was owned by the parents of an attractive young woman named Maria.

Like George, Maria was an assimilated Jew. "Maria," indeed, could not have been a common name for an Eastern European Jew in the first half of the twentieth century. Unlike George, who dropped out of school when he was eleven years old, she had completed what in America would be the equivalent of high school. Her ambition was to be a concert pianist, but she was denied admission to the music academy because of her religion. That is why she went to work in the family store. As so often happened in Hungary,

Jews could choose to be nonobservant, but the gentile world in which they lived did not fail to observe that they were Jewish.

George and Maria, who was two years younger than he, were different kinds of people. He was "a pragmatic, down-to-earth businessman, energetic and quick." He was sociable, with a wide circle of friends and acquaintances. She tended to be shy. But these traits "complemented each other," their son recalled. They got along well. They were married in 1933, the year after they met.[28] This was not a calm and quiet time in Hungary.

Economically, Hungary's interwar performance must be judged in general to have been weak. "While in the prewar period Hungary belonged to those countries whose growth rate was higher than the European average, the interwar performance lagged behind it in spite of the fact that Europe's growth had slowed down considerably as well." To put it in stark, politically incorrect terms, Hungary "was among Europe's economically backward countries."[29] Post-Trianon Hungary was stuck with an agricultural base and a paucity of natural resources.

The economic situation worsened the world over in 1931. Financial crises (in the form, for example, of the failure of Vienna's Kreditanstalt Bankverein) reverberated throughout the international financial system. Runs on banks in surrounding countries ensued.[30]

Political trouble followed hard on the heels of economic distress. Hitler's popularity soared in Germany. In Hungary also, popular opinion shifted to the right.[31] Hungary had outlawed the Communist Party, but it was active nevertheless. Four of its leaders were taken into custody. Two were executed.[32]

Horthy asked Gyula Gömbös to form a government, and he assumed office. Gömbös was an army officer during World War I, after which he turned his attention to politics. His decision to do so was not a happy one in the history of Hungary. He became the leader of an extreme right-wing faction demanding an antidemocratic, anti-Semitic dictatorship.[33]

Horthy only appointed Gömbös on the condition that he agree to play by the rules. Apparently, the admiral thought that things would be all right if a man whom everyone knew had been a right-wing demagogue for more than a decade would mend his ways. Gömbös, it has been said, "publicly renounced the vehement anti-Semitism he had espoused earlier, and his party and government included some Jews."[34]

The story of Gömbös's rise to power bears some eerie resemblance to

Hitler's. Both men had been right-wing agitators following World War I. Both represented unreconstructed, unrepentant, backward-looking elements of the population of their respective countries. Both were held in check by the relative political and economic calm of the 1920s. Neither would have experienced political rebirth had it not been for the Great Depression. Both were anti-Semites. Both took office in accord with the laws in force at the time. Both were summoned to office by men in uniform, in Gömbös's case Admiral Horthy in his capacity as regent and in Hitler's case Field Marshal Paul Ludwig Hans Anton von Hindenburg und Beneckendorff, president of Germany in the time of the Weimar Republic from 1925 until his death in 1934. In both cases, the conservative men who made these appointments or the men behind the men who made them were convinced they could control their appointees and believed the implicit, periodically explicit, reassurances that the appointees would become more tame—that they would not act the way they had always acted and that they would not be who they had always been.[35]

People with this point of view were in for a rude shock. After becoming prime minister, Gömbös "went to work at once with great energy. He began with an avalanche of social and domestic demagogy without precedent, using radio addresses and press statements." The "real aims" of this agitation were said to be "the realization of a . . . total form of fascist rule free of parliamentary trappings."[36] Gömbös "proclaimed the arrival of an 'age of reform' and the dawn of a 'new millennium.'"[37]

Under the Gömbös regime, as so often happened during dictatorships in the twentieth century, words began to lose their meaning. Thus, Gömbös denied he wanted to be a dictator but said the nation needed a leader.[38] When a man like this says "leader," he does not have in mind a middle-class, democratic conception. He is thinking of a Führer.

Gömbös paid a visit to Mussolini soon after taking office. He contacted Hitler within a week of the latter's rise to power on January 30, 1933, in the hope of achieving mutual cooperation. On June 16, 1933, he achieved the unenviable distinction of being the first foreign head of government to visit Hitler. It was Gömbös, of all people, who coined the term "Axis."[39] Gömbös's "appointment marked the beginning of the radical right's ascendancy in Hungarian politics," which lasted until the Soviets chased the Germans out of the country at the end of World War II.[40]

On October 6, 1936, one month and four days after Andy Grove was born, Gömbös died (of natural causes). Hungary, however, had already started taking steps down the road toward Nazi-style fascism. Certainly, anti-Semitism was increasing. To appease the unemployed, Kalman Darányi, Gömbös's successor, proposed a law in 1937 that would further limit Jewish participation in some businesses and professions. This was the first such law passed since 1920.[41] But it was not to be the last. In May 1938, Darányi was out, having failed to satisfy either the right or left wings of Hungary's increasingly restive political factions.

Admiral Horthy summoned Béla Imrédy to form a new government.[42] Imrédy introduced another, harsher anti-Jewish law, but he did not remain in office long enough to see it enacted. His opponents discovered evidence that one of his grandfathers was Jewish, and he was forced from office in February 1939. He was succeeded by Count Pál Teleki, who served as prime minister from February 16, 1939, to April 3, 1941, when he committed suicide. Under his leadership the anti-Jewish law proposed by Imrédy was passed. This legislation "broadened the definition of 'Jewishness,' cut the quotas on Jews permitted in the professions and in business, and required that the quotas be attained by the hiring of Gentiles or the firing of Jews."[43] The noose was tightening.

Outside of Hungary, the geopolitical situation was moving toward its climax. On March 7, 1936, Hitler remilitarized the Rhineland. On March 11, 1938, the Wehrmacht marched into Austria. Anschluss, the annexation of Austria to the Third Reich, was a bloodless triumph. No Hungarian could fail to note that Vienna, the city that had been the capital of their empire for centuries prior to 1918, was now occupied by Germany. Moreover, the world's most powerful army now patrolled Hungary's western border.

On March 13, an ecstatic Hitler was driven to Linz, his hometown. He laid a wreath at the gravesite of his parents in Leonding, a small village just west of Linz. "I shall never forget this," he wrote in a one-sentence telegram to Mussolini.[44] From Linz, the following day he drove to Vienna, where twice, once in 1907 and again in 1908, he had applied to be a student at the Academy of Fine Arts and twice had been rejected. He was received by cheering throngs, "master of this city in which he had starved in obscurity, heir to the Habsburgs his father had served as a customs officer."[45]

"There were few Jews in Linz," Hitler wrote in *Mein Kampf,* referring to his youth.[46] Vienna was the city where, Hitler wrote, he learned to become an anti-Semite:

In a short time [after my arrival in Vienna in 1907] I was made more thoughtful than ever by my slowly rising insight into the type of activity carried on by the Jews in certain fields.

Was there any form of filth or profligacy, particularly in cultural life, without at least one Jew involved in it?

If you cut even cautiously into such an abscess you found, like a maggot in a rotting body, often dazzled by the sudden light—a kike![47]

Ignaz Seipel, we will recall, an heir to the leadership of the Christian Socialist Party in Austria after the death in 1910 of Karl Lueger (Hitler's favorite mayor), had said of his party's anti-Semitism that "it was for the gutter." But now "the gutter had come to power."[48] There were few Jews in Linz in Hitler's youth. Soon there would be none there or in Vienna, where in Hitler's fevered imagination he had once seen them everywhere. "Immediately behind the German army came a large force of 40,000 police and SS [for *Schutzstaffeln,* meaning Guard Battalions—a corps whose responsibility was to do precisely what Hitler ordered] Death's Head Formations who began the systematic persecution of Austria's 300,000 Jews." The "savagery" that ensued was "uninhibited."[49] This was a pogrom the magnitude of which the world had not yet seen. It was taking place 136 miles away from Budapest, where George and Maria Gróf lived with their one-and-a-half-year-old son, Andris.

Next on Hitler's list was Czechoslovakia. The Munich Pact of September 29, 1938, stripped Czechoslovakia of the Sudetenland, a slice of territory that contained a large German population as well as valuable natural resources. Rendered defenseless by the forced cession of the Sudetenland on October 10, Czechoslovakia began to fall apart. On March 15, 1939, the German army occupied Prague and the rest of Bohemia and Moravia. Slovakia was split off from the former Czechoslovakia, and Monsignor Jozef Tiso, an anti-Semitic practicing Roman Catholic priest, became the "president" of the Nazi puppet state.

Hungary was now bordered on the west by a country that the German army occupied and that was full of ardent Nazis. Along its northern frontier was Slovakia, which, though not occupied by German troops, was controlled in all important matters by Berlin. To the south was Yugoslavia, a large part of which traditional Hungarian conservatives felt should be part of Hungary. To the east was Romania, which had made significant territorial gains at the expense of Hungary as a result of the Treaty of Trianon and which was no stranger to anti-Semitism. To the northeast, Hungary shared a short border with Stalin's Soviet Union. It is hard to imagine a more thoroughly pressured, compromised, and unsafe country in the world than Hungary in the summer of 1939. Things only got worse.

With the occupation of Bohemia and Moravia, Hitler, for the first time, extended his conquest of Europe beyond the incorporation of ethnic Germans into the Third Reich. Bohemians and Moravians were Czechs. They were Slavs with a different ethnic and cultural background from Germans.

After March 1939, with almost all ethnic Germans in Europe (one could argue about German-speaking Switzerland) plus newly acquired Czechs under Hitler's control, the forces of appeasement had run out of excuses for his behavior. His goal was nothing less than to conquer country after country and dominate Europe. After Europe, perhaps the world. You did not have to be an intelligence expert—you only had to look at a map—to see which country was next on the agenda. It was Poland.

The Western powers were slow and feckless in looking to Stalin as a counterweight to Hitler in Eastern Europe. Hitler was not slow. On August 23, 1939, the German and Russian governments announced to a shocked world that they had signed a nonaggression pact. The way was now cleared for what has been called "the fourth partition of Poland."[50]

At the border between Germany and Poland, dawn broke at 4:45 a.m. on September 1, 1939. German troops commenced the invasion of Poland.[51] Britain and France, which had drawn the line of their tolerance for German expansion at the Polish border, both issued ultimatums to the effect that if Germany did not cease hostile action by September 3, a state of war would exist between them.

2

The Grove Family, Hungary, and the Early Years of World War II

On September 2, 1939, Andy Grove and his parents were taking a walk along the promenade on the left bank of the Danube, on the Pest side of Budapest. It was a cloudy evening but warm and not unpleasant. People kept looking at the sky. The clouds were being periodically illuminated by searchlights. This was not an ordinary walk along the promenade for the citizens of Budapest. Their eyes were "anxiously following the motion of the white lines" the searchlights produced.[1]

Never was anxiety more justified. Germany and Poland had been at war for a day and a half. Unless the Germans halted their invasion, an event the most optimistic person would have had to doubt, the world would be at war once again. Normal life would come to an end.

But Andy, part of whose later fame came from his book *Only the Paranoid Survive,* paid no attention to any of the worrywarts he might have encountered that evening. He and his parents were celebrating his third birthday. "I was taking my new car out for its first drive." This birthday present "was a tiny version of a real sports car," just like his uncle Jozsi's, "except that his was white and mine was red. Red was a lot more fun."[2]

Uncle Jozsi, Maria's brother, had joined the Grófs on this particular evening. He kept egging Andy on to go faster in his toy car. Jozsi ran after little Andy "to keep me from bumping into people. Sometimes he succeeded.

Sometimes he didn't. But people didn't seem to mind. They barely paid any attention to me. They were mesmerized by those white lines in the sky."[3]

The following day, Sunday, September 3, the Germans invading Poland were gobbling up territory in large chunks. In the town of Wieruszow, twenty Jews were led to the marketplace to be shot. One of them was a sixty-four-year-old man named Israel Lewi. His daughter, Liebe Lewi, pleaded for his life. She "was ordered to open her mouth wide for her 'impudence,' and then shot through the mouth." Liebe and Israel Lewi and the other eighteen were all murdered.[4] Three million Polish Jews would suffer the same fate before the war was over. Poles kept killing Jews even after the Germans had been driven out.[5] Only Czechoslovakia stands between Poland and Hungary, and Czechoslovakia had fallen apart. One wonders what Andy's parents and his uncle were really thinking about on the evening of September 2, 1939.

George and Maria had begun their married life in George's home in Bacsalmas, just north of the border with what was then Yugoslavia.[6] Bacsalmas was not much more than a village in the countryside that had the virtue of proximity to dairy farmers whose milk George's partnership processed.

Maria was less than thrilled to move to Bacsalmas from Budapest. In a word, she hated it. She was used to nights out at concerts and the theater in a cosmopolitan, sophisticated city. "All of a sudden, she found herself in a small town out in the provinces. Not only was she living in a house with dirt floors and an outhouse, but she had to share the house with some of my father's relatives and partners. My mother was the newcomer and the outsider. She was . . . very uncomfortable with communal living."[7] It is not hard to think of better ways to begin married life.

Maria's pregnancy with Andy brought her and George back to Budapest temporarily so that she could give birth in a reputable hospital. After that, however, they returned to Bacsalmas. Toward the end of 1938, Maria got her wish. George's dairy was increasing its business in Budapest. To serve the customers, a branch was opened in the city, and George and the family moved there so he could run it. People need food, clothing, and shelter every day, so the dairy products business was not going to disappear even in dire economic times. It is still worth noting that George was growing a business when so many others were failing.

The family lived on Kiraly Street on the Pest side of the Danube. Their apartment house survives to this day; it is number 73. For part of the time the Groves lived there, during the period of Communist dictatorship that lasted de jure from 1949 to 1989, Kiraly Street was, like other thoroughfares, renamed for Soviet heroes. It became Maiakovsky Street for the Russian poet and playwright Vladimir Vladimirovich Maiakovsky.[8]

Looking back from 2001, Grove described his neighborhood and his apartment as typically middle class. The three-story apartment house was built around a courtyard. There was an elderly couple living in a ground-floor courtyard apartment who served as superintendents and performed odd jobs and various services for the residents. A balcony running along the two upper floors of the inside courtyard connected apartments.

On the ground floor facing the street, there were shops. There still are. The Elephant Furniture Store (Elefánt Bútoráruház) is there at present. This shop does not actually sell furniture for elephants, and it is hard not to wonder whether a better name might not have been selected for it. On the second and third floors there were a few apartments above the shops facing the street. These were the best apartments in the building, and the Grófs occupied one of them on the second floor.

Two rooms faced the street: the "Big Room" with its two windows and the "Little Room" with one. Maria's parents lived in the Little Room. Maria and George lived in the Big Room with son Andy's crib nearby. The apartment also had a fully equipped bathroom, including a toilet, and a tiny room where the family maid, Gizi, and her husband, Sinko, lived.

Andy Grove has not seen this apartment since November 1956. I visited it in May 2004. At that time it was occupied by a family with three children. Makeshift walls were constructed to provide privacy. Thus, there no longer is a "Big Room." One can still imagine it, however. When I visited the apartment, I was struck by how modest it was. The unit itself, the building in which it is located, and the street on which the building is located are smaller and a good deal less appealing, even on the sunny day in May when I was there, than one would expect from reading Grove's *Swimming Across*. To be sure, the apartment was not a slum, but it was rather depressing. A visit to Grove's residence today in California provides a vivid illustration of how far he has come in life.

The apartment was a lively place. People were always dropping by to socialize. Uncle Jozsi was one of them. Andy did not know what Jozsi did for a living. Whatever it was, it was not terribly impressive. "But that didn't seem to matter. There was always a warm and joyful feeling about Jozsi." He had a fraternal twin, Miklos. These, Maria's two brothers, could hardly have been more different. Jozsi "was friendly and fun, Miklos was surly and seemed to carry a dark cloud around him." All things considered, though, the apartment was a happy place.

Throughout 1939 and 1940, Hungary moved inexorably closer to Germany, a development that was not impeded by a somnolent Britain.[9] For the Grove family, the most important event of these years was the illness of their only child. Andy had contracted scarlet fever.

Scarlet fever is a streptococcal infection that usually strikes children between ages two and ten. Today it is a rare illness and can be effectively treated with antibiotics.[10] But antibiotics were not widely available until after World War II. A severe case of scarlet fever untreated could prove fatal. Little Andy was hospitalized for six weeks, where the care, supervised by a Jewish doctor, appears to have been excellent. He survived to return home for nine months of convalescence, a very long time indeed in the life of a little boy. His hearing was permanently affected. Apparently in order to deal with an ear infection that accompanied his scarlet fever, the "bones behind my ears had been chiseled away. I shuddered at that description."[11]

While Andy was resting at home, his mother bought a little hand puppet of a bear for him. You put your hand inside the puppet and moved it around. At first, Maria entertained him with it, but soon he was well enough to play with it himself. When the puppet bear was given to him, "I cut a hole in its skull behind its ears, then I bandaged it so that he looked just like me."[12] This little gesture is fraught with meaning. By replicating with an inanimate object the trauma that had been inflicted on him, Grove mastered the trauma. He normalized it. There was nothing in the least sadistic about his cutting the hole in the puppet's skull. He bandaged the hole so that it would be well, just like him. He had an ally. He and the puppet were in this thing together.[13]

Grove himself must have sensed that this gesture was important. It was sufficiently noteworthy for him to mention it in his autobiography, a brief book (290 pages with not too much print per page) written six decades after the event. Mastery of trauma is an important theme not only of *Swimming Across* but of Grove's whole life.

Interestingly enough, the two sentences following this story in *Swimming Across* are, "In 1942, when I was five years old, my father was called up into the army. He was not really a soldier; he and other Jewish men were conscripted to serve in labor battalions clearing roads, building fortifications, and the like." Another trauma was following hard on the heels of scarlet fever. Grove's father had been called up for brief stints as a laborer in the past, but this was different. "When he came home with the news," reported his son many years later but still viewing the scene through the eyes of a five-year-old, "he was trying to smile, but there was something wrong with his smile."[14] Imre Kertész begins his novel *Fatelessness* by recounting how the fictional protagonist George Koves and his family learn that his father is to be dispatched to a labor camp. There is no hysteria. Kertész, like Grove, recounts the scene with spare prose, greatly enhancing the aura of menace.[15]

George Gróf was being sent to the Russian front. International affairs had at last grabbed the Grove family, as they had grabbed the family of Israel Lewi in Wieruszow, Poland, on September 3, 1939. Would the result be the same?

The destiny of Hungary's Jews was different from that of Polish Jews until 1944 because the fate of Hungary was different from Poland's. Poland shared a long border with Germany. Much of the territory Poland occupied when Europe was reconfigured after World War I had been German during the Second Reich, which lasted from 1871 to 1918. Most galling, the "Polish Corridor," created to give Poland an outlet to the Baltic Sea, separated the great bulk of German territory from East Prussia. Poles were Slavs, an ethnic group Hitler hated, and about a tenth of Poland's population were Jews.

Geographically, Hungary was luckier, at least for the moment. Its non-Jewish population was Magyar, not Slav. Even had the Poles wanted to do so, they could never have become allied with the Germans. That was always an option for Hungary. There were reasons for Hungary to avoid Hitler's embrace. But as month followed month, the persuasiveness of those reasons diminished. Hitler's Germany seemed unstoppable. True, there was some domestic anti-German sentiment in Hungary. There were demonstrations in favor of an "independent democratic Hungary" in 1941 and even in 1942,[16] but it had already withdrawn from the League of Nations on April 11, 1939, and joined the Tripartite Pact of Germany, Italy, and Japan on November 20, 1940.[17] More menacing, membership in the Arrow Cross Party, Hungary's version of the Nazis, was increasing. Its leader, Ferenc Szálasi, had been jailed on August 16, 1938, for incitement to riot but had been pardoned on September 16, 1940.[18] On June 22, 1941, Hitler launched his invasion of the Soviet Union. Four days later, Hungary declared war on the Soviet Union as well. By then the die was cast. Hungary's fate would be determined by Germany's.

Germany foolishly declared war on the United States on December 11, 1941. In a remarkable display of provincialism, Hungary, whose politicians were acutely conscious of the disposition of each square inch of territory on its borders and of every Magyar living in Romania, Czechoslovakia, and Yugoslavia, managed to follow suit the next day.[19] We must also acknowledge, however, that there is some justice to the assessment that by 1941, Hungary "was tied hand and foot."[20]

Hungarians may not have seen any combat with Americans, but the same cannot be said with regard to the Soviets. In 1941, 40,000 Hungarian troops were shipped off to the eastern front. The Soviet Union was supposed to collapse in six weeks. It did not. The *Blitzkrieg*, or "lightning war," which had brought the Germans such spectacular success in country after country from Poland to the once great power France, traversed the thousands of miles to the great Russian cities of Leningrad (now St. Petersburg), Moscow, and Stalingrad (now Volgagrad), but it stalled out at all three. In the spring of 1942, at German insistence, the Second Hungarian Army was dispatched to the vastness of Russia. This unit was composed of 200,000 combat soldiers, 50,000 occupation soldiers, and a 40,000-man labor service corps.[21] Perhaps this was the unit into which George Gróf was drafted. These men were completely unprepared for what they faced. They found themselves stationed at Voronezh, guarding the German northern flank at Stalingrad in the winter of 1942–1943, more than eleven hundred miles away from Budapest.

The Hungarian army was already tired out by the battles it had fought to reach Stalingrad as well as by the terrible conditions of everyday life in the midst of the Russian winter. Its soldiers were the direct targets of the Soviet counteroffensive at Stalingrad that eventually turned the German flanks. In January 1943, Hungarian troops were overwhelmed at Voronezh, forty miles north of the city of Stalingrad itself. Their fate rivaled what befell the Hungarians facing the Turks at Mohács in 1526. Voronezh has justly been described as "catastrophic." "This was the greatest defeat in Hungarian military history. The whole army was lost [as an effective fighting force]."[22] After the Voronezh catastrophe, only the willfully self-deluding could deny that there was a good chance that the lightning from this particular *Blitzkrieg* might wind up striking Hungary itself. As week followed week, this eventuality became progressively more likely.

Conservative Hungarian leaders, including the aging Horthy and his successive governments, had always had reservations about Hitler's enthusiasm for war everywhere. All they wanted was a little bit of Slovakia, a somewhat larger chunk of Yugoslavia, and Transylvania returned by Romania. They just wanted to "right" the "wrongs" of the Treaty of Trianon. The result: thousands of young Hungarian men were lying dead in the snow in Russia. The lucky ones wound up in prison camps, where the conditions were unspeakable. The Soviets were quite unsentimental about the soldiers who had invaded the "motherland." As the Red Army became better equipped, organized, and trained, Germany and its pathetic allies became weaker. By 1944, they were heavily outnumbered on the eastern front. Very soon there would be nothing standing between Hungary and Soviet soldiers who felt revenge was their right.

Back at Andy's home on Kiraly Street and in the surrounding neighborhood in Budapest, the mood is difficult to capture. The fortitude of Andy's mother, Maria, was being greatly tested. Instead of happily celebrating the tenth anniversary of her wedding to a man she loved, she had seen him off at a railway station to the eastern front. George left Hungary not from Budapest but from what must have been a staging area in Nagykoros, sixty miles away, to which she and Andy traveled by train. She returned to Kiraly Street to discover that her father had been hospitalized. She and Andy visited him. He had had a stroke and was "mumbling incoherently." In a few days, he died. This loss must have been a blow to Andy as well as to his mother because Maria's father had been the "perfect playmate" for him as he was recovering from scarlet fever. Maria's brothers were also shipped off to the war. The only man left in her life was her young son, whose health was not robust.

People kept dropping by the apartment but the gaiety was gone. "Everyone," Andy recalled, "seemed preoccupied," not least his mother, who smoked and was drinking more than the others. Most of the visitors were women. The men were in that great slaughterhouse known as the eastern front. When everyone was gone, Maria would smoke and drink by herself at dusk.

In the spring of 1943, Maria received an official notice that George had "disappeared." "I didn't know what that meant," recalled Andy. "I didn't know how people could disappear." Surely, he thought, it was better to disappear than to be found dead. "But I didn't dare ask my mother." In the spring of 1943, Andy Grove was six and a half years old. He was wise beyond his years.

Maria was an astute woman, and while she could not have known with certainty how bad things really were—no letters from the front were arriving—she could have guessed that the situation was desperate. The Russians had a score to settle. The Germans were unable to protect themselves and were more than willing to sacrifice soldiers from the satellite nations.

Andy was in kindergarten in 1943. All the children in his class were Jewish, although his was not a sectarian school. One day while he was in the playground and Maria was chatting with other mothers, he heard the word "ghetto" for the first time. "They will put the Jews in a ghetto," someone said. He did not find the statement menacing. To the contrary, he and his friends all started saying, "They will put the Jews in the ghetto." The teacher was not very happy about this, but the children would not obey when she told them to stop. For weeks, the kindergartners played the "ghetto game."

Life continued in this oddly normal way. Andy got sick again. His tonsils were removed, and fluid that collected in his ears had to be drained. Again, his medical care seems to have been excellent, and his doctors and nurses were kinder and more solicitous than the average American can expect in a hospital today. His mother often took Andy to the City Park, where he enjoyed playing near an equestrian statue of George Washington.[23]

Andy started elementary school. His teacher, he recalls, was a redhead named Magda. Because he had difficulty hearing, he had to sit in the front row. Rather than this handicap making him self-conscious, he found the result quite pleasant. "[I]t felt as though she was talking mainly to me, and I loved the attention." Andy flirted with the girls in his class, and he enjoyed their attention as well.

Andy raised his hand all the time and often answered questions correctly. He basked in the praise that resulted. In June, when first grade drew to a close, report cards were handed out. He got the highest grades, pleasing not only himself but his mother.

There was another side to this coin, however. Budapest was bombed in 1943. Those searchlights that were worrying people in September 1939 were now necessary. Andy marveled at the damage just one bomb could do. An apartment house near his was hit. "It looked like a big knife had sliced off the front half of every floor. You could see into the apartments on all four stories, like a doll's house. In the back part of each room, the furniture was still in place and the pictures were still on the walls. The front part had fallen into a big heap of bricks, stones, and unidentifiable rubble."[24] He was seeing firsthand the randomness of war. Some things were demolished. Others were salvageable. How was it determined which things, or which people, were subjected to which fate?

Little Andy liked girls, and once he was building sand castles with a female playmate in the City Park. For no reason, she announced to him that "Jesus Christ was killed by the Jews, and because of that, all the Jews will be thrown into the Danube." This sent Andy running to his mother in tears. He never played in that park again. That was one of the half dozen or so statements that were seared into his memory. He never forgot what that little girl said. He never got over it. Some things one does not get over.

The true horror, however, was now clearly visible on the horizon.

On March 18, 1944, a young man named István Deák attended a sparkling party on Rose Hill, a fashionable district of Budapest. A majority of the guests were Jewish businessmen and intellectuals.[25] Such a soirée would have been inconceivable almost anywhere else between the Urals and the Pyrenees. As of March 19, it would be inconceivable in Budapest as well. Eight divisions of the German army invaded Hungary and occupied the nation unopposed.[26]

Up until that day, not only the Jews of Hungary but also liberal Christians and Social Democrats had enjoyed a unique freedom. Parliamentary government had survived, as did freedom of thought to a notable degree. Despite homegrown anti-Semitic propaganda, the Ministry of the Interior actually banned the importation of the foulest output of Germany along these lines. There was still a Zionist League functioning.[27]

Miklós Horthy would certainly by modern standards be classified as an anti-Semite. Indeed, he himself said he was. Especially when he was upset, Horthy was not above using disgusting language ("shitty Jews").[28] Far worse, he was willing to countenance the murder of Jews, at least at some times in some places.[29]

As in so many other matters, however, Horthy was consistent in nothing so much as his inconsistency. At certain times in certain settings he seemed to enjoy the company of Jews.[30] He did say that "inhumanity is alien to the Magyar character," and the net result of his ambivalence limited active anti-Semitism during his "regency."[31] When one reads about Horthy, it is difficult to escape the conclusion that he was a "mixed-up, not very bright" man[32] who did have one talent not unimportant in a political figure, which was "the ability to ingratiate himself with virtually everyone he met."[33]

By 1944, Hungary's situation had become impossible, "caught [as it was] in the vise between German and Soviet imperialism."[34] Anyone who could look reality in the face had to know that the Soviets would crush Germany in the not distant future. A separate peace was called for. However, life is lived not in the future but in the present. Germany had eight divisions that could and did roll into Hungary at a moment's notice, and Hungary had no means to resist.

Thus it is perhaps true that no one could have saved Hungary. It is not arguable that a man whose sole talent was to ingratiate himself with others was up to the task. However, for all Horthy's innumerable shortcomings, the fact is that during his long reign as regent and those of the succession of prime ministers who served under him as the head of government from 1920 through 1944,[35] Hungary became a haven for Jews.

Prior to World War I, there had developed "a silent agreement" between Jews and gentiles for the nation's modernization. The Jews accessed capital from the West; the gentiles handled politics.[36] The result for the Jews was "dazzling," and, with the important exception of the radicals on the far left, Jews were patriotic and interwoven into Hungarian society.[37]

During the eleven years from Hitler's rise to power on January 30, 1933, and Germany's invasion and occupation of its Hungarian satellite, the Jewish population actually increased. Hungary protected its Jews—not all of them, but some.[38] After March 19, 1944, this would all come to an end. With startling swiftness, Jews in Hungary were rounded up by the hundreds of thousands, shipped to Auschwitz, and murdered. Jews in the countryside were virtually wiped out because that is where the Nazis began their dreadful work. In Budapest, many survived because the Nazis did not have the time to finish.[39]

Little Andy Grove looked on as the Wehrmacht occupied Budapest on March 19:

There were no announcements and there was no fighting—they just came in. My mother and I stood on the sidewalk of the Ring Road, watching as the cars and troop carriers filled with soldiers drove by. The German soldiers didn't look anything like the soldiers who had guarded my father's labor unit. Those soldiers slouched a bit, and their uniforms were wrinkled. The German soldiers were neat and wore shiny boots and had a self-confident air about them. They reminded me of my toy soldiers; they had the same kind of helmet, the same color uniform, and the same type of machine gun. I was impressed.

Everyone on the Ring Road watched the soldiers intently. Maria grasped Andy's hand tightly. He knew that something significant had happened, but he did not really know what it was.

Accompanying the German troops was Adolf Eichmann and "a small but highly efficient special commando unit."[40] The goal of Eichmann and his assistants was to eliminate the last vibrant Jewish community in occupied Europe. They moved quickly. Deportations from Hungary, predominantly to Auschwitz, began on May 15, 1944. They were halted on July 9. By that time, according to an expert on the Hungarian holocaust, "all of Hungary with the exception of Budapest had been made Judenrein [free of Jews]."[41] The suffering, the panic, and the horror of these events equal anything that ever happened anywhere else and cannot be exaggerated.

The Holocaust had, at last, reached Hungary. Eichmann and his gruesome henchmen made up for lost time. Over two-thirds of the Jews living in Hungary were murdered. Eichmann proved to be a true monster.[42]

In the midst of the carnage that Eichmann supervised and organized, there were some people—too few, but some—who exerted themselves for the oppressed at the risk of their lives. Best known among these is Raoul Wallenberg, secretary of the Swedish legation in Budapest as of July 9, 1944. "I'd never be able to go back to Stockholm without knowing inside myself I'd done all a man could do to save as many Jews as possible," he told the Swedish ambassador.[43] Wallenberg found numerous ingenious ways to save lives by issuing official or official-looking documents. He was as good as his word. According to one estimate, Wallenberg was responsible for saving, directly or indirectly, 100,000 people or more. He did not live to return to Stockholm.[44]

Soon after the occupation, German troops were constantly seen and often encountered all around Budapest. The encounters were frightening. That summer of 1944, Maria Gróf unexpectedly shipped Andy off to Bacsalmas, the location of his father's dairy and the home of Jani, one of his father's friends. Jani was a gentile who had served as an officer in the Hungarian army before the war. Andy found the same conditions his mother had encountered a decade earlier: earthen floors, no running water, and a boring life. He did not like it any more than his mother had, much preferring Budapest. But just as suddenly as he had been shipped off to Bacsalmas, he was summoned back to Budapest by his mother. Romancz, another gentile friend of Andy's father, had heard that the Jews of Bacsalmas were going to be rounded up by the Germans and that he was safer in Budapest. This was shrewd. Had Andy stayed in Bacsalmas, the odds of his being a victim of "the final solution to the Jewish question" are great.

As Andy remembered it, life in Budapest during the summer of 1944, when he was approaching his eighth birthday, was not as frightening as it was "strange" and ever more "tense," to use his words. The radio ceased to be his toy. Now, grown-ups listened to it intently with the blinds drawn. There were occasional air raids at night. Posters showed up on walls describing anti-Jewish regulations. Stores had signs saying they did not serve Jews. Jews did not sit at the back of trams. They had to stand at the back of them. Andy has written that "We could have tried to cheat but everyone seemed to know who was and who wasn't Jewish, so it didn't seem like a good idea."[45] A half decade after it had been required in occupied Europe, Hungarian Jews still, as late as the summer of 1944, did not have to wear the yellow Star of David stitched to their clothing. That would soon change.

Stranger things were in store. A man who managed one of the shops on the first floor of the Kiraly Street apartment house began to bring flowers to Maria. The family had known this man casually for a while, but all of a sudden he had become friendlier. Andy "didn't think much of it. My mother was a beautiful woman: She had very fine features, big blue eyes, and soft brown hair. I thought giving flowers to beautiful women was what people did."

One day, this fellow came to the apartment with a box of chocolates for Andy, who loved chocolates and gleefully reported the gift to his mother. "When I told her, her eyes flashed, and in one swift, firm motion, she slapped me across my face." She grabbed the chocolates and immediately returned them. Andy was quite puzzled. His mother told him that this interloper wanted to take him and her away from Budapest back to his hometown as if they were his family. Andy still did not understand. "But," he protested, "he's already married." Replied his mother as she stared at him, "Do not under any circumstances, ever take anything from him or talk to him again."[46]

Not long after this episode, at the end of summer as Andy turned eight, he and his mother had to vacate their apartment and move into what was known as a "Star House" because a large yellow Star of David was painted above the front door. There was no room for their maid, Gizi, and since Jews were not allowed to have domestic help anyway, she returned to her home-

town. They could take nothing with them. As they were acclimating themselves to their new, rather unpleasant surroundings on Eotvos Street, not far
from their Kiraly Street apartment, they learned that they were not to appear
in public without a yellow Star of David sewn on their clothing over their
hearts.[47] "Whenever we went out," recalled Grove,

> we wore our star. But we didn't go out very much. There were few
> places we could go to, and the hours when we could be on the street
> were limited. Many stores would not serve people with a yellow star;
> besides that, it was a very strange feeling to walk on the streets wearing
> it. People avoided looking at us. Even people whom we knew wouldn't
> meet our eyes. It was as if a barrier was growing between us and
> everyone else.[48]

The world of Andy and Maria Gróf was growing ever smaller. Events in
the world outside their shrinking environment explain why. Horthy and his
prime minister, Miklós Kállay, were looking for a way out of the war. They
wanted to negotiate a separate peace with the Allies. Their problem remained
what it had been since the defeat at Stalingrad. The Russians were sure to
overrun Hungary in the near future, but the Germans were present on the
spot as of March 19, 1944. With the German invasion came not only Eichmann but a new Hungarian government, under General Döme Sztójay, a
man who did everything the Nazis wanted.[49] He was executed after the war.

On August 23, 1944, the government of the dreadful General Ion Antonescu was overthrown in Romania, and that country was out of the war.
Horthy replaced Sztójay with General Géza Lakatos in the hope of achieving
the same result for Hungary— that is, escape from World War II.

Horthy himself tried to surrender his country, but the Germans prevented him from doing so. Before removing him from Hungary they forced
him to appoint Ferenc Szálasi prime minister. Szálasi styled himself the "Nation's Leader" and had at his command a gang of hoodlums to which we
have referred previously, the Arrow Cross.[50] Thus was unleashed a campaign
of terror that compared in cruelty to anything else that took place during
World War II. With Szálasi, "the gutter had come to power" in Hungary.

Andy Grove remembers seeing the Arrow Cross thugs on the streets in
Budapest shortly before Szálasi assumed power. "They wore armbands with
their emblem, two crossed arrows, one vertical, one horizontal, with points

on both ends. . . . I didn't want to look at them; they frightened me."[51] With good reason.

Andy got sick one day, and his mother encountered a gentile friend who offered to shop for food for them. "But the next day there were loud knocks on our door." It was the police, who had come to take Maria away because she, a Jew, had obtained food with the help of a gentile. Maria's gentile friend was at risk as well. Fortunately, a neighbor spotted Maria under escort going in the direction of the police station. He had a friend there and prevailed upon him to have Maria released.

In mid-October 1944, when Szálasi's Arrow Cross took power with German support, things started deteriorating fast for Maria and Andy. Elements of the Red Army had crossed into Hungarian territory on September 23. Everyone knew they would eventually conquer the whole country. Once again, however, the future, even though it was not a distant future, did not matter. The Arrow Cross was the reality of the day. Their goal was to murder Jews. The first mass murder in Budapest took place on the banks of the Danube on November 23. Outside the capital, it will be recalled, about 430,000 Jews had already been transported to Auschwitz. Also in November, Jews were being tightly packed into ghettos and placed on starvation rations.[52] By the end of November, Andy's kindergarten chant of the previous year, "They will put the Jews in the ghetto," was proving to be true.[53] Andy's little girl playmate's remark that "all the Jews will be thrown into the Danube" was proving all too true as well.

One evening in October 1944, Maria said, "Andris, we have to get out of here." Grove does not provide us with the precise date, but it was probably around October 14. Maria had been alerted by George Gróf's sister's husband, a gentile named Sanyi, that the Arrow Cross was on the verge of taking over the city and that anyone in a house with a Jewish star over the door would be in grave danger.

During the Holocaust and in the years thereafter, a recurring theme of the conduct of the Gróf family is that when they had to get out of someplace immediately, they did so. We have already seen how quickly Maria brought Andy back to Budapest from Bacsalmas. They did not hesitate. They were not frozen by fear. Nor were they detained by denial. They knew in the twinkling of an eye that horrible things can indeed happen. Maria brought her eight-year-old son to the home of a gentile partner of her husband named Jozef. Maria boarded with a workman from her husband's dairy. The parting was not easy for Andy and doubtless hard on Maria as well.

The second time Maria was able to visit her son he was watching Jews guarded by German soldiers being led out of a Jewish house into trucks. The Jews had their hands up. No one was screaming. Everything was orderly. Andy started to cry. The sudden, unexpected appearance of his mother comforted him; but just as quickly she had to leave.

On Maria's third visit, she told Andy that they were going to relocate in a suburb of Budapest called Kobanya where Jozef's parents would take them in. She had new identity papers with a new last name for the both of them: Malesevics, a Slavic name. If anyone asked, Andy was to say that he and his mother were refugees from Bacsalmas. Their speedy response was literally vital. Maria and Andy would for the succeeding weeks be confronted with dangers that could not be anticipated and to which they would have to respond effectively in the moment. They were literally running for their lives.

Kobanya was bleak. Winter was coming on. It was dark and cold and snowy. There was a communal toilet used by both sexes. Maria warned Andy never to urinate when someone else was present. He was circumcised, and if a Hungarian gentile saw that, Andy and his mother would be revealed as Jews.

Christmas 1944. Soon after it passed, eight-year-old Andy "woke up to a strange sound. It sounded like someone was dropping planks of wood on top of each other." It was, in fact, the sound of Russian artillery. The shells were getting closer. One even hit the apartment house. The tenants decamped to the wooden cellars. Andy and Maria were to endure the Battle of Budapest, "one of the bloodiest city sieges of the Second World War in Europe."[54]

One day, the father of one of the children in the cellar gathered all the children together to recite the catechism. Andy, of course, did not know the catechism. Once again he was within a hair's breadth of exposure as a Jew. He was saved by his own quick thinking as well as his mother's. Specifically, he asked to relieve himself and ran to his mother, who loudly demanded that he help her with some chores.[55] Maria, unfortunately, was going to have more opportunities to deploy her "mother wit."

The Pest side of Budapest fell to the Red Army on January 18, 1945. Buda, and therefore all of Budapest, was occupied on February 13. Sometime shortly before the liberation of Pest, perhaps between January 10 and January 15, the Russians occupied Kobanya and specifically the apartment house in which Andy and Maria were holed up. "They came in casually," observed Andy of the Russian soldiers, "but each of them carried a machine gun."

Quite by surprise, the Grófs encountered human kindness. The leader of the platoon occupying the apartment house was a Russian sergeant who spoke German. Maria also spoke German, and she conversed with the sergeant, whose name was Haie. "I had never heard my mother speak anything but Hungarian before," remarked Andy, "so I was very impressed by how fluently she seemed to be able to talk with him." She called Andy over and asked him to recite "*Modim anachnu lach*," a Hebrew prayer he had learned at school, for the sergeant. Andy was panic-stricken. He had been warned constantly to conceal his Jewishness. His mother reassured him. "Just for now, it's okay."

The sergeant smiled as Andy recited. He was a Jew. The Germans had killed his family in Russia.[56]

Later, the Grófs had another encounter with a Russian soldier. His name was Andrei. One evening, he sat down on the corner of the bed Maria shared with her son in the cellar. He kept poking his fingers on Maria's chest and gesturing to himself. At length, Maria got out of bed, left her son with a woman in another cellar, and later returned to where she and her son slept. "I lay there, stunned and full of apprehension," Andy later wrote. "I had no idea what was happening to my mother or what would happen to us both."

Maria returned "very tense and angry" and took Andy to bed. Later, more Russians appeared. "My mother yelled at them something about how all three of the women had already done it today." They left. Andy Grove's mother had been raped. His father had disappeared. Andy was the man of the family. He had been powerless to protect her.

The next morning, Maria went with Andy to the military police. Andy had no idea what was going on. Eventually, they went to an apartment in which there were a number of soldiers as well as the military policeman with whom Maria had spoken earlier. Haie was there as well.

> My mother faced our Russian soldiers, then one after the other she looked each one in the eye and shook her head no. I was holding my breath when she faced Andrei. Andrei himself was beet red, and it looked like he wasn't breathing. After a very brief pause, my mother shook her head no. I yanked at her hand. She yanked back and said to me, "Quiet," in a fierce tone that forbade an answer.

That night, when Andy and his mother were in bed, she explained that if she had identified Andrei as the man who raped her, he would have been shot then and there. Haie had told her so. However, she had also learned—

from whom is unclear—that Andrei's friends would return to the cellar and murder everyone there. "So she had decided not to recognize him."[57]

Sometime in mid-January 1945, Haie told Maria that the Pest side of the Danube had been cleared of Germans. There was still fighting on the Buda side, but the Germans had destroyed the bridges across the Danube. This they had done to prevent further Russian reinforcements, but it also meant they themselves would never come back across the river. Armed with this knowledge, it was time, Maria told Andy, that he jettison the name "Malesevics" and become "Gróf" once again.

Andy was astonished to hear this news. "I had become Andris Malesevics so through and through that for a moment I was confused." But then "the significance of being free to use my real name engulfed me." Andy made friends easily, even in the dreadful environment in which he was living in January 1945, and when next he met his closest pal, he told him his real name and explained that he had had to change it "because I'm Jewish and they would have taken me away" if his true identity had been discovered.

His playmate told his father, who called Andy into his apartment and began peppering him with questions. What was his real name? Who was his father? What was his background? And so forth. Andy was upset but answered all the questions. The man took notes and placed them in his clothes.

When Andy left this interrogation, "I began trembling with fear and from the hatred welling up inside me." In a state of desperation, he told his mother what had happened. She reassured him that there was nothing to worry about. The Germans were gone and were not coming back. But this was another episode that Grove never forgot nor forgave.[58]

Not long after this incident, Maria decided that it was time for Andy and her to return from Kobanya to their home in Budapest. Carrying their belongings on her back, she and Andy walked ten miles through cold, snow-covered streets. The closer they got to their destination, the more evident was the extent of the ruin inflicted on the city. Andy could hardly believe his eyes. This was not the Budapest he had known. Though wide awake, he felt he was dreaming. Soon he began to feel numb, "neither particularly surprised nor unsurprised by anything we encountered."[59]

Grove's reaction to this moment is one key to his later success in life. Either because it was a natural, hardwired attribute or because it was a survival strategy that he taught himself in the face of something unimaginable, he had the ability to cushion and distance himself from an unfathomable reality. He could become numb. It was as if he was watching some other young boy walk through bombed-out streets in a movie rather than walking them himself.

The building on Kiraly Street had survived and the superintendent and his wife were still there. That was fortunate, because other people were living in the Grófs' apartment. They spent a night at what was formerly the "Jewish House" and were able to move back into their own home the next day. The place was a mess, but it was theirs, and, all things considered, they were very lucky to have a roof over their heads.

Andy's life in 1945 turned into a mixture of normality and high drama. He "desperately wanted to learn how to ride a bike." He was making new friends. He was being a bad boy on occasion and being disciplined by Maria as a result. But he accepted her discipline. If times had been normal, Andy would have been attending second grade in the winter and spring of 1945, but Maria decided to wait until the fall for him to start school again. For Andy, "It was like being on permanent vacation."[60]

Slowly, thanks in large part to the heroic work of Maria in, for example, making contact with the dairy in Bacsalmas and opening up a store to sell its products, life began to revert to a predictable routine. Things became safer. Gizi and her husband Sinko showed up and once again took up residence in the apartment.

What was missing was the presence of George Gróf. The last word Maria had received was not from her husband but about him, the official notification back in the spring of 1943 that he had "disappeared." Maria was as indefatigable in her efforts to learn what had happened to her husband as she was in everything else. She spoke to everyone who might possibly have news of him. Time and again, she met with disappointment. Andy began to get annoyed with her. "It was obvious to me that she would never get a satisfactory answer. I could barely remember my father, and now his memory, faded as it was, was tarnished by my mother's obsession." For Andy, the whole matter was just "one more thing to be irritated by."[61]

On September 2, 1939, there had been a happy celebration of Andy's third birthday. But there is no report of a ninth birthday party for him. In September 1945, Maria learned that trains were arriving from the Russian prison camp where she believed George had been held. This meant yet more walks to the railroad station pulling a by now quite reluctant Andy along. But George was not there.

George and Maria had a secret whistle, "a private signal between the two of them." One day, not long after another disappointment at the train station, Maria thought she heard it. When her husband was not to be found, Andy was irritated with her again. Then, all of a sudden, "An emaciated man, filthy and in a ragged soldier's uniform," presented himself at the door. Gizi was shocked. Maria was ecstatic. Andy "was bewildered. This was supposed to be my father, but I didn't know him. I was supposed to love him, but I wasn't sure what I felt. . . . I was embarrassed that I had been wrong [in reproaching his mother about awaiting George's return]."[62]

At first Andy and his father were like strangers, but that period quickly passed. Soon George got a good job in a government-owned department store. Maria kept working with the dairy. Visitors started to drop by the apartment again. "It was almost like before the war."[63]

Only years later did George begin to tell Andy what he had endured during the war. The troubles began with the Hungarians who guarded the Jewish labor battalions. Doubtless petrified themselves, the guards indulged themselves in an orgy of sadism. Andy wrote, "The story that was most incredible to me was how in the middle of one bitterly cold winter night, my father's battalion was made to strip naked and climb trees, and the guards sprayed them with water and watched and laughed as one after another fell out of the trees frozen to death."

Conditions after the battalion was captured by the Russians were as awful as could be imagined, with one exception—there does not appear to have been purposeful sadism inflicted by the Russian guards. The biggest problems were exposure, starvation, and the lack of medical attention. In April 1945, George wrote the following note to his family:

My dear ones: Now that it looks like the end would be here and the prospect of seeing you again, I have had another setback—a new disease, some skin ulcers. It's spreading from one day to the next. There is no medicine. They don't know how to treat it. . . . It looks like my struggles of the last three years were for nothing. And all I would like is to see you again, to know that you are alive. But I am destroyed. Just my love for you keeps me alive. Gyurka.[64]

Almost all of the prisoners died. George survived.

3

Coming of Age in Stalinist Hungary

We have to get on with our lives." That is the plaintive, emotionless statement of the uncle of the protagonist in Kertész's *Fatelessness*.[1] But how? George Koves, the novel's Hungarian adolescent, who was abducted and deported to Auschwitz and Buchenwald, had been transformed by the Holocaust. But transformed into what? He was now fatherless. How does one "get on with one's life" after experiences of the sort he had endured?

The assignment for the Gróf family was the same. They had to get on with their lives. Unlike George Koves's father in *Fatelessness*, Andy Grove's father survived the war. But when one thinks of what the Gróf family had gone through, one is struck dumb. Eviction from their home. Separation from one another. Betrayal by people they thought were their friends. Befriended by others whose willingness to risk their own safety was vital. Torture. Rape. And for some members of the extended family, including George's own mother, death in Auschwitz.

Why had all this happened? Because the Grófs were "of Jewish origin." They were not observant, but that did not matter. Being "of Jewish origin" was a condition concerning which there was nothing one could do. That alone was a death sentence. Could something as cataclysmic as this happen again? It must have been impossible to avoid asking this question, if not out loud then in one's innermost thoughts.

The Germans were driven out of Budapest in February 1945, and the war in Europe ended in May. But the conclusion of hostilities with the capitulation of the Germans and the destruction of Nazism hardly meant that a peaceful calm immediately settled over the war-torn nations of Europe. It did not even mean an end to anti-Semitism, which flourished after the war, especially in the East.

Hungary was in turmoil. Anti-Jewish riots took place.[2] But Jewishness was just one of the issues agitating the country. There was another matter causing an uproar not only in Hungary but all through Europe. That concerned settling old scores. About 10 percent of adult male Hungarians were punished in some degree for their activities during the war. These were not only small fry.

Horthy was gone, exiled to the resort of Estoril, Portugal, where he was supported by, irony of ironies, wealthy Jewish friends. It was there that he wrote his memoirs and there that he died of natural causes on February 9, 1957, at eighty-eight years of age.[3] Not all those who served under him enjoyed such a serene conclusion to their lives. Following the war, "four former prime ministers, one deputy prime minister, two ministers of the interior, a minister of finance—who had held that post in eight consecutive governments—and six other former cabinet members were sentenced to death and executed. Seven former government members were given life sentences, of whom five actually died in prison."[4]

In late 1945, the Soviet Union had about a million soldiers in Hungary, a nation with a population of about ten million. Josef Stalin, who was in a class with Hitler in his disregard for the value of human life,[5] controlled these troops and the rest of the Soviet armed forces completely. He had come close to losing the war but had emerged victorious and was now the single most powerful man in Eurasia. A word from Stalin in 1945 would have turned Hungary into a satellite. Indeed, his word probably could have turned it into a province of the Soviet Union. But for reasons of which we cannot be certain, that word was not uttered.[6]

When one thinks of Stalin, the word "compunction" does not leap to mind. In Hungary, he seized control of the levers of power that he understood so well, including the political police. "[N]o major project could be undertaken without [Stalin's] knowledge and approval, and the judicial process, too, soon bore the unmistakable stamp of Stalinist methods."[7] Nevertheless, "Hungary alone among eastern European countries was allowed to hold entirely free elections." The result was a coalition government of four political parties, the largest of which was the Independent Smallholders' Party, which encompassed craftsmen, shopkeepers, and others who simply supported "the least leftist party to emerge from the recent debacle."[8]

Any postwar government in Hungary faced an impossible economic situation. Forty percent of the nation's capital stock had been destroyed or plundered,[9] which amounted to between four and five times the national income in 1938. The bridges over the Danube and the Tisza, Hungary's second largest river, were destroyed, and the transportation infrastructure destroyed or severely damaged. Industrial facilities also suffered widespread damage, as did the housing stock, especially in Budapest.[10] Losses in terms of "human capital" were, if anything, more severe. Jews had played a vital role in Hungary's prewar economy, but by the end of the war most were in ashes at Auschwitz. Auschwitz, not Mohács or Voronezh, has rightly been called the biggest Hungarian cemetery in the world.[11] Four hundred thousand other Hungarians lost their lives as well, and the number of traumatic events, such as rape, are beyond counting.[12]

There were shortages of everything but paper money in Hungary. Inflation became so acute that, in the perhaps slightly exaggerated view of one historian, "it is still cited as the worst recorded devaluation of currency in human history."[13] One wonders whether Stalin hesitated to sovietize the economy immediately because everyone knew it would crash and burn, and it was better to let others absorb the blame.

From the point of view of the nine-year-old Andy Grove, the situation was not as complicated as it may have appeared to an outsider. "Although all kinds of political parties were operating in Hungary," he later recalled, "there was no question that the Communist Party had Russian backing. Russian soldiers still patrolled the streets. Everyone knew that the Russians called all the shots."[14] Andy began attending school again in September. He had skipped second grade because Budapest was engulfed in war, but, with the aid of a little tutoring, he was able to move directly into third grade. He attended the school attached to the Fasori Jewish boys' orphanage. Although associated with a boys' orphanage, the school was coeducational, and it did not take long for Andy to develop a "crush" on a classmate—one Jutka, with "blondish brown long hair that she wore in braids." Unfortunately, this cute little number did not notice our youthful Lothario.[15]

Through Andy's eyes, life seemed to settle back into normality. "School," for example, "was interesting enough."[16] He began to feel at home and friendly with his father, that gaunt stranger who had presented himself at his home upon his return from Russia. His father wanted him to learn English, which he found "boring . . . I didn't like the teacher or her decaying apartment. . . . But my parents had their hearts set on my participating in this stupid activity, so there was no alternative but to go along with it."[17]

Despite such complaints, Andy's life was returning to a comfortable and understandable rhythm. "Budapest, too," he has written, "was returning to a routine existence. Some of the damaged buildings were being repaired. . . . The first bridge across the Danube was restored." A parade marked the reunion of Buda and Pest.[18]

It is difficult to reconcile young Andy's perceptions with what was going on all around him. "The politics of retribution" were in full swing. Displaced persons were everywhere. Budapest was filling up with people wandering in from the countryside. The political situation was obviously unstable.

One event clearly was out of the ordinary. In August or September of 1945, Maria Gróf had an abortion. His parents later told Andy that they agreed to take this step because they did not want to bring a child into the world they saw around them. (As far as one can tell, the abortion was not the result of the possibility that Maria became pregnant because of her rape.) This event, please note, took place a few months—but only a few—prior to Andy's description of the return of tranquillity to his and his city's life. "[F]or no particular reason," Andy thought the baby would have been a girl. She was "a sister I was not to have."[19]

With this exception, for Andy it appears that the environment was becoming quite orderly very quickly. However, the parts of his narrative at this time do not quite fit together. Perhaps the stories of postwar chaos have been exaggerated and law-abiding citizens could make their way through life with a reasonable sense of security. Yet his parents did not appear to feel this was the case—if, that is, one believes Andy is accurate in his report about why the abortion took place. Maria and George Gróf were thirty-eight and forty in 1945. Perhaps they simply did not want to have another child at that age.

It is also hard not to question whether Andy really wanted a little sister. True, he has always enjoyed the company of women. He did not, however, seem to mind being an only child and thus the center of his parents' life, especially his mother's. He dedicated his memoirs to her and her alone. Although he seems to have gotten along well with his father, by his own account he did not miss him during his absence because of the war. During those days, his mother was his and his alone.

Perhaps because his parents protected him from the harsh realities around him, perhaps because he always seems to look to the future, perhaps because of a certain willful insensitivity, perhaps because of a natural optimism, Andy remembers the year from September 1945 to September 1946 as one of happiness and discovery. Third grade was problem-free. Having his father's protective companionship "felt good."[20] His biggest problem was his parents' efforts to broaden his horizons. They not only forced English lessons upon him, they inflicted piano lessons as well. He found the "big black piano [which] appeared in our living room" intriguing but he "detested" the monotony of practicing scales. He found piano lessons unspeakable. "I had put up with English without too much resistance, but piano was really too much."[21]

Andy spent the summer of 1946 in Kiskoros, a small rural town about sixty miles south of Budapest and forty miles north of Bacsalmas. Kiskoros was George Gróf's hometown, and his cousin Manci still lived there. When Andy debarked at the train station, he could not find her so he shouted, "Manci, you stupid ass, where are you?"[22] This moment was, in a small way, historic. It is the earliest documented instance of Andy's use of foul language. And this he aimed at a relative probably thirty years older than he. Manci just laughed it off. Many, many people were to follow in her footsteps. Not all of them could deal with his blithe self-expression in as jocular a fashion as she.

Andy describes Kiskoros as a shabby little village. It has been spruced up since the last time he saw it, and it is now rather an appealing small town. Kiskoros has one claim to fame. It is the birthplace of Sandor Petőfi, Hungary's national poet, whose work is known to schoolchildren as well as to adults today and has been since he composed it. Petőfi was born on New Year's Day 1823, and was killed at the battle of Segesvar on July 31, 1849, during Hungary's abortive struggle for independence from the Austrian Empire. He was twenty-six and left a young wife and infant son behind. His body lies, unmarked, buried in a mass grave. He has been a revered figure for a century and a half.

Andy visited the shrine that Petőfi's birthplace became on a number of occasions. It is a small dwelling, tastefully preserved. Once, when at the house with Manci, Andy encountered none other than Mátyás Rákosi. This was another historic moment for Andy; Rákosi was the first famous man he had ever met. The head of the Communist Party in Hungary and a favorite of Stalin, Rákosi was referred to earlier in the discussion of the 133-day Communist "Red Terror" of 1919. Like Béla Kun and so many other Hungarian Communists, he was "of Jewish origin." It was he who made the wisecrack about needing a gentile on the revolutionary governing council so someone could sign death warrants on Saturday. The name "Rákosi" is rendered "Roth" in English.

Soon Rákosi would be the nation's dictator and preside over many executions and judicial murders. When he died in Russia on February 17, 1971, he was, in the words of an historian, "unlamented by his countrymen, party members and nonparty members alike."[23]

Andy recognized Rákosi immediately. As head of the political party backed by the soldiers, he was an important man whose face was well-known. "I almost stumbled over my own feet when I saw him." Rákosi was amused by Andy's startled reaction. Andy had managed to acquire a camera, and Rákosi offered to have his picture taken. But Andy's nervous hands shook so much that "I ended up taking a picture of the sky."[24] He can hardly be blamed for his nervousness. Encountering Rákosi must have been like bumping into Caligula.

Back in Budapest, Andy's schooling continued apace. After fourth grade at his grammar school, he moved on to the Budapesti Evangelikus Gimnazium (Budapest Lutheran High School), which, despite its name and its association with the Lutheran Church, was relatively nonsectarian. This small school, unknown to the outside world, has quite a tradition of academic excellence. When you walk into its main auditorium, you pass between busts of two men. On the left is Jeno (Eugene) Wigner, class of 1920, who won the Nobel Prize in Physics in 1963. On your right you see János (John von) Neumann, class of 1921, pioneer game theorist and computer scientist.[25] Among the school's other graduates was János Harsanyi, who won the Nobel Prize in Economics in 1994.

Evangelikus was and still is a proud institution with high standards. Andy was blunt about his performance. "I was a good student."[26] He was indeed. I visited Evangelikus in 2004 and asked to see his grades. They were excellent. I also looked at the grades of other students for purposes of comparison, and

I can confidently report that grade inflation was not a problem at Evangelikus in the late 1940s. Andy got better grades than his peers.[27]

As in his previous years as a student, Andy had to sit directly in front of the teacher because of his poor hearing, the result of the infection he had contracted secondarily to scarlet fever when he was four. "My ears still drained and I didn't hear very well, but if I sat in the front row and the teacher stood right in front of me and spoke loudly enough for the whole class to hear, he was loud enough for me to hear him as well."[28]

From the scarlet fever episode onward, Grove has had to manage his body. He was unathletic. The physical exercise he most enjoyed was swimming, but his freedom to indulge was limited because he had to avoid submerging his ears in water.

Andy did not complain about his "bad hearing"—his "deafness," to use his own words.[29] He did not feel self-conscious about always having the front-row center seat reserved for him. A friend told him he compensated for his hearing by sharpening his other senses. "I had to be quicker at processing nonverbal signs and more attentive to signals, and most important, because I often understood only parts of sentences, I had to exercise my mind constantly." Thus a minus was being transformed into a plus. His bad hearing might be making him smarter.[30]

Being hard of hearing is no fun. Others have to repeat themselves when talking to you, which can be annoying for you to ask and for them to do. Conversations perfectly intelligible to others are puzzles to you. Words spoken by people behind you seem to be random sounds if you hear them at all. The word often coupled with "deaf" is "dumb." Some people are described as "deaf and dumb." Andy was "deaf and smart," not a common phrase. Young Andy successfully handled the problems caused by his hearing difficulties. As with the puppet his mother gave him following his first operation after scarlet fever, we once again encounter the theme of the mastery of trauma.

Andy's friends helped and encouraged him. One can easily imagine resentment building against the student who gets the most visible seat in the class and excels in a competitive environment despite a handicap. He was smart, hard of hearing, and Jewish. Another ten-year-old might have been "out" with those three strikes. But if Andy was hampered in his work for these reasons, he makes no mention of it in his memoirs.

There was a fourth strike:

> In the years after the war, I had gained weight. First I got pudgy, then I got even pudgier. Kids at school started calling me a variety of nicknames from Pufi (which means "Fatso") to Rofi (the sound a pig makes). I didn't like being called these names, but the more I protested, the louder the other kids shouted them at me across the schoolyard. So I resigned myself to being Pufi or Rofi. They became my names even in my own thoughts.[31]

Because Andy was not much of an athlete, "whenever teams were chosen, I was always the last kid to be picked." The heavier he became, the less athletic he was.[32]

Ten-year-old children are, to put it gently, sometimes not very nice. Calling a fat person "Fatso" is not surprising, which does not make it any more appealing. Perhaps this is how Andy's schoolmates discharged the envy and animosity they may have felt at the fact that a near-deaf Jew automatically got the best seat in each classroom and, despite his handicap, had the nerve to be smarter than everybody else.

A more interesting question is: why did Andy put on weight? From pictures, he did not appear obese, but he was clearly overweight from at least 1947 when he was eleven until about 1954 when he was eighteen.[33] By the time he was eighteen, he was trim and good-looking, and anyone who met him for the first time then would have been surprised that he had ever been known as Pufi or Rofi.

Grove gives us no clue to this question. He offers no speculation in his autobiography. There are no remarks about food cravings or attempts to diet, although he does express disappointment that activities like fencing did not help him lose weight. We are left with a passive acceptance of his getting fat and eventually getting trim again.

For someone who had battled his body so successfully from the age of four, the resignation with which Grove approached a state that is unpleasant for an adolescent boy is puzzling. Fat makes you self-conscious. It separates the real you literally as well as figuratively from your age mates. Everything becomes more difficult. You are uncomfortable all the time. You tire easily. No chair is designed for you. It is difficult to find clothes that fit. In a one-size-fits-all world, no size fits you. All his life, Grove was a self-starter, someone who made things happen. But not in this instance. And it mattered to him. He gives it space in his memoirs, and there is a picture of him as Pufi.

One can only guess what was going on for Andy. Putting on weight not only separates you from your peers, it is also a way for a boy reaching puberty to separate himself from a mother who is beautiful, accomplished, and self-assured. Neither Maria nor George said anything to Andy about his weight. They appear to have accepted it with nonchalance. Food can serve as a tranquilizer. Perhaps Andy was more nervous than he himself realized.

For some people, the "battle of the belt line" becomes a lifelong struggle. For Andy, however, the excess weight simply went away. No mention of self-control is associated with its disappearance. If ever there was a man who made things happen, it was Andy Grove. His approach to his weight problem stands in stark contrast to his approach to everything else.

As Andy and his parents were making their way through their personal lives, the political situation in Hungary was gravitating inexorably leftward. Andy was quite correct about the Communists. They held a monopoly on physical force, and they therefore "called the shots." Even though reasonably free elections were held in 1945 and the Communists were not swept into office, they could take power whenever they wished. They did not have to "seize" power. They could simply rig the political system so that the power they wielded in fact became power wielded by law. This process began in late 1946. Elections in August 1947 were a good deal less free than they had been in 1945.

By mid-1948, Hungary was effectively a tool of Moscow. In the years that followed, the vise tightened under the dictatorship of Stalin's agent, Rákosi. The approach toward the absorption into the Soviet empire was well characterized by Rákosi as the "salami" strategy[34]—that is to say, a slice at a time. Between 1945 and 1948, the Hungarian Communist Party grew quickly. Nevertheless, the judgment of one historian that "the Communists had no hope of coming to power by legal, democratic and parliamentary means"[35] appears accurate. There was a lot of anti-Communist sentiment in Hungary following the war.

As part of a coalition government, the Communists participated in passing laws that confiscated and broke up the great estates, including land owned by the Catholic Church. There was plenty of grist for that mill. In a nation of between nine and ten million, half of whom earned their living from agriculture, the thousand richest families owned a quarter of the arable land. The Catholic Church also possessed large holdings. These were broken up and redistributed to the peasantry in 1945 and 1946. Increased productivity did not, however, result. Droughts in 1946 and 1947 forced this agricultural nation to import food.

The Hungarian economy after the war faced every kind of problem. In addition to the droughts, there were shortages of raw materials, spare parts, and skilled workers. A steady descent into poverty led to the nationalization of major industries including iron, bauxite, and aluminum production in 1947 and 1948. Also in 1948, firms with ten or more employees were nationalized. The education system was overhauled. The political police either forced non-Communists into the party, hounded them out of the country, or found other means of eliminating them. The Communist Party controlled "all levels of political, social, economic and cultural life." By mid-1948, the salami had been completely sliced.[36]

There is a chapter in Dostoyevsky's *The Brothers Karamazov* entitled "For a Moment the Lie Becomes Truth."[37] For Hungary, the lie became truth during the years following the Communist takeover. Stalin knew what Hitler knew, which is that the big lie forcefully stated is disorienting. The big lie is such an affront to reality that its assertion calls reality into question. In the land of the big lie, you literally do not know what is going on.

Hungary entered that land for certain in 1949. That was when the László Rajk show trial was staged. Rajk was a lifelong Communist, and by 1949 he was Hungary's foreign minister, having already served as interior minister. At the May Day celebration in Budapest that year, he and Rákosi stood on a reviewing platform alone together, "waving to the marchers and receiving greetings—by established party tradition this meant nothing less than that Rajk was Rákosi's chosen successor."[38]

A couple of weeks after that, Rajk found himself in a dungeon run by the secret police being told to confess to "crimes" that he had not committed. At length, he did confess. He was executed in the fall.

What lesson could be deduced from this charade? If this could happen to Rajk, it could happen to anybody. No one could be trusted. Society was therefore "atomized."[39] Perhaps the real lesson was that there was no lesson. You were living on the other side of the looking glass.

Here, for example, is Andy's description of the May Day celebration in 1950: "Loudspeakers were hung from lampposts along the parade route throughout the city. They blared energetic cheers: 'Long live the Communist Party!' 'Long live Mátyás Rákosi!' 'Long live Stalin!'" Andy assumed that all this cheering was coming from Heroes' Square and that the people making all the noise were those who had preceded him there. "However, when we arrived at the square, the only people standing and waving were the Party members on the reviewing stand. None of the previous marchers had stuck around to watch. No other marchers were cheering. None of us were cheering."[40]

The cheering was coming from a recording, as if all life had turned into a sitcom with its canned laughter. Andy was asked to submit an article about the parade for a weekly magazine for young people in which he had published some previous pieces. He did not do so, leaving the task for others.[41]

The regime made it difficult to find out the truth about anything.[42] Was the harvest good or not? Was the balance between consumer spending and investment what it should be? These and every other imaginable question that had to be asked to run a country were answered in code. Nothing was debated on its merits.

This was the apogee of the "primacy of politics." "Position power" was the goal of every exercise. "Knowledge power" did not exist independent of politics. Every idea had a person stapled to it, and the wrong idea could cost a person his life. The premiership of Mátyás Rákosi was a ministry of fear.

How did the Gróf family adapt to this new reality? Quite well at first. Not long after Andy's father reconstituted himself, having returned from the war, the family's apartment once again became a lively place. Lots of people visited. Socializing was frequent and pleasant. George and Maria both went back to work for the dairy. George soon moved on to a management position at a government-owned retailer.

That was a good move. With the Communists in power by the second half of 1948, the dairy was nationalized, the result of which was the elimination of "the ready supply of fresh cottage cheese, butter, and yogurt that we were accustomed to."[43] That was not all. For the school year 1949–1950, Andy was moved out of Evangelikus to the Dob Street School. Dob Street had neither the talented faculty not the esprit of Evangelikus, but it was good enough. Andy had friends there and made the most out of what the better teachers had to offer.

In 1949, with the Communists firmly in control of Hungary, Andy had "mixed feelings" about them. "On the one hand, I felt that they saved my mother's life and my own. I was very grateful for this, and my gratitude made me want to believe in them and what they stood for. On the other hand . . . they increasingly interfered in our daily life . . . all in the name of some political philosophy that I didn't really understand."[44]

Andy sensed the chilling effect of the new regime at school. Back at Evangelikus prior to 1949, he had not hesitated to object to what was bruited about a classroom as conventional wisdom. He was always an eager pupil and enjoyed the role of contrarian. But at the Dob Street School in the Communist era the situation was different. Things were said at school with which he had every reason to disagree. However, "Contradicting a position that was even vaguely associated with the Communist Party didn't seem like a wise thing to do."[45] The "lie" was becoming "truth" in the new order, and this turnabout was going to last longer than "a moment."

At first, Andy tended to view the world through the propaganda lens of the Communist Party, although what he was seeing in some instances was difficult to figure out. Like everyone else, he was "glued to [the] radio set" when the Rajk trial was broadcast in the late summer of 1949. "I listened to Rajk's examination with morbid fascination. I couldn't understand how a man who fought against the Germans and was a member of the underground could turn against his cause and his country. But there it was: He had confessed it himself."[46]

Explanations of events under communism simply did not add up. The party line with regard to the outbreak of the Korean War provides a good example. The official explanation was that the South Korean "puppets of the Americans" had invaded North Korea. Everybody was talking about this startling development. Despite this unprovoked and dastardly aggression, the North Koreans quickly drove the enemy back.

"How," Andy asked himself, "could the North Koreans, who were caught in a surprise attack by the South Koreans, rally this rapidly and defeat an army that had the advantage of deliberately preparing for an attack for some time beforehand?"[47] This question was not merely the product of deductive thinking. Andy had lived through the Soviet invasion of Hungary. The Battle of Budapest had been fought all around him. What he was being told about Korea simply did not conform to war as he had experienced it.

Then, all of a sudden, the tide of the war turned. The Americans landed in Korea to come to the aid of their lackeys. They were accused of using what these days are known as "weapons of mass destruction." "Big ugly bugs appeared next to the maps of the [battle] front [that were posted all over Budapest], portraying the use of bacterial warfare by the Americans and South Koreans against the North." Andy had all manner of questions about Korean War reports, but he wisely hesitated to ask them.[48]

George Gróf, meanwhile, was prospering under the new regime. He was promoted out of the department store in which he had been a manager to become the director of a government-owned company that dealt with breeding livestock and with exports. He had impressive perquisites: not only an "elegant secretary" but even a chauffeur—odd accoutrements considering that the government opposed domestic help, which meant that Gizi and Sinko had to leave the Grófs' apartment.

The meaning of communism for the Grófs was not confined to Korea, a peninsula ten thousand miles away. One day, which the family was spending uneventfully, Maria was reading the newspaper when completely by chance she came across an article accusing her husband of consorting with "bourgeois elements." "Oh, my God," she said, "listen to this." Indeed they did. They were terrified. Once again, history was about to happen to them and their family.[49]

Early in 1951, Andy's uncle Sanyi, a newspaper editor, and Sanyi's son-in-law were arrested at night. "My aunt showed up at our house the next morning, frightened and utterly helpless. Nobody would say where they were taken or why. There were no charges and no one to inquire to. They were just gone."[50] This incident exemplifies life in Hungary's Stalinist period, life without the common law protections taken for granted in countries governed by "bourgeois elements." The Grófs could do nothing "except wait to see what would happen next." What happened next was that George Gróf lost his job and was informed that he would never get another that paid more than a quarter of his previous salary.

George was able to find employment, but the family's standard of living declined. Meat once a week. No more delicacies. Cheap seats at the opera. A long commute by tram, a big step down from a chauffeured car, for George. However,

> I never heard my father complain about the loss of his job. . . . In fact, I never heard him complain at all, but he became very quiet. He was a man who used to thrive on political discussions. Now he refused to discuss politics. And in any case, there was no one to discuss it with. Most of his friends still stayed away.[51]

Maria was less accepting of the political situation, but her self-mastery helped her deal with reality.

Young Andy, meanwhile, was excelling at school and at extracurricular activities. Despite the abortive foray into the world of music through piano lessons, his interest was rekindled when a friend dragged him to an open-air opera performance on Margaret Island, in the middle of the Danube. He became, to his surprise, fascinated by bass-baritone roles, and his appreciation of opera survives to this day. In addition, reading Jules Verne and C. S. Forester, he discovered what he labeled a "rich inner life," unsuspected by others. He led a rich outer life as well, writing articles for a weekly newspaper. In short, he was precocious, buoyant, optimistic, open to new experiences.

Abruptly, Andy's submissions to the weekly newspaper stopped being published. He asked the editor why and received no satisfactory answer. Then he asked his mother whether the fact that his uncle had been jailed might have something to do with it. She agreed, and a "career in journalism suddenly lost its appeal."[52]

In the fall of 1951, Andy moved on from the Dob Street School to Madach Gymnasium. Like Evangelikus, Madach was a proud institution. Grove was a discerning and demanding pupil. The instructors lived up to his expectations, and he lived up to theirs. At a parent-teacher conference, there was nothing George and Maria heard that would not have gladdened the heart of any father and mother. Mr. Telegdi, the melancholy Hungarian literature instructor, said to a meeting of all the parents, "Someday we will be sitting in Gróf's waiting room, waiting for him to see us."

The personality of Mr. Volenski, the physics teacher, was the opposite of Mr. Telegdi's. Volenski was a joyful "character" and apparently a born teacher. Andy enjoyed him and the subject he taught. On parent-teacher night at Madach, Volenski said, "Life is like a big lake. All the boys get in the water at one end and start swimming. Not all of them will swim across. But one of them, I'm sure, will. That one is Gróf."[53]

Andy Grove is a hard man to compliment. He finds "general-purpose compliments" off-putting. My guess is that he experiences them as an attempt at manipulation. Volenski's words, however, struck a deep chord and have resonated down to the present day. Grove paraphrased them for the title of his memoir, *Swimming Across,* in which he adopts the words as the master metaphor of his life. He concludes the book with:

> As my teacher Volenski predicted, I managed to swim across the lake—
> not without effort, not without setbacks, and with a great deal of help
> and encouragement from others.
>   I am still swimming.[54]

Despite the fact that his father and uncle were both *personae non gratae* with the government, Andy's teachers felt they could be uninhibited in their praise of him. As in his earlier experiences, his classmates did not resent his success. As for Andy himself, it seems impossible that anyone ever enjoyed school more.

Andy was becoming interested in chemistry. "After the fiasco of my potential journalism career, I was eager to cultivate an interest in a new profession that was less prone to subjectivity."[55] He turned out to be as good at chemistry as he was at every other academic endeavor. He taught himself how to make nitroglycerin. During his third year at Madach (he was seventeen years old at the time), his chemistry teacher, who was well aware of his prowess, asked him to show a class of thirty girls in the second year of the school how to make the compound. His demonstration was a startling success. "Bang!" he reports. "The class broke into shrieks and excited applause. I was on top of the world!"[56]

That story appears on page 156 of Grove's memoirs. What follows is his recounting of a story he wrote, entitled "Despair," for Mr. Telegdi's literature class. Although he had discarded his career as a journalist, Andy continued to write. This dual interest in technology and the arts, so rare in the modern world, he carried with him into adulthood.

Andy's story, which he submitted anonymously, caused quite a stir. Mr. Telegdi asked the whole class to read and discuss it, and it was admired. Mr. Telegdi said, "whoever the author is, I'm sure that this is not the last we have heard from him." Everyone was guessing the author's identity, and everyone was guessing wrong. Andy let the tension build. He has always been a showman. At the key moment when he had everybody's attention, he announced that the student who all were saying had written the story was right in denying authorship. Of this he was certain because he had written it.

The result of this proclamation? "Pandemonium broke out. The meeting dissolved into excited kids slapping me on the back, congratulating me, and shaking their heads in disbelief. . . . Mr. Telegdi shook my hand and repeated that he thought the story was great. . . . This was the most exciting event of my life."[57]

This passage appears on page 161 of his memoirs. Thus on page 156 Grove was "on top of the world" and on page 161 he had "the most exciting event" of his life. Not many people go through school like this. Andy's aunt showed "Despair" to a prominent writer. The response clearly illustrated a bias toward "socialist realism" on the part of this writer as well as his fear. "I was glad I liked chemistry," concluded Andy.[58]

The more Grove saw of communism, the less he liked it. There was the banging on the door by the political police in the middle of the night with the threat of being carried away to who knew where for having done who knew what. There was the "intangible but constant nagging fear." There was the continuous lie that everyone lived, the lie that they were all part of a fair and enthusiastic polity. There was the inability to square one's perceptions with reality because no one knew to whom it was safe to speak.

This lack of trust, this "atomization," is captured by a joke that Andy remembers making the rounds:

> Two men are ogling a spanking new Western car. One of them says, "Isn't this car a wonderful testimony to the technological capabilities of our friendly Soviet Union?" The other man looks at him scornfully. "Don't you know anything about cars?" The first man replies, "I know about cars. I don't know about you."[59]

March 5, 1953, Stalin died. One is tempted to say "finally died." He was seventy-three years old, not terribly aged for a political leader in the mid-twentieth century. Winston Churchill was seventy-eight years old and prime minister of Great Britain at the time. However, it seemed as if Stalin had been around forever. He had played a role in the Russian Revolution in 1917. One can date the beginning of his dictatorship of the Soviet Union from sometime between Lenin's death in 1924 and 1929, by which time all his rivals had been neutralized one way or another.

If we accept the latter date, Stalin had been the absolute master of the Soviet Union uninterruptedly for almost a quarter of a century. It needs no saying that he was a horror, arguably responsible for more death and suffering than any other person in history. Nevertheless, his presence, year in and year out, was a reality to which people under his power had accustomed themselves. Here is Andy's recollection:

> Stalin's figure had been indelibly associated with the images of the Soviet Union in my mind. The picture of a uniformed, mustachioed man with a kindly expression had been everywhere—in offices, schools, at celebrations, hung on the sides of buildings—for, it seemed, most of

my life. Even though by this time I had become deeply skeptical about the goodness of things Soviet, Stalin's death and the disappearance of that ever-present kindly face had a mixed impact on me.

I was glad and I was sad at the same time. It was very confusing.[60]

There was plenty of reason for confusion, because there was no knowing what might come next. Among the most important characteristics of a political system is its ability to ensure the peaceful succession from one head of government to the next. By that standard the political system in the United States has worked quite well, with the single exception of the outbreak of the Civil War following the election of Abraham Lincoln in 1860. To those of us brought up within the American tradition, it is difficult to imagine the situation facing the Kremlin hierarchy the day after Stalin's death. He had embodied the Soviet Union. Any discussion of who might succeed him would surely have proven fatal while he lived. Now, suddenly, a group of unlovely people named Georgy Malenkov, Vyacheslav Molotov, Nicolay Bulganin, Lavrenty Beria, and Nikita Khrushchev had to work this problem out in a life-and-death atmosphere in which trust was a complete stranger.

What transpired at first was a thaw, a loosening of the dictatorial grip over the satellites, or, as they were known in the United States, the "captive nations." The leadership of the Hungarian Communist Party was summoned to Moscow on June 12, 1953. The next day, Rákosi and seven of his comrades were brought to the Kremlin to meet with the collective leadership of the Soviet Union. They did not know the reason for this conference.

The Soviet hierarchy read the riot act to the Hungarians. The economy was performing poorly. The people were disaffected and not without reason. In a small country, there were tens of thousands of political prisoners. The terror in the terror state run by Rákosi had lost its deterrent effect because, it was alleged, of its random nature.[61] The enthusiastic loyalty of the people had to be won, not because of any particular affection for them but because without some popular commitment the economy would continue its downward spiral. Rákosi, "thoroughly humiliated," was forced to cede his position as prime minister to Imre Nagy.[62]

The result of this brutal dressing-down was amnesty for large numbers of prisoners. "The Hungarian gulag more or less ceased to exist in the autumn of 1953." Internment camps were closed. According to one report, almost three-quarters of a million people were released from confinement.[63]

These political developments had a direct impact on the Grófs' extended family. Uncle Sanyi was released from prison in the spring of 1954. His liberation was as sudden and unexplained as his incarceration had been. Sanyi endured the experience remarkably well, especially in contrast to another Gróf relative who wound up in a mental institution temporarily after his release from prison. Nevertheless, comments Grove, "at least they were out and free to settle down and get on with their lives."[64] There is that phrase again. Another unintentional echo of everyone's assignment in Kertesz's *Fatelessness*.

Perhaps there was nothing else to say or to do. However, "to get on with one's life" having experienced at first hand the worst that life can mete out requires great inner resources. Few indeed are the people who can simply forget a traumatic experience and "get on with their lives" as if it had not taken place.

Andy, meanwhile, was growing up. The school year 1954–1955 would be his last at Madach. The weight he had put on was gone, never to return. "One day at home, I caught a glimpse of myself in the mirror without a shirt on. Much to my delight, I noticed that I had muscles. I had finally lost my remaining chubbiness." Once again, a passive way to describe what for many people is difficult. No mention of ever stepping on a scale. The fat simply came and then it went.

Andy wanted to go on to university, but such a step could not be taken for granted. First he had to pass the finals at Madach, which had a reputation as a gut-clutching experience. "I was nervous. But once I faced my teachers I saw goodwill in their eyes. I realized that they wanted me to do well, and that helped me immensely."[65] He passed with ease.

Once again, however, the welcoming world within the walls of the school was not the same as the nasty world outside. Andy wanted to study natural sciences at the University of Budapest. Anyone could see that academically he would fit right in, but as always in Communist Hungary, "knowledge power" took a backseat to "position power." Andy's position was not a good one.

His first application to the university was going to be rejected because he was categorized as a "class alien." He had plenty of knowledge, but it looked like he would pay the price for this "position." The categorization was probably the result of his father's checkered career in the eyes of Hungary's capricious Communist regime since World War II. But George proved his resourcefulness at this critical moment and somehow, through the intervention of a friend, managed to get Andy reclassified from "class alien" to "other." As "other," he was accepted.

In the fall of 1955, Andy matriculated for his first year as a student at the University of Budapest. The problems he faced stemmed more from people who did not project their voices sufficiently to accommodate his compromised hearing than from the subject matter. His intellectual mastery of the material seems to have increased in this more demanding environment. Andy did not merely work his way through. He outpaced others, generating yet more "ecstatic" moments.[66] He quickly felt at home—in one particular class "more at home . . . than I ever had at Madach gymnasium."

The reason he gives for his quick accommodation is jarring. "I no longer had to be embarrassed about being a good student. At university, we were all there to learn and we all wanted to do well."[67] There is no reference in his memoirs prior to this passage about being ill at ease with his intelligence. Moreover, he was doing a lot more than schoolwork. He was becoming more deeply involved in the performing arts and honing yet further his flair for the dramatic.

Andy's first year at the university ended "with a big bang." There is that word again. But a new note now slips into his self-description. "[F]or the first time I could remember, I felt at home in a group. I was no longer an outsider. I started the summer break on a real high."[68]

Once again, we encounter a surprise. More than two-thirds of the way through his memoirs, we discover that Andy had never felt comfortable in a group. Prior to this passage, despite all the reasons why he might have felt uncomfortable—his intellectual superiority, his deafness, his weight, his religion—he never mentions any of them, or at least not after the Nazis were driven out of Hungary. What, then, is going on here?

This is mere speculation, but I think Andy was uncomfortable about being Jewish. We know that he and his family were not observant. There is no mention of participation in the most basic of Jewish rituals. Andy was not, for example, bar mitzvah. The family did not belong to a synagogue. Orthodox Jews seemed to him to come from another planet.

As we have discussed, up until the end of the First World War, Hungary was one of the best places in the world to be a Jew. Judaism was accepted by the state on an equal plane with other religions. Jews owned a disproportionate share of financial and manufacturing assets, and, rare in Eastern Europe, they were acquiring land. They ran the newspapers and played an important role in the nation's cultural life. Theodor Herzl, the founder of modern Zionism, was born in Budapest. There was an anti-Semitic backlash after World War I, but it did not last. If you were a Jew, Hungary was a good place to be relative to its neighbors until March 1944.

And yet . . .

Assimilation could never be complete. Andy could make many choices. He could have been a writer, a musician, an actor, an engineer, a scientist, and so on. He was and remains something of a polymath. He could make the choice to leave Hungary, which he would soon do.

What Andy Grove could not do was choose not to be of Jewish origin. As a Jew in the age of Hitler, he bore the mark of Cain. He could be a participant. He could even be a star. What he could never quite be was "one of the boys." Though a participant, he was also an observer. In later life, he would make reference to the Heisenberg uncertainty principle, which asserts that under certain circumstances the mere observation of a phenomenon can alter it.

At the University of Budapest, this otherness, to which Andy had not heretofore referred in his memoirs but which must have affected him, seems to have largely melted away. The reason was not only that about a third of the students were Jewish, a staggeringly high proportion considering the Holocaust and the fact that the percentage of Jews in the nation's population was far less than that.[69] It was also that he developed a friendship that spanned religious divisions. The Jewish students at the University of Budapest "as a whole mixed very well," but "close friendships did not develop."

With Andy and a student named Zoltan, the invisible wall between Jew and gentile was breached.

> Zoltan's caustic wit and his sharp insights impressed me, as did his interest in Western literature and music—he was an accomplished jazz pianist. His attempt to look Western, I soon realized, wasn't an act at all but was completely consistent with his interests. . . . [H]e openly made cynical political comments to me, [and] I found myself opening up to him more and more, too.[70]

Yet the "religious divide" or the "cultural/religious divide" (it is difficult to find the right words to describe it) remained. It was Andy who mounted a direct assault on it. He asked Zoltan point-blank whether his Jewishness posed a problem for him. Without hesitation, Zoltan responded, "Why would it bother me that you are a stinking Jew?" To which a momentarily shocked Andy answered, "Yes and why should it bother me that I hang out with a dumb goy?"

This exchange broke the ice. Andy and Zoltan then turned their newfound joking relationship into their own secret code. The initials for "stinking Jew" in Hungarian approximate the chemical symbol for bismuth. The initials for "dumb goy" match mercury. So Andy and Zoltan would say "bismuth" and "mercury" to one another when in public places. Only they knew this secret code. Grove remembers all this as if it were yesterday. On the last day of 2005, he mentioned that Zoltan was his first genuinely close gentile friend.[71]

After a summer in the Hungarian army, Andy returned to the University of Budapest for his second year, and a more eager and enthusiastic student would be hard to imagine. But during this school year, the times would once again impinge directly on his life.

Unrest in Eastern European Soviet satellites had been smoldering since the end of World War II. The first and most important example was Yugoslavia, which managed to avoid becoming a satellite altogether because of its daring and ruthless dictator, Josip Broz, who took the name by which he was known to the world, "Tito."

Belgrade was liberated by Soviet armed forces in 1944, but Yugoslavia was not completely occupied by its liberators. Tito had his own ideas about how to run Yugoslavia's foreign policy, and domestically he never bent the knee to the Russians as did the leaders of the satellites. Alone among Eastern European leaders, Tito defied Stalin and got away with it. The success of Tito complicated the position of the Soviet Union in its management of other Eastern European nations, all of which it wanted firmly shut behind what Winston Churchill famously labeled the "iron curtain."[72] Now there were two enemies—"Titoism" as well as "capitalism."

When Churchill coined the term "iron curtain," he defined the world-view of hundreds of millions of people for a generation. The world had become "bipolar"—communism versus democracy (the Western nations always characterized their pole as "democratic" rather than "capitalistic"), America versus Russia (Americans typically used "Russia" and the "Soviet Union" interchangeably).

In his list of "famous cities" behind the iron curtain, Churchill included Belgrade. But that was not true. Belgrade, Yugoslavia's capital, close by Hungary's southern border, had escaped the Soviet grasp. Tito defied Stalin, lived to talk about it, and died a natural death. His example might prove contagious.

Would "Titoism" pick up steam? This question became even more urgent after Stalin's death, with Moscow populated by a "collective leadership" of individuals not very well-known to the outside world. It did not take long before peoples in Eastern Europe began testing how ironclad that iron curtain really was. There were riots in East Berlin in June 1953, just three and a half months after Stalin's death. They were put down through Soviet power, but the genie was out of the bottle. In the words of Alexis de Tocqueville, "The inevitable evil that one bears patiently seems unbearable as soon as one conceives the idea of removing it."[73]

The eventual victor in Moscow was Nikita Khrushchev. He felt it vital to disenthrall the Soviet people from Stalin and his memory, and at the Twentieth All-Union Party Conference in Moscow in February 1956 he delivered a secret-but-not-secret speech that became a turning point in the history of communism. Entitled "The Personality Cult and Its Consequences," it was a stinging denunciation of the madness that had characterized the dictatorship of a totalitarian paranoiac.[74]

With Khrushchev's ascendancy, Stalinism and presumably the policy of the iron fist behind the iron curtain that Stalinism meant were gone. What would take its place? Would one be able to speak and act in accord with the dictates of simple common sense? Would one enjoy personal autonomy? For the satellites, such individual questions assumed national proportions. How much independence from Moscow would Warsaw, Prague, Budapest, and the rest enjoy under the Khrushchev regime? No one knew. The only way to learn would be by testing the boundaries of freedom of action. The tests began soon.

The same month as Khrushchev's de-Stalinization speech, the Stalinist dictator of Poland, Boleslaw Beirut, died, as it happens, a natural death. Under Beirut, the Polish government and society "developed the full range of Stalinist features then obligatory within the Soviet European empire: ideological regimentation, the police state, strict subordination to the Soviet Union, a rigid command economy, persecution of the Roman Catholic Church, and blatant distortion of history."[75] In June of that year, antigovernment riots broke out in Poznan, Poland. In October, Wladyslaw Gomulka was installed as the nation's new leader.

Moscow had warned the Polish Communist Party that if it selected Gomulka as its general secretary, Soviet troops would invade the country. The party selected Gomulka anyway, but Khrushchev, satisfied with reassurances Gomulka provided, kept his troops at home. Some believed the "Polish October" would lead to a general liberalization of the regime.[76]

Word of unrest in East Germany and of a "Polish October" quickly became known in Hungary. As Andy Grove was enjoying his schoolwork and flirting with cute girls, "a buzz spread through the university about a march that was being organized to express our support for the Poles."[77] Its date was October 23, 1956.

The march was to originate at the statue of Sandor Petőfi, national poet and martyr of the 1848 rebellion, and proceed to that of Jozef Bem, a Polish general who had supported the Hungarians in 1848. The event seemed spontaneous. A carnival atmosphere prevailed. The students were joined by a cross section of Budapest's citizenry. A giddy excitement pervaded the scene. "After all the years of sullen, silent May Day marches, there was something magical about a large spontaneous demonstration." Andy was swept up in the euphoria. At first.[78]

Suddenly Hungarian flags appeared from what seemed like every window in the city. But they were not the flags Hungarians had been staring at since the Communists took over. The Hungarian flag has horizontal stripes of red, white, and green. In the center, historically there had been the coat of arms of King Saint Stephen, symbol of Magyar nationalism for a millennium. The Communists got rid of that and substituted the hammer and sickle.

The demonstrators or celebrants on that bright autumn day were cutting the circular representation of the hammer and sickle out of the center of their flags. You can still see such flags displayed in Budapest today. The sight of them rendered Andy breathless. They also, however, set off an alarm for him: "Those flags were permanently altered. The act seemed unequivocal and destined to provoke a reaction. . . . I felt we had crossed a line of no return. I began to feel a little nervous."[79] The nervousness was justified. There would be gunfire before the day came to an end.

The morning of Wednesday, October 23, 1956, seemed like any other. The afternoon turned into a true and popular demonstration against the soul-destroying degradation that was Communist rule in Hungary. By the evening, working people leaving a plant named for Rákosi joined what was at first primarily a student march. Some of them took a blowtorch to a large bronze statue of Stalin, cut off its head, and spat on it.[80] Theoretically the Communist world had been "de-Stalinized" since shortly after his death. Nevertheless, this was as clear an anti-Soviet gesture as could be made short of actually shooting at the secret police or at the troops who occupied the country. That would come soon enough.

Rumors filled the air the next day, on which Andy woke up early. Gunfire persuaded him that staying at home was the best path to follow. Radio stations that had been jammed in the past, including Radio Free Europe and Voice of America, could now clearly be heard.[81] The government was petrified and scurried away. The new prime minister was Imre Nagy. The Russians evacuated Budapest. The countryside was also up in arms. For a brief moment, it looked like Hungary was to become a free country.

It was all a dream, stoked by rumors that the West would come to Hungary's rescue should the Soviet troops that had evacuated Budapest return.[82] Khrushchev correctly understood that his "position as Soviet leader, and his entire political future, were in jeopardy. . . . Surely a satellite could not be allowed to break loose from the Soviet bloc simply because its unruly youth took to the streets and denounced Soviet domination."[83] The Russians came roaring back into the country with overwhelming force on November 4 to put an end to the uprising. "I had never seen such devastation," wrote Andy, "not even from the bombing during the war."[84]

Imre Nagy, a lifelong Communist, and his cabinet took refuge in the Yugoslav embassy. Tito and Khrushchev had, however, already reached an understanding that the Russians would send their troops back into Hungary. Soviet military police arrested Nagy when he left the embassy. On June 16, 1958, he was executed. Khrushchev had proven he could be as tough as Stalin.

The Russians may have been back in charge in Budapest, but the situation in the city was not at all what it had been prior to the uprising. Both food and information were difficult to come by. The university was closed. The buzz in the air now was the possibility of escape to Austria. Andy and his parents discussed it often. Should he go or stay? If he tried to go, how would he do it? How risky was it? Was life in Budapest really so bad that the risks were worth taking? Andy liked the university, and he was carrying a torch for a girl, yet another in a fairly long line, named Vicki. Was he really willing to stake everything on the unknown? "I didn't know how to do it, and I was scared."[85]

The prospect of escape offered a lot to be scared about. The air was full of rumors and reports of rumors. Some people were making it across the border. Others were disappearing, just like George Gróf did during World War II. "Disappearing" was a bad thing to have happen to you. You might never reappear.

If he did make a dash for the Austrian border, Andy had no doubt of what his eventual destination would be. "Of course, it would be America. Or, as the Communist regime put it, 'imperialist, money-grubbing America.' The more scorn they heaped on it, the more desirable America sounded. America had a mystique of wealth and modern technology; it was a place with lots of cars and plenty of Hershey bars."[86]

The person who tipped the scales was Aunt Manci, whom Andy had once called a "stupid ass." He had learned to respect her by 1956, now that he was old enough to understand what she had gone through in her life. "She was an Auschwitz survivor and had seen the worst that could be. She was not a hysterical woman and had absolutely no reason to exaggerate."[87]

"Andris," she told him one afternoon in early December, "you must go. You must go, and you must go immediately." The Russians were summarily rounding up young people. These young people, it was feared, would soon find themselves among the ranks of the disappeared. Suddenly it seemed as dangerous to stay as it was to try to get out.[88]

The Gróf family once again was decisive. When it was time to make a move, they did so. They did not dawdle. When the three of them together agreed that Andy should make a run for the Austrian border, he spent only one more night in the apartment on Kiraly Street in Budapest. This apartment, this city, and this country were the only home he had ever known. He "silently said goodbye" to the apartment that night.[89]

Andy and his parents "were struggling with the fact that we might never see each other again." The next day the three of them parted on a street corner "as if it were any normal morning." Making a big deal out of the farewell might have drawn attention to them, which was a risk no one wanted to run. Andy met up with two other hopeful refugees, a boy and a girl, and went to the railroad station to catch a train for Szombathely, fifteen miles from the border with Austria. On the train, the three of them met another young girl who wanted to get out of the country but did not know how. They invited her to join them. Now it was two girls and two boys headed for the border with no official permission. They were repeatedly forced to trust people they did not know. The penalty for a misstep would be capture by a Russian patrol, with heaven knew what as the result.[90]

The narration of the escape across the border sounds like something out of a Hollywood anti-Nazi movie. A string of villages with unfamiliar names that had to be memorized. Nothing could be written down because of the risk of being captured. Fear of being lost amidst woods and pastures. An encounter with a hunchback in a field, who spoke in a whisper. Directions to an isolated farmhouse. A knock on the door, which is opened by a "stunningly beautiful woman" dressed in a colorful peasant garb. The next day, a guide who would show up and dematerialize like a friendly ghost. Dim lights in the distance. A whisper: "Those lights are Austria. Head toward them and don't take your eyes off them. This is as far as I go."

Stumbling across fields in the dark. Dogs bark. Suddenly a flare illuminates the sky. The four young students hug the earth. The flare burns out. Darkness again. A man appears and demands in Hungarian, "Who is there?" Why was he speaking Hungarian, a language no one could mistake for German? Then he says, "Relax, you're in Austria." Safe at last. But could they be sure?

The four were taken by Austrian police to an unheated schoolhouse where they were to spend the night. Andy did not like the situation. He was in Austria, he wanted to get to Vienna, and he did not want to follow instructions given by policemen. He and his male friend departed the schoolhouse, leaving their two female traveling companions behind, and set off for Vienna.[91]

Reflecting on his flight from Hungary four decades later, in 1996, Grove said that "the dangers involved with escaping Hungary were about equal with the dangers of staying. . . . Hungary was a pretty sad place in 1956 and there were . . . strong rumors about people being picked up, people my age, being picked up on the street and herded away and I thought it was a good time to make a run for it."

Asked how hard it was to get out, Grove said, "it was just medium-hard, but there was no way to know what it was going to be like. . . . [W]hen . . . a friend of mine and I left Budapest, we had no idea what was going to happen near the border. You know, there was no Internet in which there was a home page that somebody could tell us the border conditions of the day!"[92]

Once in Vienna, Andy navigated the unfamiliar terrain like a seasoned traveler. He sent a telegram home to tell his folks he was safe. Another telegram was dispatched to Manci's relatives, Lenke and Lajos, in New York City. Having escaped from Hungary, the next goal was to get out of Vienna, and in pursuit of that object never was a man more a "destination shopper" than Andy Grove. If that meant running all over town "like a madman" and "brush[ing] past the person whose turn it was supposed to be" in a line of anxious refugees, so be it. In the midst of all this tumult, Andy managed somehow to get inexpensive tickets to the Vienna State Opera, where he saw three productions.[93] Ever the demanding critic, he thought the performances, though good, were not quite up to what he had seen in Budapest.[94]

Grove tells us in his memoirs that on his final night in Hungary he relieved himself in the most rudimentary of outhouses. "I looked up at the bit of sky barely visible through the doorway and I thought, this is probably the last of me that I'll leave in Hungary."[95] Surely, he provides his many thousands of readers with this Aristophanic information for a reason. He defecates on Hungary as he leaves.

But as soon as he arrives in Austria, he compares Hungarian opera favorably to Austrian. Which, by the way, is a little hard to believe. Musically, Budapest is very good, but Vienna has always ranked with the immortals.

Andy has never fully come to terms with Hungary. He got out when he could and both the process and result of his escape were leaps into the unknown. He left a warm and loving nuclear and extended family and took with him a smattering of knowledge of English and German, the clothes on his back, and nothing else. He could have been captured by the Russians and imprisoned, or worse.

Andy Grove took a lot of risks in his life. However, the stakes were never higher, the penalty for failure never greater, than this risk of the flight he took when he was twenty years of age. "Andyana" Grove might have wound up in a "Temple of Doom" all his own. Robert Noyce, coinventor of the integrated circuit and cofounder of Intel, once said, "Don't be encumbered by history. Go out and do something wonderful." Grove took his advice long before it was given.

Andy remains fluent in Hungarian and will speak it on occasion. Les Vadasz, also a Hungarian Jewish émigré from Budapest, is ten days older than Andy. Les became Intel's fourth employee. For some strange reason, he is actually on the records as employee number three. For a brief moment, Intel's workforce was populated 50 percent by Hungarian Jews. When Andy first met Les at Fairchild he spoke Hungarian to him. Les, who is fluent in the language, did not initially understand because he did not expect to hear Hungarian spoken to him at a semiconductor company at 844 Charleston

Road in Palo Alto, California, by a stranger in 1964.[96] At a meeting at the University of California at San Francisco Medical School in the summer of 2004, Andy was quick to point out that a man referred to by another speaker was Hungarian.[97]

On July 30, 2004, Mr. Tamás Karman, who lives in Budapest, emailed Andy two pictures of his history teacher at Madach Gymnasium. Mrs. Edith Vasarhelyi was a very good-looking woman when she was his instructor, and because of his hearing deficit, he got a good look at her every day. As he put it, "She was close enough that I could smell her perfume. She wore open necked blouses, and from my seat, I could see her neck and the underside of her chin. I felt I was staring at her, but I didn't know what else to do with my eyes, so I stared at her neck. I was terribly embarrassed, but I was always happy when my seatmate was out sick."[98]

Hungary never completely lost its allure, and Andy always maintained a certain pride in his Hungarian background. Perhaps it was that very pride that kept him from ever going back. The thought of staying in Central Europe or going to England had no appeal for him. He was going to the United States, which is about as far away from Hungary as one could get. As he put it in a breathless letter home from Vienna, "God knows, if I have a chance I will go as far as I can."[99]

Andy's best bet for his trip seemed to be an organization called the International Rescue Committee.[100] He made his way to their offices in Vienna, and their representatives were surprised that he spoke enough English to be interviewed in their language rather than through a translator. They asked him if he had fought against the Russians in Hungary. He said that he had not actually fought. He had participated in a few demonstrations.

The interviewers were surprised at this response. Everyone else they had interviewed had fought the Russians. At least, that is what they said. "A sarcastic thought came to mind: If all these people had fought, we would have won and I wouldn't be here." Andy, however, decided to keep his own counsel, as he was "reluctant to fabricate a story for the occasion."[101] For a good example of the propaganda passing for reportage in the West and an article Grove would have hated, see Elie Abel's "Out of Hungary—Revolt of the Exiles":

Geza, a lieutenant in the regular Hungarian army at 25, has just walked across the frontier with his wife Franciszka, a registered nurse four months pregnant, and a half-dozen of the freedom fighters [the term habitually used in the West] who hurled back the Russians in a Budapest street-corner battle.[102]

This lieutenant was quoted in the article as saying that "so long as there is hope that the Russians will leave Hungary, we don't want to be too far away. If there's any possibility at all, we will go back to Budapest."[103] This was music to the ears of any Western cold warrior. Freedom fighters returning to their country to rescue it from godless communism—and not costing us any money to resettle them in our country. Either Andy had not been properly scripted or he was stuck with a script he did not want to read.

The next day came bad news. Andy learned that he was not among those selected by the IRC to be taken to America. "I felt as if someone had socked me in the stomach, then my heart started beating so hard that I could barely breathe." But he was undaunted. He rushed off "like a madman" to the IRC and cut into the front of the predictable line so that he could plead his case. His pleading was so persuasive that the IRC representatives said it was fine with them, he could go to America. "I was speechless."[104]

Many of the characteristics of Grove's life are evident in the saga of his escape to freedom. First is his willingness to take risks. The flight to a new country was fraught with them. People were being summarily and unceremoniously shot in Hungary when he, unarmed and unprotected, took off for the Austrian border. He was twenty years old, and this would be his first time out of his native land. He almost literally feels his way toward Austria, and when he arrives, he must fend for himself. This adolescent, with severe hearing impairment, now has to communicate in German and English. He could barely make his needs known in either tongue.

Second, he would not take no for an answer. When the International Rescue Committee turned down his first application for resettlement in the United States, he turned up at their offices to plead his case again. Think for a moment how difficult it can be to advocate one's own case, to thrust oneself forward after having been rejected. Grove is hindered by no such compunction. He knows what he wants, and if he has to push his way to the front of the line ahead of others equally anxious, as he did at the IRC office, he does so without a second thought. He has an innate sense of entitlement.

Third, Grove moves fast. He is decisive and effective.

Fourth, Andy is not weighed down by the past. If he has to leave "my birthplace, my family, my world" to fulfill his destiny, he does.[105] If it is safest to leave two girls behind in a schoolhouse to facilitate his flight from rural Austria to Vienna, so be it.[106]

Fifth, Andy was lucky.

On his trip to America, he was in a state of intense excitement moderated only by his intense fatigue. He seemed to feel a need to remain alert, because if he did not, the reality of his escape might be stolen from him. Perhaps his new life would dissolve like a dream upon waking and the old life reassert itself. Which was real?

The train from Vienna may have passed through Linz, Hitler's birthplace, on its way toward Germany. "The tension didn't leave me," Andy recalled, "until we got to the first stop in Germany, the city of Passau."[107] Passau is in Bavaria, just over the Austrian border. The Danube flows through Passau back toward Vienna and thence to Budapest. But the train was taking Andy in the opposite direction, through the length of Germany toward Bremerhaven, from which he would embark on his transatlantic voyage. Always in a hurry, Andy had wanted to fly across the ocean, but even his luck had limits.

At Bremerhaven, the refugees boarded a troopship that had been decommissioned after World War II and pressed back into service for the purpose of refugee transport. It was certainly no luxury liner. This was to be the ship's final voyage. Almost everything Andy encountered was new. At one point, "The thought struck me: I'm looking at England. The momentousness of everything suddenly hit me: leaving Hungary, traveling through Germany, seeing the sea for the first time, seeing England." All this was "unthinkable just a couple of weeks ago."[108] Now it was all real.

Something Grove encountered that was not new was anti-Semitism. The transatlantic voyage was long, and few if any of the passengers had experienced the open ocean previously. People became testy, and the aggravation of gentile Hungarians sometimes expressed itself in nasty and menacing comments about their Jewish fellow voyagers. A Hungarian American minister who had gone to Europe to travel to America with the refugees preached a sermon to the effect that old enmities had to be left behind in the Old World. One Hungarian, who took pleasure in sporting a hunting knife, objected to the minister's counsel. "I hate whoever I want to hate," he said. Andy stayed away from him and the other Hungarians.[109] But he never forgot this man's hatred nor that of other like-minded refugees.

4

━━━━━━━┿━━━━━━━

Andy Grove in America

The military transport *General William G. Haan* docked at the Army Terminal in Brooklyn on January 7, 1957, with 1,715 Hungarian refugees on board in addition to András István Gróf.[1] That same day, *Time* magazine published its annual "Man of the Year" issue. The selection was the "Hungarian Freedom Fighter."[2] Andy, who would be *Time*'s "Man of the Year" in 1997, did not see this particular issue, and there is no evidence any other of the *Haan*'s passengers did either. People were struggling to get their bearings in a new environment, and the task was not an easy one.

"My first impression of the United States was not very good," Andy wrote.[3] Everything seemed odd and unappealing. What impressed him in addition to the ugliness of the buildings was the plethora of automobiles and television antennas.

The refugees learned that they were going to be taken by bus to Camp Kilmer, a onetime prisoner-of-war camp in New Jersey. They were told this was a temporary arrangement, but it did not make anyone happy. Neither did the bus trip itself. The buses traversed the painfully misnamed "Jersey Meadows," a remarkably ugly, foul-smelling, dirty swamp. Someone from the back of the bus said, "This can't be true. It's got to be Communist propaganda."[4]

At Camp Kilmer itself, things began to look up. Andy was allowed to phone his Uncle Lajos in the Bronx to let him know he had reached the

United States. Lajos was delighted to hear from him and arrived at Camp Kilmer the next day along with his twelve-year-old son, Paul. The following day, Andy left Camp Kilmer to join Lajos, Paul, and Lajos's wife, Lenke, in their apartment.

Back in Budapest when Aunt Manci had mentioned her sister Lenke and her brother-in-law Lajos, there had been no little skepticism about their reliability. As it happened, they acquitted themselves admirably in every respect. They welcomed Andy into their small apartment at 165 West 197th Street in the Bronx.[5] Paul volunteered to give Andy his bed and slept on the floor. "No amount of protestation would change this arrangement," reports Andy.[6] Soon after his arrival, Andy received a phone call from his parents. It was the first time he had spoken to them since leaving Kiraly Street. Excitement and relief abounded.

Now Andy began the process of becoming an American.

Much of what he saw was startling. Lajos and Lenke both worked, Lajos at Brooklyn College and Lenke as a saleslady in a midtown Manhattan department store. Lajos took Andy to visit her at work. When they emerged from the dingy subway station, Andy

> stopped cold. I was surrounded by skyscrapers. I stared up at them, speechless.
>
> The skyscrapers looked just like pictures of America. All of a sudden, I was gripped by the stunning realization that I truly was in America. Nothing had symbolized America more to me than skyscrapers; now I was standing on a street, craning my neck to look up at them.
>
> Which also meant that I was an incredible distance from home—or what used to be my home.[7]

Grove "was astonished by the display of wealth" he saw in New York City.[8] Clearly, this was a far cry from Budapest or even Vienna. The wealth was, by and large, privately held. Not only financial assets, but the cars, ubiquitous television sets, and fancy clothes were owned by individuals. At the same time, the public arena—be it the Jersey Meadows or the New York City subway system—was in poor shape. What Andy was seeing was what John Kenneth Galbraith described as a country divided between private riches and public squalor.[9]

The United States in the 1950s was the world's leading nation in terms of wealth, military power, and therefore global influence. Alone among the major nations its infrastructure had emerged unscathed from the cataclysm of World War II. By European or Japanese standards, it had long experienced remarkably high rates of crime and violence. On the other hand, no American city had endured an ordeal of the magnitude of Warsaw, Stalingrad, Budapest, or even London in the 1940s, not to mention Hiroshima and Nagasaki.

"Everybody ought to be happy every day," said Dwight D. Eisenhower, the victorious American general who had been overwhelmingly reelected to his second term as president on November 6, 1956. "Play hard, have fun doing it, and despise wickedness."[10] It is difficult indeed to imagine such a declaration from Janos Kadar in Budapest or Nikita Khrushchev in Moscow. On its surface, the new world in which Grove found himself was one in which life was supposed to get better for everybody each day. It was a secure world. Many of its citizens felt America's preeminence was well warranted because of its righteousness.

In the upper socioeconomic echelons, the future seemed assured. You graduated from college, signed on with a big company, and climbed the ladder of success. This was supposedly the era of the "organization man," and a book by that title became a bestseller.[11] In fact, beneath the placid exterior of the big businesses a good deal of activity was bubbling, just as the placid exterior of the nation in general would burst its bounds in the 1960s.

On the day after Christmas in 1947, a team of scientists at Bell Laboratories composed of William B. Shockley, John Bardeen, and Walter H. Brattain invented the transistor. Few more important devices have ever been created. The transistor was a milestone in the "revolution in miniature" that was to characterize the world in the second half of the twentieth century.[12] All three men could have spent their careers at Bell Labs and written their own ticket. If the 1950s were so much the world of the "gray flannel suit" as they are portrayed, that is what they would have done.[13]

Shockley, however, wanted to strike out on his own. In 1955, he resigned as director of the Transistor Physics Department at Bell Labs to become director of the Shockley Semiconductor Laboratory of Beckman Instruments in Mountain View, California.[14] This was to have momentous consequences for Grove's career in less than a decade.

President Eisenhower was advising people to play hard, but Grove was more interested in working hard. "My aim was to acquire a profession that would enable me to become self-sufficient as soon as possible, so I could support myself and set aside enough money to help my parents get out of Hungary and join me in America."[15] One did not need to be a college-educated professional to earn a living in New York City in 1957. Grove was not following in his father's footsteps, for his father was not a college-educated professional. Nor, at first, did Grove pay rent to Lenke and Lajos. To the contrary, they gave him an allowance until a grant from a Hungarian refugee service enabled him to pay them for his keep. He briefly considered forgoing higher education. "I was about to forget about college when I learned about the city colleges," he said in 1960. "Friends told me that all I needed was ability. Americans don't know how lucky they are."[16]

Grove needed money to rescue his parents. But he did not need money the instant he got out of Camp Kilmer. He had the luxury of being able to accumulate intellectual capital for the sake of future production by avoiding immediate expenditure for the necessities of life. Not all penniless immigrants were so well situated.

Andy wanted to be a chemist, and Brooklyn College seemed the best place to begin his quest because Lajos had a job there. Unfortunately, the college's chemistry program did not quite fit his needs. The next stop was Brooklyn Polytechnic Institute. The problem there was that, unlike Brooklyn College, this was a private institution that charged tuition of two thousand dollars a year. "They might as well have told me it was two million."[17]

The people at Brooklyn Polytech told Grove to try the City College of New York, which, like Brooklyn College, was a government-funded, tuition-free school. It was there that he at last enrolled as a student, majoring in chemical engineering. The pace at which all this was accomplished—from Brooklyn College, to Brooklyn Polytechnic, to City College, to the World University Service, which provided a stipend for books and for living expenses, and back and forth to and from the apartment of Lenke and Lajos—was dizzying. Andy's virtually instantaneous ability to navigate the maze of New York City's subways is quite impressive. As in Vienna, he was a young man in a hurry.

Andy dove into his courses. They were not easy, especially physics. His limited language skills did not help. "I didn't know what words like 'vertical,' 'horizontal,' and 'perpendicular' meant, let alone 'isosceles triangle.'" He had never before seen a slide rule.[18] He found it a marvel of the modern world. Ironically, he and the firm he would pilot contributed to rendering this artifact obsolete.

Grove was not superhuman, and his situation took a toll. On his first big physics test, he received an F. He was accustomed to A's, and although he knew that adapting to a whole new system of education would take time, he had not anticipated such a disastrous outcome. His instructor was kind, but his suggestion that Andy drop the course made the experience even more aggravating. Andy determined to apply himself with even greater intensity. On the next big physics test, he earned an A.[19]

From then on, things could not have gone better at CCNY. As in Hungary, Andy's intellectual acumen did not apparently excite envy. He talked his way into the dreaded Chem E128 course taught by the altogether prepossessing Professor Alois X. Schmidt. He got an A. He was in need of money because his stipend from the World University Service was running out. Schmidt offered him the position of student assistant for the chemical engineering department. The pay was $1.79 an hour for a twenty-hour workweek.[20]

Other stipends and honors followed. In 1959, for example, he won the best student paper award from the American Institute of Chemical Engineers. "As a student," Grove later recalled, "it was the first thing that I ever won."[21] He was a glutton for work. The normal number of credits was sixteen. The courses were demanding—physics, chemistry, calculus. Most students wanted to bargain their course load down. Andy wanted to bargain his up.[22] That is what his freshman curriculum advisor, Professor Morris Kolodney, found most memorable: "your eagerness, and perhaps anxiety, to get your schooling under way. You came time and again with questions about the system and with a request for an outlandish credit total—maybe 21?"[23] "I used every minute to study," Grove recalled. Now and again he "rewarded myself by buying a paper cup filled with Coca-Cola from the machine in the subway station for five cents. But I tried not to do that too often because that would be five cents I wouldn't have for my parents."[24]

With the understandable exception of courses such as "Composition," "Vocal Expression," and "Declamation," Grove excelled at everything. He graduated first in his engineering class.[25]

Andy's progress through CCNY was a triumphal procession. He made friendships among the faculty that lasted for years. He has often been honored by the institution and has remembered it in his philanthropy. In 1998, he said that "a lot of what is good in America I learned at City College." It was, for him, "the quintessential American experience."[26]

In 2005, Grove gave $26 million to CCNY's engineering school, the largest donation the school has ever received. Recalling his first encounter there, he remarked, "I asked for the admissions office, and somebody sits me down, and I tell them my story. I was wondering what shoe was going to hit me in the head this time, but they accepted me with respect, without condescension. They gave me a start, and they gave it in a classy way. It's an institution that is crucial to the workings of America, and America should be proud of it. I am."[27] At the request of CCNY president Gregory H. Williams—not as a precondition for the gift—the school is being renamed the Andrew S. Grove School of Engineering.

There were a number of things Grove did not like about his bright college years. One was New York City, which he described to Kolodney as "cold and wet and ugly." This exchange took place on a particularly miserable day. He contrasted the city with Budapest, from which he only recently had been so anxious to escape, "where water and mountains meet, where the sun always shone and the wind never drove rain into your face." Untrue, of course, but that is how it seemed that day. Kolodney suggested he try California.[28]

Another annoyance dealt with Andy's name. In his classic *How to Win Friends and Influence People,* Dale Carnegie observed that nothing is more important to a person than the sound of his own name.[29] When his professors called the roll at the beginning of each class, Andy hardly recognized the sound of his. "In Hungarian, Gróf is pronounced with a long 'o'; here, everyone read my name as if it were written 'Gruff.'"[30] He told Lenke and Lajos that he liked being Andy but "hated being Gruff." They told him to change his name.

So Andy started experimenting with new names. He settled on Grove, which was, in fact, a "serviceable rendition of how Gróf was pronounced in Hungarian." He concluded his next letter to his parents with the announcement that it was "FROM YOUR SON ANDY, WHOSE NAME WILL SOON BE GROVE." He also adopted "Stephen" as a middle name, which is the English rendition of his Hungarian middle name, István.[31]

This was the third time Andy had changed his name. In Hungary, he had migrated from Gróf to Malesevics and then back to Gróf. In America, he had moved on to Grove. Professor Schmidt would have preferred that Andy "hang on to my identity and not give in to any pressure to Americanize." This is advice that he himself had obviously followed. He was Alois Schmidt, not Al Smith. But making this change did not seem to bother Andy at all. The pronunciation of his name by Americans annoyed him. This was a solvable problem, and, like a good engineer, he solved it. He was amazed at how easy it was. He did not have to fill out any forms. He simply started calling himself Andrew S. Grove. The people at CCNY could not have been less bureaucratic and more obliging. They simply crossed out "Gróf" on his transcript and wrote "Grove" above it. They did not even bother with a typewriter. They did it by hand. This change would become formal when Andy became an American citizen.[32] "Immigration is a transforming experience," Grove observed almost four decades later. This was just one aspect of the transformation.[33]

FIGURE 1

Andrew S. Gróf becomes Andrew S. Grove at CCNY

(courtesy Professor Emeritus Morris Kolodney)

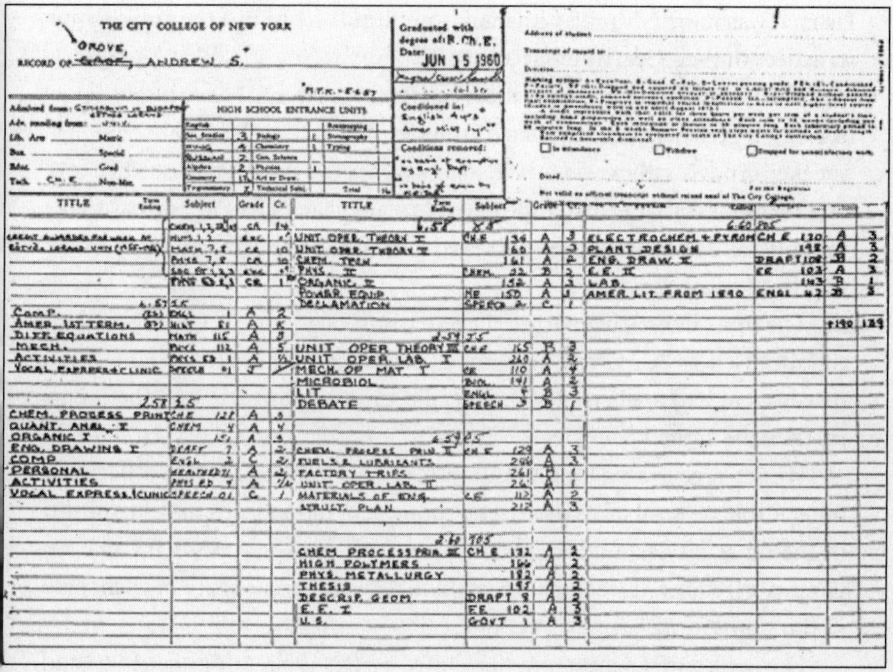

An interesting and touching sidebar to the Americanization of Andy Grove took place in 1962. Andy managed to get his parents out of Hungary that year. It was the height of the cold war, and the iron curtain was not porous, with one exception. If you were getting on in years, heading toward retirement and thus a pension, Communist authorities in Eastern Europe were receptive to getting rid of you. They wanted to keep young, potentially productive contributors to the economy. Within their respective countries, aging pensioners cost money, and if a way could be found to export those costs to the West, they went along with it. George was fifty-seven in 1962, and Maria fifty-five—not elderly, certainly not by today's standards, but old enough to get rid of if possible. George and Maria departed Hungary in 1962. Their first stop was Paris. They eventually came to Silicon Valley and lived there the rest of their lives.

While in Paris in February 1962, Andy's father wrote a highly articulate letter to the international edition of the *New York Herald Tribune,* which had a wide readership among Americans in Europe. The letter denounced Soviet anti-Semitism, made reference to his own ordeal, and sought to refute the excuse that Israel was the cause of Soviet anti-Jewish activity. To the contrary, it was merely "the way Russian Communists continue the anti-Semitic practices of their Czarist predecessors."[34]

The letter is so clearly and crisply written that it must have been heavily edited or perhaps even translated from the Hungarian by a native English speaker. Andy's father was never fully assimilated into American life, and one reason was that he had little talent for languages. His English was shaky up until his death, which must have led to an isolated life in Palo Alto, a long way from Bacsalmas.

The most interesting part of the letter is the signature. The author identifies himself as "G. Grove." In other words, Andy's father, having learned that his son had anglicized his name, did the same himself, even before he reached the United States.

We see a centuries-long tradition being exemplified in this little anecdote. A role reversal takes place. The young generation leads the old, instead of the other way around. From the day he left Hungary, Andy became his parents' caretaker. It was a relationship that generated its share of challenges in the New World.

During his first summer in the United States, 1957, Andy needed to find work, which he did by answering an advertisement for busboys at a New Hampshire resort hotel called the Maplewood. The man who interviewed him was off-putting, and Andy found himself rather anxious on the train ride up north. This was his first time away from his home away from home—that is, the apartment of Lenke and Lajos. It was his first trip out of New York City since Camp Kilmer, and it was his first encounter with a new aspect of his adopted country, Americans on vacation.

The late 1950s were the high tide of a set of resort hotels that stretched from the Catskills and Adirondacks in New York state up the Appalachian Mountain chain through the Berkshires in Massachusetts, thence to the Green Mountains in Vermont and the White Mountains in New Hampshire, finally ending at the coast of Maine. The hotels in the Catskills, such as Grossinger's, Kutcher's, and Brown's, became known as the "Borscht Belt," because they were frequented by so many nouveau riche Jewish families from Eastern Europe, whose parents and grandparents had served borscht, a kind of soup associated with peasants. Often the husband would bring his family to the resort hotel, where they would spend weeks swimming and sunning themselves while he commuted to New York City on the weekdays to run the business that paid the bills.

The commuting may not have been as common at the Maplewood, located as it was almost a full day's train ride from New York City, but the scene was probably not all that different. An army of young people was required to serve this horde of seasonal vacationers. Andy joined that army in 1957, and a bit apprehensive though he was at first, he did what he always did in new situations. He adapted quickly. He arrived around June 10 and soon thereafter started dating a girl named Audrey in a desultory fashion.

A few days later, however, he met a young woman named Eva Kastan. She was in the company of a couple of other women, and nothing in particular transpired. Not long thereafter, he saw her get out of a convertible driven by a boy. Although he was not dating young Miss Kastan at the time, he felt an instinctive pang of jealousy. He began to see her regularly. They were married on June 8, 1958.

Eva Kastan was born in Vienna in 1935. At the age of three, she and her family fled from the Nazis, who got to Austria a good deal sooner than they did to Hungary. The family emigrated to Bolivia.[35] When she was eighteen, they moved to New York City, soon settling in Elmhurst in Queens. English was thus her third language, after German, which she learned at home, and Spanish, which she learned in Bolivia. She later picked up Italian.

Fortunately for him, Andy's affection for Eva was requited. They were married in the sacristy of a Roman Catholic church in Queens. Since Eva and Andy are both of Jewish origin, this venue presents itself as in need of explanation. The Catholic wedding was in deference to one of Eva's relatives, who was a devout member of the faith.[36] Andy, in his own words, "couldn't have cared less."[37]

The couple's honeymoon consisted of a drive across the continent to the San Francisco Bay Area, taking Professor Kolodney's advice to try California. They rented a house, a cottage really, in Concord, northwest of Berkeley, for forty-five dollars a month. A small sum, but numbers like that stick in your mind when you have no money.

The original plan was that Andy would work at a Chevron oil refinery in Martinez and that Eva would work at the Sonoma State Mental Hospital. (Eva was awarded her master's degree in social work from Columbia University in June 1960.) One of the attractions of that job was that the hospital provided free housing for the staff, so they would live there and Andy would commute. This plan failed because the couple was innocent of knowledge of what it was like to get around in California. On a map, Martinez appears to be about half an hour from Sonoma. But the actual commute turned out to be three times that long, so the couple decamped to Concord. Eva gave up her job at the hospital and took a clerical position.[38]

There was not much question about making a life in California. Andy recalled driving fourteen thousand miles that first trip, three thousand out and back and another eight thousand "discovering California and that I wanted to live here."[39] "San Francisco was special. I was trying to come closer to my recollection of Budapest, and New York City was not close." He found Berkeley "gorgeous." He visited Stanford on one occasion and was distinctly unimpressed. "Actually it was pretty bad. [I]t made me appreciate how nice Berkeley is."[40]

Before he could worry himself about the relative merits of the various towns in the Bay Area, there was work to be done back in New York to finish his degree at CCNY. Grove learned a great deal there. In the chemical engineering department, his interest centered on fluid dynamics. "I got fascinated by the behavior of fluidized beds," he recalls, and he wrote an independent thesis on the topic, not a common thing for an undergraduate to do at the time.[41]

But Andy learned more than chemical engineering at CCNY. He began to get a sense of how to handle himself, of what you could do to achieve your objectives. Two of his professors had a long-term impact on "who I became [and] what I became." They were the aforementioned Alois X. Schmidt, in whose name Grove has established scholarships at CCNY, and Harvey List. "Harvey was sending me to fluid dynamics," he quipped, while "Schmidt was turning me into an asshole."

Quips aside, what Schmidt taught Grove could be summarized in one word: "Toughness." Schmidt "legitimized . . . a brusque, no-nonsense be-havior which I had no trouble adopting. Polite company frowned on those traits, but Schmidt practiced them. I thought if he can do it, I can do it, too."[42] This is vintage Grove. Schmidt taught him that it was okay to be tough in his adopted country. The message found a receptive audience.

Following the celebrated completion of his career at CCNY, the question of what Grove's next step should be asserted itself. Some of his brightest classmates were going to graduate school, but initially that was not Andy's interest. In 1957, his goal was to finish school, make some money, and bring his parents to the United States from Hungary. However, the success that he had in college, as well as the interest his studies had kindled in him, brought a change of mind. "I really liked distillation, column designs, combinations of mechanical design with fluid flow, and separation. I really warmed up to that."[43] In other words, Andy Grove discovered he was an intellectual. If he could swing it financially, with the help of summer jobs, his wife's income as a social worker, and frugality, he would go to graduate school. Once again, he would need to attend a publicly funded, tuition-free university. The University of California at Berkeley was just the spot.

Eva and Andy drove across the country again early in the summer of 1960, the third and final time they would traverse the continent by car. This time, they were moving west for keeps. They have called California home for the rest of their lives and never entertained the idea of living anywhere else. Back in December 1956, when he had just escaped to Austria, Andy, we will recall, wrote home with his characteristic effervescing urgency, "God knows, if I have a chance I will go as far as I can."[44] He was referring to his mother's idea that he go to England rather than the United States. He would have none of that. He wanted to "go as far as I can," both geographically and pro-fessionally. California was another step in that direction.

Without realizing it, the Groves were enacting one of the central themes of American history: they were westward bound. "Go west, young man, and grow up with the country," journalist Horace Greeley advised Americans 110 years before Andy Grove did just that.[45] When the Groves left New York, the "Empire State" was the nation's largest, with a population of 14,830,000. California trailed with 10,586,000, but it was growing with bewildering speed. By the end of the century, when New York's population was not quite 19 million, almost 34 million people lived in the "Golden State." Its popula-tion was greater than Canada's. Its economy was larger than France's.

The "frontier" has been one of the central metaphors of American history. The word has a meaning quite different for people in the United States than it does for Europeans. In Europe, a frontier was a border. It was a limit, an end point, a boundary that held you in, kept others out, and that you might be called upon to defend with your life. In America, frontier meant the opposite. It promised a bracing freedom from the oppressive constraints and the hierarchies of the past.[46]

Hungary is the perfect example of the frontier in the "Old World." During the course of the twentieth century it shared borders with half a dozen countries and had numerous disputes, some bloody, over where the frontier resided. To this day, both Hungarians and Hungarian Americans are not slow to express their displeasure with the frontiers created by the 1920 Treaty of Trianon.

Nineteen sixty was an election year in the United States. As Andy and Eva were driving across the country, Democratic political hopefuls were crisscrossing it in their quest for their party's nomination for the presidency. The Republican candidate was preordained to be President Eisenhower's vice president, Richard Nixon. The Democratic convention took place, appropriately enough, in California, Los Angeles to be precise. On July 13 the party nominated Senator John F. Kennedy of Massachusetts. Two days later, in his acceptance speech, Kennedy announced to the assembled throng that "the New Frontier is here."[47] It was the perfect slogan for an All-American campaign.

On May 25 of the following year, Kennedy, now president, announced to the world that part of that New Frontier was space exploration. "I believe," he told a joint session of Congress, "that this nation should commit itself to achieving the goal, before this decade is out, of landing a man on the moon and returning him safely to the earth. No single space project . . . will be more impressive to mankind, or more important for the long-range exploration of space; and none will be so difficult or expensive to accomplish."[48]

The United States had not fully appreciated that there was a "space race" during the early 1950s. But when the Soviets successfully launched Sputnik, the first man-made satellite to orbit the earth, on October 4, 1957, Americans discovered, to their utter shock and chagrin, that there was indeed such a race, and they were losing it. Sputnik has been called a "technological Pearl Harbor." Nothing since December 7, 1941, had "set off such repercussions in [American] public life."[49] These repercussions reverberated among private business as well. Some people in the electronics industry said Sputnik was the best salesman the industry ever had.[50] In line with his campaign pledge to "get America moving again," Kennedy wanted the space race to play an important role in his administration.

Bob Noyce was later to remark that the Soviets threw a piece of metal into space while the United States was the first to put a man on the moon. The space race as well as the arms race were to play key parts in the careers of both Noyce and Grove because both involved rocketry. According to one estimate, one ton of rocket fuel was required to launch a single pound of payload into space in the 1950s and 1960s.[51] Both the National Aeronautics and Space Administration (NASA) and military procurement programs were, therefore, desperate to save on weight. Both demanded high performance, and both were price-insensitive—good customers for people in the business of making electronic devices smaller and more reliable.

As Eva and Andy Grove were driving across America in June 1960, they were doubtless making use, at least for part of their trip, of the interstate highway system, an enormous public works program.[52] While certainly not without its problems, the United States was a good place to be as Andy and Eva embarked on their drive. It did indeed offer what Andy said he wanted, a career open to talent.

Before graduate school at Berkeley began, Grove took a summer job at the Stauffer Chemical Company in Richmond, California. He remembers the lab as "depressing" and "run-down." The work was boring. But Andy could find opportunities to learn even in unappealing circumstances.

> One incident stuck in my mind and had a real impact on me as a future manager. People came into work on Saturday . . . and I discovered that they sat around and bull-shitted and had an eye on the window until the most senior person's car pulled out. Minutes later, [the] next senior person pulled out; and minutes later the next one, and within ten minutes after the senior guy left the whole place was empty.[53]

Andy did not like any of his summer jobs. Boring, unsophisticated, disconnected work. Unmotivated workers. A decade later at Intel, he opposed summer jobs because he felt they would inevitably prove unsatisfactory. He certainly would not have taken full-time employment with the firms for which he worked in the summer. "It's interesting," he concluded, "to connect the dots of some of my personal experience and my strong beliefs, or obstinate beliefs, that I operated with later as a manager."[54]

It is indeed interesting to do so. Grove has thought, and continues to think, of himself as a teacher. This is a role he has played both formally at Berkeley and Stanford and less formally every day at Intel. But all his life he has also been a student—quite an apt student. From his first jobs on, he listened carefully to what people said, watched what they did, and noted the difference.

Much of what Grove learned about management came from the writings of academicians. At one point he put himself on a regimen of one management book a week. I cannot think of another executive who, in the midst of a schedule that was so packed that some would find it crushing, had the desire and the discipline to read so much about management. I have read a lot of books about management myself, and most of the few that have observations, and advice of genuine utility to a practicing businessperson are pretty dull. Nevertheless, some of these books do contain useful observations, and Grove has always been on the lookout for them. In the 1970s he read Peter F. Drucker's *The Practice of Management*.[55] He described it as Drucker's "best book . . . my favorite book," because of its description of the "ideal chief executive." This person was actually three people, in Grove's words, "an outside man, a man of thought, and a man of action."[56] He made copies of this chapter and sent one to Gordon Moore and one to Bob Noyce because he felt it so well described their troika—Noyce as Mr. Outside; Moore the Man of Thought; Grove the Man of Action.

In the interview in which Grove makes these observations, there is a brief aside, a throwaway line, that deserves our attention because it is revealing. Immediately after he describes *The Practice of Management* as Drucker's best book, Grove editorializes that Drucker published this volume "long before he writes the same thing in thousand-page versions."[57] This phrase is noteworthy because it shows Grove to be not quite capable of bestowing an unqualified compliment. There is a little dig embedded in his praise.

One often encounters this habit in conversation with Grove. He may praise something you have done, but he will often—not always, but enough that it is notable—throw a jab that tears you down. The jab hurts. Doubly so because it takes you off guard. You have, after all, just been complimented.

A man who knew Henry Ford well once observed that "in his presence no one is ever entirely at his ease."[58] This is not to compare Grove to Ford in a general sense. Ford was a monster; Grove is a charismatic man whom it is impossible to help liking. The point is to raise this issue—the sense of a man who keeps others off balance—as a theme of Grove's personality. That he shares this trait with Ford leads to the question of whether all CEOs inspire this type of feeling. Is this simply a fact of life in hierarchical business organizations? Or is it particular to Grove and, perhaps, a few others? How aware is Grove that he has the ability to make people feel uneasy? How has the ability served him in his rise to the top of Intel at a time when that position can be fairly said to have been the apex of corporate America? How has the dialectic between his remarkably effective aggression bordering on cruelty and his genuine charm and touching concern for others resolved itself as he made his way through life? How well have his person and his persona coexisted? These are issues with which we must come to terms.

But now, back to Berkeley in 1960. Not only was it a good time to be in the United States, it was a good time to be in California. And it was a great time to be a graduate student at the University of California at Berkeley, the jewel in the crown of the largest system of state universities in the nation.

What was Berkeley like for Andy? "The courses were hard," he recalls. The problem was not that they were "inherently hard" but that Andy's training did not quite prepare him for them. For a brief time he feared that he would flunk out if he didn't drop dead first. He was genuinely scared. But once again, as he always did, Andy adapted. Once he figured Berkeley out, he became a star performer. Indeed, he found it to be not as tough as CCNY.

Grove thought the students at Berkeley were not nearly as aggressive as those at City. He vividly recalls sitting in a class "utterly sunk and confused with the vector notations" he had never before seen that the professor was putting on the blackboard. He was taking notes but had no understanding of "how line two follows line one." Yet there were 80 or 90 other students in the class, watching the professor's work, taking notes, and apparently quite content with the proceedings. Andy bestirred himself to ask the professor how line two followed from line one. The professor looked at the board, realized that he had made an error, and erased it. Robotically, all the other students erased what they had just written also. Grove suddenly discovered that his classmates were not brilliant, they were simply passive.

For Grove, this was an important moment "because I discovered 'these toads don't know any more than I do. They just don't dare speak up. To hell with them.'" The contrast with CCNY was startling. "At City College, I mean, you didn't get away with anything. It was a feisty scene. You better have your act together there as an instructor, because the students will nail you." By contrast, Berkeley was much lower-key, much calmer, much less confrontational both in and out of class.[59]

Grove's recollections of Berkeley are remarkable when one realizes what was just around the corner. A mere four years later, political protests erupted there, spearheaded by a student named Mario Savio who launched the "Free Speech Movement." A student strike and mass arrests took place in the fall of 1964 on the campus, in what was to become the model for protests against American public policy at universities throughout the nation for the rest of the decade. The 1960s that people remember today were born at Berkeley in 1964, on the very campus that struck Andy Grove as so placid and passive.

Grove did encounter the turmoil on campus, but as an instructor, not as a student, and he had no patience for it. He taught chemical engineering at Berkeley after getting his PhD there. He remembers "one huge student strike" on a day that his class met.

[I]t was a big hassle driving up there for a lecture. I remember saying that if those bastards don't show up . . . I worked myself up into a fury. Finally, by the time I hit Berkeley, I had thought through that I am going to give them a pop quiz. I figured out what the pop quiz was going to be and everything. And if you are not there, you just get a zero. I went through the empty campus and people were nowhere and worked myself up into a rage. Got into the building where the class was, and I slammed the door open, and there was my whole class waiting in their seats.

Did these students show up because they knew who Andy was? Bill Lattin, later to be a top executive at Intel, remembers Andy as a strict disciplinarian. In Andy's words, "I could also put in an interpretation that engineers were always in a world of their own. They went about their education and said to hell with all this other shit."[60]

Grove may have found Berkeley "low-key" in 1963, but he himself certainly wasn't. He was at first concerned that Berkeley might not have a fluid dynamics program that was of high enough quality to satisfy him. But he learned that the university did indeed have such a program "in the form of Andy Acrivos, who was somebody to reckon with." Born in Athens, Acrivos was eight years Grove's senior. He emigrated to the United States in 1947 and became an American citizen in 1962, the same year as Grove.[61] His résumé catalogs 180 publications and 35 honors and awards.[62] In 1962 Acrivos moved from Berkeley to Stanford, where in 1988 he became an emeritus professor and also the Einstein Professor of Science and Engineering at CCNY, coincidentally tying Andy Grove's interest in fluid dynamics into a neat package.

Gravitating as he always did to strength, Grove got to know Acrivos, and the two have stayed in touch ever since. Course requirements after the first year of Berkeley's chemical engineering PhD program were vague. Grove asked Acrivos for guidance. Acrivos pointed him to a "tough, demanding" math instructor. "I took some killer courses in math," he recalls.[63]

When the time came to write a thesis, Grove had two sponsors: Acrivos and one of his colleagues. Acrivos was the experimentalist, his colleague the theorist. When I attended graduate school, the saying was that there were two kinds of doctoral dissertations: the brilliant kind and the finished kind. Grove chose to investigate a problem that was as tough as any available to doctoral students in his field at the time, the theory behind it dating back to sophisticated scholarship in the nineteenth century.[64] Another student had been working on the same problem for five years without success. But when Andy took over, things started to happen.

"I like experiments," Grove has said. "I don't like tinkering—there's a difference." His predecessor had tinkered. Andy conducted an experiment.

I went in the face of the prevailing dogma on the basis of my experiment . . . and proposed a "Gordian Knot" kind of solution that was completely against classical beliefs. I had the guts to understand . . . what the experiment was saying. I had a Ph.D adviser [a relationship Acrivos was able to maintain despite his move from Berkeley to Stanford] who, after a fair amount of due diligence, believed my data.[65]

The result? Grove coauthored four papers from that thesis, two of which appeared in the field's top journal, the *Journal of Fluid Mechanics*.[66]

But we don't need the imprimatur of refereed professional journals as evidence that Grove's thesis was first-class in every respect. Nor do we need to know that his thesis advisor, a figure of the top rank in the field, applauded it. We don't need these things because Andy's thesis won the praise of the toughest critic in the world. "This is going to sound awful," Andy told an interviewer. "It is an amazing thesis."[67] It was indeed that rara avis in the academic world, a thesis that was not only brilliant but that got finished quickly. Andy could have had an outstanding academic career, but he found the thought unappealing. He still needed money to get his parents out of Hungary, and, as he put it, "I wanted to do something useful."[68]

One of Grove's professors at Berkeley suggested he look for jobs in solid-state physics. It was a hot field. The math he had mastered under Acrivos would serve him well. Given the enthusiasm he had showed for fluid dynamics so recently, the change seems abrupt. However, Andy viewed his thesis as falling into the domain of applied physics, even though it was written in a department of chemical engineering.[69] As Acrivos himself has pointed out, one of the advantages of a firm grounding in chemical engineering is that intellectually it opens a lot of doors.[70]

When Grove hit the job market, some of the reaction that he encountered from his applications reflected skepticism because of his lack of physics training. "My background," some complained, "was not right for the job. My personality," he asserted, "you either like or hate, so that wasn't a currency either."[71] By his mid-twenties, Andy knew that people were going to react to him strongly one way or the other. And he showed no interest in modulating or cushioning the way he presented himself just because he was on the job market.

It came down to a question of Fairchild versus Bell Labs. The initial encounter with Fairchild was not encouraging. Andy contacted the personnel manager and got the brush-off because he had not yet graduated. He met this man later and described it as "dislike at first sight." Soon after that first exchange, however, he received an unsolicited letter from the head of the chemistry section at Fairchild R&D to the effect that he had discussed Andy with various faculty at Berkeley, and he appeared to fit in well with what Fairchild was doing. Bell Labs was also very interested. So was Lockheed, the big defense contractor. Others, like Texas Instruments ("I couldn't figure out why they didn't hire me") and GE ("I can't get over the fact that the guy rejected me"—both this and the previous comment coming four decades and a world of business success after the event) were not.[72]

Grove wound up mailing out dozens of applications and had a score of interviews. Despite the occasional rejection, the reaction to him was generally positive. Being wooed by the biggest and most prestigious corporations in the nation must have powerfully boosted the ego of a man who already had a not unjustifiably high opinion of himself.

Grove had been a star in school from the start, and the magnitude of his accomplishments only increased over time. He had been the center of his parents' world, and yet he had managed to separate himself from them and relocate in a foreign country successfully. The first woman with whom he fell in love had consented to be his bride. In college he was first in his class. In graduate school he took the toughest courses and excelled. He challenged authority successfully, as when he questioned what his instructor was writing on the blackboard.

Of critical importance, Grove had figured out the phenomenon of mentorship. Mentorship has two principal components. First, you as the apprentice have to select the right mentor. Second, of equal importance but usually overlooked by the apprentice, you have to make yourself worth mentoring. There is no evidence that Grove planned his mentorship strategy, and there was no one at City or Berkeley to whom he could turn for instruction on a matter like this. Often, especially in graduate school, a student can talk to his or her peers about such matters. Yet there is no indication in his memoirs or in the numerous interviews he has given that he talked with other students about who the best thesis advisor would be for him.

This is a delicate and important matter in graduate school. A great thesis advisor can be the key to a career. Why? The most valuable single piece of advice a graduate student can receive deals with the selection of a dissertation topic. There are innumerable interesting subjects to investigate in every field of graduate study from literature to physics. However, only a small subset of these are appropriate for a thesis.

Your dissertation topic must be manageable. It cannot be a life's work. It has to have not only a beginning and a middle but also an end, and the end must be within reach in a reasonable period of time.

In addition to all this, a great thesis advisor is likely to have a reputation at other institutions and in the outside world. His or her support after you have earned your degree will mean far more than that of an advisor of whom no one has ever heard because he or she has never done any important work.

Scholars who fit the description of the ideal thesis advisor are likely to be in a position to write their own ticket. They will be able to select among the students who seek their tutelage. They may decide to limit the number of students they will mentor. University administrators are unlikely to object because, due to the eminence of the scholar in question, there is the implicit threat that he or she may leave the university. A scholar who has built a powerful reputation will have no trouble finding a position at a competing institution.

Andy handled himself masterfully in the face of these challenges. First, he correctly identified in Acrivos a thesis advisor who would measure up well against the criteria enumerated above. Second, he persuaded Acrivos that he was worth mentoring. Third, he took all the tough courses Acrivos suggested. Thus, when the time came, Acrivos believed that Andy was the right choice for a thesis that was high-risk (it had defeated another student), but high-reward if completed successfully. Finally, Andy did succeed in completing it.

Thus Acrivos and Grove reaped the rewards of a successful mentoring relationship. The pair coauthored four articles that were derived from the thesis, thus advancing Acrivos's own career. For the rest of his life, he has been able to point to Grove as a student of his, which can only have added luster to his already outstanding record.

What did Grove get out of the relationship? For starters, he found a smart man who would push him to be his best. He got a thesis topic that proved ideal. It was Acrivos who steered him to it and Acrivos who was willing to bet that Andy could write a thesis others could not. When Andy started looking for work, Acrivos was a man whose words had weight. Though "normally conservative" in his evaluations, he labeled Andy a top student. He was willing to "depart from past practice" and bestow upon Andy "the strongest possible recommendation." Grove was "a truly outstanding technical person."[73] Only years later did Grove learn what a strong letter Acrivos had written. "When I first heard of that letter," he said, "I was stunned. I was kind of like, 'I didn't know you loved me.'"[74] Even more important than these considerations, Andy had learned to "manage up." He had learned how to make himself valuable to someone who was above him in an organization.

At any rate, in 1963 Andy Grove was facing a big decision. Which of the appealing offers that he had received would he accept? It came down to a choice between Bell Labs and Fairchild.

Bell Labs was the place to be in the early 1960s in the world of solid-state physics or chemistry. The company had a powerful interest in Andy. "Bell

Labs didn't write me letters. Bell Labs sent people to my lab—senior people visiting me in my lab." Their recruiter was in "selling mode." Money a problem? We'll raise your pay. Not sure whether you're more interested in chemistry or electronics? We'll figure out a way for you to do both.

On the Fairchild side of the ledger, there was Gordon Moore. Bell's recruiter was a nice guy, but he "was no Gordon Moore." "Gordon Moore asked me about my thesis, all on his own, and listened, and got it!" Grove liked Moore immediately. "He's really a smart guy—very personable, no airs. Gordon was a *big* selling factor, helping me see what I wanted to be."

It was a close call. In the last analysis, geography appears to have been the most important factor in Grove's decision of where to take his first job. "I loved it here. I didn't quite love it in Palo Alto," which Grove found a "sleepy backwater" compared to Berkeley. But Bell Labs was located in Morristown, New Jersey, a suburb of New York. In the early 1960s, Morristown was as much a sleepy backwater as Palo Alto. Moreover, it was in the New York metropolitan area, and Grove simply did not like New York at all. So Fairchild it was, and if things did not work out there, "I really had a wonderful alternative" at Bell Labs. "But were it not for the geography and were it not for Gordon [Moore], I might have gone to Bell Labs."[75]

Gordon Earle Moore, who was to become the most important man in Andy Grove's professional life, was born on January 3, 1929, in San Francisco, the closest big city with modern medical facilities to his home in Pescadero, California, an isolated little town on the coast between Santa Cruz and San Francisco. Moore has joked that Pescadero must be the only town in California in which population has declined over the past half century. Moore is one of the few outstanding successes of Silicon Valley who was born in California.

Grove described Moore as a "smart guy with no airs," and there are few people who would disagree with that characterization. Moore is what is known as a WYSIWYG—"What You See Is What You Get." Ask him a question and he'll tell you what he thinks. His answer will be brief and to the point. He does not waste words. He does not boast, although his record of achievement provides a great deal to boast about. He appears to be, that is to say, simply a regular person. That alone makes him stand out in California.

Egomania is not absent from Silicon Valley, but no one would use this word to describe Moore, who made more money from Intel than anyone else and who must be one of the few billionaires who never bought a tailored shirt. He was a small-town boy and at first a rather indifferent student. His father moved the family to Redwood City, which is located on the San Francisco peninsula between Santa Clara and San Francisco, where he became deputy sheriff. Only in his senior year at Sequoia High School did Moore begin to take his schoolwork more seriously than athletics. "I was a lazy student until my last year," he has said.[76]

When he did get interested in his schoolwork, this seemingly average boy turned out to be, as Grove described him, a "smart guy." He began college at San Jose State University but transferred to Berkeley his junior year, where he received a BS in chemistry in 1950. He was the first member of his family to earn a college degree. The next step was to the California Institute of Technology, where he earned a PhD in chemistry and physics in 1954. Upon his graduation, Moore and his family moved east so he could pursue a postdoctoral fellowship at Johns Hopkins University in Baltimore. But Moore found university life not to his liking. According to one source he too, like Grove, wanted his "work to result in something practical and useful."[77]

While he was away in Baltimore, a new opportunity to do just that developed back in Palo Alto. William Bradford Shockley, one of the three inventors of the transistor, had decided to start a company. The founding document was signed on September 3, 1955. Shockley went off on a search for the "hot minds" who would work for him.[78] One of those minds belonged to Moore, who was attracted by the prospect of "actually making a product and selling it."[79]

By the middle of 1956, there were roughly twenty people working at Shockley Semiconductor, most of them not yet thirty years of age.[80] Among these were some very "hot minds" indeed. For them the attraction was Shockley, who perhaps received a disproportionate share of the credit for the invention of the transistor. Somehow he managed to present himself to the world as an inspired lone-wolf genius, after the fashion of great inventors from times past like Edison, even though the transistor was a team effort.[81] Shockley was the magnet who drew remarkable talent to the Valley to work with silicon.

Shockley made many claims about his own genius. Ironically, one claim he did not make was being the "father of Silicon Valley." That label is sometimes attached jointly to William Hewlett and David Packard, who founded Hewlett-Packard in 1938 in a small garage at 367 Addison Avenue in Palo Alto. In 1989, the California Landmarks Commission designated that garage as the "birthplace of Silicon Valley."[82] Important to the Valley as HP became, the firm was an instrument maker in the 1950s, not working with silicon.

Robert Noyce has also often been called Silicon Valley's father. The claim in this case rests on the fact that he coinvented the integrated circuit in 1958 or 1959, depending upon how, precisely, one defines the word "invent." The other coinventor was Jack Kilby, working far away at Texas Instruments. The principal difference between Noyce's and Kilby's integrated circuits was that Noyce used a silicon substrate and Kilby used germanium. Silicon proved easier to work with and became the standard. Otherwise, the world would be talking about "Germanium Valley." The point is that it was the allure of working for Shockley that drew so many young, bright, technically gifted engineers and scientists to what as late as 1963 Andy Grove could still call the "sleepy backwater" of Palo Alto.

If Noyce is important in the story of the Valley and of Grove—and he is—that fact adds to Shockley's importance because Shockley brought Noyce to Palo Alto after attending a meeting of the American Physical Society in 1955, at which Noyce presented a paper on "base widening punch-through." Noyce was working in Philadelphia for Philco at the time. In January of the following year, Shockley phoned him and invited him to join his new company. Noyce did not hesitate. "[G]etting that job," he later said, "meant you would definitely be playing in the big leagues."[83]

Noyce met Moore at Shockley Semiconductor in 1956. Also attracted to the new company were physicists Jean Hoerni (pronounced "Ernie") and Jay Last, metallurgist Sheldon Roberts, electrical engineer Victor Grinich, mechanical engineer Julius Blank, and industrial engineer Eugene Kleiner.[84] All were remarkably talented. One would think that a firm studded with such stars would have a bright future. However, this did not prove to be the case. Like so many Silicon Valley entrepreneurs who followed him, Shockley could assemble talented people but couldn't manage them.

At first things went well.[85] On November 1, 1956, everyone at the company got a tremendous lift when they learned that Shockley had been awarded the Nobel Prize in Physics, along with Bardeen and Brattain, for the invention of the transistor. Shockley came to the lab that morning, closed up shop, and took everyone out for a champagne breakfast at Dinah's Shack on El Camino Real in Palo Alto. A photograph was taken of the event. Shockley sat at the head of the table being toasted by his employees/acolytes. Dress was informal: "This was the West, not the East. Working in a converted apricot barn (Shockley Semiconductor's headquarters) and decamping to a local greasy spoon to celebrate a Nobel Prize—this was the new way. High on achievement; low on formality and display."[86]

Beneath the gaiety, unfortunately, there was real trouble brewing at Shockley Semiconductor. It is easy to trace all the problems directly to Shockley himself. He was egomaniacal. He was very smart but would use his intelligence mercilessly as a weapon to "reduce them [people who made mistakes] almost to tears." Out of the blue, he would pepper people with pointless questions that were supposedly concocted to test intelligence but were really designed to make people squirm.

Here is an example that became well-known. One hundred and twenty-seven players enter a singles tennis tournament. Since 127 is an odd number, one contestant draws a bye on the first round. How many matches have to be played to determine the winner? The answer is 126.[87] But a bigger question is: why try to intimidate young people with such pointless exercises?

Shockley had foolish theories about how to spot and nurture intellectual capabilities. These theories would later veer toward racism. He and his company produced a lot of tension but not one unit of a marketable product. The financier Arthur Rock dismissed him as being simply impossible to deal with in the context of business.[88] As 1956 turned into 1957, a number of the most able of Shockley's employees were coming to the same conclusion.

Hoerni, Last, Roberts, Grinich, Kleiner, Blank, and Moore decided as a group that whatever dreams they had would not come true under the leadership of Shockley. There remained the question of what Noyce would do. He alone had worked out a reasonable relationship with Shockley. The seven dissidents needed Noyce. They wanted their next step to be together, as a group. Noyce seemed to have a certain something special that would make it possible for them to stay together in a company of their own.

This may have been the most difficult decision that Noyce, a man who hated interpersonal conflict so much that he fled from it more than once, had to face. He did not want to be disloyal to Shockley. Yet he knew that his seven friends were right in their assessment. At length, he agreed to leave.

But somehow, when the time came to tell Shockley face-to-face that the heart of his firm was leaving to become the heart of a brand-new company, to be called Fairchild Semiconductor, the task of bearing the bad news fell not to Noyce but to Moore, who for the only time in his life could be called "hapless" for having to do so. "I remember him [Shockley] leaving the building shortly after that with his head hanging down and kind of a beat look on his face, and I just felt terrible about it."[89] As historian Leslie Berlin has pointed out, a better label for Shockley than the "father" was the "Moses" of Silicon Valley, a title conferred by Shockley's longtime friend, physicist Frederick Seitz. He brought everyone there, but never enjoyed its fruits. His failure in business was permanent.[90]

Shockley labeled the defectors from his company the "traitorous eight." This is an intriguing phrase for a couple of reasons. One is that it has stuck. People in Silicon Valley today still know the phrase even if they may not know why, perhaps because it is sonorous. Another possible reason is that this particular phrase does not carry with it a pejorative connotation. Why not? One would think it would. After all, being a traitor is not admirable.

Let us hazard speculation on this point. Shockley himself was in no position to cast this particular aspersion. After all, he had abandoned Bell Labs because he wanted to make a lot of money.

Perhaps even more important, however, there was something almost poetically daring about numbering oneself among the "traitorous eight." Whom had they committed treason against? A man who was standing between them and the fulfillment of their destiny. Such a man gave others permission to pursue their own interest rather than to submerge it in the service of a business organization. Their action was celebrated more than condemned because, in this putative era of the "organization man," they were putting people first.

Dozens of semiconductor firms traced their origins back to that apricot barn that housed Shockley Semiconductor. So although he disappeared from the business scene, Shockley's heritage lived on.[91] Of this multitude of firms that his spawned, the highest of the high fliers was Fairchild.

Fairchild Semiconductor was founded in October 1957. Within two years, Jean Hoerni invented the planar process for semiconductor manufacturing. This vital innovation will be discussed below. Suffice it to say for now that when Les Vadasz began to appreciate what the Internet might mean in the 1990s, he said to Andy Grove, "This might turn out to be as big as the planar process."[92] Next came Noyce's integrated circuit. Then, on September 24, 1959, Fairchild Camera and Instrument back in Syosset on Long Island exercised its option to purchase all the stock of Fairchild Semiconductor.

The "traitorous eight" had been asked to invest $500 each in Fairchild Semiconductor when it was founded in 1957. Less than two years later, that

$500 had turned into $250,000, more than $1.5 million inflation-adjusted for the year 2000. No wonder so many new semiconductor firms were being founded. The "new alchemists"[93] were turning the most common of elements—silicon, nothing but sand—into pure gold.

Thus when Andy Grove met Gordon Moore in 1963, he was face-to-face with a thirty-four-year-old man who had amassed a sizable estate, although it was as nothing compared to the billions he would make from Intel. He was also facing a top technologist who was essentially the partner of Bob Noyce, who at thirty-six years of age was already a legend.

Grove was an immediate success at Fairchild. His own explanation is twofold. First, he had the technical training and ability that his job demanded. He was "[comfortable] with differential equations," and this allowed him to come up with "typical closed-form mathematical solutions" that were clear and useful.[94]

Here is Grove's description of his first week at Fairchild:

When I arrived at Fairchild on a Monday morning, my supervisor, who was an electrical engineer, gave me a problem. . . . It actually wasn't that complicated, but . . . [it did require] taking a physical problem and turning it into differential equation[s], solving the differential equations, doing a family of curves, [and] looking at a particular parameter.[95]

Somewhere during the course of his education, Grove had learned computer programming. This knowledge stood him in good stead. He analyzed data on a batch processing computer service that allowed him to create the "representation of that closed-form solution." "[V]ery few people," said Grove, "knew how to program in Fortran in 1963 at a Silicon Valley commercial company." Not that big a deal, perhaps, but Grove had the right skills at the right moment.[96]

There is a striking similarity in this incident to the career of another "Andy," Andrew Carnegie. Like Grove, Carnegie was an immigrant. His first job in the United States was in a steam-driven cotton textile mill in Pittsburgh in 1848. His next job was as a messenger boy in a telegraph office. He was so efficient that he was spotted by a man named Thomas A. Scott, who was an executive of the most important corporation in the United States at the time, the Pennsylvania Railroad.

Tom Scott hired Carnegie, to whom he soon began to refer as "my Andy," to be a messenger at the telegraph office of the Pennsylvania Railroad in Pittsburgh. One day, a major accident took place on the line. Scott was out of the office, and Carnegie could not find him. The whole railroad had come to a halt.

What could Carnegie do? It turned out that he could do a great deal. Like his latter-day namesake, Andy Grove, who had picked up Fortran programming on the side unassigned, Carnegie had not served merely as a messenger boy in that telegraph office. He had learned Morse code. No one had assigned him the task of learning it, and other telegraph messenger boys in Pittsburgh did not do so. Carnegie became good at it. He is said to have been the third person in the country who could "read" Morse code by ear, without having to transcribe rolls of dots and dashes like everyone else.

So what could Carnegie do when there was a train wreck and no one could find Scott? Here is the answer. "Finally," he tells us in his autobiography, "I could not resist the temptation to plunge in, take the responsibility, give 'train orders,' and set matters going." That is what he did—tapping out order after order and signing them with his boss's initials, "T.A.S.," rather than with his own. This was the telegraph, not the telephone. No recipient of one of those messages could know who was really sending them.

Was this risky? "I knew it was dismissal, disgrace, perhaps criminal punishment for me if I erred," Carnegie later wrote. When Scott was located, he hurried back to the telegraph office, and Carnegie explained the whole situation to him in detail. Scott was astonished. His teenage telegraph messenger had run the Pennsylvania Railroad in his absence. Carnegie himself was concerned about how his boss would react. Scott "looked in my face for a second. I scarcely dared look in his." He later learned that Scott was bragging around town about the accomplishments of "that little white-haired Scotch devil of mine." Thereafter, observed Carnegie, "it was very seldom that Mr. Scott gave a train order."[97]

Andy Grove was lucky as well as smart. "How lucky can you get?" Grove later asked of his debut at Fairchild. You show up for work on Monday, you are assigned a problem you are uniquely qualified to solve, and you devise a nonobvious solution by Friday.

Was this mere luck? Was it mere luck that Carnegie had the chance just described? Yes and no. Carnegie had prepared himself for a once-in-a-lifetime opportunity by learning Morse code and also by studying how the Pennsylvania Railroad operated. No one assigned these tasks to him, and his peers did not emulate his example.

In the same way, Grove had, by seeking challenges during his training and by doing more than he had to—specifically by learning how to program in Fortran—put himself on the right corner when luck drove by. More than that, he had, with the help of Andreas Acrivos, learned the importance of challenging conventional wisdom. Grove internalized what Acrivos taught—doing under his tutelage what he was now doing at Fairchild. "I had," he has explained, "a protector against classical dogma in Andy Acrivos." Would Grove have had the "intellectual courage" to present his ideas as forcefully as he did at Fairchild without the experience with Acrivos? "I don't know," he said.[98]

Has Grove been lucky? Yes. But as an explanation for his success, luck, though important, is hardly sufficient. When asked about Grove and luck, Michael Dell said, "He's smart; he's shrewd. No such thing as 'lucky' a thousand times in a row."[99] Grove himself coined the phrase "earned luck."[100] That is a more useful way to think about his business career.

During the summer of 1963, Grove pushed his work forward. It was strictly technical, engineering work. He was not involved in management at all. He knew nothing about it and showed no interest in it.

Through his technical work, however, he was exhibiting traits that would mark him as a manager. He wanted to be an impact player. He took great pleasure in challenging the conventional wisdom and proving himself right despite the odds. Everyone was talking about surface states, but Grove's data told him that the key to a mystery he and his colleagues were confronting was not surface states but a surface charge. "Everyone talks about surface states. Everybody talks about [the nineteenth-century scholar] Kirchoff. [But] look at the data! It says there's the surface charge."[101]

Grove presented his first paper late in the summer of 1963. "A fixed charge instead of surface states." This "sounds like a minor difference [but] it isn't." His paper was not well received. "I got nailed by all these experts who would sooner burn witches or equally burn me at the stake for being a heretic."

In high school, Grove had made himself the center of attention by writing stories like "Despair" or by his nitroglycerin experiment in a class full of girls a year behind him. In those instances, he was greeted by congratulations and slaps on the back. Grove's first experience at Fairchild also put him at the center of attention, but the difference this time was that his audience attacked him for challenging accepted wisdom.

Yet these episodes share something in common. Grove is the star of the show. He is doing the unexpected. He is fearless and conducts himself with gusto. It is his lavish enthusiasm that links these stories. It is those magic moments when he demonstrates the unexpected.

We have observed that there were two explanations for Grove's early success at Fairchild. One was his technical ability and also a cast of mind that permitted him to look at data, to stare facts directly in the face, and to prohibit theory from refracting and distorting the data before it reached him. Andy Grove never used theory as a crutch. He had such intellectual self-confidence that he believed he was as smart as the theorists who preceded him. Why rely on them when he could rely on himself? A theme of his life has been challenging assumptions, including his own.[102]

The second key to his early success was a skill he had learned long ago: "managing up." He had done this at CCNY and Berkeley. Now it was time to manage up at Fairchild. The man who was "up" and who needed to be "managed" was Gordon Moore.

Grove liked and respected Moore from the outset, and this is very important. It meant that managing Moore was almost a pleasure, rather than a task that demanded that he submerge his self-respect and hide his true feelings. For his part, Moore liked the way Grove worked right away.

Just as Thomas Scott had "my Andy," Moore had a "my Andy" of his own. The backgrounds and personalities of Moore and Grove could hardly have been more different. Grove was the extrovert, a combative man who was unabashedly ambitious. As he matured, these traits would transform themselves into a controlled flamboyance, if that is not an oxymoron.

Moore—just your average, "aw shucks," down-to-earth billionaire—was different from Grove in almost every way. Moore avoided conflict when possible, but he faced it when he had to. He was in no sense a coward, and, indeed, at times he has been bold. His statement of what came to be known as Moore's law in 1965 was daring and has exercised a fundamental influence on the industry.[103]

Nevertheless, Moore is essentially a quiet man. His first impulse is to listen and evaluate and only then to speak. Of the triumvirate that created Intel (Noyce, Moore, and Grove), Moore was the least interested in the limelight. In interviews, he responds frankly and accurately, but he rarely elaborates.[104] He does not tell you more than you ask. He seems to live in a "yes, no, or maybe" world. He is a true technologist. It is hard to believe that he would willingly be drawn from this great love to management.

I once asked Moore why he hired Grove. The two men were and are different in general and in every particular. Moore is a tall man, which somehow makes his relative silence the more surprising. Grove is slim and of average height. He was still hard of hearing in 1963 and wore prominent hearing aids. Not until further operations in the 1970s and 1980s would his hearing approach normal. Moore wears a hearing aid now, but did not in the 1960s. Grove wore thick glasses with thick frames.

Grove was from Hungary; Moore was a native Californian. Grove was blunt; Moore was careful and considered. Grove used foul language; Moore, raised in a churchgoing home, did not. Grove was of Jewish origin; Moore was Protestant. Grove sometimes raised his voice and, interestingly, has been perceived over the years as shouting more often than he actually has because his words have often been painful to hear. Sometimes this was purposeful. Sometimes it was the result of his temper and temperament. No one would ever have said such things of Moore.

It is noteworthy that the feeling one experiences in the presence of Moore and Grove is quite different. Grove once said of Moore that "he was kind of Uncle Gordon."[105] That avuncular relationship does seem an accurate description. Moore and Grove seem to come not merely from different cultures, but also from different generations. One is surprised when one remembers that Moore is only seven years and nine months older than Grove.

When I asked Moore why the differences between him and Grove exercised no influence on his decision to hire Grove, he leaned back in his chair, clasped his hands behind his head, smiled, and declared, "It didn't matter." What did matter was that Grove was obviously savvy from a technological point of view. For the sake of due diligence, Moore wrote Acrivos about his potential new employee. Acrivos responded with a handwritten note in red ink across the typescript of Moore's letter that Grove was exceptionally able and Moore would be lucky to get him.[106]

That was all that mattered. Grove was a rare talent. Cultural differences did not count in the "republic of technology" that was emerging in Silicon Valley.[107]

In fact, the differences between Moore and Grove worked to their mutual advantage in what was to become one of the most fecund business partnerships of modern times. All his life, Grove has been looking for something solid, for the "real thing." Moore filled that role. In a melodramatic world, he was calm. He liked doing what he liked to do, and he hated doing what he did not like to do—hated it so much that he simply did not do it. Gordon Moore did not put himself forward. His undeniable talent—"genius" might not be too strong a word—is what put him forward.

At Fairchild, Moore was the manager of engineering from 1957 to 1959 and the director of research and development from 1959 until he left to found Intel with Noyce in 1968. But apparently, despite his titles, Moore did not do much "managing" or "directing." There was, for example, a serious problem with the head of the physics department, where Grove was assigned, at Fairchild in the summer of 1963. His name was Tom Sah. "I was amazed," Grove recalled, "in reading Gordon's description of the problem of Tom Sah, because I was very angry and my colleagues were very angry. . . . Gordon was Tom Sah's boss, and Gordon always looked like he never heard us complaining. . . . He just chose to detach himself from it [and] never did anything about it." Sah eventually quit.[108]

This was merely a taste of what was to come. If you were going to manage up and Moore was the man who was up, you were going to have to learn how to get the most out of his strengths—and there was a great deal to get—and how to deal with the fact that there were aspects of business management that he simply ignored. "[T]here was absolutely no discipline," observed Grove of the Device Development Lab. "There was no internal discipline to the place; and there was no external discipline or expectations that were put on the lab and . . . on the manufacturing organization to support the lab."[109] Too bad. Deal with it.

There was not only the issue of managing one's way through an unmanaged organization, but also the question of how to get the best Gordon had to give. Grove has offered the following as the "secret of my success" in his early years in the semiconductor industry: "recognizing Gordon's facial reactions better than anybody else." It is not clear the extent to which this remark is tongue-in-cheek.

Here is what he meant: "I would be [running] a meeting and people would be bashing each other's heads and all of that . . . I look at Gordon . . . something is wrong. So I'd yell, 'Stop! Gordon, what's bothering you? . . . Shut up! Gordon, tell us whatever you wanted to tell us. . . .' [S]omebody had to stop the traffic."

When the traffic was stopped and Gordon spoke, what he had to contribute was usually "the right answer . . . the right comment, the right concern." Grove was the traffic cop, making way for "access to Gordon's insight." Moore understood this and appreciated it. He once said to "his Andy," "You know me better than my wife [or at least] as well as."[110]

How does one find the right mentor? There is no more important question for an ambitious person in a hierarchical organization to answer. Precisely how do you go about making yourself worth being mentored? This Grove did with regard to Moore in two ways. First, he quickly learned that it was pointless to confront Moore with a certain set of managerial problems. They would make him uncomfortable, and he would simply ignore them. Worse, he might resent the person who was asking him to face them. Second, he spotted in Moore someone whose technical ability was second to none but who at times had to have his insight coaxed out of him. Grove helped Moore be his best.

A noteworthy aspect of the relationship between the two men was that they occupied different professional and emotional spaces. They were not competitive, which perhaps is one reason why they seem to be separated by a generation. Their talents complemented each other perfectly. When one succeeded, the other did too. Lock and key.

"Gordon was then, and continues to be, a technical leader," Grove has concluded. "He is either constitutionally unable or simply unwilling to do what a manager has to do." If you sought his advice, you would receive it, and it was usually worth seeking. "But would he interfere in some conflict between X and Y and Z? Not on your life."[111]

When it came to management, the same could be said of Moore's boss— really his nominal boss because they were more like partners than superior and subordinate—Robert Norton Noyce. In the summer of 1963, Noyce was the golden boy of Silicon Valley.

Noyce was born in Burlington, Iowa, on December 12, 1927, so he was about two years older than Moore and nine years older than Grove. He was the third of four sons of Ralph and Harriet Noyce. Noyce's father was a Congregational minister, as were both his grandfathers. In the first thirteen years of his life, the family lived in six different towns, widely dispersed but all in Iowa, as his father moved from tending one flock of parishioners to the next. One of Noyce's earliest memories was of the Great Depression. Although the family was not impoverished, there were times that Ralph Noyce was paid in kind rather than in cash.

The last of the six towns in which Noyce lived during those first thirteen years was Grinnell. This was the home of the Iowa Conference of Congregational Churches, and Ralph Noyce became the "associate superintendent" of one of the least hierarchical of religious denominations. Grinnell was also the home of Grinnell College, among the gems of higher education in the United States. Founded in 1846, Grinnell has achieved an enviable and deserved reputation as a first-class college that just happened to grow in the midst of the vastness of the American prairie. Noyce always loved both the college and the town. One Silicon Valley journalist has described Grinnell as "Noyce's first—and perhaps only—real home."[112]

Noyce was resourceful, talented, and adventurous. He had a strong dose of playfulness, and he liked to "tinker." He did not see his tinkering as anything noteworthy. "It was just sort of the way life was. Dad always managed to have some sort of workshop in the basement. And it was the usual rural environment of harvesting in the summer and canning in the winter."[113]

Years later, the writer Tom Wolfe would see more in this activity than a way to pass the time. In 1983, Wolfe published a lengthy article in *Esquire* magazine entitled "The Tinkerings of Robert Noyce: How the Sun Rose on The Silicon Valley."[114] This article went a long way toward glamorizing Noyce, the man with the "halo effect" and the "Gary Cooper smile," as well as Silicon Valley itself. Note the use of the article "the" in Wolfe's subtitle. As late as 1983, the development of a unique subculture of technology on the peninsula ("peninsula" is a more accurate description than the commonly used "valley" for Silicon Valley) south of San Francisco was still not that well-known to the general readership of a magazine like *Esquire*. It needed to be specified. No one refers to Silicon Valley that way now.

As with Moore but unlike Grove, it was only toward the end of high school that Noyce "began to feel that maybe I had [a] little bit more than average ability."[115] While in high school, he had already enrolled in courses at Grinnell.

When Noyce graduated from high school, his family once again decided to move. He, however, stayed behind to study at Grinnell College. By chance, his physics professor, Grant O. Gale, for whom he had served as a babysitter, was one of the best-informed men in the world on the development of the transistor. A classmate of Gale's at the University of Wisconsin had been none other than John Bardeen, who, along with Shockley and Brattain, invented the device. Gale had kept up with Bardeen and his work, and he obtained two transistors in 1948, while Noyce was an undergraduate. Noyce worked with Gale on the transistor and was thus among the first to encounter its limitless potential.

It has been observed that one test of the importance of an invention is the variety of uses to which it can be put. A general-purpose device such as the steam engine, for example, could pump water from coal mines or power locomotives. Likewise, the transistor could touch so many appliances of daily life that it constituted "not simply a new sort of amplifier, but the harbinger of an entirely new sort of electronics with the capacity not just to influence an industry or a scientific discipline, but to change a culture."[116]

For Noyce the next stop after graduating Phi Beta Kappa from Grinnell was the Massachusetts Institute of Technology, where, it turned out, no one knew as much as Gale did about transistors. He wrote a thesis that was as close to the field as he could get.[117] He excelled at MIT, as he had at Grinnell. As had been true all his life, he indulged in a lot of extracurricular activities. He joined a group that sang madrigals. He acted in college theater.

Like Grove a number of years later, Noyce was offered a position at Bell Labs. Like Grove, he turned it down, as he did GE and RCA, in favor of "lowly Philco."[118] Journalist Michael Malone said that Noyce preferred being a big fish in a small pond. This enabled him "to wear many hats, including those of both scientist and businessman, and be able to hop around to different projects."[119]

Noyce enjoyed hopping around. "I don't run large organizations well," he once said. "I don't have the discipline to do that, have the follow through."[120] It is not surprising that he became a pilot, and as soon as he could afford his own airplane he bought one. There was more than just a touch of mania to this man.

Noyce was spirited out to Palo Alto by Shockley, and he was spirited into Fairchild when the seven defectors convinced him to become the traitorous eighth. The seven defectors well knew that actually to start a new company required financing. To obtain the requisite funds, they needed someone capable both of understanding the new technology and of showing an appealing face to the often unforgiving world of the money men. Noyce was ideal. It was he who would serve as "Fairchild's public face."[121]

The touch of magic attaching to Noyce has often been remarked upon. There was a certain flair that drew attention to him and inspired confidence.

He was intensely competitive and had to lead. The other seven were in the market for a leader. The fit was perfect. Almost everyone whom Noyce encountered fell under the spell he so effortlessly cast. Almost everyone.

Andy Grove's first encounter with Bob Noyce took place seven days after he arrived at Fairchild. Noyce, who at the time was vice president and general manager of Fairchild Semiconductor,[122] had for some unknown reason read the report that Grove had written by the previous Friday on the problem he felt himself so fortunate to have been assigned his first day on the job. Noyce wrote Grove a note to the effect that "I just read your report on MOS [metal oxide semiconductor] capacitors—very nice work." It was signed simply, "Bob."[123] "I thought I'd died and gone to heaven," said Grove. He was really startled that the general manager of the company, Moore's boss in effect, read technical reports over weekends.[124]

When it came to managerial abilities, however, Grove found Noyce sorely deficient. He was particularly incensed at Noyce's willful ignorance of the havoc that a man named Wilson, one of two division managers at Fairchild, was wreaking. He reported directly to Noyce. According to Grove, he was an alcoholic. "The reason Fairchild disintegrated," Grove has said,

> was because neither Bob nor Gordon was capable of removing a Wilson, who was staggering in at eleven o'clock for a nine o'clock meeting breathing alcohol. I mean, it wasn't subtle. Nor is it hearsay. I cooled my heels in Wilson's office for two hours before he showed up, with a huge technical problem involving recall of integrated circuits on a major scale.[125]

"I had witnessed," Grove goes on,

> Bob Noyce being absolutely inactive and paralyzed as the Wilson/ Fairchild [situation] was disintegrating. Because I subbed for Gordon at Noyce's staff meetings a number of times and it was awful. So this was a long time from that one-line compliment. I had very little appreciation for Bob.[126]

Noyce was not a good manager. Everyone, including him, knew it. But Moore was not a good manager either, in Grove's view. Nevertheless, Grove could forgive "Uncle Gordon" but not Noyce. What explains this state of affairs?

The relationship of Grove to the two men becomes even more mysterious when one learns that he developed a casual social friendship with Noyce, but not with Moore. Noyce taught Grove to ski. "My wife and I got along with his first wife, and our kids are similar ages."[127] As for Gordon and his wife, Betty, Grove says, "We never socialized with them." In 2004, after working closely with Moore for over four decades, Grove said of the Moores that "I actually have no idea what their social life is. I don't know anyone who socialized with them."[128]

Grove's feelings toward Noyce are complicated, and they have changed over the years. It is true that when Moore told Grove that Noyce was going to join him in founding Intel in 1968, Grove groaned and clearly expressed his displeasure. Moore had to reassure Grove that Noyce "was better than you think," or words to that effect. It says a lot that after half a decade of working for Noyce, Moore had to offer Grove this kind of observation. Grove's editorial reaction to Moore's comment—"blah, blah, blah"—made it clear that, in Grove's words, "my reaction to Bob's presence was not very good."[129] Both at Fairchild and at Intel, "I was not a Bob Noyce fan."[130]

Why not? Everybody else was. People came from far and wide to spend half an hour with him. Japanese visitors would not wash their hands for a couple of days after shaking hands with Noyce. He was good enough for Moore. And one of Noyce's greatest fans was another icon of the Valley, Steve Jobs. Noyce, who liked to fly his own plane, once almost crashed with Jobs aboard, but they both took it in stride. When Jobs learned of Noyce's sudden death from a heart attack on June 3, 1990, the news was little short of devastating. "I almost lost it," Jobs said in something of a reverie.[131]

Jobs was saddened that Noyce died as young as he was (he was sixty-two) but glad he died the way he did. Suddenly. Of a heart attack with no hint of its approach. Noyce had gone for a swim, felt tired after it, and lay down on a couch in his home. He never arose. Jobs said that Noyce was such a physical man that it would have been awful to watch him die of a wasting disease. He added, "There was a touch of Errol Flynn in him."[132]

The relationship between Grove and Noyce becomes still more intriguing when we take into account the fact that Grove appreciated Noyce's strengths. Noyce was "a very smart guy. [He had] lots of ideas, some of which are brilliant, most of which are useless." This sounds like damning by faint praise, and it would be from anyone but Grove. This was Grove's idea of a compliment. Moore felt the same way, but expressed the idea differently. Noyce, he said, had "many ideas, some of them good."[133]

Noyce, according to Grove,

> was perfectly tolerant of you[r] picking the gems . . . and throwing the rest . . . away. He was very approachable.
>
> Bob was a mystery. Not a mystery, a paradox. And very private. Approachable the first inch and after that you don't go any further. But the first inch was good enough to charm every customer [and] every partner.

And to inspire general adulation. Moreover, Noyce put up with Grove. He "would tolerate me saying, 'That's bullshit.'"[134] Not every boss would take this from a subordinate he could fire in an instant. Such language must have caused at least a little cognitive dissonance for a man who everyone else said walked on water.

It is noteworthy that in 1984, Grove took a special interest in cementing Noyce's relationship with Intel. "I had a 1:1 ["Intel speak" for a private, face-to-face meeting] with Bob, relative to his future at Intel," Grove told Moore. "I was very emphatic that we needed him, and that we needed to tie him into things in a more systematic fashion. I think Bob really wanted reassurance that he was wanted here. . . . It was an excellent discussion."[135]

What Grove did with regard to Noyce was rationally to evaluate his strengths and weaknesses. Few others did. They saw him through the gauze of his special mystique. It has been said of Steve Jobs that there is a "reality distortion field" in his presence.[136] Grove was not subject to this phenomenon in Noyce's case.

All of which brings us back to our earlier question. Why was Grove immune to Noyce's charm? There are a couple of reasons. First, Grove hates to be manipulated. People who have worked closely with him have marveled at the tenacity with which he pursues reality. Mere charm will not get you very far with him.

Second, and perhaps more important, Grove and Noyce had more in common than Grove himself might appreciate. They both aspired to positions of leadership. They both enjoyed the special aura that surrounds special people. They both have been show-offs. They have loved the limelight. They both were performers. Noyce loved to act, and he enjoyed singing madrigals with groups he organized. Grove has a deep, sonorous voice, believed in "strategy by speech making," and possessed a superb and carefully crafted public presence. Grove loved opera from his youth and is more than a little knowledgeable about it.

Grove and Noyce were both, in a sense, magnified men. Both were "operatic" in a way. Both craved attention. No one would make the same statements about Moore. It is difficult to imagine him singing madrigals or practicing strategy by speech making.

It was because Grove has always been a ham that he recognized and saw through the ham in Noyce. There was probably some jealously in this relationship. Grove had to be the star of the show, but so did Noyce. Two stars can't get top billing.

What saved the relationship was that both Noyce and Grove recognized the other's talent. Moreover, Grove did develop a genuine interest in the practice of management that Noyce did not possess. Management bored Noyce. So did corporate strategy.

One of the few people other than Grove who was not smitten by the man whom Arthur Rock called "impossible not to like"[137] was Elizabeth Bottomley Noyce. She met Noyce when he was a graduate student at MIT. He was acting in a musical staged at Tufts, and she was a costume designer. That was in 1953. Boston was full of graduate students, and perhaps she did not recognize that this particular one was bound for glory.

At any rate, in 1974, twenty-one years and four children later, Betty Noyce had had enough of being married to a great man. To the outside world, Noyce seemed perfect. As one executive at Intel said, "Bob could stand up in front of a roomful of securities analysts and tell them we were facing a number of major problems in our business, and the stock would go up five points." But this perfect face to the outside world could not find peace at home. After a "monumental row," Bob and Betty Noyce decided to divorce. They split Noyce's Intel stock fifty-fifty.[138] Noyce's troubled personal life is deftly described in Leslie Berlin's outstanding biography of him.[139]

Noyce remarried the following year. His second wife is Ann S. Bowers, who at the time of their courtship was the head of human resources at Intel.[140] She felt she could not keep that position while married to the boss, so she moved on. Her next position, as it happens, was at Apple, where she met Steve Jobs. Sometimes, Silicon Valley seems like a small town.

The same year that Noyce remarried, he became chairman of the board of directors of Intel. Gordon Moore became president and chief operating officer. His second in command was Grove. In 1979, Noyce became vice chairman of the board, Moore became chairman and CEO, and Grove became president and chief operating officer.[141]

By the late 1970s, Moore and Grove were managing Intel on a day-to-day basis. Noyce was an important presence both because of his charisma and because he was a major stockholder. However, by 1979, he was becoming more an "industrial statesman" than an executive at Intel. This is a trend that continued up until he died.[142] As for the actual management of the innards of Intel, Grove was the man to see. That is what the newly recruited John Doerr, today one of America's leading venture capitalists, was told as early as 1974.[143]

Arthur Rock, the financier who provided the seed money for Intel, remarked in January 2000, "In order to succeed, Intel needed Noyce, Moore, and Grove. And it needed them in that order."[144] He could not have been more right. Noyce jump-started the company. He was the man the bankers banked on. Moore was the master technologist. And Grove, who is as technologically capable as anyone who has worked in the Valley, is the man who married that technology to managerial excellence and created an extraordinarily magnetic corporate culture.

Grove was remarkably hardworking, and he demanded his place in the sun. In 1967, the year he almost left Fairchild out of frustration with the lack of managerial rigor, he published *Physics and Technology of Semiconductor Devices*.[145] One need merely turn the pages to see that this book is going to have a limited readership. In 1983, he published *High Output Management*.[146] It is inconceivable that either Noyce or Moore could have written *High Output Management* or that they would have wanted to.

Amidst luminaries like Noyce and Moore, Grove created a unique position for himself. Noyce was the technologist who came to speak for the industry in Washington, D.C., and around the world. In 1988, out of a sense of duty and despite the fact that he did not want the job, he became CEO of the industry consortium known as SEMATECH. Moore was the consummate technologist. Moore's law will be discussed presently. For now, let us summarize it by saying that it posits that the number of transistors and other electrical devices that can be fit onto a silicon chip doubles every year and a half.

Andy Grove became the technologist who knew how to run a business.

In 1983, Michael Malone wrote of Noyce that "he has come as close to immortality as any [other] engineer."[147] But he achieved that exalted status largely outside of Intel, with which he was certainly still very much connected, but with whose daily management he was really not involved. It is Grove, not Noyce or Moore, who was selected as *Time* magazine's "Man of the Year," and Grove whose name became a byword in the business world for effective management.

Grove would have been dissatisfied with anything less. Yet these accolades might well have been denied him had the "immortal" Noyce wanted to run Intel during the late 1970s and early 1980s—had he, that is, wanted to be as much a presence inside the company as he was outside it. We will never know, but in that case, I believe Grove would have left Intel.

5

"A Hotheaded 30-Year-Old Running Around Like a Drunken Rat," or Andy Grove Comes to the Valley of the Heart's Delight

Eva and Andy Grove moved from Berkeley to Palo Alto late in 1962. They rented a house for six months, but the landlord was impossible. In March 1963, they moved in with Eva's aunt and uncle, who also lived in Palo Alto. That did not work out well either. Eva's aunt was problematic to live with. The next stop was a house at 3011 Ross Road in Palo Alto. This is a small dwelling not too far west of the freeway, U.S. 101 (or just 101 to the natives).

The Ross Road house was the first home Andy and Eva owned. It is a modest but comfortable dwelling on a small lot abutting a creek. They purchased it for $25,000. Later they bought the house next to it for the same amount. Andy's parents lived in the first when they came to California. The second house was used by Maria's caregiver following her husband's death. After her death, it was rented. The Groves lived at the Ross Road house until moving to a spacious and beautiful home in an exclusive town in the Valley.

Those who knew the Valley before it was developed—when it was known as "the Valley of the Heart's Delight"—wax rhapsodic about its exquisite beauty. Fruit trees were everywhere, "[filling] spring days with white blossoms and summer evenings with bees and the sweet scent of ripening fruit."[1] Terri Murphy, who succeeded Karen Thorpe as Grove's administrative assistant at Intel, moved to the Valley as a child. She remembers walking to elementary school in the 1960s past the plum orchards. "Ate fresh plums in the morning for breakfast. It was awesome. Just literally picked them off the tree. It was great!"[2]

The Valley is in one of the five regions in the world with a "Mediterranean" climate.[3] The temperature is moderate year-round. Descriptions bring to mind Shakespeare's final play, what historian Leo Marx called his "American fable,"[4] *The Tempest*. From Miranda, this famed, ecstatic utterance:

> O, wonder!
> How many goodly creatures are there here!
> How beauteous mankind is! O brave new world,
> That has such people in't!
>
> (act 5, scene 1)

The "brave new world" is so "beauteous" that even the monster Caliban is moved:

> Be not afeared; the isle is full of noises,
> Sounds and sweet airs, that give delight and hurt not.
>
> (act 3, scene 2)

One Calar Louise Laurence, a resident of the Valley in the pristine days prior to the explosion of business activity, wrote the following verse about "this veritable paradise":

> Orchard after orchard
> Is spread before the eyes
> With the whitest of white blossoms
> 'Neath the bluest of blue skies.[5]

Not Shakespeare, admittedly, but touching in its simplicity. The pristine beauty of the preindustrial Valley was deeply moving to many who knew it.

"Be not afeared," advised Caliban, and there is no reason to believe that Eva and Andy were anything but optimistic as they settled in Palo Alto. Andy preferred Berkeley to Stanford, but that did not matter for now. What mattered was that soon after the Groves moved into the Ross Road house Eva became pregnant. Their first child, Karen, was born the day after Christmas in 1963. Their second child is also a daughter. Robie (a diminutive for "Roberta") Grove was born on October 10, 1966, while the family was still living in the Ross Road house and Andy was still at Fairchild.

As it always did, work mattered a lot to Andy. He threw himself into his job with an intensity suggested by the title of this chapter, which, by the way, is his own description of himself at the time. Great things had already been achieved at Fairchild. What might be next?

There was, during the 1950s, a gold rush into the semiconductor industry. New firms materialized like mushrooms after a spring rain. By one count, there were twenty-five new entrants between 1951 and 1959.[6] By another reckoning, eighty-six new firms entered the industry between 1954 and 1971.[7] This latter figure refers to firms entering "the transistor business."[8]

These numbers encompass the United States alone. They do not take into account activity abroad, which was to become important in the 1970s and 1980s. In addition to newly founded companies, established electronics firms were creating semiconductor divisions. The ten leading merchant semiconductor companies in 1960 were: Texas Instruments, Transitron, Philco, General Electric, RCA, Motorola, Clevite (the first "e" in the name of this firm is long), Fairchild, Hughes, and Sylvania. "Merchant" firms are those that sold to others. Two firms that manufactured semiconductors for their own use only and thus are not classified as merchants were AT&T, in 1960 the largest corporation in the United States, and IBM, soon to solidify its position as the towering giant of the computer industry.[9]

Entry into this industry was facilitated by the technology policy that AT&T adopted. It patented the transistors developed at Bell Labs, which was one of its subsidiaries, but it nevertheless allowed easy access to its proprietary knowledge. The company believed that the more people working on transistor and allied semiconductor technology, the greater that technology would benefit the telephone. In the words of one executive, "We realized that if this thing [the transistor] was as big as we thought, we couldn't keep it to ourselves and we couldn't make all the technical contributions. It was to our interest to spread it around. If you cast your bread on the water, sometimes it comes back angel food cake."[10] Whether this proved wise policy for the American telephone monopoly is unclear. We can, however, be fairly sure that if AT&T had vigorously defended its transistor patents, they would have proven a powerful barrier to the creation of all these new semiconductor firms.

In a gold rush, a couple of people get rich. Most do not. Many of the new entrants got out of the industry soon after starting up. Some of the established electronics firms also exited. Speaking generally, from a financial standpoint, semiconductors were not attractive. Industry profitability was below the all-manufacturing average in the United States at least from 1967 to 1977 and probably for a longer period. Companies were competing away their profits in a search for growth that demanded investment in research and development and in manufacturing facilities.[11]

This was the context in which Andy Grove found himself when he went to work at Fairchild. The company needed to break away from the pack, to establish itself as a leader, and to create barriers to new competition that would enable it to reap the rewards of its work in terms of high profits.

Founded in 1957, Fairchild had gotten off to a running start. The essential dilemma faced by semiconductor manufacturers during the late 1950s was how to mass-produce reliable devices. In the R&D labs, under carefully controlled circumstances, any one of a number of companies was capable of producing a semiconductor. Hurdles of theory had been cleared. The issue was not what new theoretical knowledge was needed. It was, rather, how to solve practical problems that bedeviled semiconductors on their way from research and development to factory production. The slightest impurity would ruin a chip, making yields low and costs high.

The problem of maximizing the number of problem-free semiconductors on each silicon wafer as it made its way through the factory—the maximization of yield per wafer start—was more of an engineering challenge than a problem of pure science. Two key developments at Fairchild in 1958 led to increased productivity, to a higher yield per wafer start. One of these was Jean Hoerni's planar process. Prior to the planar process, the state of the art in semiconductor manufacture was the mesa process. As the name suggests, the mesa process entailed building devices that were layered, almost in a sedimentary fashion. The problem was that the critical junctions of differently treated meeting points of silicon were exposed and thus subject to contamination.

The planar process, as the name suggests, led to a flat semiconductor. It looked under a microscope like a plane rather than like a mountain, as did a mesa semiconductor. With a flat semiconductor, the silicon junctions could be protected by allowing a coating of silicon dioxide to grow on the surface.

Without this breakthrough, it is hard to see how what came next, Noyce's integrated circuit, would have been possible. It was Noyce who, to use Leslie Berlin's words, was able to "determine a practical and profitable way to use the planar process."[12] The integrated circuit was the result.

Noyce came up with the integrated circuit as the solution to what he viewed as a "stupid" problem. It was a production problem, and this is how Noyce conceptualized it: "Here we were in the factory that was making all these transistors in a perfect array on a single silicon wafer, and then we cut them apart into tiny pieces and had to hire thousands of women with tweezers to pick them up and try to wire them together."

Speaking of Fairchild's production system, he asserted, "It just seemed so stupid. It's expensive, it's unreliable, it clearly limits the complexity of the circuits you can build." The solution to the problem was not to cut the wafers apart, but that was not immediately apparent.

However, once Hoerni had reconfigured the semiconductor from mountain (mesa) to plane (planar), new opportunities presented themselves. A planar semiconductor was, certainly compared to the mesa, a two-dimensional device. Why not run wires across the top of it? Better yet, since any wire, no matter how small, would take up space, why not use metal to print "wire" on the silicon dioxide coating of the planar semiconductor? If positive and negative regions of a transistor could be so connected, why not connect transistors with resistors, capacitors, and other electrical devices? It turned out that one could integrate electrical devices on a single planar chip and connect them with wires printed on the silicon dioxide that coated the silicon of which the chip was made. This was the integrated circuit with a silicon, as opposed to germanium, substrate.[13]

"[A]ll the bits and pieces came together" for Noyce early in 1959. On January 23 of that year, he recorded a lengthy entry in his lab notebook that described what was to become the integrated circuit.[14] Jack Kilby at Texas Instruments came up with the design for an integrated circuit with a germanium substrate virtually simultaneously. How important was this invention? Kilby was awarded the Nobel Prize in Physics for it in the year 2000. Had Noyce lived that long, he undoubtedly would have shared in the prize. But Noyce died in 1990 and the Nobel Prize is not awarded posthumously.[15]

The planar process and Noyce's integrated circuit help explain why Fairchild was able to hit the ground running and rank eighth out of the dozens of companies producing semiconductors, including some large, established firms in 1960, just three years after it was founded. Another reason for Fairchild's quick start was the fact that the traitorous eight migrated to it from Shockley Semiconductor as a group. They had worked together previously.[16]

In January 1958, Fairchild's marketing manager noticed an article concerning problems IBM was having with a fire control system it was building for the air force's big bomber, the B-52. Noyce and Sherman Fairchild decided to bid for the business. Fairchild Semiconductor, though a tiny start-up, was not unknown to the behemoth IBM. That is because Sherman Fairchild sat on IBM's board. He held that seat because he possessed the largest block of stock in IBM in private hands. That was because when IBM was formed by a merger of three companies in 1911, his father, George Winthrop Fairchild, was chosen to be its chief executive officer.

One try. One win. IBM chose Fairchild to produce 100 transistors at $150 a unit. The transistors were ready to ship in just under a year. By the end of 1958, Fairchild was selling 7,000 devices a week and was beginning to look like a going concern.[17]

When Andy Grove arrived at Fairchild, a number of characteristics of the company and the industry had already manifested themselves. First, in the midst of this era of the "organization men," few indeed were the people in this industry who felt any loyalty to an organization. Often a useful teaching question in a business school classroom is: "What holds a company together?" In Silicon Valley in the late 1950s and early 1960s, whatever held companies together did not seem as powerful as the forces ripping them apart.

Fairchild gave birth to the so-called "Fairchildren," engineers who saw Fairchild as a mere way station in their careers. In February 1961, Jay Last, Sheldon Roberts, and Jean Hoerni left the company to form a semiconductor division of Teledyne, a Los Angeles–based firm that itself had only been founded the previous year by Henry Singleton and George Kozmetsky. This trickle of talent from one firm to another would turn into a flood. In 1969, there was a semiconductor industry conference in Sunnyvale, north of Santa Clara and south of Palo Alto in the heart of the Valley. Four hundred people attended. Over 90 percent had graduated from what by then was coming to be known as "Fairchild University."[18] Tom Wolfe, in his famous article on Bob Noyce's "tinkerings," asserted by the end of 1983 that "Defectors (or re-defectors) from Fairchild started up more than fifty companies" in the semiconductor industry.[19] Alfred D. Chandler Jr., the nation's leading business historian, has written that the problem with Fairchild "was that it produced entrepreneurs, not products."[20]

Meteorologists refer to a "microclimate" as a small zone in which the climatic conditions differ from those in the larger surrounding area. Silicon Valley was developing into its own "microeconomy," where the "heroes are the successful entrepreneurs who have taken aggressive professional and technical risks."[21] In this microeconomy, you were more loyal to your network than to your company, and you were more likely to change jobs than carpools.[22] The network thrived around after-hours places that were "in," such as the Wagon Wheel or Rickey's.

Some scholars have seen in this microeconomy a unique hothouse environment for nurturing new technology. Of one thing we can be certain: descriptions of Silicon Valley are the polar opposite of the "eastern establishment" version of technology as embodied in the company of companies in the industry of industries, the International Business Machines Corporation.[23] At IBM, you and your employer owed one another a great deal. There were rules and procedures through which the mutual debt could be discharged. The defining characteristic of Silicon Valley when Andy Grove was hired at Fairchild was that there were no rules.

If mobility between companies was the first lesson Andy learned, the second was that Silicon Valley companies were not very well managed. The third was that good management was vital because of the precision the products of the Valley demanded. Without good management, you would never get a device from a lab to a fab. Without good management you would always find yourself selling not what customers wanted, but what you made too much of.

In 1963, Andy Grove was a young man in a hurry. He doubtless exaggerated for effect by calling himself a hothead running around like a drunken rat. But he did want things to move. He wanted action. Waiting two hours for an alcoholic to show up at an important meeting was simply unbearable.[24]

Grove was competitive, and he was ambitious. He was not bending the old elbow at the Wagon Wheel, and he was not losing sleep about his network of contacts in the industry. We see his competitiveness as soon as he arrives at Fairchild. Here is how Grove describes early interactions with his peers there:

> We started collaborating by literally running into each other in the cafeteria. . . .
>
> "Hi, I'm so-and-so. What are you doing?"
> "I'm working on an MOS capacitor."
> "Gee. That's funny. I'm working on the MOS capacitor, too."

Andy editorializes that at this stage of the encounter, "Claws come out." But then he proceeds:

"Well, what do you do?"

"Well, I'm trying to grow pure oxide."

A further editorial comment from Andy: "A sigh of relief." The conversation continues:

"I'm trying to analyze the theoretical capacity."

Then Andy's final comment: "The other guy relaxes."[25]

Stories of life in Silicon Valley from the mid-1950s to the mid-1980s, such as Tom Wolfe's article, are replete with instances of competitors cooperating and of swapping trade secrets over a beer after hours. What they underrepresent is the amount of competition between engineers working for the same company of the type that Grove narrates. One develops a picture of an environment where you were more likely to find friends outside the company for which you worked than within it. If you did find collaborators within your own firm, it was by chance. By and large, semiconductor startups in Silicon Valley simply did not "do" management.

The annual reports of Fairchild Camera and Instrument Corporation, of which Fairchild Semiconductor had been a division since 1959, did not break out results by division. However, merely reading the description of the semiconductor division's new products and the speed with which it was outgrowing even recently built facilities leads to the conclusion that this division was growing very fast.[26] Growth this rapid without skilled management invites waste and even chaos.

Grove, meanwhile, must have been busy every waking moment. While at Fairchild, he completed and published the four articles from his doctoral dissertation that we have mentioned above. From 1963 to 1968 (the year he left Fairchild) inclusive, he authored or coauthored twenty-six more articles, and he filed for two patents.[27]

This would be enough to keep most people busy. But not our Andy. While he was working at Fairchild, despite the fact that Fairchild was so frustrating it seemed to be working against him, while he was writing all these articles, while, not incidentally, he was raising a family, he was also teaching a graduate course in semiconductor device physics at his alma mater, the University of California at Berkeley.

Even all this was not enough. Grove turned his course at Berkeley into a textbook. The system he used to write this book was first to prepare a lecture, then, after delivering the lecture, to go home and speak it into a Dictaphone. That material would be transcribed while he was preparing his next lecture. Then there would be final edits. Thus Grove would simultaneously be working on, say, lecture number three, preparing the preliminary edits on lecture number two, and preparing the final edits on lecture number one.[28]

The result was *Physics and Technology of Semiconductor Devices,* a 366-page text targeted at seniors in college and first-year graduate students in electrical engineering and materials science. In the past, Grove explains, "most, if not all" books on the subject concentrated on what was most important for germanium alloy devices. But during the 1960s, silicon semiconductors and integrated circuits made by the planar technology became more important than germanium. Although the general principles involved in the use of silicon and germanium were similar, when one got down to specifics, there were differences. "To render a problem tractable, we must concentrate on its most important features. What is important for an alloy germanium diode, for instance, may not be important for a planar silicon diode." This book was perhaps the first to focus specifically on planar silicon devices.[29]

Carver Mead, who was already well-known for his work on VLSI (very large-scale integration) circuit design, and who was to become a world-famous computer scientist, couldn't say enough glowing things about *Physics and Technology.* "I have reviewed the book in some detail," he wrote, "and believe it is in a class by itself. The very clear, simple treatment of recombination-generation centers effect on the p-n junction and transistor is a truly outstanding achievement. . . . In addition, the treatment of surface effects and the MOS [metal oxide semiconductor] structure are absolutely unique, embodying the latest and best work in the field, much of which was done by the author and his co-workers."[30]

The obvious question is, why was Grove doing so much extra work? He had no interest in a career in academics, which would have been his for the asking. He tells us that things at Fairchild were, by 1967, bad and getting worse. He could not apply his "energy . . . [to] products" because the company had become dysfunctional. So he poured some of that creativity into his course, which he was finding "very enjoyable."[31]

The rise and fall of Fairchild Semiconductor took place so fast that it is hard to comprehend. Founded in 1957, it had made Moore and Noyce financially better off in just two years than either of their fathers ever were in their whole lives. Noyce responded to a lull in the market in 1964 with an aggressive price cut. This put Fairchild on top in terms of integrated circuits sold, and the market as a whole grew dramatically.

From January to October 1965, the stock price of Fairchild Camera and Instrument, the parent company of Fairchild Semiconductor, shot up by almost a factor of five, from 27 to 144. Noyce became a vice president of Fairchild Camera and Instrument. With the spectacular growth, however, came intractable problems. The biggest of all was the gap between R&D and manufacturing, a gap "which had been growing for years and by 1965 yawned positively cavernous."[32]

The unreliability of Fairchild as a semiconductor supplier became obvious quickly. Charlie Sporck, the new manufacturing manager, tried to make the company cooperate with itself. He was a tough businessman in the "kick ass and take names" tradition, but whatever he tried was too little and too late. Fairchild's record of meeting promised delivery dates was abysmal by the end of 1966. In March 1967, Sporck gave up in frustration and walked out. Within six months, thirty-five other Fairchildren decamped to Sporck's new firm, National Semiconductor. In October 1967, Fairchild Semiconductor posted a monthly loss for only the third time in its decade-long history.[33]

Sporck wanted Grove to come with him to National, and Grove was sorely tempted. In fact he told Gordon Moore that he was going to leave, news that Moore greeted by becoming choked up. Moore went to Noyce about it, and Noyce went to see Grove at his office in R&D.

Noyce turned on the old charm, but that never impressed Grove. What did impress him was the statement that they wanted Grove to stay and that he should name what it would take to keep him. "Are you serious?" asked Grove. Noyce was, and that is how Grove became assistant director of research and development at Fairchild Semiconductor, reporting directly to Moore.[34] Grove's "fundamental assumption" in making this move was that he would succeed Moore.[35] It was a position he would not hold for very long.

The problem was not that the new job did not suit him. On the contrary, although parts of his new job were dull, he did speak with Moore about substantive matters almost daily, and these encounters were invariably productive. The problem was that the job was about to disappear.

Here is Grove's description of how that came to pass. There was a conference in either May or June, June is Grove's best guess, of 1968 on solid-state devices. Grove arrived a day prior to Moore, who was stuck in meetings at Fairchild. When Moore did arrive, Andy played his accustomed role, "busily updating him" about what had gone on at the conference.

But Grove could see that Moore was distracted. Grove probed, and Moore said to him, "I've decided to leave Fairchild." "What are you going to do?" a suddenly very excited Grove asked. "I'm going to start a new semiconductor company," said Moore. Without hesitating one second, Grove blurted out, "I'm going with you."[36] Grove was never actually asked to join Intel. He invited himself.

How did Moore react? "Gordon didn't say no. I don't remember what he said. I mean, he didn't exactly hug me. But then he hasn't exactly hugged me or anyone else in my presence, then or any other time. So we start feverishly talking about what was to be Intel."[37]

What Moore was thinking we will never know. Grove recalls that not too long into this feverish discussion, Moore let the other shoe drop. He announced that Noyce was coming too. The phraseology was something like, "By the way, Bob Noyce is joining as my partner." To which Grove responded, "Oh."[38] Andy Grove was probably the only person in the industry who would have responded this way. Noyce was, after all, Noyce. The company was his initiative. He was, literally, money in the bank, because there was probably not a venture he could have dreamt of for which Arthur Rock would not have found the funding. Grove had to reconcile himself to news that would have excited anybody else.[39]

Why did Noyce decide to leave Fairchild and found his own company? We cannot know with certainty. We do know the following. The CEO of Fairchild Camera and Instrument was fired after the poor financial record of the third quarter of 1967 was reported. His replacement was a temporary CEO with little power. An "office of the chief executive," consisting of four persons, one of whom was Noyce, was created. It was, apparently, assumed that when the time came to select a permanent CEO, Noyce would get the nod. He was, however, passed over. For Noyce, who had already been thinking about leaving Fairchild, that was the trigger that got him to think seriously about founding his own company.[40]

For the above to be true, one has to assume that Noyce's objection stemmed from the injury to his ego. It is hard to believe that he really wanted to be the CEO of Fairchild. Everyone—Moore, Sporck, Grove, Noyce himself—knew that he was not a good manager.

Noyce wanted freedom. That is why he flew his own plane. He craved what was new. He had a limited attention span, especially for meetings with eastern businessmen discussing accounting profits. If he had been offered the position of CEO of Fairchild, he would, it appears, have taken it. But he would not have liked it. He probably would not have been very good at it, and he probably would not have lasted too long in it.

Bob Noyce touched the careers of many people. He imparted to them a sense of possibility and of fun in one's work that they cherished for the rest of their lives. He helped people aim higher than they otherwise would have. It was he who told anyone who would listen not to be encumbered by history. "Who, me?" one can almost hear some young person saying. "Yes, you." If the word "inspiration" means anything, Bob Noyce embodied it.

It is hard to believe that Noyce really wanted to move to Syosset, New York, and run Fairchild. It is not hard to believe that he did not want to have Fairchild Semiconductor, which he doubtless regarded as his company, run by Fairchild corporate back east. He did not like those people. He did not respect them. He felt they were out merely to manipulate a technology about which they had no understanding in order to balance the miserable performance of other divisions in the company. If Noyce were not to become the boss, that meant that he was going to have a new boss. Why put up with that aggravation?

What is really incomprehensible is Fairchild's allowing Noyce to go. He was the biggest single asset the company possessed. Sherman Fairchild should have gone to Noyce the same way Noyce went to Grove in 1967, and he should have said the same thing: "What will it take to keep you?" Everyone in a position of responsibility should have known that entrepreneurship had become a way of life in Silicon Valley and that Noyce was just one phone call away from becoming the CEO of his own company. If and when Noyce left, the people at Fairchild should have known that he would not leave by himself.

Leslie Berlin has observed that "Without Moore . . . Noyce could not have been Noyce, and 'his' successes could never have been achieved." The idea upon which Intel was built was Moore's. "We were working," he later recalled, "in the laboratory on the ideas of semiconductor memory and I remember commenting to Bob that this was one of the first ideas I'd seen in a long time you could probably start a new company on."[41] This was in 1967. Moore was merely musing. He did not suggest that he and Noyce drop everything and start their own firm. Thoughts like that were Noyce's department.

Noyce was thinking of launching a new company by early in 1968. Moore may have been happy in his laboratory, but if Noyce were going to leave, that meant that if he did not go with him, he (Moore) would have a new boss. He had worked closely with Noyce since they met at Shockley more than a decade previously. There was no telling with whom the Fairchild parent might replace Noyce at its semiconductor division. With Noyce's decision to leave Fairchild, Moore was faced with a fact. That fact was he would soon be working at a different company. Without Noyce, Fairchild Semiconductor would not be the company it was with Noyce. To stay with Noyce, on the other hand, meant leaving Fairchild. The question was, which new company did Moore want to work for? Unsurprisingly, he chose the man over the organization and went with Noyce.

Change was in the air in 1968. In May there were riots and strikes in France, which threatened the stability of the regime of Charles de Gaulle. In August, the "Prague Spring," the attempt by Alexander Dubcek and other liberals in Czechoslovakia to create what came to be known as "socialism with a human face," was crushed by the Soviet Union under Leonid Brezhnev. This was the most direct assertion of Soviet power in Eastern Europe since the failed Hungarian revolt in 1956 provided Andy Grove his window to escape to America. China, meanwhile, was in the midst of the Cultural Revolution, a convulsion with an incalculable cost in human suffering.

On China's southern border was Vietnam, and 1968 was the turning point in the disastrous Vietnam War. The North Vietnamese and Vietcong launched the Tet offensive on January 30. It was a military defeat but, far more importantly, a stunning psychological victory over the United States. In April, violent riots broke out at Columbia University in protest to the Vietnam War and other issues. More riots took place on college campuses the following month.

On April 4, Martin Luther King Jr. was assassinated in Memphis. Senator Robert F. Kennedy, campaigning for the Democratic Party's presidential nomination, was in Indianapolis at the time. He delivered the news to a hushed and shocked group of African Americans.

On the evening of the California Democratic presidential primary,

June 5, the winner, Robert F. Kennedy, was shot in the Los Angeles hotel that housed his campaign headquarters. He died the following day. In August, riots accompanied the Democratic National Convention in Chicago, an event that became probably the most raucous political gathering in the nation since the Democratic convention in Charleston, South Carolina, in the spring of 1860, on the eve of the Civil War.

Anger, confusion, at best unease, seeped into many American institutions in 1968—companies and families, as well as universities and political parties. Noyce did not have children of draft age that year, but it would be surprising if a man like him was unaffected by such events taking place all over the world.

In early July, Noyce and Moore made a change of their own. They resigned from Fairchild, a decision that would eventually lead to their both becoming enormously wealthy. In terms of obtaining funding and attracting talent, the company they founded got off the ground as easily as any company can.

For financial backing, Noyce made that one phone call mentioned earlier. "Bob just called me on the phone," said the omnipresent venture capitalist Arthur Rock. "We'd been friends for a long time.... Documents? There was practically nothing. Noyce's reputation was good enough. We put out a page-and-a-half little circular, but I'd raised the money even before people saw it."[42]

Intel was incorporated on July 16, 1968. In an effort to decode this tumultuous year a quarter of a century later, a columnist in *Forbes* said that only two great events took place. The founding of Intel was one of them.[43] On August 2, the *Palo Alto Times* featured the firm in a front-page article. Unsolicited, Noyce and Moore "began to receive résumés, calls, and letters of application from talented engineers all over the industry who knew of Noyce's work on the integrated circuit or of Moore's achievements at Fairchild. Finding good employees willing to join a start-up—usually one of the hardest tasks facing most entrepreneurs—was clearly not going to be a problem."[44] Moore later said, "It was easy to finance Intel" and to hire the talent the company needed.[45]

Noyce and Moore did not have to find the first of the "good employees" they hired. He found them. That, of course, was Andy. Just as Noyce could not have been Noyce without Moore, Moore could not have been Moore without Grove. No one could have known this in July 1968, but Grove was both able and willing to make the transition from technologist alone to technologist and business manager. Moreover, he became not only a manager, but a strategist second to none. He became as good at business as he was at technology.

What would have happened to Intel without Andy? In all probability the company would have failed. How do we know? Because America's corporate graveyard is stuffed full of semiconductor companies, some of which attracted first-class engineering and scientific talent. Where are they now? Advanced Micro Devices (usually referred to as AMD) survives and recently it has stolen a march on Intel. It is gaining market share at this writing. However, to paraphrase Dr. Johnson, a fly may sting a horse, but the fly is still a fly and the horse is still a horse. AMD and other domestic competitors in the semiconductor business are tiny compared to Intel.

In the semiconductor industry, management talent has been harder to find than engineering talent. By becoming a brilliant manager, Grove differentiated himself and his company. All this was in the future. Up until the year Intel was founded, Grove had shown no interest in business management. All his writing dealt with technical subjects. He was, after all, an engineer. He was a very good engineer. Perhaps brilliant. But there were a lot of brilliant engineers in Silicon Valley. There were not a lot of brilliant managers. There were even fewer brilliant managers who were also engineers.

The fact that Intel was "managerially challenged" was immediately apparent in a number of ways. Noyce and Moore had decided to launch their own company. But they had neglected to think up a name for it. They had a number of ideas: "N.M. Electronics"—somehow lacking in sex appeal. "Moore-Noyce"—sounds too much like "more noise." At length they settled on Intel, a word that was short for "integrated electronics" but that also suggested "intelligence."[46]

The fourth employee at Intel was Leslie L. Vadasz. Born in Budapest ten days after Grove, on September 12, 1936, Vadasz escaped at the same time Grove did, during the autumn uprising of 1956. Coming to North America via Canada and studying electrical engineering at McGill University in Montreal before moving to the United States, he worked at Transitron in Wakefield, Massachusetts, on the well-known technology corridor along Route 128, which surrounds Boston. Unimpressed by Transitron, he made the trek west to the Valley of the Heart's Delight. He wound up in R&D at

Fairchild in 1964, which is where he met Grove. It says something about the management of this start-up that Grove and Vadasz were assigned incorrect employee numbers. Somehow, through some misunderstanding, Vadasz became Intel employee number three and Grove number four even though Grove hired Vadasz.[47] It is indicative of the combined management talent of Robert Noyce, Gordon Moore, Andrew Grove, and Leslie Vadasz that among them they were unable to accurately count to four.

6

"Off and Limping"

Summer 1968 in Silicon Valley. Noyce and Moore have a company of their own. They each bought 245,000 shares at $1 per share, and Rock bought 10,000 shares at the same price. Additional investors were invited to purchase 250,000 additional shares. These, however, were more expensive. They were priced at $10 per share. Even at these prices, investors were turned away at the door. By the 1990s, this company would be celebrated in the popular press as essential to the future of the nation and the world.

In January 2000, I asked Arthur Rock if he was surprised at the behemoth Intel had become. When I asked this question, Intel's market capitalization was about $425 billion. At the height of the great bubble, it surpassed half a trillion dollars. At this writing, Intel's market capitalization has declined to about $101.6 billion. (All market capitalizations are accurate as this book goes to press. They will most likely be different as you are reading it.) Rock's immediate response was that of course he was surprised. No one starts a new venture expecting a success of this magnitude. I never had the opportunity to discuss this company with Noyce, who died just as it was beginning its decade of greatness. There is, however, every reason to believe that Moore and Vadasz would have agreed with Rock. As for Grove, as late as 1994 he "still thought of us [Intel] as a creative, dynamic start-up that had just grown a bit bigger than the other creative, dynamic start-ups."[1] Thus did some of the most intelligent businessmen in the world march backward into the future!

The Intel story has, during its almost four decades on the corporate landscape, been about many things. One part of the story is control. By starting their own company, Noyce and Moore took a leap. Most start-ups fail. But it was a leap they felt worth taking because it would give them control over their own destiny. They would not have to answer to a parent firm full of executives who did not know the difference between a silicon chip and a potato chip. Was Noyce worried? Probably not. Worrying was something he delegated. Was Moore worried? "I wasn't very concerned about it," he has said. "Changing jobs in our industry is fairly common, and I was sure if this didn't work out I could find something else to do, so I didn't consider it much of a risk."[2] As Noyce's biographer Leslie Berlin has pointed out, Noyce and Moore had already participated in two start-ups, Shockley Semiconductor and Fairchild Semiconductor. The latter of these was, despite its troubles, a success that had made both men wealthy.[3]

What about Andy?

Andy was petrified.

In his own words:

> I was scared to death. I left a very secure job where I knew what I was doing and started running R&D for a brand new venture in untried territory. It was terrifying. I literally had nightmares. I was supposed to be director of engineering, but there were so few of us that they made me director of operations. My first assignment was to get a post office box so we could get literature describing the equipment we couldn't afford to buy.[4]

Grove had marketable skills, but he also had a family of four to support. What if this company failed? Worse, what if the company succeeded, but he failed? It is worthwhile remembering where he had come from to get to where he was.

Americans of Moore and Noyce's generation were brought up to believe that, despite the Great Depression, which came to be viewed as a strictly contained aberration, history was a tale of progress. Each day, in some way, things got a little better. Furthermore, reality would bend to your will. If you worked hard and did right, you could do what you wanted to do and be what you wanted to be. Certainly there could be surprise setbacks. There could be Pearl Harbors. But these would, with effort, inevitably be followed by an American general dictating terms to a beaten enemy aboard a gigantic battleship securely anchored in the port of the enemy's capital city. "[W]e will win," the great heavyweight champion Joe Louis said of World War II, "because we are on God's side."[5] That settled that.

Now recall Andy's background. His native land was in the habit of losing wars rather than winning them. Members of his religion had historically been persecuted, and during his early life there had been a concerted effort to annihilate them. Relatives of his and of his wife had died in Auschwitz. As Grove recalled recently, "My father's mother and his half-sister (Manci's mother) perished in Auschwitz, and my father's two brothers were captured by Nazis or Fascists but [we] don't know what happened to them, and my uncle Jozsi was killed, but we don't know what happened to him either."[6] Grove knew only too well that sometimes your worst fears really do come true. He was a man determined not to become a victim.

Initial fear was usually Grove's response to a new challenge. He was frightened at CCNY and at Berkeley. It says a lot about him that he never let fear prevent him from giving his all to something new.

I said earlier that an important part of the Intel story was control. The very reason Intel was founded was control. Noyce especially and, because of Noyce, Moore as well, had to be free of Fairchild's control. They owned almost half the stock of the start-up. At last they had self-control.

Andy Grove has, during the past decade or so, routinely been described as "one of the founders of Intel." This is true in the sense that he was the third person to go to work for the firm. It is, however, untrue in terms of ownership and therefore of the potential for economic rewards. He was not invited to buy any of those $1 shares. Apparently it was Arthur Rock who prevented him from doing so.[7] There was a bright line separating Grove from Noyce, Moore, and Rock. He was an employee. He worked for a wage. Noyce and Moore were wage-earning employees too, of that "nonperson person" called a corporation. But as the corporation grew, presuming that it did, they would have real wealth. Grove would have a higher salary. He would also become wealthy through grants of stock options. However, his financial assets would not approximate those of Noyce, Moore, or Rock.

Neither Noyce nor Moore could be fired. The same could not be said of employee number three and every employee after him. He was an employee at will. He trusted them—or, to be specific, he trusted Moore. But listen to this: "Owner-run companies are often run in an arbitrary, dictatorial way. In fact, often that is what limits their growth." These words are Andy Grove's.[8]

In 1997, an author named Tim Jackson published an anti-Grove book entitled *Inside Intel*.[9] Here is what Jackson had to say about the selection of Grove to run the factory. Noyce and Moore "could have hired just about anyone they wanted within fifty miles" for that job. Choosing Grove "was so bizarre that it mystified most of the people who were watching the new business take shape." The newly appointed director of operations was "a guy who had no manufacturing experience at all—who was more a physicist than an engineer, more a teacher than a business executive, more a foreigner than an American."[10]

Let's examine this indictment. It is true that Grove had no manufacturing experience, and he was in charge of manufacturing very sensitive devices. He was indeed a strange choice for this job. In fact, he was not initially chosen for it. He was supposed to be director of engineering. At a start-up, however, you do what needs to be done, not necessarily what you have been trained to do or what you have had firsthand experience doing. Grove had probably never purchased a post office box either, but the company needed one, so he got one.

"More a physicist than an engineer." That is simply incorrect if what is meant is theoretical physicist. In 1999, I referred to Grove, in conversation with him, as a physicist, and he immediately corrected me.[11] His training made him familiar with experimental physics, but he never considered himself a scientist, certainly not a theoretical physicist. This point has been made to me more than once about all of Intel's early executives. They were not hard scientists. They were far more concerned that things worked than they were with why things worked. To illustrate this attitude, consider the following observation. "While it was several years before we understood the physics involved [in a complicated problem]," Gordon Moore once wrote, "that was not important at the time. What was important was that we had a reproducible process to make contacts to our transistors."[12]

Embedded in this discussion, however, is a point about Grove and his career the importance of which cannot be overemphasized. He never stopped growing. He never confined himself to one specialty. In 1997, he said, "I went from chemistry, to chemical engineering, to applied physics, to solid state device physics to manufacturing, all in a 10- to 12-year period."[13] After manufacturing, Grove could have added that he migrated to management, from there to leadership of Intel, to spokesperson for high technology, to expert on corporate governance, to, arguably, the most admired business leader of his era. Even within the technical world, he kept learning more and mastering different fields as circumstances demanded. Had he not been able to do so, he would not have succeeded as Intel's general manager.

To choose one example, at a key moment in Intel's history in the mid-1980s, the company was forced out of the memory chip market, as we will soon see, and made the decision to concentrate its energies on selling micro-processors to the personal computer industry. Gordon Moore presciently observed, "You know, if we're really serious about this, half our executive staff had better become software types in five years' time."[14]

This was necessary because a microprocessor is a more complex device than a memory chip, and, unlike memory, it has a software component. As Grove explained, "Memory chips are, by and large, all alike. . . . [T]hey are basically interchangeable." By contrast, microprocessors "have the equivalent of software built into the silicon chip. They are quite unique, and there is a whole lot of intellectual property involved in that software," some of which is known as micro-code.[15]

For Grove, "the implication [of Moore's statement] was that either the people in the room needed to change their areas of knowledge and expertise or the people themselves needed to be changed."[16] Grove, needless to say, would change his area of knowledge so he did not wind up becoming one of the people who were changed. Moore's "observation captured the essence of a strategic change in the workings of the company that, in turn, precipitated career inflection points for quite a few people, including myself."[17] It was time for Grove, the ultimate autodidact, to teach himself about software.

"More a teacher than business executive," to return to Jackson's observations. By 1968 Grove had taught for a number of years at Berkeley. He could only be said to have been a "business executive" for the less than one year he spent as assistant director of R&D at Fairchild.

From Grove's point of view, however, being a teacher was a key part of being an executive. He has always conceived of himself as a pedagogue, and he has recommended to other chief executives that they make time in their schedules for graduate-school-level teaching.[18] *Qui docet discet* is the Latin maxim. He who teaches, learns.

Jackson's final observation is the most noteworthy: "more a foreigner than an American." This comment stands out like a sore thumb. It has nothing to do with Grove's ability to discharge his responsibilities. And it simply could not be more wrong, more at variance with the spirit and reality of what it means to be an American.

Grove's life story is a microcosm of "Americanization," itself an odd word that has few counterparts. There is no "Hungarianization." Read the world-famous poem "The New Colossus," engraved on a tablet within the pedestal on which the Statue of Liberty stands. The Statue of Liberty has become a symbol of the United States—in the words of the poem, the "Mother of Exiles." "Send these, the homeless, tempest-tost to me, / I lift my lamp beside the golden door!"[19]

Becoming an American certainly was not like this for everyone. It was not like this for Africans, stolen from their native land and enslaved in the United States and elsewhere in the Western Hemisphere from the seventeenth through the nineteenth centuries. No "golden door" for them.

But for the Andrew Carnegies and Andrew Groves of this world, the golden door was real. Grove was constantly amazed that no one held against him the fact that he was not native born. No one held against him the fact that he was of Jewish origin. All the things that had happened in Hungary— the phony parades, the mysterious newspaper articles that denounced you, the disappearances of people—all of these things were absent from Grove's life in the United States. There was no need to develop a coded language to protect you from the authorities. Your background did not come between you and your ambitions. You were not "encumbered by history." The detritus of the Old World was automatically cancelled out. What mattered, as Gordon Moore so well understood, was whether you could do the work that the future demanded.

Complaining that Grove was "more a foreigner than an American" has a distinctly odd ring to it.[20] Once Grove became an American citizen, which he did in 1962, he was as American as anybody else.[21]

One more observation. Moore and Noyce knew something about Grove that others did not. He had never failed. He had always exceeded expectations. What could this man not do?

It is true that Grove was thrown into the deep end of the pool. Noyce and Moore may have been full of self-confidence, but, at least for a time, they may have had more confidence in Grove's ability to do anything to which he put his mind than did Grove himself. As Grove said, he was having nightmares. Here is one that he recorded in his notebook for February 20, 1970.

Nightmare:
Intel is one-half of old house; other half empty. I walk in empty house half; viscious [*sic*] dog jumps out of closet & attacks me. Incident repeated two more times—then I wake up. [22]

What are we to make of this dream? For Grove, the answer is simple. It is an expression of the anxiety he was encountering on the job. The dogs, he explained, have names like Moore and Noyce and Vadasz. They want to know why he is not getting his work done on time and to specification. This dream, which Grove remembers vividly despite the fact that it took place decades ago, was a living illustration to him of just how tough his job was in 1970.[23]

Grove is adamant about his interpretation. Perhaps he is right. After all, it is his dream, his special creation. It is easy to imagine that a man struggling and suffering this intensely for the good of the company might feel internal permission to demand that everyone else struggle as hard and put up with equal suffering to see to it that the work of Intel got done. A man willing to absorb so much himself might feel justified in dishing out plenty of discipline to slackers. Grove is uniquely effective at punishing others. Benjamin Franklin wrote that there were no gains without pains.[24] There would be plenty of pains to accompany the gains at Intel.

Despite the fact that Grove refused to entertain any further interpretation, one can be forgiven for speculating about other meanings this dream might contain. Dreams have their own rules. Even the dreams of engineers.

The first observation that needs to be made is that in talking about this dream, Grove repeatedly referred to dogs in the plural. Yet in his notebook, he refers to "dog" in the singular. He used the plural despite the fact that he and I had the text of the dream as he recorded it in front of us as we discussed it.

Second, it is rare that men or women who achieve the heights Grove did in business record their dreams. Why that is I do not know. The titans of industry have often dreamed big dreams in the sense that they have imagined themselves leading giant organizations that change the world. The business leaders who have succeeded in their quests have seen their dreams come true. Many of them succeeded beyond their wildest dreams. But if these people had an active dream life, evidence of it has not survived.

Taking the dream literally, it is not surprising that Grove should associate Intel with an old house. The company's first headquarters was in a cramped building on Middlefield Road in Mountain View in Silicon Valley, not far from Fairchild, in what was formerly a Union Carbide facility. "Spartan" is the adjective usually used to describe it.

Intel's headquarters have always been spartan. Even when the company became rich and many of its employees millionaires because of the spectacular appreciation of its stock, the ambience of the Robert Noyce Building in Santa Clara is very spare. Everyone, including the CEO, has a cubicle. There are no offices. There are no decorations. There is nothing to delight the eye. It is not an "old house." The lobby has just been refurbished. However, it is distinctly utilitarian.

This arrangement was not an accident. In its early years, Intel grew so quickly that it made sense to move cubicle dividers around rather than to knock down walls. But there is more to the story than utility alone. These spare surroundings were a statement. The statement was: We are concentrating on our work, not wasting time and money on overhead. We have a target. That target is the technological frontier. In the quest for that particular frontier, "position power" did not matter. The coin of the realm was "knowledge power." It was not who you were or where you were on some organization chart, but what you knew or what you could contribute to the solution of a problem that counted. Not only does everyone have a cubicle at Intel to this day, there are also no executive elevators, executive washrooms, or reserved parking spots. "If you come late," Noyce once said, using a prairie metaphor to highlight the contrast between the prairie virtues of the Valley and the excesses of the eastern establishment, "you just have to park in the back forty."[25]

This was quite a dramatic contrast to the lavish offices of successful large companies in other parts of the country, especially in finance in the East. This atmosphere created a powerful element of self-selection. If you thought the point of succeeding in business was to get a big office with fresh flowers and a glorious view and that traveling first class was de rigueur, you would not look at Intel twice. If you like egalitarian surroundings, Intel was for you. Karen Alter, a graduate of Radcliffe and the Harvard Business School, who became an Intel marketing manager, worked on Wall Street before encountering Andy. Much to her surprise, she took a job at Intel, and the corporate culture was one of the reasons. "It's . . . you go to any Intel office around the world, and it feels like Intel. And Andy stands in line in the cafeteria with— same as anyone. There are no executive parking spots. People don't fly first class." The "cubicle thing" mattered a lot to her as a point of pride. "Michael Dell doesn't do this. Larry [Ellison of Oracle] doesn't. Bill Gates probably doesn't." Ellison is famed for his lavish wardrobe. Andy is informal.[26]

Sean Maloney, presently executive vice president and general manager of Intel's Mobility Group, joined Intel in 1982. He is English. "When I joined Intel," he recalled, "British industry was still extremely hierarchical, to a large extent class-based. There were enormous class divisions. Intel was this almost quasi-egalitarian company, which immediately energized me. . . . I turn up, I'm an engineer, and the managing director has the same car as me. I said to him, just casually . . . 'I'm amazed you've got the same car as me,' and he stopped, turned around, looked at me from behind, and said, 'I think your butt's the same size as mine, isn't it?'" British companies were peopled by clock watchers, but "Intel was an entirely different culture—very non-hierarchical, very fast-moving, completely, completely passionate."[27]

Grove was the man most responsible for establishing Intel culture. "Corporate big shots have big corner offices, right? Not Intel CEO Andy Grove. His cubbyhole is only slightly bigger than his coworkers', and working there, he says, 'is a little like having coffee in the square of a European village.'" *Fortune* magazine constructed an index in 1993 of return to shareholders per square foot of CEO office space. Grove led the pack by far, as Intel returned $1.64 per square foot of his cubicle.[28]

Let us return to Grove's dream. Intel is half of an old house. But that is not the half Andy walks into. He enters the other half, the half that is empty. One feels a palpable resonance with his first home on Kiraly Street in Budapest. This was an old flat in a small apartment house. It too was spare. It too was old. Andy remembered it vividly as having two parts, not quite equal halves: the Big Room and the Little Room.

What is his assignment in the dream? Is he supposed to enter the Intel half of the house? Is he supposed to fill up the empty half he has entered? This engineer who has always been able to focus like a laser has no directions and no instructions.

Whatever assignment our dreamer has, he must first overcome a major obstacle to achieve it. A vicious dog jumps out of a hiding place, a closet, and attacks him. This keeps happening until he wakes up. The terror in this dream refuses to go away.

There is no resolution. The dream ends in medias res—in the middle of things. Does the dog's attack succeed in preventing Grove from achieving his unspecified goal? Does it keep him from getting to the Intel half of the house? Does it push him out of the half he has entered? Does it injure him? Does it destroy him? Does he fend it off successfully? We do not know. The dream repeats itself. It does not resolve itself. It demands that its message be attended to, but it conceals that message from the dreamer.

A question that begs to be asked is: who or what is that dog? You can find more than one psychiatrist who will tell you that the vicious dog is Andy's father. At first, this strikes one as a startling suggestion. It is true that when George Gróf miraculously reappeared at the door of the apartment on Kiraly Street (pops out of a closet?), he looked so dreadful after his ordeal that one could without a great leap liken him in his young son's eyes to a mangy cur. Andy was in no big hurry for his father's return, which he had viewed as an impossibility. Each trip his mother took to the train station was a fool's errand from his point of view. Once his father did reestablish himself as the head of the house, Andy no longer had sole possession of his mother. Nevertheless, with the exception of one incident when young Andy overturned a raft on which his father was lounging on a Hungarian lake,[29] there is very little in his memoirs that suggests unresolved Oedipal issues. Which does not mean such issues did not exist.

Grove treated, and was treated by, his father with kindness and respect. When he approved of something his son did, his father "would come up behind me and gently whack the back of my head three times, saying, 'Good, son,' while patting my head."[30] A mad dog would be a clever way for Grove's unconscious to disguise his father from him.

The possible interpretations of this dream are endless, but let us consider one more. What if the dog was Andy himself?

Once again, one would not think this plausible. Grove is one of the most focused people you are likely to meet. This is a trait that almost everybody who has dealt with him discusses. When you speak with him, he will immediately stop you if you wander from the issue at hand. In a meeting, he insists that all participants sit around a table, and the rule is that you can discuss only one thing at a time. You cannot deal with Andy Grove without becoming more disciplined in your approach to problems. Many people are grateful and will forever be grateful to him for this gift.

Grove has accomplished so much in his life that it is hard to conceive of him as torn by inner conflict. It is hard to describe his leadership of Intel, indeed, his whole career there, without using the word "vector." One reason is that he himself used it. Robert A. Burgelman, the Edmund W. Littlefield Professor of Management at Stanford's Graduate School of Business and a man who formed a unique alliance with Grove, has this to report:

> Grove described his strategic leadership as *vectorizing* Intel's strategy-making process. A vector—a quantity having direction and magnitude, denoted by a line drawn from its original to its final position (*Oxford English Dictionary*)—seems an apt metaphor for Grove's efforts to align strategy and action to secure and exploit Intel's preeminence as supplier of microprocessors in the PC market segment.

Next, an exceptionally important observation: "By creating a strategy vector, Grove was able to drive Intel in the intended direction with a total force equal to all the forces at its disposal."[31]

What does this mean? It means that Grove was able to organize all the forces at his command and see to it that they were all moving in the same direction. I would take the liberty of amending Professor Burgelman's featured sentence slightly. Intel, under Grove's leadership, moved with a "total force" that was *more than* "equal to all the forces at its disposal." Part of the reason that Grove's tenure as CEO was so spectacularly successful was that under his leadership two plus two equaled not four, but eight. The atomic reactor named Intel went "critical" under Andy Grove. He was the Enrico Fermi of the business world. Grove removed the cadmium rods inhibiting Intel, and new sources of power were unleashed and then channeled—vectored, if you will.[32]

Is it possible that a man who could be such a unifying force during a time of disruptive change could harbor within himself demons of his own creation? Did he have to fight IBM, Microsoft, *plus* a monstrous dog that stood between him and his goal? Was that dog some combination of him and his father saying, "By what right do you saunter into the promised land? Look at how I was tortured. Look at the millions of Jews just like you who were murdered for no other reason than that they were Jews just like you. By what right do you enjoy the freedom to exercise your talent to the fullest, while they were slaughtered? Why are you, Andy Grove, in the Valley of the Heart's Delight and not Liebe Lewi, shot through the mouth for her 'impudence' in the godforsaken town of Wieruszow in Poland? Your uncle Jozsi, your mother's brother, who accompanied you on your third birthday in your toy red sports car on the banks of the Danube on September 2, 1939— he died during the war.[33] Why is it that he died and you lived?"

All mere speculation. Grove has had dreams that were clearly about the Holocaust, as have many other Jews, including those born after the event and who lived in nations where anti-Semitism never approached the European extremes of the Nazi era. Perhaps the inner conflict expressed by this particular dream was no more complicated than his interpretation of it. We are still left with a man who had to master his own powerful emotions as well as an uncooperative body in order to accomplish his ambitions.

"He who overcomes others is strong, but he who overcomes himself is mightier." These are the words of John Henry Patterson, founder of the National Cash Register Company, one of the most successful businessmen in American history, and not quite sane.[34] Patterson's dictum is applicable to Grove. He could master himself. There was a lot to master. That gave him permission to master others. To direct them. To be demanding of them.

Once Grove got past that ferocious dog, what was he going to be producing in the factory? What business was Intel going to be in? Moore told Noyce in 1967 that semiconductor memory was a product you could build a company around. That turned out to be true. However, "semiconductor memory" is a term that encompasses an array of possibilities. Intel had to make specific choices among this array. It had to manufacture and sell specific products, not merely develop interesting general ideas. It was the penchant for ideas rather than products that drove Andy to distraction at Fairchild, which, he said, was more like a university than a company.[35]

There were two processes by which semiconductor memory chips could be built in the late 1960s. The traditional method was known as bipolar. A newer and promising method was called MOS (for metal oxide semiconductor) technology. MOS was slower and more difficult than the bipolar process, but it possessed the signal advantage that it could produce chips more densely packed with transistors than the bipolar method.[36] Moore was not one to gamble. "We started out," he said, "with deciding to develop technology for semiconductor memory. We did not want to choose between bipolar and MOS process technology, so we tried both."[37] As late as February 27, 1969, a morning staff meeting was devoted to the question of deemphasizing MOS in favor of bipolar. The decision, according to Grove, was "no, at least not now."[38] It is noteworthy that the bipolar versus MOS debate was one concerning which reasonable people could take either side at that late date.

The charge has been made that "Intel was *founded* to steal the silicon gate process [a promising method for MOS technology] from Fairchild."[39] A variation on this theme is: "What [we] brought with us was the knowledge that [we] had seen some built, and the knowledge of the device physics. . . . We didn't bring with us recipes, mask sets, device designs, that sort of stuff. . . . What we brought was a lot of knowledge."[40] Leslie Berlin dismisses the idea that Intel stole trade secrets from Fairchild. It took a full year for Intel to make silicon gate work. That year would not have been necessary if the manufacturing process had already been perfected. If Intel was based on stolen intellectual property, Fairchild would have sued, an option that it considered but rejected.[41] In his authoritative account of Intel's history, Robert Burgelman does not entertain the thought that the company was born under an ethical cloud.

In his reminiscences of Fairchild, Gordon Moore acknowledges the company's "contributions to the understanding of MOS structures," and he also credits it with the "first commercial introduction of a MOS transistor." Nevertheless, Moore points out that "Fairchild never was a major participant in the market for MOS devices." Why not? One reason, which Moore does not mention, is that with the founding of Intel, much of the knowledge of MOS technology left Fairchild. Another reason, which Moore does mention and which deserves emphasis because of the twists and turns the industry would experience in the 1980s, was "Fairchild's great success in bipolar circuits." The market for integrated circuits was growing quickly in the late 1960s. Fairchild was holding its own with its bipolar product. The difference between bipolar and MOS was sufficiently significant that a foray into the latter would have sucked resources from the former.

We have here an interpretation of Fairchild's failure that is at variance with Grove's. Grove, who was an expert in the MOS process and its advocate at an early stage, saw Fairchild's failure as a result of its lack of management discipline. As far as he was concerned, it was simply too damned difficult to do anything right at that company. Moore does not address organizational issues in his discussion of Fairchild. To him, Fairchild's essential problem was that it was expending all its effort competing with what, in hindsight, we now know was a superannuated technology.[42]

Fairchild was like a toy rocket, which soars into the firmament only to flame out. Silicon Valley would see many similar phenomena in the future. There are two points about Fairchild's history that deserve emphasis.

First, planar technology and the integrated circuit were major developments that opened new technological doors and increased the performance of the end product for which they were purchased. However, not everybody was happy about their introduction.

The objection was not solely that they were more expensive by orders of magnitude than the devices they were replacing. It was also that the integrated circuit represented vertical integration. Prior to its introduction, customers "designed the circuits they needed from off-the-shelf transistors, resistors, and capacitors that they bought from manufacturers like Fairchild." Now, however, the Fairchilds of the world were "designing and building standard circuits that would be sold to customers" as a finished product.[43] They were able to charge more money because they were adding more value. According to one trade journal, "Equipment manufacturers fear that full use of microcircuits [integrated circuits] will mean they will be doing little more than putting small cans on circuit boards and then putting their name on it."[44] Furthermore, as soon as these "microcircuits" became available, people started to design products around them. Each "can" produced would have certain characteristics and specifications. Therefore, to change the nature of the microcircuit would mean that other companies would have to change the "cans" they were marketing. The inertial forces were strong.

This dynamic became a signature of the electronics industry. As one member of what has been called the "value stack" expanded its activities, other members might be in danger of being commoditized. It is not that far from "putting cans on circuit boards" to putting boxes around a microprocessor and an operating system. Once you commit to certain components, switching costs can be noteworthy.

Grove has used the term "complementor" to describe a company that you need in order for your business to have any value but from which you do not buy and to which you do not sell. "Each company's product works better or sometimes only works with the other company's product. Cars need gasoline; gasoline needs cars."[45]

It is inconceivable that General Motors would start refining and retailing gasoline or that ExxonMobil would go into the automobile industry. In the world of electronics, however, complementarities among firms in the value stack are blurred. In a sense, although the Intel/Microsoft duopoly was the story of complementors—Intel handled the hardware, Microsoft the software—it also was the story of two firms competing for margin dollars generated by the computer in your home or office. Intel today employs more than ten thousand software engineers. Microsoft, with the strongest balance sheet in the business world, has kept and will continue to keep a wary eye on its "complementor" in the vertical value stack of personal computing.

One more observation must be made before leaving the discussion of Fairchild. Ever since the invention of the transistor, change in the world of electronics has been continuous, quick, and, at times, fundamentally disruptive in spite of the inertial forces inhibiting it. Electronics firms have had the exceptionally demanding assignment of balancing commitment to the present technology with the flexibility necessary to adapt to, or even to create, a new technology.

It is difficult for a company to abandon a product or a process with which it is comfortable even if that product is certain to lose favor in the marketplace. To choose one example, Firestone kept investing in bias-ply and bias-belted tires even when these investments could never pay off. When Firestone switched to radials, it did the same thing. It made investments that simply could not, under any reasonable set of assumptions, be worth the capital. Equally egregious was BF Goodrich, whose executives understood that the radial revolution meant the end of seventy-five years of business as usual but who were nevertheless unwilling to form a joint venture with Michelin, which was an ideal way out of an impossible situation. All the U.S. tire manufacturers found the radial revolution so threatening that they simply denied its power. Their executives and shareholders paid the price for their myopia.[46]

If the "human, all too human"[47] tendency is to use denial to permit yourself to stick with what you are familiar and comfortable with and what you have designed your commitments around, how much more difficult it is to change when you see no crisis on the horizon, when it appears that things are going well, when problems that may be looming in the future are based upon guesswork and speculation? It is in this context that Moore's observations about "Fairchild's great success in bipolar circuits" is so important. Fairchild certainly had experienced its ups and downs in the decade from its founding to the time of the defection of many of its top people to Intel. Nevertheless, it was a successful company, and its success was, according to Moore, based on bipolar technology. That was difficult enough to manage. Why change? Intel could afford to experiment with the commercialization of the silicon gate MOS process because it had nothing to lose. Even so, remember that it began by using both processes.

In one of the few documents prepared at Intel's founding, apparently by Arthur Rock, potential investors were informed that

> Intel expects to pursue development and production of Large Scale Arrays, utilizing both MOS devices and Bipolar transistor technologies. It is not expected that the company will produce any of the types of integrated circuits now on the market, but rather will seek to extend the technology to higher levels of integration.[48]

Intel thus announced to the world that it planned on being a leading-edge technology company. It was going to produce a new kind of LSI (large-scale integration) circuit. Its target market was not any application for which semiconductors were at the time being used in volume. Therefore, its competitors were not really semiconductor companies in business when it was founded.

Rather, Intel was going after the market for computer memory. This was the idea that Gordon Moore had said you could build a company on. Intel aimed to put that proposition to the test. It had chosen a big target.

There were no personal computers in 1968, nor were there minicomputers. The industry was dominated by gigantic mainframe machines. IBM had announced the introduction of its 360 in 1964. This product offered the customer soup-to-nuts computing power. The 360 was the quintessence of a vertically integrated, proprietary product. Its very name, 360, suggested its all-encompassing ambition. The 360 encircled all the customer's data needs, just as 360 degrees defines a circle.

The standard technology for the memory function in mainframe computers was "magnetic core." It was a well-understood and "well entrenched" technology. "Magnetic core memory was a complex product in which rings of magnetic metal were woven together with interlocking strands of copper."[49] Intel was not attacking a competitor currently in the market, it was attacking a whole new class of products for which semiconductors had not customarily been used previously. This was "intermodal competition." In order for it to succeed even in getting the attention of firms the size of IBM and its competitors, it had to offer a product that was not just a little better, but an order of magnitude better than what was already on the market. To escape the pull of commoditization, Intel planned on being a moving target. It would invent, price high, skim the cream, and move on to the next invention before competition drove prices down on its products.

Moore thought first-mover advantages were very valuable in his industry. Here is the analogy he liked. Think of a rifleman who shoots at a blank wall, finds the bullet hole, and then paints the target around it. "He always hits the bull's eye." The second rifleman has to hit a specific spot already defined by the first.[50]

Sounds good. But you better make sure that blank wall is the right one. Otherwise, your bull's-eye will merely prove that you have succeeded in becoming number one in a game of one.

Before a company can craft a strategy, it has to craft itself. It has to put itself together from the boardroom to the post office box. Let's take a quick look at Intel from top to bottom as it set sail in 1968. There were six members of the board at the company's inception. Arthur Rock was chairman. Other members who were not operating executives were Gerard Currie, who ran Data Technology; Max Palevsky, president of Scientific Data Systems, another Rock creation, which would soon be sold to Xerox for more than $900 million; and Charles B. Smith, representing the Rockefeller family.[51] From within the company came Noyce, whose title was president and treasurer, and Moore, the executive vice president. An article in *Fortune* magazine in 2004 described Intel's board of directors at that time as among the most active in business.[52] Nineteen sixty-eight was a different world in business and at Intel. The board went along with whatever the corporate officers wanted, even when early results were losses. That year, Intel lost about a half million dollars, and there is no record of any complaint from the board.[53]

There were, however, clear attempts to show the board that the company was making progress. On March 19, 1969, Grove recorded in his notebook, "This has been one hell of a month." Preparations for the March board meeting did not make it any easier. For example:

3/7–3/9   *Fri–Sunday*

- Feverish activity, e.g., [Gene] Flath starting at 4:30 A.M. Saturday to finish B[oard] of D[irectors] runs, while solving high point → contact → metal etch problems.

- Electroglass blows Fri 5 P.M., fixed Saturday, blows again Monday, fixed again.

- Lack of reading identified as due to old mask error.[54]

Despite the "feverish activity," the board of directors' meeting on March 12 was "gloomy."[55]

But then things started to look up. Two days after the board meeting:

- Bin 1 '1101's appear, first 5, then 9, then 27 per wafer.
- General euphoria descends on everybody.[56]

The world of Intel's start-up was one of high ups and low downs.

Practices that became institutionalized at the mature Intel can be traced back to its earliest days. Intel has a system of staffing called "two in a box." Important positions are filled by two executives rather than one, who are chosen in such a way that their strengths complement one another.

The first two executives in a box were, unsurprisingly, Noyce and Moore. Their titles and employee numbers (Noyce was number one, Moore number two) suggested that Moore reported to Noyce. In fact, they were equals in terms of their share ownership and in their direction of the company. Noyce, always thirsting for freedom, wanted to be able to "take off without severe guilt feelings about leaving a job undone." He could do that because he had in Moore a man who dotted i's and crossed t's. Noyce loved the spotlight. Moore did not seem interested in it.

Noyce was a great recruiter, "the Pied Piper," according to Roger Borovoy, who was a lawyer at Fairchild and eventually came over to Intel in 1974. "If Bob wants you to come, you come."[57]

It is one thing to hire people, another to keep them working for you. Arthur Rock was not happy that there were in the Valley so many "millionaires who did nothing for their company except leave after a short period of time." The solution lay in a compensation scheme designed to keep them. That meant granting stock options generously, but in such a way as to render them worthless if the grantee did not stick around for as long as management desired.

Yet another characteristic of Intel that a number of authors have commented on was its secrecy—a supposed change from the openness of the Valley's early days. Here is a passage from Tom Wolfe's article on Bob Noyce that characterizes his view of Silicon Valley in the 1960s. "The new breed of the Silicon Valley lived for work," he wrote. Sometimes he would bring work home.

Or else he would leave the plant and decide, well, maybe he would drop in at the Wagon Wheel for a drink before he went home. Every year there was some place, the Wagon Wheel, Chez Yvonne, Rickey's, the Roundhouse, where members of this esoteric fraternity, the young men and women of the semiconductor industry, would head after work to have a drink and gossip and brag and trade war stories.[58]

There was to be a lot less gossiping and trading of war stories in the world of Intel. Employees were told specifically to stay away from the Wagon Wheel. Trade secrets were to be kept secret.[59] The Valley was going corporate, a western version of corporate, but corporate all the same.

In order to keep secrets, Intel had to have secrets worth keeping. An internal report in November 1968 described the MOS/Silicon Gate Research as "off and limping," but that very phrase could have been applied to the company as a whole.[60] Intel's first product was a 64-bit bipolar SRAM (static random access memory) chip, introduced in 1969, which, according to Burgelman, "found some small initial markets."[61] This description does not sound like the company was setting the world on fire.

What was Grove up to during the early days of the start-up? His notes to himself make it look like he was doing everything. Here is the entry for August 2, 1968:

WHERE DO WE STAND?

Summary #1

PERSONNEL
- Systems-man search well underway. One man probably found (Hoff)
- IE probably found (Belleville)
- Electronics tech. probably found (Brasseur)

→ *Needs now:*
- vacuum tech
- process tech

- secretary (Jean leaves in two weeks) (JC)
- Engineers → start hitting TI (GM)
- Review of all applic. at end of week

MISCELLANEOUS

- Name, logo, postcards, filing system for personnel & catalogs; phones: OK

→ *Need:* office furniture (JC)

EQUIPMENT

- Masterlist prepared
- ICE list received
- Catalog file about 50% complete; another 30% requested
- Electronic lab, mask design, evaluation lab: ordering started, probably complete weekend.
- Furnaces: ready for selection & order

→ *Needs Now:*

- Investigate epi reactor situation (AG, GM)
- Investigate mask aligners, (EF) arrange for trials
- Investigate vacuum equipment (GM)
- Investigate assembly equipment (AG)
- lay out hoods, request bids (EF)
- get literature on masking room equipment (EF)

DESIGN

Activity ready to start this week.

→ - Define set of characterization devices (AG, LV, EF)
- Let them out, have them cut (LV, AG)
- Start thinking about I (LV)[62]

What is remarkable about Grove's notes on the early days of Intel is the variety of tasks he was called upon to undertake. He is thinking and doing everything, from engineering drawings, to cost accounting, to staffing the company, to ordering office furniture, to asking questions that ought to have simple answers but might not (e.g., "What happens to those prototype products later? Where do they go?")[63]

Clear from a reading of these notebooks is that nothing got done by itself. Andy was in the trenches mounting charges and fighting off the countercharges launched by the forces of entropy on a dozen fronts.

At Intel, there was not a lot going on to make one optimistic in those first few months. A recession in the computer industry in 1969 didn't help matters. By the fall of 1968, head count at the company was thirty. In September of the following year, Intel introduced its first MOS chip, the 1101. It was a flop, unable to compete in the mainframe market.[64]

An internal document from early 1970 contained the phrase "Management Near Panic." It was the workforce that should have been even nearer to panic. Ten percent of those people the company had been so busy hiring were laid off by June.[65] There was a lot of pressure and tension for quite a while after Intel opened its doors. "We have to prove something," said Les Vadasz, "or else, are we faking it?"[66]

"Are we faking it?" Not a nice question for proud people to be asking themselves. Only results would show whether they were "faking it" or not. The phrase came from Paul Simon's song "Fakin' It," which appeared on Simon and Garfunkel's 1968 album *Bookends* and was still quite well-known in the early 1970s.

Decades later, Grove remembered how that song and those verses "haunted me." He had convinced himself that the failure of Fairchild to function properly was the fault of a dysfunctional organization. An important reason for his wanting to be a part of Intel was that with organizational problems solved, he would be part of a team that would manufacture and market great products people would use. But the plethora of problems with early products at Intel tormented him. They forced him to ask whether Fairchild's problems had migrated with him and others to Intel. He felt like that song was written for him, or aimed at him.[67] "If at Intel we can't make it," Grove asked himself, "how could I look myself in the mirror?"[68]

In October 1970, Intel came out with its third product, the 1-kilobit

1103 DRAM (for dynamic random access memory, pronounced "D-RAM"). This represented a demonstrable, step-function improvement over its predecessor, the 1101 SRAM. The 1103 put Intel on the map. The difficulties involved with this product, however, can hardly be overstated. As Grove said, during the period in which Intel was struggling to get the 1103 into production, he was "scared shitless." When asked by an interviewer a decade later if there had been production problems with the 1103, his response was simply, "Oh, God."[69]

When the 1103 got itself out into the hands of customers, one found ample reason for Grove's fears. After thousands of units had been shipped, it turned out that, in Grove's words, "under certain adverse conditions the thing just couldn't remember."[70] Yet that was supposed to be its sole function. Nothing daunted, the company continued to sell the product. In the summer of 2004, Grove delivered a presentation to a couple of hundred Intel manufacturing managers. He introduced himself as Andrew S. Grove, and, recalling the early days of the company, told them that the "S." stood for "ship the shit."[71] He might have been thinking of the 1103.

The problems with the product were never completely fixed. Ed Gelbach, Intel's marketing vice president in the 1970s, said that the 1103s "never did work in the customers' systems exactly right, but they worked." According to Moore, the 1103 "was one of the most difficult-to-use integrated circuits ever produced."[72] If one were writing the story of a semiconductor company that failed, it would be easy to point to the 1103 as the prime cause. A proud slogan of Intel during this era—you can still see it at the company's headquarters—was "Intel Delivers," an effective battle cry during an era in which so few semiconductor companies were reliable.[73] When one considers the 1103, however, the obvious question is: "Delivers what?"

For all its many flaws, the 1103 delivered a lot of bang for the buck. It had the power to compete successfully against magnetic core memory and was soon to displace it. Two years after its introduction, the 1103 was the biggest-selling semiconductor in the world.[74] It established Intel as the memory company—*the* memory company.

In 1971, Intel went public. This was also the company's first profitable year. The source of the profit was an arrangement to license the production of the 1103 to another company, Microsystems International, Ltd., of Ontario, Canada, the manufacturing subsidiary of Bell Canada. The extraordinary income resulting from that license was $1,427,504. Total revenues in 1971 were $9,411,821, more than double the $4,241,253 in 1970. The loss of $969,915 in 1970 turned into a profit of $1,051,080 the following year, a profit made possible by the almost $1.5 million Microsystems International license.

How does technology change? This question probably has as many answers as there are people who have asked it. There are almost always barriers to the adoption of new technology. Among these is that there are usually people making a living with the old technology, whose livelihoods will be threatened by the new. This, unsurprisingly, was the problem faced by Intel with its 1103. It was going to displace magnetic core memory and with it a lot of hard-won expertise.

In Moore's view, the very difficulty of using the 1103 actually facilitated its adoption. What explains this paradoxical turn of events? According to Moore:

> There was a lot of resistance to semiconductor technology on the part of core memory engineers. Core was a very difficult technology and required a great deal of engineering support. The engineers didn't embrace the 1103 until they realized that it, too, was a difficult technology and wouldn't make their skills irrelevant.[75]

Is it possible that the problems with the 1103 actually worked to facilitate its acceptance in the marketplace? Moore says so, and he was in a position to know.

One is reminded of the story of the introduction of the instant cake mix. This story may be apocryphal. But if it is not true, it ought to be, and the fact that it is so well-known says something about change in technology.

Apparently, General Mills many years ago came up with an instant Betty Crocker cake mix.[76] The cake mix was exceptionally easy to use. That turned out to be a problem. Women using it felt they were not really giving enough of themselves to their families. In response to this reaction, General Mills, so the story goes, reformulated the cake mix to require a little more effort on the part of the cook. This supposedly assuaged guilt and increased sales.

Returning to the 1103, we may well ask why Intel would have licensed this product to another company. They did this for the best reason in the world. They had no choice. In Moore's words, "[I]t was standard procedure in the semiconductor industry that no company would design in your product without a second source. The nominal reason was that the customer wanted to have a guaranteed supply. The unstated reason was to have price competition. Especially as a small company, we had to second source our memory."

This custom of "second sourcing" was a barrier to technological change. You, as Intel, bear all the risk of creating a new product. You do all the design work. Then, somehow, you manage to transfer the design you have created in the R&D facility to the manufacturing site, known in the industry as a "fab," for "fabrication" facility. It was this handoff from R&D to manufacturing in quantity that had proven so terribly difficult not only at Fairchild but at other semiconductor firms as well. Gremlins repeatedly would ruin a chip that went into mass production despite the design looking so promising in the R&D laboratory.

It took time to fully appreciate how easily a chip could be contaminated. Step by step, Intel developed fabrication sites that are today astonishing moonscapes. The word "clean" fails to describe how pristine these fabs are. The absolute necessity for precision in every step of mass production and for clean rooms that would make a brain surgeon envious help account for why fabs have become so expensive. At this writing, a new fabrication facility costs between $3 billion and $4 billion. That is the cost of the building alone and does not count the many millions needed for machine tools.

In 1971, no one at Intel realized the lengths to which the company had to go to mass-produce semiconductors with high yields. Here is Leslie Berlin's description of the "seat of the pants" approach to manufacturing in mid-1971:

> The fab at 365 Middlefield Road (Fab 1) had grown haphazardly in an effort to keep up with demand without incurring the expense of moving the biggest pieces of equipment. Flames shot from ungrounded sealers. Ovens were used to re-heat food for potluck dinners. Roof timbers cracked because the roof was overloaded with process equipment. Sump pumps flooded. An alloy furnace blew its cap so often that employees began a contest to predict how far the cap could travel. At one point, a backhoe sat in the rear of the fab, poised to begin expansion work, but contaminating the facility in the meantime. More than one fab employee recalled late-night parties that ended only when the security guard barked, "All the drunks, out of the building!"[77]

Given this situation, it is no wonder that, according to Moore, the people at Microsystems International, from whom Intel, due to the second-sourcing rule, could keep no secret, "said that they ran Intel's process better than Intel did." "[T]hey were probably right," said Moore. After all, this was a unit of Bell Canada. One doubts that drunks were being kicked out of their production facilities by security officers.

To add insult to injury, in order to train the licensee in the complexities of the 1103, Intel had to dispatch the most skilled people it had up to Canada for long periods. "The *crème de la crème* of the company's technical force . . . moved to Ottawa," said Grove. The "B team," in which Grove included himself, "had to keep going with the production RAMs and the technology development . . . with all the best people being gone for months at a time."[78]

The license was negotiated by Noyce and Moore. Grove was opposed to it. Even with everyone whom Intel had recruited since its inception working on the 1103, the company's ability to push this product out the door was "so tenuous" that sending the "A team" to Ottawa to set up Microsystems International in business "might," Grove feared, "jeopardize our existence."[79]

There was, however, a second reason that Intel set up Microsystems International as a second source for the 1103. Intel needed the money. The company was in the red from its founding in 1968 through 1970. The million and a half dollars from that license meant profitability in 1971, which meant the company could go public that year.

Thus, the license was a good news/bad news story. The good news was that Intel made money that it needed very much at this moment in its history. The "bad news was that the competitor [Intel created through the license] had higher yields than we did" because the A team was up in Canada while the B team was toiling away with nail-biting tension back at Fab 1 on Middlefield Road in Mountain View in the Valley.[80]

The second-sourcing agreement was time-limited. In other words, Intel only had to share its crown jewels with Microsystems International until December 31, 1972.[81] After that date, any improvements that Intel made in product or process were its to keep.

The original process for 1103 production was designed for chips on wafers that were two inches in diameter. At some date after the expiration of the information-sharing agreement, Intel decided to shift the manufacture of the 1103 to wafers that were three inches in diameter. The company could process chips more economically on a larger wafer.

The Canadian second source had little choice but to follow suit. Otherwise, the prices for its product would not be competitive with Intel's. However, since the information-sharing agreement had lapsed, the Canadians were, as Moore explained, "on their own." And they could not handle the new wafer size. As a result, Intel's "products were designed in, so when [large orders] came in we were the only ones shipping." Moore concludes by saying, "That was luck! And this was a very profitable part of our story."[82] Intel's 1972 *Annual Report* featured a circle three inches in diameter on its cover. A wafer this size could contain "more than twice the number of memory circuits of 2-inch wafers now in production."[83]

The 1103 was a profitable product, and the 1970s as a whole proved a very good decade for Intel. Sales rose from $9.2 million in 1971 to $854.6 million in 1980 and profits from $1 million to $96.7 million. The compound annual growth rates for sales and profits were 66 percent and 65 percent respectively. Return on assets was 6.9 percent in 1971 and 12.6 percent in 1980. Return on equity was 7.6 percent in 1971 and 22.3 percent in 1980. One could hardly have asked for more.

If the 1103 was such a gold mine, why didn't other companies copy it and enter the market? According to Berlin, its initial headaches helped it once again. The 1103 "was so terribly difficult to reverse engineer that Intel had almost no competitors" for years.[84]

Was this really "luck," as Moore suggested? Intel's people spent a lot of time in Ottawa with Microsystems International. They must have had a pretty good idea of what this company was and was not capable of doing without their help. It is not hard to believe that Intel engineers realized that the shift from the two-inch to the three-inch wafers was difficult. Intel could manage it, but without Intel's help, Microsystems could not. Indeed, executives at Intel were not that worried over competition from Ottawa once the license ended. Nor was their major concern the other semiconductor startups in the Valley such as National Semiconductor, the firm Charlie Sporck founded when he left Fairchild in 1967, or Advanced Micro Devices (AMD), the firm Jerry Sanders founded when he left Fairchild in 1969. Bob Noyce was an early investor in AMD.[85]

Why, then, was Intel in such a hurry to move from a two-inch to a three-inch wafer? This transition was accomplished as quickly as possible at the cost of increasing the strain on Intel's manufacturing capabilities, and specifically on Grove, whose responsibility it was to make manufacturing work. At one point, the two-inch and three-inch production lines were running simultaneously in Fab 1. This was a 25,000-square-foot facility that housed not only manufacturing but the rest of the company as well. It was about this time that Andy had his dream of vicious dogs. Nevertheless, whether it was best described as "orchestrated brilliance" or "controlled chaos," the job was getting done.

Why push so hard to make the leap from two inch to three inch? Because Intel was worried about a potential new entrant into its semiconductor memory market. This was a competent company known for its aggressive competitive behavior. "They ate babies with nails there," said Grove. He was referring to Texas Instruments.[86]

Headquartered in Dallas, Texas Instruments was no start-up. It had been founded in 1930. Jack Kilby, coinventor with Bob Noyce of the integrated circuit, worked there. They had deep knowledge of semiconductor technology. In 1970, when tiny Intel lost almost a million dollars, TI posted $827.6 million in sales and employed 44,752 people. It had the resources to swat Intel like a little gnat. Intel had to keep buzzing fast to prevent that from happening.

The development of the 1103 and the ramp-up to mass production have a lot to teach us about Intel's policy toward competition. Specifically, it did not want any. It wanted to innovate constantly, make the most of each technological advance, and then quickly move on to the next one. This meant a high R&D budget, but the money was well spent if it resulted in high-margin new products. The goal was to get rid of companies that had entered its market, like Microsystems International, but even more important, to prevent entry by big, aggressive companies with expertise and organizational capability, like Texas Instruments.

Some of the new employees peopling Intel were particularly talented. "Based on its deep competencies in silicon technology," Burgelman has written, "Intel was a wellspring of technical variations that created new business opportunities in its early days." Two unplanned products in 1971 were the EPROM and the microprocessor.[87]

Dov Frohman, another alumnus of Fairchild, "turned a previously intractable technical problem into a new product."[88] In the course of trying to figure out the cause of the failure of a certain percentage of Intel's chips, Frohman invented a new kind of chip. Unlike the standard ROM (read-only memory), Frohman's EPROM (erasable programmable read-only memory, pronounced Ee-prom) could easily be programmed by an engineer. Frohman demonstrated his chip to Moore, and "Moore did not need to see [the] demonstration twice."[89]

With the EPROM, Moore saw that "the prototyping cycle for a new computer product would be cut from months to hours."[90] EPROM "quantities got to be pretty high," said Moore. "We ended up hiding this as well as we could. EPROM was our most profitable product line through 1985."[91]

The microprocessor was conceived by Marcian E. "Ted" Hoff, and here we see serendipity at work with a vengeance. A Japanese manufacturer of desktop printer-calculators named Busicom was planning a complicated new product. Attracted by Noyce's reputation, they approached Intel with a contract that called for a set of twelve chips for their machine. The assignment to design the set of chips was given to Hoff, a postdoctoral fellow at Stanford when Intel hired him in 1969.

Hoff and Noyce were both unhappy with the proliferation of special-purpose integrated circuits. For Busicom, Hoff developed an elegant solution. Instead of twelve chips, he would do the job with four. The calculator would be supplied with one memory chip, one chip for storage registers, and a third to hold the program. The fourth chip was a "strikingly new design" from Hoff: "a general-purpose processor circuit that could be programmed for a variety of jobs, including the performance of arithmetic in Busicom's machines." Because Hoff could put "all the logic circuitry of a calculator's central processor unit . . . on a single chip," circuit design became far simpler than before.[92]

Unlike the EPROM, the utility of the microprocessor was not immediately apparent. Intel came close to giving the rights of its design to Busicom for a few thousand dollars.[93] For a decade, the microprocessor Hoff developed along with fellow Intel engineers Federico Faggin and Stan Mazor,[94] found a variety of niche markets. Only with the coming of the age of the personal computer in the 1980s did it become apparent that this device was worth tens, perhaps hundreds of billions of dollars. Its value today is incalculable. The world of the twenty-first century is unimaginable without it.

But all that was in the future.

7

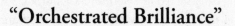

"Orchestrated Brilliance"

When one looks at the Intel of 1971 and 1972, what is most impressive is the variety of activities under way. Here is how Grove described the challenge of manufacturing the 1103.

> Making the 1103 concept work at the technology level, at the device level, and at the systems level and successfully introducing it into high volume manufacturing required, if I may flirt with immodesty for a moment, a fair measure of orchestrated brilliance. Everybody from technologists to designers to reliability experts had to work to the same schedule toward a different aspect of the same goal, interfacing simultaneously at all levels.[1]

Intel had, by 1971, hired dozens of people "because of their expertise in a sliver of technology." Grove's job was to manage these people so that they would all contribute to the creation of the 1103, which Grove later described as "this flimsy, flimsy device" that became the first mass-produced DRAM and remained the only one successfully mass-produced for some years.[2]

If all Intel did was manufacture the 1103, it would, one feels, have been enough. But the company was doing a lot more. It was manufacturing new products both at the components and systems levels. It was using both bipolar and MOS technology. MOS technology especially was a moving target. Change was constant and welcomed. Intel was committed "to volume production in order to achieve early cost reduction."[3]

Production facilities had to increase to accommodate this fast-growing business. A new fab was opened in Santa Clara, south of Fab 1 in the Valley, in June 1971. An assembly plant was built in Penang, Malaysia, and another facility was being constructed in Livermore, California.

Not only did this increasing variety of products have to be manufactured, they had to be sold. According to its initial public offering prospectus prepared in mid-October 1971,

> Intel products are sold directly from its facility in Santa Clara, and through regional sales offices near Los Angeles, Boston, New York, and Minneapolis, and in Brussels, Belgium and Tokyo, Japan. Sales are also made through four independent distributors with over 40 locations in the United States and Canada, one independent distributor in Japan, and approximately 13 sales representatives in the United States, 13 in Europe and the Middle East, and one in the Far East. Approximately 83% of all sales to date of Intel products were made to customers in North America, 12% to customers in Europe and the Middle East and 5% to customers in Japan. Typically, independent distributors handle a wide variety of products, including those competitive with Intel products.[4]

Sales in 1970 were made to over five hundred customers. That number was almost to double by the end of 1971.[5]

In addition to all this, Intel decided to begin consumer product marketing through the purchase of Microma, which sold watches. As always, new technology was going to provide the competitive advantage Intel sought. Microma made solid-state quartz watches with liquid crystal displays. In 1972, the company moved into a new 21,000-square-foot factory in Cupertino, a town in the Valley that would soon become the home of Apple Computer.

"Andy and I," Gordon Moore said at an interview of both of them, "have a completely different view of [Intel's] start-up. We were both there, shared a lot of experiences. To me, it was amazingly smooth. We did things on time and on budget and everything ended up working." After this statement, Moore asked, "Andy, what's your description of it?"

Grove immediately responded, "It was pure hell." Problems came in all sizes, both technical and interpersonal. Getting product out the door was very stressful. This stress had to be handled by "a bunch of . . . strangers without any team spirit or trust." There was plenty of "backstabbing [and] fighting," and it took a long time before something approaching teamwork was achieved.[6] "I wouldn't want to relive those early years for anything," Grove remarked in 1986.[7]

How could the same event, the Intel start-up, be viewed so differently? One reason is that Moore and Grove are two very different people. Moore is, or at least seems to be, calm by nature. Grove is volatile. He has a very short fuse, and nothing seems to stand between his feeling an emotion and his blunt expression of it—at least nothing at Intel. Grove has carefully cultivated his self-presentation to the world outside.

The different perceptions also arose from the different roles the two men played. Moore always stayed close to the technology, to the exclusion of other concerns. He was older than Andy, and he held a major share in the ownership of the company.

It was Grove, from the beginning, who could rightfully have displayed the famous sign that Harry S. Truman put on his desk not long after becoming president: "The Buck Stops Here."[8] Speaking about managing Intel, Moore observed, "You look at the problems that are current at the time, and you try to come up with some kind of creative solutions for them. Or you turn them over to Andy, one or the other."[9]

Moore said that when Intel was founded, "We really thought that Andy's eventual position in the company would be as chief technical officer."[10] However, Andy simply had to deal with managerial problems. Moore had the option of passing them along to Andy. Andy did not have the option of passing them along to anyone else. If he did not learn how to manage this business, it might turn into another Fairchild.

For all the technical brilliance at Intel, there was precious little knowledge of business management. There were 1,002 employees at the company at the end of 1972, and to the best of my knowledge not one of them had earned an MBA. There seems simply to have been the assumption that the company could manage itself.

But Intel was already a global business by the end of 1972. It manufactured one of the most demanding product lines of any company. Its marketing was also highly complex and had grown haphazardly. For Intel to succeed as a company, marketing and manufacturing had to work in as coordinated a fashion as the fab that produced the 1103. This was not going to happen by accident.

Grove was a technologist. There was nothing in his background, in his studies, or in his publications that gave any indication that he had an interest in business management as a discrete endeavor. He did know enough about business to know that management mattered. For him, the Fairchild experience was a lesson in "how not to do it." He was bound and determined to make Intel different.

One can trace his developing interest in management by examining his notebooks. On September 19, 1968, for example, he records not only progress toward goals, but a brief note "On Progress Reports."[11] He was showing an interest in the reports themselves, not just in what they reported. This is followed three days later by a notation about how opinions seem to have the ability to take the place of facts. Next comes this: "The formal decision making process is usually only the protective covering for a much simpler *informal* process."[12] What prompted that observation, one wonders? Is the informal process really much simpler? Isn't it, by its nature, unknowable by the decision makers because of its very informality . . . its formlessness? Who has talked to whom about what? Am I "in the loop" or not? Despite such questions, Grove has not changed his view. "People kind of know the answer, and they manage the arrangement of facts so that the formal process validates what they want to do anyway." "More often than not," he believes, informal conclusions drive formal processes, rather than formal processes producing conclusions.[13]

By mid-November, Grove was looking for a structural solution to a problem that had bedeviled him at Fairchild, the handoff of a product from one expert to another. Thus we find the following entry in his notebooks:

11/14/68

QUALITY/RELIABILITY

- The best person to worry about product quality first is the designer.

- As the product goes into mfg [manufacturing] and the designer takes on a new product design, he loses interest.

- A third independent body should take over the quality control function from the engineers, at that stage.

- To insure meaningful results & determinations, and rapid feedback, he should be closely related to both the design & the processing groups (e.g., interchange of personnel).

- To insure external auditing, their books should be open to examination by general mgmt [management].[14]

Grove appears to be suggesting that one approach to the problem of the handoff is to avoid a complete break between design and manufacture. There will be a third party involved in shepherding a product from one stage to the next. People will be stapled to their products. Records will be kept so that "general management"—the first time I have seen him use that term—can see what is working well and what is not.

In March 1969, Grove cut out and taped into his notebook a report of a presentation made by the assistant secretary of the navy for research and development at a luncheon of the IEEE, the Institute of Electrical and Electronics Engineers. The speaker decried the rise of "systems engineering" at the expense, he felt, of managerial expertise. "We have forgotten that someone . . . must be in control and must exercise his management knowledge and understanding to create a system. As a result, we have developments that follow all of the rules, but merely fail." In an early exhortation to what came to be known as "management by walking around," the speaker warned, "A project manager who spends his time in his management information center instead of roving through the places where the work is being done is always headed for catastrophe."[15]

For July 4, 1969, Grove pasted in his notebook a clipping from *Time* magazine. Above it, he printed "MY JOB DESCRIPTION?" The clipping was a brief description of the responsibilities of a motion picture director:

> **Vision to Inspire.** Any director must master formidable complexity. He must be adept at sound and camera work, a soother of egos, a cajoler of artistic talent. A great director has something more: the vision and force to make all these elements fuse into an inspired whole.[16]

Grove was experimenting, poking around, about possible selves as a business manager. We will never know, but I doubt that anyone else at Intel, or in the whole semiconductor industry, cut out that clipping and inquired of themselves rhetorically whether or not this was their job description.

On February 26, 1970, Grove devoted a page, complete with a graphic illustration, to the "Peter Principle." This is the famous idea that nothing goes right because people are promoted to their level of incompetence. That is to say, if you do a job well, you get promoted one rung up the hierarchy. If you do that job well, you receive another promotion. However, if you do not do well in the job into which you have been promoted, your reviews by your superiors will be negative, and you will not be promoted again. Therefore, everyone is promoted out of jobs at which they excel and stalled in jobs at which they are mediocre at best.[17] The phenomenon described by the Peter Principle has been a central concern for Grove throughout his career as a manager.

By 1971, flow diagrams and even organization charts begin to appear in Grove's notebooks. On May 18, 1971, he observes, "I think we rely too much on our ability to engineer ourselves out of trouble, and do not concentrate on running a smooth ship."[18] This is as clear a snapshot of an engineer thinking managerial thoughts as one is likely to encounter.

On September 10, 1971, we are treated to:

Grove's Thoughts on Management:

Management is the art of absorbing a task in one lump from above; cutting it into smaller lumps and pushing them down one level in such a way that if the members of the lower level each take one of their own lumps, the mother lump automatically gets done.

A poor manager is one who (1) does not transmit his tasks downward; (2) does not partition his lump well; (3) does not make sure each of the sub-lumps gets done.

For effectiveness, each layer should transmit its lump downward very rapidly.[19]

Interpersonal conflict was sharp during the tense early years of Intel. For example, the October 1969 review of an engineer "turns into 6 hours of delirium; never the same after that: blowups, fights . . ."

In February, Bruce MacKay (pronounced "Mackeye"), Intel employee number fifty, announced that he had decided to quit. MacKay, a Briton who had come to Intel by way of Bell Canada and Texas Instruments, was persuaded by Jerry Sanders to join AMD. He gave Andy his reasons for jumping ship in no uncertain terms:

2/8/70

SOME OF MACKAY'S COMMENTS

Re me:

— Too mild, not demanding enough.

— Do not appreciate the work of foremen, do not visit them often enough.

  Dropping mfg no's from Prog. Report—one example of this.

— Our organization is loose and undefined; no job descriptions exist. . . . I am "not a production man."[20]

MacKay was not alone in charging that Grove, the man in charge of production, was "not a production man." There were constant comparisons to Charlie Sporck, the consummate "production guy." On the other hand, Andy was hearing from Les Vadasz that "Your favorites [are] the production guys. . . . [Y]ou lost interest in engineering."[21] Andy was getting it from both directions. But MacKay must be unique in charging that he was too mild and undemanding. He could not allege that Andy was unpersuasive, because Grove succeeded in convincing him to turn Sanders down and remain at Intel.

The criticisms got Andy thinking. A "production man." "Is there such a thing, really?" he asked himself. As if to reassure himself, he quoted Moore: "There are people who gravitate to the heart of any problem immediately." Such people would do well at anything. Nevertheless, Grove continued to experience self-doubt in his production role.[22]

By February 1970, Grove was describing "Rock Throwing" as "the symptom of the Intel disease." "Do we," he asked himself rhetorically, "get super critical when we are not sure of our own performance?"[23] Grove, a man who presented himself to the world as self-confident and masterful, had to, like the rest of us, deal with self-doubt. "How am I doing?" he wonders. "I think OK, but I did strain in the past 2 weeks."[24]

While Grove was managing manufacturing at Intel, the idea and the image of Charlie Sporck came to play an important role in his life. Sporck seemed to epitomize "the operations guy that I aspired to become. Without my knowing him particularly well at the time, he became a role model. He cast a big shadow over my life without ever knowing that he did so."[25]

Charles E. Sporck was born in the small town of Saranac Lake, nestled amid the Adirondacks in upstate New York, in 1927. He graduated from Cornell with a degree in mechanical engineering and went into the manufacturing training program at General Electric. He spent almost a decade with GE before spotting an advertisement in the *New York Times* that Fairchild had placed for a production manager. He joined Fairchild in October 1959.

Sporck has described himself as "not a scientist type at all." "I'm more blue collar."[26] He is a big man, six feet five inches tall, with a thick mustache. He developed a reputation as a pretty tough guy, rough around the edges, who was at home on a factory floor no matter who comprised the workforce. What Bruce MacKay was saying to Grove was that he knew Sporck, nine years older and eight inches taller than Grove, and that "You ain't no Charlie Sporck."[27] Not the kind of message designed to make one's life easier.

Grove's first entry in his notebooks dealing at length with organization appeared on January 10, 1970.[28] For the next two years, he sketched charts of the organization and how it should operate in the future. He was turning his training as an engineer toward management in his effort to become a true "production man."

What was the cause of the "Wafer-Fab Woes" that he wrote about on August 15, 1971?[29] Was the problem rapid growth? Was it poor organizational structure? Was it people not stepping up to assume new roles as the company grew? Was it Grove himself?

A question to ponder: I knew [the nature of a particular problem in] early June. Yet I could not induce [the manager] to step in, much as I tried. Why?—[the manager] clearly cannot direct himself. If I cannot direct him either, should I not replace him?

But with whom? How?[30]

A lot of questions. Not a lot of answers. "I am too damned busy!" he confides to his notebooks on March 12, 1972.[31] But why? Is the problem rooted in organizational structure? Is it a people problem? Is it both? How can it be solved? Manufacturing was not the only problem.

The issues encountered on the marketing side of the street were, if anything, more searing. Noyce hired Bob Graham, who had worked at Fairchild before leaving in 1965 for a semiconductor company in Florida, to run marketing. Graham joined Intel in late September 1968. Grove simply could not work with Graham. Noyce and Moore were going to have to make a choice. They made the only choice they could. Graham left the company.[32]

Grove may have been absorbing a lot of criticism, some of it personal, but he was not above dishing it out. And he was not above dishing it out to people more powerful than he.

On June 3, 1971, he wrote the following to Bob Noyce:

I view the 1103-1 situation as Intel's biggest management blunder, with you being the principal. . . . [The 1103-1 was, according to the Intel data sheet, "the high speed version of the standard 1103.]

You are human, like the rest of us. You are entitled to make your mistakes, like the rest of us. But I think you should also have to face them like the rest of us have to otherwise you will keep going on making them!

I see [the 1103-1 story] as a continuation of a philosophy of yours which you once expounded to me . . . : "You can be conservative about it [a problem with a product], and you will never be wrong. But you will also not be using what you have to full advantage." This is a philosophy of yours you have used throughout the time I have known you. You specifically used it in [the] case of the "-1." When late last year, O'Hare commented that we should not be selling what we don't have, with specific reference to the "-1," you sharply disagreed. You said, it is very important to get the design cycle started. You were heavily involved, personally, in getting the design cycle started at Data General, at the time.

Please understand: I don't blame you for this philosophy. The whole thing was nothing but a calculated risk. Except, in this case, I think we lost. And that is all right also if somehow the fact that we lost is fed into and stored in your mental computer to be used in future risk appraisals. What is not all right is for you to indulge in a cheap game of rationalization. Because in that case, you—and therefore we—will have profited nothing from this whole affair.

. . . [Y]ou very much dislike defensiveness in others. I know of no better way to combat it than for you to be brutally honest and be ready to fully . . . accept blame for your own mistakes.[33]

It is safe to say that no one other than Andy Grove spoke to the godlike Bob Noyce this way.

A key stage in Grove's development into the business leader he became is his re-creation of himself as a "production man," in addition to remaining the technologist that he was formally trained to be. Gene Flath, an émigré from Fairchild's manufacturing operations, agreed with MacKay that Grove "was absolutely not a processing or a manufacturing oriented person; he was still very much an R&D person."[34] Grove had a distance to travel before he could win the respect of his colleagues in his new role.

During 1971 and 1972, Intel's manufacturing processes began to improve. Training programs were initiated. In the face of a lot of doubt, Grove was proving to the world of Intel that he could learn a whole new trade on the job. Fab 2 in Santa Clara was far more efficient than Fab 1. Fab 3, which opened in Livermore, California, in April 1973, was more efficient still.

From then on, Intel manufacturing was on a roll. More plants opened. The relationship between R&D and manufacturing, which had driven everyone crazy at Fairchild, was being hammered into shape at Intel. By 1974, nobody was singing morose songs about "Fakin' It" anymore.[35]

Andy Grove had proven he could solve what up to that time had been the most obdurate problem in the semiconductor industry: transforming concept chips in the lab into mass-produced items coming off the assembly line in the fab. He had hired more key people at Intel than anyone else.

In 1974, Arthur Rock stepped down from the board chairmanship to become vice chairman. Noyce took his place. Moore became president and CEO. Grove, the vice president of operations, took a seat on the board, a seat he would hold for thirty-one years. Two decades previously, he had been an eighteen-year-old living in Budapest with one year to go before entering the University of Budapest. Now he was a vice president and member of the board of a company in California that was beginning to attract some attention. He had proven himself to be the indispensable man in what, in less than fifteen years, would become the indispensable company. He was on his way, even despite the fact that 1974 was to prove a tough year for Intel.

8

The Long and Winding Road

The general management of a business involves making plans, allocating resources to turn those plans into reality, recruiting and training new hires, monitoring performance, determining compensation, and in general coordinating the company. General management involves more tasks than just these. Library shelves groan under the weight of books about what it means to manage. At a minimum, we can say that managers make plans and try to achieve them.

Unfortunately, life does not always cooperate. Life, as John Lennon said, is what happens while you are making other plans. Human beings cannot be predicted as phenomena in engineering and the sciences can be. The business organization is a construct composed of lines and boxes. But the people in those boxes do not always behave as the general manager wishes. Moreover, the company as a whole can find itself affected by circumstances beyond anyone's control. Thus, the manager finds him- or herself dealing with a never-ending tension between opposing needs, for predictability and flexibility.

In 1973, the challenge at Intel was to deal with growth and increasing complexity. Sales skyrocketed from just under $23 million to almost $65.6 million. Profits almost tripled from $3.1 million to $9.2 million.[1] By October, Intel's product catalog was an inch thick.[2] A new marketing manager, Ed Gelbach, had been hired away from Texas Instruments and was doing what he could to whip that function into shape. He decided to get rid of distributors and establish a company-owned salesforce.[3]

"The human cost of such growth is high," Grove commented in his notebooks in November. "The obvious part of this is that people [have] to work hard." Less obvious were the potential strains caused by the organizational changes that growth demanded.[4]

Various people—Les Vadasz, Federico Faggin (another émigré from Fairchild), Bill Regitz (from Honeywell)—were being given new responsibilities or giving up old ones. Human beings, not electrons, were living through this changing environment. The big question was the extent to which these individual human beings "can successfully absorb new jobs, tasks, or increased complexity in old ones."[5]

Here is how Grove conceptualized the issue of growing with your job.

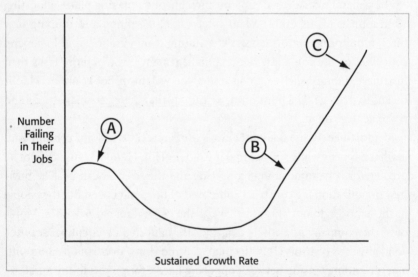

Figure 2
Growing with Your Job

Source: "Intel; A.S. Grove, 11/1973–." (Document in author's possession)

Those in category A were hiring mistakes. Those in category B were stalled out. Only with category C do we find "all kinds of growth capability."[6]

"The point," according to Grove, is that "there is a growth rate at which *everybody* fails, and the whole situation results in . . . chaos."

I feel it is my most important function as being the highest level manager who still has a way to judge the impending failure level of people to identify the <u>maximum growth rate</u> at which this wholesale failure phenomenon begins.

This maximum growth rate is not necessarily the level we want to operate at. Instead, we want to operate at a level where we can match the failure rate with external additions:

FIGURE 3

On Growth

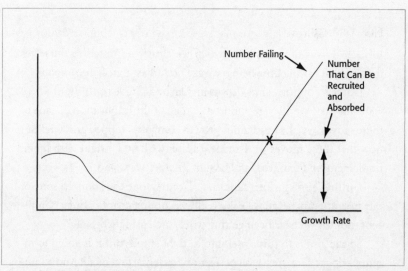

Source: "On Growth," November 10, 1973; "Intel; A.S. Grove, 11/1973–." (Document in author's possession)

As a technologist, Andy could play the role of individual contributor through the exploitation of his intellect. As he became a manager, however, his role within the organization broadened. He had to understand what architecture the organization needed, and he also had to master the more subtle and difficult task of figuring out how flexible the people were with whom he had to work. He needed their commitment in order to leverage his power to achieve his goals. He needed to be persuasive as much as commanding, and the way he himself behaved would serve as a powerful cue to others in the organization.[7]

There is one guaranteed cure for the problems of growth. That cure is decline. As late as May 1974, business across the semiconductor industry was strong. But then the picture, according to *BusinessWeek,* "suddenly and dramatically changed. . . . The rapidly deteriorating marketplace caught nearly everyone by surprise."[8] All the companies in the industry closed plants and first furloughed workers, and eventually had to lay off people in large numbers.

Intel was hit as hard as everyone else. You can manage a company, but it is very difficult to manage major market trends.[9] Intel closed two plants for a week before both July 4th and Labor Day. This was just the beginning.[10]

Here is Grove's assessment of the situation in the summer of 1974:

NON-GROWTH . . .

July, 1974, was the month in which we clearly admitted to ourselves that, at least for the time being, we are no longer a growth company.

[After recounting shut-downs and layoffs, Grove continues:] These were not easy. We all were almost ashamed of the implication of each of these moves: we, the prodigious growth company stopped growing! But now that these moves were made, I think we'll do all right with them, implementing them well, and benefit in other ways, too.

For this "growth-interruption . . ." came none too soon. In spite of our best attempts at it, we were really becoming chaotic. In fact, in recent months we have been getting worse increasingly rapidly.

So the aim is to turn Intel into a "tight ship." And it is going to require a dogged insistence on perfection from me, first of all! And an unending pool of energy to transmit that!

We need financial measures to spur us & monitor our progress![11]

If Grove thought there might be opportunities in a slower-growing Intel, the second half of 1974 would give him the chance to test his theory. The industry collapsed into the worst slump ever. By the end of the year, Intel had fired fully 30 percent of its thirty-five hundred employees.[12]

The turmoil of 1974 had repercussions on Intel that are felt down to the present day. The layoffs took a tremendous toll on everyone. You can see the sadness on the face of Gordon Moore, a man who does not wear his heart on his sleeve, when he recalls them even now. Arthur Rock, who knew Noyce well and was deeply fond of him, believes these layoffs robbed him of the fun of running the company. He actually considered merging Intel with another firm.[13] This was Intel's first brush with mortality. It would not be its last.

According to Rock, Noyce "really and truly did not like to tell people their shortcomings, demote them, or especially, ask them to leave. That aspect of being CEO just tore Bob apart."[14] Noyce decided not to sell or merge Intel when Moore "suggested I might like to try running Intel for a while."[15] Noyce was happy to give Moore the chance and to "kick himself upstairs," as *BusinessWeek* put it.[16]

It was no secret to anyone, including Noyce, that he was not an effective manager. Firing people is painful, but if you can't do it, you can't function effectively as a CEO. Combined with the necessity of firing so many people, Noyce's personal life was coming apart. After twenty-one years of marriage, he was divorced. Nineteen seventy-four was a tough year for him, and it was his last year of intimate involvement in the daily affairs of the firm. Those affairs would now be in the hands of the vice president of operations and new member of the board, Andrew S. Grove. In addition to the mass firings, some new people were hired. Two are particularly important.

Craig R. Barrett joined Intel as a technology development manager. Barrett was born in San Francisco in 1939 and attended Stanford, from which he received his BS, MS, and PhD in materials science. He was a tenured associate professor in that subject when he decided to sign on with Intel. He is widely admired for his management of Intel's fabs and became famous for his "copy exactly" method. Barrett succeeded Grove to become the company's fourth chief executive officer in 1998.

Paul S. Otellini, another member of the class of 1974, was also born in San Francisco. He graduated from the University of San Francisco and then from business school at Berkeley. He remembers conditions well when he received his MBA. "[T]here was a recession. . . . Jobs were not plentiful, certainly not the kind of jobs people would have hired MBAs for."

Otellini wanted to work for a technology company. He could see that Fairchild was going nowhere, a shadow of its former self. So it came down to a choice between Intel and AMD. "I liked the spunk of AMD, but I liked the quality of people at Intel. Actually the AMD offer was more money and more stock than Intel, but I chose Intel for the people and the job opportunity."[17]

A friend of Otellini's took the AMD job he turned down. His friend was laid off in the summer of 1974 as the depression in the industry became more severe. Intel, however, in the belief that young people "were the way of bringing new ideas into the company," kept them onboard. "I remember," said Otellini, "it was a bit macabre, but the desk I was assigned when I got in after orientation that morning had been occupied by someone who had been laid off."[18]

In May 2005, Paul S. Otellini became the fifth chief executive officer of Intel, succeeding Craig Barrett. It is an odd coincidence that three of Intel's five CEOs were born in San Francisco, odd because California, until late in the twentieth century, was more a place to which people moved than in which people were born and raised.

The Intel of which Otellini took command was a very different company from the one into which he was hired. In 1974, the company posted sales of $135.5 million and employed 3,150 people. Thirty-one years later sales were about $35 billion and the head count approximately 85,000. Getting to numbers of that magnitude meant traversing a long and winding road.

If all one looked at were the financials Intel reported in 1974, the year seemed good. Sales and profits doubled. However, the text of the *Annual Report* for that year warned, "These results alone . . . do not truly reflect the course of the year." The bottom fell out of the memory market in the third and fourth quarters.[19] The struggle was more apparent in the numbers provided by the 1975 *Annual Report.* Sales inched forward, but earnings declined for the first time in the history of the company.[20]

A reorganization of the top management of Intel took place in April 1975. The repositioning of Noyce, Moore, and Rock did not, according to *BusinessWeek,* "signal a management upheaval or change in corporate direction." Noyce planned to devote three-quarters of his time to Intel and the rest to outside activities, including his beloved alma mater, Grinnell, where he was a trustee.

The elevation of Grove, however, did matter. He was "a tough operating type" who now had broad responsibility, including for the company's "troubled Microma digital watch-making subsidiary. . . . Under Grove, Microma will be expected to grow up fast."[21]

"I like my job, my peers, my subordinates," Grove observed in a cryptic entry in his notebooks, but "I do not like working for them!" These remarks were made at the end of 1973, when things were still rosy. One of the aggravations of his situation dealt with money. "Right from start, felt disproportionately comp'd (stock). Even now, aggravated by comments like salary comparison."[22]

Eleven months later, Grove listed "my financial position" as first among a list of worries.[23] It was during the following month, however, that he really began to feel tested. This was the month that the restructuring of top management was announced.[24] "It's hard!!!" Grove exclaimed to himself. A man who had worked hard all his life noted that "I don't think I have ever worked this hard before!" The date of this entry is December 25, 1974. Merry Christmas.

"But," Grove goes on, "I can't give up; not yet anyway. If by 2Q the market is going to be as bad as we now think it will be and [Microma—the watch division] doesn't break even, I'll change my vote to shutting the shit pile down. In the meanwhile, if there ever was a case for MBO [management by objectives], this is it!"[25]

Nineteen seventy-four turned out to be as deranged a year as 1968. The world economy had to adjust itself to the oil shock following the Yom Kippur War in 1973. Confidence was profoundly shaken in the United States by the only forced resignation of a president in American history, as Richard Nixon was compelled to give up his office in August as a result of the Watergate revelations.

The world of which Intel was a part had not straightened itself out by 1975. "The recession, which hit most of the semiconductor industry about mid-1974, has proven to be deeper and more persistent than previous dips," according to the *Annual Report*.[26] No early end to the slump in electronics was predicted.

However, the "microcomputer" offered a ray of hope. The company sometimes used the words "microcomputer" and "microprocessor" interchangeably. At other times, it referred to the microprocessor as a type of microcomputer. In either case, by the mid-1970s, Intel realized that the microprocessor was a product with real potential. What was not clear as yet was where that potential lay.

Intel products, particularly the 8080 family, have become industry standards. Some of our competitors have decided to become alternative sources to our products rather than to develop and support a microcomputer family of their own. This action strengthens the position of the Intel designs as standards and makes them acceptable to some large potential users who require multiple independent sources before making major product commitments. While alternative sources increase the pressure on prices, particularly in times of excess production capacity, we feel that over a period of time their existence is more of a positive than a negative for Intel.[27]

Did the executives at Intel really feel that multiple sourcing was "more a positive than a negative" for them? Perhaps they did in 1975, when the company was seven years old and the industry was depressed. We must keep our eyes on this issue of second sourcing, however, because a decade after these words were written, there was no talk at Intel about its putative positive aspects.

Nineteen seventy-five was Grove's first full year as a member of the board of directors. There was nothing he did not know about Intel, and he kept Moore abreast of developments with regular memoranda. Here is what he wrote on Friday evening, June 6, 1975:

> Welcome home! You absolutely, literally, positively could not have chosen a better/(worse) week (depending on point of view) to be gone. Aside from the fact that May fell $1m short, Univac put us on total shipment hold, the ITT inspection team angrily walked out of the plant, one of our ex-employees was shot and killed in a robbery, the 19-year-old son of another one committed suicide, Helen Hoover had a heart attack, Dick Boucher [in charge of Microma] and I almost came to blows over the board presentation and various aspects of the plan, what was left of the week was pretty routine.[28]

No wonder that Grove wrote to Moore when he returned from another vacation that "It seems to me that Intel should contract with you not to go on vacation—the world invariably seems to turn into a piece of shit while you're away."[29]

One of America's leading historians in the twentieth century, Richard Hofstadter, observed that he never really knew what he thought until he tried to record his thoughts in writing. Grove was similar. Hofstadter's comments resonate with historians, but it is a rare business executive who uses writing to help him or her think through problems. Grove has written all his life, from "Despair" through dozens of books and articles to *Swimming Across*. He has written for publication, and he has written for himself. He has not used ghostwriters. The volume of his writing must be unique among top executives and is particularly noteworthy given his professional training. Grove migrated from Greek letters to Roman, from equations to prose.

On May 16, 1975, Grove wrote about a thousand words to himself. "I hope . . . that by setting my thoughts in writing . . . I can converge to a steadier and clearer picture in my head." Not yet forty years of age, he had seen a lot of different business situations, not to mention political regimes. What he discovered was that nothing is easy.

"Our naïve and evidently erroneous belief" was that growing at top speed "was particularly difficult, and that once this growth stopped" life would get a little easier. "[I]t didn't work out that way." Growth was "a lot of work," but it hid a lot of sins. "[B]ecause of supply-limited situations one can get away with doing fewer things and less perfectly." When you are growing, you are working very hard, but "while the growth mode may be hard on one's physique, it is relatively easy on one's mind."

In the "non-growth mode," you figure that you have the chance to do all the things that you swept under the rug when times were good. You could reduce costs in manufacturing, accelerate engineering, and explore new businesses. In reality, however, "Getting into new business is a complicated phenomenon where the directions can change fairly rapidly as one feels one's way, realigning emphasis . . . means shuffling people about and having people stagger under the same load that their predecessor, who had done the job for years, would have been able to handle with ease."

The result is that whether one is growing fast or not, certain problems do not get attended to properly, or the people assigned to them are not right for the job. These sleeping problems awaken eventually, sometimes with a seeming suddenness even though they may have been festering for a long time. The result is a high-stress environment in which people are constantly dealing with emergencies. "The overwhelming problem that I see at Intel today," Grove wrote, is that top and middle management were being "driven into saturation."

Grove was constantly struggling to find the right people to put in the right organizational framework so that problems could be properly antici-pated and needless crises averted. Overwork had been a theme of his com-ments about Intel from the company's inception. Every time a solution was attempted, new problems would crop up. Key people might leave.[30] New hires might disappoint. Add to that the unanticipatable, such as the fire that burned down the Penang assembly plant,[31] and general management begins to present itself as quite a problem.

In the meantime, while you are fighting the forces of entropy in your company, the rest of the world is hardly standing still.

> This year, or in some cases last year, competition arrived and very logically went after the most visible segment, the large account. The large accounts, who now have alternatives, have started to move toward those alternatives with a resulting loss of standing, if not business, for us. In retrospect, that seems to have been unavoidable, but we were too skimpy, too busy, and too smug with our success to have anticipated this trend . . .[32]

The numbers Intel recorded for 1975 were disappointing. Sales were up slightly. Earnings were down almost 18 percent. In a stock market that by more recent standards was placid, Intel's shares gyrated wildly in price. In the third quarter of 1974 alone, the stock's high was $66 a share. Its low was $16. In a company where a lot of people received stock options, such swings had to have had an impact on people's moods.

In 1975, the gyrations in share price were less drastic. The first quarter came close to the third quarter of the previous year, with a low of 21 and a high of 53. But for the remaining nine months the trend was steadily upward from a low of 54 in the second quarter to a high of 88 in the fourth. Wall Street was showing a good deal of confidence in this company.

In 1975, Intel handled itself the way it was to do in future cyclical downturns. It increased its investments in R&D and other corporate functions. As the stories of Craig Barrett and Paul Otellini show, it kept hiring new people even as it had to let others go. Sales and earnings skyrocketed in 1976, growing 65.2 percent and 54.9 percent, respectively. By year's end, Intel employed 7,347 people, up 60 percent from the previous year.[33]

Memory products continued to be the mainstay of the company. However, second only to memory was the microcomputer/microprocessor family of products. "In only five years since Intel introduced the microcomputer concept, microcomputers have grown to rival memories in market size and importance in electronics."[34] Intel established a microcomputer division to act effectively against heightened competition. In charge was a PhD in electrical engineering who came to Intel from Hewlett-Packard, William H. Davidow.

In August 1975, Grove wrote that if he were to give an after-dinner speech, he would say that "we have continued to make progress toward a universal level of mediocrity." The better performers and the lesser were regressing toward an undistinguished level.[35]

A few months later, Grove wrote one of his most upbeat reports to Moore:

Welcome back! This time I think we are going to depart from the pattern of a disaster letter greeting you. With the stock flirting with the $100 level, how could anything be wrong? In fact, things are in reasonable shape even beyond that.

Sales were solid. Various reorganizations were proceeding surprisingly smoothly, especially in manufacturing. Reorganizations always stimulate insecurity and some discontent, but "I am hoping that the present stock price will counterbalance some of the emotions." "Other people," Grove wrote, "like Fairchild, reorganize in the depths of despair; we tend to do it the other way around."

Even in his uncharacteristically cheerful mood, Grove could not tell a happy story about Microma. Intel's foray into watches, its first and its last attempt at consumer product marketing, was thrashing about. Every new idea cost money and produced disappointing results.[36] There was a constant drumbeat of bad news about Microma in Grove's correspondence.[37] Dick Boucher, the executive Andy had put in charge of Microma, does not have happy memories of it. It was a "difficult business" lacking "a good product plan." They "didn't have any controls . . . within the company. The inventories were all over the place. The products were somewhat mediocre." Noyce and Moore had bought Microma, Boucher said, "presuming it was a technology company. And the watch business is not a technology business." It is consumer marketing, like jewelry. "So here you've got technologists running a consumer business."[38]

On November 18, 1976, in the midst of a spectacular year, Grove recorded the "ASG outlook." It was not good. "[D]issatisfied w/overall co. performance (hence: me!) ↔ frequently depressed; thoughts of bailing out (giving up)."[39]

This note is revealing for a number of reasons. First, Grove is prone to dissatisfaction. He is a critic. He knows that bad things can come true. Second, he identifies intimately with the company. If Intel is performing poorly, then: "hence: me!" He always understood that he had to lead by example. The speed of the gang was the speed of the boss. Sometimes the degree of concentrated effort required got to him. Even Andy could get depressed. Two weeks prior to this notation, he remarked to himself that Intel stock was at its 1976 low. The price of the stock and his mood were probably not unrelated.[40]

"In many ways 1977 was a difficult year," we are told by the *Annual Report*. Many a company would covet such problems. Sales were up by more than $56 million and profits by more than $6 million. These increases of 25 percent and 25.8 percent, respectively, were not as sharp as some years, but they were better than others. The stock price eased downward from its 1976 performance, but not terribly. The price of a share ranged from a high of 57 in the first quarter to a low of 37.5 in the third quarter.

The company was growing in numerous ways. Employment rose to 8,100. R&D spending was up. A revolution appeared to be under way in the "continuous interaction between circuit requirements, basic science, and process technology."

> Quantitative changes finally result in a perceived qualitative change. The average number of transistors in the eleven LSI [large-scale integration] memory components and the ten microcomputer components Intel introduced in 1977 was greater than the number of vacuum tubes in the early electronic computer, EINAC [*sic*; ENIAC], which was the most complex piece of electronic equipment built just 30 years ago.

Moore was quoted in *Fortune* in 1973 as saying, "We are really the revolutionaries in the world today—not the kids with the long hair and beards who were wrecking the schools a few years ago."[41] This observation has been quoted numerous times. It is so unlike Moore to have made such a truculent declaration—even the article that quotes him described him as "normally taciturn"—that I asked Grove what prompted it. Grove, who knows Moore as well as he permits himself to be known, responded that he did not believe Moore ever said it. Even if he did not, the fact is that it was true. Quantitative changes were turning into qualitative changes. Intel was developing technologies at such a rapid pace—a record number of new product introductions in 1977—that it was in the process of changing the world.[42]

In one product category, Intel finally admitted defeat. "We abandoned the digital watch and watch module business including the closing of our Microma subsidiary, the transfer of most of the people to other divisions of Intel, and the disposal of Microma's assets."[43]

Intel had gotten into the watch business in 1972. Try as it might, the company could never make a go of it. According to Grove, "We went into the business because we thought we had a unique combination of capabilities: the CMOS [complementary metal oxide semiconductor] chip, the liquid crystal display, and assembly facilities. We got out when we found out it was a consumer marketing game, something we knew nothing about."

Especially distasteful was the cost of advertising. Intel ran a grand total of one television commercial for Microma. It cost $600,000. "Just one ad," bemoaned Grove, "and poof—it was gone."[44] Moore continued to wear his Microma, his "$15 million watch" as he called it, for years. "If anyone comes to me with an idea for a consumer product, all I have to do is look at my watch to get the answer."[45]

The Microma diversion has actually proven quite important in Intel's history for two reasons. What holds a company together? This is an especially urgent question in the world of job hopping in which we live today. Note that when Intel shut down Microma, it managed "the transfer of most of the people to other divisions of Intel." It is easy for the casual reader or even for the serious investor to skim such a passage. However, it was a powerful statement that the company was making not only to Microma's employees, but to everyone else: "You matter to us. If you give us your best, even in a losing cause, we are going to do what we can for you. We won't throw you out on the street if we can help it."

"We put together the 'end of business plan,'" recalled Dick Boucher. This meant dealing with customers "and also guaranteeing that we would place our people." With the exception of some individuals who were let go for cause, Boucher working with Grove found appropriate positions within Intel for those who had tried so hard at Microma.[46]

People are much more likely to sacrifice for a company like that than for one that is cold-blooded. Unbeknownst to anyone in 1977, the 1980s would provide plentiful opportunities for self-sacrifice. A whole breed of people were being developed who "bleed blue," the color of Intel's logo.

Second, it is possible that Intel's failure with Microma resulted in a lesson the company learned too well: "We better stay away from consumer products," the company told itself, "They are not in our genetic code." Grove agrees. In April 2005, he commented, "All our subsequent consumer products efforts were half-hearted."[47] "Half-hearted." Despite having by the 1990s one of the most famous names in business, Intel has never sold directly to consumers. The Intel name is therefore a very large underutilized asset.

As these words are being written, the iPod is one of the hottest products in the United States. It is produced by Apple and is the brainchild of Silicon Valley living legend Steve Jobs, who is a friend of Andy's and who was interviewed for this book. Why wasn't the iPod an Intel invention? Ask people in the Valley that question, and you get a consistent answer. It is that they (or we, if you ask someone at Intel) don't market consumer products. If you ask the next question—"Why not?"—you get a blank stare. They (or we) just don't. Microma is one reason. There are others. If ever there was an illustration that a company's history matters, it is Microma.

Nineteen seventy-eight was Intel's tenth anniversary. Sales increased 41.8 percent to $400.6 million. Profits were up 36.4 percent to $44.3 million. Expenditures on research and development were up 48.1 percent to $13.4 million. Employment was up to 10,900. Sharp increases were recorded in every category where you would want to see them. These increases were both in real and percentage terms. Intel's growth was accelerating even though the base of that growth was increasing in size.[48] A decade previously, Intel had been founded by two men with an idea. At the end of 1968, it had no sales, spent a half million dollars, and employed a mere handful of people.

The company appeared poised for even greater growth. In the semiconductor memory industry, judging from "the phenomenal growth of the number of memory bits shipped, the market . . . seems nearly unlimited." Intel was the innovator. "[Nineteen seventy-seven] saw the establishment of the HMOS (High-speed Metal-Oxide-Semiconductor) technology in the high-volume production of the 2147, a high-speed 4K static memory offering access and cycle times of 55 nanoseconds. This product has been the key to large contracts with several computer manufacturers."

The EPROM, that happy accident which was the fruit of Dov Frohman's fertile mind back in 1971, maintained the lead in a product category Intel created. "In 1978 the 32K EPROM was introduced, enhancing Intel's position as the leading supplier of these components."

Intel's other happy accident from its earliest years, the microprocessor, was being labeled "the most significant development since the transistor" and the "miracle chip." The microprocessor was being employed in a variety of ways undreamt of when it was created. Les Vadasz's favorite example was the bacon package. Prior to the microprocessor, the last strip of bacon in a shrink-wrapped package was never the size of the others. It was smaller and scrunched, if that is a word, up. It looked like an orphan. Using a microprocessor, bacon packagers were able to make each strip of bacon of equal length and width.[49]

Intel's *Annual Report* for 1978 does not mention Vadasz's bacon slicer, but it does enumerate "appliance controls, games, educational toys, heating systems, burglar alarm systems and telephone dialers, among others." This list is followed by a particularly noteworthy sentence: "The home computer offers more capability by far than the first giant computers and is priced to reach the hobbyist."[50]

This is the first mention I have seen in any Intel published document of the "home computer." There was as yet no official inkling that there would be a market for the "home computer" other than the "hobbyist," although some executives did guess that something very big was just over the horizon. Intel in 1978 was as high-tech a company as any in the world, but the potential commercial applications of its technology were not quite appreciated at the upper reaches of the corporation.

One reason that few at Intel guessed what the personal computer would come to mean is that one person who believed in it had left the company. Armas Clifford "Mike" Markkula was an early employee and yet another émigré from Fairchild. Bob Graham had hired him as a product marketing manager for memory chips. When Jack Carsten was promoted past him, Markkula surprised everyone not just by quitting Intel, but by retiring.

At Intel, Markkula apparently was not terribly impressive. He "was always very nice to me, but I didn't have much use for him," recalled Grove.[51] Impressive or not, Markkula could spot a winner when he saw one. He acquired all the Intel stock he could. When the company went public, he became a millionaire and retired at the age of thirty-three.[52]

Markkula met Steve Jobs through a venture capitalist named Don Valentine, who had also worked at Fairchild. When Markkula saw the Apple I in Jobs's soon-to-be-famous garage, it was love at first sight. The Apple I "was what I had wanted since I left high school." It was better than the Corvette he had bought with his Intel stock. He decided to underwrite a loan to Apple for a quarter of a million dollars.[53]

That was in 1976. Two years later, Andy Grove "picks up one of those pink message slips from my secretary. My secretary gives it to me with a big grin. It says, 'Mike Markkula, Apple Computer, please call him back.' I said, 'Apple Computer??' . . . I thought it was a joke."[54]

Andy visited Markkula at Apple and met "the two Steves"—Steve Jobs and his partner, Steve Wozniak. Markkula wanted Grove to join the board of directors. Grove turned him down. He did, however, buy 15,000 shares of stock.[55]

"That's how much I knew in '78," said Grove. Nevertheless, "I guess the incident left an impression because I started paying more attention to those little computers."[56] He certainly did not focus on them. But they were on Grove's radar screen. Just barely. Intel was the home to his concentrated attention. Apple was a not uninteresting sideshow.

Nineteen seventy-eight must have been a great year to be at Intel, but you would not know it from reading Grove's notes and memoranda. "[W]ith our operating managers being busy with operating, planning does not get sufficient emphasis," he complained.[57] Once again, in June, there was another refrain of the chorus about overwork. How could they grow "in spite of an increasingly over-burdened management structure?"

Grove's answer was that "the time has come for us to establish an honest-to-goodness corporate staff." The staff would be made up of top-flight operating executives who would serve for a limited period prior to returning to line management. The role of the staff "would be to deal with longer-term issues, especially those that cross divisional boundaries."[58]

Early July found Grove musing to himself about what was missing at Intel that prevented it from reaching a billion dollars in sales. His answer: "'Oomph' and Administration." When Intel was small, an individual or a small group could provide the "oomph," the initiative and enthusiasm, that the company needed to do its work. All the "oomph" in the Intel of 1978 was concentrated in its top managers, and they were used up by their day-to-day responsibilities. Short-term concerns customarily drove out long-term thinking and planning.

When Grove looked at the ranks of middle management, the picture was bleak indeed. "The middle is populated by the passive introverts—honest, competent, decent, well-meaning work-oriented people who just can't tolerate controversy." The result: "Shit rises uphill." "The depressing thing about it is that it is impossible to change people's personalities," and very difficult to change behavior closely linked to fundamental personality traits.

Intel had "to upgrade the oomph quotient" of its middle managers. But how? Andy had two ideas. One was to put "aggressive and enterprising individuals" from lower in the ranks on a fast track. The second was to "[modify] the criteria" when hiring, and value more highly entrepreneurial qualities "at the expense of competence and integrity—and that [would be] a goddam pity."

It is not clear why Grove thought there might have to be a trade-off between "oomph" on the one hand and "competence and integrity" on the other. This is the only such observation I have found in his writings and speeches. My guess is that it was made out of frustration rather than because he was willing to compromise on either one of these two qualities.

The other barrier between Intel and a billion dollars in sales was administration, an issue that could be broken down into two parts. First, Intel's technically competent people tended to lack administrative skills. The company had only itself to blame. Administrative ability had been viewed as a "nice to have" rather than a "need to have" and had been sacrificed as a result.

The second aspect of the administrative barrier was more profound. There was, in Grove's view, an "absence of strong administrative systems throughout the company." This was a big problem because "the conceptual expertise [to create such systems] is missing in the company." Intel could turn to McKinsey, the well-known management consulting firm, but "I would hope we should be able to do better." Andy had to admit, however, that "I don't even know how to begin to go about it."[59]

Late August found Grove in a rage. Manufacturing was undisciplined. Marketing was "abominable!" "I think I was totally wrong a month ago," he told Moore, "in perceiving improvements in our 'get organized' campaign. If anything, things are getting worse. . . . If I truly had the guts, I think what we should do is put on a total hiring freeze until we get our nose above the shit level."[60]

Despite the constant drumbeat of Grove's criticism, the news during the course of 1978 was so consistently good that even he took a moment to savor it. "We seem to have developed an attitude of self-flagellation that has reached such an extent that we don't even recognize when we as a group do something good," he wrote to the company's top executives. Now, where, one wonders, might that "extreme Sado-Masochism" to which he referred have come from?

In a thoroughly uncharacteristic tone, Grove had nothing but good things to say about Intel's direction in October 1978.

> To a large extent, I think we owe our success not to luck but to a culture of problem orientation, of being critical of ourselves and thereby urging ourselves and our organizations to perform better and better. This virtue, however, can be carried to such an extreme that it can bring about our own paralysis through self-doubt. . . .
>
> So let's try to keep our perspective and permit ourselves to enjoy the fact that . . . we have never yet in our history had a problem we didn't solve.[61]

We see here in chrysalis the beginnings of what was to become the powerful and clearly articulated "Intel culture."

Intel's 1978 sales entitled it to a place on the Fortune 500 for the first time. It ranked 486. This was as nothing compared to the next year. Sales and profits in 1979 soared to $663 million and $77.8 million, respectively. Once again, Intel experienced accelerating growth, 65.8 percent in sales and 76.5 percent in profits, on top of an ever-growing base. Employment increased about 40 percent to about 14,300. Intel was becoming a genuinely big company now, 368 on the Fortune 500. Its market capitalization more than doubled from $638.43 million at the end of 1978 to $1,392.93 million a year later. For purposes of comparison, the average market capitalization of firms listed on the Dow Jones Industrial Average increased from $805.01 million to $838.74 million.

Prices for Intel's products had remained high all year because demand far outstripped the forecasts at the year's outset. The industry was constrained by supply shortages. If you are going to have a problem, that is one which many businesspeople would select.[62]

On the national scene, the temper of the times was not nearly as aggressive and optimistic as it was at Intel. On July 15, 1979, President Jimmy Carter delivered what has been called "the most important speech of his presidency." This was the "malaise" speech, which did not actually use the word "malaise," the definition of which many Americans probably did not know. It is formally known as Carter's "Crisis of Confidence" speech.

The president bemoaned a "nearly invisible" problem. "It is a crisis of confidence. It is a crisis of confidence that strikes at the very heart and soul and spirit of our national will." One could see it "in the growing doubt about the meaning of our own lives and in the loss of a unity of purpose for our nation."[63] Punch-drunk from the second oil shock, Carter painted a maudlin picture of a nation that had lost its spiritual way and was mired in a materialism that was destined to prove ungratifying.

One of the speechwriters noted that "it was more like a sermon than a political speech. It had the themes of confession, redemption, and sacrifice. He was bringing the American people into this spiritual process that he had been through."[64] Unfortunately for Carter, the American people were in no mood to take his rather depressing spiritual journey. They were more receptive to the soon-to-be-heard mindless happy talk of Ronald Reagan about "morning in America." With the best of intentions, Carter only succeeded in getting himself blamed for any sourness that might have been present in the national mood.

At Intel, the mood was anything but sour. Nevertheless, upbeat feelings were modulated by some caution. According to the 1979 *Annual Report,* the year was "a complicated period in Intel's history." On the one hand, there was continued and widespread talk of a global recession. On the other, the daily reality was that product was flying out of the fabs and commanding fancy prices. The result: "We found ourselves proceeding full-speed ahead—with caution, a difficult balance to maintain."[65] Even Andy was not immune from what must have been a sense of euphoria at the company. On July 3, he wrote one of his regular "While You Were Away" memoranda to Moore. "I have no major catastrophes to report. This must be some kind of a first."

If there was room for complaint, no one could find it as surely as Andy, and 1979, record year or not, was no exception. Once again, middle management posed a dilemma. "[T]here may be a fair number of middle managers that are struggling and losing faith in themselves." Grove suggested that Moore provide some encouragement. Nevertheless, one has to ask why the middle managers would not have been thrilled with the company's performance. Was there something wrong with the way they were being selected? Or did Intel have a systemic problem that robbed talented people of their potential? There was no clear answer to that question.[66]

Nineteen seventy-nine was also a special year for Grove's own professional progress. Way back in 1967 when Noyce had persuaded him to remain at Fairchild rather than join Charlie Sporck, who was leaving to head up National Semiconductor, he did so with his "fundamental assumption" that he would succeed Moore as head of research and development. In 1979 Grove did succeed Moore, but to a different position in a different company. Grove became president and chief operating officer. Moore moved up to chairman of the board and chief executive officer. Noyce became vice chairman of the board.

At the age of forty-three, Grove was running one of the most important companies in the world. His first year as COO was a resounding success. He was pictured in the *Annual Report,* full-bearded, next to the clean-shaven Moore. Andy had arrived.

Had Intel arrived? It had learned as a corporation how to do things that all corporations must do if they are to succeed. Two of these deserve special note. First, Intel had learned how to grow. Second, it had learned how to compete.

In 1971, Intel carried $3.6 million on its balance sheet for property, plant, and equipment.[67] By 1979, that figure had increased by two orders of magnitude to $217.4 million.[68] Fabrication facilities were expensive. During the 1970s, the semiconductor industry became capital intensive.

Manufacturing at Intel began in Fab 1 in Mountain View. Fab 2 opened up on Intel's Santa Clara campus in 1971, a campus which today is 115.5 acres. Clean-room standards became stricter. No more putting pizzas on top of diffusion furnaces to keep them warm. But the hair and shoes of people working there were uncovered. The smocks worn were not as clean as they needed to be.

A big step forward was taken with the opening of Fab 3 in Livermore, California, in April 1973. It was here that the now familiar "bunny suit" was introduced. "The bunny suits and the whole routine were a huge joke around the company for years," according to manufacturing manager Gene Flath. "In fact, people used to find excuses to visit Fab 3 just so they could put a bunny suit on."[69]

Fab 3 was also important because it introduced the "McDonald's approach" to erecting fabs. They were to be made as similar as possible. In the world of "McIntel," exact replication would mean that products from each fab would be indistinguishable from one another. Fabs 4 and 5 both came online in 1979, each more efficient and more expensive than their predecessors.[70] From humble beginnings, manufacturing was well on its way to becoming one of Intel's competitive strengths.

As manufacturing at Intel was growing up, so was marketing. The idea of attacking core memory in mainframe computers with the 1103 DRAM proved a winner because, despite this product's problems, it was far more economical to use than the existing alternative. When Intel turned a profit and went public in 1971, it was successful, but it was still a small company. It "benefited from the benign neglect" of other firms.[71]

By the mid-1970s, however, the days of coming in under the industry's radar were gone. Intel's growth was well-publicized and was proving "an embarrassment" to large semiconductor manufacturers around the world. "The list of competitors poised for attack was more than a little daunting: Texas Instruments, Motorola, National Semiconductor, Philips, Siemens, Nippon Electric Corporation (NEC), Hitachi, and Fujitsu, among others— the Billion Dollar Club of the semiconductor industry."[72]

By late in 1979, Intel "was under full siege." At stake was the fate of the 8086, which Bill Davidow labeled, with some hyperbole, "the linchpin of the entire corporation." The principal attackers were Zilog and Motorola. Motorola was especially problematic. Far larger than Intel, it was a proud company with a rich history. Worst of all, the microprocessor it had positioned against the 8086, its 16-bit 68000, was believed by many to be a technically superior product.

The 8086 sales team at Intel was stricken, its morale "shattered." "It was demoralizing to have one customer after the next lecture you about your employer's failures and your competitor's strengths. Many customers actually relished the opportunity to stick it to the famous Intel."[73] Yesterday's feisty underdog had, it seems, become today's oppressor, ripe for a comeuppance.

Field sales was aware of the problem Intel faced, but, according to a sales engineer in the Hauppauge, New York, headquarters of Intel's Atlantic Region, "the message wasn't getting through to management on the West Coast." On November 2, 1979, the manager of the Atlantic Region "fired off" an eight-page telex detailing the difficulties. Coincidentally, an equally impassioned memorandum was sent by a field applications engineer working out of Denver. Intel was in a life-and-death struggle to establish the standard for the 16-bit microprocessor market. The future of the microprocessor business and the collateral sales that business generated were at stake.[74]

Now the message did indeed get through to the West Coast, and "the executive staff meeting the following Tuesday couldn't have been more unpleasant." Davidow "either volunteered or [was] asked" by Andy to fix the problem. The result was Operation CRUSH.[75]

Davidow put together a talented team that set an outrageously aggressive goal: two thousand design wins. The goal, the name, the team—aggression was written all over this effort. Andy Grove was and is a tenacious and pugnacious man. Operation CRUSH was the perfect expression of his conception of business as a contact sport.

The target was Motorola. The 68000 might have been technically superior to the 8086, but Davidow figured out a way to make that undeniably important fact irrelevant. What mattered was not the design of a chip but the total bundle of benefits the customer received with the purchase. Here, Intel had the edge. According to Davidow, "Intel had great customer service and support. We could assure a customer's success with our device. By comparison, choosing the Motorola path clearly presented a risk to the customer."[76] Hovering over the entire effort was Andy. Since "subtlety is not one of Andy's strengths," when he said that Operation CRUSH would go on as long as it took to win, the team knew he meant it.[77]

Intel found the winning ground: the total bundle of benefits. The technique was a spectacular success. It surpassed the impossible goal of 2,000 design wins. It achieved 2,500.[78] One of those proved to be more important than the other 2,499 combined.

When you are facing an impossible challenge, you attempt the impossible to meet it. Among Intel's field sales engineers was a gentleman named Earl Whetstone. Heavily into the "I'll try anything" mode, he decided to pitch the Intel 8086 to the world's largest and most sophisticated information processing organization, the International Business Machines Corporation. IBM epitomized the computer industry as it had been for at least two decades: vertically integrated and proprietary. Whetstone was a pipsqueak in the land of the giants. Intel's market capitalization at the end of 1980 was $1.7 billion. IBM's was $39.6 billion. IBM manufactured most of its microelectronics in-house. Never in its history had it gone to an outside vendor for such a key ingredient of one of its machines.

Timing is everything. Whetstone knocked on the door of "Big Blue" at precisely the right moment. IBM welcomed him cordially. They were open-minded and also very secretive as he and his team worked with their technical people. At length, Whetstone, with the help of Paul Indigo, made the sale.[79]

No one at Intel and no one at IBM knew the significance of this particular design win. According to Moore, "Any design win at IBM was a big deal, but I certainly didn't recognize that this was more important than the others. And I don't think anyone else did either."[80] Whetstone said that a great design win would result in the sale of ten thousand units a year. But the IBM win grew to tens of millions of units annually.[81]

According to journalist Michael Malone, "With the IBM contract, Intel won the microprocessor wars. And the victory was due to Operation CRUSH."[82] This is a remarkable fact. In 1979, when Operation CRUSH was conceived, no one knew there was a "microprocessor war." Intel's top brass understood that Motorola was attacking an important Intel franchise and that they had to fight back. No one dreamt, however, that this contract would be a defining moment in the history not only of Intel and not only of microprocessors but of the whole information processing industry, arguably the most important industry of the second half of the twentieth century. Intel was "just another component supplier" in the eyes of IBM in 1981.[83] In 1996 this particular component supplier rocketed past IBM by almost $30 billion in market capitalization.

We have previously encountered Grove's phrase "earned luck." Let us see if we can deconstruct the IBM design win in order to determine what part of it was "luck" and what part of it was "earned."

It was lucky that in 1980 IBM was willing to consider an outside source for the microprocessor for the line of personal computers it was developing. This unprecedented openness had nothing to do with Intel and everything to do with IBM's history up to the time of the sale. Specifically, Apple Computer was getting a great deal of publicity, and IBM did not even field an entry in the desktop computer product category until 1981. It had to move quickly and therefore outsourced the heart and soul of its new machine as it had never done with its old ones.

Intel was lucky to be in the microprocessor business at all. It had almost signed away the rights to the product after it was created. With the benefit of hindsight, it is easy to see how important the microprocessor was, even in the 1970s.

From a technical standpoint, management did see the mircoprocessor as a "major breakthrough." The dilemma was that no one knew what it was good for. It was a solution in search of a problem. Planning for the 80286, the next step up from the 8086, began in 1978. That year, the 286 team conducted "extensive field interviews" to help it create the product's features. These interviews uncovered more than fifty possible applications. Of these fifty-plus markets for the 286, the personal computer did not even make it onto the list!

According to Moore,

In the mid-1970s someone came to me with an idea for what was basically the PC. The idea was that we could outfit an 8080 processor with a keyboard and a monitor and sell it in the home market. I asked, "What's it good for?" And the only answer was that a housewife could keep her recipes on it. I personally didn't see anything useful in it, so we never gave it another thought.[84]

Bill Davidow referred to the 8086 as "the linchpin" of all of Intel. But he wrote that in a book published in 1986. By then, it was clear that if Intel were to survive, microprocessors would play the central role in the corporation. It is doubtful, however, that when Operation CRUSH was conceived in 1979, anyone was thinking such thoughts. At the end of the day, microprocessors were nice to have; but remember that Intel saw itself as the memory company—*the* memory company.

This part of the IBM design win is luck, but a lot of it, the preponderance, was "earned." Intel was big, but it was still hungry. The problems with middle management of which Grove had consistently complained had been solved to such a degree that in those instances in which Intel did not outengineer its competitors, it could outmarket them. Marketing muscle was what Intel proved it had with Operation CRUSH. It was not selling a "device." It was selling what in modern parlance would be labeled a "solution."

Finally, and critically important, top management was able to listen to the managers in the field. Top management was able to respond when middle managers sent up flares that something was wrong. Intel was not too big to listen. It was not too big to admit when news was bad. But it was big enough to marshal the resources necessary to solve big problems.

On Friday, November 2, 1979, Intel's headquarters in Santa Clara received alarming communications from Don Buckhout on Long Island and

Bert Hill in Denver. How long did it take to get action? The following Tuesday, November 6, a distinctly "unpleasant" meeting of Intel's executive staff took place. Grove must have been in a rage. That was the day Operation CRUSH was born. Massive retaliation in less than a week.

If you want informative people around you, you must listen when they tell the truth. You can pay them no higher compliment. The word will get around the company quickly that you don't murder the messenger.

In spite of the great IBM design win, "1981 was a very difficult year for Intel." For the first time in the company's history, both sales and profits declined, sales by 8 percent and profits by a whopping 72 percent. Industry overcapacity had resulted in plummeting prices for large-scale integration memory components. Intel's market capitalization also fell sharply. It was down 43 percent. An indication of the year's problems was the institution of the "125 percent solution." Salaried employees "voluntarily" worked an extra 25 percent in order to accelerate new product introduction.[85]

Sounding an unaccustomed upbeat note amid the bad news, the *Annual Report* observed that "the slowdown has given us the opportunity and the motivation to increase the overall efficiency of the entire company." This sentence could have been taken right out of Andy's notes to himself from half a decade earlier.[86] His belief was that you should fix the place up when things slow down. His complaint was that that did not happen. According to the *Annual Report*, it did in 1981. Intel made use of the opportunity to refresh and overhaul its operating and administrative infrastructure.

The 1980s, however, were to prove an era of sharp ups and downs for which no one could have planned. In the middle of the decade, Intel could have failed. By decade's end, the company had managed to put itself on a growth trajectory matched by few other large companies ever. Before it reached the heights, however, it marched through the "valley of death."

In 1982, sales reached an all-time high, just short of $900 million. Profits rose to $30 million, up from the previous year, but only because of a change in taxation. Pretax profits dropped as "Intel's business continue[d] to be affected by the depressed world economy and strong international competition, particularly in the memory components area."[87]

The year started off strong, and Intel responded by increasing head count and opening new facilities. But the improvement in business "turned out to be a mirage," and the actions the company had taken to grow with the market "proved to be premature and not easily reversible."[88] Intel was manufacturing a set of products that were becoming progressively more complex. The company could not turn on a dime. The United States had fallen into the grip of the Reagan recession, the worst economic slump since the Great Depression of the 1930s. U.S. GDP fell 1.9 percent, from $5,291.7 billion in 1981 to $5,189.3 billion in constant 2000 dollars. The semiconductor industry was particularly hard hit. Each glimmer of light raised hopes but turned out to be a false dawn.

"[Nineteen eighty-two] was a terrible year," Andy confided to his notebooks, but in the next line he asked: ". . . or was it?" This is vintage Grove. He questions everything. "For the s/c [semiconductor] industry, it was the third year of recession." But at Intel, things were not really all that bad. Revenues were up about 15 percent, shipments about 30 percent. It remained profitable "(barely . . .)." Market share was up. "[G]ot financing for the next 3–4 years (IBM)."[89]

A word about this last notation is in order. Grove wrote in a memorandum to Moore on February 19, 1982, "Nobody has tried to acquire us. Too bad. During the last two weeks there were definitely several days when I would have sold out at $25."[90]

It is hard to know how seriously to take this remark. Business was not good, but it was not terrible. Though only forty-five years of age, Grove was thinking about retiring. If Intel had been acquired, his holdings would have become sharply more valuable. Nevertheless, control of Intel had from the beginning been a passionate concern of its founders. Were they really prepared to trade that control for more money?

At any rate, Intel's 1982 *Annual Report* put the agreement with IBM this way: "IBM and Intel agreed that IBM would buy $250 million of newly issued Intel stock. IBM has agreed to a 30 percent maximum limitation to their ownership of Intel stock and to other limitations designed to assure Intel's independence."[91]

This investment was big news. According to a securities analyst at investment bank Hambrecht & Quist, an influential financial force in Silicon Valley at the time, "This is the most significant development to hit the U.S. semiconductor industry in the last decade." In the view of *Fortune,* it was a "bonanza" for Intel that would give it "the financial muscle to compete against big corporations like Texas Instruments and Motorola and especially against the Japanese, who have been invading the chip market."[92]

The deal rated a front-page headline in *Electronic News,* in which it was asserted that IBM's "unprecedented move" would help Intel through a cash squeeze and guarantee the health of a company upon which IBM "is becoming increasingly dependent for microprocessors, memory parts and MOS technology."[93] Grove denied there was a cash squeeze, but he welcomed the investment. "We need not just money," he said, "but the certainty" that Intel could launch major, long-term investments without having to worry about each quarter's results.[94]

The 1980s were the era of hostile takeovers in American business. When recently asked whether Intel was concerned about a hostile bid at the time, Grove's response was, "Only me."[95] The idea made it into press coverage.

> Although Intel officials strongly deny that the firm was in danger of being taken over by any company, the infusion of cash from IBM will assure that the funds Intel needs will not have to be raised in the open market through a public stock offering. Analysts also note that IBM's minority interest in Intel would be a classic "shark repellant" that would deter potential acquisitors from attempting an unfriendly takeover.[96]

According to one estimate, by 1984 IBM had invested $400 million in Intel, amounting to 20 percent of the company's equity. It did not go further. IBM sold all its Intel stock in 1986 and 1987 for $625 million. The sale was as newsworthy as the purchase had been. The *Wall Street Journal* reported that some analysts believed the sale meant that Intel was in trouble. An insider, IBM, was "dumping the stock."[97] According to historian Alfred D. Chandler Jr., IBM sold its Intel stock not as a no-confidence vote but because by the time of the sale, "Intel's survival seemed secure."[98] Perhaps this is part of the reason why Andy wrote of 1982 in his notebooks that "Maybe it's not so bad."

On top of everything else, Grove observed, "I wrote a book (I am very happy with it)." Among Andy's other hopes for 1983 were a billion dollars in sales, a "cogent defensive strategy in memories and an offensive one in MC [microcomputers] → systems." He wanted "A good sabbatical—for Intel (smooth) and one for me (a taste of life w/o structured work)." He wanted one more thing: "Book on best-seller list!"[99]

What did 1983 offer to compare to these hopes? Financially, Intel really came through. Sales and profits both hit records. Sales rose by a quarter to $1,121.94 million. Whatever problems of "oomph and administration" that had been keeping Intel from breaking the billion-dollar mark had apparently been solved. Profits skyrocketed to $116.1 million, up 286 percent.[100] Market capitalization more than doubled to $4.6 billion. Grove began his "Welcome Home" memorandum to Moore on July 14 by saying, "Congratulations! The good news is that while you were gone, you became ~$68 million richer."[101] According to the *Annual Report,* "The explosion of personal computers and other office use products certainly is a major source of the unusual order strength but by no means the only one."[102]

All businesses have problems all the time. It is in the nature of the corporation for this to be so. Given that fact, the problems Intel faced in 1983 were an appealing set with which to deal. The company had spun around 180 degrees from the miseries of the previous year. According to the *Annual Report,* "our outlook changed extremely rapidly from strong concern over the possibility of a deepening recession to a focus on increasing output at the maximum rate. Our employees started the year with a temporary pay cut and freeze that was phased out by mid-year."[103]

If you have to have problems, capacity constraint is preferable to a shuttered plant, and capacity was the issue agitating Grove by July. "We are deeply production limited," he told Moore in July. "Short term . . . it's test; beyond that, fab."[104] The word "paranoid" was being attached to the company as early as February 1983,[105] but what Intel was most worried about by the summer was allocating the products that were being sucked out of its plants. Fear of something real is not paranoia. It is rational. "The short-term allocation methodology essentially honors existing backlog, establishes reserves after that, and goes on the basis of loyal customers for the rest of it," Grove told Moore.[106]

An executive from IBM called Grove and asked, "If John Opel called you, could you get us more devices this year?" John R. Opel was the CEO of IBM in 1983. He was a geniune big shot at the time. His company owned 20 percent of Intel.

Andy's response to this question was, "The only way we could do that is by taking more away from others. Since I ❤ our other customers as well, I told him no. We *must* be steadfast."[107] By "we," Andy meant Gordon. A number of times in one memorandum, Grove urged, "Please don't be a softie," and "Please hold strong." As for himself, he assured Gordon concerning one issue that "I served notice that I will act like Attila the Hun."

It is indeed better to have too much than too little business. However, as Grove realized when he began to become a manager, the problems associated with growth were quite real. Your customers depended on you, and you wanted very much to be dependable. Imagine what would happen today if Intel had to inform a major customer that it would have to limit purchases of its microprocessors. No matter what the reason, be it an unexpectedly sharp spike in industry demand or an earthquake that put an Intel fab out of commission, a vital business relationship would be in danger of a rupture. Trust would be violated. Worst of all, other companies would detect an opportunity to enter Intel's market.

Perhaps, wondered Andy, Intel should engage a second source to help out its pleading customers. Intel's Japanese SCS ("Strategic Capability Segment")[108] came up with a couple of ideas Andy liked. Maybe Intel could find a manufacturing subcontractor, "a company that would be a manufacturing source . . . for us," while they sold the product themselves. The 286 microprocessor, meanwhile, "needs a prestigious architectural (vs. manufacturing) source." Mitsubishi would be a "likely candidate" for manufacturing, Fujitsu for architecture.

"Since there is such an enormous interest in becoming our approved second source," Andy told Gordon, "we should go out and entertain proposals from the various Japanese companies on this." The winner had to pass three tests:

Step 1: Royalty for past sins.
Step 2: Promise not to do it again.
Step 3: Bid for futures.[109]

It says a lot about the extent to which Grove believed Intel had seized the strategic high ground that he felt he could dictate terms to giant corporations.

Grove concluded by, among other things, telling Moore, "A chapter of my book was published in *Fortune* and got good reception from the outside world." He added tongue-in-cheek (one assumes), "I'm thinking of making it mandatory reading for sabbaticals."[110]

Looking back at 1982 on January 2, 1983, Andy had written, "Let '83 be no worse!" Looking back on 1983 on December 26 of that year, he was fairly well pleased. Intel beat the billion-dollar sales mark for which he had hoped. "Strategies are good." One middling comment: "Book on local best seller lists but *not* on national. This is a mixed result."

The "Hopes for 1984" that Grove recorded on the day after Christmas in

1983 included "Intel > $1.6B, and 20% pretax" and "Start a new & different personal 'project.' . . . Examples: a new book, a bus. school course, (hah . . .), start a fund."[111] Some of these ambitions were realized.

Intel's sales and profits soared to new records in 1984. Sales rose 45 percent to $1.629 billion, placing Intel at 226 on the Fortune 500. Pretax profits did not quite reach Grove's 20 percent goal, but net after-tax profits increased 71 percent to $198.2 million. Intel's compound annual growth rate in sales and profits from 1981 to 1984 was 27.4 percent and 93.5 percent respectively.

Behind Intel's fantastic performance was the fact that IBM had selected its microprocessor as the hardware for its new "microcomputer," which quickly became known simply as the "PC" for "Personal Computer." Had IBM chosen a different firm to provide the microprocessor for its PC, it is possible, indeed probable, that Intel, despite its proud history and all the brilliance of its engineers, would not have survived into the 1990s.

IBM introduced its PC in 1981. Some of its champions had been predicting "a dramatic explosion in demand" as soon as Big Blue's product hit the market. No one, however, anticipated how quickly this product would gain market acceptance. IBM's manufacturing facilities could produce a PC in forty-five seconds. It was not fast enough. In the first five months of 1983, PC sales equaled the previous year's total. Sales were so high that by the end of 1983, IBM's PC division alone, had it been an independent firm, would have been listed on the Fortune 500. In 1984, IBM PC sales were estimated at $5 billion, which would have made the division number 75 on the *Fortune* list.[112] Each one of those little boxes contained an Intel microprocessor.

Although Intel's overall performance in 1984 was spectacular, "the year ended on a down note."[113] Demand suddenly softened. Nevertheless, the twelve months as a whole were excellent.

Unfortunately, the same could not be said for 1985. "It was a miserable year for Intel and for the rest of the semiconductor industry," the *Annual Report* frankly announced. Few in the industry would disagree. "It's been a stinko year in the semiconductor industry," observed *Industry Week,* with "plant closings, layoffs, pay freezes and reductions." A projected 22 percent growth in the global semiconductor market had turned into a 17 percent decline.[114] The softness in the market in the fourth quarter of 1984 intensified, and prices went into free fall.

Sales at Intel fell 16 percent to $1.365 billion. Only during the first quarter did Intel record an operating profit. For the year as a whole, "net income . . . essentially disappeared," plummeting to $1.57 million.[115] Even that meager result was not generated by operations. Intel lost $60.2 million from operations in 1985, but that was offset by $54.7 million in interest income and a $7 million tax credit.[116] What did this mean for the company? "[L]ayoffs, plant closings, salary cuts and time off without pay, as well as delaying the completion of new facilities."[117]

Intel was being attacked on all sides and from all directions. From Europe and especially from Asia, large electronics companies were muscling into its markets. Domestically, small start-ups were carving out their own niches. Intel certainly could not be accused of avoiding reality, however unpleasant. The company was looking facts in the face. The facts were: no place to run, no place to hide. The news was grim, and there was no "happy talk" about what was on the horizon. "[Nineteen eighty-six] will probably be another tough year."[118]

The willingness to face the bad news lent credibility to the news that was not bad. Despite the miseries of this miserable year, there was progress to report. To the classic business school question—Are we doing today what will enable us to succeed tomorrow?—Intel could legitimately answer "yes." The company economized everywhere, but not in R&D. There, spending increased. In the factories, new levels of productivity were achieved.

A new product was introduced that was to prove the most important in the company's history. "The high point of 1985 was the introduction [in October] of the 80386, an advanced 32-bit microprocessor that is completely software-compatible" with Intel's previous microprocessors. Early indications were that this product had a great future.

Just two short years earlier, things had looked great. But in 1985, there was no more speculation about a happy future. To be sure, there was plenty of speculation, but of an altogether different kind. Bill Lowe, head of IBM's PC business, asked Grove in November what would happen if Intel went bankrupt. What would happen if a foreign company, such as Hitachi, bought 20 percent of the company? Such concerns would have been unimaginable so recently.

Nineteen eighty-six—the dark night of the soul at Intel Corporation. The forebodings of 1985 were fully borne out by events. Sales slid to $1.265 billion. The company lost over $173 million. This was Intel's first year in the red since 1970, when it was still in start-up mode. It was Intel's first money-losing year as a public company. Its Fortune 500 ranking slid to 256. Its market capitalization was down to $2.438 billion.

"We're pleased to report 1986 is over." With that sentence, containing a hint of wit, a sober-looking Moore and Grove began the *Annual Report*. What caused such dreadful results?

The culprit was the PC boom. Demand exceeded everyone's expectations, and Intel built capacity and grew in every way that it could to meet that demand. The bubble burst at the end of 1984, and "Intel was left with an overhead structure appropriate to the $2–3 billion company we wanted to be rather than $1.0–1.5 billion company we were becoming."[119]

It has been said that things always seem darkest just before they become completely black, but Intel made no such concession. The company adopted what might be called a countercyclical approach to public announcements: warning of potential problems when things were going well; pointing to hopeful signs when they were not.

What was hopeful in 1986? First, as just noted, Intel continued to do in the moment what would enable it to succeed in the future. It increased spending on R&D. Second, it reengineered its product offering, exiting unprofitable lines and focusing on promising ones. Third, the company implemented the advice Grove confided to himself in his notebooks about "Non-Growth" companies on August 11, 1974, and again on May 16, 1975. That is to say:

> We concentrated [during 1986] on strengthening relationships with our customers. We significantly improved delivery performance and started programs that enable customers to forego incoming inspection of Intel products, the latter made possible by our high product quality.... [C]ustomer satisfaction indicators have improved markedly....
>
> Intel is well positioned to grow.... Our product portfolio, manufacturing infrastructure, and customer relationships are all better than they were two years ago.[120]

The "Management Report" in the 1986 *Annual Report* contained a "postscript" from Intel's chairman, Gordon Moore. He announced that although he would remain chairman, Andy Grove would become chief executive officer in April 1987. "Andy has been at Intel since the beginning, and as president and chief operating officer, he has been one of the principal architects of this company's growth, direction, and character. . . . He is an extraordinarily talented manager."[121] Back at Fairchild in 1967, Grove had operated with the "fundamental assumption" that he would succeed Moore. Now, in a much bigger and more important corporate context, that assumption was borne out once again.

The picture the press painted of the challenges Grove faced was not particularly heartening. He had to "restore Intel to financial health." This would not be easy. He had two big problems. One was the Japanese, whose low prices had "battered" the company. The second was IBM, which was "becoming annoyed by the growing number of IBM clones using Intel parts." IBM's share of Intel's sales had plummeted from 20 percent in 1985 to 6 percent in 1986. What if IBM substituted its own microprocessors for Intel's? What if they redesigned their PC so that Intel's chips were no longer the standard? How about Grove himself? He "would have to give up much of the personal power he wields as president and chief operating officer if he wants to decentralize the company and make it more responsive to shifting technologies." Was this new approach something he was capable of adopting?[122]

9

Andy Grove in 1986: At Work and at Home

As early as 1982, Andy Grove began thinking about retirement. In November of that year, he taped an article from the *San Jose Mercury* into his notebooks entitled "Retirement Game: Knowing When to Quit." The subtitle provides the gist of the story: "As in Athletics, Your Career Is Judged by Your Exit. . . ."[1] Notes about succession planning began to surface in the notebooks late in 1983.[2]

Grove turned forty-six on September 2, 1982. By common standards, that is an early age for a healthy man to quit work. It is especially early when one considers Grove's commitment to Intel and his remarkable energy level. Life in Silicon Valley in the 1970s and 1980s was, however, quite different from life in corporate America in prior years. We have already encountered Mike Markkula, who retired, albeit for a short period, at the age of thirty-three.

Grove was a man of appetites and yearnings. He wanted to be not only a corporate executive, but also a public figure in the context of the business world. He never had the slightest interest in holding public office, either elected or appointed.

Andy had family responsibilities. There were four mouths to feed and two children to educate in Grove's nuclear family in the 1980s. He had succeeded in extricating his parents from Hungary. By the 1980s, they were living at the house at 3011 Ross Road in Palo Alto. In the mid-1970s, Andy, Eva, and their daughters moved into a spacious house in a quiet and appealing town in the Valley. Andy was financially responsible not only for his nuclear family, but also for his parents and for Eva's mother, who had moved to Palo Alto in 1965. He sent money back to relatives who had remained in Hungary. We can thus conclude that by the mid-1980s, Andy was financially secure.

Grove brought discipline to what was once a "cowboy" industry, semiconductors. Wal-Mart's founder, Sam Walton, said, "We always have tried to make life as interesting and as unpredictable as we can, and to make Wal-Mart a fun proposition."[3] Ever since Intel was born, Grove labored to do the reverse. I have never heard anyone describe Intel as "a fun proposition."

There was altogether too much fun in semiconductor companies in the Valley for Grove's taste. Too much drinking, although we should note that Andy was not bashful about having a couple of scotches at a recruiting dinner. Too much swapping of trade secrets. Too much sleeping late, which Grove found unacceptable even if followed by a late night at work. To push a quality product out the door demanded focus and concentration. That meant organization and adherence to schedule.

A symbol of the discipline Grove introduced was the "Late List," which he created in 1971. From then until 1988, if you showed up at work after 8:05, you had to sign in. This went for everyone, including the CEO.[4] One Intel employee was quoted in 1983 as having "seen vice presidents sprinting across the parking lot to make it." Said Grove, "We may have some millionaires around here, but they're the kind of guys who get up at 5 AM to meet with the swing shift."[5] This is the sort of thing that by 1985 made Grove known as one of the nation's toughest bosses.[6]

According to Grove critic Tim Jackson, the Late List, even though one's name on it generated no sanction, made a lot of people angry. "The idea," according to Jackson, "was strongly opposed by most of Intel's management and also by the human resource department." Federico Faggin saw it as a symbol of "regimentation" as Intel grew.[7]

Grove was quite unapologetic. He wanted to whip Intel into fighting trim. The Late List was one of his tools. It is, moreover, worth mentioning that the man who institutes such a program is bound by it. When he put pressure on Intel's employees, he put greater pressure on himself. He, above all others, could not afford to be late. That adds stress to your evenings and your mornings.

Grove believed that everything should be measured, quantitatively if at all possible, and that everything should be improved every day. Ranking and rating systems were used to evaluate all managers. In the words of Dennis Carter, a top executive with Intel who had served as Grove's "technical assistant," the evaluation of each manager against previously established objectives was a priority task. "If you are unprepared in a review meeting to talk factually about the employees you are reviewing, you are bludgeoned. I don't think anything we do is taken more seriously."[8]

Note that word "bludgeoned." Grove created a tough environment at Intel. One of the precepts of Intel culture was, and still is, "constructive confrontation." There has unquestionably been a great deal of confrontation at Intel over the years. Whether all or most of it has been constructive is a question concerning which reasonable people differ.[9]

As proponent and also product of this culture, Grove had to hold himself to the highest standard of all. He was known for his relentless drive to get at the truth behind business issues. He has always maintained that at Intel, arguments center on issues, not on the people involved in discussing them. Not everyone agrees. There are plenty of people at Intel who have experienced Grove's deep dive into the truth as, whether he intended it to be or not, a direct attack on them personally.

Grove himself, in calmer moments, has acknowledged that he has an impact on people that he does not fully understand. In the early 1980s, a staffer sent him a plaintive note beseeching him to "Say something nice!" He posted it on his cubicle wall. Apparently he needed help remembering.[10] That sign still remains in Grove's sparse office, encased in plastic on top of his cubicle wall.

Speaking of Frank Gill, a senior executive in the 1990s, Grove said, "I sensed that he was petrified, turned into mush with respect to the networking business. I still don't understand why he would be intimidated by me." Gill took exception to this characterization. This episode illustrates that Grove did not fully, consciously grasp that sometimes his verbal pyrotechnics could generate confusion and pain.[11] I brought Grove's statements about Gill to Grove's attention, and he said he simply could not understand Gill's feelings toward him.

The bottom line is that Andy Grove's Intel was a pressure cooker. It is not surprising that even he should find himself looking for a way out. Perhaps retirement was the valve that would release all that pent-up energy, anxiety, and anger.

Or perhaps just the idea of retirement served that purpose. Into the early 1990s, Grove thought about retirement on multiple occasions. When he became CEO in 1987, he said he was planning to retire at the age of fifty-five. In 1991, he said that he had changed his mind. He also said that he had been advised not to name a retirement date when he did so in the 1980s. He regretted not taking that advice and decided never again to announce his retirement far in advance.

Even at the time of this writing, in 2006, after Grove has stepped down as chairman of the board of Intel, he cannot quite bring himself to leave the company. He has become a "senior advisor" and maintains his cubicle on the fifth floor of Intel's headquarters building in Santa Clara. He has business dinners and is in regular email contact with Intel's current CEO, Paul S. Otellini.[12]

In 1986, Grove was on sabbatical from Intel. This sabbitical was a three-month break rather than a full year as it is in academic life. Moore asked him to cut his sabbatical short and help the company through its troubles.

What was Moore asking Grove to come back to? When Grove was at Intel in the mid-1980s, what did a week in his life look like? "How you handle your own time," he has written, "is, in my view, the single most important aspect of being a role model and leader."[13] How, then, did he handle his own time? We know what "one of my busier days" looked like because he has recorded an example in his book *High Output Management*.

A DAY FROM MY LIFE	
Time and Activity	Explanation (Type of Activity)
8:00–8:30 Met with a manager who had submitted his resignation to leave for another company.	I listened to his reasons *(information-gathering)*, felt he could be turned around and saved for Intel. Encouraged him to talk to certain other managers about a career change *(nudge)*, and decided to pursue this matter with them myself *(decision-making)*.

Time and Activity	Explanation (Type of Activity)
Incoming telephone call from a competitor.	Call was ostensibly about a meeting of an industry-wide society, but in reality he was feeling out how I saw business conditions. I did the same. *(Information-gathering)*.
8:30–9:00 Read mail from the previous afternoon.	I scribbled messages on about half of it, some of which were expressions of encouragement or disapproval, others exhortations to take certain types of action (*nudges*). One was the denial of a request to proceed with a particular small project *(decision-making)*. (Of course, *information-gathering* took place in all of these cases, too.)
9:00–12:00 Executive Staff Meeting (a regular weekly meeting of the company's senior management). Subjects covered at this particular one:	
—Review of the prior month's incoming order and shipment rates.	*(Information-gathering)*
—Discussion to set priorities for the upcoming annual planning process.	*(Decision-making)*
—Review of the status of a major marketing program (scheduled subject).	This came about through a prior decision that this program was faltering and required review. We found it was doing a little bit better than before *(information-gathering)*, but the presentation still elicited a lot of comments and suggestions *(nudges)* from various members of the audience.

Time and Activity	Explanation (Type of Activity)
—Review of a program to reduce the manufacturing cycle time of a particular product line (scheduled subject).	The presentation indicated that the program was in good shape. (It represented only *information-gathering;* no further action was stimulated.)
12:00–1:00 Lunch in the company cafeteria.	I happened to sit with members of our training organization, who complained about the difficulty they had in getting me and other senior managers to participate in training at our foreign locations *(information-gathering).* This was news to me. I made a note to follow up with my own schedule, as well as with my staff, and to *nudge* them into doing a better job supporting the foreign training program.
1:00–2:00 Meeting regarding a specific product-quality problem.	The bulk of the meeting involved getting sufficient information on the status of the product and the corrective action that had been implemented *(information-gathering).* The meeting ended in a *decision* made by the division manager, with my concurrence, to resume shipment of the product.
2:00–4:00 Lecture at our employee orientation program.	This is a program in which senior management gives all professional employees a presentation describing the objectives, history, management systems, etc., of the company and its major groups. I am the first lecturer in the series. This clearly represented *information-giving,* and I was a *role*

Time and Activity	Explanation (Type of Activity)
	model not only in communicating the importance we place on training, but also, by my handling of questions and comments, in representing, in living form, some of the values of the company. The nature of the questions, at the same time, gave me a feeling for the concerns and understanding level of a large number of employees to whom I would not otherwise have access. So this also represented *information-gathering,* characteristic of the "visit" type in its efficiency.
4:00–4:45 In the office, returning phone calls.	I disapproved granting a compensation increase to a particular employee, which I thought was way outside of the norm (clearly a *decision*). I decided to conduct a meeting with a group of people to decide what organization would move to a new site we were opening in another state. (This was a *decision* to hold a decision-making meeting.)
4:45–5:00 Met with my assistant.	Discussed a variety of requests for my time for a number of meetings in the upcoming week. Suggested alternatives where I *decided* not to attend.
5:00–6:15 Read the day's mail, including progress reports.	As with the morning's mail reading, this was *information-gathering,* interspersed with *nudging* and *decision-making* through my annotations and messages scribbled on much of it.

Grove counted twenty-three "separate activities in which I participated" in the day he has just narrated. The day "ends when I'm tired and ready to go home." It does not end when he is finished, because "a manager's work is never done."[14] He has described a busy, ten-hour day. But it is not a "gut-clutching" day. There are a great many people in this world who would envy being able to have a day that "ends when I'm tired." Why should a yearning for retirement enter into the thinking of a man living this life?

This is not all that one finds appealing. In not one of these twenty-three "separate activities" is Grove doing something because he is being ordered to. No one tells him what to do. He does a lot of things, but he is the person who decides what he will do. He dances to no one else's tune. "Oh, it's so fun to be on the top!" he once wrote Moore.[15] Unquestionably, there are worse jobs in the world.

What is missing from this outline is the passion, the "flow of self,"[16] that Grove invests in each of these twenty-three episodes. Also missing is how much you have to know about one of the most complicated businesses in the world to live this day successfully.

Let's take a look at Andy's first half hour at work. The day does not get off to a great start. Someone whom Andy wants to stay at the company has already resigned. To reject Intel is to reject Andy. So he has to sell Intel to an unwilling buyer. He had to know a lot about who this man was, what he did, what he might prefer, and whether he would be accepted by his new colleagues to know if the "career change" within Intel that Grove was proposing would work.

I have been informed by people other than Grove that on many issues, Tim Jackson's *Inside Intel* is not a reliable source. It is therefore with caution that I provide Jackson's account of the conversation Grove had with Federico Faggin when Faggin decided to leave Intel in 1974. Once it was clear that Faggin's decision was final, Grove sent him "on his way with a dismissal that amounted almost to a parting curse. 'What will you do if you leave Intel? . . . You will leave no heritage for your children. Your name will be forgotten. You will fail. You will fail in everything you do.'"[17] Jackson described these words as having an "almost medieval brutality." Faggin's own account is a little less melodramatic. In a 1995 interview, he said, "Andy even . . . you know . . . when I left . . . when I had my sort of 'exit interview' . . . no actually he was still trying to make me stay but he intimated that I would leave no heritage to my children if I leave Intel." This statement was followed by laughter.[18]

Perhaps this story is apocryphal. Perhaps something like it took place, but it has been embellished in the retelling. Whatever the truth of this particular encounter, we can say that Grove has "separation anxiety." He does not like to travel. He dislikes being away from his wife, Eva. When his mother was elderly and living alone as a widow in Palo Alto, from 1987 to her death in 2002, Grove phoned her every day. Maria Gróf and Andy and Eva had a relationship that was not an easy one when she immigrated to the United States. Maria became cantankerous with age, a mood that intensified with the death of her husband in 1987. Nevertheless, Andy phoned her every day. Only when seen in the light of this separation anxiety can we appreciate the courage it must have taken to flee Budapest, leaving his parents behind, in 1956.

This is an admittedly long way of saying that his first task of the day might not have been all that pleasant. Was the next? He receives a phone call, apparently unscheduled, from a competitor. What ensues is a "virtual conversation." The two speak in code. Both talk about a trade association meeting, but both wanted to find out the other's view of "business conditions." Grove's antennae are out during every minute of this discussion. Not a word passes his lips without being filtered through the test of: how will this word benefit Intel?

A similar story could be told about the remaining twenty-one encounters of this day. It was a demanding day because Grove demands a great deal of others and more of himself. Thoughts of escape into retirement are not, therefore, surprising.

Despite the high stakes of Grove's job and the intensity he brought to it, he had a rich home life. True, the Grove family considered Intel almost like a third child. Nevertheless, it was a child that was put in its place.

Andy was usually home for dinner. He was usually available to be with Eva after dinner. He might make a phone call or two about business, and, especially if he were recruiting a promising hire, he might go out to dinner on a weeknight. But as a rule, he was at home in mind as well as body during weeknights.

Grove rarely went into the office on weekends. He had a study in his home and he used it, but he did not usually work seven days a week. He made an effort to "be there for the girls" as they were growing up.

Andy accompanied Eva and Karen when the time came for her to select a college. She settled on Berkeley, where she majored in mechanical engineering. She then went on to Stanford, where she earned an MS in the same subject.

Robie was more oriented toward the theater. She loved to perform. When she was in second grade and Karen was in fourth, they both had roles in the school play, *The Sound of Music.* Andy and Eva saw multiple performances.[19]

After graduating from high school, she went to the University of Washington and majored in theater. To the relief of her parents, she developed an interest in physical therapy, in which she received a master's degree from the University of Puget Sound.

Both children and their families vacation periodically with Andy and Eva. Both are involved with their parents in the philanthropy of the Grove Foundation.

I am not suggesting that the Grove family was friction-free and that no member ever had a problem. I do want to assert that Andy has been a devoted family man. His home has been a haven in a world that, if not heartless, was at times not very nice. He had four weeks of vacation a year, and "he took them," according to Eva.[20] He had periodic sabbaticals from Intel, and he took them as well.

Were there exceptions in business emergencies? Yes. Moore asked him to cut his sabbatical short in 1986, and he did so. But Grove did not sacrifice his family to his job. I have seen the family albums. The Groves knew how to have fun. Given who he was at work—the tension, the effort, the conflict—the extent to which he was able to compartmentalize work and home is enviable.

10

"The Valley of Death"

Gordon Moore had a small wooden plaque that had etched on it:

This is a profit-making organization. That's the way we intended it. . . .
And that's the way it is![1]

It certainly did not look that way in 1986 with the loss of $173 million. With the benefit of hindsight, we know that Intel pulled out of this dive dramatically in 1987. Sales soared 51 percent to $1.9 billion. The profit picture was equally exciting, hitting a record $248 million.[2] Market capitalization increased by almost $2 billion to $3.328 billion. In 1987, Intel placed 200 on the Fortune 500, higher than ever before. We know today that Intel reached the precipice in 1986 but was able to leap it and continue its climb the following year. No one was arguing with Moore's sign displayed in 1987.

Life, however, is not lived in hindsight. What if the collapse of 1986 had continued into 1987? If the company experienced another 7.3 percent decline in sales, they would have dropped to $1.172 billion, well below the level of 1984. If the company's losses had continued at the 1986 rate, it would have been close to $350 million in the red, losing almost a million dollars a day. Its market capitalization would have fallen to $1.767 billion. Intel's situation would have been dire.

On May 10, 1940, Winston Churchill became prime minister of Great Britain. He was sixty-five years of age and had been written off politically on innumerable occasions. Britain was facing a threat to its existence as acute as any in its long history.

Churchill greeted his new position not with anxiety, but with its opposite. He went to bed on May 10 with "a profound sense of relief. At last I had authority to give directions over the whole scene. I felt as if I were walking with destiny and that all my past life had been but a preparation for this hour and for this trial."[3] This kind of Shakespearean language does not typify Grove's self-expression, but it might well have captured his feelings. In Grove's infancy and childhood, Admiral Miklós Horthy had delighted in parading around in his admiral's regalia mounted on a white stallion. I doubt that any individual could have been further from Grove's conscious thoughts in 1986 than Miklós Horthy. Yet such display makes an impression on young boys that can be enduring.

During the Seven Years War (1756–1763), William Pitt the Elder, First Earl of Chatham, was Britain's secretary of state. As such, he was in charge of military affairs. When he was reelected to Parliament in 1758, he declared, "I am sure I can save the country and no one else can."[4] Was Andy thinking such thoughts as he was called back from his sabbatical? He probably was not thinking of either Pitt or Churchill, much less of Horthy. But the images and declarations may have been in his mind. Andy is a knowledgeable, liberally educated man with a sense of history and a remarkable sense of the moment. Now it was his turn, not Art Rock's (Intel's banker), Bob Noyce's (Intel's image to the outside world), or Gordon Moore's (Intel's greatest technologist). It is especially worth commenting that Moore did not ask for Noyce to come back. He was not the man for this kind of situation.

Now it was Andy's turn, and he was going to make the most of it. He knew, and others did too, that he could save the company and that no one else could.

Grove has cautioned against drawing sharp distinctions between "management" and "leadership." One hears arguments in the academic world about management being "transactional." Management concerns itself with the myriad activities that, when undertaken effectively, keep the corporation running and increase its profitability.

Leadership, one can argue, is "transformational." The leader drives the company in a whole new direction. The leader is charismatic and inspirational. His or her impact helps people exceed their own expectations of themselves.[5]

The problem with these definitions is that, in Grove's words, "there is an implicit value judgment that suggests that leadership is better than management. In reality, you need both capabilities." Grove believes that "the same person should be able to do transactional jobs when those are needed and transformational jobs when those are needed. . . . A tennis player has both a forehand and a backhand. Not all tennis players are equally good at both, but we don't talk about backhand players and forehand players."[6]

True. Indeed, if anything, Grove's career indicates a bias toward management and a skepticism that borders on the acute when it comes to leadership, especially charismatic leadership. He and others in the company were proud when *Dun's Review* named Intel one of the "five best-managed" companies in the United States.[7] There was no similar survey on the "five best-led" American companies.

Grove's efforts, more than anyone else's, put Intel deservedly on that list. John Doerr said that Grove made Intel the best-managed technology company in the world.[8] The semiconductor industry had historically been plagued by poor management. Grove was determined to see Intel break that mold. Remember that Grove's first full-time experience in a corporation was at Fairchild Semiconductor from 1963 to 1968. If ever a company was "over-led" and "under-managed," it was Fairchild. Grove blamed Noyce, the perfect example of a charismatic leader, for that state of affairs.

If people were going to say nasty things about him because of his Late List and other such devices to instill discipline at Intel, Grove could not have cared less. He did not need the affection of Intel's workforce. What he needed, what he demanded, was that Intel's employees manage their work lives rigorously.

Grove's first book not on a technical topic, *High Output Management*,[9] is all about management, not leadership. The book makes reference to "leadership," but only in passing. The words "charisma," "transformation," and even "strategy" do not appear in the index. The first two chapters concern themselves with running a restaurant called "Andy's Better Breakfasts." The chapter titles are "The Basics of Production: Delivering a Breakfast (or a College Graduate, or a Compiler, or a Convicted Criminal . . .)" and "Managing the

Breakfast Factory."[10] He did not have a chapter on "Leading the Breakfast Factory" or "Transforming Andy's Better Breakfasts into Chez Panisse."

Even conceding these points, the fact is that in 1986, Grove acted as a "leader," if that word has any meaning. In February and March of 1986, he had been skiing in St. Anton in Austria and at Lake Tahoe in California. This earned, private time had been interrupted, as he returned to Intel a week early. This gesture alone was noteworthy.

Grove is doubtless correct that a businessperson should manage when management is called for and lead when leadership is called for. Two sides of the same coin. Backhand and forehand. However, if one looks at business history, one will find precious few executives who are equally good at both these tasks. To use Grove's own metaphor, it is not easy to hit a winning backhand if you have spent your life on the tennis court running around that backhand to hit a forehand at every opportunity. In 1986, Grove had to be downright ambidextrous.

Enough of metaphors. What did Grove do? To make a long story short, he presided over the creation of a new product line for Intel. Under his leadership—his management also, but preeminently his leadership—Intel exited the memory business and became a microprocessor company. Or, as he put it, "The most significant thing was the transformation of the company from a broadly positioned, across-the-board semiconductor supplier that did OK to a highly focused, highly tuned producer of microprocessors, which did better than OK."[11]

This is a long story that should not be made short. Intel's success at navigating a major technological discontinuity in its industry is a remarkable saga of the confluence of technological imperatives, economic globalization, human knowledge (how people learn), and human passion (how people feel).

Who worked at Intel? Why was the company founded? Why did people continue to work there when they were economically secure? Were Intel employees "mercenaries" or were they "marines"? To return to a question we have asked twice already, what holds a company together?

Companies have to make money or they will die. Intel was founded to make money. During its existence, it has been one of the world's most profitable corporations, and it has made a lot of people rich. "From its founding, Intel . . . had a strong profit and shareholder-value orientation and the finance group held a prominent position within the company."[12]

Intel's founders were, however, motivated by more than money alone. One could argue that for them, money was like air. You have to have air to breathe, and you have to breathe to live. But you don't live so you can breathe. That is not the purpose of your life.[13]

What was Intel's corporate purpose? If you read the company's reports and listen to the speeches of its leaders over the years, themes that recur constantly are technology and revolution. Intel wanted to change the world through developing new technology. Gordon Moore, the man with the "profit" sign, was also the man quoted in the *Dun's Review* article just mentioned saying, "We're in the business of revolutionizing society."[14] At the Intel Sales and Marketing Conference in 2000, Andy Grove took questions from the floor about the company. One salesman asked, in front of an audience of thousands of employees, what Andy thought were the most important technological developments of the second half of the twentieth century. He said the most important was atomic weaponry. The second most important was the democratization of information. In that second category, he said, Intel had played a not insignificant role. Indeed, with the benfit of hindsight we can say that Andy Grove, Bill Gates, and Steve Jobs are the three most important figures in the computer revolution that has swept the world.

Did Grove really mean what he said? Without question. Did his saying it on the spur of the moment before thousands of his troops constitute an act of leadership? Intel's minions in the audience certainly thought so. From the beginning, Intel's founders evinced "a strong appreciation of the importance of technical depth and excellence."[15] These were proud people. We know from private papers that were never meant to be seen by the outside world that the thought that they might be "faking it" when it came to technology haunted them in the early years. Remember the phrase "bleed blue." Intel's culture has exerted a very strong pull. People have worked harder for that company than sane people should.

Intel began as the memory company. Its beginning was not easy. Looking back on it in 1996, Grove wrote that much of what became Intel culture was forged during the frustrations of those early years. "[S]truggling with this tough technology and the accompanying manufacturing problems left an indelible imprint on Intel's psyche. We became good at solving problems." Also came a results orientation and "constructive confrontation."[16]

By the end of the 1970s, Intel's people were feeling pretty good about life. There were competitive battles, and Intel did not win every time. But "[w]e won our share."[17] In the 1980s, however, a new kind of competition entered the semiconductor memory market.

Japanese companies had been exporting products to the United States since the 1950s. By chance, their earliest exports used semiconductors. These were cheap transistor radios. Early Japanese automobile exports were laughed off American highways. From 1950 through the mid-1970s, the Japanese were easy to underestimate—and Americans did. By 1980, however, in a whole range of products, from automobiles to consumer electronics to semiconductors, they became a lot harder to underestimate. By the time the Japanese challenge was recognized, it was already too late for many American-based companies to compete effectively against them in our own home market, much less abroad. Thus begins the economic globalization aspect of our story.

In Grove's assessment, the Japanese were a pleasure to have around in the late 1970s. They helped out when Intel could not keep up with demand. Seemingly overnight, however, Japanese competitors appeared to have transformed themselves from docile puppies to ferocious pit bulls. In one paragraph of one of his books, Grove twice describes them as "scary." Huge facilities housing floor after floor of skilled engineers working on tomorrow's technology. Rock-bottom cost of capital made possible by the intricate highways and byways of "Japan, Inc." In addition to this was the fact that their product quality was suddenly superior.[18] For Grove, the "insidious" Japanese attack on the American economy featured "these humongous companies with their humongous factories trying to take a major share of whatever we have left away from us."[19]

As if all this were not enough, the Japanese had learned what aggressive marketing was all about. "Win with the 10% rule," announced one memorandum. "Find AMD [Advanced Micro Devices] and Intel sockets. . . . Quote 10% below their price. . . . If they requote, go 10% AGAIN. . . . Don't quit until you WIN!" Intel had been so proud of its Operation CRUSH in 1979 and 1980, which had achieved so many design wins against Motorola's arguably better product. Now the shoe was on the other foot. Giant Japanese firms with superb products, high volumes, and privileged access to capital were mounting their own version of Operation CRUSH against not only Intel but the whole American semiconductor industry, and they were winning.

In 1985, as Figure 4 below illustrates, the Japanese suppliers overtook the American industry in global share of market for semiconductors. The Japanese seemed to have discovered a whole new way to compete. Market share was everything. Profitability could wait.

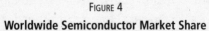

FIGURE 4
Worldwide Semiconductor Market Share

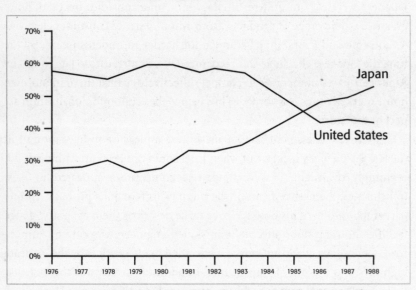

Source: Andrew S. Grove, *Only the Paranoid Survive: How to Exploit the Crisis Points That Challenge Every Company* (New York: Doubleday, 1996), p. 86.

How do people react when they find themselves facing a fact that is too terrible to be true? They deny it. If something is too terrible to be true, then it cannot be true, because if it were, things would be too terrible. Intel's executives, their high IQs to the contrary notwithstanding, were no different from other human beings in this regard. "This had to be wrong," they told themselves. "As people often do in this kind of situation," Grove later wrote, "we vigorously attacked the ominous data."[20]

When the evidence became too overwhelming to deny, Intel fought back. However, as is so often said of generals, it was fighting the last war. Anything it could do in the memory market, the Japanese were able to do better. The competition was not even close.

The numbers were really bad. Figure 5 shows the percentage of Intel's revenues derived from memory chips and logic chips (i.e., microprocessors). The sustained slide in memories as a percentage of Intel's sales began in 1978.

Figure 5

Memory and Logic as a Percentage of Intel's Sales

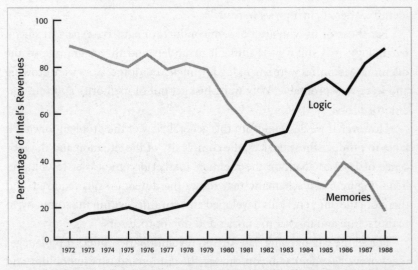

Source: Robert A. Burgelman, *Strategy Is Destiny: How Strategy-Making Shapes a Company's Future* (New York: Free Press, 2002), p. 93.

The lines of the chart on Figure 5 crossed in 1982. Intel became a microprocessor company at that time and has been ever since. In 1980, Intel's worldwide market share in DRAMs was under 3 percent.[21]

Given these facts, why was the decision to exit the DRAM market so difficult? And there is no question that it was difficult—"traumatic" is the word usually attached to it by the people who lived through it. At this point, we must deal with the ways in which people know things and come to terms with reality.

"Managing," says Grove, one of the most rational managers in the history of business, "especially managing through a crisis, is an extremely personal affair." From a personal point of view, Intel's top management generated quite a few reasons to stay in the memory business. In truth these were not reasons. They were rationalizations. But that is apparent only in hindsight, which, as we have already had occasion to observe, is not how life is lived.

DRAMs were the spoiled darling of Intel's product line. "The bulk of the memory chips [i.e., DRAMs] development took place in a spanking new facility in Oregon. The microprocessor technology developers had to share a production facility—not even a new one at that—with the manufacturing folks at a remote site. Our priorities," Grove explains, "were formed by our identity; after all, memories *were* us."[22]

For those of us who are not semiconductor engineers expert in silicon technology, it is still a little difficult to understand the magnitude of the dilemma. Memories were shrinking for Intel. Microprocessors were growing and were very profitable. Why wait? Just get out of memories and into microprocessors.

However, if we descend from this general view of the problem to what it takes to produce these devices, the complexity of the situation and the reticence of Intel to abandon the memory market become easier to comprehend. Figure 6 is a schematic that shows the different skills required, and therefore the different skills developed and rewarded within the company, to manufacture and market memories and microprocessors.

For all the talk of being data-driven revolutionaries, Intel's top management proved as adept as anyone in, say, the fashion industry in bobbing and weaving in the face of brute facts. Up until 1984, the microprocessor business had been so good that it had served to obscure a lot of problems the company as a whole faced. But when the tide of the semiconductor business began to recede, the shoals that could wreck the good ship Intel had to be dealt with.

Writes Grove:

We had meetings and more meetings, bickering and arguments, resulting in nothing but conflicting proposals. There were those who proposed what they called a "go for it" strategy: "Let's build a gigantic factory dedicated to producing memories and nothing but memories, and let's take on the Japanese." Others proposed that we should get really clever and use an avant-garde technology, "go for it," but in a technological rather than a manufacturing sense and build something the Japanese producers couldn't build. Others were still clinging to the

FIGURE 6

The Differences Between Memories and Microprocessors

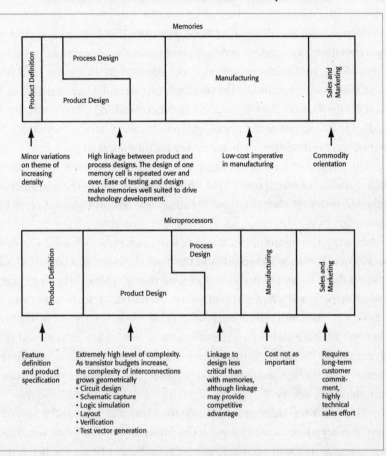

Source: Robert A. Burgelman, *Strategy Is Destiny: How Strategy-Making Shapes a Company's Future* (New York: Free Press, 2002), p. 58.

idea that we could come up with special-purpose memories, an increasingly unlikely possibility as memories became a uniform worldwide commodity.[23]

While all these options were being chewed over, money kept flying out the door. "We had lost our bearings," Grove said. "We were wandering in the valley of death."[24]

Two beliefs that Grove said were "as strong as religious dogmas" made it more difficult than it otherwise would have been to get out of a product that any objective outsider could see was a loser for Intel. One of these "dogmas" was that memory was Intel's "technology driver." Note the phrase "technology development" under "Product Design" in the "Memories" section of Figure 6. Because memory devices were easier to test than other Intel products, they were traditionally the products that were debugged first. The lessons learned could then be applied to other products. Intel's identity was rooted in its excellence in technology. In its industry, technology and testosterone were linked. Real men live on the technological edge.

The second dogma dealt with marketing. Intel owed it to its customers and therefore its salesforce to field a full line of products. The customers demanded one-stop shopping, and if Intel could not provide that service, its customers might defect to someone else who would.[25]

At one point in mid-1985, after a year of "aimless wandering," Grove said to Moore, "If we got kicked out and the board brought in a new CEO, what do you think he would do?" Moore immediately replied, "He would get us out of memories." "I stared at him, numb, then said, 'Why shouldn't you and I walk out the door, come back, and do it ourselves?'"[26] Note the word "numb." We have seen it before. Andy was "numb" when he returned to his apartment in Budapest from where his mother and he had been hiding in January 1945. Once again, he could "cushion and distance himself from an unfathomable reality."[27]

This was a real moment of truth in the history of Intel, and it should be part of every management course at our business schools. Grove was able, by self-creating new management, to adopt a different frame for his decision making. He was no longer the actor. Now he was the audience. The audience was so displeased with the actor that it would give him the "hook" if it could. He was no longer the subject. He was the object. He got outside himself and looked at the situation as a fantasized, rational actor would.

This was a cognitive tour de force. It was made possible by Grove's capacity to frame issues differently from the way others do.[28]

Grove said that even after this moment of clarity, effective action was inhibited by the intensity of emotion around this product and around the thought that Intel had been beaten at its own game. When he started talking about jettisoning memories, "I had a hard time getting the words out of my mouth without equivocation."

How do you get something like this done? Once you know that you have got to get rid of a product, how do you implement the decision? When I started teaching at the Harvard Business School more than a quarter of a century ago, a businessman said to me that if you are going to cut off a dog's tail, it is best to cut it right at the torso rather than half an inch at a time. The observation struck me as quite uncalled-for and even sadistic. We were talking about business, not the mutilation of animals. The point he was dramatically making was that if you have made a tough decision, you should implement it cleanly, completely, and without hesitation. The pain will only be greater if you move in stages.

Intel moved in stages, as if its executives were working their way through a trance. At one point, Grove, to his own amazement, allowed another executive to persuade him "to continue to do R&D for a [memory] product that he and I both knew we had no plans to sell."[29]

At last, at long last, Intel got out of the memory business. It had taken three years.[30] A decade later, Grove recalled that the mechanics of getting out of that business were "very hard." It was a "year-and-a-half-long process of shutting down factories, letting people go, telling customers we are no longer in the business, and facing the employees who all grew up in the memory business, who all prided themselves on their skills and those skills were no longer appropriate for the direction that we were going to take with microprocessors."[31] The wounds remained always fresh for Grove. No matter what success Intel achieved, he never ceased to believe that what had happened before could happen again.

Lessons learned? For Grove, the whole memory episode reinforced in his mind the importance of middle management. "While [top] management was kept from responding by beliefs that were shaped by our earlier success, our production planners and financial analysts dealt with allocations and numbers in an objective world."[32] So it was simply vital to have the ranks of middle management populated by top-flight executives and then to pay careful heed to what they say and do.

Second, in Grove's words, "It is always easier to start something than to kill something."[33] Therefore, you better be very careful about what you start. That is, however, another example of a lesson that may have been learned too well. With the triumphant exception of microprocessors in personal computers, Intel has not set the world on fire introducing new products into new markets.

Third, when your failure has been of the noble variety rather than the result of stupid mistakes, you as the top manager have to figure out a way to keep the talent that was involved in that unavoidable failure in the company.[34] This is the Microma story once again, but the stakes were higher. The DRAM technology development group was unquestionably highly talented. "The DRAM TD group led the company in linewidth reduction. They were already developing a 1-micron process while the logic group was still developing a 1.5-micron process. Sunlin Chou and his group were widely regarded as Intel's best resource for process development."[35] Grove had hired Sunlin Chou at Fairchild in 1964 and always held him in particularly high regard.

What is called for in situations like this can legitimately be denominated as something more than management. What is called for is leadership. "So I went up to Oregon," Grove tells us. Oregon was the headquarters of the DRAM team. The team was worried about its future, not without reason.

Grove gathered them into an auditorium and delivered a speech whose theme was "Welcome to the mainstream." Intel was making the transition from a memory company to a microprocessor company. In fact, the transition had already been made for Intel by marketplace realities. Although this group had not been involved in microprocessors, there was plenty of room for them, and the company would do what it could to help them make the contribution Grove knew they could.

The speech "actually went a lot better than I had expected." Grove's audience, knowledgeable people below the ranks of top management, had seen the handwriting on the wall and wanted some resolution of the situation.[36] Thus Grove narrates this story as one in which "the CEO is the last to know" what others inside and outside the company had already figured out. Perhaps. However, that would not be the case as Intel moved self-consciously forward as a microprocessor company.

11

"The PC Is It"

Andy Grove officially became president and CEO of Intel on April 23, 1987. He replaced Gordon Moore as chairman of the board in the spring of 1997. From the spring of 1997 to the following year, Grove was both Intel's chairman of the board and CEO. In May 1998, he relinquished the position of CEO to Craig Barrett while remaining chairman of the board until 2005. This decade proved as eventful as any in Grove's life.

Eva's father died in 1963, but her mother, who also moved to Palo Alto, lived until 2003. George Gróf, "Gyurka," was in frail health by the 1980s. He was not adept at languages, and his English was passable, but nothing more. Nevertheless, photos of him at family gatherings show a smiling and relaxed man. As the years passed, his health, especially the condition of his heart, deteriorated. In 1987, on the eve of his son's greatest professional success, George Gróf passed away. Andy regrets that his father did not live to see the magnitude of Intel's achievement during his leadership of the company.[1] His mother did. She died in 2002.

Outside of Grove's family, outside of California, outside of the United States, events were taking place of world-historical importance. Berlin was bisected by a giant, formidable wall, which had been erected on the night of August 13, 1961. As the years passed, the wall was fortified and strengthened. It symbolized the division of the world into two hostile camps led by the Soviet Union and the United States. None of us who saw that wall and toured

East Berlin through "Checkpoint Charlie" will live to forget it. Two different armed forces and political philosophies met there in an atmosphere of mutual hostility. It was a powder keg. A careless match could ignite World War III and the end of the human race.

The wall was backed up by machine guns and watchtowers. Almost two hundred people were killed trying to escape over it from East to West. It was literally cast in concrete. It was a palpable symbol that civilization existed on a precipice because of a division between peoples that everybody thought was permanent.

At 10:30 on the evening of November 9, 1989, the inconceivable happened. A moribund, politically bankrupt East German regime simply gave up the ghost. The wall was breached. By the end of the year, communism had collapsed in what was once the Warsaw Pact. Grove's birthplace, Hungary, became a free country. At least one of his relatives, whose husband had been killed following the 1956 revolt, visited him in California.

By the end of 1991, the Soviet Union itself had disintegrated. The Baltic states, the former "Soviet republics" of Central Asia, and even the Slavic Soviet republics of Belarus and Ukraine had become independent. The Soviet Union—the mighty superpower whose Red Army had turned back Hitler's Wehrmacht at Moscow, Leningrad, and Stalingrad and occupied Berlin in 1945; whose armed forces backed by missiles and ten thousand nuclear warheads had menaced the West for decades; whose scientists and engineers had launched a satellite before the United States—had lost the cold war. To the generation of baby boomers who had grown to maturity following World War II, such a turn of events was unimaginable. But it happened. It was true. And it mattered.

With China slowly turning its back on communism in everything but name, and with India moving away from its previous policy of autarchy, the whole world was coming to accept Western-style market mechanisms. Globalization now meant a lot more than North America, Western Europe, and Japan. This had major implications for all of business. Intel was certainly no exception. Indeed, as early as 1987, 39 percent of Intel's sales were outside the United States.[2]

During Grove's tenure as CEO, the upheaval in the computing industry matched in its context the dramatic changes taking place in the world at large. When Grove took over, the computer industry was still dominated by

IBM in mainframes and the Digital Equipment Corporation (DEC) in minicomputers. A DEC minicomputer was a large machine and not to be confused with the "personal computer" that was soon to wind up on everybody's desk.

By any measure, IBM was the behmoth of the industry. Its sales in 1987 were a record $54.2 billion. Profits, at $5.3 billion, did not reach record levels that year, but they were up half a billion dollars from 1986. Neither was market capitalization of $72.2 billion a record, but it too had increased from the previous year. Intel's comparable numbers were $1.9 billion, $248 million, and $4.3 billion, respectively. Thus, IBM, which was Intel's biggest customer, recorded profits in 1987 that were a billion dollars higher than Intel's market capitalization. And Intel, under Andy Grove's direction, was about to poke Big Blue, as IBM was known in those days, in the eye.

IBM was the purest example of what Grove called the "vertically aligned" model of the computer industry. It had

> its own semiconductor chip implementation, [built] its own computer around these chips according to its own design and in its own factories, develop[ed] its own operating system software (the software that is fundamental to the workings of all computers), and market[ed] its own applications software (the software that does things like accounts payable or airline ticketing or department store inventory control). This combination of a company's own chips, own computers, own operating systems and own applications software would then be sold as a package by the company's own salespeople.[3]

"Note," Grove points out, "how often the word 'own' occurs in this description." Not by accident. This was the "proprietary" business model that IBM perfected with the introduction of its 360, announced in 1964. This was also how DEC, Sperry Univac, and Wang did business.[4]

This business model propelled DEC to become the largest employer in the Commonwealth of Massachusetts, where it was headquartered, in the mid-1980s. In 1987, DEC hired the *Queen Elizabeth II* to sail into Boston Harbor for a celebration of how wonderful the company was. As late as 1990, a book about DEC's founder, Ken Olsen, was published, entitled *The Ultimate Entrepreneur*.[5] The title was not meant to be taken ironically.

This is the business model that created great corporate empires and immense personal wealth. This was the industry's dominant design when Grove became CEO of Intel. But not when he stepped down.

During the eleven years that he was Intel's CEO, Grove made his share of mistakes. He was also lucky, making some guesses that could have turned out not as well as they did.

Above all, however, Grove was shrewd and astute about the one issue concerning which he had to be right. Grove understood that "The PC Is It."[6] This insight should not be taken for granted. The PC was launched into the stratosphere at the beginning of the 1980s by IBM. What followed was a classic bubble. "We have a lot of capacity just around the corner," Gordon Moore told *BusinessWeek* in September 1985.[7] It turned out to be too much capacity. As Moore explained to the New York Society of Security Analysts on February 13, 1986, the overbuilding of 1984 and 1985 resulted because "we were trying to respond to seemingly insatiable demand."[8]

It is an extraordinary challenge to manage through a bubble. The biggest problem is that you do not know when you are in the midst of one. You find yourself in the grip of a herd mentality. Every signal says, "Get big, fast." Normal metrics for analyzing a business are thrown out the window. All of a sudden, everyone is saying that something special, unique in history, is happening. You can jump on the train or be left behind. If you object that demand cannot continue to grow at the pace you are seeing, or that assets are being overvalued, you are met not by an argument but by an assertion. It is among the most dangerous assertions in business. "This time," you are invariably told, "it's different." There is something new under the sun, which means that old metrics don't matter.

Maybe the assertion is true. Maybe "it," a new technology or a new business model, really is new. But maybe not. If not, you are going to wind up building a lot of useless facilities, chasing a "ghost market."[9] If so, if there is a new market, the very fact of its novelty renders planning difficult. If you don't hire enough people and build enough capacity, you are going to lose market share to a more aggressive competitor. If you overshoot the mark, even if there really is a new market, you are going to have to shutter plants and fire people, and you may find yourself in financial trouble. In 1985, according to *BusinessWeek,* when Intel began to lose money, Grove "shut down eight plants and cut [the company's] workforce by 30%."[10] By year's end, Intel had posted an operating loss of $60 million, its first since 1971. Profit margins had suffered a "precipitous decline" of 15 percent for the year and 25 percent for the fourth quarter.[11] Apparently Intel was falling behind in its "mad dash to keep up with Japan."[12]

In the midst of a bubble, there is a great deal of noise. New companies are being founded almost, it seems, by the hour. You can't walk into a hotel or restaurant without seeing fevered, whispered discussions about new business breakthroughs. The impulse to follow the crowd is overwhelming.

Meanwhile, other events are rocking your company. In Intel's case, the whole drama of the loss of the DRAM business coincided with the slump in the personal computer industry. But the loss of the DRAM business did not also mean the loss of EPROMs. In this segment of the memory market, Intel continued to make money.

In addition to all this, life happens. Remember that Andy Grove's father died on April 27, 1987, four days after Andy became CEO of Intel.

It was up to Grove to organize the company so that it could capitalize on the opportunity presented by the rise of personal computers. Despite overshooting the mark in the early 1980s, and, as a result, overinvesting in property, plant, and equipment, Intel had to avoid the "once bitten, twice shy" syndrome. It had to marshal all its resources to win a battle for the desktops of America and the world. Because the truth is that something fundamental really had changed, and the advantage would fall to the firm that could exploit that change.

Business in the late twentieth century turned out to be all about information. Information processing became the essential infrastructure of the era. The computer was to the United States of 1990 what the railroad was to the United States of 1890. It was the backbone of business.

By its willingness to open up its personal computer to outside vendors, IBM made a decision that spelled spectacular success in the short term, but disaster down the road. This was indeed a one-time change. It ranked in importance with the standardization of railroad gauges at the end of the nineteenth century. How was Intel to capitalize on it?

First, the company had to recognize the magnitude of the opportunity it faced. In his analysis of Tolstoy's view of history, Sir Isaiah Berlin divided people into two categories: the hedgehog and the fox. The fox knew many things. The hedgehog knew one big thing.[13] In 1987, Grove had to be both hedgehog and fox. The one big thing he had to know was that "The PC Is It." The many other things he had to know would enable him to capitalize on that one big fact for Intel.

In both these roles, Grove succeeded. He was hedgehog and fox. He figured out how to do the right things right. We have seen how Grove himself thought "the CEO was the last to know" about the necessity for exiting the DRAM business. Robert Burgelman, a longtime student of Intel who is as skeptical as any scholar about the ability of business executives to pull rabbits out of hats, agrees with Grove about the DRAM market story.

When it came to microprocessors and personal computers, the situation was quite different. "Andy Grove's decade as CEO of Intel Corporation," Burgelman has written, "was a rare case in which a company leader successfully set strategic intent and created a process for its relentless and successful pursuit."[14] Everybody's dream—the right strategy and effective implementation—came together in this decisive decade.

Up until 1985, it appeared that Intel's biggest problem with microprocessors was posed not by its domestic competitors nor by its giant customer, IBM. Figure 7 illustrates global share of market for microprocessors.

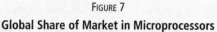

FIGURE 7
Global Share of Market in Microprocessors

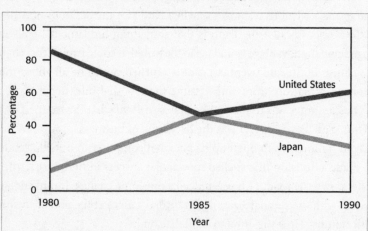

Source: Robert A. Burgelman, *Strategy Is Destiny: How Strategy-Making Shapes a Company's Future* (New York: Free Press, 2002), p. 136.

A glance at Figure 7 up until 1985 looks a lot like Figure 4 (p. 204). Japanese manufacturers are knocking the socks off of American companies. Intel's marketing manager for the 386, Claude M. Leglise, said of the Japanese chip makers, "They're awesome competitors."[15] But suddenly, things turned around. Why? What happened?

"We learned," said Grove, "that we had to get around the companies that had subjugated us in DRAM." Note the verb "subjugated." The Japanese had done more than beaten Intel at a game that it once owned. They had "subjugated" the company. They had rendered it subservient.[16] Intel was in business to make money, but its people were marines as well as mercenaries. Losing hurt so much that you had to bend every effort to see to it that it did not happen again.[17]

"We learned," continued Grove, "that high market share was critical for success, and that to get market share we had to be willing to invest in manufacturing capacity. Such investments involve big bets because they have to be made in advance of actual demand. We learned that commodity businesses are unattractive, so we didn't want to license out our intellectual property anymore."[18]

Here was Intel's strategy clearly laid out. Some aspects were familiar from the company's history. Intel had always been a manufacturer, for example. Now, however, it was going to set a new standard.

Addressing the New York Society of Security Analysts in February 1986, Moore said that the "level of competition" in manufacturing had "obviously increased" recently. The Japanese focused on it, and their success was clear. In the past, Intel's "emphasis was on competing in process technology superiority and being one generation ahead of the rest of the world. Our cost reduction efforts were principally technology driven: shrink to tighter dimensions and go to higher integration."[19] In other words, Intel was competing by following the roadmap laid out by what everyone but Moore referred to as Moore's law.

Intel had no intention of letting up on this dimension, but it did intend to focus on manufacturing more prominently than in the past.

We are doing a lot to improve our general manufacturing technology. We are automating. . . . We are acquiring manufacturing technologies through partnerships, and we are studying what others are doing. We have made tremendous advances over the last 12 months in equipment utilization, yields and the productivity of our direct and indirect work forces.[20]

Back in June 1980, Grove saw an NBC documentary entitled *If Japan Can, Why Can't We?* He told Moore it was "fantastic . . . and I will propose to mount a corporate crusade around it."[21] Grove showed this documentary at Intel, and it had an impact. In 2005, he received an email from an employee at Fab 7 who still remembered it.[22] Unfortunately for Intel, Japan could do what Intel could not in terms of both cost and quality in the DRAM business. The company was determined that history would not repeat itself in microprocessors. Figure 7 shows that Intel succeeded. Intel did what the American automobile industry failed to do. It beat the Japanese at their own game. The different fate of these two industries is a vivid illustration that there was nothing inevitable about Intel's success.

It may also be true that the rules of the game the Japanese were playing, at least in the semiconductor industry, were changing. Bob Noyce was deeply involved in organizing the industry against Japanese competition. He met with Grove to discuss the subject late in 1986.

Grove told Moore that his meeting with Noyce

was very useful and interesting. . . . He gave me an interesting insight. The previous Japanese strategy was, "[D]ump, no matter what it costs, because then you can take over the market and get your return." With the Koreans around, their opportunity to get their return is gone. . . . Therefore, inevitably they will have to alter their strategy because it is deadly for them.[23]

If manufacturing was one leg of the three-legged stool that comprised Intel's strategy, marketing was the second. Moore told the New York Security Analysts that Intel intended to be "the vendor of choice." Customers were narrowing the number of companies from which they made their purchases. Intel planned to be first in line because of superior customer service and product quality. Intel's quality was already so high that its products could be shipped directly to factories rather than being cleared first by inspectors. Said Moore, "[W]hen a company can ship directly to a customer's manufacturing line, the customer will have a difficult time replacing that vendor."[24]

The third leg of Intel's strategy was, in Moore's words, "extending our architectural leadership."[25] This goal requires some explaining.

Microprocessors have a set of instructions through which they are accessed by software writers. These "instruction sets" differ from one another in significant ways. Thus software could be written to run on Intel's x86 family of microprocessors, but that same software would not function on, for example, Motorola's 68000 series.

To win the microprocessor wars, your goal is to have your product with its particular specifications accepted by as many software programmers as possible. The more who write for your chip, the more valuable your chip will become. This business was characterized by what came to be known as "increasing returns to adoption." In Robert Burgelman's words:

> Achieving a high installed base was the key to setting in motion the virtuous circle associated with increasing returns to adoption. The high installed base of a technological platform motivated the development of software applications. The availability of software applications increased the value of the platform. The increased value of the platform attracted more users and hence increased the installed base. Increasing returns to adoption created a winner-take-all competitive situation.[26]

Competition in microprocessors was even more complicated than this description suggests. There was not only competition among architectures, there was also competition within them. Because of the power relations in this industry, when relatively small suppliers such as Intel sold product to giant companies like IBM, the suppliers were forced to license their designs to at least one other manufacturer. We encountered this in 1971 when Intel was forced to license the 1103 DRAM chip to Microsystems International, Ltd.

Multiple sourcing for a single chip design was not necessarily all bad, even from Intel's point of view. It had the effect of drawing more attention to the architecture and legitimizing it. OEMs demanded it. Intel attorney Tom Dunlap estimates that there were about a dozen second sources for Intel's early microprocessors around the world. Craig Barrett not only agrees, he points out that the multiple sourcing applied to Intel's other products as well. He estimates that the 1103, Intel's first successful DRAM, was announced by a dozen or more companies soon after Intel introduced it.[27]

Each big OEM, according to Dunlap, wanted a second source in its own country. "IBM wanted a U.S. second source. NEC wanted a Japanese second source. Siemens wanted a German second source. . . . Our preference was not to sell our technology for money. We preferred to get products in return." This was how the 8080 and 8085 were managed. With the 8086, Dunlap explained, this was looking like an expensive way to do business, and the number of second sources was trimmed down.[28]

Intel introduced its 286 in 1982, but as late as 1986 Moore said that it was "still hard to find a system that uses the full capability of the 80286. People use it as a fast 8086 rather than using a lot of its special features because the software is not available yet."[29] Perhaps if more companies were manufacturing the 286, more software engineers would have exploited it more fully.

That said, licensing a microprocessor had a lot more to be said against it than for it from Intel's point of view; and Moore and Grove were well aware of that fact. It meant doubling the competitive battles you had to fight. You had to win among architectures, and then you had to win within your architecture. Looking once again at the microprocessor chart (Figure 6, p. 207), licensing meant that you had to share almost everything you had done to bring a new product to life—product definition, product design, process design, and manufacturing—with at least one competitor. Each one of these four stages gave you an opportunity to create competitive advantage. As Dennis Carter pointed out, each stage was becoming more expensive as the features of the microprocessor, following Moore's law, became more sophisticated. "The cost of the 386, for instance, was over $100 million compared with about $50 million for the 286. The value added of design had become larger than the value added of manufacturing [as Figure 6 illustrates]. Yet, the second-source manufacturers did not have to incur any of these design-related costs."[30]

Licensing all that "intellectual property," as Grove observed, meant that you were turning your product into a commodity, and Intel had learned from the DRAM debacle that "commodity businesses are unattractive." Craig Barrett agrees, and cites the actions coming out of this viewpoint as a major reason for Intel's success. "Other people kept beating their brains out with commodity products that were multi-sourced—the DRAM guys, the SRAM guys, the embedded controller group, and so forth. We walked away from commodity businesses and the military business—business after business—and we just kept pushing our resources in this one area; and that one area [the microprocessor in the PC] happened to grow to be the biggest consumer market."[31]

There are, in fact, numerous ways to differentiate your product through marketing. Intel would soon create some new ones in its industry. Meanwhile, however, putting a competitor into business meant competing primarily on price. Intel wanted to decommodify its products so it could control its price. Multiple sourcing had the opposite effect. On balance, therefore, second sourcing was a practice that Intel wanted to terminate. The question was: how?

The "Valley of Death," which is the title of the previous chapter, was a phrase that Grove himself used in his most famous book, *Only the Paranoid Survive*.[32] Given the plant closings, the attendant firings, and the miserable financial performance in 1985 and 1986, the metaphor is appropriate. As Moore, a man not known for his sense of irony, said to the New York Society of Security Analysts in the winter of 1986, "Looking at 1985—for I hope the last time—this is the trend in revenues over the year. You can see this would be a smooth curve if we could only reverse 1984 and 1985. The wrong year came first!"[33] As we know, 1986 was to be far worse still.

Grove wrote to Moore that he attended a CTMG GOR (Intel speak for "Corporate Technology and Manufacturing Group" "General Operations Review") in the fall of 1986, and it was "the most miserable meeting I've sat through in recent memory. We have truly major problems piled on top of each other."[34] There was plenty of reason for gloom.

One must resist the almost unconscious predisposition to allow hindsight to determine our view of history. Events now in the past were once in the future. In other words, it takes an act of will to keep in mind that just because things turned out in a certain way, that is the way they had to turn out.

The story both of Andy Grove and of the company to which he devoted his professional life have implausible aspects that deserve emphasis. Grove could have died of scarlet fever when he was four. Had he, it certainly would not have been surprising. Had he died in Auschwitz along with some of his aunt Manci's relatives, it would not have been surprising. Nor would it have been surprising had he been killed during the Communist era. Arguably, it is more surprising that he survived.

It is more surprising that Intel survived in 1986 than people usually think. Following World War II, the United States was an economic colossus capable of being challenged by no one. Slowly, as the non-Communist world began to rebuild itself, American industrial hegemony was subjected to successive challenges. First, it was in the low-value-added, labor-intensive industries such as apparel and textiles. By the 1970s, foreign competition had invaded industries in which the United States had been dominant for more than half a century, such as steel and automobiles. Foreign companies overwhelmed American firms in industries that had been invented in the United States and were technologically sophisticated, such as consumer electronics. American firms not only failed globally but in the home market. Today, there is not one television manufactured in the United States by an American firm. This future would have been hard to imagine when RCA's boss David Sarnoff demonstrated the television at the New York World's Fair in 1939 or when RCA brought color television to market in the late 1950s.

"They said it couldn't be done" was the lead phrase in a 1993 article in the *San Francisco Chronicle*. They said that "the U.S. manufacturing sector had lost its edge and could never rebound in world markets. But Silicon Valley . . . has proven the doom-and-gloomers wrong."

In 1980, 57.2 percent of the world's semiconductors were produced in the United States, while Japan accounted for 27.4 percent. Just six years later, Japan surpassed the United States, by 45.9 percent versus 41.5 percent. In 1993, the United States accounted for 43.6 percent of global semiconductor output compared to 40.2 percent from Japan. The 1993 results, not those of 1986, are what are remarkable. This is a performance equaled by few other industries. Once the slide begins, it is difficult to reverse.

"If Japan can, why can't we?" Grove asked along with others back in 1980.[35] It turned out we could. "[N]ow it's normal business," said Grove in 1993. "Having been burned by the Japanese once," he added, "we are much tougher now. It was a horrible experience and we won't forget it."[36]

On the other hand, in some ways the "valley of death" metaphor is slightly misleading. The phrase is taken from Alfred, Lord Tennyson's poem "The Charge of the Light Brigade." The poem memorializes an assault made on October 25, 1854, by the 661 or 673 (accounts vary) men of the Light Brigade of the British cavalry into the teeth of the Russian guns during the battle of Balaclava in the Crimean War.

The charge was the result of a series of mistakes. In Tennyson's poem,

> "Forward, the Light Brigade!"
> Was there a man dismay'd?
> Not tho' the soldier knew
> Some one had blunder'd:

Indeed, someone, it is not clear who, had blundered. The Light Brigade never had a chance, facing, completely exposed as it was, Russian cannon on three sides. As Tennyson wrote,

> Cannon to the right of them,
> Cannon to the left of them,
> Cannon in front of them
> > Volley'd and thunder'd;
> Storm'd at with shot and shell,
> Boldly they rode and well,
> Into the jaws of Death,
> Into the mouth of Hell
> > Rode the six hundred.

Despite the manifest stupidity of the charge, it was carried out with incomparable bravery and without a murmur of complaint:

> Theirs not to make reply,
> Theirs not to reason why,
> Theirs but to do and die;

"*C'est magnifique*," observed a French field marshal, "*mais ce n'est pas la guerre.*" ("It is magnificent, but it is not war.") One hundred thirteen men were killed, two hundred forty-seven wounded. For nothing.[37]

Before proceeding, it is impossible to avoid observing that this poem encapsulates the opposite of the tenets of Intel culture. Not a man was "dismay'd" even though many knew that "Some one had blunder'd." Whoever that someone was obviously had "position power" that trumped the "knowledge power" of those who could see that six hundred men were about to deliver themselves into a meat grinder. No one spoke up to point out the absurdity of the situation. They were not supposed either "to make reply" or "to reason why." Their job was "to do and die." Even if they had occupied the ground they fought for, the game was not worth the candle.

That is the essence of the difference between the "valley of death" the six hundred rode into and the "valley of death" in which Intel found itself in 1986. The six hundred would find no prize worth winning. But if Intel could manage its way through its valley of death, it would discover "broad, sunlit uplands" of profit and market dominance.[38]

Even as Intel marched through its valley of death, a lot of people thought it would reach those sunlit uplands. To be sure, these were particularly low moments at the firm. But for the most part, they were well handled. An examination of Wall Street analysts' reports during 1985 and 1986 reveals that they universally recommended that their investors accumulate Intel shares.[39]

A vital part of Intel's strategy for climbing out of the valley of death was serving as the sole source for the new microprocessor it introduced in October of 1985, the 80386.[40] This decision constituted a revolution in the industry. It took guts to make it and to make it stick. This decision was a turning point in the history of the company and the industry. Although not fully recognized at the time, it marked a pivotal shift in power from IBM to Intel.

The sole-source decision was a gamble. Looking back on it from 1999, this is what Grove said to Robert Burgelman's class at Stanford:

> You're sitting in a room with IBM purchasing executives who purchase more of any one item in one month than all of your total production for the year, and they ask, "Who is your second source?" Weigh in the balance: what good is the 386 if IBM doesn't adopt it?[41]

This was a pretty scary prospect, a real "moment of truth" for Intel.

Grove discussed this moment of truth with me in 2005. Even that far removed, you can feel the tension he felt. There was another side to the question of the value of the 386 if IBM did not adopt it. That was: what was the value of the 386 if, in order to secure IBM's adoption of it, we have to back down from our sole-source strategy?

There is a revealing passage in Grove's *Only the Paranoid Survive* that bears directly on this point and more generally on how Grove feels a company should be run. He begins by observing that the world-renowned management consultant W. Edwards Deming said it was important to stamp out fear in companies. Of all the assertions with which to take issue, this surely must be among the most unlikely. But Andy did. Andy came out in favor of fear:

> The most important role of managers is to create an environment in which people are passionately dedicated to winning in the marketplace. Fear plays a major role in creating and maintaining such passion. Fear

of competition, fear of bankruptcy, fear of being wrong, and fear of losing can all be powerful motivators.[42]

It is true that fear can be a powerful motivator. But it is a dangerous emotion. The line between instilling fear of failure as a motivational technique and simply being mean is a thin one indeed. Even if Grove himself could walk that line and separate the "good fear that motivates" from the "bad fear that paralyzes," how sure could he be that people brought up on such a diet would be able to walk that line as well as he? There are other ways to lead. Why not focus on the joy of success rather than the fear of failure? In Grove's view, the fear of failure was more effective. Was this because the price of failure during the first two decades of his life was so high, literally life itself? Was it because this is who the man is, and he would have been this way if he had been born in Iowa like Noyce, or California like Moore? We will never know.

What we do know is that, not only in his early years, but as a business executive, Andy Grove knew fear. This fact comports ill with the image he has shown to the world. The Andy Grove who "took on prostate cancer" and had the courage to publish an article in *Fortune* about it does not seem fearful. A fearful patient would trust his doctor, close his eyes, and hope for the best. The man looking out at us on *Time*'s "Man of the Year" cover for 1997 does not seem fearful. Nor does the man who spent his life thinking "out of the box," challenging received wisdom. But there can be no doubt that Grove knew real fear.

"How do we cultivate fear of losing in our employees," he asks rhetorically in *Only the Paranoid Survive*. His answer: "We can only do that if we feel it ourselves."

It is fear that makes me scan my email at the end of a long day, searching for problems. . . . It is fear that every evening makes me read the trade press . . . and . . . tear out particularly ominous articles . . . for follow-up the next day. It is fear that gives me the will to listen to Cassandras when all I want to do is cry out, "Enough already, the sky *isn't* falling," and go home.[43]

Is this what business really is? It does not sound like much fun.

This is certainly an unorthodox attitude. Although it is doubtless true that plenty of managers use fear to motivate, I cannot think of one who has publicly extolled its utility as a business tool. Is Andy simply making explicit what others do? Is he making a virtue of necessity? In other words, is he saying that because of who I am and what I have been through, I have to feel fear? That it is a blessing, not a curse, because it makes me a better manager? If I can stand it, you can too. It will make you a better manager as well.

At any rate, in 1986 Andy had every right to be frightened about the fate of the 386. He was the one who had to face IBM's purchasing people. He was the one who had to tell them something they did not want to hear. There would be no second source for the 386. This was bad news for AMD as well and resulted in a legal action that lasted into the 1990s. But IBM was a bigger problem.

Intel did have a story to tell IBM, the essence of which was that Intel could serve as its own second source. The company had worked so hard in the early 1980s to perfect its manufacturing capability that it felt that, acting alone, it could satisfy demand. In Craig Barrett's words, "Our quality thrust of the early '80s began to pay off in improved consistency on the manufacturing line and overall better product quality." Barrett also asserted that the lessons learned from previous products led Intel to believe "that we could accurately forecast demand for the 386 and put sufficient manufacturing capacity in place." He was right. Intel never missed a shipment of the 386, despite having no second source agreement.[44] Furthermore, by 1988, Intel had fabs in Albuquerque, New Mexico; Aloha, Oregon; Chandler, Arizona; Livermore, California; and in Jerusalem. So no customer could complain that a vital supplier had all its plants located on one of the earth's most active fault lines. The belief had always been prevalent at Intel that you cannot save your way out of a business downturn. You had to invest your way out of it. That practice served the company well at this point.

Nevertheless, all this might have sounded like so much white noise to IBM. The fact that Intel would never miss a shipment could be known after the fact, not prospectively. Anyway, the demand for a second source only partially dealt with the security of supply, as everyone in the industry well knew for years. It also dealt with forcing price competition on your vendor. As Moore put it, the nominal reason for multiple sourcing in the early years of that practice was that semiconductor companies were not very reliable. They "had a bad habit of losing the recipe." In other words, they would produce a device for, say, three months, and then suddenly things would go wrong and deliveries would stop. "Of course," Moore added, "the unmentioned reason was that with multiple sourcing [the OEM] can get much better pricing, particularly with a high fixed cost industry like semiconductors."

Intel, Moore said, attacked the nominal reason for the OEM demand for a second source by building more fabs, not on fault lines, to supply product to customers. The new Intel policy was multiple sources but from different fabs within a single company. Now "at least we could plaster over what they were claiming was the major problem. And we did, and we still do that with our 'copy exactly' philosophy." There are numerous sources within the company for individual products.[45] IBM might well wonder what would force prices down if Intel was competing only against itself.

It should be said that no less an authority than Craig Barrett observed that there was some pretty tall hustling to get the 386 out the door in quantity. At the time, "copy exactly" was still more of a goal than a reality. The truth, said Barrett, was that insistence on sole-sourcing that product was a pretty "ballsy" maneuver by Andy. He took a big chance. Things easily could have failed to work out.[46]

Nineteen eighty-six proved to be the critical year in Intel's history. The company stood fast. There would be no second source for the 386.

The great fear about IBM did turn into reality. IBM was in no hurry to purchase the 386. It fell victim to its "mainframe mentality." IBM controlled the mainframe market and operated on the principle that it was better to "be right than be early." However, according to journalist Paul Carroll, "the PC business wasn't at all like the mainframe business. It was better to be early than to be right. And no customer would wait for any manufacturer, not even IBM."[47]

It was at this critical moment that the method of IBM's entry into the personal computer business came back to haunt it. Giant though it was, IBM did not monopolize the desktop segment of computing. Because it had outsourced the operating system to Microsoft and the microprocessor to Intel in order to speed its market entry, these two critical components of the personal computer were no longer proprietary

What really mattered from Intel's point of view was the birth of the IBM "clones." A clone worked just like an IBM PC. Sometimes it even worked better and cost less. It had the same ingredients. Manufacturers of IBM clones in the mid-1980s included Zenith, Tandy, Epson, Osborne, Acer, and at least a dozen other companies. Dell was founded in 1984 when Michael Dell started putting together computers in his dorm room as a freshman at the University of Texas at Austin. He soon dropped out of college, and the $1,000 company he founded has grown to a market capitalization of about $49 billion.[48]

In the mid-1980s, however, the IBM clone on everybody's mind was not Dell, it was Compaq. Founded in 1982 by three former engineers at Texas Instruments—Rod Canion, Bill Mutro, and Jim Harris—Compaq was created on the idea that the company could make a portable PC that could run IBM software. The first portables were unwieldy on a good day. They were known as "luggables." But Compaq caught on. In 1986, just four years after its founding, sales hit $625 million.[49]

Now let us return to Andy Grove's critically important question: what good was the 386 if IBM did not adopt it? The answer was that it was still worth a great deal. IBM wanted to hold off on its purchase of the 386. But Compaq proved "a willing customer." In September 1986, it introduced its Deskpro 386, stealing a march on "Big Blue."

This looked like a big deal, and it was. Here is how Paul Carroll described it:

[L]ittle Compaq . . . slapped IBM in the face by coming to New York City, in the middle of IBM country, to stage an extravagant announcement of a PC that used the next-generation Intel 80386 chip and that operated several times as fast as IBM's most powerful machine. . . . As lasers flashed around the room in a Manhattan disco, it was clear that customers loved the additional horsepower in the Compaq machines.[50]

All of a sudden Compaq was more than a maker of clones. It was marketing a better personal computer than IBM. Its sales in 1987 doubled to $1.2 billion on the strength of Intel's microprocessor.[51] Compaq had gone from a start-up to a billion dollars in sales faster than any other company in history.[52]

In *Only the Paranoid Survive*, Grove writes at some length about the "strategic inflection point," an idea he introduced that has gained currency in the business world. In mathematics, "we encounter an inflection point when the rate of change of the slope of the curve (referred to as its 'second derivative') changes sign, for instance, going from negative to positive. In physical terms, it's where a curve changes from convex to concave, or vice versa."

In business, Grove explained, "a strategic inflection point is when the balance of forces shifts from the old structure, from the old ways of doing business and the old ways of competing, to the new." How do you know when you have reached a strategic inflection point? It is, unfortunately, very difficult to answer that question, even in hindsight. The strategic inflection point can sneak up on you, preceded by vague forebodings and the uncomfortable sense that things are not proceeding in your business as they should.[53]

In September 1986, the whole computer industry marked a strategic inflection point. When Compaq bought the 386 for its Deskpro personal computer, IBM ceased dictating the pace of change in the industry. For IBM, more than for any other company in the computing industry, the strategic inflection point had been reached. The slope of the curve changed sign from positive to negative.

From an historical point of view, the roots of this event can be traced back to the 1970s, during which time IBM stubbornly refused to believe that there was a real market for or real money in personal computers. It could be traced to August 12, 1981, when IBM introduced its own Personal Computer, the two most important components of which, the operating system and the microprocessor, were outsourced. It took less than a year for the clone market, led by Compaq, to get venture capital funding. Its growth was explosive.

If strategic inflection points are difficult to pin down even with the benefit of hindsight, no wonder they are so hard to predict. If analysts did not understand that IBM was no longer the master of its fate in 1981, they certainly should have when Compaq bought the 386 in 1986. Yet IBM's market capitalization actually increased from $68.8 billion in 1986 to $72.2 billion in 1987.

Why? Because human beings are . . . human. They march backward into the future. When you uttered the letters IBM in 1987, what came to mind were the great days of the IBM 360. The problem is that eventually reality catches up with everybody. IBM's market capitalization in 1991 was $28.8 billion. It lost money, as it did in the next two years as well. What IBM's top brass in the 1970s and 1980s did not know was the one thing they had to know.

The PC Is It.

12

———— ✦ ————

"Awesome Intel"

Some Wall Street analysts did begin to catch on and to understand what the 386 sole-sourced could mean to Intel. In the words of one report, "The Intel 80386 32-bit microprocessor is going to do for desktop computing what running water did for mankind." Quite a claim! "That is, bring users out of the cold dark woods and indoors into a whole new world of powerful computing, making computers as easy to use as brushing your teeth." Perhaps not the world's greatest simile, but this analyst seemed at a loss for words. "[J]ust open any magazine or newspaper," he said, "and the headlines spew the virtues of this part to computer users everywhere."[1]

The "virtues of this part" to Intel were manifest because of its sole-source policy. The only license was to IBM, which was permitted to manufacture some of the 386s it needed for its latest personal computer. Despite this license, IBM bought most if not all of its 386s from Intel anyway. Only Intel could sell the device to any other company. Intel had a monopoly, "with gross margins likely to exceed 90% and pretax operating profits exceeding 35%."[2]

Intel had put itself in a position to print money. Sales in 1987 of $1.9 billion represented a new record and were 51 percent higher than the previous year. The $173 million loss of 1986 turned into a $248 million profit, also a record. Intel was not merely basking on the sunlit uplands, it was astride the commanding heights of its industry. At $4.3 billion, its market capitalization was as high as it had ever been, with the exception of $4.6 billion in the wonder year of 1983. The company's winning strategy was being executed to perfection.

Intel was becoming an ever more complicated company to run. The microprocessor bonanza was driving the business. The Compaq sale had proven critical, as did the new relationship with IBM. In the early 1980s, computer people did not talk about competing against IBM as much as they did about operating within the "IBM environment."[3] That was about to change. No one was "subjugating," to use Andy's word, Intel anymore.

The company was organized into six operating groups. These were: the Microcomputer Components Group, the Systems Group, the ASIC (Applications Specific Integrated Circuit) Components Group, the Components Technology and Manufacturing Group, the Sales and Marketing Group, and the Administration Group. Each of these was staffed by Intel veterans. Each reported directly to Grove as CEO. Each had its representatives at the SLRP (Intel speak for "Strategic Long Range Planning," pronounced "slurp") meeting, at which Intel executives made presentations concerning the state of the business and challenged one another's ideas about the future.

Robert Burgelman has written that "Grove was perhaps the first CEO to clearly see the strategic implications of the transformation of the computer industry from vertical to horizontal."[4] That knowledge enabled him to organize Intel to capitalize on a process that others were only dimly aware was taking place. Grove usually winces at the word "vision" ("too lofty for my taste"),[5] but in this context it is the best descriptor of the role he played. All his knowledge of technology and all his knowledge of the wider world served him well in helping him arrive at this insight.

It is intriguing that as Intel's products followed the inexorable dictates of Moore's law and became continually smaller and more intricate, Grove's view of his responsibilities became broader. The 386 microprocessor contained 275,000 interconnected transistors. A staggering number. Try counting a tenth that high. By May 2005, Grove had grown from the new CEO of a $2 billion company to a world-renowned business statesman. In the meantime, Intel's products had shrunk to an unimaginable size. The most intricate Itanium microprocessor today contains 1.75 billion transistors interconnected in twenty layers on a chip the size of your thumbnail.

One has to examine Grove's own notes to get a sense of the myriad details involved in running Intel in the late 1980s. The company was exceptionally complex and, as Grove understood better than anyone else, it had the chance, as of 1987, to become one of the most important companies in the world. He had to keep everyone's eye on the ball while managing day-to-day problems and opportunities and by separating challenges that were real from those that merely seemed to be. Intel's corporate structure and its long-range planning process were the levers of power he needed to achieve the audacious goals he set for the company.

The senior vice president and general manager of the Microcomputer Components Group was David L. House. House graduated from Michigan Technological University in 1965, where he majored in electrical engineering. Noting the college he attended is worth doing. Noyce, Moore, and Grove all graduated from tier-one universities, but that should not obscure the fact that a lot of people who helped build Intel did not. Michigan Technological University is located on Michigan's Upper Peninsula in one of the more obscure corners of the United States. Wedged in between Lake Superior and Lake Michigan, the Upper Peninsula looks like it ought to be part of Wisconsin. It seems that a cartographer's hand must have slipped when that border between the two states was drawn.

Why mention this? Because an exceptionally large number of Intel's top people came from institutions of higher education that do not rank near the top in terms of, for example, difficulty of admission. Tom Dunlap, for example, who served as chief counsel for Intel for more than two decades, received his law degree from Santa Clara University. Pat Gelsinger, Intel's first chief technology officer, received an "associate's degree" from Lincoln Technical Institute in Allentown, Pennsylvania, in 1979. I mean no disrespect when I say that until I met Pat Gelsinger, one of the smartest, hardest-working, and most sincere individuals I have ever encountered, I had never heard of Lincoln Technical Institute. When Intel interviewed on his campus, Gelsinger had no intention of moving out west. He is devoutly religious, the author of two books—one is highly technical and deals with programming the 80386 microprocessor, the other is *Balancing Your Family, Faith & Work,* which deals with how he manages a packed life while always keeping his commitment to God, which he sees as uppermost in his life and that of his family.[6] The thought of this man spending his professional life around people who are not strangers to swearing and drinking and for some of whom the marriage vows are honored more in the breach than in the observance is a little hard to take in. Yet Gelsinger "bleeds blue" as much as anyone else at Intel.

There are a lot of people with backgrounds like this who put in decades

At the age of four, Andy was stricken with scarlet fever. As a result of a secondary infection, he almost lost his hearing. The bandages are evidence of the first of many operations that succeeded in saving it.

This is the last picture of the Grove family before it was split up by the Holocaust. George and Maria know what is coming. Young Andy does not. The expressions on the three faces and the body language speak volumes.

Not until 1944 did Jews in Hungary have to wear the yellow star of David on their apparel. Here is a picture of Maria, Andy's mother, wearing one.

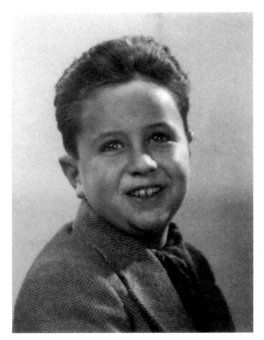

This is a picture of Andy as "Pufi," a Hungarian word that can be translated as "fatso" in English. Andy unaccountably put on weight after the war.

By the time he had reached 18, Andy had taken the weight off and remained trim for the rest of his life.

In the summer of 1956, Andy saw service in the Hungarian Army. You can see him standing on the far left.

The year 1957 found Andy in New York City studying for his classes at the City College of New York. The apartment is in the Bronx.

Andy Grove, New Yorker.

An enthusiastic Andy with his beautiful bride, Eva, at their wedding reception on June 8, 1958.

In 1963, Andy was awarded his Ph.D. in chemical engineering from the University of California at Berkeley. His parents, whom he had managed to get out of Hungary, attended the ceremony.

The beginnings of Intel in 1968.
Courtesy Intel Corporation

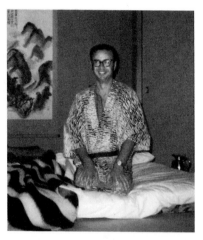

Andy's first trip to Japan in June 1970.

Intel established an assembly facility in Penang, Malaysia, in 1971. Muddy going at first. However, the government was very cooperative, and infrastructure problems were solved.

Bowers Avenue in 1973. Intel has moved to Santa Clara.

Courtesy Intel Corporation

In September 1975, Andy took a business-building trip to Europe along
with other Intel executives. On the far left is the young John Doerr.

Andy Grove, Bob Noyce, and Gordon Moore in 1978.

Courtesy Intel Corporation

...the same three men - Andy Grove,
...ight) - continue to lead Intel

A quarter of a century later, Andy is pictured with the photo of the previous trio on the occasion of Intel's thirty-fifth anniversary.

Courtesy Intel Corporation

Intel's board in 1989. Standing on the far left is Arthur Rock. Standing next to him is Les Vadasz. Seated in front of Vadasz is the thirty-four-year-old Harvard Professor David B. Yoffie. Grove, Moore, and Noyce are in the center.

Courtesy Intel Corporation

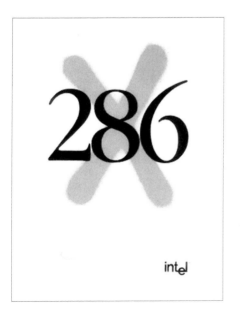

The famed "Red X" campaign of 1989.

Courtesy Intel Corporation

Competitors' dream, 1994. Intel Inside a hearse in front of the offices of NexGen.

Andy's visit to China in 1994. This is a seminar in Beijing on September 4.

Eva and Andy with Sean Maloney on the Great Wall of China, September 1994.

Andy with Dennis Carter on the
Great Wall during the 1994 trip.

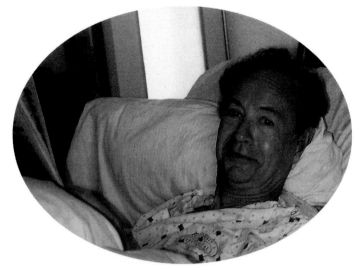

Treatment for prostate cancer at the Swedish Medical Center in Seattle.

Telekom 95.
Andy with Nelson Mandela.

Andy giving Warren Buffett a computer lesson in 1997.

Andy in China once again, 1998.

Speak no evil, see no evil, hear no evil.
Andy with Gordon Moore and Craig Barrett, 1998.

Courtesy Intel Corporation

Three who made a revolution. Andy with Steve Jobs and Bill Gates.

Was wir von
Silicon Valley
lernen können

ProShare beams
Andy to a European
seminar, October
1998.

Andy featured
in NASDAQ
display, April
2000.

*Courtesy Intel
Corporation*

Gordon Moore,
Craig Barrett, Andy,
and Paul S. Otellini
at Intel's thirty-fifth
anniversary, August
2003.

Courtesy Intel Corporation

Andy with Jean Jones, who was present at the creation in 1968.

Andy at Intel's International Sales and Marketing Conference (ISMC),
appearing precisely as he did many years earlier, February 2004.

An informal Andy Grove returns to CCNY on August 22, 2005. When he went back downtown, he took the subway.

Andy in 2006 side by side with his picture in 1968.

Andy in his cubicle at the RNB in Santa Clara, 2006.

at Intel. Grove felt he did not need credentialing institutions to help him evaluate the people he hired and promoted. As always, he wanted to know what the individual had to offer, not whether he or she had gone to Harvard or Stanford.

Dave House was yet another member of the class of 1974, hired, like Barrett and Otellini, when others were being fired. After graduating from college, he went to work for Raytheon in the Boston area and earned a master's degree in electrical engineering at Northeastern University. His first job at Intel was as "manager of applications," and for the next twenty-two years he took on ever-greater responsibility for microprocessors. In 1996, he left Intel to become president of Bay Networks, which merged with Nortel, of which he became president in 1998.[7]

House was thus in charge of Intel's crown jewels, its microprocessors. In 1987, those jewels were shining brightly. "The 80386 . . . has been successful beyond our most optimistic forecasts," declared the *Annual Report*.[8] Design win after design win, award after award, adoption by such major players as Compaq—that was the story of the 386 in 1987.

The two other senior executives in the Microcomputer Components Group were Lawrence R. Hootnick and Albert Y. C. Yu. Hootnick graduated from MIT with a degree in industrial management and earned an MBA from the University of Maryland. Yet another member of the class of 1974, he was at Intel for eighteen years. He was senior vice president of finance and administration before becoming senior vice president and general manager, operations, of the Microcomputer Components Group. At one period in the mid- and late-1980s, Hootnick, like a number of others including House, was given to believe that he might someday run Intel. That was a future that was not to be.[9]

Albert Y. C. Yu was born in Shanghai in 1941. He holds a BS from Cal Tech and a PhD from Stanford. His business career began at Fairchild, which he left to join Intel in 1972. He rose to the position of senior vice president for microprocessors at Intel before retiring in September 2002.[10]

The charter of Intel's Systems Group was to broaden the company's participation in the microcomputer marketplace by selling "single-board computers, software and hardware development tools, personal computer enhancements, networking products and scientific computers."

Les Vadasz was the senior vice president and general manager of the Systems Group. The following year, in 1988, he would take a seat on the board, which he held until his retirement in 2003. He is presently involved with a number of high-technology companies in the Valley. He and his wife, Judy, are the proprietors of a magnificent 205-acre estate in Sonoma, about forty miles north of San Francisco. Vadasz Vineyards was cash-flow positive in 2005.[11]

Second in command at the Systems Group was Keith L. Thomson, who joined Intel in 1969. In 1987, his title was vice president of Intel and general manager of operations for the Systems Group. He retired from the company in 1998, after managing Intel's Oregon operations. Since then, he has pursued various technological and philanthropic activities.[12]

The third of Intel's six divisions was the ASIC Components Groups, run by Vice President and General Manager Richard D. Boucher. In the 1970s, Boucher had been stuck with the hapless job of trying to turn the misbegotten Microma watch business into a valuable property. Back in 1975, Grove told Moore that he and Boucher "almost came to blows" over a presentation to the board of directors.[13]

Boucher was incapable of doing the impossible. Microma failed. But it was a "noble failure," not a "stupid mistake." Grove knew it, and he was impressed by Boucher's efforts to find appropriate jobs for those who had labored so hard to make this born loser win.

While he was in the process of shutting down Microma, Boucher asked Grove what his own chances of staying at Intel were. Grove figured them at 40 percent but told Boucher 10 percent because he did not want to make a promise he could not keep. Boucher spent the rest of his career serving Intel and Andy and was undyingly loyal to both.[14] ASICs were a fairly new market for Intel. The goal of the division was "to allow customization of products for our customers' specific needs."

At the Components Technology and Manufacturing Group, the boss was Senior Vice President and General Manager Craig R. Barrett. Born on August 29, 1939, in San Francisco, Barrett holds three degrees from Stanford. His PhD is in materials science, concerning which he is the coauthor of a textbook[15] and numerous technical articles. He was a track star as an undergraduate and remains physically prepossessing and, although soft-spoken, somewhat intimidating. Like Grove, he was hired as a technologist, a job he took when Intel was a small company in 1974. He left a tenured associate professorship at his alma mater, one of the world's premier universities. This was not an intuitively obvious career move in the early 1970s.[16]

Also like Grove, Barrett moved from technologist to operations. It is to him that Intel's manufacturing prowess is usually credited. He instituted the "copy exactly" approach, meaning that each manufacturing facility should be precisely like every other. No "empowered" workers shutting down production lines on his watch. Barrett understood the received wisdom about how to run a factory and ignored it.[17] The result was that manufacturing became one of Intel's most important competitive strengths. Barrett deserves a lot of the credit. "I'm the master mechanic. My job," he said, "is to get my fingernails dirty and make sure the products move through the factories."[18]

Barrett joined the board in 1992 and became the presumptive successor to Grove when he was named chief operating officer the following year. In 1997 he became Intel's fourth president and CEO. He relinquished those positions to become chairman of the board on May 18, 2005.

The Sales and Marketing Group was the fifth Intel division. Its "objective was to establish an atmosphere of mutual trust; our customers had to trust we would meet our commitments, and we had to count on them for realistic, short-term assessments of their needs for scarce products."

At the helm was Vice President Frank C. Gill, an electrical engineer from the University of California at Davis. Gill joined Intel in 1975 and was, like a number of others, at one time thought of as a possible heir to Grove. He retired from Intel in 1998 to pursue a variety of high-technology projects in Oregon.[19]

Under Gill was Vice President and Marketing Director Ronald J. Whittier. An alumnus of Berkeley, Stanford (where he earned a PhD in chemical engineering), and Fairchild, Whittier joined Intel in 1970. He spent three decades there and is presently involved in technology and philanthropy.

Finally, there was the Administration Group, run by Vice President Robert W. Reed, another member of the Intel class of 1974. Reed's group was charged with collaborating with Intel's five other groups "to raise the money, hire the staff, build the buildings, run the computer and communications systems and provide the other administrative support a growing, successful company needs." Reed served as Intel's chief financial officer from 1983 to 1991 and left the firm in 1996 to pursue other technological interests.[20]

Ten senior executives ran Intel's six divisions the year Andy Grove became president and CEO. Among them, they had 148 years of experience at Intel. In other words, these ten men had worked for an average of just under fifteen years each at a company that was only nineteen years old. Judging from this list, it would appear that the "organization man," who was supposed to have been born in the East after World War II but to have disappeared somewhere between New York and the Valley of the Heart's Delight, was being reincarnated at Intel. All these executives owed their careers and their wealth, which was already considerable in some cases, to Intel and to the man who ran it. They knew they would share in the success of the company and in the success of the man at the head of the company.

Not all these people liked one another. But Grove's managerial ability turned them into a team. He could soothe egos and cajole artistic talent. He had "the vision and the force to make all these elements fuse into an inspired whole."

They all knew who Andy was. In the words of a financial analyst who covered Intel, Andy was a carnivore "who would be safe in a cage with a man-eating tiger" because he "would probably eat it."[21]

Not everyone in 1987 was impressed with Intel. The fact is that it was the sixth largest semiconductor company in the world in 1982, but had slid down to number twelve by 1986. It had been kicked out of the DRAM market. As Moore remarked in November, "Intel introduced the DRAM. We used to have a 100% share of the market. And we went from 100% to 0% over time." That was one historical vignette that could not be allowed to repeat itself. As an executive at L.M. Ericsson, the big Swedish telephone company, said, "Intel used to be the innovator in so many markets. And now, what do they have? Only microprocessors."[22]

Saying in 1987 that all you have is the microprocessor is a bit like saying that all Henry Ford had in 1908 was the Model T. The microprocessor at the dawn of the PC world was a nice thing to have. The question was: given the fact that Intel had lost out in DRAMs, that it was big, and that like any big company it was bureaucratic, could it hold on to what it had in the microprocessor and exploit the kind of opportunity that does not present itself often in the life of a company?

Grove's answer was emphatic. Intel may have become a big company, but it was going to prove an "agile giant."[23] In Grove's view, Intel had the strategy it needed and the people to execute it. This would not be easy. Grove's memoranda to Moore in 1987 are, while basically upbeat, especially considering the worldview of the author, replete with problems. Of those, the most worrisome was posed by AMD. They wanted to second-source the 386.

Grove would have none of that. The AMD dispute dragged on for years. But Intel could not afford to give in on sole sourcing. It was a pillar of the reborn company's strategy.

We cannot bid farewell to 1987 without noting that it saw the publication of Grove's third book, *One-on-One with Andy Grove: How to Manage Your Boss, Yourself, and Your Coworkers*.[24] This book is a compendium of letters that newspaper readers wrote to Grove concerning issues in the workplace, his responses to those letters, and his commentary on the managerial issues each correspondent raised. The impetus for Grove's column was a request from the editors of the *San Jose Mercury News*, a request that he himself inspired, that he write "a weekly question-and-answer column on the subject of managing."[25]

Why write such a column? It certainly was not for the money, if he was paid at all. By 1987, when all these columns, which at their peak were syndicated in a dozen newspapers, were published as a book, the result was a volume of 235 pages. This is a lot of text, and it took a lot of thought. Grove deals with the most difficult and sensitive problems faced in the workplace. What do you do when you hate your boss? How do you hire? How do you handle performance reviews? What do you do if someone with whom you work has a personal habit, such as loudly chewing gum, that drives you crazy? How do you fire people?

Writing this book took time. There was no topic too sensitive for him to discuss. There is, for example, a chapter entitled "Women in the Workplace: No Longer Separate but Not Yet Equal." It potentially exposed Grove to criticism on all kinds of fronts.

Grove wrote the columns that became this book in part because he wanted to settle old scores, and now he had the opportunity. He tells his readers that when he was fourteen years old and living in Hungary, his potential career in journalism was blocked by a Communist regime that stood for everything he despised.[26] This was news to Grove-watchers. *Swimming Across* was not published until 2001. At any rate, what was denied him in Hungary, which was still part of the Communist bloc in 1987, was not only permitted but invited in his adopted country. This column was an opportunity to right a wrong he had suffered many years earlier.

Second, Grove had done a lot of thinking about management, and, what is more, he had done a lot of managing. As a young man, he thought of management as a waste of time.[27] By 1987, he had come to feel that it was interesting and that there were good and bad ways to do it. He had something to say about it, and Grove is not a man to be told to be quiet.

What, then, is the message of this book? Andy offers five principles at the conclusion: "Enjoy your work," "Be totally dedicated to the substance of your work, to the end result, the output," "Respect the work of all those who respect their own work," "Be straight with everyone," and "When stumped, stop and *think* your way through to *your* own answers!"[28]

Grove constantly encourages his readers to walk a mile in someone else's shoes. He cautions against the belief that there are "magical" solutions to intractable problems. He comes close to saying that honesty is the best policy.

What saves this book from being pedestrian or reading like a recycled version of Benjamin Franklin's 1757 essay "The Way to Wealth" is that it is artfully and thoroughly grounded in examples.[29] Honesty often does turn out to be the best policy, but what Grove appreciates is how difficult honesty can be. The truth can hurt, both for the person speaking it and the person hearing it. Nevertheless, it is the responsibility of the manager to be truthful with his or her people even though it is often tough. "Steel yourself to be truthful and consistent."[30] Moreover, every employee has "the right to be managed."[31] Grove sticks to "suggestions that have been proven in real life."[32] That is what makes this tome vibrant reading. What is in this book is genuine.

People close to the company had been dreaming big dreams for Intel for a long time. Indeed, they were dreaming big dreams since before the company was founded, ever since Moore remarked to Noyce back in 1967 at Fairchild that replacing magnetic core memory with semiconductors was an idea you could build a company around. In 1988, two decades after it was founded, those big dreams started coming true in a big way. The company's *Annual Report* for that year was more unabashedly upbeat than any other in the history of this, the company that celebrated paranoia.

"Intel's 20th anniversary year was an outstanding success," the *Report* announced in its first paragraph. Sales of $2.875 billion "set a new record, growing 50% or better for the second consecutive year." Intel moved up another 50 spaces in the Fortune 500 ratings, now ranked as 150. As far as profits were concerned, it also set a record: $452.9 million represented an increase of 83 percent over the previous year. This being Intel, there was the inevitable note of caution. "Our business weakened in the last quarter of the year . . . and we started 1989 in a cautious stance."[33] That said, the authors of the *Annual Report* could only with difficulty contain themselves.

The key to Intel's success was "the enormous popularity of our 386 microprocessor. It has emerged as the standard for a new generation of 32-bit personal computers that are bringing unprecedented power to desktop computing."[34] Unit sales of personal computers at 9,425,000 in 1988 were up 7.7 percent from Intel's money-losing year of 1986. Dollar sales of personal computers were up 6 percent from 1986. Intel's 386 was the favored microprocessor of the overwhelming majority of these new machines. Despite the greatly enhanced computing power the 386 made possible, the average selling price of a personal computer actually declined slightly from $2,687.58 in 1986 to $2,649.34 in 1988.

At the end of 1988, Intel employed about 20,800 people. This was up from the 19,200 employed in 1987, but well down from the all-time peak of 25,400 in 1984. Sales in 1984 were about $1.6 billion. Productivity per employee had thus more than doubled from about $63,000 to over $138,000 in just a few years.

On March 9, 1988, Moore received another of the "Welcome Home" memoranda that Grove had been preparing for him for so many years. This one was as good as it gets. Under the heading "BUSINESS," Grove was short and sweet. "In a word, it continues good."

Many things have been said of Andy Grove, but I have nowhere seen anyone assert that he does not worry. "When you left [for your sabbatical], I was trembling in my shoes about the 386 demand collapsing," he wrote to Moore. "It hasn't, and it doesn't look like it's about to. . . . Bill Lowe [in charge of IBM's personal computer business] *twice* made a public statement in the last few weeks to the effect that by 1989 the 386 will be *the* standard processor across IBM's entire personal computer line, including their entry-level computer!"[35]

In *One-on-One*, Grove adopts the definition of "managing" as "getting things done through other people."[36] Grove devotes a whole chapter to "Managerial Leverage" in *High Output Management*.[37] "What particularly confounds most new managers," he wrote, "is the huge variety of *people issues* that take up so much of their time and attention. They complain that they can't do any 'real work' because so much of their time is spent sorting out personnel problems, reconciling disagreements, orchestrating the workers and their work. In time they will come to realize that this is what *managing* is all about."[38]

A great deal of space in Grove's memoranda to Moore over the years dealt with just such "people issues," and the prosperity of 1988 did not cause them to disappear. People were coming to Intel and leaving despite the fact that the company still needed them. Some, having left, intimated that they might like to come back. There were problems with titles for executives. Money was often an issue, and sometimes this took the form of arguments over the EB (Intel speak for employee bonus). Occasionally, suboptimal personnel decisions were made because of the press of other business. Never satisfactory, but such is life.

Grove had to testify in the arbitration case forced by AMD because of Intel's refusal to second-source the 386. "First," Grove wrote Moore, "there was preparation; then I was on for a week; then a judge had the flu and I was placed in suspended animation; then I got back and finished as AMD's witness. . . . I still have to get back on for my 'direct,' but it will be as part of the Intel case."[39]

Grove said he thought he did well because he was well prepared. The man who prepared him was Tom Dunlap, the chip designer who got his law degree at Santa Clara University over Grove's protests. Dunlap attests that Andy made an effective witness.[40] Grove knew this dispute was going to take a long time before it was resolved, and he told Moore that he felt "you will need to testify. This whole case is very heavily impression-based. I would like the judge to see you. I think you will make an exceptionally good impression on him (he likes fishing, by the way . . .)."[41]

Management thus dealt with people. It dealt with products. It dealt with lawsuits. It dealt with competitors. It dealt with industry associations. It dealt with things that just sort of happened, such as

> The smell in SC6 ["SC" is Intel speak for Santa Clara]
> You [Moore] just left when this affair erupted. It was bad news. There was nobody around to take charge of the situation. We ended up evacuating all of the SC6 for two days while we investigated the building in infinite detail. We ended up finding nothing, moving back in so we could all move out again.[42]

There were dozens upon dozens of issues with which management had to deal in order to run Intel. Most they got right. Some they got wrong. But the biggest challenge of all, the mastery of the microprocessor in the personal computer, they simply could not have handled better. The world was waking up to that fact by 1989.

Andy Grove has always enjoyed managing the press. He gets a kick out of publicity for his own professional accomplishments, and he takes pleasure in angling for the best coverage for Intel. The first portrait of Grove in the *New York Times* was published in 1977. He had been profiled before, but this was the first article devoted to him in America's "newspaper of record." The article describes Grove as "bronzed [and] side burned," and the picture that accompanies it makes him appear more like a refugee from the 1960s than from Hungary. He has a full head of long hair and a mustache and is wearing a rather loud, checked shirt with a very wide collar.

In this article Grove described Intel as a producer of "high technology jelly beans" and said it had much to learn from the standardization mastered by McDonald's, the leading producer of "medium technology jelly beans."

> When McDonald's wants to grow, it doesn't increase the size of its outlets; it just adds new franchises. That is exactly the principle we have adopted. We add production capacity in modular increments. Each module is meant to be identical to every other module in the same way each McDonald's is the same.[43]

This new kind of manufacturing needed a "different breed" of people to make it work.

> The wild-eyed, bushy-haired boy geniuses that dominate the think tanks and the solely technology-oriented companies will never take that technology to the jelly bean stage.
>
> Likewise, the other stereotype—the straight-laced, crew-cut, sideburn-and-mustache-free manufacturing operators of conventional industry—will never generate the technology in the first place. Our needs dictated that we fill our senior ranks with a group of highly competent, even brilliant technical specialists who were willing to adapt to a very structured, highly disciplined environment.[44]

Grove was always gifted at analogies, and the "McIntel" one stuck. Intel experienced its share and more than its share of manufacturing challenges.

Fab 1, the converted Union Carbide plant on Middlefield Road in Mountain View, had been a mess. Fab 2 in Santa Clara, Intel's first greenfield plant, had also, to understate the case, "experienced numerous difficulties." Fab 2 was a story of "struggle, struggle, struggle" for a long time.

With Fab 3, which opened in Livermore, California, in April 1973, that would change. When Fab 3 started up, everyone, literally, was reading from the same page in identical binders. In future fab start-ups, the "McDonald's approach" meant that each new fab would be as much like its predecessor as possible. According to Keith Thomson, "Every McIntel wafer looks and tastes the same wherever it is made."[45] Craig Barrett would perfect this approach in the context of a far more complex company with his "copy exactly" method.

Grove must have been pleased with this article with the possible exception of the description of him as the "least widely known" of the three people responsible for founding Intel. It would take some time, but he would change that.

On April 3, 1988, an article appeared in the *New York Times* that Grove has commended as the first piece in the general circulation press that showed a firm grasp of what was going on in the information technology industry. It was entitled "An 'Awesome' Intel Corners Its Market." The reporter was Andrew Pollack. "The personal computer industry and Wall Street," Pollack wrote, "are waking up to the fact that Intel has one of the most lucrative monopolies in America [in its 386]." Because it sole-sourced the 386 and because no competing chip ran the standard software, the whole industry, with the exception of IBM, which could produce its own 386 for some of its own needs, had to buy from Intel. The IBM license was not an immediate problem. IBM would not be able to produce its version of the 386 until 1990. Meanwhile, it too had to buy from Intel. "[Intel's] got a lock on the market," one analyst is quoted as saying. "It's awesome how well they are positioned," declares another. Analysts were predicting sales at Intel to grow 40 percent and profits to better than double.[46]

Competitors, according to this article, were especially unhappy because of the sheer luck, in their view, involved in Intel's preeminence. "Archrival" Motorola had introduced its 68020 two years before the 386, and "some engineers believe it is superior." But because of that design win at IBM for the 8088 way back in 1980, the industry, with the exception of Apple,[47] "standardized around that. The PC industry is now locked into the Intel architecture, which is best suited to running the MS-DOS and OS/2 operating systems."

Luck? Grove did not deny it. Luck alone. No. "There is such a thing as luck and then you grab it and exploit it," he said.[48] Meanwhile, Intel was not waiting for the attacks it knew would come. Rather, it was introducing new, enhanced versions of the 386, flanking products that would provide a presence in workstations and "the higher reaches of the computer industry." Intel was in the process of changing itself from a semiconductor company to, quoting Grove, "a company that produces stuff for microcomputers."

Intel planned gradually to lower the price of the 386, thus increasing sales volume and discouraging new entrants into its market. It was also going to introduce a variety of microprocessors aimed at various markets, including one for embedded controllers, one which used elements of the new and potentially threatening RISC (reduced instruction set computing) technology, and a "stripped down" 386, which was inexpensive but also lacking some of the key properties of its upscale sibling. Intel was also in the systems business, selling circuit boards and, in some cases, complete computers. This business was growing at a rapid clip. Intel aimed to sell more chip sets for clones of one of IBM's products.

Perhaps most important, Intel wanted to sell even more chips for the personal computer. An indication of what the PC business had meant to Intel in the 1980s is that the earliest IBM PC contained $20 worth of Intel chips. The Compaq Deskpro 386 had $800 worth.

No one was describing Andy anymore as the least well-known of Intel's founders. Rather, he was "[s]trong-willed and blunt talking." Grove had made it known that he would retire at fifty-five, and the *Times* article speculated about his successor. The names mentioned were Dave House, Larry Hootnick, Craig Barrett, and Les Vadasz.

But Gordon Moore, who certainly knew his man in this regard, said that Grove's retirement at fifty-five was "as likely to be adhered to as the 55-mile-per-hour speed limit."[49] As Craig Barrett said in mid-1993 when Grove was fifty-six and at the height of his powers, "Andy Grove has not been very good at forecasting his retirement."[50]

Nineteen eighty-nine was another strong year for the company. Although the leap in financial performance that characterized both 1987 and 1988 was not repeated, Intel was busily positioning itself for future prosperity. Sales of $3.1 billion represented a healthy increase of 9 percent over the previous year and set a new record. Profits did not keep pace. At $391 million, they were down 14 percent from the peak level of $453 million the previous year. Nevertheless, 1989 was the second most profitable year in Intel's history.

The *Annual Report* for 1989 was upbeat despite the softening in the bottom line. "[R]evenue gains from increased unit volumes were moderated by changes in product mix and lower average selling prices, including price declines on proprietary products following a normal product maturity/pricing trend." Add to this charges of $44 million incurred by the shuttering of two older fabs, in Livermore and Santa Clara, which could no longer be run economically, and you have an explanation for the profit performance that did not bode ill for the future.

There was plenty of room for optimism going forward: "[I]t was an extraordinary year for new product introductions." Most important among these were probably the i860 high-performance RISC microprocessor and the i486, the new addition to the x86 family, "a 32-bit processor that offers high-performance and is compatible with the $30 billion of software written for earlier versions of the x86 architecture."[51]

The i486 contained more than a million transistors and had taken 130 person-years to design. Development costs were estimated at $200 million. This compares to 80 person-years to design the 386 and development costs half as large. As with the 386, Intel was the sole source for the i486 and remained so for four years.[52] Volume shipments of the i486 began in the fourth quarter of 1989, which may help explain the generally positive tone of the *Annual Report.*

Certainly Wall Street had no complaints about the company. Its market capitalization climbed to $6.341 billion. This represented an increase of almost 50 percent over 1988. It outpaced the rate of growth of the Dow Jones Industrial Average and represented an all-time high for Intel. The best was yet to come.

The most important single event for Intel in 1989 was the introduction of the 80486 microprocessor at a trade show called COMDEX on April 10. COMDEX, which stands for Computer Dealer Exposition, had been held in Atlanta during the 1980s. In 1989 it was moved to Chicago because larger facilities were necessary to accommodate the expected 60,000 visitors.[53]

Gordon Moore was justified in his assertion that "The star of the show is the 486 microprocessor. . . . Five years ago it was inconceivable that we could make such a chip. This is a monster."[54] Bill Gates agreed. According to him, "The 486 chip is a fantastic advance." Compaq CEO Rod Canion called it "a huge leap forward in performance.... The 80486 is clearly taking things well beyond the PC range and moving us into the minicomputer market."[55] Grove remembers Canion saying that the 486 would provide a stable computing platform for the next decade. Grove characterized Canion as an "understated, low-key, computer guy," and he was impressed with the sweeping nature of Canion's observation, which, by the way, turned out to be accurate.[56]

Canion's sentiments were shared by others. According to a *New York Times* article, "A number of industry executives said the effect of Intel's i486 would be far greater than that of the 80386. The Intel and other competing 32-BIT chips will create a class of desktop computers that will be increasingly indistinguishable from more expensive mainframe and minicomputers."[57]

If this were true—indeed, if anything like this were close to being true—it meant that the whole information processing industry was on the cusp of a revolution. This was the transformation of the industry from vertical to horizontal referred to earlier, caused by a fundamental change in the price/performance equation. If you could do with a desktop machine what used to require the power of a minicomputer, that threatened DEC's flagship product line. If you could do what used to require a mainframe, it was a dagger pointed at the heart of IBM's most profitable business. All this was a little hard to believe.

Jim Cannavino, head of IBM's Entry Systems Division, said of the 486, "It's not just what Intel did, but what they didn't do. They didn't compromise compatibility one little bit."[58] What Cannavino meant was that every software program that had been written for the 386 would also run on the 486. The importance of compatibility had been impressed upon Intel by IBM years earlier. In the words of Paul Otellini,

We didn't really understand the importance of compatibility between different generations of processors. I remember a meeting in 1982 with Don Estridge who was running the IBM PC division. We had just finished the 286 and were shipping it to IBM. Estridge called Gordon [Moore] and me up to San Francisco and lectured us on the importance of compatibility—the 286 was not strictly compatible with its predecessor. As a result of this experience, we finally got it. Backward compatibility is really critical.[59]

IBM played "chicken" with Intel when the 386 was introduced. Big Blue lost because Compaq bought it, and Big Blue had to follow suit. This time, there was no such charade. IBM was first in line to buy the 486, thus hastening its own inevitable downfall as a great corporation and moving in the direction that it occupies today as being just another big company that has its good years and its bad years.

At one point during the COMDEX show, Grove found himself seated between Cannavino and Canion. It turned out that these two men, one the head of IBM's PC division and the other the founder of Compaq, at the time IBM's leading PC competitor, had never met. Grove introduced them to one another. It was a memorable moment for him. He later told Moore, "We were a second-class chip supplier to the Burroughses and the Univacs of the world. And now here we are. . . . We are *it*."[60]

Stock options have long been the mother's milk of Silicon Valley, so the reaction of analysts on Wall Street to the 486 was vitally important. Intel could not have asked for more. Plaudits came from everybody: Merrill Lynch, Smith Barney, Shearson Lehman Hutton, Prudential-Bache, Donaldson, Lufkin & Jenrette, and Salomon Brothers.[61] Everybody had nice things to say about the 80486 and about the company that made it.

Decisiveness and focus became the hallmarks of Grove's tenure as CEO. Another Andy—Andrew Carnegie—used to say, "Put all your eggs in one basket and then watch that basket."[62] Grove lived by that rule.

Running Intel in the 1980s meant living on the edge. Exiting DRAMs, sole-sourcing the 386, CISC versus RISC (which we will discuss in a later chapter)—the wrong decision, or even more insidiously, the right decision poorly implemented, could have hobbled Intel. There were always firms nipping at its heels that could have gone after more vital organs had Intel slipped. AMD was engaged in a blood feud with it. Motorola was in the midst of the same quandary with regard to RISC as was Intel. What if it decided to bet on CISC, and RISC turned out to be the technology of the future?

There were new entrants into the industry. Cyrix Semiconductor was created in 1987 by defectors from Texas Instruments. It entered the microprocessor business in 1991.[63] T. J. Rodgers founded Cypress Semiconductor, of which he is still CEO, in 1982. He was quoted in the press in 1990 as predicting that Intel faced "a decade of eroding market share."[64] This was obviously a self-serving prognostication, and it could not have turned out to be more wrong.

No one, however, could have been sure of Rodgers's miscalculation at the time. Even if Intel outpaced Cyrix, Cypress, National, Motorola, and Texas Instruments, there was always the question of IBM. "I never understood that company, and I never will," Grove wrote Moore back in 1986.[65] By 1990, it appeared that no one, including IBM's own executives, understood the company. It was drifting toward Niagara Falls.

Even if domestic competition could be kept at bay, what about the Japanese? They had driven Intel out of DRAMs. Why would history not repeat itself with microprocessors? If the Japanese themselves were threatened by the Koreans, were not the Americans equally threatened, especially with the rise of Samsung? The 1990s were to be the years of Intel's greatness. But there was nothing guaranteed about that.

All companies, but especially those in high-technology industries, are in a war for talent. You have got to recruit the best people you can find, and then you've got to hold on to them. Through its practice of redeployment, Intel showed in deeds not words that it wanted to keep good people and would go to considerable lengths to do so. Thus, those involved in the abortive RISC effort were redeployed. This is one way among many to create a workforce and an executive corps peopled, to revisit a metaphor, not only by "mercenaries" (Intel had to make money) but also by "marines" (Intel had to stand for something—that something was changing the world through technology).

Grove became more interested in history as his responsibilities at Intel increased and as Intel grew. During the 1990s, he said repeatedly that in the world of technology, anything that can be done will be done.[66] This is a simplification of a complex phenomenon, but let us accept it as true for the sake of discussion. What this truth leaves out is the dimension of time. When is it that technology will advance? Intel wanted to bring the world the technological future. It had to make money doing so. In order to manage technological change profitably, Intel had to give the world the future on schedule.[67]

13

Intel Inside

During the 1990s, it all paid off. All the effort, all the aggravation, all the small steps that made Intel a more muscular company—all paid off.

Intel, and in some important measure because of Intel, Silicon Valley, became famous. Andy Grove, the penniless immigrant from a small, backwater Communist country, became *Time* magazine's "Man of the Year" in 1997. Three years later he was awarded an honorary degree from Harvard.

The 1990s were also to prove a decade of unprecedented professional and personal challenges. The RISC/CISC war was a brush with what might have been a disastrous strategic error. The Pentium flaw threatened the foundation of Intel's greatness. On a personal plane, Grove was diagnosed with prostate cancer in 1995. Once again, he was at war with his body. Once again, as when he had scarlet fever at the age of four, it was a life-or-death struggle.

By 1990, Grove had completed the transition from technologist alone to a man who was at home with technology but who was also a master manager. The number of American business executives who crossed that chasm is not large. Alfred P. Sloan Jr., who created General Motors during its great days, is one. George Eastman, founder of Eastman Kodak, is another. However, the fact that you can name a couple of standouts shows how few there have been. Far more common are the engineers who never master the art of management or the managers who are technologically illiterate. Grove combined technology and managerial ability with the fact that he was a natural leader. Once he became president and CEO of Intel he had the perfect platform from which to display all these talents.

What, precisely, is a business leader? How does the business leader differ from the business manager? Grove has always disliked such distinctions. He was strongly oriented toward output. Output requires goals, measurement, system, evaluation, and concentrated attention to detail. All such tasks are more commonly associated with management than leadership. At the minimum we can define a leader as someone who has followers. Grove did. He still does. He is a charismatic figure. His dislike of that description only increases its accuracy.

By the 1980s, as we have seen, Grove's view of Bob Noyce's utility to Intel had changed. As "Mr. Outside," Noyce could play a useful role by deploying his prestige in the public arena to defend the American semiconductor industry from being overwhelmed by "Japan, Inc." He was also important if for no other reason than that he continued to hold a lot of Intel stock.

In 1987 and 1988, the federal government agreed to fund the semiconductor industry consortium, SEMATECH. Its purpose was to help the industry pool its resources without the threat of antitrust prosecution in order to disseminate best practice and fend off the Japanese challenge. Government-sponsored industry associations for such purposes do not have a track record of success in the United States. SEMATECH desperately needed a healthy dose of prestige. This it received when, on July 27, 1988, the announcement was made that Bob Noyce would serve as its CEO.

Noyce was sixty at the time and enjoying semiretirement with his second wife, Ann Bowers. He took the position out of a sense of duty to the industry and to the country. Noyce brought instant prestige to SEMATECH. As one editorial put it, "When an infant business needs credibility, there's nothing like hiring a legend."[1] Grove said he was a "mensch" to take the job. In other words, he was a "stand-up guy" to involve himself so intimately in such a tough and potentially unrewarding endeavor.[2] Noyce and Ann moved to Austin, Texas, where SEMATECH was headquartered. She got a job with the then virtually unknown Michael Dell.

Noyce had two goals for his tenure at SEMATECH. He wanted to secure continued support from Washington and continued commitment from the companies involved. By the spring of 1990, he felt his goals had been achieved, and he informed the SEMATECH board that he intended to step down as CEO.

On June 1, 1990, he was celebrated at SEMATECH with "Bob Noyce Day." T-shirts featuring Noyce's likeness and the phrase "Teen Idol" stenciled on them were distributed to everyone. A good time was had by all.

On the morning of June 3, Noyce went for a swim in his pool. Feeling fatigued afterward, he lay down on a couch in his home. He never arose. His fatal heart attack was sudden and shocking. A comprehensive physical examination the previous week had suggested no problems. But he was a heavy smoker, which may have contributed to his early death.

Memorial services were held both in Austin and San Jose. Apple Computer, which at the time bought no microprocessors from Intel,[3] issued a statement that described Noyce as "one of the giants in this valley who provided the model and inspiration for everything we wanted to become. He was the ultimate inventor. The ultimate rebel. The ultimate entrepreneur."[4]

The people at the top in Silicon Valley know each other. Steve Jobs, Arthur Rock, Bob Noyce, David Packard—and a host of other people who, while not as well-known, are very important and wealthy and have known each other for years. They have invested in one another's funds and in one another's companies. They have made money together.

Bob Noyce was the first of the men at the top of this small town to die. His death was so unexpected. He had been so vibrant. It was not easy for the villagers of Silicon Valley to understand his passing.

Noyce's death was gracefully noted in Intel's 1990 *Annual Report*. The company's headquarters building in Santa Clara was named for him, the Robert Noyce Building, known in the company as RNB. How appropriate. At his death, Intel's employee number one became a three-letter acronym.

The other news delivered in the 1990 *Annual Report* was a good deal more positive. "Excellent acceptance of our products and strong growth in all geographies helped to produce record results."[5]

Sales climbed by one-quarter to a record $3.921 billion. At $650 million, profits were two-thirds higher than the previous year and also a record. Intel moved up to number 119 on *Fortune*'s list of the nation's 500 largest companies. At $7.7 billion, Intel's market capitalization set a new record. This was an increase of more than a fifth over the record year of 1989. The increase took place as the Dow Jones Industrial Average lost over 4 percent of its value. What explains this performance?

"Demand for 386/486 microprocessor family products exceeded supply." That was true because Intel had won the standards war. Its architecture was now the platform on which other companies in the computer value stack were building their businesses. In the words of software entrepreneur Philippe Kahn, "If you're going to learn only one instruction set, it's going to be the Intel x86."[6] The industry demanded "compatibility, upgradeability, and connectivity." Intel delivered.[7] None of this was easy. Nothing happened automatically. Intel really was on top of its game in 1990.

A major theme of Intel's history since its transformation from a memory company to a microprocessor company was the effort to capture the value it was creating. Remember, Intel was the technology company that generated profits. Those were its twin goals, and they were equally important.

Everyone in its own and related industries and on Wall Street was well aware of Intel by 1990. That was not, however, true of the world outside. Intel was a business-to-business marketer, not a consumer products marketer. The Microma experience had left a heavy imprint on top management. Intel was a company of engineers selling to other engineers products the technical complexity of which is difficult for the layperson to grasp.

How did such a dyed-in-the-wool, business-to-business marketer develop a brand and a slogan to go with it—"Intel Inside"—that became one of the most widely known worldwide? The story of Intel Inside begins with a man named Dennis Lee Carter.

Dennis Carter was born and raised in Kentucky. He attended the Rose-Hulman Institute of Technology in Terre Haute, Indiana, from which he received a BS in electrical engineering and physics in 1973. He went on to earn a master's in electrical engineering in 1974 from Purdue, which awarded him an honorary doctorate in 1996.

Carter's first job out of Purdue was with the defense contractor Rockwell International. It was there that he got experience using Intel's early microprocessors. He loved the technology, but he found himself equally enamored of business. "I was often pulled out to the customers to explain to them the technology we were designing, and I liked that role."[8]

Carter's interest in business resulted in his enrolling in the Harvard Business School in the fall of 1979. Interestingly enough, what made the deepest impression on him was not the coursework in marketing or production. It was a finance class taught by Professor Henry Reiling called "Tax Factors in Business Decisions." Carter never forgot how Reiling concluded that course. "When you look for your first job," he advised, "find a job where nobody knows exactly what you're supposed to be doing. If they don't know what you're supposed to be doing, they won't know what you're not supposed to be doing. As a result, you can do anything you want, and you can take risks."[9]

The jobs most sought after by newly minted MBAs when Carter received his degree in 1981 were with consulting firms and investment banks. He had no inclination in either of those directions. He wanted to work at a high-technology firm. Vinod Mahendroo, a Harvard Business School MBA from the class of 1978, was recruiting from Intel, and he persuaded Carter to come out to Santa Clara. Like so many other midwesterners, Carter thought he would spend perhaps two years on the West Coast before moving back home. But once he came, he stayed.

Carter joined Intel in 1981, and in 1985 he found an opportunity to get the kind of job Professor Reiling had described. In the mid-1980s, Intel decided to hire "technical assistants" for their top executives. The idea came from IBM, which had such a system. At Intel, the hope was to pick promising people, give them plentiful exposure to the responsibilities of a senior manager, and then see what happened. In short, the job of "technical assistant" would be made up as the two people involved went along. It was undefined, giving the person who held the position room to shape it. This position still exists at Intel. Andy Grove knew Carter from some of his work on memory chips. He interviewed several people to be his TA. Carter got the offer.

Be careful what you wish for. At first, the job was massively disappointing. Carter was not much more than a "gofer"—"go for" this and "go for" that. He felt like a glorified, and only slightly glorified, secretary.

But soon it became apparent that Carter and Grove made a potent combination. Carter's responsibilities grew as his abilities asserted themselves. "I loved the job. It was a great job." The idea was to hold the job for two years, but Carter held it for four and a half. "In the end, he [Grove] literally had to throw me out of his office."[10]

Before being thrown out of the TA's job (to be replaced by Paul Otellini, now CEO of Intel), Carter had spotted a problem with the relationship between two of Intel's own products, the 286 and the 386. Specifically, the 386 was having trouble replacing the 286 in the marketplace. The 286 was too popular, and the 386 was viewed as so powerful that it was only appropriate for highly sophisticated tasks.

Carter believed that this situation arose because of the changing decision-making process for the purchase of personal computers. The move to the 386 was not dependent on design engineers at original equipment manufacturers. The focus had shifted to the marketing side of the OEMs. The marketers were making the decision to stick with the 286 rather than migrate upstream to the 386 because their assessment was that their customer, the end user who actually bought the personal computer, was not asking for the processing power that the 386 provided. Carter made this case to Grove. Andy responded that Carter might be right. The question now was what to do about the situation.

Carter's response was that Intel had to go to the end user and convince him or her that the 386 was the product to demand. The end user would look for the 386 in his or her PC and thus pull the product through the distribution channel rather than Intel's trying to push it through. A little graphic from a beginning marketing course will illustrate what Carter had in mind.

FIGURE 8
Push Marketing Versus Pull Marketing

Push Marketing	versus	Pull Marketing
Intel's 386		Intel's 386
↓		↑
OEM		OEM
↓		↑
Retailer		Retailer
↓		↑
End user		End user

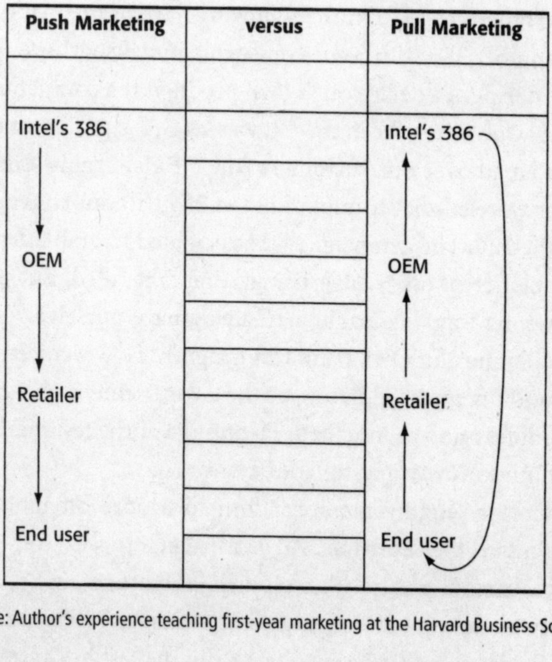

Source: Author's experience teaching first-year marketing at the Harvard Business School.

Remember that end-user marketing was not looked upon kindly at Intel in 1989. Actually, that's putting it mildly. It was "anathema."[11] However, Grove proved, as he often did, that he was willing to challenge his own assumptions and everyone else's. Moreover, the end user being targeted was at least as likely to be a corporate IT ("information technology") manager as a member of the general public. This situation was not a replay of the Microma watch experience.

Carter was going to have to go out into the field and demonstrate with field-based data, rather than what you could gather around the office, that "pull" marketing would provide the punch the 386 needed. Carter accepted the challenge. It was, in fact, this project that finally ended his tenure as Andy's TA. "So," Carter recalls, "I go form a team of five very brave people who are going to do this thing that everybody in Intel is glowering at."[12]

Carter's approach was nothing if not bold. For a variety of reasons, he chose Denver as a test market. He did not have much time. The announcement of the 486 was just months away. "So our little crack team flies into Denver, and the only kind of media we could buy on short notice are newspapers and billboards." The copy was arresting. On one page of a newspaper advertisement would appear "286" in black ink with a huge red "X" seemingly spray-painted over it. On the following page of the newspaper would appear the number 386 with some copy explaining its virtues.

This was daring. To deface one's own product! If a competitor had done so, it probably would have been sued. It was, as Grove put it, "unprecedented for us to lob an ad over our customers [the OEMs] against our own product."[13] Carter worried that it might kill the 286 without convincing people to move to the 386. The campaign "was calculated to grab attention, to cut through the clutter of other advertising," Carter recalled. But if consumers took it the wrong way, "we could actually damage ourselves." Dave House called it the " 'Eating Our Own Baby' Campaign."[14] However, perhaps because of the clear and unequivocal nature of the advertisement, the message penetrated the public mind as intended. The results of the test market were unmistakable both to Grove and to House.

Grove wrote a lengthy memorandum to Moore on June 9, 1989, in which he discussed the "End-User Ad Campaign."

Dennis, in his new job, is moving with great speed toward running a test ad. The latest is that he is going to run the test in Denver to help move the market to 32 bits [from the 16-bit 286 to the 32-bit 386]. It's a controlled experiment all set up very thoughtfully and professionally, but done in a hurry, because if it works and we do it on a bigger scale, it has to happen in the next few months in order to have an impact on the PC selling season this year. The ad is imaginative—strikes me even as brilliant—but bold and aggressive. It has been blessed by all the top guns in marketing, including Gelbach, who was consulted as a disinterested bystander.

"I predict," added Grove, "you'll hate it."[15]

Whatever Moore's feelings toward what came to be known as the "Red X" campaign, they could not have been too negative. The campaign was rolled out nationally. It served as "a vivid signal that Intel was ready to cannibalize its own products, and that the end-users, and by implication the OEMs, should follow Intel's lead."[16]

As Burgelman says bluntly, "It worked."[17] Sales of the 386 skyrocketed. Moore's law was not an inevitability. It was not like gravity. It was an expression of what would be possible in the future if the future unfolded as the past had. In order for this "law" to become a reality, Intel had to drive the market forward. It had to move a whole environment—suppliers, distributors, consumers—to the next level of complexity. The Red X campaign is an example of how Intel managed its market. Rich Lovgren, associate general counsel for the always complaining AMD, said, "Intel doesn't have customers—they have hostages."[18] Managing a market cost money. Intel put $5 million behind the Red X. It had proven it could speak directly both to IT professionals and even to consumers.

Branding, it has been said, is one-half finance and one-half romance.[19] That is to say, it costs money to brand a product. However, brands are "co-created." It is not only the company selling the product but the customer buying it that creates the brand. This was what Roberto Goizueta, the CEO of Coca-Cola from 1981 until 1997, said he learned from the failed effort to change Coke's formula in 1985. Coca-Cola shared "ownership" of its brand with the people who drank it.

With the 386 SX, a product-line extension of the 386, Intel accidentally discovered that it had a brand on its hands. "Kids, teenagers, would walk [into consumer electronics] stores saying, 'I want a radio with this 386 SX in it because it's cool.'"[20] Somehow, the 386 SX was a name that caught on. It was not in any radios, but some people obviously thought it was. Carter began to wonder about how brandable Intel's products were.

Intel sells components, ingredients that go into a box like a computer or some other container such as an automobile. The idea of ingredient branding was fairly new in 1990. Nutrasweet, the artificial sweetener, had successfully created its brand with a campaign that began in 1981, but there were few other examples.[21]

Think about buying a personal computer. You cannot tell where the microprocessor is inside that box. Even if you opened up the box, you might find it difficult to put your hand on it. Most computer users do not know what a microprocessor actually does. Thus the barriers to creating a valuable brand were not insignificant. Unfortunately, Intel in 1990 had neither a marketing structure nor an advertising agency capable of addressing this issue.

However the potential rewards of branding the microprocessor were very great. A brand reassures the customer. It eliminates search costs. It creates a bond with the buyer. James E. Burke, the CEO of Johnson & Johnson from 1976 to 1989 and the man who saved Tylenol despite its being poisoned in 1982 and again in 1986, has said that if you want to find out how valuable a brand is, go out and try to buy one. He defined the value of a brand as the capitalized value of the trust between the company and the customer.[22] Not easy to quantify, but a genuinely important asset in the fight for dollars within the value stack of an industry. Carter wanted a brand for Intel.

To achieve his goal, Carter scoured the country looking for answers. He found one in an unexpected place. He approached John White, a partner in a small advertising agency in Salt Lake City. "I described the strategic thing we're trying to do," Carter recalled with his characteristic urgency. "This is what we want to be. We want to make the processor more prominent in the computer. It's really important. It's invisible. People don't know about it. They don't know us. How do we do this?"[23]

Carter's goal was not just to increase the sales of a class of product, for example the 386 over the 286, but to increase the sales of Intel's products within that particular class. When Intel introduced the 386, the first 32-bit microprocessor, it was, as we have discussed at length above, the sole source for that product.[24] In 1990, however, its monopoly was lost. "AMD Ends 386 Monopoly," announced the *Microprocessor Report,* an industry newsletter, on November 28. "The most valuable monopoly in the history of the semiconductor business is about to end."[25] This development did not threaten

Intel's future as much as the headline implied. "Intel will lose some business to AMD, but it is unlikely that the company will be hurt badly. To the extent that Intel has not been meeting 386 demand, AMD could ship some 386 chips without affecting Intel at all."[26]

AMD introduced its first genuine imitation 386 in 1990. By 1992, as Intel was busily at work trying to move the world to the 486, AMD had achieved a market share in the 386 class microprocessor of greater than 50 percent.[27] If Intel wanted a brand, that brand could not be called 386 or 486. You cannot trademark a number.[28]

After Carter's explanation of what he wanted and what function the microprocessor performed, White suggested the following slogan: "Intel: The Computer Inside."[29] Slowly, in Carter's hands, this phrase became compressed to "Intel Inside."

Carter advocated a complete marketing program aimed at the end user. He wanted mass-market advertising, and he also wanted cooperative advertising with OEMs. In other words, Intel would pay part of the cost of an advertisement placed by a computer manufacturer if the advertisement included a small notice that said "Intel Inside" and if the computer itself had a sticker that said the same thing.

If you are manufacturing computers, your reaction to Intel's proposition is likely to be mixed. Intel's money to help you advertise your product you will gladly accept. However, Intel's brand in your advertisement and on your computer itself might dilute the value of your brand by cluttering it up. Carter understood this. "We need to be friendly, and the sticker needs to say 'Intel.' But it can't be the corporate ID."[30] Look at the "Intel Inside" sticker that is on your PC right now. You will see that the word "Intel" is written in a style different from what was the corporate logo, with its distinctive dropped "e," until the new CEO Paul Otellini had that logo changed and the dropped "e" removed in January 2006.

Here, then, were the basics of the "Intel Inside" program. Carter put all the pieces together and presented it to top management. "Everybody looks at it in disbelief. 'This is crazy. What are you doing? This is nuts.'" More than one executive could not understand "why in the world our OEMs would want to participate" in such a program.[31] Andy said it was brilliant and that Carter should make it happen.[32]

This is the story of how a semiconductor start-up run by technologists reached out directly to consumers and established one of the world's best-known brands. The campaign debuted in April 1990, and the company did not look back until Paul Otellini's restructuring of the company and the attendant reengineering of its marketing after he became CEO in May 2005. From 1990 to 1993, Intel's Corporate Marketing Group spent half a billion dollars to build the brand in the minds of end users. The lion's share of this staggeringly large sum went to "Intel Inside."[33] There is a persistent myth, believed even by Intel executives, that the idea for "Intel Inside" came from Intel's Japanese operations, where the slogan for Intel's products was "Intel In It." When I told Carter that numerous people still hold this view, he was incredulous. However, he quickly rallied and observed that "stories live forever."[34]

The "Intel Inside" slogan was to prove of inestimable value. The wealth of Bill Gates and the power of Microsoft asserted themselves in the 1990s. Gates became rich beyond imagining, and Microsoft developed the strongest balance sheet in business, which it still possesses. "Intel Inside" endowed Intel with an identity beyond the confines of the world of high technology. The company became famous. The pulling power of the slogan with consumers helped prevent Intel from being swallowed up by the machine Gates was constructing. It proved valuable abroad in ways that had not been anticipated. By the end of 1991, 342 OEMs were involved in the "Intel Inside" program. The logo appeared on about three thousand pages of advertising placed by these companies.

Success spawned further effort. Intel sponsored television advertising in 1991 aimed at the end user. The goal? To educate consumers "about the easy upgradeability offered by many new Intel 486 SX CPU-based PCs."[35]

Silicon Valley is a complicated place, and it is about many things. All would agree, though, that one central preoccupation is with growth. Getting big is more important than being big. Getting bigger is also more important than being big. It is not accidental that Paul Otellini made growth a central theme of his early weeks as Intel's CEO. He announced aggressive growth targets for what is already a very large company.

Growth matters for any number of reasons. First, it increases your opportunities as an employee to assume a more important position and command a higher salary. You can have more prestige and more fun and make more money.

Second, growth has a direct impact on compensation. A stock option is a grant to buy a share of stock at the price the stock sold at when the grant was made. In other words, if you are granted a stock option when the stock is selling at $20 per share and five years later the stock is selling at $100 a share, that option gives you the right to purchase a share at a fifth of its current price. Stock options are more complicated than this, but suffice it to say that if you work for a company that grants them, you have a very strong interest in seeing that company's stock rise as steeply as possible as quickly as possible.

With this in mind, let us ask how Intel had done as of December 31, 1990. The company went public at $23.50 a share in 1971. Between then and the end of 1990 the stock split eight times in such a way that your one share had turned into thirty-eight shares. The compound annual rate of return was about 24 percent. This compares to a compound rate of return of 6 percent posted by the Dow Jones Industrial Average. Ten thousand dollars invested in Intel in 1971 would have been worth almost $600,000 at the end of 1990.[36]

Among Intel's strengths, according to Wall Street analysts, was its management. "Drs. Moore and Grove make an ideal team." Craig Barrett's elevation to a three-person "office of the president" boded well for the future. "Dr. Barrett," explained one analyst, "was largely responsible for remaking Intel from a mediocre manufacturing company to a manufacturing giant, able to hold its own with the best in the world."[37]

Interestingly enough, this same bullish analyst (for Prudential-Bache Securities) saw as the "most important risk" facing the company "the tremendous animosity among its customers." A clear explanation for the cause of this animosity was not offered. Indeed, neither was any proof brought forward that it existed. It was merely asserted.[38]

Angry or not, Intel's customers kept buying its products, and investors kept buying its stock. Sales and profits were both up 22 percent in 1991 to $4.8 billion and $819 million, respectively. Intel moved up to number 106 on the Fortune 500. Its market capitalization at the end of the year was $7.68 billion, up 21 percent from 1990. All three numbers set records. Intel passed Motorola as the nation's largest semiconductor manufacturer. For the first time in its history, more than half its sales came from abroad.[39]

Intel was becoming a really big business, with a suite of products superbly positioned for growth. "Intel," according to an analyst in late January 1991, "is clearly one of the most important and dynamic companies in the world, as [its] innovation has changed the world in which we live."[40] The semiconductor industry as a whole would continue to experience cycles. Intel, however, seemed poised for secular growth. Why?

According to the 1991 *Annual Report,*

It's historic: for the first time a stable 32-bit microprocessor architecture spans the entire range of computing options. What this means for systems manufacturers and their customers is unquestioned compatibility, upgradeability, and connectivity throughout their product lines. The Intel 386 and Intel 486 architecture protects manufacturers' and PC users' investment for the future.[41]

14

"We Almost Killed the Company"

A ndy Grove's decade as chief executive officer of Intel can usefully be divided into two parts. The first part lasted from 1987, when he got the job, to about 1993. The second was from 1993 to his relinquishment of the position in the spring of 1998. Nineteen ninety-three was a turning point because by that time, the choice among three paths Intel could have taken had been firmly and clearly made. Those three different paths had to do with product policy.

A key question all businesses face is what markets they elect to serve with what products. In the late 1980s and early 1990s, Intel confronted a fork in the road with regard to product policy. One direction suggested that it continue to develop the x86 architecture in its microprocessor business. Another suggested that it turn its attention to a new microprocessor architecture that was attracting a lot of publicity. There was also a third choice, to pursue both architectures simultaneously.

In 1989, Grove was fully aware of the competitive threats to Intel's growth. On his mind were Sun Microsystems with its SPARC chip, MIPS with a new chip of its own, Motorola introducing the 80040, NEC from Japan with its V33,[1] and "clones" including Cyrix, IIT, NexGen, and Chips & Technologies. Also lurking about was that problem of which Intel has never been able to rid itself, AMD. The issue that was convulsing Intel in 1989 and the years immediately thereafter was: what attitude should it take toward RISC? Should RISC architecture be regarded as Intel's friend? Was it worth a major investment? Intel's x86 architecture was based on CISC. Would the success of RISC threaten all Intel had put into CISC?

The RISC/CISC debate would be decided by Grove. Intel, while he was CEO, was a top-down organization. Which is not to say that Grove stifled controversy. To the contrary, he encouraged argument. Indeed, when you are with Grove, it is with difficulty that you can avoid an argument. But you had better be prepared to defend your point of view with data and with passion, or he will run right over you. He will, however, change his mind in the face of a superior, data-driven point of view. So arguing with him is worth doing if you are sure you are right. There were to be plenty of arguments about RISC and CISC in Intel's future.

Grove's decision was not going to be made easier by his own knowledge base. "Architectural discussion," he has said, "is, of all the various aspects of my work, that for which I am least competent." This controversy, therefore, took place in an arena in which Grove felt "very out of my element."[2] Grove is human, and insecurity about his intellectual mastery of an issue does not make him easier to deal with. "If he is confused," one Intel executive has said, "he gets tougher."[3]

Let us begin by describing the difference between CISC (complex instruction set computing) and RISC (reduced instruction set computing) at the most general level. We can start with a definition of an "instruction set."

An instruction set, or instruction set architecture (ISA), describes the aspects of a computer architecture visible to a programmer, including the native datatypes, instructions, registers, addressing modes, memory architecture, interrupt and exception handling, and external I/O [input/output] (if any).

An ISA is a specification of the set of all codes (opcodes) that are the native form of commands implemented by a particular CPU design. The set of opcodes for a particular ISA is also known as the machine language for the ISA.[4]

This is quite a mouthful. To simplify, an instruction set is "All the commands that [a computer] can carry out directly in one step."[5] It is a group of commands that tells a microprocessor what to do. The instruction "ADD," for example, would generate a series of zeroes and ones that would result in addition. A complex instruction set describes precisely what it is, a set of many instructions. A reduced instruction set, to state what must be approaching the obvious, contains fewer instructions.

The number of instructions embedded in the architecture of a microprocessor turns out to be matter of great importance. CISC microprocessors are extraordinarily complicated artifacts. The real estate on a tiny microprocessor is expensive. Intel's great competitive strength by the late 1980s lay in the mastery of that complexity and in the ability to turn out these chips on a mass basis in expensive fabrication facilities.

What would the microprocessor world look like, however, if, instead of mastering complexity, you simplified the task? That was the promise of RISC. It turns out that many of the operations that complicated microprocessors made possible were seldom used. If the instructions enabling those operations were eliminated, the chips would be far simpler to design and manufacture. The operations a RISC chip did perform would be more efficient than a CISC chip because it would have to jump through fewer hoops to get the job done. The operations that RISC could not perform, it was theorized, could be written into software if it were necessary.

Here was the choice. RISC chips could perform a smaller number of operations than CISC. However, those operations could be performed very well, and the chip itself was simpler to deal with than CISC.

In looking for an analogy, consider the following. The MinuteClinic is a health care delivery company, staffed largely by nurses, that treats only the most common ailments.[6] It turns out that these ailments account for a remarkably disproportionate number of hospital visits. Like strep throat, they are well-known and are relatively easy to diagnose and treat. The MinuteClinic works because of the truth of an old saying, "Rare things in medicine are rare."[7]

Compare this to the Massachusetts General Hospital. It is "general," indeed, treating a staggering variety of health problems. Often these problems require a highly trained team of physicians as well as medical equipment and a large physical plant. It is easier to make money picking the low-hanging fruit.

The first RISC processors showed up in IBM's laboratories in the 1970s. It was not until the new architecture was adopted by some Silicon Valley companies, however, that it began to attract a lot of attention.

Sun Microsystems was founded in 1982 by four graduate students at

Stanford, hence the name Sun, for "Stanford University Network." The most public of these four has been Scott McNealy, for many years the CEO of what has become a troubled company. (He relinquished this position in 2006.) Convinced that Intel was overcharging for the 386, he decided that Sun should develop its own microprocessor. It would be designed in accord with RISC architecture.

Active in RISC was another Silicon Valley start-up, MIPS (for "millions of instructions per second") Computer Systems. Today known as MIPS Technologies and quite different from its original incarnation, MIPS is headquartered in Mountain View, between Santa Clara and Palo Alto. The company was founded by, among others, a Stanford computer scientist named John L. Hennessy. In 1981, Hennessy and a team he assembled began intensive work on RISC. In 1984, he brought this expertise to MIPS. A decade later, he coauthored a standard text on RISC, *Computer Organization and Design: The Hardware/Software Interface.* And in September 2000, he became Stanford's tenth president.[8]

An extraordinary oddity of the April 1989 COMDEX show discussed in the previous chapter is that there is one voice missing from the copious press and analyst coverage that event attracted. Moore is quoted, Gates is quoted, Canion is quoted, Cannavino is quoted. Everyone is quoted except Grove. Not once in all the clippings I have gone through does he speak out. This cannot be an accident. Andy was not bashful.

In the midst of the accolades for the 486, in Grove's mind there was the looming issue of the rise of RISC architecture. What role would RISC and CISC play in Intel's future? No question was more hotly debated at the company in 1989 and immediately thereafter. This quandary was probably one reason for the uncharacteristic silence of Grove at the COMDEX show.

You do not have to look far amid the press coverage of the microprocessor business in 1989 and 1990 to get a feel for the momentum behind RISC. "CISC will barely make it to orbit, but RISC is going to the moon," said one chip designer. "The 486 is the golden age of CISC, but it'll also be about the last one."[9] "[T]he interest in RISC as a commercial computing platform has never been greater."[10] "The Intel 586 will be the last great CISC chip."[11] "You'll buy a PC in the year 2005 with a MIPS chip and your neighbor will buy one with a SPARC chip."[12]

The rise of RISC posed a dilemma of critical dimensions to Intel. The "awesome" Intel that cornered the market Andrew Pollack described in the

New York Times in 1988[13] cornered a market defined by CISC architecture. Among the reasons the market was cornered was that, in addition to Intel's expertise in the design and manufacture of astonishingly complex microprocessors, a "vast library" of software applications for such purposes as word processing and database management had been developed to operate with the x86 architecture during the 1980s following the hallowed Intel design win for IBM's PC.[14]

How vast was this library? Estimates in 1989 ranged from 25,000 to 50,000 applications.[15] Many of these applications had been around for a while. They had been used extensively and debugged. Thus, tens of thousands of software engineers had over the course of a decade written millions of lines of code to conform to the instruction set of Intel's microprocessor architecture.

That was why it was vital that successive generations of microprocessors be backward-compatible. All the software written for the 286 had to run on the 386. The software for both had to run on the 486. This "unquestioned compatibility, upgradeability, and connectivity" was what the 1991 *Annual Report,* quoted above, referred to as protecting the investment of OEMs and end users.[16] If the claims of the RISC camp were true, this huge barrier to entry disappeared more quickly than you can press the delete key on your computer's keyboard. That is why "RISC is viewed by new entrants in the computer market as a way to effectively challenge makers of machines using existing chips."[17]

"Inexorable" and "inevitable" migration of technology is much easier to spot in hindsight than before the fact. Because of its efficiency made possible by its relative simplicity, RISC architecture first became popular with sophisticated computer makers running complicated or highly repetitive applications. But you could tell a plausible story in 1989 and 1990 that what the sophisticated consumer wanted today the mass market would want tomorrow. In the words of a top executive at Hewlett-Packard, "Work stations can run high-end applications that would drag a PC to its knees quickly. We'll always see the work station at the leading edge, pushing the state of the art. Eventually, people are going to want to see those things on dealer shelves and we'll end up calling them PCs."[18]

If this expert was correct, RISC was the future. CISC was in the position of the buggy whip manufacturer in 1908, the year the Model T was introduced. But what if he was wrong? If Intel jumped to RISC, it would be as powerful an endorsement as the new architecture could win. If it did not jump to RISC and RISC was the future, Intel would wind up in the "dustbin of history."[19] But if RISC was not inevitable, then endorsing it was the worst possible business decision. This was Andy Grove's decision to make. It was as tough a call as the memory exit or the decision to sole-source the 386.

In the face of a new technology that poses a fundamental threat to the established business model, the incumbent often greets the new entrant with denial. The radial tire revolution mentioned earlier is a good example. Incumbents first denied the superiority of the radial tire to what they were producing. Next they panicked and tried to produce radials of their own on the cheap, with equipment that had been designed for a different kind of tire.

We see the same thing happening at Intel, where the "official corporate strategy" was not to endorse the movement to RISC but rather to stick to the CISC x86 architecture that was making Intel so awesome. As Robert Burgelman explains, "Intel's top management called RISC 'the technology of the have not.' And the strength of the organization's aversion to RISC architectures was demonstrated by the corporate argot, YARP, for Yet Another RISC Processor."[20]

Despite this attitude, Intel began to flirt with RISC seriously. On August 19, 1988, Grove visited Burgelman at his office at Stanford's Graduate School of Business. The discussion dealt with the possibility of writing a case about Intel. "[O]ne of the strategic issues on Grove's mind," Burgelman reports, was whether Intel should start a "RISC branch."[21]

Grove "seemed to be leaning fairly strongly against starting such an option."[22] The company's 1989 *Annual Report,* however, featured a picture of three chips. Most prominent was the company's flagship, i486, fully "compatible with the $30 billion of software written for earlier versions of the x86 architecture."[23] Also on the cover, however, was an i860 RISC chip. Introduced in February, the i860 was being used by customers "to build supercomputers, workstations, graphic subsystems and accelerator boards, and in other applications where number-crunching ability is paramount."[24]

Burgelman was surprised to see this, given his discussion with Grove.[25] One can only imagine the surprise experienced by those people who had invested $30 billion to develop software compatible with the x86 architecture. After all that trash talking, Intel's commitment to a RISC processor must have been very unpleasant for a lot of people to discover. What did it portend? Did Intel harbor the belief shared by others that RISC architecture would migrate down from the upper reaches of supercomputing to the PC on your desktop?

The appearance of Intel's RISC processor has a remarkable history, unearthed by the research of Robert Burgelman. It is worth retelling in some detail because it illustrates how things happen in the real world of the corporation. The question we must answer is: how did a despised product architecture that was a threat to the "awesomeness" of Intel wind up being designed and manufactured by Intel?

First of all, RISC architecture and what became the 860 had a talented, determined, and clever product champion named Les Kohn. Kohn had come to Intel in 1982 from National Semiconductor, and he brought with him the belief that "RISC architecture has some definite technical advantages."[26] Which it unquestionably did. The question was always whether those technical advantages were worth the diversion of resources required to develop a product the potential success of which would be a mixed blessing, to say the least. For Kohn, the answer to this question was yes.

Before proceeding, one might ask why a microprocessor engineer who was attracted to RISC would have gone to work for the most CISC-loyal company in the industry. The answer may lie in the year he joined Intel. In 1982, the controversy between RISC and CISC had not quite progressed, or degenerated, into the "religious war" it was to become. The 286 was introduced that year, but that had to be backward-compatible only with one generation of product. Nothing like $30 billion in x86-compatible software had yet been created. In other words, the situation was still fluid. This is an illustration of how fast things happened during the 1980s. In 1988, an advocate of RISC architecture would have been a good deal less likely to join Intel than in 1982. By 1993, there would have been very little opportunity indeed.

At any rate, Kohn was at Intel, and he wanted to work in RISC. He tried promoting his ideas through the standard channels for four years and got nowhere. In 1986, however, when it became clear that Intel's next microprocessor, that is, the 486 (the 386 had been introduced in 1985), would have a million transistors on board, he took a different tack. He developed more "aggressive goals" in his next proposal. Thinking big often paid off at Intel. He got some higher-ups interested.

Then came the question of how this RISC processor was to be positioned. Here, Kohn straddled a fence. The 860 was to be "a coprocessor for the 80486," an "accessory" to it. At the same time, it was to be thought of as a "stand-alone processor."[27]

The idea of a "coprocessor" was appealing. When Intel brought out the 386, it also brought out a math coprocessor named the 387. The company viewed this as a niche product for customers who had mathematically intensive requirements. The 387 was priced high and generated a lot of profit dollars. This association, therefore, was a happy one.

On the other hand, Kohn and his team "made sure it was very different from the x86 family so that there would be no question in the customer's mind of which product to use."[28] The 860 was definitely a RISC chip, different from Intel's standard offering, but not all that much more different than the very profitable 387 was from the 386. Kohn wanted Intel to be able to tell itself what made it comfortable to think about the 860.

Kohn's group made some presentations to large companies that were well received, presentations to a "whole group of customers who did not previously talk to Intel because they were more interested in performance than compatibility. 3D graphics, workstation, and minicomputer accounts all got very interested." The favorable reaction of these customers was transmitted to top management, and this flow of information played a key role in selling the RISC chip to Intel. According to Kohn, new potential customers praising the chip to Intel's leadership was critical "because at a technical level, senior management are not experts."[29] In 2005, I showed Grove that phrase. He agreed with it.

As the movement behind the 860 picked up steam within the company, Intel began to discover firsthand the problems involved in supporting two different microprocessor architectures. "Distinct CISC and RISC camps— situated on different floors of the same building—had formed," according to Burgelman's research, "and they were competing for the best engineering talent." Rumors began to circulate in the industry that Intel was going to veer from the x86 path toward RISC after the 486. Such rumors had the potential to loosen Intel's hold on its most loyal PC customers.[30]

"Everybody is at a crossroads," said the marketing director of LSI, Logic's microprocessor group, which produced RISC products.[31] It was not going to be possible to support both architectures. It was too expensive. The task of managing two sets of software suppliers was immense and easily underestimated.

Then there was the marketing perspective. Dennis Carter was horrified at the thought that Intel might call the 860 the 486r. The company would thus have two types of 486s—a 486r (RISC) and a 486c (CISC). Carter "became pretty hysterical" about that possibility. The whole point of a brand is to reassure the customer and eliminate search costs. Yet Intel was on the point of claiming that two incompatible products, its RISC and its CISC chips, were variations of one product, the 486.[32] This kind of confusion was pure poison. You can create a brand, but then the brand winds up defining you.

Intel wandered around in this wilderness for over a year. In February 1991, Grove said to Burgelman's MBA class that he was soon going to give a speech to software developers. "What," he asked, "should I tell them?"

> I have three options. I can tell them that we lean heavily on x86, that the x86 is forever. Or I can tell them that RISC is important and that Intel wants to be the premier company in RISC. Or I can tell them we will support both CISC and RISC and let the marketplace sort it out, just trust us.[33]

It is not easy in a company full of engineers who "want to make a dent in the world"[34] to champion, as even the general circulation press was putting it, the "old processing technology" in its effort to "beat back a challenge."[35] Dennis Carter was willing to play that role. He had an ally in Craig Kinnie, one of the "superheroes of Intel."[36] Kinnie is an engineer whom Grove had asked to establish the Architecture Develoment Lab that grew into the Intel Architecture Lab in Oregon. Carter remembers, as do Grove and Kinnie, the three of them arguing over CISC and RISC at the entry to Grove's little cubicle on the fifth floor of the Robert Noyce Building. Arguing with Grove is not easy. Carter, who had worked closely with him as his TA for four and a half years, and Kinnie, were up to the task.[37]

Some time after Burgelman's class in 1991, Grove reached a decision. Intel was going to stick with CISC architecture. "It was a confusing period for Intel," Grove told Burgelman. "The i860 was a very successful renegade product that could have destroyed the virtuous circle enjoyed by the Intel architecture. . . . Intel was helping RISC by legitimizing it."[38]

Grove's comment is so important that it is worth rereading. On his watch, Intel almost took a wrong turn of historic proportions. RISC turned out to be, if not a "ghost market," clearly not worth the sacrifice of the legacy software for the x86 architecture. The i860 did not develop into a profitable product.[39]

Two questions assert themselves. First, how did Intel, one of the world's best-run companies, come so close to the edge of the cliff? Second, why was it able to stop itself before committing suicide?

The memory and RISC episodes have a good deal in common. Both the move out of memory and the RISC initiative bubbled up from within the lower ranks of the corporation. Neither resulted from a strategic initiative planned at the top after surveying the opportunities and problems Intel faced. Both violated what, for lack of a better word, might be called the "meaning" of the corporation. Intel meant memory, but it had to exit the business. Intel meant x86 CISC architecture, but some talented people in the corporation felt it had to move to RISC.

Juxtaposing these two stories illustrates how difficult it is to develop general rules for running a business. Most people would favor an empowered, talented workforce showing initiative. Grove himself often said the strength of a company is its middle management. What Les Kohn and his team did was thus what Grove advocated.

Perhaps all that can be learned from these two stories is that it is better to be right than wrong. Grove said something close to that when he told Burgelman that "not all paradigm shifts are paradigm shifts."[40]

To this day, Grove holds himself responsible for the wrong choice Intel almost made. He is both angry and puzzled that he came so close to giving away what proved to be one of the most valuable franchises in business history. He has said that he is willing to accept the praise he has received for managing the move from memories to microprocessors, but "in this case, I'm a bum."[41]

Grove wrote about the great RISC/CISC war in *Only the Paranoid Survive.*[42] "Looking back at these debates," he wrote, "I shake my head about how I could have even considered walking away from our traditional technology that then had, and still has, phenomenal headroom and momentum."[43] In 2006, a decade and a half after all this took place, RISC/CISC is as fresh today in Grove's mind as if it had all happened yesterday. He is still eating himself up about it.

The chapter in *Only the Paranoid Survive* in which Grove covers this subject is entitled "'Signal' or 'Noise.'" That is the big issue concerning information about one's business. Can we push this subject a little harder and see whether we can get beyond the irrefutable proposition that it is better to be right than wrong? "Most strategic inflection points," Grove warns, "instead of coming in with a bang, approach on little cat feet. They are often not clear until you can look at the events in retrospect."[44] There are no easy answers. There are, however, important questions you can ask to help you get closer to the truth of the matter.

"Is your key competitor about to change?" Grove often used the "silver bullet" test with himself and his company. "[I]f you had just one bullet in a figurative pistol, whom among your competitors would you save it for?" That should be an easy question to answer. If it starts becoming more difficult, think signal, not noise.

The second question deals with your prime complementor. Does the company that has traditionally mattered the most to you still do? Or are you seeing a change?

The third test harkens back to Grove's earliest concerns in his quest to transform himself into a manager. It is a variation on the "Peter Principle." "Think about it. You and your management have both been selected by the evolutionary forces of your business to be at the top of your organization. Your genes were right for the original business." However, the very factors that made you right for the business you grew up in might make you wrong for the other side of the strategic inflection point. A key sign: are people whose clarity and shrewdness you used to depend on now no longer quite "getting it"?[45]

Beyond these particulars, there is a more general, systemic way to save yourself from the kind of fateful error that Intel almost made. Today, many of Grove's suggestions would be collected under the general category of Intel culture. "[B]reak down the walls between those who possess knowledge power and those who possess position power." Muscle build middle management. "If you are in middle management, don't be a wimp."

Cultivate Cassandras, advised Andy. Cassandra, in Greek mythology, was the most beautiful of the daughters of King Priam of Troy. Her beauty caught the eye of the god Apollo, who bestowed upon her the gift of prophecy. Unfortunately for Cassandra, Apollo did not give her this power for nothing. He demanded what in our day would be called "sexual favors" in return. When Cassandra rebuffed his advances, Apollo added a curse to his gift. Cassandra would always speak the truth, but never be believed.

The "Cassandras" that Grove had in mind had the first quality, truth-telling. It was vitally important that, unlike the Cassandra of Greek mythology, Intel's Cassandras be paid heed. They were most likely to come from middle management. Being younger and having logged fewer years with the company than top managers, middle managers were less genetically predisposed toward the old ways. Being "on the front lines," they were more likely to sense danger quickly.[46] It is to "Cassandras," especially Dennis Carter and Craig Kinnie, that Grove gives the credit for bringing him back from the brink of disaster.

15

Cultivating the Creosote Bush

On June 25, 1991, Paul Otellini delivered a luncheon presentation at a conference in New York City, hosted by the Wall Street brokerage house Bear, Stearns & Co., on trends in the PC industry. There were four hundred to five hundred people present in an amphitheater setting. Otellini was, at the time, Intel's vice president and general manager, Microprocessor Products Group (following the reorganization referred to earlier).

"Every time I appear in public," he said, "I get asked the RISC/CISC question, and it's getting to the point where it's an interesting question, but I think not entirely appropriate as things are moving on."

Otellini then showed a graph that, in his view, demonstrated

that the 286, 386, and 486 generations had a given level of performance increase along a fairly predictable line. We were doubling performance every 18 months fairly predictably now for three generations. [Here we see Moore's law at work.]

And the RISC guys have been saying publicly that the x86 is out of steam. And their view of our performance kind of peaks off. "Yeah, they can do one more generation, but there's a cap [on] their performance."

Then Otellini delivered his, and Intel's, response to the RISC advocates' view of the development of the microprocessor industry. "[A]s we implement more and more of the high-performance architecture capabilities into the x86 architecture, we don't see any capping off of performance."[1]

Sometime between Robert Burgelman's class in February 1991 and Paul Otellini's statement in June of that year, Intel had made the decision to stick with the CISC x86 product roadmap. To be sure, the controversy surrounding the relative merits of RISC and CISC architecture continued, but the die was cast. In a 1991 SLRP presentation, Grove put up a slide that announced that "RISC Is Pushed Out. . . . Technically Strong but Fragmented."[2] In 1992, he referred to the fact that MIPS had been bought by Silicon Graphics and that SPARC, Sun's RISC entry, had not proven successful as a stand-alone product. "And the PR tide has turned! (finally!)"[3]

The i860 was not successful because, according to Burgelman, the market became fragmented "as every workstation vendor decided to develop its own RISC processor."[4] Claude Leglise was the manager in charge of dismantling the RISC operation. "I went from 225 employees to 3 in about 90 days." However, as had become the custom at Intel, most of these people were placed elsewhere within the company.[5]

Les Kohn and others who worked closely with him left. Kohn went on to a successful career designing microprocessors for Sun. By 1992, RISC was a dead issue at Intel. Grove announced at the SLRP that year that 90 percent of the microprocessor business was being captured by Intel Architecture. "This Is a BIG WIN For Us!!!" The "merchant RISC" business, he told his executives, "is dead."[6]

Reviewing Intel's history at the 1992 SLRP, Grove saw three phases. The first was Intel as the "LSI [large-scale integration] Company." This lasted until the disaster of the mid-1980s drove Intel out of memory. Next came the "Microcomputer Company," which performed brilliantly. However, it was still a component supplier. In March 1991 a judge ruled, "The combination 386 is not entitled to trademark protection, and in consequence there can be no infringement." This decision "allows AMD to market its chip as the Am386, which is the most natural designation for the product. Even more importantly, however, it allows computer system vendors to use AMD's chip in products with names such as 'Deskpro 386.'"[7]

Protection of the brand was as important as protection of Intel's intellectual property if it were ever to control its destiny. The 486 was not, as claimed at the height of the RISC wars, the last of the "golden age" of CISC.

Nor would the "Intel 586 be the last great CISC chip." There would be no Intel 586. "Jungle Rules Prevail!" Grove told his troops in 1991. Of course, there are no rules for "Groping in the Jungle" other than one Andy quoted from Paul Otellini: "Grab a Vine!"[8] Thus it was time once again for Intel, a company that could reinvent itself, to undergo yet another transformation. This would be to a "branded products company." It was there, in that new part of the jungle, that Intel would look for a vine to grasp that would keep it above the forest floor.

One of the declarations on the cover of the company's 1992 *Annual Report* is: "What's New? Intel Is." This statement and the company's journey toward moving itself closer to the consumer is worth a moment's reflection. Intel's world was one of mounting tension in 1992. True, the company was doing very well. But a lot of other players in the industry were not. IBM, for example, lost just under $5 billion that year. Other companies such as DEC were experiencing increasing difficulties. Change was in the air.

Even though the landscape was changing, it was still quite a leap for Intel to transform itself into a branded products company. Ever since the Red X campaign, Intel had done well talking to end users. Nevertheless, no one in senior management had any experience in a consumer products company. Intel was not a firm to hire an executive from, say, Procter & Gamble to help its top people figure out how to achieve their new positioning. Intel has always been a company of self-taught individuals. They had taught themselves a great deal over the years. They could, they felt, learn this too.

When Grove reviewed Intel's progress toward its new destination in the summer of 1992, he realized he and his colleagues had a long road to travel. If they were going to navigate their strategic inflection point successfully and wind up as a branded products rather than microprocessor company, a

> corollary to this transformation is that a similar reordering/molting of our marketing activities needs to take place. As I see it, we need to make a transformation from a company that largely lives by OEM marketing (engineers selling to other engineers in conference rooms) to a company that does its business by both OEM marketing *and* end-user marketing (communicating through indirect means to millions of users whose attention to our message is, by necessity, very brief). I think this need to do the *hybrid* of both types of marketing is highly unusual (unique?).

In Grove's eyes, Intel had to think anew and act anew. The implementation of these new ideas would be through the medium of the company's organizational structure, which, as he saw it, was quite unfit for the task. "As it stands today, a malicious competitor could not have jumbled us more than we are. Everybody feels responsible for everything; everybody consequently second guesses everybody else."[9]

What vine, to use Otellini's observation, was the newly invented "branded products company" going to grab? What brand would Intel choose for its flagship product? What process would it employ to select that brand?

Once Intel executives decided that "586" was not the name to choose, Dennis Carter asked a member of his group, Karen Alter, a 1990 graduate of the Harvard Business School, to come up with an answer to these questions. She did not hire an advertising agency. She managed the process herself.

"[E]verybody had an opinion," said Carter. Names "came from all over the place," including employees, customers, and students from all over the world. The list was narrowed to ten that passed the necessary legal hurdles and "seemed plausible." Then Andy called a meeting with engineers and managers who would have some sense of ownership over the new processor. Andy made it clear that he and Dennis would make the decision, but before doing so he wanted to hear what everybody had to say.

The names were presented, the pros and cons were discussed, but no consensus was arrived at. So Grove and Carter conferred with one another. On a Friday afternoon, Grove opted for "Pentium," and Carter agreed. Grove flew to New York City to announce the name of the product on Lou Dobbs's *Moneyline* on CNN. Over the weekend, Carter found himself getting pretty nervous about whether they had made the right choice, "but Andy never wavered!"[10] That is why there would be no product called a 586.

If this sounds simple, it was not. There is emotion attached to a name. One reason Intel did not want the Pentium brand announced in front of a large audience is that no one wanted to risk the possibility that the name would be greeted by boos and catcalls or, even worse, laughter.

People in the industry had gotten comfortable with the progression of numbers from 286 to 386 to 486. This was supposed to be the 586. Very few people at Intel knew the name until Andy announced it on television. When he did, Karen Alter recalls that "there were people who were upset within the company." She answered a lot of complaining emails. "[W]hen all the engineers heard it, they hated it. They really got upset that they ruined their product." That attitude softened with time as "people kind of got used to it, because familiarity is a big thing, and it wasn't so bad. And then their friends at other companies started telling them they thought it was sort of cool. So over the course of two months it went from bad to cool."[11]

Intel's performance during the "branded products company" era—and I should note that when I told Grove he had said this in 1992 he replied that he should have used the singular ("product" rather than "products")[12]—was noteworthy for any number of reasons.

First, Intel was managed with clarity. Grove had set his sights on the ownership of the desktops of the world. The vehicle for owning those desktops was the personal computer industry. More often than not, it is the assembler rather than the component supplier that winds up making the lion's share of the profits in a product's value chain. Not in this case.

Even though very few end users ever actually bought a microprocessor from Intel, it was Intel that came to own the customer relationship in the course of the 1990s. As Grove himself remarked in his 1992 SLRP, there were "few success models" for what Intel wanted to do.[13]

What were Intel's strategic objectives? Grove enumerated them with his customary precision:

1. Win in all Segments of Personal Computing by Staying Ahead of the Evolving PC Market.
2. Move the Market to the Next Wave of CSC Applications by Offering Products at All Levels. [CSC stands for "computer-supported collaboration."][14]
3. Manage Intel Inside and Intel Brands for Significant Return and Long-Term Advantage.
4. Be Better and Faster Than Our Competition by Doing the Right Things Right.[15]

The second point that needs to be made is that, as Burgelman has observed, "Seldom has a CEO achieved such complete success in aligning strategy and action."[16] It is possible that "never" should be substituted for "seldom." Grove's intensity was directed as much toward implementation as it was toward strategy. Implementation was, he recognized, a key limiting factor in setting strategy because "strategy cannot be better than its execution."[17] The relationship between "think" and "do" was as tight during Grove's decade as Intel's CEO as it ever was anywhere else.

Let us take just one part of the picture to illustrate this point. Intel's advertising as measured in March 1988 generated 16 percent awareness. By February 1992, that awareness number was up to 67 percent.[18]

Sales and profits both set records again in 1992. Sales of $5.84 billion were up 22 percent from 1991 and placed Intel at number 93 on the Fortune 500. Profits at $1.1 billion were up more than 30 percent and breached the billion-dollar barrier for the first time.[19] "It was a stunning quarter," management told the company, "one of those unusual times when just about everything was going right." The reward: a bonus for everyone of more than three weeks' pay.[20] Rocketing past three other companies, Intel became, also for the first time, the world's largest semiconductor manufacturer. Consider where it had been just six short years earlier.

Intel's market capitalization soared to $18.1 billion, a jump of over 80 percent. With so many stock options out, numerous employees must have become multimillionaires in that single year. Many other companies did not fare quite as well in 1992. The Dow Jones Industrial Average climbed 4 percent. The Standard & Poor's 500 was up just slightly more. The market capitalization of the once great IBM plummeted over 43 percent, giving up a staggering $22 billion.

Headlines in the 1992 press featured such items as "Cypress [Semiconductor] Stock Takes 20% Dive: Quarterly Profit Lower Than Expected"; "Battered C&T [Chips & Technologies] On the Ropes"; "Slump Hits Japanese Electronics"; "They're Slashing As Fast As They Can: The PC Price Wars Are Escalating, and There's No End in Sight"; "Acer [a Taiwanese computer company] Is Still Searching for the Password to the U.S."; "Low-Cost PC Makers Have Come on Strong But Difficulties Loom"; "[Motorola's] 88000 Line's Momentum Erodes"; "SGI [Silicon Graphics] and Mips: Lots to Prove"; "Compaq Backs Out of Deal with ACE [an alliance formed to establish a RISC standard] Ally SGI"; "Why Ace May Be in the Hole"; and others.[21]

Thus, Intel's success was hardly the result of a rising tide lifting all boats. Everybody else seemed to be sinking, and no one as quickly as the computer manufacturers themselves. "INDUSTRY BLOODBATH," announced Grove. Bullet points in his SLRP presentation included "PRICE, PRICE, PRICE" and "PC manufacturers will kill for 5¢." Grove's presentation featured a collage of newspaper advertisements of the crudest kind featuring price above all else.[22]

An important move in the corporate hierarchy at Intel took place officially on January 4, 1993, when Executive Vice President Craig Barrett was named Intel's chief operating officer. Barrett "has been managing Intel's internal day-to-day operations for the past three years," and this promotion recognized his accomplishments in that role. Although the promotion only became official just after the turn of the year, Barrett was featured in the 1992 *Annual Report* along with Moore and Grove as a member of "Intel's Executive Office."[23]

Barrett thus became Grove's successor publicly. This was an important moment. Grove had been considering not only Barrett but also Dave House and Frank Gill as candidates to succeed him as we have noted. Others mentioned in the press over the years included senior vice presidents Les Vadasz, Laurence Hootnick, and Jack Carsten.[24]

House had for years been a key player in the all-important microprocessor business. In the middle and late 1980s, Grove guessed House would be next in line, but questions about him began to develop in Grove's mind around his management of the sole-sourcing of the 386 and the RISC/CISC issue thereafter. Grove developed "a bit of concern about his guts. House's courage. Not physical courage, because he's a daredevil, but strategic courage." House understood computer technology, and Grove found him easy to work with. Eventually, however, he came to feel that House was not the man to lead the company.[25]

Grove was very enthusiastic about Frank Gill. He still considers him "the second best sales manager in Intel's history," behind only Ed Gelbach. Gill "was tough—they called him Sluggo in his old territory in the Midwest—he rose through the ranks."[26]

Something went wrong with the relationship between Grove and Gill that mystifies Grove to this day, some unknowable thing. Grove feels that whatever happened took place despite his high regard for Gill.[27] Meanwhile, "Barrett was coming on stronger and stronger, so there was no question."[28]

It was Craig Barrett who, later in the decade, developed the metaphor of the creosote bush. Though born in San Francisco and a loyal product of Stanford, he moved to Arizona. Unlike Grove, who disliked travel and preferred to be home for dinner at seven o'clock, Barrett was on the road all the time. When he was not traveling, he commuted from his home in Arizona to Silicon Valley, where he kept an apartment.

A lot of Arizona is desert country, intensely beautiful to some, forbidding to others. In the Arizona desert grows a plant called the creosote bush. It has come to dominate large swaths of the local landscape "due in part to its tenacious competitiveness—the creosote's roots starve grasses and release toxins that kill its woody neighbors."[29]

The creosote bush is a case of survival of the fittest. If you are a plant and want to survive in the desert, it serves you well to have roots that collect all the moisture nearby and release toxins as well. You do not want other plants competing for that scarcest of resources. With the immediate neighborhood cleared of competition, you can grow large and live long.

Barrett likened the ascendancy of the microprocessor at Intel to the creosote bush. The microprocessor was extraordinarily demanding in terms of talent and capital. If you wanted to get ahead at Intel, the microprocessor business was where you wanted to be. That was the crown jewel. By 1992 it was clear that if Intel mastered this product, a fortune lay at its feet. The result was that attempts to develop new businesses within the company or acquire new companies from related industries either failed or were not attempted.

Read about Intel, ask Andy Grove today what the secret of its success has been, and it is not hard to arrive at an answer. That answer is "focus," both as a noun and a verb. Intel could focus. Intel had focus. It was a focused company. The focus, after the RISC sideshow was put to bed, was on the growth and management of the x86 product roadmap. So successfully and so creatively was this strategy executed that a mere quarter century after its founding, in the midst of the most turbulent of industries, Intel grew into one of the most profitable companies in all of business history.

However, the creosote-bush factor exacted a price. As profitable as it was, Intel missed opportunities in both hardware and software to become more profitable still. It was a hedgehog of a company, not a fox.[30] It knew one big thing, not many things. Intel grew by being a one-trick pony. The trick was a rich one. But what would its next trick be?

16

That Championship Season

In 1993, Intel reached its twenty-fifth birthday, and it published an oversized, 11-by-14-inch brochure to mark the occasion. The cover of the brochure was silver, since the twenty-fifth is the silver anniversary. Given how Intel performed that year, it might well have been gold.

Almost 30,000 people worked for Intel at the end of 1993. Fewer than a hundred were employed there a quarter of a century previously. Of those who had joined in 1968, eight remained. They were:

George Chiu, senior engineer, Package and Assembly Research
Nobuko Clark, tech specialist in California Technology Development, Quality and Reliability
Andy Grove, president and CEO
Tom Innes, general manager, Intel Connectivity Division
Ted Jenkins, vice president and director, Corporate Licensing
Jean Jones, executive secretary
Gordon Moore, chairman
Les Vadasz, senior vice president and director, Corporate Business Development[1]

Intel in 1968 had been an upstart start-up trying to sell semiconductors to IBM. Now in 1993 it had journeyed to the center of the "new computer industry" and become one of the world's most important companies, even more important for its technology than its profitability. Intel, Microsoft, and Apple were the three key companies in the creation of the new computer industry. Andy Grove, Bill Gates, and Steve Jobs were the three most important people in this turn of events.

Its silver anniversary was an outstanding year for Intel. Sales rose by 50 percent to $8.78 billion, placing Intel at 56 on the Fortune 500. Profits more than doubled to almost $2.3 billion. Thus profits in 1993 were well above sales in 1987, the year Andy became CEO.[2] According to *Fortune,* Intel's 26 percent return on sales made it "the most profitable company of its size in the world."[3] Market capitalization was up over 40 percent to $25.93 billion, far outpacing the Wall Street averages. Nevertheless, Intel's stock commanded a low price/earnings ratio, 10.7 compared to 20 for the S&P 500, in May 1994. The reason was competitive threats, but some analysts saw in this low price/earnings ratio a great investment opportunity.[4]

In May, Intel introduced its new Pentium processor. This is what would have been the 586 if you could trademark numbers. Customers bought it so quickly that the "Pentium processor has enjoyed the fastest production ramp of any [other] new processor generation in our history. . . . Market acceptance of the Pentium processor has been excellent, with more than 150 systems introduced to date."[5]

"Pity poor Motorola," was the first sentence of a trade journal article in July 1993 on what was once a great powerhouse of a company in this market. "Even though the chip maker has two corporate PC giants in its corner— Apple and IBM—it now has the unenviable task of trying to persuade the PC community that the trio's PowerPC microprocessor is a match for Intel's awesome [there is that word again] Pentium, which in the past few months has been on more magazine covers even than Princess Di."[6] How, this article asked, could Motorola match Intel's $200 million microprocessor advertising budget? With such a small installed base, how could it gain a bigger share of the PC market?[7]

There were, unfortunately for Motorola, no answers to those questions. In allying itself with Apple and IBM, Motorola was chaining itself to anchors rather than hitching its wagon to stars. Both firms were in a lot of trouble in 1993. Both continued to embrace the vertical, proprietary model of the PC industry that Andy Grove knew to be the past, not the future. Both IBM and Apple would pay the price for their myopia.

Asked about the PowerPC, Grove, with an uncustomary nonchalance, said, "It is a very competent chip as far as I know, but there is hardly any software available to run on it. So what good is it? . . . The high-technology market is littered with the carcasses of good technical ideas because no one could find a use for them."[8] A remarkably unparanoid assessment of a chip that was "smaller than Intel's best, cheaper to manufacture, and comparable in power."[9] But Grove was right.

Motorola's problem with its PowerPC chip extended to its partners. Apple Computer, the company that seemed to have been designed to show the world that the counterculture of the 1960s could become the corporate culture of the 1970s, was on the verge of failure. Steve Jobs, who symbolized the idea that business could be fun, had been forced out of the firm in 1985 by the man he had hired to run it, John Sculley, formerly a top executive at PepsiCo.[10] Jobs would triumphantly return as Apple's CEO in 1997.

Sculley got the ax in 1993 at a time when the firm seemed to be flirting with complete failure. According to journalist Michael Malone, "There are in the story of high technology a number of men who grew great companies into even bigger companies, but because of mistakes and missed opportunities, ultimately destroyed them, leaving them rotting, sinking hulks." The fate of these people was "to become invisible." That is what John Sculley is today in Silicon Valley, while Steve Jobs, master of the second act, is back on top at Apple.[11] No one speaks Sculley's name in the Valley these days. By contrast, Jobs, a college dropout, gave the commencement address at Stanford in 2005.[12] He made more than $3.4 billion in the stock of Pixar, which Disney had no choice but to purchase in January 2006. His comeback was beyond imagining when Apple was flopping about in the early and mid-1990s.

Apple's troubles were small, because Apple was small, compared to what was going on at IBM in 1993. This company had been the dictator of the world of information technology since at least the 1950s, and perhaps, depending upon how one chooses to read history, since as far back as the 1930s. The United States has never produced a prouder company. Pride went before a fall in 1993.

The company's sales hit an all-time high of $69 billion in 1990. Profits, at $6 billion, were way up from the previous year but considerably below the peak of $6.58 billion in 1984. That was also the strongest year for market capitalization, at the dizzying heights of $95.6 billion. In the early 1980s,

IBM employed 407,000 people. Now, however, the sins of the past caught up with Big Blue.

Frank T. Cary became CEO in 1973 and served until 1981. It was thus on his watch that the disastrous method of entry into the personal computing business took place, although it would be years before the implications of outsourcing the most valuable components of the personal computer were appreciated. In the early 1980s, IBM's PC business looked like another home run for Big Blue. *Time* magazine selected the personal computer as the "Machine of the Year" for 1982. "If any three letters can be considered synonymous with computers, they are IBM," declared *Time*.[13] But the star of the issue was probably the charismatic twenty-seven-year-old Steve Jobs.[14]

Cary was succeeded by John R. Opel, who served as CEO from 1981 to 1985. It was while he was running the company that it purchased a fifth of Intel. Once again, if all you looked at were the numbers, Opel, like Cary, seemed to be a hero. By Paul Carroll's estimate, IBM was taking in 70 percent of the earnings of the entire computer industry during these years.[15] There would, however, be a high price to pay soon enough for the company's bloated bureaucracy and for its fundamental misperception of the future of the information technology business.

The chickens began coming home to roost during the tenure of John Fellows Akers. Akers was an intelligent, talented, decent man who had never known failure. With a "firm jaw and sniper gray eyes," this Yale graduate and navy fighter pilot looked like "the CEO from central casting."[16] Year after year of his tenure, however, things at the once great firm continued to deteriorate. Without necessarily showing it to the outside world, he was by small steps becoming a desperate man.

Akers seemed to have lost the connection between words and deeds. Steeped in the IBM tradition of "Ever Onward" optimism, he kept predicting turnarounds, issuing hopeful forecasts, and announcing the "Year of the Customer," as if such activity could substitute for rather than supplement performance.[17] One thing IBM did not do was cheat on its accounting, a practice that became all the rage in the era of Enron at the end of the 1990s. The result was that invariably there would be a wide gulf between what Akers said and what the company had to report in the following months. For 1992, he was predicting a profit of $3 billion. This would have been a welcome turnaround from the previous year's $2.8 billion loss.

Unfortunately, Akers ran straight into the words/deeds problem. IBM lost $5 billion in 1992, which is notably different from making $3 billion. The board of directors finally had to face the fact that Akers had to go. He was more than ready to step down. "I watched him suffer under the pressure," said Jim Burke, the retired CEO of Johnson & Johnson who served as lead independent director of IBM during this crisis. "You could feel the stress."[18]

Akers's tenure as CEO of IBM must have been dreadful beyond description. Paul Carroll, who covered IBM for the *Wall Street Journal* during the Akers years, wrote bluntly that he left the company "with the worst record of any chief executive" in IBM history. All his life he had worked for IBM. When he made it to the top, he could do nothing other than preside over a corporate catastrophe of biblical proportions. "He didn't create most of his problems," said Carroll, "but it was in his power to solve many of them and he didn't. He wrestled with the problems. He talked about them a lot. Eventually, he articulated what most of the problems were and took tentative steps toward fixing them. But he repeatedly came up a day late and a billion dollars short."[19] Carroll concluded by speculating that IBM might regain profitability "but it will cast nothing like the shadow it has cast over the computer industry and the world economy during the past eighty years."[20]

Industry experts Charles H. Ferguson and Charles R. Morris published an even more scathing critique in 1993, *Computer Wars: How the West Can Win in a Post-IBM World*.[21] They laid the blame for IBM's collapse squarely on management's doorstep:

> General Motors slipped in all aspects of its business—technology, design, production, management. IBM's problems can be pinned much more directly on its management; during its fifteen-year slide, it possessed much of the world's best computer technology, it invested massively, and in key computer components, its manufacturing and process technologies matched any in the world. But IBM's managers were very late to understand the fundamental changes afoot in the industry, changes they had often initiated, and IBM quickly slipped from being market leader to an also-ran in a broad range of products.[22]

Akers resigned on January 26, 1993, before a successor was named. All the publicity surrounding this event did not make locating a successor easy.

The head of the search committee was Jim Burke, and he apparently talked to a lot of people before selecting Louis V. Gerstner Jr. to recommend to the board as IBM's next CEO. An engineering graduate from Dartmouth and, like Burke but unlike any previous IBM CEO, a graduate of the Harvard Business School, Gerstner had no previous experience in the computer industry. He was, however, unquestionably smart and tough. He had made partner at the consulting firm McKinsey very speedily and had moved on to head American Express and then RJR Nabisco. He was fifty-one years old when he took the helm at IBM, a job that a decade previously people would have killed for but that was hard to give away when Gerstner got it.

Gerstner was not the board's first choice, and when offered the job, he said he repeatedly turned it down. At length, however, he accepted it. On Friday, March 26, 1993, he was introduced to the press as the successor to Akers. "Short, round-faced, and pudgy," Carroll reports, Gerstner "would be played by Danny DeVito in any movie."[23] He was also a very able businessman and apparently oblivious to the opinions others held of him.

Gerstner officially took the helm on April 1. That day marked the real end of the Watson era at IBM, which had begun back in 1914 when Tom Sr. was chosen to head the company. His oldest son, Tom Watson Jr., died on the last day of 1993. Gerstner would thus be the first CEO of IBM to have the freedom to do his job without Watson looking over his shoulder. The company was in a lot of trouble. "Only a handful of people understand how precariously close IBM came to running out of cash in 1993," Gerstner later wrote.[24] The company lost the staggering sum of over $8 billion that year.

In the midst of all this turmoil, to expect to wrest control of the microprocessor from the company that Intel had become was to expect much. The PowerPC was, as Grove said, "a very competent chip." Its fans were a good deal more enthusiastic. "The PowerPC's raw performance has the competitive juices flowing among the allies [Apple, Motorola, and IBM]," reported the *Wall Street Journal* in March 1994. The developers "staged a celebration in which a roomful of IBM and Motorola engineers cheered wildly as a mock PowerPC battleship sank Battleship Intel."[25] You do not have to look far to find headlines in 1994 in the trade and business press such as "IBM, Compaq Edging Away From Intel Chips; PowerPC Called Force Behind Big Blue's Move,"[26] and "PowerPC Consortium Challenges Intel With the Fastest PC Chip Yet."[27]

Thus Motorola's two partners, Apple and IBM, were not well positioned to help it regain its lost leadership in the semiconductor industry. IBM survived and is today still a major force in the global information technology business. Many other once great companies, such as DEC, did not survive.[28]

As the late Professor Theodore Levitt of the Harvard Business School said years ago, any product that does not sell is not a product. It is a museum piece. The problem with the PowerPC lay not in its design or production, in which its three-company consortium had invested a fortune by 1994. The problem lay in marketing it. One aspect of the marketing problem was that the three consortium partners had different goals. There were, in fact, different goals within IBM. "IBM's strategy is the riskiest and most conflicted one of the PowerPC partners," according to the *Wall Street Journal*, "because its success depends solely on taking business away from makers of Intel-based computers running on Windows—including IBM."[29]

An even bigger problem was the software. Ninety percent of it was written for Wintel (which will be discussed presently), comprising a "vast universe." When discussing ACE (Advanced Computing Environment), which was a larger alliance designed to break Intel's hammerlock on the microprocessor business, a Hewlett-Packard vice president said, "This is what the Germans would call 'Die Eier-legende Wollmilchsau': An egg-laying wooly milk pig. It's what happens when you try to put together many different animals. You don't know what you'll end up with."[30] The problem for the PowerPC was that there was *eine Eier-legende Wollmilchsau* within IBM all by itself. The time to beat Intel at its own game had long passed by 1993.

In his SLRP presentation on April 11, 1994, Grove used a clipping from the *San Jose Mercury News* that had run three years previously. The title was, "Setting Up a Challenge to Intel: 21 Firms Unite to Create a New Computer Standard."[31] Above the headline was a photograph of five industry executives: Rod Canion, Bill Gates, Doug Michels (cofounder with his brother Larry of a company called the Santa Cruz Operation, or SCO, which supported the Linux operating system), Bob Miller of MIPS, and the venerable Ken Olsen, founder of DEC. On the next page of Grove's SLRP presentation, he has the same headline and accompanying photograph with the word "GONE" over the pictures of everyone but Gates. Canion was fired in 1992. Olsen, who was described in *Fortune* in 1986 as "arguably the most successful entrepreneur in the history of American business,"[32] was forced out of the company he created in 1992 as well. Times were changing fast.

Soon after assuming his new position on April Fools' Day 1993, Gerstner scheduled a series of meetings with industry heavyweights. Among these was Grove. Sean Maloney, who today is an executive vice president of Intel and the general manager of the company's Mobility Group, was Grove's technical assistant at the time, and he remembers vividly how hard he had to work to prepare Andy for that meeting. Nothing he delivered was good enough. Work led to work and more work until Grove was satisfied that he had material to put before Gerstner, whom he had never met.

Here is how Maloney describes the experience:

Andy said to me, "I want you to tell me what to say to Gerstner." So I got a team together, and we did an in-depth financial analysis of IBM. We looked at it from every angle. Up, down, in, and out. Very smart people in the group. I think the smartest people in this company. We came back with something, and Andy said, "No. This is inadequate."

After about a month of this, he said to me one evening, "I'm bitterly disappointed. This doesn't go anywhere." It was immensely frustrating and personally very frustrating. I had worked so hard on it for a month. In reality he was right. On the edge of desperation, we went back into the room over a period of three or four days. It seems completely obvious now but it wasn't at the time. We finally came to the conclusion that IBM needed to become a services company. The financial reason for that was that we looked at the ongoing cost of IBM's competing with Microsoft at the operating level, and we decided they couldn't compete. They couldn't afford to develop their own hardware, the sums didn't add up. Subsequently, Andy went to Gerstner and said, "You need to become a services company." And of course IBM basically became a services company. Which may have had nothing to do with Andy's visit, but that was the direction IBM took.

Maloney's experience with Grove on this assignment was not unique.

The lesson of all of that was that he was completely demanding to the level of pushing you right to the brink. I learned a lot. If you're an athlete, you don't want a coach who says, "Hey, way to go, awesome dude, attaboy." You want the person who pushes you beyond the beyond, and that's what he did. That's what he did routinely with the people who worked around him. He had a sentence that he wrote in *High Output*

Management, his first management book, which is, "The job of a manager is to elicit peak performance from subordinates"—and that one sentence summarized, in my view, much of the brilliance of what he did. He would get the best out of every individual. He may piss them off, which he frequently did, but he got the best out of every individual. . . . He was a chili pepper. He was in your face the whole time.[33]

There is a revealing anecdote that highlights Grove's approach to those who worked with him. It is said—and perhaps this story is apocryphal, but it is useful for our purposes now—that when Henry Kissinger was national security advisor, he told an assistant to prepare a report. The assistant worked very hard on it and submitted it. Four hours later, Kissinger summoned him to his office and, clearly annoyed, said, "Is this the best you can do?"

The assistant sheepishly took the report and went back to work. He submitted it a second time only to receive the same question from Kissinger. Then the assistant resubmitted the report. Kissinger once again snarled, "Is this the best you can do?" By this time, the assistant's firmly submerged pride poked through his timidity and he managed to respond, "Yes. It is." To which Kissinger said, "Okay, I'll read this one."

I began to tell Grove this story, and he stopped me. "I have heard that, and I hate it," he said. Grove read the reports submitted to him and provided detailed critiques. He did not play what he viewed as a cheap game. Testimony from others is unanimous on this point. Grove provided detailed annotations on the detailed annotations of material submitted to him.[34] He was deeply involved in works in progress. He always demanded more of himself than he did of others.

Armed with Maloney's painstakingly prepared report, Grove met with Gerstner not long after Gerstner became CEO. "I talked with Gerstner," Grove emailed Barrett on June 4, "and agreed to meet in NYC in a few weeks—just him and me. Subsequently, dinner was set during PC Expo. Keep your fingers crossed."[35] Their two companies were moving in opposite directions. Intel was becoming more "awesome" by the day. As for IBM, questions were being raised about whether it should be broken up into separate firms.

This is how Gerstner recounts the meeting with Grove. It was, he has written, "perhaps the most focused" of the dozen or so meetings he was having with industry leaders.

In his wonderfully direct style, Andy delivered the message that IBM had no future in the microprocessor business, that we should stop competing with Intel with our Power PC chip, and that unless this happened, relationships between the two companies were going to be difficult. I thanked Andy, but, having no real understanding at that point of what we should do, I tucked the message away.[36]

This is a pretty meager report about an encounter Grove felt was important. Doubtless Grove also told Gerstner that IBM did have a future in services. His thinking was powerfully influenced by a void he felt existed in 1993 in what he consistently called the "new computer industry." We have seen this phrase before. What precisely did it mean?

The new computer industry was an "industrial democracy. It resists central guidance." Nevertheless, the products the various players provided had to work together if the computer was going to perform the tasks for which it was purchased. The products were integrated. Your Intel processor could work with your Sharp display, your Conner hard disk, your memory from Toshiba, your U.S. Robotics modem, Microsoft's operating system, and so forth.

This integration, however, was engineered "just well enough to sell. We have to have a minimum of integration to survive, but doing more is a luxury. That's why these products—chips and programs and computers—are not integrated enough to be easy for people to use." Andy said it took him forty hours to get his first laptop to work. If that was true for an engineer who knew the industry as well as anybody, it was no wonder that the average consumer found the PC infuriating.

It was precisely because of this "industrial democracy" with its less than fully satisfactory integration that there was "a huge business opportunity for the old mainframe and minicomputer companies. Their very structure forced them to develop expertise at integrating layer after layer of technology into large-scale systems that work. The demand for that expertise is enormous, because the horizontal industry arrangement obviously doesn't satisfactorily resolve the issue of systems integration."[37]

There had been talk within IBM of the opportunity presented by the service side of the industry as early as 1984. Akers's predecessor John R. Opel received an internally prepared report on computer services that year and pigeonholed it. In mid-1987, Akers received a staff report emphasizing software, services, and systems integration at the expense of the slower-going hardware business. He did more than nothing but clearly not enough about these recommendations.[38]

Gerstner did many of the things his predecessors, shackled by the past and perhaps limited by their own attitude, did not do. IBM is today a very large company in terms of employment, and sports a market capitalization of $115.9 billion, higher than Intel's.

From Gerstner's point of view, his remarkable achievement in turning IBM around had nothing to do with his interaction with Grove. When asked what role the changing relationship between IBM and Intel played in IBM's rebirth, he responded simply, "NONE." "As I pointed out in my book," Gerstner said, "Andy's primary message was that IBM should get out of the microelectronics business and rely completely on Intel for this technology. This suggestion was no more or less self-serving than those offered by most of the other CEOs [with whom I met in my early days as IBM CEO], all of whom came armed with agendas for advancing their own company's position vis-à-vis IBM."

Asked whether Grove made suggestions with which he did not agree and which he did not follow, Gerstner was more than a little direct in his response:

> Obviously, I did not follow Andy's advice, and thank goodness. Many of the key achievements IBM made in the ensuing 10 years were highly dependent on our semiconductor technology (e.g., the turnaround of the mainframe business, the replacement of Sun as the leader in Unix servers, the development of a unique position in the Game Machine business, etc.).

Gerstner's overall evaluation of Grove was clear-eyed and modulated. "My view of Andy has always been that he has all the tenacity, toughness, competitiveness, and focus of most of the successful leaders in the computer industry, without the bluster, arrogance and ego that characterize so many of them."[39]

While IBM was enduring its own dark night of the soul and its survival was in doubt, Intel was rocketing forward. The price of its stock was behaving very well. Morgan Stanley initiated its coverage of Intel on August 27 and its report was strongly bullish. Not all such reports are reliable. Within a decade, the relationship between research and investment banking at firms such as Morgan Stanley would become quite a scandal. History proved this report to be particularly prescient.

Even though Intel was selling at its fifty-two-week high, it was neverthe-less a "buy." It was selling at a 30 percent discount to the market on 1993 earnings prospects, a valuation that reflected "more fear than opportunity." The basis of that fear seemed to be the company's endless legal entangle-ments. Intel "is currently involved in no less than 11 separate lawsuits, all of which involve [its] microprocessors."

Unfavorable results from some of these legal matters might prove trou-blesome. But look at the big picture. The PC would not exist without the mi-croprocessor. Intel owned that business, and there was plenty of reason to believe that it would continue to do so for years to come. Computing was now a mass-market proposition, and Intel was at its center. Intel was a mov-ing target, and the margins its products commanded were luscious.

A whole environment was being created around Intel's products.

Looking ahead, the power of the microprocessor will continue to in-crease, systems will become even easier to use, and the enormous in-stalled hardware base will continue to attract new software and new applications. . . .

More than ever before, Intel stands at the heart of the information processing revolution. It controls the dominant architecture in com-puting, and, with the help of both software vendors that design prod-ucts for its growing installed base and aggressive pricing by its systems customers, it is continuing to expand its markets. Intel's ultimate target is information processing, where many of the needs of users have not yet been translated into products.[40]

The future was limitless.

From Grove's point of view inside Intel, the news was both good and bad. A variety of technical problems, especially dealing with the ramp-up of Pen-tium production, demanded attention. Relations with customers were mixed. Relations with EDS and Incredible Universe seemed good. Yet more promis-ing was the situation with Dell, which in 1993 was still a small player. Compaq, at the time, was viewed as the "invincible upstart" of the PC industry.[41] Grove told IBM's president Jack Kuehler that his company "is dead in the water on Pentium, and will almost certainly lose market share as a result."[42]

Grove saw plenty of opportunities to manage Intel itself better. "I ragged on them," he said of his performance at an executive staff meeting in the summer of 1993.

> I see no real improvements in the discipline of our doing business: Organization redundance is large, external meetings—proliferate and go into them unprepared with me doing last minute temper tantrums—like at the FAE [Intel speak for field applications engineer] conference, except we have "a major meeting a month" now in effect. My rule was that if you can't handle them, we shouldn't take on organizing any more meetings. . . .
>
> Lots of discussion about orientation, etc. Question to you [to Craig Barrett]—how did we lose this so badly in the last several years. We used to have a pretty good training culture.[43]

Andy Grove was not a man easily satisfied. There was always room for improvement, always grounds for complaint, which sometimes degenerated into cavil.

An issue that grew in importance as IBM's power waned was the relationship between Intel and Microsoft. As we know, Grove conceived of Microsoft as a "complementor," that is, a firm to which Intel did not sell and from which it did not buy, but whose conduct was essential to its business.

An equally reasonable way to think of Microsoft, however, was as a competitor for the profit dollars that were generated by the sale of every personal computer. Say, for example, that the price of the average PC in 1993 was $3,000. How much did the company assembling that personal computer—Compaq, Dell, Gateway, the other clones, or IBM, which had become no more than a clone in the PC market—have to pay Intel for its 486 microprocessor, and how much did it have to pay Microsoft for its Windows 3.1 disk operating system? The line between hardware and software may seem bright. In fact, it is not. Intel and Microsoft were to spend the 1990s testing the boundary between the two of them.

"Last weekend one phone call with Gates," Grove wrote Barrett on June 14, 1993. "Exchange of pleasantries, threats . . . he threatened me a bunch of times with everything from disembowelment upward. We are now pissing at each other's pants legs in all kinds of different areas."[44]

17

The Buck Stopped There:
Bill Gates and Andy Grove

One problem with using money as a metric for your success in life is that there is always somebody who has more. Unless, that is, you are Bill Gates. Born on October 28, 1955, eight months almost to the day after Steve Jobs, Gates was a billionaire by the age of thirty-one, said to be the youngest self-made billionaire in history. In 1992, when he was thirty-six, he was the richest man in America. His liquid assets came to about $6 billion. He had already spent about a half a billion dollars on various toys and trinkets.[1] Soon, he would be the richest man in the world.

Bill Gates, William Henry Gates III to be precise, was born in Seattle, to which his great-grandfather on his father's side had migrated in the 1880s. His great-grandfather on his mother's side was in Seattle by 1906. Both were well-established men.

Bill's father was a successful attorney. His mother, Mary, was a schoolteacher who was bright, sharp, and good-looking. Gates was the second child and the only boy in the family, sandwiched between two pretty sisters, Kristianne, born in 1953, and Libby in 1964.

Bill was six when the Seattle World's Fair was staged. Inspired by the "New Frontier" spirit of the conquest of space, the fair's enduring symbol has been the "Space Needle" that still marks the city's skyline. It has a revolving restaurant, which is patented. The goal of the American science exhibit was "to stimulate youths' interest in science," and science was everywhere.

NASA was represented, as were electricity and computers. General Electric and IBM had big footprints at the fair. Gates was captivated. This was "a huge event, a neat deal. We went to every pavilion."[2]

It became very obvious very early that Bill Gates was very smart. By the time he was nine, he had read the *World Book* encyclopedia cover to cover. His fourth-grade teacher estimated that his IQ was between 160 and 180. When he took the SATs, he got an 800 on the math test and on five achievement tests. His verbal SAT was in the low 700s.[3] He liked playing games and was good at them. He was interested in making money at an early age. Arrogant even as a youngster, he believed that rules did not apply to him. "He was a nerd before the term was even invented," said a teacher.[4] He did not care.

One of his classmates at Lakeside, the exclusive private school that Gates attended from seventh to twelfth grade, described him as "an extremely annoying person. He was very easy to sort of dislike. And I think that probably me and lot of people took a little extra pleasure in sort of bumping him while passing him in the hall and basically giving him a little bit of a hard time. . . . In public school, the guy would've been killed."[5]

Lakeside, however, was not a public school, and Bill Gates did not ever seem to mind if he annoyed other people. He was able to make enough friends to satisfy himself. In eighth grade in 1968, Gates encountered at Lakeside what he never would have found at a public school at that time, a computer terminal. He quickly mastered BASIC (Beginner's All-Purpose Symbolic Instruction Code) and discovered that software, a word that hardly existed at the time, was terrific. "Programming was exciting; it was smart; it was addictive."[6] Gates and his friends, one of whom was Paul Allen, two years older than he and destined to become one of the world's richest people, developed an obsession with computers.

Gates and his friends became involved with a company called the Computer Center Corporation (C-Cubed). The first rule of C-Cubed was "Anything goes."[7] That ruleless rule was the guide for much of Gates's early life with computers. Perhaps the phrase should be amended. For Gates, a more appropriate motto would have been "Anything goes for me but not for you."

Early in the computer revolution, numerous adults were stumped by the question of why anyone needed this device, particularly in their home. This is a question that never crossed Gates's mind. Almost at first sight, the computer set off numberless business ideas for him.

Computers cost money, and in the late 1960s and 1970s, access to them cost money. Charges were based on the amount of time you used. Gates, however, was a good deal smarter than the people who created the methods for measuring time used. From the beginning, he had quite an interest in taking money in, which was matched by a lack of interest in paying it out. His sudden transformation into a philanthropist shows that the accumulation of money for its own sake could bore even him.

In the fall of 1973, Gates went to Harvard. It was there that he discovered he was not the smartest person in the world. That discovery, however, did not affect his self-confidence, nor did it mute the nasty side of his personality. He was on fire about computers. There would be one in everybody's home soon enough, he was convinced. This was at a time when they were all but invisible at Harvard.

While at Harvard, Gates used a great deal of time on the DEC PDP-10 at the university's Aiken Computation Laboratory, where he was viewed as "a hell of a good programmer" and "a pain in the ass."[8] A number of his activities attracted the attention of the university.

[A]lthough other people were writing resumes and even books on the computer, they weren't exactly monopolizing the machine. Nor were they using the PDP-10 for commercial projects. Nor were they inviting off-campus friends, nonstudents such as Paul Allen, to join them at all hours of the night in the computer center. Nor were they using the Defense Department's unclassified ARPANET, the first nationwide computer network, to store some of their commercial efforts on a machine hundreds of miles away at Pittsburgh's Carnegie-Mellon University.[9]

Harvard did not think this was funny, and Gates had to do some fancy footwork to prevent himself from getting kicked out. The pattern of his later behavior was clearly evident in his youth. Bill Gates took what he wanted and settled up with the "authorities" later, if at all.

It is not easy to know how to think about Gates's "less-than-spotless past when it came to computer freebieism."[10] His transgressions against honest behavior can be traced back to his first encounter with computers, when he "[manipulated] accounts on a time-sharing system" when he was in eighth grade.[11] All of us have episodes from our youth that we would be happy not to have broadcast to the world. Balzac wrote that behind every great fortune is a great crime. Gates accumulated the greatest fortune of his era—

according to Forbes, he was worth about $18.5 billion by the time he was forty years old and, a staggering $85 billion in 1999[12]—and surely the "crimes" he committed were small, not great.

Moreover, there was something about the "new computer industry" that seemed to encourage theft. Steve Jobs once said, "When we were developing the Macintosh we kept in mind a famous quote of Picasso: "'Good artists copy, great artists steal!'"[13] These seem to be words the industry lived by. Somehow what was being stolen did not feel like private property. Youngsters should have a right to computer time. To grab some without paying for it is something Gates would do in a flash, whereas we are probably safe in assuming that he would not have robbed a candy store in Harvard Square just because he thought he could get away with it.

Three important events transpired for Gates before he dropped out of Harvard in his junior year. First, he met Steve Ballmer. Microsoft's Web site says of Ballmer, "Variously described as ebullient, focused, funny, passionate, sincere, hard-charging and dynamic, Ballmer has infused Microsoft with his own brand of energetic leadership, vision, and spirit over the years."[14]

Here is how Gates's biographers Stephen Manes and Paul Andrews describe the Steve Ballmer that Gates met at Harvard:

> Down the hall from Gates lived a math-science student who was as straight-arrow and outgoing as the typical Currier bunch [Currier is the undergraduate residential house in which Gates lived] was nerdy and introverted. Steve Ballmer, a big, bluff Detroiter with a high forehead and the mood swings of a manic-depressive, was the ultimate social guy, Mr. Extracurricular Activity, with fingers in every pie from the football team, which he eventually managed, to the literary magazine, of which he eventually became publisher. Yet somehow he and Gates got along, a Mutt and Jeff collaboration cemented by mutual tastes in movies and mutually snide, cynical senses of humor.[15]

Ballmer finished his college education and then spent two years at Procter & Gamble before going to Stanford's Graduate School of Business. Gates hired him at Microsoft in 1980. He has been the CEO of the firm since January 2000 (Gates is chairman of the board) and is today among the world's richest people.

A big problem for a person like Gates is finding peers with whom he can forge relationships.[16] Spoiled, smart, fearless, ambitious—who could keep up with him? He met one such person at Lakeside, Paul Allen, equally smart but with a softer personality and more likable. He met another in Steve Ballmer, who, unlike Gates, actually knew something about running a business when he showed up at Microsoft.

The second important development while Gates was at Harvard was the publication of the January 1975 issue of *Popular Electronics* magazine, on the cover of which was the Altair. The man who spotted it when it became available in December and ran over to see Bill Gates to talk about it was Paul Allen. Allen had dropped out of Washington State University after his sophomore year and had taken a job as a computer programmer with Honeywell in Billerica, Massachusetts, not far from Boston. He was spending a lot of time on Harvard's PDP-10 with his buddy Bill. Suddenly, the Altair burst upon the scene.

Manes and Andrews make a convincing case that the "Altair was certainly not the first personal computer."[17] But that did not matter as much as the fact that "the Altair put it all together in a way that none of its predecessors had managed." For Gates and Allen, it was a gift from the gods. They were not interested in hardware, and now the Altair had taken care of their hardware needs. It was up to them to write software that would run on the Altair so that the thing would be more than a mere box. That they set about doing, at a pace which "feverish" hardly describes.

Gates and Allen had decided to build a computer of their own back in 1972. The goal was to process data given to Gates concerning automobile traffic. He and Allen bought their first microprocessor for this computer, the Intel 8008. It cost $360, which Gates thought was pretty high. The name of the company Gates and Allen created was Traf-O-Data, and it is fair to say that nothing went right with this venture. Manes and Andrews believe that the Traf-O-Data failure "soured" Gates and Allen on hardware. Other people should take care of that. They would be software entrepreneurs.[18]

The Altair was a kit produced by a company called MITS, an acronym for Micro Instrumentation and Telemetry Systems, located in Albuquerque, New Mexico.[19] Gates, Allen, and another friend at Harvard put together a version of BASIC that would run on Altair by February 1975. Allen flew out to Albuquerque to demo it for the owners of MITS, Ed Roberts and William Yates. By March 1, Paul Allen was the vice president and director of software at MITS.[20] Gates and Allen had developed the first programming language for the Altair 8800.

Gates paid a visit to Albuquerque in March. He, Allen, and their Harvard friend Monte Davidoff spent the summer there. Gates and Allen decided to become partners, supplying MITS with software for the Altair.

> Although the informal partnership with Allen had initially been fifty/fifty . . . Gates bargained for a change. The partnership was restructured on a sixty/forty basis—with Bill exacting the larger share by reminding Paul that he remained a full-time salaried employee of MITS. Their initial investments were $910 and $606, respectively.[21]

The returns on these investments were to be considerable.

Gates and Allen signed a contract, after a bout of aggravation of the sort which always attended Gates, on July 22, 1975, with Ed Roberts to supply BASIC for the Altair. "Microsoft was not yet an official partnership. It was not even a name that had appeared anywhere in public."[22] The Gates and Allen partnership, with the ownership renegotiated again, to 64 percent for Gates and 36 percent for Allen, was signed on February 3, 1977.[23]

It is worth reflecting on the differences between the childhoods of Gates and Grove. Gates was born both to wealth and privilege. His prominent family was well-connected. For example, when he spent three weeks in the spring of 1971 as a legislative page in the halls of the state capitol in Olympia, as sister Kristi had done before him, he roomed in the governor's mansion. Daniel Evans, the incumbent, was a friend of the family.[24] The Gates family belonged to a Congregationalist church. There is probably no job-seeker in American history who has encountered prejudice because of that affiliation.

In every way, Gates was to the manor born. One could easily see a child with his socioeconomic profile settling down to a comfortable, secure life as a country club Republican, with all the money, golf, and alcohol that a well-off person might need.

What is intriguing about Gates is his intense desire to make money for its own sake. He did not want to buy things of which he was deprived. He craved money nevertheless with the voracity of the great nineteenth-century robber barons. He was rude and selfish, but he was also fearless. The thought of modulating his personality in order to ingratiate himself or at least to be less offensive never seemed to have entered his mind. Gates has spent a lot of his life offending people, and, with the sole exception of the antitrust establishment of the federal government, he never paid a price for doing so. He had an innate sense of belonging to the world in which he lived, coupled with an overwhelming ambition to write the rules of whatever activity in which he was involved. Put this together with native ability as impressive as anyone else who ever went into business, and you have a potent brew for success.

It hardly needs saying that the differences between Gates and Grove in the first two decades of their respective lives were immense. Grove's very survival was repeatedly at risk. He saw firsthand the depths to which human beings could sink and the depths to which they could be driven. When he was twenty, he was a stranger in a strange land, feeling very lucky to be in America. When Gates was twenty, there was nothing he had to which he did not feel perfectly entitled. By the 1990s, these two very different men were joined at the hip.

There was a perfectly dreadful motion picture made in 1958, the kind of movie only Stanley Kramer could direct, called *The Defiant Ones*. Tony Curtis, who, as chance would have it, is the Jewish son of a Hungarian tailor, played John "Joker" Jackson, and Sidney Poitier played Noah Cullen. These two men, Jackson a white racist and Poitier an African American, escape from prison, but they are handcuffed to one another. The movie recounts how the physical bond of those handcuffs becomes a metaphorical allegiance that is stronger than their racial antipathy. Each has the opportunity to abandon the other, but they choose not to. The pair wind up being recaptured by the authorities because of the loyalty that develops between them. The late African American actor/comedian Godfrey Cambridge parodied this story by having the Poitier character wave "Bye, baby" to Curtis and leave him to his fate.

By 1993, Intel and Microsoft were handcuffed together. Their relationship turned into a bilateral monopoly and constituted one of the great profit engines in history. However, the phrase applied to so many situations was perfectly applicable to them. They could not live with one another, but they could not live without one another. IBM's historic blunder of outsourcing the operating system for their PC to Microsoft and the central processing unit to Intel had commoditized the PC. By the mid-1990s, profits for PC manufacturers were so meager that three phone calls to a help desk from a customer would wipe them out for a sale.[25] In a commodity business, the low-cost supplier is king, which explains the success of Dell and the fact that IBM sold off its PC business.

IBM's exit and the magnitude of Dell's success were in the future during the 1980s. The information technology industry was still in thrall to IBM, which seemed to hold all the high cards. It had the money. It had the reputation. It had the history of success. Unfortunately, it was so hidebound that there was no chance it could understand the forces it had unleashed. Nor was it possible for it to understand the new type of businessperson that it had invited into its industry. There was no chance that it could grasp the motives and methods of Andy Grove. Bill Gates was utterly beyond its ken. It was difficult enough for Gates and Grove to achieve an understanding of one another.

In 1978, Microsoft moved from Albuquerque to Bellevue, Washington, just east of Seattle. This was home territory for both Gates and Allen, and both far preferred it to the New Mexico desert. They thought about relocating to Silicon Valley, which Gates found particularly appealing. But the Valley posed some noteworthy problems for a small software start-up with a handful of employees. Compared to Seattle or to Dallas, the home of Radio Shack, "[h]iring might be simpler in Silicon Valley, but keeping employees would clearly be harder, a major consideration in a business where the primary assets walk out the door every night or, in Microsoft's case, the wee hours of the morning." Housing prices were and are very high, which meant Microsoft's salary expenses would have to be high as well. All told, suburban Seattle seemed like a better bet, and that is where Microsoft's headquarters have been from that day to this.[26]

This decision turned out to be not unimportant. When it was made, no one realized that Microsoft would ascend to the heights that it did. A few years earlier, just after the company got started, Gates remarked to Allen that if they were successful they might employ twenty people someday.[27] What the decision meant was that neither Gates nor his minions would become creatures of Silicon Valley. When combined with the fact that Microsoft was self-funded and grew through retained earnings with minimal venture capital involvement, the difference in how its executives viewed the world when compared to those at Intel and Apple and, in recent years, Google, Yahoo!, and eBay was heightened.

Writing of the early 1980s, Gates's biographers Manes and Andrews say, "Venture capitalists were getting a lot of use out of Microsoft's door, in both directions." VCs were telling Gates that they could take Microsoft public and make him rich. They then observe:

That was not the way to get to Bill Gates. Gates was already rich. With the upper-crust kid's disdain for mere lucre—not that he'd ever turned it down or given much of it away—Gates saw himself as a mover, a shaker, a builder, a leader, the smartest of the Smart Guys.

Nevertheless, one venture capitalist did manage to ingratiate himself with Gates by avoiding talk of going public and discussing instead computer architecture. This VC was David Marquardt whose firm, Technology Venture Investors, was located in Menlo Park in Silicon Valley. Marquardt helped in Microsoft's incorporation in 1981. His firm was allowed to purchase five percent of the company's stock for a million dollars. Microsoft didn't need the money; the cash went straight into the bank.[28]

There has not been much love lost between Silicon Valley entrepreneurs and Microsoft. In the Valley, Microsoft came to be known as the "Evil Empire," a label borrowed from *Star Wars*. For their part, the top people at Microsoft have little affection for Valley-based firms. It is alleged that in November 2004, Microsoft CEO Steve Ballmer frothed at the mouth about Google. He is reported to have "picked up a chair and [thrown] it across the room, hitting a table in the office. . . . Ballmer roared: 'F****** Eric Schmidt [Google's chairman and chief executive] is a f****** p******. I'm going to f****** bury that guy. I have done it before. I will do it again. I'm going to f****** kill Google.'"[29]

Fortune magazine reports that Gates and Grove first met in the summer of 1978. The article observes that Grove did not give the encounter "a second thought." Intel was well-known by this time, and Grove was an established figure in the world of high technology. *Fortune* described Gates as "a scrawny, callow computer programmer" and Allen as "his burly, bearded partner." "Just another scruffy wonk with big ideas and a squeaky voice. At least the other guy looked old enough to drive."[30]

The article is probably right in asserting that Grove did not give this meeting a second thought. If you talk to him now about the relationship between Intel and Microsoft, he has only a vague recollection of what might have been this meeting. He does say that Microsoft began to appear on his radar before 1980.

Intel had worked in software during the 1970s. It actually had written an operating system called ISIS;[31] but the product, although Grove thought it was pretty good, was never vigorously promoted by the company and died on the vine. Intel had also written a number of "compilers." A compiler is a software program designed to translate a program written in a high-level language into a set of instructions that can be followed by a microprocessor. As far as Grove was concerned, Intel had developed a good suite of compilers.

In spending time with Intel's field salesmen, which Grove liked to do because they served as a distant early warning alert of what was going on in the marketplace ("snow melts at the periphery," as he has written),[32] he began hearing complaints from Microsoft's development systems group, which doubtless originated with Gates, about Intel's compilers.

Intel got out of the compiler business. This was, Grove later rather ruefully reminisced, "the first drop of salt water which tells you what you're going to see when the sea is going to engulf you."[33] It "is the first conscious memory I have about Microsoft f****** with our strategy."[34]

In the early 1980s, during the great explosion caused by the spectacular sales of the IBM PC, Grove does not recall a lot of conflict with Microsoft. He was fully occupied with dealing with the Japanese challenge, exiting memory, and introducing the 386 on a sole-source basis. Microsoft had nothing to do with these activities.

Grove was certainly aware of Microsoft by the early 1980s. It began to grow quickly for precisely the same reason Intel did: the announcement of the IBM Personal Computer on August 12, 1981.

At the end of 1979, Microsoft had been a partnership with twenty-eight employees and sales of roughly $2.4 million. It had offered a variety of programming languages, mostly for OEM customers, and a tiny assortment of lowball packages for end users. Just two years later, Microsoft was a corporation with venture capital funding, sales of $16 million, 130 employees, over $1 million in the bank, and the broadest product line in the microcomputer software business: languages, operating systems, application programs, even hardware. The IBM deal and MS-DOS [Microsoft Disk Operating System] had completed Microsoft's transformation from a little language house to [a] "one-stop shopping" center.[35]

Through the 1980s, Microsoft's big problem was not Intel, it was IBM. Outmaneuvered and outsleazed, IBM lost the operating system battle to this once tiny company. In 1986, when IBM already owned 20 percent of Intel,

Gates and his friends suggested it buy 30 percent of Microsoft. "It was a real turning point," observed Gates, "when IBM said no."[36] Had IBM kept its 20 percent of Intel and had it purchased and held 30 percent of Microsoft, the industry and the whole world on which the industry exerts such a large impact would be very different. This is just another of the many "would have," "could have," "should have" encounters that IBM had with history during the 1980s. Of all the numberless mistakes IBM made in its dealings with Microsoft, this was the biggest.[37]

Bill Gates was the individual most responsible for IBM's decline in the 1980s and early 1990s. He was extremely smart, nimble, and very tough. He was beyond intimidation. He represented a phenomenon that most IBMers simply could not comprehend.

Microsoft moved to the campus it currently occupies in Redmond, Washington, near Seattle, in February 1986. The next month, Gates finally took the company public. At Goldman Sachs, executives told Microsoft's top people that the company might be the "most visible initial public offering of 1986—or ever."[38]

The magic moment took place when the markets opened on March 13, 1986. Microsoft CFO Frank Gaudette described the experience as "a shark frenzy. The phones were ringing at such a dramatic pace only for one subject— Microsoft stock."[39] When the sun set on March 13, Bill Gates was worth $311 million in Microsoft stock. The $1.7 million he received for stock he sold at the initial price of $21 hardly seemed mentioning. The stock's price at close of trading was $27.75, up over 32 percent from the morning. Gates, meanwhile, still owned 45 percent of the company.[40] He was thirty years old. March 13 was a triumph of epic proportions.

Meanwhile, back in Westchester, the folks at IBM could not process all this news. They

> couldn't understand. They felt sure they were more important than anyone from this little company way off in the Pacific Northwest. Some IBM executives also felt they had created Microsoft and wondered why they hadn't become wealthy, too. The IBMers couldn't see that being smart wasn't enough, getting a big office at IBM wasn't enough, working hard and following the rules wasn't enough.[41]

Bill Gates was writing his own rules.

Through the 1980s, Gates viewed hardware not as a business worth entering but rather as a tool that, with each incremental improvement, made it possible for him to leverage the software Microsoft turned out.[42] It was software that was going to put a computer on every desk and in every home. "We're still not at the stage," Gates said in 1981, "when I'd tell my mother, or some naïve person, just go out and buy one of these machines. In a couple of years we'll achieve that real peak—to fill that gap and feel like it's a real tool."[43]

Microsoft's relationship with IBM during the 1980s is endlessly complex. Microsoft had to do a lot of things right, and IBM had to make a lot of mistakes in order for David to kill Goliath in that decade.

The essence of IBM's error was that it entered into a joint development agreement with Microsoft to create an updated PC operating system, called OS/2. However, this agreement ignored Windows altogether.[44] Windows did not seem like much in its early years. It was announced in 1983, but it did not reach the market until 1985. By 1989, however, Windows 3.0 was announced, much to the anger of IBM. Microsoft's new operating system, which it alone owned, took the market by storm. There was nothing IBM could do to stop it.

Appealing to the nontechnical public because of its ease of use, Windows 3.0 swept the field. From 1990 onward, Microsoft in software and Intel in hardware dominated the PC market. Their bilateral monopoly came to be called "Wintel." In order for Wintel to function, Intel and Microsoft had to cooperate. In order for these two companies to cooperate, Gates and Grove had to get along with one another.

18

---•---

Wintel

Through the early and mid-1980s, the relations between Intel and Microsoft seem to have been cordial enough. Hardware and software were different parts of the information technology forest. Japanese competition continued to be a major problem for Intel but is not mentioned in discussions of Microsoft. On the other hand, the companies did have one common problem: how best to manage IBM?

Probably between 1985 and 1987—Grove is not certain of the date although he remembers the room in which the meeting took place (it was a conference room in Santa Clara 4 on the Intel campus)—Gates came to seek Grove's advice. We have, he said, Windows, and it is moving along quite well. Gates sketched out its progress on a blackboard as Grove looked on. But IBM, Gates explained, did not want him to proceed down the path of further Windows development. He wanted to know Grove's views about what he should do.

"Yours truly," recalls Grove with more than a touch of irony, delivered a lecture to Gates. "Bill," he said, "you are not a vassal of IBM. You're an independent company and you should stand up and be counted and do what's right for you." As Grove observes, "I gave a f****** pep talk to the man who was to become the terror of the industry!"[1] This encouraged him to do what he wanted to do anyway. As we have seen, Microsoft stood up to IBM and won.

This encounter may have been the high point of the relationship between the two men and their two companies. Once they had to deal with each other as "complementors," things became a lot more difficult. Part of the reason was technical. The line between hardware and software shifts.

Part of the cause of the difficulties between Intel and Microsoft was personal.

Grove and Gates shared certain traits: both were tough, combative, and highly aggressive competitors. The inevitable conflicts that arose from these two leaders were affectionately described in the popular press as "squabbles of an old married couple." The relationship was cyclical in terms of trust, rotating from stable, to bad, to worse, and at its worst . . . "seemed like two porcupines trying to mate."[2]

Emblematic of the interpersonal dilemma was a dinner at Grove's house in Silicon Valley. The purpose of the dinner was to iron out some technical issues that had arisen between the two companies.[3]

In the late 1980s, Grove had begun to educate himself about software. He visited various executives including Philippe Kahn of Borland, Jim Manzi of Lotus, and Larry Ellison of Oracle. "One of the secrets of business," Grove has observed, "is that people will teach you by selling you. They aren't selling product, but they want you to support them and they want you to appreciate them."[4]

The most telling visit was to a man named Fred Gibbons who published software manuals.[5] A perplexed Gibbons told Grove that he did not know what to tell his subscribers. They were asking whether they should support OS/2 or Windows, and Gibbons had no authoritative answer for them. Gibbons's subscribers, independent software vendors, did not have the resources to support both.[6]

Grove came back from that meeting with the feeling that Windows was going to win. At the time the conventional wisdom was that OS/2 was "real software" and Windows mere "tinkertoy." But that is not the way the world looked to Grove after his meetings. So strategically he wanted to move a little closer to Microsoft.[7] Ironing out some technical issues was a step in that direction. Dinner at Grove's home seemed like a congenial setting. Unfortunately, the evening was not a success. As Grove put it, "Personally, we had a little hiccup."[8] Indeed, the dinner has become something of a legend.[9]

There must have been a good deal of tension in the air to begin with.

Gates felt that Intel was using Microsoft's intellectual property in a product he believed was competitive with Microsoft. Grove knew nothing about this except that Gates had called Gordon Moore and had a fit about this issue. As Grove said, Gates "reamed Gordon out like a plugged toilet."[10]

Moore hardly knew Gates, and after this rather startling phone call, he went to Grove and said, "I don't know what the heck is going on. Please take care of this." Moore was "a little shaken up," Grove recalls, by this encounter with "the trailer of the future Gates."[11]

Then came the dinner. Gates arrived at Grove's home with Jim Harris, a former Intel executive who at the time managed Microsoft's OEM business. Grove was joined by Bill Lattin, vice president and director of Intel's software group, the man who had audited Andy's course at Berkeley back in the 1960s. Eva Grove was not present. Andy suggested that the evening might be difficult, and they agreed that she would dine with her mother. The discussion became fairly heated. "The thing that really kicked me into high gear," recalls Grove, is that Gates said that something Intel was doing was "actionable." What Gates meant by this word was that whatever was being discussed was something concerning which the people involved could take action. But Grove was not sufficiently familiar with the way Gates used words to understand him that way. He thought, perhaps having somewhere in his mind the knowledge that Gates's father was a lawyer, that he was being threatened.

"I reared up from the table," remembers Grove. "Do you mean to threaten me with legal action at my own dinner table?" he hissed at Gates.[12] The ensuing uproar was such that "the caterer peeked into the dining room to see what the ruckus was all about."[13] An episode like this can simply kill an evening. "I was the only one who finished my salmon," said Grove.[14]

It took a while for Grove and Gates to have their next meeting. Eventually they did, and by the early 1990s they got together a couple of times a year. There were multiple points of contact at various levels within the two companies.

Intel and Microsoft had some interests in common. Both benefited from the sale of every PC because they both had virtual monopolies on their contributions to the finished product. However, these two companies had different cost structures. They managed technologies that were ready for the market at different speeds. Even if their CEOs got along as well as two people could, conflict was inevitable.

It is not an accident that Microsoft became the world's most valuable corporation. The company recognized the characteristics of the software side of the "new computer industry" and exploited those characteristics with focus and ruthlessness. It is also no accident that Bill Gates was able to hold on to so much stock. Paul Allen, who retired from Microsoft in 1983 after being diagnosed with Hodgkin's disease, and Steve Ballmer also became billionaires thanks to Microsoft's stock.

What, then, are the key characteristics of the industry in which Microsoft found itself once it had greatness thrust upon it by the fact that IBM chose it to provide the operating system for the PC and also, crucially, by the fact that IBM permitted Microsoft to license that operating system to other manufacturers? One such characteristic can be highlighted by a joke from the 1990s:

Q: How many Microsoft executives does it take to screw in a lightbulb?

A: None. Bill Gates will just redefine Darkness™ as the industry standard.[15]

Standards are critical. "We look for opportunities with network externalities," Gates has said, "where there are advantages to the vast majority of consumers to share a common standard."[16] If there were a common operating system platform, any company or any individual entrepreneur could write a software program designed to the specifications of that standard and know that it would work.

With the exception of Apple, which, at least until its recent purchase of Intel microprocessors rejected the Microsoft standard and managed to survive as a niche player in the computer industry, all PC makers ship their product equipped with Microsoft's Windows operating system. The result is that if an independent software vendor, or ISV as it is known in the trade, wants to create and market a PC software application, it knows how to make that technically possible. ISVs can afford to spend a lot of money developing programs because they know that if they are successful, their programs have the potential to be distributed to almost every PC in the world.

The "network effects" made possible by a standard operating system proved so powerful that this is a "winner take all" business.[17] Microsoft won. And it took all.

Microsoft's ability to establish MS-DOS in the early 1980s and then

Windows by the end of the decade as the industry standard did for it in software what the establishment of the x86 standard in microprocessor architecture did for Intel in hardware. It provided a powerful barrier to the entry of new competition because billions of dollars had been invested by ISVs, as well as by Microsoft itself, in writing software programs that conformed to the standards established by Windows. Billions more would have to be spent to "port" that software (i.e., to make the software work properly) to a new operating system. These switching costs made it almost impossible to attack Microsoft successfully unless a major technological discontinuity developed. The Internet was just such a discontinuity in the early and mid-1990s. That is why Microsoft had to bury Netscape even if it meant using predatory practices and violating the antitrust laws to do so.[18]

The combination of network effects and the implications of the need for standards meant that there were increasing returns to adoption of Windows. That is to say, Windows was unlike, say, an automobile. If you double the number of automobiles produced, their price is going to drop because there is no reason to believe that demand will rise commensurately. Windows, by contrast, became more valuable the more copies were installed. In that way, it is like the telephone. Yours is more valuable if I have one. Thus, at the operating system level, Microsoft was in a race to get big fast, and it did.

Operating systems are expensive to develop. The cost of a major upgrade to Windows today would be about $2 billion and would take about four years. In 2004, Microsoft spent $7.78 billion on research and development, over 20 percent of sales. This is a very large amount of money. For purposes of comparison, Intel spent $4.78 billion, or 14 percent of sales. IBM, which before the dawn of the new computer industry dominated research and development, spent at its peak $5.7 billion, which, while very large in absolute terms, amounted to only about 5.4 percent of sales and had to be spread over a much broader product line than Microsoft or Intel.

In addition to its operating system, Microsoft's other principal profit center was its applications software. Applications, which are what the consumer actually uses on a computer and sees on the desktop, include such products as Word, Excel, and PowerPoint. These three products are the best-known components of what has been bundled together as Microsoft Office. They also absorb R&D dollars, and they also are market leaders.

A simplified view of a personal computer is to conceive of it as a set of layers. The applications are on top and are visible to the consumer. Instructions the consumer transmits to the applications are communicated to the operating system software. The operating system directs the hardware to perform whatever tasks are necessary to get the job done. The hardware then communicates to the operating system, which communicates to the application delivering, if all goes well, the service that the consumer desires.

Microsoft was dominant in a number of the most important software applications. It owned the standard operating system. A major reason for the astounding profitability of this company is that its manufacturing and distribution costs were negligible. Once its software was designed, Microsoft spent next to nothing producing it. In 2004, it carried $2.3 billion on its books for "property and equipment, net." This amounted to a mere two and a half percent of total assets of over $92 billion.

When it came to distribution, the story was even happier. Distribution costs were very low, especially to OEMs. Microsoft simply shipped a master disk to, for example, Dell, and Dell reproduced it. The marginal cost of an extra sale was precisely zero. Thus, if Microsoft charged, say, $60 for each operating system that Dell loaded onto a computer it sold, Dell would pay Microsoft $600 if it sold ten computers in a year.[19] If Dell sold a hundred computers, it would pay Microsoft $6,000. Every penny of that added revenue fell directly to Microsoft's bottom line.

When it dawned on Andrew Carnegie how much money he was going to make from his steel mills, he exclaimed in ecstatic wonderment, "Where is there such a business!"[20] Bill Gates had found one. At the close of the twentieth century, he possessed a business model second to none, anywhere, ever. Their businesses made both Carnegie and Gates the richest people in the world during their eras.

Intel was also fabulously profitable, but, unlike Microsoft, it actually manufactured a product. Microsoft sold information. Intel sold microprocessors. In 2004, Intel carried $15.8 billion on its balance sheet for "property, plant, and equipment." This equalled almost a third of its total assets of $48 billion. Those fabrication facilities cost real money. They had to be kept running full and steady.

When considering Intel's performance in the Wintel "partnership," it is not easy to know what the right question is to ask. Is this the story of how Intel not only survived but prospered in the same industry in which Microsoft had killed or marginalized so many other companies? Or is this the story of how Intel missed opportunities to use its corporate capabilities more effectively to leverage its strengths? Intel faced no threat that Microsoft would backward integrate into the microprocessor business. The expenditures for facilities and expertise made no sense. There was, however, a threat that Microsoft might support a microprocessor made by a firm other than Intel. Indeed, Microsoft played a fleeting and unwelcome, from Intel's point of view, role in its RISC/CISC decision by joining the ACE consortium that backed the development of a RISC chip.[21]

To be sure, Intel and Microsoft shared some goals. Both wanted to see more personal computers sold. They also, however, had a built-in conflict. As Professor David Yoffie has put it, "[I]n an ideal world, everyone wants their competitors to price as high as possible, but they want complementors to price as low as possible." You want your competitor to price high so you can too. But you want your complementor to price low so that you can extract as much value from the end product as there is to be had. "[C]omplementors, like competitors," Yoffie observes, "are competing over who gets what share of the pie and . . . competition between complementors can be just as intense as [between] direct competitors."[22] Grove suggested that the differences between Intel and Microsoft "occur because our business priorities are fundamentally different. We sell a new chip with a new computer; we don't sell many replacement chips or upgrades. Bill sees a big installed base to take care of."[23]

Through Windows, Gates had his fist on the neck in the hourglass of information technology. His very name seems like it comes from a Dickens novel. Gates was the gatekeeper. It was he who decided what went into and what came out of the PCs of the world. He was technology's version of Cerberus, the three-headed doglike monster that, in Greek mythology, guarded the entrance to Hades, through which all souls had to pass. Taming Cerberus was the twelfth and most difficult of the labors of Hercules.[24] How could Intel tame the Cerberus it faced? Was it worth even trying?

Intel's attempts to break out of the computer and reach the end user without paying a toll to open Windows were unsuccessful. One example is the story of Native Signal Processing (NSP). NSP was a result of Intel's desire to see the creation of "MIPS [millions of instructions per second]-sucking applications" for the PC. "This is a critical point," David Yoffie has explained. "Intel needs applications that require more and more processing power; otherwise it will not be able to sell new processors."[25] Although both Intel and Microsoft wanted improvements in the performance of the PC so that they could render obsolete the products consumers already owned and give them a reason to trade up, there was no reason to believe that the improvements each company developed would work well together. The question of who would reap the lion's share of the rewards for such upgrades always loomed. Moreover, the development cycle for each company had a tempo of its own. The improvement of the performance of the PC was a highly technical proposition, challenging the talents of the most able engineers in business. Coordinating the timing of the upgrades in PC performance between the worlds of software and hardware undertaken by two companies whose relations ran the gamut, as we have noted, "from stable, to bad, to worse"[26] was problematic in the extreme.

To achieve greater control over its destiny, Intel established the Intel Architecture Lab in Oregon, where it has become the largest private employer. As Yoffie points out, "Intel feared that the PC platform was moving slower than its ability to develop more processor power. Rather than idly wait, Intel was determined to eliminate potential roadblocks itself."[27] Established in 1991, the mission of the Intel Architecture Lab "was to tackle PC platform problems as well as create newer applications and more advanced computer peripherals that would inspire new ways to use the PC."[28] NSP was one of these initiatives. The Intel Architecture Lab began work on it the year it was founded.

Yoffie describes NSP as "a specialized software technology and applications program interface that would help developers build applications with advanced video and graphics capabilities without the use of special signal processing chips."[29] Of crucial importance to the relationship between Microsoft and Intel, NSP did not require software developers to use Windows. It enabled them to bypass the operating system and deliver instructions directly to the microprocessor. (See Figure 10.)

According to Yoffie, Intel's executives managed to convince themselves that NSP would serve Microsoft's interests as well as theirs. The logic ran as follows. For Intel,

by having more functions performed by the software [embedded in the microprocessor], NSP gave PC buyers a greater incentive to buy faster microprocessors. On the other side, NSP acted like an operating system that facilitated speedier development of better multimedia applications. Intel management argued that new multimedia standards could help grow the market for Microsoft products.

In 1995, Grove was hailing NSP as the future.[30]

The people up in Redmond did not see things that way at all. Yoffie says they were "livid." Intel was "trespassing into Microsoft territory." Adding "salt to the wound," NSP had been developed as an extension to Windows 3.1 just as Microsoft was releasing Windows 95. This was a good example of the problem of coordinating product launches by two companies that were in theory "complementors." Windows 95 had its own set of intractable problems that had nothing to do with anything Intel was undertaking.

FIGURE 10

The Relationship Between NSP and the Operating System

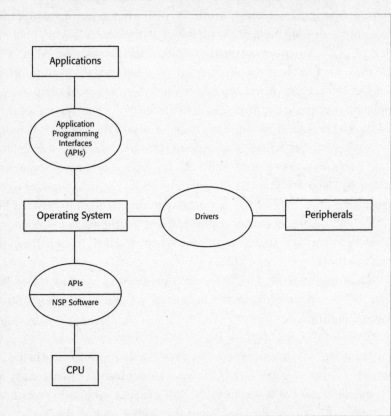

Source: David B. Yoffie, Ramon Casadesus-Masanell, and Sasha Mattu, "Wintel (A): Cooperation or Conflict?" Harvard Business School Case No. 704-419, rev. March 16, 2004, p. 21.

Even if there were not a coordination problem in this instance, Gates would have been enraged by NSP. Intel, in his view, had no business monkeying around with software. This looked to him like forward integration into his domain. The fact that Intel "pitched NSP to system makers independently of any collaboration or cooperation with Microsoft further [positioned] NSP as competing software." This was pure poison from Microsoft's standpoint.

On its side, some of Intel's most talented technical people in high executive positions were sick of seeing their creativity hamstrung because of Microsoft's monopoly.

> Even when Microsoft didn't have a competing technology, Intel engineers accused Microsoft of "preannouncing" future software to freeze the market and prevent Intel's solutions from becoming a standard. . . . [I]n an internal document titled "Sympathy for the Devil" [the name of a song by the rock group the Rolling Stones], Intel vice president Steve McGeady wrote that Intel was tired of Microsoft's . . . tweaking Intel's standard interfaces to create advantages for its own software rather than maintaining fair and easy access to all software developers.[31]

For Gates, the NSP issue was starkly simple: "[W]e are the software company here, and we will not have any kind of equal relationship with Intel on software."[32] Gates made it clear to Grove personally, to Intel generally, and to the whole PC industry that he would do anything to kill the NSP initiative at Intel. He succeeded.

Speaking of NSP in 1996, Grove said that what mattered to Microsoft the previous year was the launch of Windows 95. Chip performance was "of secondary importance" in this new product launch. "It's not that we had a different notion of the goodness of enhanced multimedia performance [which NSP would have enabled]," Grove said. "We just had different senses of urgency."[33] There is that issue of timing the coordination of innovation again.

With the bluntness that was his trademark, Grove explained, "I admit we were dumb enough not to understand that the software we developed was actually contrary to some of the features of Windows 95. And hence came all that crap."[34] In retrospect, Grove believes the NSP initiative was a mistake, given the realities of the relative power and expertise of Microsoft and Intel in the early and mid-1990s.

Gates, of course, was delighted that Intel dropped NSP. He said to Grove, "Look, we don't disagree with your guys. We think they're smart. But this stuff does not work well with Windows 95." Intel, Gates told Grove, "deserves a lot of credit for stepping back" from NSP.

"We didn't have much of a choice. We basically caved," replied Grove.

"No, no, you didn't cave. Come on. If Intel had shipped that NSP stuff, you wouldn't have done yourselves any favors."

"We caved," Grove said again. "Introducing a Windows-based software initiative that Microsoft doesn't support . . . well, life is too short for that."[35]

What did this all mean? Steve McGeady's view is that after 1995, Microsoft was in the driver's seat in the PC industry. Intel, he said, "had moved from being a powerhouse in the industry to being a pig [strapped to] the back of Microsoft's bicycle."[36]

Is McGeady correct in his belief that Intel had been the channel commander in the PC industry up until the mid-1990s when the mantle passed to Microsoft? Or, better put, when Microsoft seized it? As late as the last day of trading in 1996, Intel's market capitalization was higher than Microsoft's. If we look at the years during all or part of which Grove was Intel's CEO, 1987 through 1998, Intel's market capitalization exceeded Microsoft's five times: in 1987, 1988, 1989, 1993, and 1996.

There was a time in the late 1980s with the spectacular success of the 386 that according to Grove, "when you asked someone what kind of a computer he had, the first thing he tended to say was 'I have a 386'—which was the microprocessor chip inside the computer—and then he would go on to identify the computer manufacturer, what kind of software it had, and so on. Computer users knew instinctively that the identity and class of the computer were determined more than anything else by the microprocessor within. This was obviously good for us."[37] This may well have been true then. It is doubtful that it was true a decade later. It is not true today.

In 1997 and 1998, as the great dot-com investment bubble inflated, Microsoft's market value far outpaced Intel's. The difference was over $40 billion in 1997 and almost $150 billion the following year. Intel's performance was spectacular in absolute terms but not relative to Microsoft.

Could or should Intel have done anything differently to outpace its Redmond rival? A tough question to which we will return.

After all the *Sturm and Drang* between Grove and Gates, their relationship matured remarkably. On June 15, 2006, Bill Gates announced that he would terminate his daily responsibilities at Microsoft over a two-year period in order to devote himself to the charitable foundation he had established with his wife, Melinda. The next day he received the following Andy-gram:

> Good move. Congratulations and good luck
>
> a

19

The Pentium Launch: Intel Meets the Internet

Intel introduced the Pentium processor on March 22, 1993. Following the product roadmap Gordon Moore laid out in his pathbreaking article in 1965, the Pentium contained a staggering 3.1 million transistors on a device "[t]hinner than a dime and small as a postage stamp"[1] that was "capable of executing more than 100 million instructions per second."[2] "Intel's newest manufacturing technology," the company proudly announced to the world, "is a state-of-the-art four-metal-layer 0.6 micron process, meaning that the etched features on each chip are less than 6/1000 the width of the average human hair."[3] The microprocessor had moved into the realm where human imagination is challenged.[4]

From a technical point of view, not every knowledgeable analyst was overwhelmed by the Pentium. In the words of one, the Pentium "wasn't exactly a blockbuster by the standards of its RISC contemporaries." According to this commentator "the main thing that the Pentium had going for it was x86 compatibility." That was, however a very big thing indeed. "Intel's decision to make enormous sacrifices of performance, power consumption, and cost for the sake of maintaining the Pentium's backwards compatibility with legacy x86 code was probably the most strategically-important decision that the company has ever made."[5]

Intel could have built a more technically efficient microprocessor than the Pentium if it were beginning with a clean sheet of paper. But of course it was not. Fidelity to the x86 architecture, although it may have slowed progress on strictly technical dimensions, was an absolute business necessity. The rapid market acceptance of the Pentium illustrated satisfaction with whatever compromises were necessary to maintain the integrity of the x86 platform.

Figure 11 shows the speed with which the Pentium took off. The Pentium was not merely another product. It was news and received its share of free publicity. It was, for example, featured on the cover of *Fortune* for June 14, 1993, accompanying a story on the "new computer revolution."[6]

FIGURE 11

Pentium Output Compared to Previous Intel Microprocessor Product Launches

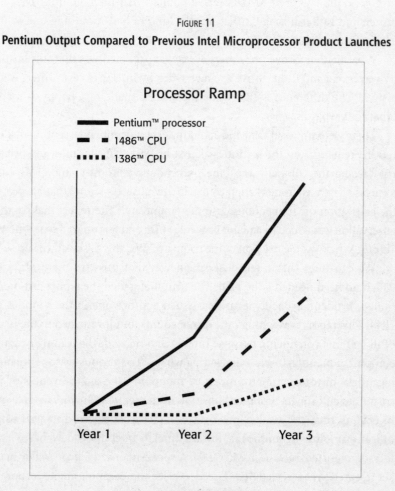

Source: *Intel Annual Report,* 1993, p. 2.

Things appeared to be going as well as even the most paranoid, least optimistic Intel executive could have hoped. The Pentium helped 1993 to be the championship season that it was, and it seemed to be doing the same for 1994. Until October 30. October 30, 1994, is a date which will live in infamy in the annals of Intel.

Fully to understand why the events of that day and of the ensuing weeks unfolded as they did, it is useful to recall earlier remarks about how Intel was viewed by others. Grove knew there was plenty of hostility to his company beyond the confines of Intel. He never thought of business as a popularity contest, and when it came to hostility he was quite skilled at giving as well as he got. So if a lawyer at AMD asserted publicly that Intel did not have customers but rather hostages,[7] that was the kind of bad-mouthing one could expect from a competitor.

What neither Grove nor others at Intel appreciated was that this hostility was broad and deep. Grove was awestruck by Intel's success. Others were as well. The difference is that while the success made him happy, it made others angry.

There were straws in the wind about the extent of anti-Intel sentiment. Recall the remark from the securities analyst in 1991 that the "most important risk" facing the company was "the tremendous animosity among its customers."[8] There is no marketing course in any business school that advocates the cultivation of "tremendous customer animosity." The report making this observation was issued by a major brokerage firm and was undoubtedly known at Intel. What was the reaction of the company? Was this a "signal" or "noise"?

We can infer that Intel's assessment was that this was mere noise to which no heed needed to be paid. The firm that issued the report just mentioned, Prudential-Bache Securities, issued another one in the summer of 1994. This report was wrong on a dozen counts, but it returned to the issue of ill will in a convincing passage. Intel's relations with the leading original equipment manufacturers were getting worse. "For various reasons, including Intel's historical [microprocessor] monopoly, the aggressiveness of its corporate culture, its dominant position in the semiconductor market, and its envious financial results, Intel's customer base has always displayed a significant amount of animosity toward Intel."[9] Intel "is widely hated and feared," reported *Fortune* in May 1994. A spokesman at a Silicon Valley market research firm asserted that "Greed, avarice and paranoia are its corporate culture."[10] The situation was deteriorating.

The events set in motion by what happened on October 30 show what can transpire when you mistake a signal for noise. On that day, Professor Thomas Nicely, a mathematician at Lynchburg College in Virginia, sent an email "to a number of individuals and organizations" about what seemed to him to be a problem with the Pentium. His email was addressed to "Whom it may concern," and the subject was a "Bug in the Pentium FPU [floating point unit]." "In short," Professor Nicely wrote, "the Pentium FPU is returning erroneous values for certain division operations."[11]

Bugs were nothing new in computer technology. The word "bug" was first used back in the late 1940s and early 1950s with reference to the ENIAC and the Univac. These gigantic computers were constructed without transistors. They used vacuum tubes instead. The vacuum tubes generated not only a lot of heat, they were very bright as well. The light attracted moths and other insects. Debugging a computer first meant sweeping off the floor the insects that had been attracted by the light and killed by the heat of the vacuum tubes.

The word "bug" lived on, although it came to have a different meaning. By the late 1950s, it referred to a flaw built into the hardware or software of a computer. Bugs were and are common. The computer is such a complicated creation and can do so many things that it can make mistakes beyond counting. Some of these mistakes are only discovered when a particular element of the hardware or software has been on the market. It is not always possible for a supplier to verify that every possible operation a computer can perform will be completed accurately. Therefore, some problems come to light only when the machine has been in use and a customer tries to perform an operation the computer should have been able to handle but could not.

Even after a new chip hits the market, testing continues. In the case of the Pentium, Intel "continued to perform trillions of random mathematical operations" in the search for bugs.[12] A five-and-a-half-billion-dollar testing industry had grown up to "exterminate these bugs."[13] *BusinessWeek* speculated that the Pentium may have been more extensively tested than any other chip in history.

The Pentium was a vitally important product for Intel. "[F]ast, powerful, and three times as complex as the 486," it went from design to sales in two years, half the usual development period.[14] Intel was proving its mettle as a learning organization. More difficult assignments were being dispatched more quickly than less difficult ones had been previously. The Pentium was targeted at a range of products from the household PC, the most quickly growing segment of the PC market, all the way to the computation-intensive workstation market in businesses. This was Intel's answer to the PowerPC.

The intensity of Intel's search for flaws in the Pentium bore fruit in June 1994, thirteen months after shipment of the product had begun. An error was discovered in dividing certain numbers with decimal points, known as "floating points." Thus, the number 4 is an integer without a decimal or floating point. The number 4.1 has a decimal, referred to as a floating point.

To speed up division involving floating points,

the Pentium employed an algorithm that calculated quotients by re- peatedly estimating successive digits of an answer. . . . The process in- volved looking up numbers in a table containing 4,000 entries in a part of the chip known as the floating point unit, or FPU. . . .

The look up table was supposed to be identical to the one used in In- tel's 486 chip, but in the process of transferring the table from the 486 to the Pentium, five of its 4,000 entries were omitted due to human error.[15]

Ironically, the floating point feature had been viewed as a "major advance" of the 486 when it was introduced in 1989 over its predecessor, the 386. "Code written for the 386/387 combination will run on the 486. The major difference is that since the FPU [floating point unit] is on [a] chip, off-chip delays are eliminated, speeding up processing."[16]

Thus the Pentium performed improperly under certain circumstances involving division with long numbers. This lengthy explanation of the problem from a Harvard Business School case study provides an idea of how complicated these chips are.[17] What Professor Nicely discovered, among other things, was that although multiplying 824633702441.0 times 1/824633702441.0 should equal 1 ("within some extremely small rounding error," Professor Nicely explained), this exercise in multiplication did not generate the answer 1 if you used a computer with a Pentium processor. In- stead, it resulted in an 18-digit fraction—0.999999996274709702. No one could mistake that for 1. It lay outside the "extremely small rounding error" for which Professor Nicely made allowances. In a word, it was just plain wrong.[18] The specific problem occurred in the division of the number 1 by 824633702441.0. That is why this is a problem in division. That decimal be- tween the last 1 and the zero is the floating point.[19]

Professor Nicely, by chance, actually first encountered the Pentium bug in June 1994, the same month Intel's engineers did. For four months, he searched for answers to what appeared to be an intractable conundrum. It was not until October that he came to believe the problem was with the Pentium. On October 19, he got in touch with the retailer who had sold him his computer, but the retailer knew nothing about the bug he described. He then got in touch with Intel technical support, which took six days to inform him that they could not help him. A decade later, in 2004, Nicely wrote that "Even more baffling, Intel failed to warn their tech support desk to immediately report any external complaint about the bug, so that it could be given special handling."[20] On October 30, he dispatched his email.

Intel, as mentioned, had come across the problem that caused Nicely's incorrect results back in June. They found the cause, determined to fix it in the next version of the chip, and also decided it was not worth mentioning to customers, distributors, or OEMs. The company issued "errata sheets" that described bugs in its microprocessors to distributors and OEMs, who had to sign a nondisclosure agreement. Information about the flaw was not, however, even distributed through this method. Why not? Because the problem seemed so small, certainly in comparison to bugs in previous chips, that, as Grove said in December, "We couldn't imagine anyone ever running into it."[21]

Grove later described this as "a minor design error . . . which caused a rounding error in division once every nine billion times." That meant "that an average spreadsheet user would run into the problem only once every 27,000 years. . . . This is a long time, much longer than it would take for other types of problems which are always encountered in semiconductors to trip up a chip." So Andy and Intel decided to fix it when the opportunity arose and, meanwhile, just "[go] about our business."[22] That, however, turned out not to be possible.

A new method of communicating was developing quickly in the early 1990s. Depending upon how you look at it, the roots of the Internet can be traced back to 1958.[23] By the early 1990s, it began to take off. Online chat rooms and newsgroups proliferated, as did the use of electronic mail, which, like television, was first demonstrated publicly, by IBM, at the New York World's Fair in 1939.[24]

As a result of Nicely's emails, news of the Pentium flaw was posted by November 3 on two Internet forums, CompuServe's Canopus and comp.sys.intel. Comp.sys.intel was a newsgroup devoted to Intel products but neither maintained nor formally monitored by the company. It was "obscure" and "frequented by a few technicians interested in discussing Intel-related hardware issues."[25] It was about to become a lot more important.

Nicely's original emails set in motion a noteworthy chain of events. One of his emails went to an author of computer books, who forwarded it to a software executive in Cambridge, Massachusetts. He, in turn, posted Nicely's email on CompuServe's Canopus forum and within a day there were ten confirmations of the error. The managing editor of the *Electronic Engineering Times,* Alexander Wolfe, read the Canopus posting and published an article about this development in his trade journal.

The article could hardly have been fairer or kinder to Intel. The headline—"Intel Fixes A Pentium FPU Glitch"—announced not only that there was a problem, but that the problem had been taken care of. The problem was described as a "glitch," which sounds like something well south of a disaster. Before this story was over, the Pentium flaw would be compared to the poisoning of Tylenol in the 1980s.[26]

The body of Wolfe's article quoted an Intel engineer to the effect that the glitch "was a very rare condition that happened once every 9 to 10 billion operand pairs." (An "operand" is a "quantity on which a mathematical or logical operation is performed.") A spokesman for the company stated that "this doesn't even qualify as an errata [*sic,* erratum]. We fixed it in a subsequent stepping [i.e., version]."

Wolfe reported that Intel "confirmed that it had updated the floating-point unit (FPU) in the Pentium microprocessor" to "correct an anomaly that caused inaccurate results on some high precision calculations." The "glitch" had been discovered by the company "midyear." This certainly sounds like no big deal.

Intel's statements to Wolfe were not quite accurate. The "glitch" had indeed been discovered "midyear," but it had not been "fixed in a subsequent stepping." The remedy for the flaw required adding a couple of dozen transistors to the Pentium. The corrected version of the product would become available after the next stepping, but that would not take place until early in 1995. Meanwhile, Intel would continue to ship flawed Pentiums. Only when the flaw became public did Intel change its plans. Even then, the change came in stages. Sometime in November, Intel began shipping debugged chips, but only to customers with exacting technical requirements. As reported by Wolfe in his nonhostile, noninflammatory article in the *Electronic*

Engineering Times on November 7, Intel seemed quite dismissive—"doesn't even qualify as an errata."

In the late 1930s, when he suddenly burst upon the movie world as a star, the actor Errol Flynn delivered a Christmas broadcast to his native Australia. One of his remarks was, "If there's anyone listening to whom I owe money, I'm prepared to forget about it if you are."[27] Intel seemed to be taking a similarly cavalier attitude toward its customers. To all who purchased a flawed Pentium, we're willing to forget about it if you are.

Intel's customers were not willing to forget, and they did not accept the company's reassurances. Engineers, mathematicians, and other quantitatively technical people began running experiments of their own. Their findings were not pretty. According to some calculations, Pentium failure was going to be a good deal more serious than Intel suggested. Moreover, in the words of one scientist, "the real difficulty is having to worry about this at all. There are so many other things than [*sic*] can go wrong with computer hardware and software that at least we ought to be able to rely on the basic arithmetic."[28]

Despite this manifest dissatisfaction, the chorus of complaint was still rather muted. Intel touched the lives of a lot of people by late 1994, and it is a safe bet that only a very small percentage knew there was a Pentium problem in mid-November. On the sixteenth, Andy Grove was the keynote speaker at COMDEX, the big computer trade show held in Las Vegas that year. There was not much talk about a Pentium flaw at the convention.[29] Grove certainly did not mention it in his address, in which he spoke of the Pentium confidently and proudly.[30] The press was out in force for this event and not one of the 175 representatives of the Fourth Estate asked Grove about this problem.[31]

The "Internet discussion came to the attention of the trade press," Grove later wrote, "and was described thoroughly and accurately in a front-page article in one of the trade weeklies." This is a reference to Wolfe's article in the *Electronic Engineering Times*. "The next week," Grove continued, "it was picked up as a smaller item in other trade papers. And that seemed to be it."[32]

Grove discovered that that was not it on the morning of November 22, the Tuesday before Thanksgiving. The morning began uneventfully enough. He co-taught his class on strategy with Professor Robert Burgelman at Stanford's Graduate School of Business. As was their practice, Grove and Burgelman graded the students on class participation immediately after the session. On this particular day, "[t]he process was taking a little longer than usual . . . and

I was about to excuse myself to call my office when the phone rang. Our head of communications wanted to talk to me—urgently. She wanted to let me know that a CNN crew was coming to Intel. They had heard of the floating point flaw in the Pentium processor and the story was about to blow up."[33]

This is how the information got to Steve Young, a reporter for CNN. A number of people who worked with Young sent him emails about the Internet postings concerning the Pentium. Reporters were just beginning to monitor Internet newsgroups for leads, and here, some of Young's friends felt, was one worth following up on. Young started receiving anonymous phone tips. Next came a call from NASA's Jet Propulsion Laboratory in Pasadena. Now he became seriously interested. The following day, Wednesday, November 22, CNN's *Moneyline* led with a segment on the Pentium. It was, Grove says, "a very unpleasant piece."[34] He was right. It was.

Young said that Intel discovered "the problem early this summer and removed it." As we know, that was only half true. The flaw was not removed. The history of this inaccuracy is not knowable. Was it an honest error by an Intel spokesperson? Was it an intentional falsehood? Did Young misunderstand what he was told? In any case, even accepting the inaccuracy, Young stated that "the bug is in at least 2 million chips," which presumably meant that two million computers were compromised.[35]

Young's telecast showed Intel once again being dismissive of the flaw. Stephen Smith, identified as "Pentium Engineering Manager," said, "If you measure the distance from the Earth to the sun, the one part [presumably he is referring to the defect] is on the order of feet, a few feet of difference relative to the measured distance between the Earth and the sun."

Young said that Intel had received only one complaint but that CNN had been in touch "with a dozen Pentium customers . . . who [have] lost confidence and there are hundreds of worried messages on the Internet." Despite the public relations fracas on the Internet, Intel would not issue a Pentium recall. "It says if a worried customer wants a replacement chip, Intel will decide if the customer really needs one."[36]

The CNN *Moneyline* report was picked up by newspapers around the nation, and soon by the press around the world. None of the stories were helpful to Intel. "Television reporters camped outside our headquarters," recalled Grove. "The Internet message traffic skyrocketed."[37]

Grove himself posted a message on comp.sys.intel on November 17. Being who he is, he faced reality: "[I]t's clear . . . that some of you are very angry at us." He apologized twice. However, the master communicator did not communicate masterfully in this message. What was required was something brief and clear, such as, "We apologize. We will replace every Pentium, no questions asked." Instead, readers got a lengthy message that varied in tone between common parlance and technical specifications. Grove himself must have sensed that his message was not as effective as it should have been. "Sorry to be so long winded," he wrote in the penultimate paragraph.[38] In spite of the continued drumbeat of criticism, "all tangible indicators," he later wrote, "from computer sales to replacement requests—showed that we were managing to work our way through this problem."[39]

The "tangible indicators" proved misleading. At this critical moment, Intel paid the price for the animosity of its customers. On December 12, IBM issued a press release that was also posted on the Internet. The headline read, "IBM Halts Shipments of Pentium-Based Personal Computers Based on Company Research." That morning Intel's stock plummeted from 67⅞ to 58¼ in an hour. The NASDAQ halted trading, hoping that a little breathing room would stabilize the situation.

This was a remarkably hostile gesture on IBM's part. If you need any proof that business can be tough, here it is. The hostility was evident not only in what IBM did, but in the way it was done. An IBM senior executive explained, "We believe no one should have to wonder about the integrity of data calculated on IBM PCs." Although this statement was issued by an underling, the action had been personally approved by Lou Gerstner.[40]

No one could argue with a company's desire to protect its customers by refusing to incorporate components of questionable quality in its product. But there was more going on than merely the pursuit of this laudable goal. One indication of the undercurrents at work was published remarks earlier in the year that "clearly IBM wants to wean itself from Intel microprocessors" and that "IBM is very, very committed to PowerPC."[41] In the words of an industry analyst, "If you believe [mathematical accuracy] is the only reason for [IBM's] announcement, I've got a bridge to sell you."[42]

Unmistakable proof that IBM's action was designed as much to stick a thumb in Intel's eye as it was to protect its customers was that it did not provide Intel with any advance warning of its decision. Intel's executives learned about it when the rest of the world did. Not long after the announcement, an IBM executive sent a fax to Intel explaining that no one had been able to find Andy Grove's phone number over the weekend.[43] This is such a lame explanation that one wonders why the fax was sent. Grove's home phone number was published and listed in the phone book.[44]

Lou Gerstner is a resourceful man. If he wanted to get in touch with Andy Grove on Saturday, December 10, or Sunday, December 11, it is difficult to believe that he could not have found a way to do so. If this capability really did elude him, IBM could have waited one more day. Halting shipments on the thirteenth would have served whatever purpose needed to be served as well as doing so on the previous day.

IBM's method of announcing the shipment halt was designed to inflict the maximum amount of discomfort at Intel headquarters at Santa Clara, and it succeeded. Given the three-hour time difference between East Coast and West Coast, Intel's employees began showing up at the Robert Noyce Building to discover their stock had fallen out of bed before they had gotten out of bed. This could not have done much for morale two Mondays before Christmas.

In his book *Who Says Elephants Can't Dance?: Inside IBM's Historic Turnaround*,[45] Gerstner makes no mention of the Pentium flaw or the manner in which IBM handled it. The book is neither comprehensive nor terribly enlightening, so this absence is not a surprise. Gerstner does, however, mention Grove among four of "the great CEOs I have known."[46] Great or not, when Gerstner saw the opportunity to whack Grove, he took it.

"All hell broke loose again" following IBM's announcement, Grove commented. "The phones started ringing furiously from all quarters." For years, ever since 1986, everything at Intel had been sunshine. Now a big black cloud covered the sky. People felt the chill not only at work but at home. Everyone was depressed.

As for Andy,

> I wasn't having a wonderful time either. I've been around this industry for thirty years [he wrote in 1996] and at Intel since its inception, and I have survived some very difficult business situations, but this was different. It was much harsher than the others. . . . I felt we were under siege—under unrelenting bombardment. Why was this happening?![47]

What was happening was that Intel had changed, the world's view of Intel had changed, methods of communicating that view had changed, and Intel's conception of itself had not kept pace.[48] The very talent that had enabled Grove and Moore to realize in 1985 that they had to get out of the memory business had disappeared by 1994. There is no application during this episode of that remarkable test Grove had proposed in 1985. "If new management were hired, what actions would the new team take?" Success had gone to everyone's head. They did not realize it. No one thought to ask this vital question.

Intel had grown spectacularly in the intervening years. Much of this growth was the result of grabbing along with Microsoft a leadership position in an industry in the midst of explosive growth. "The PC Is It!!" However, as Grove had confided to himself in his notebooks two decades earlier, "there is a growth rate at which *everybody* fails."[49] Intel had passed that point.

Much of that growth had taken place at the expense of other companies in the value chain. Discussing IBM's shipment halt, one of its executives was still complaining about what was by then the long-running Intel Inside campaign. Through it, he said, Intel was claiming that purchasers of IBM PCs were Intel's customers. "These are *our* customers," he insisted. "We're Intel's customer."[50]

The next Monday, one week after the IBM's bombshell, "we changed our policy completely," reported Grove. "We decided to replace anybody's part who wanted it replaced, whether they were doing statistical analysis or playing computer games." Finally, decisiveness! This was the first time since Professor Nicely's email that Intel got ahead of the publicity cycle. At last, Intel's top executives were making news, not just responding to it.

"This was no minor decision," Grove said, and he was right. No planning had been undertaken to implement it. How many chips would be returned? Who would staff the phone banks to handle the inevitable flood of questions that would inundate the company? Where would the replacement chips come from, given that there was little excess capacity in the fabs?[51] How much would all this cost? Intel would have to make up the answers to these and a host of other questions as it worked its way through this process.

The press release was issued on December 20: "Intel Adopts Upon-Request Replacement Policy on Pentium(™) Processors With Floating Point Flaw; Will Take Q4 Charge Against Earnings."[52] "Dr. Andrew S. Grove," not "Andy" in this announcement, had the following to say:

The past few weeks have been deeply troubling. What we view as an extremely minor technical problem has taken on a life of its own. Our OEM customers and the retail channel have been very supportive during this difficult period, and we are very grateful. To support them and their customers, we are today announcing a no-questions-asked return policy on the current version of the Pentium processor.

Our previous policy was to talk with users to determine whether their needs required replacement of the processor. To some people this policy seemed arrogant and uncaring. We apologize. We were motivated by a belief that replacement is simply unnecessary for most people. We still feel that way, but we are changing our policy because we want there to be no doubt that we stand behind this product.[53]

Actions speak louder than words. The fact was that, although it had taken him more than a month and a half to reach the correct answer, Grove was offering a no-questions-asked product replacement program. Anyone who asked could obtain a new Pentium that did not have the floating point flaw at no cost. This was not an inexpensive decision. "Ultimately, we took a huge write-off—to the tune of $475 million. . . . It was the equivalent of half a year's R&D budget or five years' worth of the Pentium processor's advertising spending."[54] No doubt about it, half a billion dollars is a lot of money.

Perhaps people simply reacted to the "no questions asked" policy and did not read the text of the press release too closely. When you do, you discover that it is too long ("We apologize. We'll replace every one without question" would have done fine), it is not quite accurate, and it adopts a querulous tone that ill befits an apology. Graciousness was called for.

To be specific, the announcement says that Intel's OEM customers have been supportive. That simply was not true. If IBM had been supportive or taken no action at all, the odds are that a no-questions-asked recall would not have taken place.

The problem, according to the statement, is that "an extremely minor technical" shortcoming had "taken on a life of its own." Following the apology is the assertion that Intel felt that a replacement was "simply unnecessary for most people. We still feel that way." Thus Intel was telling consumers that they wanted something they did not need, but the company had decided to indulge their irrationality. The whole statement lacks the consumer point of view. "This consumer, this end-user, who for whatever reason had spent money to have the latest, most advanced chip, didn't want it flawed— and certainly didn't want to be told that his or her work, whatever it was, wasn't sophisticated enough to merit a perfect chip."[55]

If you are going to spend this much money to fix a problem, you want to wring every ounce of goodwill from the gesture. Grove finds it difficult to give ground in the heat of battle, however, and this phraseology was the result. We know better, he was in essence saying, but we'll do it your way.

One posting on comp.sys.intel the day of the press release captured the dilemma.

Does anybody else think that Intel's apology sounded a tad insincere? I wonder if they have really learned their lesson?

> When in the future we wish to deride
> A CEO whose disastrous pride
> Causes spokesmen to lie
> And sales streams to dry
> We'll say he's got Intel Inside(™).[56]

"What a year," is how the letter "To our stockholders" began in the 1994 *Annual Report*. For the Pentium, this year was "the best of times . . . and the worst of times."[57] Nothing to complain about on the top line of the income statement. Sales surged to $11.5 billion, an increase of 31 percent over 1993. Despite this jump, an increase of 9 percent greater than the 22 percent annualized growth rate over the preceding decade, Intel's Fortune 500 ranking declined from 56 to 90. Profits declined three-tenths of a percent to $2.288 billion, which would not have been the case had the Pentium recall not become a necessity. Earnings per share edged up four cents to $5.24.[58] Market capitalization also increased slightly, 2 percent, to just under $26.5 billion. The financial consequences of the recall certainly were not happy, but neither were they devastating.

Nevertheless, the whole experience was a bitter pill to swallow. "What was hardest to take," Grove later wrote, "was the outside world's image of us." He wanted the world to look at Intel as he did: as a vibrant, upstart innovator at the cutting edge of technology. "Yet now the world seemed to view us like some typical mammoth corporation. And, in the public view, this corporation was giving people the runaround."

Amid the blizzard of blistering attacks on Intel, there was one newspaper article of which Grove approved. He still recalled it vividly in 2005, eleven years after it was published.[59] The author was T. R. Reid, and his article was published in the *Washington Post* the day after Christmas in 1994.

Reid argued that Intel's "surrender" in the "Great Pentium War" was "a victory of public relations over common sense." Millions of people who would never encounter "the obscure math bug" might wind up getting new chips. This action set "a new standard for PC equipment: perfection, or complete replacement." "I wonder," he added tellingly, "how many other companies will really be willing to meet this high standard."

IBM forced the recall upon Intel. Now "the same rules are going to apply to any IBM product." But that was not the real problem. IBM was big and could afford a product recall if one were necessary. The more important problem was that of "smaller PC firms and software companies that can't afford to ship a whole new product for free to anyone who asks." If "innovative, dedicated" start-ups are driven out of the industry, "the PC business is going to get safer—and duller—real fast."[60]

After Grove brought this article to my attention, he said with a certain dejection that unfortunately Reid was forced to recant. On February 6, Reid published an article in which he declared, "I stand corrected, criticized, cudgeled, crunched and categorically castigated by readers from coast to coast who did not agree—not even a little bit—with my recent column defending Intel Corp. in the matter of the Great Pentium War."

The argument of Reid's numerous critics was that companies were obliged to sell products that operated properly or replace them. It came down to honesty. Reid admitted to being won over by this point of view in its "stark simplicity." "I've come to the conclusion that the readers were right and I was wrong. . . . So you can call this column an 'upgrade'—and a free one at that."[61]

What happened? Grove asked, and why did it happen at this juncture?[62] After the event, when the fury of battle was no longer upon him and he was able to let his pensive side assert itself, he came up with two answers to his own questions.

First, the Intel Inside program had succeeded to a remarkable degree. Intel's research in 1994 showed that recognition of the Intel logo ranked with such consumer products as Nike and even Coca-Cola.[63] This is another one of those developments in Intel's history that never should have taken place. How could the manufacturer of a component buried inside a computer that the consumer never saw and that most people did not understand become this well-known?

Unexpected though it may have been, Intel had become a consumer product marketer with a global brand. Unlike Nike and Coca-Cola, however, no one at Intel had any experience at brand management. Intel executives quickly recognized that a brand is a valuable asset when things were going well. When things did not go well, however, Grove saw firsthand how "our merchandising pointed the users directly back to us."[64]

The second explanation upon which Grove alighted was "our sheer size. . . . And we were still growing fast—faster than most large companies. We had become bigger than most of our customers, companies that I remembered from our earlier years at Intel to be monumentally large corporations. At some point along the way, like a kid who suddenly looks down at his father, our sizes reversed."[65] Here, then, we have another case of marching backward into the future.

There was a third factor at work in the Pentium flaw story, and its impact is difficult to evaluate. That is the Internet.

Professor Nicely set this whole train in motion with emails that he dispatched on October 30. Email is transmitted from sender to recipient via the Internet and indeed has been viewed as the Internet's first "killer app"—that is, the first use, or application, of the Internet that was magnetic in attracting users. Email has proven itself to be a vital new way to communicate and is now used by millions if not billions of people around the world multiple times every day.

Recall Grove's comment concerning the PowerPC microprocessor. The world of high technology "is littered with the carcasses of good technical ideas because no one could find a use for them."[66] It is very easy for technologists to fall in love with what they are doing and forget that what they are doing has to do something for a customer that the customer is willing to pay to have done. They mistake the world of business for an engineer's sandbox. This is precisely what the Internet was not, and email proved it.

Email was something people wanted with a passion. It was an Internet application that customers pulled out of technologists, rather than a product technologists had to push onto an unwilling or puzzled market. It ranks with Web browsers (Netscape was the first, but was overwhelmed by Microsoft's Internet Explorer) and search engines (of which Google is king of the hill at present) in turning the Internet into the all-purpose appliance that, once having appeared, people could not figure out how they managed without.

An illustration of how important email has become is one of the stories coming out of the prosecution of Microsoft for violating the antitrust laws by the antitrust division of the Justice Department of the federal government during the latter half of the 1990s. The government demanded a great many documents, and Microsoft produced them. "Remarkably," according to two reporters for the *New York Times* who covered the proceedings, "the most damaging documents—the ones that galvanized the resolve of state and federal prosecutors nationwide—were written months after the first government request arrived, months after Microsoft's leaders knew that everything they were writing was likely to wind up in plaintiffs' hands."[67]

It is more than remarkable, it is incredible that executives at Microsoft would continue to write emails that they knew could and would be used against them in litigation that would determine the future of the company. Why on earth did they do it? According to William H. Neukom, Microsoft's chief counsel, email was essential to managing Microsoft, and effective management of the company would not be possible unless email communication was honest and blunt. He said, "Email is a big part of how we run this company, and candid, frank, open email communication is a big part of our efficiency."[68] Bill Gates's father, who, remember, was a successful lawyer, said that Neukom and his staff should have warned Microsoft's executives to be careful about what record they were making through their emails from as early as 1990, when the government started taking an interest in Microsoft's conduct. But no education program was instituted.[69]

What is it about email that is so appealing, that turned it literally into a "killer app" in Microsoft's case? This is not an easy question to answer. One observation we can make is that if you think of all the ways that human beings have of communicating with one another, running the gamut from intimate, face-to-face conversation between two people to a television broadcast aimed at many millions, email is something new under the sun. It establishes a new, and to many people, uniquely comfortable distance between people. Unlike traditional mail, often referred to as "snail mail" these days, email appears instantaneously on your computer or your PDA. If you are online, you can read it and respond. Your correspondent does not know if you are online, so you have the option of not responding without giving offense or of responding at a later time.

On the other hand, if you or your email correspondent are online simultaneously, you can carry on a dialogue in typescript almost as quickly as if you were conversing face-to-face or over the telephone. You can also send attachments containing presentations or pictures to your correspondent instantaneously.

Unlike a phone call, there is an impersonality to contact through email that can be especially user-friendly if you are getting in touch with someone you do not know. Also unlike a phone call or a face-to-face conversation, email can be asynchronous. Two parties do not have to be present simultaneously in order to communicate. In an increasingly globalizing economy, this is a noteworthy advantage over a phone call. You are able to communicate with business associates in India while working half a world away in Silicon Valley without inconveniencing them.

Unlike a telephone call, email permits you to express your complete thought precisely without being interrupted. You do not have to respond in the moment, so you can take time to consider what you want to say and how you want to express yourself. An email conversation is thus more relaxed.

In the early 1980s, when email first started to be used in some corporations, one began to hear about the "paperless office." "Paper-free in 1983" was the battle cry of the Reliance Insurance Company of Philadelphia.[70] We are not there yet. Like voice recognition, it is a goal we appear to be approaching asymptotically. Nevertheless, the fact is that email does not require paper. Your computer keeps the record of what you have sent and received.

In addition to point-to-point communication, email facilitates point-to-mass communication. A newsgroup such as comp.sys.intel was both. By sending an email to its site, you could respond to a previous email and also make a statement that everyone with access to the site through the Internet could read. The number of such people was rapidly increasing. In 1994, 5 percent of American households had Internet access. The following year that figure increased over 50 percent to 8.2 percent. It continued to rise quickly.[71]

This new way of communicating provided an answer to the question of why one should gain access to the Internet. The Internet created a platform for user-created content delivered in a new way. It created new communities, such as the group of people who monitored comp.sys.intel.

There is one final aspect of the spread of email that is more than incidental to its popularity. If you are part of an organization that subscribes to an email service, your emails are free, whether personal or business-related. Because you view them on a screen, there is no need to purchase stamps or stationery.

What role did email specifically and the Internet in general play in the story of the Pentium flaw? Professor Nicely used it to inform various people that there was something the matter with his microprocessor. It is easy to send multiple emails. No paper to xerox. No envelopes to seal. No stamps to buy. The message was transmitted in a matter of milliseconds. The people whom he contacted proceeded to contact others by email. By November 3, two newsgroups, Canopus and comp.sys.intel, carried postings on the Pentium flaw. This all took place very quickly. There was no reaction from Intel, nor was there an indication that anyone in authority at the company was monitoring news about it in what has come to be known as "cyberspace."

The managing editor of *Electronic Engineering Times* did read the story, but the article he wrote merely suggested that a problem had been found and fixed. Intel did have a spokesman comment for this article. His use of "errata" when he should have said "erratum" may not have inspired confidence in some, but the issue seemed settled.

It seemed settled, that is, until CNN showed up, very uninvited, at Intel's door in Santa Clara. Now there was no choice but to respond. The information had reached CNN's reporter through emails from colleagues who monitored Internet sites. Those sites did not go away. They were not thrown out with the trash. They remained alive and available, ticking time bombs.

CNN's report was picked up by the general-circulation press. A bit earlier, Grove posted his first notice on comp.sys.intel, apologizing for any inconvenience the controversy may have caused. After that, the storm seemed to abate, and there is no reason to think that Intel would have changed its policy to one of no-questions-asked replacement if nothing further happened.

But something further did happen. IBM caught Intel by surprise—Intel's unpreparedness is a theme in its management of this dilemma—by issuing a press release and posting it on the Internet announcing the shipment halt. By now, people were beginning to make jokes about the Pentium. For example:

Q: Why did Intel call this chip the Pentium instead of the 586?

A: Because if they had stuck with numbers they would have had to call it the 585.9999999.

This kind of mockery is deadly for a brand.

Only on December 19, when Intel announced its no-questions-asked recall policy, did the company get ahead of the carpet bombing it had been suffering. Even that change did not quiet all complaints immediately, but it did put them on the road to their ultimate extinguishment. The brand survived and today remains one of the strongest in the world.

Early in this episode, Craig Barrett had suggested that Intel simply give a new chip to anyone who asked for it. "And I said no!" recalled Grove. "I mean, that's ridiculous! Where do we stop? Then somebody's not going to like something else about it. Do we just forever replace chips? I mean, we've got a specification, the stuff meets specifications."

For Grove, the problem was one of point of view. "I'm inside my skin. I'm inside this company. I've dealt with quality problems for 30 years and that's not how we deal with quality problems. You analyze them and you go into the factory and explain it to the customer." For Grove, decision-making was dictated by his attitude. "I was being self-righteous. 'I'm right, I'm right, go away,' that kind of thing. It was largely an attitude issue and it was largely me."[72]

There are few people who were at Intel during the great Pentium flaw episode who would disagree with Andy's assessment. So often during his career, both before and after this incident, Grove's greatness as a manager has been a story of point of view. He has been able to abstract himself from the passions of the moment and be not only a participant but an evaluator, not only the actor on the stage but a member of the audience.

For some unknown reason, he was not able to adopt that special perspective this time. Perhaps, subtly and without realizing it, his perspective had been warped by the success he and Intel enjoyed from his ascendancy to the position of CEO in 1987 to late 1994 when this storm cloud burst.

Perhaps Grove had committed the cardinal sin of the engineer by falling in love with the product rather than the customer. One of the reasons he was so determined to sole-source the 386 back in the mid-1980s was that "Finally we had a real winner of a device."[73] This was in stark contrast to the general view of the 8088, which despite its fabled design win at IBM, was, even at Intel, viewed as a technically inferior product. A week prior to the design win, an Intel executive called the 8088 "the Edsel of microprocessors."[74]

If the road from the inferior 8088 to the winner 386 was a long one, the road to the Pentium was as well. Everything surrounding the Pentium launch—the naming of the product, its announcement—had been a celebration. Now this great new product was being trashed by some mathematical calculations at IBM that were incorrect and a horde of Internet addicts and reporters who knew nothing about the product.

There were plenty of reasons to get upset, but merely getting upset never solved a problem. Grove needed to rise above this situation and was unable to do so. He "kept thinking like an engineer and waded into the online mob himself, as though it were purely a technical debate."[75]

Karen Alter was there, saw it all, and couldn't get over the turmoil. Walter Mossberg of the *Wall Street Journal* told her that he had seen Watergate and Intel's cover-up was worse. As for Andy, according to Alter, "he couldn't believe, on the one hand, that people were so stupid. And at the same time, he was so furious at a couple of his general managers, who never really recovered in his eyes, that they had let the flaw get into production, that they hadn't found it earlier. . . . He was just mad. He needed to be mad at somebody."[76]

Another key executive who was present at the time has a different recollection of the same events. According to him, Andy publicly exonerated the engineers involved in the problem. This executive remembers Andy saying that you don't punish people for making mistakes; you admit the mistakes and correct them. Which is what he personally did with regard to the flaw (although, as this executive observed, it took a couple of months).

Perhaps, most important, Grove "couldn't believe that things were not in his control. . . . [He] just had no ability to control it. He freaked out. He was just a mess."[77] The hero of this story turns out, in Alter's opinion, to be Craig Barrett, "who has ice in his veins. He just stepped up and got us organized. . . . Okay, we have to build a machine to deal with this. We had a press machine and a Wall Street machine, and an OEM communications machine." Craig said the company would redesign what needed to be fixed and "get the new thing into production while not screwing everything up in the marketplace."[78]

In retrospect, can we say that this is a story of the power of the Internet? Perhaps. Intel would have probably toughed it out with its old policy had it not been for IBM's action. Nevertheless, a review of the chain of events leading to IBM's shipment halt does show the Internet playing an important role at a number of key moments.

Grove certainly decided to pay closer attention to it. Asked by Harvard Business School casewriters, by email, whether Intel was going to monitor the Internet more carefully, Grove replied, "Yes. We are much more active on the Internet and also on on-line services. These turn out to be very powerful ways to deliver customer support to a segment of our end customers. We also have plans to use the WWW [World Wide Web] more actively."[79] Grove had already begun dividing companies into two categories: those that used email and those that did not.

As he put it,

> Companies that use email are much faster, much less hierarchical. . . . From the moment you [use email] yourself, you're available to anybody and everybody. The elimination of the screening process in my email . . . tends to lead to . . . a more democratic way of operating. . . .
>
> How will this change companies? There are two companies—one that operates this way and one that doesn't, competing with each other.

After imagining these two hypothetical competitors, Grove asked the key question: how will the company that does not use email "stick around"? "[Y]ou're either going to do it or you disappear."[80]

The Internet was a signal, not noise.[81] The story of the Pentium flaw deserves a chapter in any history of the Internet just as it does in a history of Intel and a biography of Grove.[82]

20

---✦---

Life Is What Happens While
You're Making Other Plans

In 1993, the physician whom Grove and his family had been seeing for two decades retired. So they had to find a new physician. Andy's administrative assistant, Karen Thorpe, "got a kick out of this process, because he just interviewed doctor after doctor. Most people would not have been so systematic. They would have gotten a recommendation from a friend or something like that. Anyway, he finally chose this one young doctor."[1] In the autumn of 1994, Andy had an appointment with this new young doctor for a routine physical. Grove was fifty-eight years old and felt perfectly healthy.

The doctor ordered that a PSA test be run. PSA stands for "prostate specific antigen." Most men over fifty have this test taken regularly. To Grove's recollection, this was the first PSA he had ever had drawn.

The healthy prostate gland emits PSA in small amounts. An elevated PSA is probably, not certainly, evidence that something is provoking the prostate that should not be. That something may be, but is not necessarily, cancer. Acceptable levels of PSA at the lab that processed Grove's blood work ran from 0 to 4. Grove's result was 5. "It's slightly elevated," said his doctor. "It's probably nothing to worry about, but I think you should see a urologist."

The doctor did not treat this as an urgent matter, so Andy did not either. In the fall of 1994, he had plenty of urgent matters at the office. He did, however, mention this finding to his younger daughter, Robie, who has an advanced degree in a health care field. (His older daughter, Karen, has a master's in mechanical engineering.) She put him in touch with a physician who had just finished an article on testing for prostate cancer. The article led to a phone conversation that led Grove to the conclusion that PSA tests were not a good idea. "[M]y eagerness to see a urologist, not very high to start with, waned some more."

Early in 1995, Grove had another sabbatical planned, during which he was going skiing and working on a book. The PSA question wended "its way back to my consciousness." He logged on to CompuServe to find out more about it. A decade earlier, he might have phoned a friend with access to a library in order to learn more about PSA testing. But in 1995, the Internet was upon us, and Grove had just had a lesson about its reach and richness through the Pentium flaw episode.

CompuServe was the largest online service in the United States by the mid-1980s. It was a closed, proprietary environment that you could join by purchasing an account at a computer store to log in.[2] You got online through a dial-up modem, and you were charged an hourly rate. The charges dropped sharply in the early 1990s, from $10 to $1.95 an hour, and usage increased rapidly. By April 1995, CompuServe had three million subscribers. It has been described in the early 1990s as "enormously popular, with hundreds of thousands of users visiting its thousands of moderated Forums, forerunners to the endless variety of discussion sites on the Web today."[3] One of those users early in 1995 was Andy Grove. He visited the forum on prostate cancer, "where patients and relatives of patients swapped stories, asked questions of each other, and gave answers. The term PSA was mentioned in every message."

Grove printed out a paper posted by the chief of urology at Stanford. From it, he learned that two hundred thousand men had been diagnosed with prostate cancer in 1994. Thirty-eight thousand were expected to die of it. The treatment options, as his daughter's physician friend had said, "were all lousy." Most common was surgery. "It's major surgery, with a long recovery period and pretty bad side effects. . . . I read a posting on the forum by an airline pilot who had undergone this surgery and was bitter beyond words. He claimed that it cost him his health, his job and his marriage, and that it ruined his life."

Grove's most important lesson was that PSA was a tumor marker. A higher number meant a larger tumor. He decided to have the test performed again. Not trusting to its accuracy, he decided "to test the tests." Samples of his blood were sent to two different laboratories. The results illustrated what many of us have had occasion to learn. We are all one lab report away from catastrophe.[4] Six point zero was the result from one lab, six point one from the other. Something was provoking the prostate to release greater levels of PSA. In a situation like this, cancer is a prime suspect.

The next step was an appointment with a urologist, who performed a manual examination and detected nothing unusual. He also biopsied some tissue.

Andy's administrative assistant from 1985 to 2000 was Karen Thorpe. Highly competent, this former high school physical education teacher took Andy's calls, including calls involving doctors and dentists. Shortly after he chose his new physician, she noticed that he started receiving phone calls from different doctors. "In the back of my mind, I thought, 'I haven't heard this doctor's name before.' And he would say, 'If doctor so-and-so calls, get me out of my meeting, OK?' So I knew that it was important."[5]

One day, Grove has written, Thorpe's "face appeared in the conference room window. I could see from her look that it was the call I was expecting." It was his urologist. "Andy you have a tumor. It's mainly on the right side; there's a tiny bit on the left. It's a moderately aggressive one. There are only slim odds that it has spread."

I once said to Grove that the day you are told you have cancer is the worst day of your life. He disagreed as far as he was concerned. Some people reading this page have heard these words—"you have cancer"—about themselves or a loved one. Whether or not it is the worst day of your life, what ensues is not a conversation you forget.

Grove saw his urologist soon after the phone call. "He sat me down and told me my options: surgery, radiation, cryosurgery (in which the tumor is destroyed by freezing it), and, finally, doing nothing and playing the odds." What were those odds? As we have noted, 200,000 diagnoses; 38,000 deaths. After lung cancer, prostate cancer is the second leading cause of cancer deaths among men. Men are one-third more likely to contract prostate cancer than women are to get breast cancer.[6]

Andy's urologist told him that "surgery would have a pretty good chance of getting rid of [his] tumor." The chances of success with other treatments, the doctor implied, were lower. Was there a danger of complications with surgery? "Don't worry," said the urologist, "we can do something about each of those."

Andy "wanted to know more." He made appointments with a number of physicians who were expert in this field. "I also decided to dust off my research background and go directly to the original literature." He began "plotting and cross-plotting the data from one paper with the results from another." Eva was doing a lot of library work to assist in this information gathering.

At work, Grove continued his usual pace. Only one person at the office knew of his diagnosis, Karen Thorpe. "It got to the point," she recalls, "where I just knew something was wrong." At length, she asked him if he was all right. He mumbled something and then told her he would talk to her.

Grove told her all about the situation and asked her to keep it strictly confidential. Thorpe is someone who is capable of keeping confidences. It took Grove a while, she recalls, "to know the scope of it and to know what he was going to do. He proceeded to come in every morning with the graphs he had made the previous evening. And so every morning we'd do a little rundown on his prostate cancer." Thorpe was "very much in the loop" as far as the disease was concerned, but no one else at Intel was.[7]

Grove found the numerous medical studies he assembled to be "overwhelmingly confusing" at first. "But the more I read, the clearer they got, just as had been the case when I was studying silicon devices [in the mid-1960s]. That added a strange element of enjoyment to a process that was, overall, very scary."

The more deeply Grove researched prostate cancer through interviews, through listening to tapes of meetings with titles such as "Prostate Cancer Shootout," and especially through reading technical journals, the clearer it became to him that there was nothing that could be called general agreement on how this illness should be treated. Each approach had its own adherents. Once a researcher became a member of a particular congregation he rarely converted to a different denomination. Instead, he would do more research to prove his assumptions.

There is sociology, politics, and money involved in clinical and academic medicine, just as there is in everything else. Physicians and scientists are human. They develop emotional attachments to certain approaches to problems. They desperately need grants, and the number of proposals submitted vastly exceeds the number funded.

After listening to the tape of the "Prostate Cancer Shootout," a distressingly flippant title for a meeting about a life-and-death issue, Grove "could sense the undercurrents of strong disagreement, couched in polite, faux-respectful terms." Perhaps "shootout" was, if unfortunately cute, the proper metaphor for that meeting. People did not seem to approach the topic with an open mind, anxious to be convinced if they should change their point of view. They came to say what they had said in the past and would say in the future. "The tenors always sang tenor, the baritones, baritone, and the basses, bass."

When one is facing life-and-death medical choices, disagreement among doctors can drive you to despair. You don't expect miracles, but you do want to make the choice that gives you the best chance of survival with the fewest side effects. At all costs, you want to avoid looking back upon a choice you made and saying, "If only I had approached this differently." You do not want to be in the position of that airline pilot whose posting Andy had read on CompuServe who survived the disease but whose life was ruined by side effects.

How do you make the right choice? You have two types of data at your disposal. One is anecdotal. You can talk to people who have had your illness or to doctors whose specialty it is. In the age of the Internet, you can gather such information from a chat room in cyberspace.

Anecdotes are useful. They demonstrate that extreme cases, though rare, are real. What happened to that airline pilot might happen to you. But it also might not. This is a weak reed upon which to lean.

Then there are studies in peer-reviewed academic journals. These studies must satisfy certain rules. Often they are based on a sample of patients and adhere to accepted statistical guidelines in the analysis of the data gathered. This sounds good; but in instances in which there is not a consensus, these studies can generate confusion. They are next to impenetrable to the layperson. Most troubling, *you* are not a large sample. *You* are an individual. These studies leave the reader with probabilities. But how do you make a choice on the basis of probabilities when you may die or the quality of your life may be ruined even if you survive?

Let us take a simple, nonmedical example to illustrate just one aspect of the dilemma. Suppose you listen to three weather forecasts. One says there is a 30 percent chance of rain, one 50 percent, and the last 70 percent. What conclusion can you draw from such data? Perhaps you should conclude that there is a 50 percent chance of rain. What does that mean? It means it will either rain or it will not, which you knew before the forecast. What proof can be offered that the 50 percent probability was accurate? What if it does rain the following day? For all you knew, the forecast was wrong. Perhaps the chances of rain were really 100 percent, and that was the accurate probability.

When the outcome of your decision is not whether or not to carry an umbrella but whether you will live or die, such questions take on a compelling urgency that is difficult to communicate to those who have not been through the experience. Often, the patient selects a physician who, for whatever reason, has gained his or her trust, and the patient then does what the expert recommends. Grove, however, was not a man to take issues such as this on faith. "As a patient whose life and well-being depended on a meeting of minds, I realized I would have to do some cross-disciplinary work on my own."

What Grove discovered was that the PSA test was the key to the early detection of prostate cancer and to its recurrence. Understanding the significance of the PSA test also helped Grove understand the technical papers he was studying. An ultrasound reading indicated that there was a 60 percent chance that his tumor had metastasized, that is, spread, beyond the prostate gland itself. This is a very bad development. Metastatic cancer is far more difficult to treat than is a tumor in a defined and confined location.

Through his studies, Grove learned that this information should not have come as a surprise. In one of the papers he came upon, he found a table that correlated a set of diagnostic findings prior to treatment with the extent of the disease as it became known after surgery. The table showed that for a PSA of 6, there was a 60 percent chance that the tumor had metastasized. The research on a large patient population thus supported the findings of the ultrasound on patient Andrew S. Grove.

Further research indicated that prostate cancer tended to recur more frequently in patients with higher PSAs when first diagnosed. All forms of treatment had a better chance of eliminating the disease if it were caught early. Putting all the data together, Andy calculated that surgery did not cure everybody. His "recurrence rate in ten years worked out to about 40%. I wasn't crazy about those odds."

Then there was the issue of side effects. Examination of this evidence provides a good example of the problems confronting a patient trying to make decisions based upon medical literature. "According to the surgeons who write papers," Andy found, "the side effects were not so bad." Surgeons and patients, however, tend to evaluate side effects quite differently. "Minor" surgery has been defined as "surgery that happens to somebody else."[8]

When Andy found the results of "a study that questioned a large group of patients directly," the answers were "alarming." "The reports of incontinence and impotence were dramatically worse . . . leaving me to wonder whether patients described these things more pessimistically to a third party than to their doctors, or whether patients in the second study were more representative of the work and results of urologists all over the United States, as compared with leading practitioners." Either way, the articles left Andy anxious to explore other treatment options.

What about radiation? The side effects seemed to be less severe, but its efficacy was hard to evaluate. Most urologists assumed that surgery was the best option. Andy did not like "assumptions." The results of this particular assumption was a "selection bias." "[Y]ounger and healthier patients [with smaller tumors] are selected for surgery, leaving the older, less healthy patients with more advanced tumors to make up the bulk of the patient population that undergoes radiation therapy. The results in the latter class are, of course, worse—reinforcing the spiral that sends the early-stage patients to surgery and the later-stage patients to radiation."

However, Grove found that a sufficient number of patients had overcome this selection bias to make outcome studies on healthier subjects who selected radiation possible. When the PSA was low because the tumor was discovered at an early stage, radiation results were much improved. "When I took the radiation treatment data [on early-stage patients] and compared them with the surgical data, matching the initial PSAs of the patient populations as best I could, the outcomes were not that different, at least at five years after treatment." This kind of data was not yet available ten years out.

Grove was having to undertake these comparisons because they were not a part of the work of the medical researchers themselves. It was standard practice in semiconductor research to compare your results with others. In medicine, by contrast, researchers "tended to publish their own data; they often didn't compare their data with the data of other practitioners, even in their own field, let alone with other types of treatments for the same condition. So I kept on doing cross comparisons."

There were, Grove found, two approaches to radiation therapy. One consisted of "bombarding the area of the prostate, selectively causing more destruction of the cancerous cells than of the healthy ones." The second involved "implanting radioactive seeds directly into the gland." The problem with this approach was that it had in the past been difficult to guarantee that the seeds were implanted at the key positions. If not placed properly, parts of the tumor would be untreated and would therefore grow and metastasize.

By 1995, however, new imaging machines enabled doctors to place the seeds more precisely where they were needed. The seeds remained in the body, releasing radiation for between six and nine months until they decayed. Seed therapy, or brachytherapy to use its technical name, could be supplemented by bombardment by external radiation, to make sure all the bases were covered.

Grove could not find much published information on radioactive seed therapy so he phoned the technical support group of the company that made the product. He got a lot of good information and useful leads for more data. Then, in the midst of this process, a paper was published that contained the first data on how patients fared with this approach ten years out. The result? Outcomes from seeds and surgery "were very, very similar."

Instead of resolving issues, Grove's search for information only led to further complexity. He received word of "yet another procedure, a variant of the seed technique called high-dose radiation. In this technique, a highly radioactive seed is attached to a wire that is momentarily inserted into the patient's prostate . . . under local anesthesia. The results . . . seemed even better than with regular seed therapy, especially when it came to side effects."

These findings were sufficiently intriguing to warrant a trip to two physicians in Seattle, one of whom left the seeds in, the other of whom used high-dose radiation with the seeds inserted and then removed. What appealed to Grove most about the high-dose radiation was that it was "customizable to an individual case."

This is what every patient dreams of, personalized medical treatment. You could irradiate the tumor while minimizing the exposure of surrounding organs to radiation, thus minimizing side effects. "I sat in [this doctor's] office absorbing the elegance of this technique." Grove then asked this doctor a question doctors hear often: if you had what I have, what would you do? The doctor pondered for a moment and then replied, "I would probably have surgery." This response would drive a lot of people to distraction. The doctor who specialized in radiation for his patients would choose surgery for himself! Grove does say he was "utterly confused." On the brighter side, he had gathered "some unpublished data from the two seed doctors that I could add to my charts."

There was one more approach that appeared on Grove's radar. This was cryosurgery, which used tools and techniques to freeze the tumor. There were no reliable data on this approach, and from what Grove was able to gather, the side effects were serious. This, therefore, he was able to eliminate.

Yet more information indicated that hormone treatment could shrink the tumor. Since smaller tumors were always preferable under any treatment approach, Grove began this regimen. The side effects, "supposedly temporary," were mild diarrhea and a loss of interest in sex. After all this information seeking, treatment had begun.

Meanwhile, Grove kept seeing surgeons to gather yet more information. The three he consulted "were ferociously opposed to the combination radiation therapy, or any radiation therapy whatsoever." One brought up the possible need for a colostomy if radiation were selected, which "scared me enormously." Another argued that radiation would not result in a PSA of zero as surgery often did. "This puzzled me. Since some PSA is generated by the prostate itself and radiation does not destroy the prostate tissue, why shouldn't the patient end up with some PSA after treatment?"

Grove then observes, "The conversation got so heated that my question was never answered." Why such heat? One can speculate that the strain of all this work and the parade of horribles that were being marched past Grove were beginning to take a toll on his nerves. He was probably beginning to take a toll on the nerves of the doctors he was consulting. Most, not all, physicians and even more—once again, not all—surgeons encounter very few patients like Andy Grove and are quite alien to "Intel culture." Physicians and surgeons are used to having "position power" with regard to the people they treat. They are the "doctors." Patients are "patient." Their names are preceded by the honorific "doctor" and followed by the letters "MD." You are merely "Mr.," presuming you are a man, and even if your name were followed by "PhD," as was Grove's, you were not a "real" doctor. Especially in hospitals, you are often summoned to the inner sanctum of a doctor's office by a staff person who bellows out your first name to a waiting room full of anxious people. So much for patient confidentiality. You see doctors when they have time to see you, not the other way around.

It takes many years of formal, demanding training to achieve the eminence of the people Grove was seeing. They not only learned the old rules, they conducted studies that broke new ground. It is rare for them to encounter a patient like Grove who became a self-taught oncologist and cared nothing for position power. He went to the primary data, constructed his own charts, and expected a give-and-take between equals. One of the most startling aspects of this story is that Grove seemed more confident of his knowledge of the pros and cons of various treatments of prostate cancer than he was of microprocessor architecture during the RISC versus CISC controversy. I discussed what I considered this odd discrepancy with Robert Burgelman. In his view, the explanation is that the RISC/CISC issue was one among a welter of business issues that intruded on Grove's attention. The prostate dilemma was a matter of physical survival and therefore was in a class by itself.[9]

At any rate, following his visit to the surgeon that concluded unsatisfactorily with an unanswered question, Grove returned to one of the radiation oncologists. "To my surprise, he took a very evenhanded and unexcited position on the controversy" between surgery and radiation. He told Grove he had never encountered the need for a colostomy. Perhaps this procedure might have been necessary during the early days when excessive radiation might have been employed. Yet this was the man who had told Grove that in his position he would have surgery. "Why?" Grove asked him. "You know," he replied, "all through medical training, they drummed into us that the gold standard for prostate cancer is surgery. I guess that still shapes my thinking."

By July 1995, it was time for a decision. Grove took a long bicycle trip with his wife and some friends, during which he drew up a "balance sheet" assessing the pros and cons of all the approaches about which he had so painstakingly gathered information.

"One of the arguments that surgeons tended to make against radiation was that the long-term results—that is anything longer than ten years—were not as good as in surgery. That wasn't obvious from the data. PSA had only been around for ten years, so as far as I was concerned, both surgery and radiation had relevant data only for ten years or less. . . . But it occurred to me that if combination radiation, which looked better to me than external radiation by itself, only gave me ten years of freedom from disease, I could buy myself a ten-year reprieve relatively inexpensively, considering that it's a lot less onerous treatment." And who knew what breakthroughs in therapy might take place in a decade?

This line of thinking was only convincing if the combination radiation generated results as good as surgery in the first place. "All the surgeons said it didn't. The radiologists shyly suggested it did. I fell back on my data. I looked at my plots. The data said the treatments were the same—maybe even better for seeds." Grove "decided to bet on my own charts" and opted for high-dose radiation.

The procedure for the implantation of sixteen tubes through which irradiated needles were to be inserted into Grove's prostate would take place at a Seattle hospital beginning at 5:30 on a Tuesday morning. The previous day at work was packed, "which was wonderful: I didn't have a chance to think about Tuesday at all. But when I settled in on the late evening flight, the workday behind me, no computers, no phones, the anxiety hit. Although my wife was with me, I didn't feel like talking."

Over the next forty-eight hours, Grove was wheeled into the radiation room four times for insertion of radioactive seeds through the tubes. Various calculations were performed concerning the placement of the seeds and the duration that they should remain in the tubes. These calculations were performed on a computer. Grove asked about the microprocessor. It was a 286, which Intel had introduced in 1982 and discontinued in 1992. Not even a 386, introduced in 1985, never mind a 486, introduced in 1989, or a Pentium, which debuted in 1993.

On Thursday, Grove was discharged. "Altogether, I was out of work for three days." Nothing else happened until a few weeks later, when the external radiation began. This was undertaken at a local hospital and lasted for twenty-eight days. It was annoying and fatiguing, necessitating shorter workdays and afternoon naps. Then it was over. "I was done. No more hormones, no more radiation, no more naps." He suffered no side effects. No urinary incontinence. No impact on sexual function.

Andy Grove may yet have a recurrence of prostate cancer. He may die of the disease. But at this writing, more than a decade after the procedure just described, his PSA is normal and stable. There is every reason to believe he has been cured.

What lessons did Grove learn from this experience? Well-intended, well-informed physicians are likely to advocate the particular therapies around which they have built their careers. Therein lay a trap the patient had to avoid. "Investigate things, come to your own conclusions, don't take any one recommendation as gospel." Grove quoted a famous urologist: "[W]hen faced with a serious illness beyond our comprehension, [each of us] becomes childlike, afraid, and looking for someone to tell us what to do. It is an awesome responsibility for the surgeon to present the options to a patient with prostate cancer in such a way that he does not impose his prejudices which may or may not be based on the best objective information."

The story of Andy Grove and prostate cancer does not end here. Grove has always cultivated the press." Public relations," he has said, "is not an event. It's a process."[10] He paid special attention to *Fortune* magazine, and it was its pages wherein he decided to tell his prostate cancer story, from which the account in this chapter is drawn.[11] According to *Fortune*'s managing editor, John Huey, Grove "comes forth on this *Fortune* project with sincere reluctance, mostly because he is an intensely private man who strives to keep his personal and professional personas separate. Moreover, he has no interest ... in stirring up controversy with the medical establishment. So why," Huey asked, "do it?"[12]

Why, indeed? There were a lot of good reasons not to publish this article. Grove was at the height of his fame and power when this piece appeared. He was at the helm of a company that was at the center of global high technology. Intel had almost 50,000 employees at the end of 1996. Thousands more had worked at the company and moved on but remained on good terms with the executives there. Some people working for Intel had to be dealing with prostate cancer when the article came out. Many of those that were not must have had relatives and friends who were battling the disease. Now, all of a sudden, the leader of their company turned out to have dealt with the same horrible illness. Why not get in touch with him and ask his advice?

This question included far more than Intel employees. *Fortune* has a wide readership. Grove was world-famous. His picture on the magazine's cover made him seem so decent, so straightforward, so accessible. Not, perhaps, the same image as the average surgeon. Why not contact him?

People did, in large numbers. Grove told Karen Thorpe that he could not both run Intel and serve as a consultant on prostate cancer. As of May 13, 1996, she found herself with a new assignment.

"You can't imagine," Thorpe said, "how many phone calls came to our office from men who had prostate cancer." The calls came from people Grove knew and people he did not know. "They read the article and they called. They just called Andy Grove's office, and they got me," Thorpe said. "These people ... when you answered the phone, you could tell by their voice that it was another prostate cancer individual. Most of them would hem and haw. They wouldn't come right out and say, 'I read the article in *Fortune* magazine.' Half of them got the wrong magazine. They would say

Newsweek or *Forbes*. Then I would say, 'I think you're talking about the prostate cancer article in *Fortune*.' 'Yes. Yes. Yes,' would come the reply.

"Sometimes," continued Thorpe, "it wasn't the man himself but his wife who was so concerned. Some of them hadn't actually read the article. They had only heard about it. We offered to fax it or mail it to them. I had a list of doctors with their phone numbers who did the procedure Andy had in different parts of the country. I would fax this information out or mail it or sometimes just give it out over the phone.

Thorpe found herself empathizing with some very frightened and confused people. There were lots of inquiries, and it took a lot of effort. Especially when you consider that working for Andy was already a full-time job.[13]

Publishing this article turned Grove into the "poster boy" for prostate cancer. This generated a lot of work. It also has to have had the effect of keeping it on his mind. The article came out less than a year after his treatment was completed. There was no guarantee that his own illness would not recur. Only probabilities, which are not easy to rely on when your life is at stake. There were other arguments against writing this article. "I'll tell you," Karen Thorpe said, "that a lot of people in public relations at this company did not want him to write that article." They were worried about its potential impact on the price of Intel's stock.[14]

Grove wrote it because he had something to say. It was Grove who approached *Fortune* about the idea for this article. He was on a panel with some other CEOs and with John Huey, the managing editor of the magazine. Grove took Huey aside after the panel and broached the subject. Huey immediately grasped the impact this article might have. A decade ago, men were more reluctant to discuss prostate cancer than is the case today. To have a man of Grove's stature tell his story was a tremendous opportunity for *Fortune*, well worth the eight thousand words and extensive graphics the magazine allowed it. Huey himself was no stranger to cancer. His first wife died of it.

The United States was not the Hungary of Grove's youth. If he wanted to say something, he could. What he wanted to say was that every man over the age of fifty should know his PSA. It was an invaluable data point from which lifesaving action could develop. "PSA tests are a godsend. They give you the next best thing to not having cancer: They give you time."

There was a bigger message, which transcends the issue of prostate cancer. This bigger message deals with a way of living life. Specifically: Face facts. Take action on the basis of the facts you face. "I shared what happened to me and what I'd learned with a handful of friends and close associates. I learned that three of them had elevated PSAs. They were riddled with anxiety but hadn't done anything about it. I ran into another friend who had two relatives with prostate cancer, which greatly increases the likelihood of his getting it himself. Yet he hadn't had a PSA test."

Long ago, at his mother's knee in Hungary, Grove had learned that denial does not change reality, but it can make reality deadly. When his aunt Manci said to him in 1956, "Andris, you must go. You must go, and you must go immediately,"[15] he too may have been "riddled with anxiety," but he did do something about it. He acted. He left. It is quite possible that Grove's article helped people take action that might have saved lives.

The prostate episode provides us with a valuable avenue to learn about how Grove attacks a problem. First, he forces himself, as we have just observed, to face facts.

Second, he goes to a great deal of trouble to be certain that what passes as a fact deserves to be so regarded. Remember how he had his PSA tests performed at two labs, rather than one. When the results came back as 6.0 and 6.1, he could be pretty certain that his PSA was indeed rising. There could be no blaming a result on a lab error. In this way, Grove protected himself from the human desire to deny bad news.

Third, there is nothing he will not do to get the facts. When he could not find what he wanted to know about irradiated seeds in the published literature, he phoned the company that produced them.

Fourth, when it comes to the analysis of facts, Grove takes nothing on faith. Whenever possible, he gains access to raw data and analyzes the findings himself. That is what he had been doing at least since his doctoral dissertation.

Finally, Grove showed by his approach to prostate cancer that uncanny ability to abstract himself from a situation and view it objectively. Grove is most effective as a manager when he is able to be both the actor in a play and a member of the audience watching it. As an actor, he is the subject, the center of attention, who interprets the situation in the play as he sees it and acts his role accordingly. As a member of the audience, Grove adopts a wholly different point of view. He watches the other actors, the scenery, the lighting, and so forth through a different lens. The process of data gathering and especially data analysis helped him achieve this dual point of view. Those graphs made his situation objective.[16]

To be sure, this was very much about him. *He* was the patient. It was *his* tumor that had to be treated. That is why it was true personalized medicine. But it was also about line graphs and histograms that captured the experience of many other men facing not completely dissimilar situations who were treated at a half dozen different hospitals.

In a way, this was the 1985–1986 exit from the memory business all over again. Andy and Gordon made the decision, but only after they engaged in the exercise of abstracting themselves from the issue first. What if the board fired us and brought in new management? As soon as this key question forced the two of them to see the world through a new lens, to adopt a different point of view objectively and without the legacy of history, the answer became clear.

When Grove has not done as well as he might have with regard to business issues, one reason is that he has been unable to adopt this objective point of view. Intel may have been right and its critics wrong from a technical standpoint with regard to the Pentium flaw. However, Intel had passed the moment where a question like this could be settled by a technically rational response. What Grove had trouble appreciating in this instance was that the subjective perceptions of others, however misguided from his point of view, had become the objective reality with which he had to contend.

Taking a step back and evaluating Grove's experience with prostate cancer over the course of a decade, what conclusions can we draw?

Grove's analysis led him to choose a treatment option that was not preferred by most physicians who dealt with the disease. Even one of the doctors most committed to radiation therapy told Grove that in his position he probably would have surgery. Surgery was indeed viewed as the "gold standard." That was true, in Grove's view, for the wrong reasons. Specifically, the patients most likely to do well were encouraged to have surgery, so a selection bias was built into the data that Grove had to account for. Grove was and is an inveterate contrarian. Telling him something is the "gold standard" won't impress him.

Grove's treatment would appear to be a success. Would the same results have been achieved through surgery? We do not know. Might the disease recur? One cannot know that for certain either. Grove phoned me on October 2, 2004, the first anniversary of my wife's death from ovarian cancer, and said in passing that he thought he would eventually die of prostate cancer.[17] I mentioned this to his wife, Eva. Her response: "He'll die of something else."[18]

Grove's condition is presently monitored by Dr. Peter R. Carroll, the Ken and Donna Derr-Chevron Distinguished Professor of Urology at the University of California at San Francisco (UCSF). With Dr. Carroll's encouragement, Grove and other men have formed a "Prostate Advocacy Group" at UCSF of which Dr. Carroll, whom Grove once described as his idea of a leader, is also a member.[19] UCSF undertook a major fund drive early in this decade. Grove was asked to chair it, and he did. The goal of $1.4 billion was reached a year ahead of schedule.

Looked at from one point of view, this story is an inspiration. "[F]aced with a serious illness beyond our comprehension," this particular patient did not "[become] childlike, afraid, and looking for someone to tell [him] what to do." He showed that the most emotional of decisions, those concerning life and death, could be made on a rational basis.

Looked at from another point of view, this story is frightening. If this is the kind of effort and dedication that we all need to get proper medical care, what are our chances of doing so successfully?

Two footnotes.

First, a fact-checker on Grove's article at *Fortune* was a twenty-four-year-old kid just out of Williams College. As she was going over the article, she checked the charts and graphs Andy had so laboriously prepared. She found what she believed to be a mistake.

Think of this. A cub reporter finds an apparent error in technical work dealing with a very sensitive subject and written by an accomplished engineer who was also one of the world's leading CEOs. This particular CEO is famed for his bluntness and for not suffering fools gladly. What should the fact-checker do?

She told him her opinion. I don't think Andy was happy to hear her views, but knowledge power trumps position power in his world. So although he was a big shot and she was a zero, he rechecked the data she thought he had graphed improperly. It turned out she was right.

This cub fact-checker is Bethany McLean, and this encounter made her name at *Fortune*. McLean has become quite well-known. She is the lead author of the bestselling book on the Enron debacle, *The Smartest Guys in the Room*.[20] This outstanding book was made into a movie in 2005.

Bethany McLean is a smart young woman who majored in math at Williams and must have done her homework. Her comments on Grove: "[H]e is the extremely rare person who is brilliant, very successful, and very strong-willed—yet also immediately able to admit when he's wrong. When the story was going to print, he called my editor to ask where my reporter's credit was."[21] Andy gives credit where credit is due.

Here is how Andy himself narrates the encounter:

This is what happened.

Bethany was a researcher (those days they called them "reporters") assigned to my story. She was methodically going through factoids and all went well until she claimed she found an error in one of my graphs that I constructed from published data. After some back and forth, I conceded the point and nursed my wounded pride (the back and forth was heated at times).

After I recovered, I wrote her one of my handwritten notes, thanking her for her thoroughness.

During my next visit to Fortune a number of months later, I found out that the note and Bethany were much talked about. I asked to see her and in fact was introduced to her. In the process, I found out she was a boxer. Had I known that, I would have backed down earlier.

I was not surprised when she turned out to be an early debunker of the Enron financials.[22]

A second footnote.

The Fortune article must have been read very widely, if not universally, at Intel. Every reader would have learned that the CEO lost a grand total of three days of work while battling prostate cancer. This information must have had the effect, at least in some instances, of making an employee think twice before calling in sick because he or she had the sniffles. Grove has said that he did not intend that result, if it in fact did occur.

21

The Darwinian Device

On Tuesday, October 3, 1995, Andy Grove shared the stage of the PALEXPO conference hall in Geneva, Switzerland, for the opening ceremony of TELECOM 95, the Seventh World Telecommunications Exhibit, Forum, and Book Fair, with, among others, Nelson Mandela. Mandela, one of the most important political leaders in the twentieth century, was the key figure in bringing about the peaceful conclusion of apartheid in South Africa, of which he, a man who had been imprisoned for twenty-seven years, was elected president in 1994. The previous year he was awarded the Nobel Peace Prize.

In his address, Mandela declared that "in the 21st century, the capacity to communicate will almost certainly be a key human right. . . . I would wish to emphasize the importance [to] young people [of] the information revolution. Many of us here today spent much of our lives without access to telecommunications or information services, and many of us will not live to see the flowering of that information age. But our children will. . . . And it is our responsibility to give them the skills and insights to build the information societies of the future."[1]

This conclave in Geneva took place only a few weeks after the completion of the irradiation of Grove's prostate, but nevertheless, he looked terrific. Dressed in a brown suit with a rather elaborate corsage on the jacket's left lapel, Grove began his presentation by expressing gratitude at the invitation to address the telecommunications industry. He, after all, was from the computer industry (he no longer referred to Intel as a supplier of components to the industry), and as such was an outsider. But it is noteworthy that it was Grove, not Gerstner from IBM; Eckhard Pfeiffer, CEO of Compaq; Michael Dell; or Michael Spindler, CEO of Apple, who was speaking for the computer industry. Not so long ago, the PC had been "It." Now it appeared that Intel, not the original equipment manufacturers, could lay claim to being "It." The conference described its attendees as "communications specialists, manufacturers, operators, users, businessmen, telecommunications service providers, industrial and financial leaders, scientists, regulators, [and] equipment suppliers." Computers were not mentioned.[2]

This conference was a major event, with 133,000 visitors. Over a thousand companies mounted exhibits, and these were not cardboard cutouts from the local science fair. The exhibits of companies the size of, say, Motorola might cost a million dollars. In short, TELECOM 95 was a globally high-profile event. Andris Gróf had come a long way from Kiraly Street in Budapest.

What did Grove have to say when he took center stage? In his view, the telecommunications industry had reached a "strategic inflection point," a phrase he would make famous with the publication of *Only the Paranoid Survive* the following year. The telecommunications strategic inflection point was brought about by three forces: deregulation, increased competition, and digital technology. Working together, Grove believed, the computer and telecommunications industries could create a new infrastructure that would transform the global landscape of business, of the professions, of the academy, in short, of everything. It would impact people at play as well as at work.

To illustrate his point, Grove began his presentation with a high-risk, technology-intensive "demo." It consisted of a consultation in real time between two physicians in South Africa. The selection of South Africa was not accidental. Grove knew he would be preceded by Mandela. One of the physicians was located in Tintswalo Community Hospital, a rural health care facility located in Acornhoeck, and the other at the Johannesburg General Hospital. Both their faces were visible on the computer screen onstage, and this screen was projected to the huge display at the rear of the stage so as to be visible to the whole audience.[3]

In addition to the faces of the doctors, one could also see the image of an

X-ray of the patient whom they were discussing. After the doctors briefly conversed with one another, Grove introduced himself to them by way of his computer on the stage and asked them how they were managing with this technology.

Following this demo, Grove explained to the audience that computing power was increasing while its price was decreasing. As a result, it could be used, with the help of the telecommunications industry, to usher in a new era of interactive communication. People could talk to each other, see one another, and work with documents or artifacts such as that X-ray all at the same time despite being separated physically by a room or by ten thousand miles.

The next demo was with a Japanese saleswoman for Kawashima textiles. First on a desktop PC, then on a wireless notebook computer, Grove and the saleswoman spoke to a textile designer in Kyoto, Japan, about the carpeting in a hotel room. Grove asked for the color of the carpeting to be changed. The saleswoman told the designer in Japan of Grove's wish and the carpet's color was changed immediately with seeming magic.

The third demo picked up on Mandela's comments about the uses of communications technology for the world's youth. Forty-five percent of the 60 million PCs that Grove estimated would be sold in 1995 would be going into the home. Young people such as Clovis Casali, whom Grove visited onstage, could speak, see, and play games, such as Monopoly, on a board they could see on their computer screens, with friends around the world.

The theme of Grove's presentation, and of the whole conference, was "Smart Connections to the World," and Grove's goal was to show how close technology was to the achievement of those smart connections. He estimated that almost 20 million computer users were already connected through proprietary services such as CompuServe, AOL, or Europe Online or through the Internet, which he said might constitute the most important development of his business life and was likely to lead "to real ubiquity" in connectedness.

The computer was evolving before everyone's eyes, and this is why Grove labeled it a "Darwinian device." It was adapting to the demands of the environment.[4] Computers began their existence as tools to analyze quantitative data, as hyper-efficient number crunchers. They were still needed for that purpose, but by the mid-1990s the world was demanding that they provide access to information. That was one reason why the Internet, especially after the World Wide Web was put on it, became so important. Furthermore, it was in the nature of things, as Grove remarked later, that communications would be a larger market than computation. "We all communicate even if we don't all compute."[5]

The information, or "content," available through the Internet was quickly coming to consist of more than that professionally created through corporate Web pages or online encyclopedias. Grove's thesis was that the environment was calling in the mid-1990s for the transmission of user-created content. That is what his three onstage demos showed: people in real time communicating with each other. Looking at each other. And looking at documents, such as X-rays, or hotel rooms, the decor of which could be instantaneously transformed, or of games like Monopoly where one move could follow another.

That "Darwinian device," the computer, was ready. Grove was making an implicit appeal to the telecommunications industry to do its part and meet computers halfway. Issues such as bandwidth and the completion of networks that "last mile" to the homes of literally billions of willing consumers were the next challenges to be met to make possible both the reach and the richness of the communications experience that was now technically within the grasp of the human race for the first time in history.[6]

Grove did not mention an Intel product named ProShare during his presentation, but it was very much on his mind. In fact, he used it in his demos. ProShare was a system devised by Intel in the early 1990s and officially launched in January 1994 that was designed to do what Grove was showing the world in his TELECOM '95 speech.

Grove told Robert Burgelman that ProShare "came together bit by bit. It started in 1987 with our purchase of [a company] that produced special video-processing chips. We had this idea of applying video technology to the PC but nothing ever seemed to come out of it." There was a lot of talk, but the chain of ideas from "rich email" to videoconferencing did not seem to go anywhere.

In 1991, Andy was scheduled to give the keynote speech at COMDEX. He had decided to fish rather than cut bait with ProShare, and the COMDEX presentation would get this fishing expedition going. The presentation was designed to provide a vision of the "New Computer and Communications Industry."

As was so often the case, the Grove style was "show first, then tell." The result had him striding around the stage from one workstation to another showcasing a vision as he delivered the COMDEX presentation in a large auditorium in Las Vegas. Grove, as we know, dislikes the word "visionary," but that was the role he was playing for the sixty-one minutes he spoke at COMDEX on October 21, 1991, with the eyes of the industry glued to him. He was describing his view of the direction of the personal computer industry.

The animating idea for this complicated presentation was a single, clear thesis set forward with a broad stroke. The first decade of the PC era had changed the way we as individuals worked. The accomplishments had been outstanding. Every time the PC encountered a limitation, technology rose to the occasion and overcame it.

Had the PC really helped us as managers run our businesses more efficiently? Not yet, in Grove's view. What did it mean to run our businesses better? It meant running them faster, getting information where it was needed quickly. More quickly than the competition. That is what would prove to be the competitive advantage of the future, and it was a goal that required numerous companies from different areas of the industry to coordinate their efforts. It was that simple and that complicated and provided Grove with the title of his presentation: "The Second Decade: Computer Supported Collaboration."[7]

This presentation seemed smooth as silk, but only because a great deal of work had gone into it. COMDEX '91 became known around Intel as MOAD, the Mother of All Demos.[8] Toward the conclusion, Grove thanked the thirty-six engineers from the fifteen companies who had put in a lot of time and effort to make his demos work as well as they did.[9]

Characteristic of the Grove style, a simple expression of gratitude carried with it multiple meanings. All these big, important companies that were listed at the end of the presentation did not lend their support to it out of the goodness of their hearts. They did so because Intel was important. Their cooperation, Grove has said, signaled that the industry "implicitly accepts that Intel is in the center of the computer industry—for example, who else would have been able to bring all those participants to the same speech. Careful to show but not call attention to it—key element of my style if there is one (complete opposite of Gates)." Two other elements of this presentation that Grove thought important were, first, that "collaboration is essential," and, second, "never miss a dig." This refers to the fact that he launched some wisecracks at IBM and Apple.[10]

COMDEX '91 was an event with real impact. "People ate it up!" Grove told Burgelman. "We made a video of the demonstration; over 20,000 copies of that tape [were] requested."[11] To Grove this was the future.

Not until 1993, however, did Intel swing into high gear behind videoconferencing. This new application for the PC was not going to develop by itself. Intel had to give it a very firm push. That began in 1993 when Grove approached Pat Gelsinger, one of the two senior programmers of the 386 who at the time was working on the Pentium Pro, the successor to the Pentium and a product on which Intel's future depended, and told him to lead Intel's charge into the world of PC communications. This personnel move was "controversial," said Grove. "But in many ways this is the test of it. We can't expect to succeed if we aren't willing to put our best people on the project."[12]

Gelsinger knew there were high hurdles to jump in order to turn the product idea in Grove's head into a reality. A "cultural shift" was necessary so that people would come to view the PC as a videoconferencing device. Technically, "the communications infrastructure has to continue to evolve. The RBOCs [Regional Bell Operating Companies] and Interexchange Carriers . . . need to continue to upgrade their networks to make digital phone lines generally available."[13]

It says something worrisome about Grove's grasp of the challenge ahead that he apparently did not appreciate the enormity of the problem of the unavailability of the telephone network to deliver what videoconferencing needed in order for it to become a mass-market phenomenon. He was enchanted by the opportunity before him. "This is a brand new market. There's just something about live video on a computer screen. I can't walk away from it."

Andy Grove has always been at his best when he has been able to step back and objectify the situation he faced. That trait made him a hero in the memory exit of 1985–1986, and it accounts for his remarkable management of his prostate cancer. When he loses that perspective, as he did in the case of the Pentium flaw, he can run into trouble. He seems to have believed that the RBOCs would view videoconferencing as a "killer app" powerful enough to prompt them to spend the billions of dollars it would cost to upgrade their phone lines. How much research was behind this assumption? Not much, if any.

ProShare—Intel's videoconferencing system—was introduced to the public in January 1994. An estimated $8 million was spent on advertising.[14] There was plentiful free publicity too. Grove appeared personally on CNN's *Moneyline* and CNBC's *Business Insiders*. The product was also mentioned favorably and treated as news on ABC's *Good Morning America* and on local television news broadcasts such as WJLA-TV in Washington, D.C., and KNTV in San Jose.

A careful look at the coverage of this new product announcement should have been somewhat disquieting to the public relations people at Intel. The problem was not with the reporters. They could not have been softer or more deferential. The problem was that the value proposition of ProShare was difficult to communicate in a sound bite. On one program, it appeared that ProShare could be transmitted directly to the home, through preexisting phone lines. On others, Intel said you needed ISDN lines. These, it turned out, were not available.

Grove explained that all that was necessary was to complete the last little distance to your home. The phone companies had not yet done that because there had been no reason to do so. ProShare was the application the phone companies had been waiting for. Undoubtedly, that is what Grove, Gelsinger, and others believed. The question we are left with is, what formed the basis of their belief? Had they canvassed the CEOs of the RBOCs? It appears not.

Intel made it clear to the world that it was putting everything it had behind ProShare. At its peak, seven hundred people were on the team. "There was no doubt on the part of anybody about Intel's commitment," said Gelsinger.[15]

ProShare failed. Why? The root cause was that the mass market had no trouble "walking away" from what Grove had found so enchanting. In Burgelman's words, "the market for the product did not materialize as expected." The RBOCs did not build their digital connections to the home, a development on which "Intel had initially been crucially dependent." Even when the technology came to permit the use of existing equipment, however, the market remained unenthusiastic.

In 1996, the effort behind ProShare was sharply curtailed. Pat Gelsinger got a new assignment, and a skeleton crew of sixty remained to manage the product. Speaking to his Stanford Graduate School of Business class in 1998, Grove said ProShare had cost three-quarters of a billion dollars and gobbled up five years.[16]

"We assumed," Grove told the class, "that just because it could be done technically there would be high demand. I was an enthusiastic user and supporter, but I've stopped using it. The novelty wore off. It was difficult to set up and so forth."[17] Grove assumed he had an iPod. He wound up with an

Edsel. Furthermore, his statement seems directly to contradict what he has often called "Grove's law," which was that whatever could be done technically would be done. ProShare required no technological breakthrough, but it was not going anywhere.

"We did all the things required for strategic leadership, it's just that we were wrong."[18] No one would argue that it is better to be right than wrong. One could argue, however, about whether or not Intel had done "all the things required for strategic leadership." Grove, famed for his clarity, did not mastermind a clear product launch. When asked about details, Intel spokespeople and Grove himself did not have a crystal-clear set of memorable responses. There was no all-encompassing phrase. No "Intel Inside."

Intel had not conducted market research for ProShare. "Who the hell are you going to ask?" exclaimed Grove. ProShare, after all, was something new.[19] It is unquestionably difficult to conduct research to estimate demand for a new product. But measures can be taken, and they were not. Nor was enough work undertaken to figure out how important a problem the underpowered telephone network posed.

To add a layer of irony, although Grove had stopped using ProShare in 1998, he was using it again by the summer of 2005. He has it in his home, and he was quite pleased to demonstrate its use. Once he made the adjustments necessitated by the fact that his house is inside the Intel firewall, which he had momentarily forgotten, the product worked well.

It is arguable that the cost of the failure of ProShare was high. Not solely the money. Nor just the prestige. This was Microma on steroids, on a huge scale; but the Intel of the 1990s could take these slaps and recover more easily than the Intel of the 1970s could absorb Microma.

To understand the true cost of the failure of ProShare, it is worth thinking of what might have happened had it succeeded. There would have been a whole new confidence in dealing with issues involving software, networking, and building collaborative programs among companies. Intel would have had a real "MIPS-sucking application," to use David Yoffie's phrase, to generate demand for ever more complex and expensive microprocessors.

In 1998, when Grove told those Stanford students that ProShare had run out of steam, Intel was on top of the world. ProShare's failure served to root the creosote bush even more firmly in Intel's world. This was the company that made a fortune selling microprocessors in PCs. Shoemaker stick to your last.

Yet great things were happening in Silicon Valley in the late 1990s that demanded a high degree of comfort with software and also with the consumer. New platforms were being created on technology Intel had pioneered to permit the creation of new "consumption communities."[20] eBay was founded in 1995 in San Jose, the same year that Yahoo! was incorporated in Palo Alto. Steve Jobs returned to Apple in Cupertino in 1997, and Google was incorporated in Menlo Park the following year. In the hardware world, there was a moment when Intel could have bought Cisco Systems for $200 million.[21] Cisco had been founded in San Jose back in 1984. Its market capitalization at this writing is over $100 billion.

Late in 1999, Grove said to Burgelman that "I have been rabid about four things in my career at Intel: motherboards, Intel Inside, chipsets, and videoconferencing. What if I had been equally rabid about networking? Intel could be a very different kind of company." (Chipsets "perform essential logic functions" surrounding the microprocessor. Motherboards combine "microprocessors and chipsets to form the basic subsystem of a PC or server.")[22] Grove here is his own most astute critic.[23]

It must also be said, however, that business was going well in the mid-1990s and that no individual or company is right about everything. As the computer, that "Darwinian device," made its way from the office to the home, it took ever more profitable Intel chips along with it. Moreover, "New PC communications applications and emerging markets," Intel told its shareholders, "are driving increased demand for our microprocessors."[24]

In October 1995, one analyst observed that "Despite repeated threats of competition from direct x86 competitors as well as various RISC architectures, Intel has delivered on its aggressive product plans [in the microprocessor business] while its competitors have repeatedly fallen short. The combination of good execution and the advantage of scale that it enjoys in both production volume and R&D budget has Intel sitting in the catbird seat for the foreseeable future." It was very hard "to compete against Godzilla."[25]

Godzilla had a very good year in 1995. Sales of $16.2 billion were up 41 percent from the previous year, as Intel moved back up to 60 on the list of the Fortune 500. Net income of $3.57 billion was up almost 56 percent, and earnings per share rose 54 percent. Market capitalization soared over 75 percent to the unheard-of heights of $46.6 billion, an increase of an order of magnitude from the year Grove became CEO. A lot of Intel executives with stock options were accumulating personal fortunes.

The 60 million PCs sold in 1995 represented an increase of 25 percent over the previous year. The reason was that this Darwinian device was migrating into the new world of communication. The PC was the "predominant gateway" to the Internet and the booming World Wide Web. "We believe," explained the 1995 *Annual Report*, "that this easy-to-use graphically based Internet interface will continue to attract new users and investments in the PC communications world, helping to expand the PC's role as a consumer communications device and driving future PC sales."[26]

This was nothing but good news for Intel because it viewed those PCs as the distribution mechanism for its microprocessors. Apple, which was steadily shrinking into an ever-smaller niche, was the only important desktop computer manufacturer that cleaved to the old vertical model of the industry and did not endorse the x86 architecture. As for everybody else, the Pentium was now "the processor of choice in the mainstream PC market." Nineteen ninety-five also saw the introduction of the next-generation microprocessor, the Pentium Pro. Developed in record time, it hit the market less than three years after the Pentium was introduced.

The *Annual Report* touted ProShare under the headline "Smart Connections."[27] "Smart Connections to the World" was, of course, the theme of TELECOM 95.

The 1995 *Annual Report* also featured, among a catalog of a great deal of information about Intel's progress, a full-page photograph of twenty-two Intel executives. Twenty of them were "Corporate Officers," and the remaining two were "Appointed Officers," which was one step down in the hierarchy. "We are particularly proud," according to the *Report*, "of our management team, which we believe is one of the most seasoned and stable groups in the industry." The twenty-two managers pictured had been with Intel for a total of 443 years, for an average slightly in excess of two decades per person.[28]

What statement was being made by this photograph? The semiconductor industry of the 1950s and 1960s had a reputation as a "cowboy" industry.[29] When Tom Wolfe wrote his famous article on the "tinkerings" of Bob Noyce, he described an environment in which people were more likely to change jobs than carpools. This easy mobility and transparency have been cited by scholars as a hallmark of Silicon Valley, one of the key characteristics that differentiated it from other industry clusters.[30]

There was nothing undisciplined about the presentation of the executives in this picture. It was a men's club. Only one woman, Carlene Ellis, the vice president and director, Information Technology, was present. Everyone wore a suit and, with the exception of Ellis, a tie.

What was pictured was an organization, peopled by organization men, with one woman. They were not elderly, but this was no children's crusade either. Most were in their forties or fifties. This could have been a set of IBM executives from the 1950s or 1960s. Your money would be safe in the hands of such managers. The child's play of the past was dead and buried, at least in this company.

22

"What Are You Paranoid About These Days?"

A note—no a chorus—of self-congratulation was presented to the public in Intel's *Annual Report* for 1996. It was, to be blunt, "another outstanding year."[1] It was "another fantastic year."[2] The self-congratulation was not conceit. It was well warranted. Old records were smashed. New records were set.

Sales of $20.8 billion were up 29 percent over the previous year. Net income of $5.2 billion topped the record of the previous year by almost 45 percent. Earnings per share rose at the same rate. That all-important indicator both for shareholders and for a management team supping at the trough of stock options, market capitalization, more than doubled from the previous year's peak to the dizzying heights of $111 billion. In total return to shareholders, Intel ranked first among the nation's top 100 firms by market capitalization. Intel had known high growth rates in the past. However, it was a relatively small company in those times. In 1996, it was the forty-third largest company in the United States in terms of sales. It employed 48,500 people.

If you had bought 100 shares of Intel stock back at its initial public offering in 1971 and held them through the ten times the stock had split by the end of 1996, you would have owned 15,188 shares. The hundred shares in 1971 would have cost you $2,350. The 15,188 shares you owned at the end of 1996 would have been worth more than $2 million.[3] You would thus have enjoyed an appreciation in your investment of three orders of magnitude. It does not get much better than that.

Nothing had been inevitable about this spectacular performance. Nineteen ninety-six, for example, was "a year when most of the global semiconductor industry [was] enduring a painful slump."[4] AMD and Cyrix, small domestic competitors of Intel, lost money that year on their microprocessor operations.[5] Revenue for the semiconductor industry as a whole, after growing an average of 21 percent annually from 1986 to 1995, was down 9 percent.[6]

Driving this spectacular year for Intel was the continuing surge in the sale of personal computers. Seventy million of them were sold globally in 1996. Between 80 and 90 percent of these had Intel microprocessors inside. Intel's margins on these devices hovered at around 60 percent.

Intel was continuing to flog ProShare. It reported that Intel Video Phone with ProShare technology could now deliver "quality video communications over ordinary telephone lines."[7] So the "last mile" problem of ISDN telephone line connections apparently had been largely solved. Nevertheless, ProShare stubbornly refused to gain the kind of market acceptance that Grove had envisioned for it.

On the manufacturing side, the story was happier. Fab 12 in Chandler, Arizona, came online. Less than twenty-three months were required from groundbreaking to operation for this facility, which was a record for Intel. Craig Barrett, the company's chief operating officer, deserves primary credit for this achievement. An emphasis on competing through capacity had been one of the cornerstones of Grove's strategy since the decision to sole-source the 386 in the mid-1980s, if not earlier. Barrett was completely in tune with this approach. His "copy exactly" method[8] made it possible for Intel to become a remarkably efficient producer of one of the world's most complicated artifacts.

The 1996 *Annual Report* made explicit what everyone had by then assumed with regard to corporate succession. Barrett, who was anointed Grove's successor when he was named Intel's executive vice president and chief operating officer back in 1993, moved a step closer to the top spot. It was announced that as of May 21, 1997, he would become president of Intel while remaining COO. Grove would become chairman of the board on that date and remain CEO. Moore would become chairman emeritus. The three would continue to work together as the members of the "Executive Office" of the corporation.[9]

Intel continued during 1996 to look for markets for its most advanced products. The company wanted to get into PC servers. It continued to talk about "connectivity," now with "connected CD-ROMS" that would "provide powerful solutions to the bandwidth-clogging frustrations of the World Wide Web."[10]

In the cause of networking, this engineering-driven company even made a foray into Hollywood. Intel worked with Creative Artists Agency, in what must have seemed to both parties an odd partnership "to expose actors, directors, writers, and musicians to the potential of new media on networked PCs."[11]

During 1996, equity analysts were tripping over themselves to recommend purchase of Intel stock. According to one, "We believe that Intel is a tough competitor and is positioned to maintain its dominant market position for the foreseeable future. We believe that Intel views all competition, both existing and emerging, as credible and serious. *It is the paranoia that is ingrained in Intel culture that has motivated the Company to attack its own product line with new products before its competitors get a chance.*"[12]

Intel had it all, the analysts agreed. Architectural leadership: "Intel has the enviable position of being the architectural driver for the PC market." The company's architecture was the standard for the PC, a standard that it might well have sacrificed had it opted for RISC over CISC. Manufacturing capability: "Intel has the expertise and experience of manufacturing leading-edge technology in high volume." Brand recognition: "'Intel Inside' . . . has successfully created brand preference for a technical product."[13]

Everyone knows that nothing is constant except change. Everyone also knows that institutions tend to resist change. Why, then, did Intel, quite a big company by 1996, embrace it?

Woven into the fabric of the whole semiconductor industry was Gordon Moore's famous law. Back in 1965, it will be recalled, Moore observed that during the history of the chip, the industry had managed to double the number of electrical appliances—transistors, capacitors, resisters, diodes—"crammed" onto a small sliver of silicon approximately every eighteen months. To everyone's amazement, that historical trend projected into the future continued to hold true. Back when the world was young, in 1978, Intel introduced the 8086. This device was home to 29,000 transistors. The top-of-the-line Pentium in June 1996 carried 3.2 million transistors. Along with this staggering increase came far greater computing power. The 8086 had a MIP (million instruction per second) rating of .75. The Pentium, eighteen years later, sported a MIP rating of 325.[14] As the cost of instruction per second declined, whole new applications for the computer, hitherto undreamt of, were born. Moore had published his "law" in an article in *Electronics* magazine on April 19, 1965. The magazine no longer exists. Moore's law lives on. Everybody in the industry read about Moore's law. Everybody knew about it.

It had, however, a special impact on Intel because that was where Moore worked. To this day he and his foundation own two and a half percent of the company, which is why he is among the world's richest people. Moore did not have an office. Like everyone else at Intel, he had a cubicle. Drop in anytime. You might on any given day find yourself walking into the Robert Noyce Building with him from Intel's parking lot. No spaces were reserved for executives. You could have lunch with him in Intel's spartan cafeteria. In the old days, this was called "lunch with the bunch."[15]

Moore's law mattered at Intel to a greater degree than anywhere else because you saw its author around the place all the time. His presence was a constant reminder that change—substantive change, not the chrome and tailfin variety that ruined the American automobile—was real. It was inexorable. You could predict its occurrence with geometric certitude. Intel could not be the institution that resisted change. It had to be the institution that mastered it. According to the equity analysts and according to its own *Annual Report,* this is precisely what it was doing.[16] It was, therefore, not only "paranoia" that drove Intel "to attack its own product line." It was the terrifying treadmill of Moore's law. It was a treadmill on which you could not push a "stop" button. You couldn't even lower the speed. But stop moving, even slow your pace, and you would fall off the edge of the world.

Intel had to keep moving because of Moore's law, but not because of Moore's law alone. "Paranoia" had its part to play. Nineteen ninety-six turned out to be a very big year for Grove as an author. "Taking on Prostate Cancer" appeared in *Fortune* on May 13 and became one of the most important articles ever published in the magazine. In September, Doubleday released what was to become Grove's classic statement on strategy: *Only the Paranoid Survive: How to Exploit the Crisis Points That Challenge Every Company.*

Why did Grove write this book? We know that he was a born writer. His total output of published work, if one includes his technical book and articles, exceeds a thousand pages. He kept notebooks for himself to clarify his thinking.[17] For decades he wrote lengthy, astute, and often funny memoranda to Gordon Moore designed to encapsulate the state of the business.

But why this particular book at this particular time? In his acknowledgements, Grove states that he "had no intention of writing a book on this subject until Harriet Rubin, from Doubleday, sought me out and convinced me that I should do so."[18] Rubin founded Currency Books, which was the Doubleday imprint under which *Paranoid* was published, in 1989.[19] She must have been very persuasive. Andy Grove was a busy man when he was working on the book. He had recovered from treatment for prostate cancer the previous year. His *Fortune* article was generating endless inquiries about how to deal with the illness. Not incidentally, he was running Intel, which was growing at a wild pace and having its greatest year ever.

However Rubin and Grove made contact, she was knocking at an open door. When Grove had something to say, he said it. The days of being stifled by Soviet communism were long passed. Indeed, by 1996 when *Paranoid* was published, the Soviet Union had disappeared. Grove was not only very much still around, he was at the pinnacle of his power and fame. He had always wanted to teach, and he felt he had learned some things worth teaching.[20] The message of *Paranoid* has been discussed above.[21] We have covered the concept of "strategic inflection point" and the dilemma of "signal" versus "noise" and the importance of "Cassandras" in our discussion of the RISC/CISC controversy. Let us now, therefore, look at this book more broadly. What is *Only the Paranoid Survive* really about?

The book is about change and gathering the information to make the right changes at the right time. His whole career at Intel, Grove had been haunted by the "Peter Principle." He wrote about this in his private notebooks way back on February 26, 1970.[22] The term is not actually mentioned in *Paranoid*, but the spirit of the concept pervades the book. How can you manage change if you do not have accurate, reliable, and, especially, timely information?

For starters, Grove demands that we face a cruel reality about change. People, especially senior people, don't like it. "With all the rhetoric about how management is about change," he declares, "the fact is that we managers loathe change, especially when it involves us."[23] Senior managers succeeded in the world as it was. The temptation to fall prey to "the inertia of success" is overwhelming.[24] To admit that change is necessary "[entails] some personal risk." You have to swallow your pride and admit your ignorance.[25] This is not comfortable for a senior person used to being right and accustomed to the praise of courtiers.

Like it or not, to deny the need for change is to invite catastrophe. Moreover, "timing is everything."[26] In the words of Royce Yudkoff, managing partner of ABRY Partners, a highly successful private equity firm, "Don't tell me *what* is going to happen. Tell me *when* it is going to happen."[27] Getting the timing right was a devil of a problem. You usually got the information you needed later than you should have—"the leader is often the last of all to know."[28] Once the information reached you, there were a boatload of reasons and rationalizations to deny the necessity of change. Grove used himself as an illustration: "Looking back over my own career, I have never made a tough change, whether it involved resource shifts or personnel moves, that I haven't wished I had made a year or so earlier."[29]

How do you know what to do? We have already seen Grove's emphasis on listening to middle managers on the front lines of the company and on cultivating "Cassandras" who will tell him unpleasant truths. There is no easy answer to this question. In *Only the Paranoid Survive,* Grove proposed a two-step process and devoted a chapter to each: "Let Chaos Reign" and "Rein in Chaos."[30] Always the phrasemaker, "Let chaos reign, then rein in chaos" became, according to Robert Burgelman, one of Grove's "favorite expressions."[31] What does it mean?

When facing a strategic inflection point forces you to deal with "strategic dissonance," that is, saying one thing but doing another, then you know the time has come to experiment. "Loosen up the level of control that your organization normally is accustomed to. Let people try different techniques, review different products, exploit different sales channels, and go after different customers. Much as management has been devoted to making and keeping order in the company, at times like this they must become more tolerant of the new and the different. Only stepping out of the old ruts will bring new insights."[32]

What would be an example of letting chaos reign? Grove does not cite it in his text, but the "Red X" advertising campaign qualifies. This was certainly "out of the box" thinking for a company that from its Microma watch experience had nothing but bad memories of communicating directly to end users. Intel had to move the industry from the multisourced 286 to the sole-sourced 386, perhaps the greatest strategic inflection point since the demise of the vacuum tube, and new action—not just new thinking but new action—was called for.

Another example of letting chaos reign was Grove's prostate research. Notice how many different avenues he walked down before choosing the route he took. Note how, in the first phase of his research, he allowed information to lead to more information and complexity to increase.[33] This is difficult enough when you are facing a business problem. When you are facing a life-threatening medical challenge and you want someone to tell you what the right road is, this approach demands a high degree of self-control.

Grove's pugnacity leads him to place tremendous value in taking action. In a speech to four hundred executives on November 14, 2005, Grove defined strategy in one word: "action." "In a single word, strategy is action. Strategy is not what we say. Strategy is what we do."[34] "Be quick and dirty," he went on to say. "Engage and then plan. And get it better."[35]

The time then comes to "rein in chaos." Decisiveness is vital in your determination of the company's new direction. Crystal clarity is called for. You need to develop a vocabulary to rally the troops. "You need to answer [key] questions in a single phrase that everybody can remember and, over time, can understand to mean exactly what you intended."[36] Just as "Intel Inside" answered a host of questions for the end user, "The PC Is It" answered a million questions for Intel as a company.[37] When the time came for a decision with regard to prostate cancer treatment, he never looked back.[38]

Evidently, reining in chaos is a good deal more difficult than letting chaos reign. The chapter on bringing order back to the company is slightly more than twice as long as the chapter on permitting disorder. In the process of reining in chaos, there is a powerful tendency to hedge your bets. To that approach Grove is unequivocal: "No." "Hedging is expensive and dilutes commitment." You need "exquisite focus." Without it, you will always be looking for a way out rather than a way to win.[39] "If you're wrong, you will die." At least you will go down fighting, having a chance to win. "[M]ost companies don't die because they are wrong; most die because they don't commit themselves." Because of internal divisions, you divide your forces in the face of the enemy.[40]

When Grove took that great leap into the unknown with his historic decision to sole-source the 386, he jumped without knowing whether a net, in this case Compaq, would catch him. Intel was biting its collective fingernails before Compaq put the 386 into its Deskpro, forcing IBM to follow and forever changing the structure of the information technology industry.

An even greater fear than whether the customers would buy the product or Intel would be ambushed by the companies that had served as its previous licensees was Grove's concern about Intel itself. He would lead the company to the promised land of freedom to price in such a way as to reap the rewards of the research and development work needed to create breakthrough products. What if the company did not follow?

Intel's own people were Grove's greatest concern in the sole-sourcing decision, especially early on. Some salesperson may have already made a sale with the promise to his or her customer that there would be a second source for the 386. If the salesperson lost that sale because of the sole-source decision, that was money, in the form of a commission, out of his or her pocket. Some business development manager might have initiated an arrangement with the same presupposition and encountered the same problem.

Grove felt that these deals based on multiple sourcing did not make sense and had to be stopped. He feared that some people at Intel would not have the fortitude to stick to the new sole-sourcing policy. Indeed, one senior executive appeared to waver in his commitment to the sole-source decision. Grove has that snapshot in his mind to this day. That particular executive, Dave House, had been a candidate to succeed Grove as CEO. He was not after this episode.

Grove continues to believe that you have to plunge ahead, not look back, and make the best of it. Others wanted to negotiate better terms and continue to second-source. This is a time when one's mettle is tested. What "proclivity toward risk" must one have to be a leader? Do you value winning *your* way so much that you are willing to take a chance of losing everything? Or do you feel that if you have a chance of losing everything, maybe it is time to see if you can make a better deal within the existing framework?[41]

Grove said he didn't fear "publicly losing" as much as "losing by giving up." In the early days at Intel, he became concerned that one of the company's lawyers was making too many deals. "I made him put into his 'key results' to sue some number of people during the next time period. I wanted him to get out of the habit of settling everything. Because if you settle everything you're leaving money on the table. The tendency that I was fighting in him was that if he settles, he never loses. If he takes a dispute to trial, he may win but he may lose; and if he loses, everybody knows it. I don't care about that—specifically, the act of losing in a public way as opposed to losing by giving up."[42]

Roger S. Borovoy, a well-known patent attorney, came to Intel from Fairchild at Noyce's urging in 1974 and served as chief counsel until moving on in 1982. At one point, he was confronted with the choice of paying $250,000 to license a patent or going to litigation, the result of which could be either paying half a million dollars or no money at all. Borovoy told Grove he thought the chances of Intel's winning were "better than fifty-fifty." Grove told him to "Go for it." He did, and he lost.

To Borovoy's surprise, Grove congratulated him even though Intel had to pay its adversary half a million dollars. "Roger," Grove is quoted as saying, "we were in litigation. You fashioned a clever settlement where you paid what you thought was reasonable. . . . Better than that—when the other side offered to split the difference, you were willing to go for a full victory anyway."[43]

In this instance as in others, Grove preferred a public defeat to the private compromise, even at the cost of a quarter of a million dollars. He wanted to establish a reputation for Intel as a fighting firm. True, this was a defeat. What we can never know is how many suits were never filed because Intel's potential adversaries knew that it was willing to fight rather than settle. This is therefore a perfect example of a "noble failure" rather than a "stupid mistake."

Grove was a very public chief executive. "Throughout his tenure as CEO," Burgelman has written, Grove "was a very articulate spokesperson for Intel and became one of the most quoted CEOs of the late 1980s and 1990s." He won a lot of awards that "were no doubt highly personally satisfying [to him] as an individual," but, Burgelman explains, there was more than ego gratification to the publicity.[44]

Grove was a masterful manager of the press, which gave him the chance "to communicate Intel's strategic intent [not only] to the world [but also] to Intel's employees."[45] The press helped him both to manage the perceptions of the world at large and to lead the people inside his own company. Remember how vital he thought it was to have Intel's troops close behind him as he sole-sourced the 386, especially toward the beginning of that shift in strategy. Grove told Burgelman that he "was convinced that Intel's employees were more likely to believe statements about Intel's culture when they saw them published by outsiders."[46]

Only the Paranoid Survive, as was true with so many of Grove's undertakings, served multiple purposes. It told the outside world what Grove was thinking about the industry and his company. Since by 1996 Intel was sufficiently important to influence its environment with its actions, *Paranoid* took the world as it was and made it more so. It told the world inside Intel what the views of its CEO were. It gratified Grove's desire to be a public figure within his orbit—that is to say, his ambition related strictly to business. A job like running SEMATECH, the industry consortium funded by the government in the late 1980s to assist the semiconductor industry in its battle against Japanese manufacturers, would have been out of the question for him. Noyce took the job reluctantly, and Grove sent him an encouraging note for doing what he would never have done.[47]

In addition to all this, the book satisfied Grove's desire simply to teach. He wanted to tell the world what he had learned about strategy. There was always part of Grove, a small but important part, that was deeply attached to academic inquiry. Look at the notes to *Paranoid*. They are filled with scholarly references to the work of business academicians. Grove was probably the most well-read CEO in academic business literature in the country. "Intel is a schoolish company," he said.[48] It certainly had a schoolish CEO while he ran it. There is an element of *ars gratia artis* in all his writing.

Grove's book tour began on September 10 at 6:30 in the morning with an appearance on *Bloomberg Business News*.[49] The innumerable Q-and-A sessions are instructive. Grove was asked the same questions repeatedly in different broadcasts. Naturally, he provided the same answers, not quite word for word, but close enough. When one reads the transcripts, the first impression one gets is that this is a process that could become boring very quickly.

The good news was that Intel was prospering in September 1996. Thus one broadcaster began by saying that "Intel yesterday hit another 52-week high, up 2¼ to 83½, and . . . Intel's CEO is touring the country publicizing his book." Once again, multiple purposes are served by a single effort. Intel, its CEO, and his book all receive publicity at once.[50]

Interviewers also often noted that *Time* magazine had recently named Grove one of the ten most powerful men in the country, a list on which President Clinton and Disney's Michael Eisner also appeared. That gave rise to the following exchange on one program:

INTERVIEWER: Boy, that's some pretty tough company you have got there, President Clinton and Michael Eisner! How does it feel to be one of the ten most powerful men in the country?

GROVE: I haven't changed since the article came out! [June 17][51]

INTERVIEWER: You are still the same old guy, huh?

GROVE: That's right; actually, older.[52]

Grove was invariably asked about the book's title, which in itself makes for an interesting story. His first idea was to choose a title built around one of the concepts in the book, such as the "strategic inflection point." Harriet Rubin, who "sought me out and convinced me" to write a book about his ideas concerning managing change,[53] also suggested that the title he liked was not going to sell many books.

Rubin kept pushing Grove for another title. The process reminded him of a management parable. A father says to his son, "Bring me a rock." The son goes to a nearby riverbank, gets one, and brings it back. "Not that one. Another one." The kid scurries back to the riverbank and returns with another rock. The father is displeased again. The process repeats itself. The point? The father, or in Grove's case the publisher, didn't know what he, or in this case she, wanted. He just knew he wanted something different. At length, Grove came up with "only the paranoid survive." "It didn't have much to do with the book," he said, "but it was the title she wanted." Grove was then put in the position of having to justify it in the text as well as in interviews.[54]

The title is undeniably catchy. But there may have been a price to pay for it. "Paranoia" is a complicated word. For psychiatrists, it is a clinical disorder characterized by delusions.[55] The key word here is "delusions." That is what makes paranoia an illness.

The word also has a meaning in common parlance to the effect that the paranoid person worries a lot, indeed, too much. A person labeled "paranoid" in common conversation would be a person who worries to an unreasonable degree that the world is out to get him or her. Once again, the key word is "unreasonable." Is Grove telling us through the title of his book that it is reasonable to be unreasonable? Is the title meant to be taken literally?

Here is the explanation Grove gave to one interviewer: "At some point many, many years ago . . . I used that phrase ["only the paranoid survive"] internally, but I must have used it in an interview and in [the] course of time, the press . . . associated it with me as my trademark phrase, which to some extent it is. I feel one has to be constantly alert in business to the unexpected, so it's sort of my motto."[56]

To another interviewer, Grove said, "If you want to maintain your success, you have to dodge the bullets that come from your competitors. Most importantly, you have to dodge the most dangerous threat to your business, which is when your environment changes in such a way that the whole rules of the game get changed, and all of a sudden you find that your business is in a different game than it used to be before."

One of the dilemmas of being interviewed about a book you have written is that often the interviewer has either not read or not understood the book. He or she is guaranteed not to have thought about it deeply. When you are being interviewed on live radio or television, you have to be on your toes, and not just for tough questions (you are lucky if you get those) but for questions that are orthogonal to the message of your book, irrelevant, uninformed, or simply stupid.

In this interview, the anchor followed up on Grove's description of dodging bullets by citing the Pentium flaw episode as a successful example of avoiding disaster He then mixed that up with the concept of the "strategic inflection point." He misunderstood Grove's point completely, and Grove had to straighten him out immediately.

"Well, first of all, we didn't dodge a bullet; we were hit by a bullet." This was the heart of Grove's argument. It zipped right by the interviewer. "The strategic inflection point," Grove went on to say, "took place [earlier], when, in the perception of the public, we became a supplier to the consumers who buy computers. We didn't realize it in time, so when we hit a problem with our product, we continued to pursue resolution . . . as if [Intel] was still an engineering company selling to other engineers." However, Intel itself and the rules of the game it was playing had changed. Intel had become "a consumer company supplying consumers, and we didn't adapt, and it took us a very bitter experience—lots of bad publicity, financial consequences—to learn that lesson."[57]

What can we learn from this exchange? First of all, if you are going to go on a live medium for an interview, you have to be ready to assume the role of interviewer as well as interviewee.

Second, it matters that Grove begins *Only the Paranoid Survive* with the story of the Pentium flaw. That fact guarantees that interviewers, some of whom are only going to read a few pages of the book, are going to ask him about it immediately. He thus forces himself, through the book and through conversations about it, to relive an episode in Intel's history that turned out badly and for which he was at fault. Every such discussion has to have brought back memories that were both vivid and bad. Why should a man in Grove's position put himself through this?

I am often asked to compare Grove to other well-known business executives, such as Alfred P. Sloan Jr., the man who built General Motors during its glory days, which are becoming increasingly difficult to remember as the once great company experiences mounting difficulties. In 1964, Sloan published *My Years with General Motors*.[58] The book became a bestseller and has remained in print ever since. But in all its 522 turgid, dull pages, Sloan devotes in this book only a brief passage to the birth of the United Automobile Workers and the unionization of the plants of General Motors.

Sloan glosses over the relations between workers and managers at his plants. No one in the autumn of 1936 thought an industrial union had a prayer of organizing GM. The company was staunchly anti-union, it was making a fortune even through the Depression, and it was paying its workers well, 25 percent above the all-manufacturing average in the United States. Squirreled away on page 475 of Sloan's endless book are the following observations:

> We knew that some political radicals regarded unions as instruments for the attainment of power. But even orthodox "business unionism" seemed to us a potential threat to the prerogatives of management. As a businessman, I was unaccustomed to the whole idea. Our early experiences with the AF of L [American Federation of Labor] unions in the automobile industry were unhappy; the chief issue with these unions became organizational. They demanded that they represent all our workers, even those who did not want to be represented by them. Our initial encounter with the CIO [Congress of Industrial Organizations] was even more unhappy; for that organization attempted to enforce its demands for exclusive recognition by the most terrible acts of violence, and finally seized our properties in the sit-down strikes of 1937. I have no desire to revive the bitter controversies that arose over these early encounters with labor organizations. I mention them merely to suggest one of the reasons why our initial reaction to unionism was negative.

Sloan's mismanagement of labor relations was his greatest failing as a business executive. His egregious mistakes in this area saddled GM with a workforce that was both high-cost and highly adversarial. That dreadful combination is killing GM right now.

What, then, do we see when we compare *My Years with General Motors* to *Only the Paranoid Survive*? Sloan himself had learned nothing from the conflict with the UAW [the United Automobile Workers, which was affiliated with the CIO]. He did not even want to talk about it. Grove, by contrast, put the Pentium flaw front and center in *Only the Paranoid Survive*. That is why every interviewer asked him about it. These questions forced Grove personally to experience the incident again, to rework it in his own mind, and to educate all the listeners or readers, as the case may be, about what went wrong and the new point of view that was required to avoid similar errors.

There is a difference between one executive trying to forget mistakes and another trying to face them, however unpleasant they may be, and minimize the chances of their recurrence. Remember that many Intel employees were doubtless among the readers of *Only the Paranoid Survive*. We see the difference between one executive, Sloan, who felt that the world stopped turning with GM's success, and another, Grove, who felt that "Intel has always been one wrong answer away from disaster—and that a closed mind is a trap door to the abyss."[59]

The world of Andy Grove was not a comfortable one. An interviewer said, "[The] title of the book is *Only the Paranoid Survive*. That sounds a little scary. What does that mean?" Grove responded, "Business is scary." It wasn't scary to Sloan. Grove continued, "Business consists of your trying to do something other people can't do, and other people trying to do something you can't do. And if you're not looking over your shoulder, they may just sneak up on you and do it."[60] "[Y]ou are always in danger," he said to another interviewer. "You are in danger of competitors, you are in danger of new ways of doing things, but most importantly, you have a danger that the way you have conducted your business . . . is going to lose relevance."[61] If this is the way you view business, then perhaps this book's title is justified. It certainly attracted attention, and it was scary. Both were among its goals.

Nevertheless, one feels that the title came with a price. The book's title is indeed so catchy—it is inconceivable that Alfred P. Sloan Jr. would have chosen such a title—that it detracts ever so slightly from the message. The thought that the author may be kidding wends its way into one's mind when one hears the title. It takes a moment to realize that this book is as serious and more straightforward than anything Sloan wrote. The review in *Forbes* suggested that Grove would "go down in history as the man who made paranoia respectable. With the publication of his new book, the affliction's no longer a psychosis. It's a survival trait."[62]

Tom Brokaw interviewed Grove on MSNBC on September 24, 1996. Brokaw said, "[Y]ou came here as an immigrant from your native Hungary, you have had enormous business success and with that comes great wealth. Has that changed your life at all?" Grove responded that "I live more comfortably. In that sense, of course it did. I'm enjoying my life but I've always enjoyed my life. I think I'm basically the same person I was thirty years ago."[63] Arthur Rock agreed: "Andy has been exactly the same person," he remarked. "He hasn't changed. That's the beauty of it. He has no airs."[64]

This particular paranoiac was able to enjoy his life. "Can Grove finally relax?" asked two business school professors. Their answer: "Afraid not." They could find plenty for him to worry about.[65]

"What are you paranoid about these days?" asked an interviewer on September 23, 1996. The Internet was on everyone's mind at the time, and Andy was no exception. "I don't want to miss the opportunity that the Internet provides. . . . We have the potential in the PC industry to become the center of entertainment for all consumers worldwide." It would be a tall order to persuade consumers to migrate from their television sets and newspapers to their PCs. For this change to take place, PCs had "to become more consumer friendly and . . . more compelling." This would constitute a major transformation. The reward made the effort seem worthwhile.[66]

Andy being Andy, he did not confine his views of the competition between television in particular and the PC to the print medium. On CNN, he said, "I see a lot . . . that threaten[s] our ambition." "Such as?" he was asked. "Television sets." Asked for an explanation, he said it was "[a] terrible thing to tell you on the television," but the PC was competing with TV for the disposable hours of consumers. By the time this interview came to its conclusion, one of the interviewers said, "We're paranoid about *you*."[67]

Andy was asked more than once whether his book had any lessons for "individuals who are trying to dodge bullets in their careers." He had been giving career advice for years, both in his "one-on-ones" at Intel and in print. This is what he had to say in 1996. "An individual's career is like a business. It's your business, what you do—and my business, what I do—and we both own our little businesses. In the same way as businesses become obsolete or irrelevant, individual skills and capabilities and activities can become irrelevant also. Nobody's going to look after you as well as you can and should [look after yourself]. . . . And we have to treat this as a business problem. We have to manage our careers as a business with its own strategies and adaptations."[68]

Tom Brokaw asked Grove if he wished there was more discussion about "cyber technology" in the current 1996 presidential campaign. The response was vintage Grove. Direct. Blunt. Evincing no desire to please his interviewer. "Not really," he said. "I think it would be . . . a bunch of drivel." "It wouldn't make any difference?" Brokaw tried plaintively again. "No, I don't think so," came Grove's response.[69]

Only the Paranoid Survive was republished in 1999, and there was a significant addition to the book. A new chapter called "Career Inflection Points" warned that such events are "caused by a change in the environment [and] do not distinguish between the qualities of the people that they dislodge by their force."[70] Since in the case of an individual's career as with a company "Timing Is Everything," you want to be prepared to make the changes that are coming upon you well in advance of facing the proverbial pink slip. You want to change "in your own terms."[71]

This chapter is invaluable not only for the advice it proffers but also because it opens a window into how Grove thinks. First of all, "career inflection points," just like corporate "strategic inflection points," can happen to anyone. Just because you may be very good at what you do, you can't allow yourself to start thinking that it "may happen to others but not to me." Working "inside an organization, you're often sheltered from . . . the world at large." That shelter is illusory. If the environment changes, you may find your old skills irrelevant. How do you break through the cognitive barriers to thinking outside the box about your professional future?

What Grove proceeds to offer is a recipe for how he managed the various cognitive triumphs that characterized his own career. The key is to get outside of yourself. Just as if you were the CEO of a corporation, you must objectify the situation. As has been emphasized previously, you have to play two roles—subject and object, actor and audience. But how?

"Go through a mental fire drill," Grove advised, "in anticipation of the time you may have a real fire on your hands." There are plenty of "helpful Cassandras" around. In this instance, they "are likely to be concerned friends or family members who work in a different industry or competitive environment and deduce winds of change that you don't sense yet." Cultivate such people and listen closely to them.[72]

It is up to you to "get in shape for change." Hence, Grove recommends, perhaps without realizing it, doing exactly what he did, as documented in his notebooks. "Picture yourself in different roles."[73] Recall how, way back in July 1969, Grove cut out an article about the job of a motion picture director and printed above it in his notebook, "MY JOB DESCRIPTION?" This took place just as he was embarking on his personal reinvention, from technologist to manager.[74] "Conduct a dialogue with yourself about how you suit those roles. *Train your brain* in preparation for the big change."[75] All this had to be done with clarity and conviction. None of it was easy.[76] One feels Grove is writing his own autobiography.

One feels this even more powerfully in reading the final two paragraphs of the last chapter of the second edition of *Paranoid*. "It's a bit a like emigrating to a new country," writes Grove. "You pack up and leave an environment you're familiar with, where you know the language, the culture, the people, and where you've been able to predict how things, both good and bad, happen. You move to a new land with new habits, a new language, and a new set of dangers and uncertainties." Grove knew whereof he spoke.

"At times like this," he went on, "looking back may be tempting, but it's terribly counterproductive. Don't bemoan the way things were," he advises, perhaps with his own parents in mind. "Things will never be that way again. Pour your energy, every bit of it, into adapting to your new world, into learning the skills you need to prosper in it and into shaping it around you. Whereas the old land presented limited opportunity or none at all, the new land enables you to have a future whose rewards are worth all the risks."[77]

23

✦

The Year of Decision

Nineteen ninety-seven was yet another year of records for Intel. Sales soared 20 percent over 1996 to $25 billion, leading to a ranking of 38 on the Fortune 500. It was 200 on that list a decade previously when Grove became CEO. Market capitalization set another record of $114.7 billion. This was an increase by more than a factor of 25 from $4.3 billion in 1987. Thanks to stock options, scores of people at Intel were multimillionaires, far richer in 1997 than they could have imagined when Grove took office. Profits skyrocketed to $6.9 billion, 35 percent above the previous year's record.

During his book tour for *Only the Paranoid Survive*, Grove was asked why he continued to work. He certainly didn't need the money. "I mean," asked the interviewer, "how much does staying on top mean to you, and if it means a lot, what is your motivation? Why stay in this competitive, constantly changing environment?" Grove replied, "'Staying on top,' what that means to me is being in a position to have a measure of influence on shaping the future. . . . I have certain beliefs [about] what this future might look like and . . . [w]hat we might do with our technology" to make this vision a reality. "That's very exciting stuff!"[1] This does not sound like the statement of a man ready to step down as CEO. But 1997 was a "career inflection point" for Grove.

On Wall Street during the course of the year 1997, analysts were not of one mind about Intel, although the climate of opinion was positive. Among the critics was Krishna Shankar from Donaldson, Lufkin & Jenrette. He was concerned with a slowing PC market in Europe, which accounted for 25 percent of Intel's income; a weakness in higher-priced PCs, with their higher-margin Intel chips; in the United States an unwillingness to upgrade PCs in the corporate sector; and a belief that in the consumer market it was unlikely that the PC would become, as Intel envisioned, "an all-inclusive consumer entertainment center to be found in every living room."[2]

John M. Geraghty, analyst for Credit Suisse First Boston, whose parent company purchased Donaldson, Lufkin & Jenrette in November 2000, recommended Intel as a "buy" the month after the Shankar report. "The financial press has begun noting that the profitability of Intel is now approaching that of the best companies in the United States," he wrote. "We have previously noted that the company's substantial cash flow enables it to fund a capital spending program that is more than 10% of that spent by the entire semiconductor industry. In sum, Intel has one of the best businesses and strongest competitive positions in any industrial segment." Almost in the spirit of "only the paranoid survive," he added, "This can change." The overall message was, however, upbeat.[3]

Later in the year, Wall Street analysts became more cautious. According to Ken Pearlman of CIBC Oppenheimer, most of them were lowering their ratings and estimates. He, however, felt "relatively optimistic about the stock. In his view, Intel was "better positioned than many believe," and this was a good time to buy.[4]

Back in March, Alan Rieper of Deutsche Morgan Grenfell had noted an interesting legacy effect that he believed tended unreasonably to drag down the price of stocks in this industry. "The sharp decline in semiconductor shipments in 1985," he wrote, "has depressed the P/Es [the price/earnings ratios] of the larger semiconductor companies, including Intel, ever since. Despite the superior performance of the industry in the ensuing recovery, especially during the industry growth acceleration in the early 1990s, fears of another major mishap reminiscent of 1985 have resulted in relative P/Es for these stocks well below their pre-1985 highs. . . . Intel's growth in sales and operating earnings has accelerated in the 10-year period 1986–95, from the rate achieved in the 10 years immediately prior to the 1985 industry collapse." But Intel's price/earnings ratio did not follow suit. Rieper believed that "the stock is still being punished" for the sins of 1985–1986. Not until 1996 did Wall Street "begin to pay for Intel's superior record." This was the first time in seven years "that it achieved even a modest premium P/E to the S&P 500. We believe the company's track record and prospects should command an even higher premium."[5]

For Grove as CEO, 1997 was the most public year of what had already been a life spent to a not insignificant extent in the public eye. As noted above,[6] he became chairman of the board as well as CEO in May 1997, at which point Moore became chairman emeritus. For one last time, he had followed in Gordon Moore's footsteps. Grove delivered more than one hundred speeches in 1997, publicizing Intel's view of the PC business and talking repeatedly about "MIPS-sucking applications" that would exploit Intel's most advanced and profitable microprocessors. One of these speeches was at the World Economic Forum in Davos, Switzerland, on February 3. This is the only time Grove appeared at this high-profile annual conclave.

When Grove was on the road, his days were packed. The day of the Davos speech, for example, began with a meeting at 7:45 in the morning and ended with a working dinner that concluded at 10:00 p.m. His keynote address was delivered from 8:30 to 9:15 a.m. He was accompanied by Eva, as he was on a number of trips that year, which doubtless made the experience easier and more enjoyable. As with so many of Grove's presentations, this one featured live "demos." There is always the chance that something will go wrong.[7]

If it was a strain for Grove to work as hard as he was, it did not show. From his youth in Hungary, he had learned to manage an audience. By 1998, when he would turn sixty-two on September 2, he was a masterful communicator and seemed completely at ease. This may have been an illusion. One executive who got to know him at about this time recalled that when Andy and Eva were driving into San Francisco one day, he pulled over and asked her to take the wheel, saying, "I'm just so tired."[8]

Grove not only ran Intel; as CEO he represented it. He had been running the company, according to one contemporary, from as early as 1972 and more clearly by 1975 when he officially became "executive vice president."[9] It should be said that when he began "running the company" depends upon what one means by that phrase. Grove himself has said that Intel never was a one-man show. He and Gordon Moore had a lifelong, intriguing, mutually dependent relationship.

Although Moore does not appear old for his chronological age, he seems to come from a different era from Grove. In a way he does. He had already participated in two start-ups prior to Intel (Shockley and Fairchild),[10] and one of these (Fairchild) had some very successful years. Moreover, he lacks completely that exotic air with which Grove's accent endows him. His relationship to Grove was more like that of a father than a brother. As late as December 5, 2005, Grove wrote Moore, in response to a complimentary email, "Seriously, your compliments still matter a great deal to me. Thank you."[11] Gordon Moore was progressively disengaging from business during the late 1990s. This was a fact. Grove had followed Moore—mentor and father figure—step by step.[12] It is perhaps true that Moore's disengagement was one factor in Grove's thinking about his own future.

Nineteen ninety-seven was a glittering year for Grove. In addition to Davos, there was Herb Allen's annual gathering of the elite in Sun Valley, Idaho, in July. Andy Grove, who as a boy was too nervous to photograph Mátyás Rákosi at Sandor Petőfi's home and memorial in Kiskoros in Hungary, met with the president of the United States, in the company of other CEOs, for more than an hour on June 4. Next that day came meetings with the leadership of the Congress, as well as a one-hour meeting with Secretary of the Treasury Robert Rubin. He met with former President George H. W. Bush for an hour at his home in Houston on April 8.

Heads of governments, heads of the world's most important corporations, Nobel Prize winners—if not Grove's daily fare, he spent a lot of time with such people. He was Intel's ambassador. There was probably no important person in the world who would not have returned a phone call from Andy Grove in 1997.

This is heady stuff. However, as so often has been the case in Grove's life, many wheels were turning at once. Moore's presence was receding. Grove felt that Craig Barrett, whom Intel had hired back in 1974 and who had done such an outstanding job in manufacturing, deserved his chance as Intel's CEO. There was only a three-year difference in age between the two. Grove asked Barrett if he felt he was ready to become CEO. Barrett responded that he was prepared to play any role deemed best for the company.[13]

There were other, more strictly personal considerations that were affecting Grove. His parents were long-lived, but he had prostate cancer in 1995. Cancer punctuates your life. Ask anyone you know who has won a bout with prostate cancer how he feels the evening before his regular PSA is to be drawn and what it is like waiting for the result. By 1997, Grove was having his PSA drawn three times a year. "It's an unusual thing," he said. "Most cancers don't have scorecards, but here you go and give blood, and a day later they tell you the rest of your life basically. I worry about it the last month of the four. It's not logical, but it's very observable and real. When I enter the month of the test, my stress notches up. And then as I get closer, I get more nervous. And then when they draw the blood, it's unimaginable—a new level of anxiety starts, and it continues until I get my results back."[14] Grove seems to have been more nervous before the thrice-a-year checkups than he was about the original diagnosis and treatment in 1995.

When Tom Brokaw interviewed Grove in 1996, he said, "You stunned the business world when you wrote a very compelling story about conquering prostate cancer." Grove challenged that statement because "No one ever conquers prostate cancer. I have prevailed so far and I hope to prevail further, but that word makes me uncomfortable."[15] We all know we are mortal, but when you have had prostate cancer, you hear the clock ticking more loudly.

Other developments exercising an influence on Grove's point of view came from family and friends. His first grandchild was born. Grove did a lot of traveling in 1997, and although it was all first-class, luxury, limousine, private plane, and so on, it still meant time away from home. His grandchild would only be a child once. How much of her childhood would he miss?

Eva and a friend she had recently made, Denise Amantea, were also asking Andy how much longer it made sense to keep up the pace.[16] It was clear that 1997 was going to be another record year for the company. Eva and Andy had come an awfully long way together. Why not shift gears? What more mountains were there to climb?

Toward the end of 1997, *Time* magazine contacted Andy about doing a story on him. He agreed. As they undertook their work, the reporters made it clear that this was going to be a major story. Sometime in December, it became obvious that *Time* had selected Grove as its "Man of the Year."

Time began selecting a "Man of the Year"—the title was changed to "Person of the Year" in 1999—in 1927. The magazine was founded by Henry Luce and Briton Hadden in 1923. Hadden died young, in 1929, and Luce (1898–1967), his Yale 1920 classmate, became the top person at *Time* and *Life*. The impetus for the "Man of the Year" idea was that the week after New Year's Day was usually slow for news, and this feature would liven it up. The magazine selected and profiled a "man, woman, couple, group, idea, place, or machine" that, as the editors put it, "for better or worse, has most influenced events in the preceding year."

Time's editors have repeated endlessly that the key criterion is influence, not whether the influence was for good or evil. Adolf Hitler was selected in 1938. Nevertheless, "the title is frequently mistaken as being an honor, . . . reward or prize."[17] That mistake is not surprising. Most of the choices, especially in recent years, have been admirable people.

Moreover, it is undoubtedly a distinction to be selected as "Man" or "Person" of the year. You are chosen. Others are not. The year begins with you on the cover of a magazine that received a lot of attention through much of the twentieth century. One must keep in mind that the Internet was still in its infancy when Grove was selected. *Time* was a good deal more important then than it is in the context of the explosion of the media that has taken place during the early years of the new century.

Given all he had done in his life, one could well ask why Grove would care what the editors of *Time* thought about him. The fact is that he did. So did his family and his friends. This is a man whose life had been full of struggle. *Time*'s selection of him shone forth as a vindication. In 1997, Tim Jackson published *Inside Intel: Andy Grove and the Rise of the World's Most Powerful Chip Company,*[18] a book highly critical of Intel as a company and of Grove as an executive and as a person. Once again one can ask: in light of the life he had led, why should Grove care about Tim Jackson and his book? The answer is that he cared because he is human.

Time trumped Tim. But it was more than that. We have seen that the very day Grove landed on American shores on January 7, 1957, *Time* came out with its "Man of the Year" issue. The "man" selected was the collective "Hungarian Freedom Fighter."[19] Forty-one years later Andrew Stephen Grove (né András István Gróf) was *Time*'s selection.

The articles accompanying *Time*'s cover story on Grove and especially one of the authors exercised an important influence. The title of the cover story was "The Microchip Is the Dynamo of a New Economy . . . Driven by the Passion of Intel's Andrew Grove." The author is Walter Isaacson. He noted that 1997 was "a year of big stories," but the biggest was the "new economy." At the center of that was the "microchip," that is, the microprocessor; and at the center of that was Andy Grove.

Here was Isaacson's take on Grove's character. He had a paranoia stemming from his youth, the "entrepreneurial optimism" of the immigrant, and "a sharpness tinged with arrogance" resulting from having "a brilliant mind on the front line of a revolution." He combined "a courageous passion" with "an engineer's analytic coldness."[20] Grove was indeed both passionate and clinical. His ability to combine the two has been one of his signal strengths.

To call him "tinged with arrogance" is, however, not quite right. He is neither modest nor immodest but has an accurate view of what he does well and where his weaknesses lie. He knows he has made mistakes in the past and can make them in the future, which is why he so vigorously questions his own assumptions. I brought to his attention a famous quotation from a letter Oliver Cromwell wrote to the General Assembly of the Church of Scotland in 1650: "I beseech you, in the bowels of Christ, think it possible you may be mistaken." His response: "That . . . quote is priceless!"[21] He knew it applies to everyone, including him, who is more certain than they should be that they have answers to difficult questions.

The thesis of the Isaacson piece was that the microprocessor was "like the steam engine, electricity and the assembly line—an advance that propels a new economy." One reason for selecting Grove as "Man of the Year" was that it was he who had made Moore's law come true. Remember, Moore's idea that semiconductor productivity could increase at the astonishing rate it did described a possibility, an opportunity, not a certainty.[22] To make this dream come true required superlative business acumen. That is what Grove provided.[23]

"Vindication" is again the word that comes to mind. In his early years at Intel, when he was doing a great deal of the heavy lifting, Grove was receiving precious little public credit for his achievements. After Bob Noyce's divorce in 1974 and remarriage the following year, he played a progressively less important role in the company. In the words of Noyce's biographer, Leslie Berlin, "By all rights, the attention paid to Noyce when he was president of Intel should have shifted to Moore, and possibly to Grove, after 1975."[24]

That, however, is not what happened. Intel's public relations agency, run by Valley personality Regis McKenna, set out to "put a human face" on the company, and the human McKenna chose was Noyce. The less work Noyce did at the firm, the more attention he received in high-profile publications including *Business Week* and the *New York Times*.[25]

Moore noticed this but could live with it. It got on Grove's nerves, however. At one point, Eva Grove took it upon herself to phone Noyce at the office and talk to him about the situation. She told Noyce that she knew he "appreciated Andy, but I think he's not feeling he's getting the recognition, he's not getting the chance to be out there and to be recognized on the outside. And I said people are talking to him, and I'd just hate to see him leave Intel. And I don't think he wants to leave Intel. But he just might."[26]

Eva said that the conversation was brief and that Bob "was encouraging and positive." This phone call may have been one of the factors motivating Noyce to get in touch with McKenna. There was a worried sound in his tone when he said that "Andy feels like Gordon and I get all the credit. We have got to make Andy more visible, and we've got to give him more credit." McKenna told Leslie Berlin that he phoned the same reporter who had written a story about Noyce in late 1976 about the newsworthy aspects of Grove's life and career. McKenna reported to Berlin "with satisfaction" that the result was the article on Grove as "High Technology Jelly Bean Ace" in the Sunday New York Times.[27] "That article launched Andy," claimed McKenna.[28]

By 1997, there was no need for this kind of activity to generate press coverage for Grove. He was at the center of Intel, at the center of the Valley, at the center of technology. He seemed to be at the center of the future.

Grove had always kept his private life private. He did not discuss his youthful encounters with fascism and communism. When asked about his past, he clammed up, as Terry Gross found out when she interviewed him on Fresh Air. Commenting on that interview recently, he said, "frontal assaults don't work well with me."[29]

There was, however, something quite remarkable about how Josh Ramo interviewed him for the "Man of the Year" piece. Somehow, he established an environment in which Grove felt he could tell his story. As we know, "timing is everything," and Ramo was interviewing Grove at a high point in his career and in his life. Without the special touch of a gifted reporter, the opportunity might have been squandered. To be sure, Grove remained "protective" of his family. He asked that neither the names nor occupations of his two daughters be mentioned in the article. Nevertheless, his daughters were interviewed, and I believe this is the first time they were publicly quoted about their father.

This is what they had to say. According to Karen, referred to in the article as "his older daughter," "He was a wonderful father." Robie, the "younger," said, "Being Andy Grove's child isn't for the faint of heart. But if you can roll with it, it's great." Grove took the girls on his travels abroad when he could, but there was no free ride. They were required to write reports on the countries they visited. Their reward was a nickel a page. "That's how we'd get our spending money. Luckily, [our] grandparents would kick in a little more."

Ramo portrayed Grove as a devoted family man. He "has always been fully flushed with fatherhood." And "[h]is marriage to Eva—the daughters call her 'Eva the saint'—has been the essential constant in Grove's life. He is clearly still nuts about her. There is a world-worn gentleness in their touch. She takes care of him: lays out his breakfast, orders the small details of his life, helps him find whatever he needs. Grove's big eyes—which in meetings can penetrate the skull of an unprepared executive at 50 feet—are at their softest when he rests them on Eva." Andy and Eva were married in the torrent of youth. The forty-seven years they have spent together have drawn them closer. His understanding of how lucky he is to be with her and the ways he shows it are touching.

Ramo wrote that the Groves "today are worth 'north of $300 million.' He could almost not care less. Grove doesn't spend his money on planes, giant homes or fast cars. He lives on a relatively modest scale." Moore was reported to possess $7 billion in Intel stock. In sum, this was the most personally revealing article that ever appeared about Grove, who said that Ramo started early, and he didn't try to break down doors. "It was more like a flirtation."

The selection as "Man of the Year," the manifest success of Intel, Barrett's readiness to take the helm, the urging of Eva and of Denise Amantea—all combined to prompt Grove to take the fateful step. After thinking of stepping down for so many years, he finally decided that now was the time.

He was later quoted to the effect that trading the CEO's job for board chairman "was one of the most wrenching transitions of his life."[30] That is not, however, what he remembers it as being, nor is it the way people who knew him when he made the decision remember it. Grove stepped down because it was time to do so.

24

"Frozen in Silicon"

The official announcement was made on Thursday, March 26, 1998. "Intel CEO Andy Grove Steps Aside; A Founding Father of Silicon Valley," reported one of hundreds of headlines around the country and the world.[1] The Groves were at one of their vacation homes when the news was released. Andy went into town to scan the coverage. He was on the front page of every newspaper he saw.

Reporting for the *Washington Post*, Elizabeth Corcoran wrote, "At the heart of the computer is a single silicon chip, the microprocessor. And at the heart of Silicon Valley is the man who made the lion's share of those chips, Intel Corp. chief executive Andy Grove." Grove was sixty-one. Barrett, to whom he was "turning over the daily reins of the company," was fifty-eight. "The whole Intel experience was patterned after Andy," Barrett commented.[2] He was right.

How can we evaluate Grove's decade-long leadership of the company? In financial terms, as we noted at the beginning of this book,[3] Intel with Grove at the helm could hardly have done much better.

In strategic terms, Intel was a struggling company when Grove was recalled early from his sabbatical to save it. The seemingly unstoppable Japanese juggernaut had crushed its memory business. That product line was where the company not only had its brains but also its heart. Microprocessors beckoned, but change is always hard, especially so in this instance when the thought of being driven out of memory caused cognitive dissonance throughout the organization that generated one reason, or rationalization, after another about why Intel had to stay in it. Moreover, where was the guarantee that after chasing the Americans out of memories, the Japanese would not proceed to chase them out of microprocessors?

Grove has written that the CEO is often the last to know about the challenges his or her company faces. That certainly was not true in this case. Grove built the bridge across the technological chasm between memory and microprocessor, and the Intel army marched behind him. Unlike Gates and Allen, unlike Jobs, unlike even Noyce, Grove was not an early convert to the idea that the future of the world and of Intel lay in mass-marketed personal computers. Nor was Grove an early cheerleader for microprocessors. "Microprocessors meant nothing to me [in the early 1970s]," he told Leslie Berlin. "I was living and dying on two points of yields in memory."[4] Once he "got it," he got it like no one else. "The PC Is It" was something this CEO understood in all its implications. Soon thereafter, Intel, which could have failed in the face of the Japanese onslaught, became "awesome."

The decision to sole-source the 386 proved a masterstroke. This ranks high among the most important strategic moves in the history of the computer industry. The success of the 386 not only as a technical device but as a marketing strategy was complete.

One success after another followed close on its heels. The 486, Intel Inside, the Pentium—the sum total of all these initiatives put Intel squarely in the middle of the "new computer industry." It was a hardware world, and it was Intel's hardware that defined that world. Thanks to Moore's seminal insight in 1965, just one year after the IBM 360 debuted, everyone at Intel knew that change had to be part of the company's DNA.

Intel made ever more complex chips for technical and business reasons. As we have noted, Grove believed that from a technical standpoint, anything that could be done would be done.[5] This is not to say that life on the cutting edge of technology was easy. A semiconductor fabrication facility is one of the most complicated and exacting manufacturing operations ever created in the whole history of the world. One of the mottoes of Craig Barrett, the manufacturing genius of the company during Grove's tenure as CEO, was that complexity was never an excuse. "We've outlawed [that] word," he has asserted. That is to say, if there was a problem in a fab, the explanation that the task at hand was terribly complicated was never satisfactory.

Everything they did in the fab was terribly complicated.[6] John Doerr, who spent six years working at Intel in the 1970s before joining the venture capital firm Kleiner, Perkins, said that "Andy Grove had no tolerance for people who were late or meetings that ran on without a purpose. It wasn't that he was a hard ass. It's just the nature of their business. There's no room for error."[7]

When you measure width in fractions of a micron—a human hair is about 75 microns in diameter[8]—you get a sense of the precision required in this business. Remember that Intel was mass-producing its microprocessors, not just crafting one at a time in the pristine serenity of a laboratory.

In addition to the belief that if Intel did not drive the technology forward, someone else was destined to do so, the company viewed technical change as its friend. Substantive change in performance meant that the computer you had on your desk would become obsolete. You would need a new one. When Grove was being treated for prostate cancer, the Seattle hospital where he received his treatment was using computers with the Intel 286 microprocessor. Three years out of date by the time Grove was treated, a computer powered by a 16-bit 286 CPU simply could not do things that a 32-bit 386 could do.[9] It could not, for example, run Microsoft's breakthrough Windows 3.0, introduced in 1990.

Intel's enemy, indeed the enemy of all new technology, is the phrase "good enough."[10] That is why Grove recommended to the thousands of people who attended Intel's annual Sales and Marketing Conference in 1998 that if they were to read one business book the following year, that book should be what has become a classic work by Professor Clayton Christensen of the Harvard Business School entitled *The Innovator's Dilemma: When New Technologies Cause Great Firms to Fail.*[11] The thesis of Christensen's book is that high-technology companies tend to get too close to their most demanding customers. To satisfy these customers, to make higher-margin products themselves, and to challenge their own ingenuity, these technology suppliers migrate upmarket, producing ever more sophisticated and expensive products at steadily higher prices. This product policy leaves an opening for a new entrant to the market who produces a less sophisticated device that is sufficient for the needs of most users and is much less expensive. Not a great product, but "good enough" and a lot cheaper.

This dynamic has always posed a threat to Intel. To see how real the threat is, look at the computer on your desk. Other than processing email, searching the Web, and, perhaps, using Excel, what needs that are really urgent for you does it satisfy? If you could buy a gadget for a small fraction of the price that served solely to get you to the Internet, would you prefer it? Intel's product policy has been purposefully broadened to protect the company against a new entrant's gaining a foothold with inexpensive products, achieving economies of scale, and moving upmarket.

One way to assess the record of a CEO is to look for the disasters that did not take place on his or her watch. Being outflanked by a cheaper product is one such example. Another is RISC. Grove was tempted, but he didn't take the bait.

Speaking of him strictly as a manager, the impact of Grove on Intel, therefore on the Valley, which is so widely populated with Intel alumni, and therefore on high technology in twentieth- and early twenty-first-century America has been immense. "At Grove's core," according to the *Washington Post*'s Corcoran, "is that driven sense of discipline—the determination to drill down into the details, to persevere."[12]

There were instances in which Grove drilled down with excessive abandon. "Sometimes even he recognized that he had gone too far," Ramo wrote in *Time*'s "Man of the Year" essay. "After I cooled down, I apologized," Grove observed of one of his own outbursts. "But by then it was too late. A loyal, experienced and valuable manager had been so hurt that no apology could get through to him."[13] Whoever this manager may have been, he is not alone. There are plenty of people at Intel who have been wounded by Grove's words.

Rob Walker, who conducted a number of interviews for the "Silicon Genesis" oral history project, made the following comment when speaking with Federico Faggin. "Well, I noticed that change at Intel in the culture. It used to be that when Noyce was very active in the company, there would be a meeting and Andy Grove would start off on one of his diatribes and Noyce would say 'Andy, shut up.' And that was sort of the end of it. So he was able to hold him in check and then as Noyce semi-retired and became vice chairman, a lot of the decency went out of the company."[14] It is hard to believe that Noyce ever told Grove to "shut up." Noyce was not that direct. Furthermore, he needed Andy very much. But that remark is on the Web for anyone to see, and Tim Jackson's screed about Grove is easily available for anyone to read.

The simple, sad truth is that Grove's sharp tongue has hurt a lot of people. Some bear grudges they will not forget. Barrett remarked that "Occasionally we . . . suggest [to Grove] there may be an alternative to grabbing someone and slamming them over the head with a sledgehammer."[15]

Grove had anger attacks. Why were they so effective at turning so many people "into mush"?[16] Not an easy question. There was never any physical menace. Grove himself is not a big man, and no one has ever alleged that he picked something up and threw it across a room, much less actually at someone. Grove has told me that although people have perceived him as shouting, in fact he seldom raised his voice. I told him that although he may not often shout, his voice does tend to rise an octave when he is frustrated.

Grove's impact lies not only in the fact that he is both smart and relentless. It also resides in a certain pattern that asserts itself when you get into an argument with him. You can feel quite trapped. He not only argues, he seems to be able to control the terms of the debate. You can feel yourself being maneuvered into agreeing that he is right and you are wrong. Once that point is reached, he becomes dismissive.

A close analogy may be losing a chess game. You may have played for hours. You have given it all your concentration. But you feel inexorably driven toward losing because you have to play by rules you did not make, and your opponent is better at this particular game with these rules than you are. When, at length, you resign, it can be a miserably destructive experience. To deal with Andy at work, you simply have to get past this dynamic. You have to know what you are talking about. You have to give as good as you get. You have to have an inexhaustible appetite for such jousts, because he does.

For those who made it past "the Grove treatment," the commitment they developed to the man, not to the company but to Andy personally, is hard to overstate in its intensity. I have spoken to dozens of present and, especially, former employees of Intel who were there during the Grove era. The variety of backgrounds from which they come is remarkable. The gratitude they feel toward him, from far down in the ranks to top people who are today very wealthy, is hard to communicate. They feel he got the best out of them they had to give. Sometimes he wrung it out of them. They discovered that they were better, smarter, more skilled, more effective, more able to concentrate than they had dreamed they could be prior to falling into his orbit.

For this set of people, Grove was genuinely charismatic. He touched something in them that was beyond the rational. Some of these people do not like one another. They were held together by a sense of fealty, for lack of a better word, to Grove. These people who passed the Grove test share a trait in common. They have an edge. You feel it when you speak to them. Man or woman, religious or atheist, from whatever part of the country or the world, engineer or not, soft-spoken or not—they all share this edge. The Intel edge of the Andy era. It made the company great.

Now let's look at the other side of the ledger. "My personality," Grove well knew, "you either like or hate."[17] For some very talented people, the answer was "hate." They left. Intel lost their services. "Former Intel executives are plentiful in Silicon Valley, some because they had had enough of the Intel way."[18]

It must also be said that in the war for talent, Grove was no slouch. When John Doerr told him back in 1980 that he was leaving Intel to join Kleiner, Perkins, where he created a legend of his own, Grove offered him what appeared to be a promising new job to keep him at the company. Doerr said, "He reaches inside of you and pulls your heart out and puts it in front of you."[19]

Also on the other side of the ledger were the products that flopped. Among these, the most painful and perhaps the most expensive was ProShare. Grove had been passionate about it. This product was "one of the largest commitments ever made by Intel in a non-microprocessor area." Seven hundred people and three-quarters of a billion dollars later, by 1998, Grove had to admit failure. He did not use the phrase, but he was chasing what at the time was a "ghost market" with this product.[20]

It is not uncommon for big companies, especially if they are still run by entrepreneurs, to make big bets on big products. ProShare failed, but it was a failure Intel could afford. Arguably, it was the kind of failure Intel could not afford to avoid if it were to push the envelope to grow its business.

If we were to seek one instance of a single, discrete management blunder during Grove's decade as CEO, that would be the handling of the floating point flaw. There was something about this episode, hard to put one's finger on it, that disarmed him. According to Josh Ramo, Grove "was floored" by the uproar. He went on a family ski trip at Christmas of 1994, in the midst of the fracas. It didn't help, as he "grimly [rode] the lifts for three days." One of his daughters observed, "He had really punched himself in the face. We were all like, 'This too shall pass,' but he just went inside himself."[21] His other daughter does not remember things this way.

Karen Alter, the sharp-witted Harvard Business School MBA whom Andy lured to Intel, was in marketing working with Dennis Carter and Pam Pollace, head of public relations, when the Pentium flaw became news. Some part of the disorientation caused by the event was that it was among the first news stories driven by the Internet. All kinds of rumors were circulating in cyberspace and then being picked up by the mainstream media, which, anxious not to be scooped, reproduced them as facts. Suddenly, especially after the IBM shipment halt, Intel found itself adrift in a storm-tossed sea of misinformation.

This was the only time that Alter, who retired from Intel in 2000 but remains friends with Andy, saw him freeze. She said it was like watching Gregory Peck in the famous and unaccountably popular 1949 movie *Twelve O'Clock High*. Peck plays the "hard-ass" General Frank Savage assigned to whip into shape the 918th Bomber Group, which is beset by low morale. Peck/Savage is tough as nails and cares nothing for personal popularity. He succeeds in his mission but the end of the film finds him overwhelmed by the reality of war and death, and he breaks down.

Most of all, Alter believes Grove could not deal with the fact that the incident had spiraled out of control so quickly. It seemed that all the moving parts were obeying an unfamiliar set of rules. "I was thick-headed," Grove said in an interview in 1996. "I don't know how to say that differently."[22] Once again, Grove is his own shrewdest critic. "Thick-headed" is not a phrase commonly associated with him.

Talk to Grove today about this episode, and he gets angry quickly. "To think," he says, "it was actually compared to Tylenol," the Johnson & Johnson analgesic that was poisoned in 1982 and 1986, resulting in the deaths of eight people. He is right. Dennis Carter was asked to compare the Pentium flaw to Tylenol by the *New York Times* on December 14, 1994. Carter was not happy with the question. He responded that "in the Tylenol case, people were dying. . . . With Pentium, you have a one-half of 1 percent error that might occur—might occur—once every 27,000 years. This is a non-issue. Comparing this to Tylenol is totally inappropriate."[23] Grove still protests—correctly, but not relevantly—that not one hair on anyone's head was harmed by the flaw.[24]

Craig Barrett emerged as the real hero of the Pentium flaw story. Barrett approached this as just another business problem. He stepped in and took charge, with Andy's blessing. Intel eventually emerged bloodied, to the tune of its $475 million write-off, but unbowed.[25] David Yoffie believes that "the irony of the Pentium floating point episode is that it generated enormous brand recognition for Pentium. Once the flaw was fixed, the combination of brand strength and renewed confidence in Intel helped drive the rapid conversion from the 486 to Pentium."[26]

What else can we find on the negative side of the ledger during Grove's tenure as CEO? Grove has prided himself on being an institution builder. When asked by a reporter recently how he would like to be remembered, he replied, "As a guy who had a lot to do with Intel."[27] He had a passionate desire to know not only the products Intel manufactured but the people in the company . . . their strengths and weaknesses . . . their personal ambitions and willingness to sacrifice for Intel . . . their hearts, as Doerr said, as well as their heads. He wanted argument, controversy, fearlessness, commitment. He wanted all these things to be woven into the fabric of the company.

By the time Grove stepped down as CEO of Intel, he had been running the company for over two decades in fact if not in name. His knowledge of its people, processes, and products was unmatched. He had seen good times and bad times. He had survived the product flops prior to the success of the 1103 DRAM, as wretchedly temperamental as that product was. He had lived through the layoffs of 1974, the "125 percent solution" of 1981 during which employees were asked to work an extra two hours a day with no pay raise, the dark days of 1985 and 1986 when Intel shuttered seven factories and was forced to fire a third of its workforce, the Pentium flaw, and a myriad other problems.

Meanwhile, through storm and stress, the company grew to become a behemoth, one of the largest in terms of market capitalization in the world. It came to dominate its industry. Intel set the hardware standard for the post–mainframe computer era. Grove both ran the company and represented it to the world. His people saw him everywhere—in his cubicle in the RNB, in newspapers and magazines at their newsstands, on the shelves of their bookstores, and on television. With his leadership, Intel had beaten the Japanese, it had beaten Motorola, it had beaten the dozens of semiconductor start-ups that were born at the same time Intel was, it had beaten IBM, and it had not been beaten by Bill Gates. On the personal front, Grove had beaten cancer.

Given a record like this, it is perhaps not surprising that a cult of personality grew up around Grove. "You know," he said to a reporter recently, "I'm not a hog. The last person I would like to kid is myself. I may stumble here and there, but I really try not to kid myself."[28] Comments like this only intensified the aura of magic that came to surround him by the late 1990s.

There were people at the firm more devoted to him than to Intel. The very magnitude of his success made his successor's job all the more difficult.

The transition of power from one CEO to the next is among the most important responsibilities of the outgoing CEO and the board of directors. In this case, judging from the press, the transition went smoothly. Most commentators expected it.[29] Only one clipping that I have seen mentioned health as a possible reason for Grove's departure. "He had a well-publicized bout with cancer in 1994–1995," wrote Kevin Maney in *USA Today*, "but is not stepping down for health reasons."[30] "Are you going to write another book?" Maney asked Grove. "Nooooo," came the unequivocal reply. "Books come at the same rate as CEOs at Intel."[31] This was a forecast that would be proven incorrect in three years.

What would Grove's new role be? He was already chairman of the board, so part of his new role would be a continuation of his previous one. Maney asked Grove what Intel's number one challenge was, and he answered, "Growth. And the industry's growth. We have a supreme internal machinery for fine tuning and delivering microprocessors. Our presence in the marketplace is as large as it's ever been. But as the industry fragments into servers and low-cost clients and mobile computing, it's not getting easier but harder to push the envelope. That's why I'll spend more time on it, but it's Craig's challenge as well."[32] According to Arthur Rock, "We need someone who is going to spend more time on operations and how the business is done, while Andy spends more time figuring out where it's going."[33]

What role would Andy play as chairman while Craig was CEO? Would the board become more or less active? Would anything of consequence happen at Intel of which he did not personally approve as long as he was chairman? Would Andy play the role solely of evaluator? Or would he be an initiator as well? "It's too much in his blood to walk away," said one financial analyst. "It would be an enormous loss if he walked away. He will still be the godfather of the PC for some time to come."[34]

"I have thoroughly enjoyed being Intel's CEO for the past 11 years," Grove explained, "and now I would like to focus more of my time on broad strategic issues concerning the industry and Intel. Craig and I have had a long working relationship and I look forward to a smooth transition as I continue my work as chairman." The problem was that Grove was an impact player in the nation and the world. Barrett was a man to conjure with as well, but his reputation was much more restricted to the company and the industry.

When Noyce stepped down, there was Moore. When Moore stepped down, there was Grove. All three were powerful presences in the world of high technology. All were present at the creation of Intel in July 1968. All had impressive reputations by the time they took the helm. "The transfer of power [from Grove to Barrett], although planned, is a symbolic changing of the guard for Intel, for the chip industry, and for just about everyone who uses a personal computer," according to one journalist.[35] Would anyone be speaking in such terms about the transition from Barrett to his successor when that time came? During interviews I often asked what Intel would have been like without Grove. Many people found it impossible to answer that question. This is what Moore said: "Without Andy Grove, Intel might have been a less intense, more friendly company, but it would also be a smaller, less profitable company."[36] This is a noteworthy observation from the man Grove chose as his surrogate father. If ever there was a moment at which one should say something nice or nothing at all, surely this was it. The phrase "more friendly company" could have been dropped, and no one would have missed it. However, Moore, in his distinctive way, said what was on his mind whether it was for public or private consumption.

Grove got a kick out of being listed among "America's toughest bosses" in a *Fortune* article in August 1984.[37] He was much less well-known then. By the late 1990s, headlines such as "Attila the Hungarian" were, one senses, beginning to wear a little thin.[38]

In his own comments about Barrett, Grove was consistently gracious and upbeat. "Craig is more purposeful, more organized—and tougher—than I am," he told an English business publication. These attributes of his had worked wonders for Intel's operations during the previous ten years. "He transformed Intel from a medium manufacturer to an outstanding one. He is now ready to exercise those qualities on business matters as well, hence his promotion to president."[39] One financial analyst commented that Barrett "smiles a lot more and is more diplomatic."[40]

The same day that Intel announced the change in the executive suite—one should say the executive cubicle—it also announced a 100-million share buyback program. The financial markets took it all in stride. Intel's shares rose 1.938 to close at 78.1875.[41]

The news media, however, were not as warm and welcoming as the market. They "were happy to take Intel down a few notches." Grove was "a tough guy, hard to criticize and legendary in the industry. If you wanted to run a hatchet piece on Intel, you had to think you were smarter than Grove." This was an assumption few were willing to make. When Barrett took center stage, he did not inherit his predecessor's aura. "The media doled out heaping scoops of pain and anguish for Craig Barrett. You almost had to feel sorry for him."[42]

Craig Barrett was Andy Grove's handpicked successor. He was as smart as anyone. He knew the company as well as anyone. He was capable of prodigious amounts of work and was willing to travel far more than Grove. Nevertheless, we are left with the question of whether he was the best choice for the job. Grove could have chosen anybody. Why Barrett?

Smart. Tough. Direct. Results-oriented. Calm in crises. Unflappable. Highly intelligent. Ambitious. Utterly devoted to the company—its products and its culture. A known quantity of proven ability. All these things could be said of Craig Barrett at the time he was chosen to lead the company. What more could one want?

Perhaps nothing. Nobody was questioning Barrett's discharge of his responsibilities on, say, August 31, 2000, when Intel's market capitalization hit the truly incredible height of half a trillion dollars. But when the bubble burst, Intel's stock tanked along with it. Intel could buck a trend in 1996 but not in 2001. If you had invested in Intel on the day in May 1998 when Craig Barrett became CEO and sold that investment in May 2005 when he was elevated to the chairmanship of the board, you would not have made any money.

Is that Barrett's fault? Is it Grove's fault for selecting Barrett? Is it Grove's fault for remaining on the board and looking over Barrett's shoulder during his tenure as CEO? Is it the board's fault for going along with the selection?

Looked at from another angle, are Barrett, Grove, and the board all to be applauded? Almost every publicly traded company in the country, especially those in technology, benefited from the bubble when it was at its peak and was clobbered when the crash came. If you plot the price of Intel's stock against the performance of AMD, Texas Instruments, the Philadelphia Semiconductor Index, the Dow Jones Industrial Average, the NASDAQ, Cisco, and Microsoft, the graphs all look similar.

It was Barrett's astuteness, toughness, and exceptionally hard work that kept Intel in the game and positioned the company to ride out the violent gyrations of Wall Street. Grove believes the way Barrett handled the bust after the boom was his finest performance.[43] Intel is today a pillar of a whole new economy, with manufacturing capability second to none. It throws off

FIGURE 12

The Performance of Intel Stock in Comparison to Relevant Benchmarks

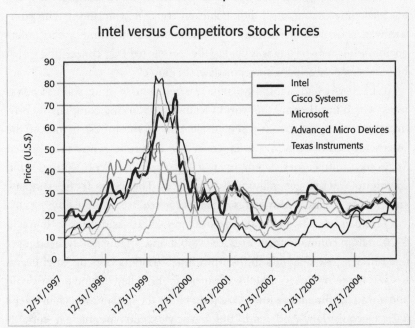

cash at an astonishing rate, permitting a great deal of flexibility in facing the future. It is impossible to look at Intel's financials and its strategic position today without seeing a very strong company.

Given the macroeconomic forces, a stock market that in the short term is driven by the famed conflict between fear and greed and is governed more by rumor and herd instinct than by a rational appreciation of business fundamentals, and given further the unprecedented national and global developments that rocked the nation and over which no business executive could have any control—the contested presidential election of 2000, the astonishingly successful terrorist attacks of September 11, 2001, and the pointless and painful replay of Vietnam in Iraq—one can make a strong argument that Intel is to be congratulated rather than criticized. Compare it to whole industries—automobiles, airlines—and it looks very good.

And yet . . .

Speaking to Robert Burgelman late in 1999, Grove indulged in some speculation on "what might have been." "There was a time," he reflected, "when I could have flipped a switch between videoconferencing and networking. I was funding both opportunities. Much more funding was going to videoconferencing, but I didn't chicken-choke networking."[44] The problem was, as Grove conceded in 1999, "the market didn't want" videoconferencing, while networking was vital to the "connected PC," concerning which he had been evangelizing since the dawn of email.[45]

What Grove had in mind when he referred to networking was Cisco Systems, which has become the world's leading networking company by producing routers that are an essential element of the infrastructure of the Internet. Cisco Systems was founded by two computer center managers at Stanford: Sandy Lerner (women play a larger role in Silicon Valley than in corporate America generally) and Len Bozak. The name of the company comes from the last two syllables of San Francisco.

"We considered—halfheartedly—buying Cisco," said Grove. "It was a $200 million company then." It is a $108 billion company today, headquartered in San Jose, a stone's throw from Intel's headquarters in Santa Clara. Cisco is the second most valuable company in the Valley, behind only Google and ahead of third-place Intel. "We didn't have the distribution channel for a Cisco acquisition," Andy said. "But maybe we could have made it work."[46]

And maybe not. Intel's track record in acquisitions has been miserable. Perhaps Intel would have smothered Cisco if it had been acquired. We will never know, but you can almost hear Grove sigh as he thinks about this particular "might-have-been."

The fact is that Intel's growth has been, in by far its greatest part, internal. It has not been able to grow by acquisition. Usually, internally generated growth is a sign of strength. Intel is indeed a strong company with a robust business model. However, there is a problem if it cannot spot a company like Cisco, which fit so well Grove's vision of the future, buy it, and integrate it successfully.

This, then, belongs on the negative side of the ledger of Grove's leadership of the company. Cisco is close enough to Intel's business that it could reasonably be considered a related acquisition. Companies whose businesses were less related but which were deeply involved in markets that Intel wanted to penetrate were unthinkable as acquisitions.

Grove told Burgelman in 1999 that a proposed acquisition of a company called Fore Technologies was placed before the board and voted down. Grove abstained. This, he said, "was the only time the board rejected management's recommendation." In retrospect, Grove agreed with the board's decision.[47]

What deserves emphasis is that "management," in the above quotation, meant Craig Barrett. This was the first proposed acquisition he put before the board, and the directors rejected it. This result could not have presented itself to Barrett as a vote of confidence in him, nor could it have whetted his appetite for bringing more candidates for acquisition to the board. It is an illustration of the difference between the standing of Grove and Barrett in the eyes of others. It is hard to believe that the board would have rejected anything Grove proposed when he became CEO in the spring of 1987.

Why has Intel failed to acquire companies that might have helped it grow in new directions? The answer is a combination of ingredients. One was Intel's uniquely powerful culture. If you were in, you belonged. If you were not, getting in was very difficult. Another was the "creosote bush." Grove himself has complained more than once that the sinews of Intel's power did not extend sufficiently far from what it knew best. Its power in microprocessors had been repeatedly demonstrated. The farther you strayed from that bright-shining star, the weaker the gravitational pull became. On December 7, 2005, in a class he taught with Robert Burgelman at Stanford, Grove was asked whether a big company was better off attempting an acquisition or using "internal venturing" to develop new products and prevent them from being marginalized. With characteristic bluntness, Grove responded that Intel had been "shitty" at diversifying no matter whether through acquisition or internal venturing. The reason was a combined lack of "strategic recognition" and "strategic will." Whatever Intel tried did not, after a year or two, look as good as the microprocessor. The result was that the company consistently gave up too soon.[48]

Finally, there was the fact that, as John Doerr said, the nature of Intel's business meant there was no margin for error.[49] If you were going to be the king of the microprocessor hill, you had to devote yourself to that goal. Intel did, perhaps to a fault.

There was a larger issue about Intel's future as the 1990s drew to a close. Intel's top people knew well that the Internet was the future, and they had known this since 1995 if not sooner. Netscape, another Valley start-up, located in Mountain View, had its initial public offering on August 9, 1995. The price of the stock soared from 28 to 58 on that single day. One journalist has called this "the unofficial launch date for the bull market in high-tech stocks."[50] That date might have been a little early to locate the beginning of the Internet bubble, but it certainly mattered. People in the know understood that the world of high tech was now in the grip of something altogether new and important.

What no one at Intel really understood was what the dawn of the Internet age meant. The ramifications of the Internet are not yet fully known, and the odds are they will not be known for decades. It is a sobering thought that it required about a hundred and fifty years for the world to appreciate the ramifications of the steam engine.

This much we do know. The existence of the Internet has permitted the rise of a new set of companies with previously undreamt-of business models to high market capitalizations faster than ever before in history. Foremost among these is Google.

Google opened its doors, or more accurately its door, in a garage in Menlo Park in the heart of Silicon Valley in September 1998. The following February it moved all eight of its employees to University Avenue in Palo Alto. On August 19, 2004, Google had its initial public offering. The stock quadrupled in price from that day to Christmas of 2005. The cofounders are Lawrence E. Page, known to everyone as Larry, and Sergey Brin. Page was born on March 28, 1973, in Ann Arbor, Michigan. Brin was born in August of that year in Moscow. Page and Brin met at Stanford. As of the end of 2005, they were, at the age of thirty-two, in possession of more financial assets than the Harvard University endowment. Harvard has been saving up since 1636. Google's market capitalization at the end of 2005 was $127 billion. The world had never seen anything like this happen so quickly. Page and Brin bought a Boeing 767 for themselves. Needless to say, it is fully equipped with a gymnasium. Brin especially likes the StairMaster.

Google was not the only miracle of Silicon Valley to be created during the Internet age. Yahoo! was also founded by two Stanford graduate students, David Filo and Jerry Yang, in January 1994. Its current market capitalization is $37.6 billion. eBay, surely one of the strangest companies in the history of capitalism, was founded on September 4, 1995. Its current market capitalization is $33.4 billion. eBay is located just south and east of Intel in San Jose. Yahoo! is just north and west in Sunnyvale. Google is just north and west of that in Mountain View. Among them, these three companies have a combined market capitalization of more than $180 billion, with well over half of that accounted for by Google.

We have not even mentioned Oracle. Founded in 1977, it has made Larry Ellison one of the world's richest people. Its sparkling cylindrical buildings in Redwood City are the first glimpse you get of what Silicon Valley has in store when you drive south from the San Francisco airport on U.S. 101. After a lengthy battle, Oracle acquired PeopleSoft in 2005. It claims to help "more governments and businesses around the world become information-driven than any other company."[51] Its market capitalization is $79.3 billion. Intel's market capitalization at present is $101.6 billion.

Wealth in unimaginable sums has been created on all sides of Intel. Some of that wealth was in the form of high-technology hardware, the best example being Cisco's routers. Some of it was in the form of high-technology hardware sold to consumers.

The outstanding example of a home run in consumer hardware is yet another product of the special genius of Steve Jobs. Jobs, the avatar of the new world in which we find ourselves, cofounded Apple Computer in 1976 when he was twenty-one years old. In 1985, he was forced out of the company, but he returned in triumph in 1997. In 2002, Apple brought out the iPod, and it took the world by storm. A company whose obituary had been written many times, Apple now has a market capitalization of $53.9 billion and sports a price/earnings ratio of 29.5. A share costs $63.40 as opposed to $6 at the beginning of 2000.

If Silicon Valley were to be named today, it would not be called Silicon Valley. There is plenty of money being made in hardware, from routers to products such as the iPod that a consumer walks into a store to buy; but the real revolution for the past half decade is in software. Silicon is the infrastructure. The two freeways that run the length of the peninsula from San Francisco to San Jose—U.S. 101 (the Bayshore Freeway) and Route 280 (the Junipero Serra Freeway, or merely "280" to the locals)—are the silicon of Silicon Valley today. They are not where the mystique is to be found. They are the roads that take you to where the mystique is to be found—San Jose, Sunnyvale, Cupertino, Mountain View, Palo Alto, San Bruno, Redwood City, and the home of so many venture capitalists on Sand Hill Road in Menlo Park. Just as there is plenty of money in hardware, there is also plenty left in silicon. But how much magic and mystique remains in the silicon of Silicon Valley? Perhaps the time has come to reposition microprocessors as software frozen in silicon.

25

Andy Grove—Ex-CEO

A ndy Grove's prestige only increased with each year following his stepping down as Intel CEO in 1998. In 2000 he received an honorary doctor of laws degree from Harvard. This is the highest honor that the nation's
oldest university can bestow.[1]

In 2001, not that any further evidence was necessary, he proved his attributes as a polymath once again with the publication of *Swimming Across: A
Memoir*. This book chronicles the harrowing first two decades of Grove's life.
He met with a lot of rejection from publishers who wanted him to tell the
world the secrets of business success. Rather than do that, he wrote the book he
wanted to write. The result is a masterpiece, unlike anything else ever written by
an important American business executive. This is a book that will live long after the standard business biographies and autobiographies are forgotten.

Barrett travels so much and Grove dislikes travel so much that Andy may
have spent more days at corporate headquarters, at least in 1998 and 1999,
than did Craig. Nevertheless, Andy's interest did begin to diverge from mainstream Intel. His concerns with health care grew as he became more involved
with prostate cancer issues and also became closer to the University of California at San Francisco's medical center.

In the year 2000, a new reason arose for Grove to interest himself in the
health care system. While Andy was out for a walk on Cow Hill in Palo Alto
with a friend named Barr Taylor, a Stanford psychiatrist whom Grove had

met when he first moved to Silicon Valley in 1963, Taylor noticed that Grove had a slight tremor in his right hand. He suggested this was a symptom calling for attention.

Grove was eventually diagnosed with Parkinson's disease, often referred to by those afflicted with it simply as PD. Parkinson's is a brain disease caused by the death of brain cells producing a substance called dopamine. The results of the loss of dopamine are, according to the National Institute of Neurological Disorders and Stroke of the U.S. National Institutes of Health, four principal symptoms: "tremor, or trembling in the hands, arms, legs, jaw, and face; rigidity, or stiffness in the limbs and trunk; bradykinesia, or slowness of movement; and postural instability, or impaired balance and coordination." Eventually, victims of this disease "may have difficulty walking, talking or completing other simple tasks."[2]

PD is a progressive disease. Symptoms become more severe with time. "[T]he shaking, or tremor, which affects the majority of PD patients, may begin to interfere with daily activities. Other symptoms may include depression and other emotional changes; difficulty in swallowing, chewing, and speaking; urinary problems or constipation; skin problems; and sleep disruptions."[3] Some 40 percent of Parkinson's patients are clinically depressed.[4] There are about one million people with PD in the United States today.

Thus the man who had been battling his body since the age of four had, at the age of sixty-four, a new front on which that battle had to be fought. There is no cure for PD, but there is treatment that can be very effective in mitigating its symptoms. A drug called levadopa, often referred to as l-dopa, can help brain cells produce dopamine. Unfortunately, treatment with levadopa diminishes in efficacy over time.

Although Parkinson's disease cannot be cured, it can be managed. Its management demands a lot of time, energy, concentration, and intelligence. For example, the patient may want to put off taking l-dopa for as long as possible. The drug is not effective for every patient, although it is for most. However, from the time you as a PD patient start using l-dopa, the clock starts ticking. When it stops working, there is no effective second-line treatment.

There is real hope that medical research may develop a cure for Parkinson's. Deep brain stimulation (DBS) works in some cases to activate dopaminurgic activity by brain cells still capable of it. DBS is a surgical procedure, and its very name suggests the risks involved.

Another highly promising avenue of research involves stem cells. Properly introduced into the brain, stem cells appear capable of creating dopamine-producing brain cells. There really does seem to be a chance that a breakthrough on any number of fronts might lead to an alleviation of suffering from PD.

On one aspect of PD all doctors are in agreement. Its course is difficult to predict. If it moves fast, it can savage your body, impact your cognitive skills, and contribute to death by generally weakening you and leaving you vulnerable to opportunistic infections such as pneumonia. If it moves slowly, you may not even notice you have it for a time. According to one estimate, half the people in the United States who have PD do not yet know it. Andy probably had it for at least six months before Barr Taylor diagnosed it. The tremor in the hand is likely to be the first symptom.

When my late wife and I met with Andy and Eva Grove in May 2003 to discuss the writing of this book, Andy's PD symptoms were obvious but not extreme. They progressed through 2004. Grove, who in his "geek" years in the 1960s wore thick, dark-rimmed eyeglasses, had shifted to contact lenses by 1985. By 2004, he switched back to eyeglasses, his tremor having made it difficult for him to put contacts in his eyes. He wrote and typed hardly at all. His computer is equipped with voice-recognition software. His voice grew softer and more difficult to hear. He walked more gingerly. His face began to take on a frozen, masklike quality, a symptom typical of PD.

Grove was spared some of the illness's symptoms. There was no cognitive impairment. His analytical powers and remarkable memory remained intact. He did not suffer from depression. He attacked PD the way he attacked every obstacle to a happy life. He took action. He exercised regularly. He hired a speech therapist. He established a nonprofit foundation to fund research into PD that he believed showed promise. He maintained a positive attitude and did not lose his sense of humor.

There was one dramatic moment when the symptoms interfered with his ability to speak in public, a talent that he had honed over the years and for which he was naturally gifted. It was at the Intel Sales and Marketing Conference in Anaheim, California, in February 2005. Intel had begun the practice of convening its sales and marketing team annually when the company was founded. The first few gatherings could be held at the office because the company was small enough to permit that. Then the annual ISMC was moved up to a San Francisco hotel. The first real off-site meeting was in Monterey, California. Noyce flew Andy there in Noyce's plane. Showing, as

Andy later said, the spirit of adventure on which Intel prided itself, Noyce let Grove take the controls. Showing the prudence on which Intel also prided itself, Grove remarked, Noyce took the controls back well before landing.[5]

Grove had attended every Intel ISMC. This one, in February 2005, would be his last. It was held in a huge auditorium in which were gathered more than forty-five hundred Intel salespeople and marketers. Grove was planning on introducing Eva to them and asking her to come forward and say a few words. This was unbeknownst to her. He was going to "cold call" her. After bidding this group his final farewell, he planned to introduce the CEO who was going to succeed Craig Barrett in May, Paul S. Otellini.

Like all Grove's presentations, this one was complicated. Everything seemed okay at the rehearsal, but as the time for the presentation approached, Grove realized that he was not going to be able to turn the pages he would bring with him to the podium. He seems suave and relaxed in front of an audience, but that is the art that conceals art. This was a big night, an important night. As the adrenaline began to flow more freely, it increased the intensity of his tremor. He was no longer able to grasp and hold a piece of paper.

Grove was in a room backstage. He started to concentrate very hard to figure out what to do. Paul Otellini stuck his head in to wish the "boss," as he called Andy, good luck, but Andy was so preoccupied that he could not respond gracefully and felt guilty about that later. Andy's technical assistant, the omnicompetent Julie Coppernoll, showed up, diagnosed the problem, and came up with a solution. The papers Andy was going to use as notes had to be consolidated flat on the podium so Andy did not have to turn any of them. It was a brilliant idea, but Andy was going on in ten minutes. Was there time to get this done? Andy was probably as nervous and as distressed at that moment as at any other time in his adult professional life.

Coppernoll succeeded, and Andy mounted the rostrum to give one of his finest presentations. Eva was cold-called and played her role like a professional. Andy concluded by asking rhetorically, "Can anybody doubt that Paul Otellini will be the greatest CEO in the history of Intel?" He left the stage to applause and cheers and was succeeded by Otellini.

Soon after this episode, Grove vacationed in Hawaii with Eva. He began to take l-dopa, and the medication had a remarkable effect. His gait steadied, his face became as supple as ever, and, with the help of his speech coach, his public presentations improved dramatically—so much so that in a cover story on changes at Intel, *Business Week* referred to a speech Grove delivered on October 20 by saying that "Grove's deep baritone . . . pierced the expectant silence." Grove did not merely speak, according to this article, he "boomed."[6]

There was a noteworthy difference between the way Grove handled prostate cancer and Parkinson's disease. With prostate cancer he went public. He joined the board of the Prostate Cancer Foundation, formerly CapCure, founded by Michael Milken and of which Milken, who has been diagnosed with the illness, is presently chairman.

Grove's Parkinson's disease was kept as confidential as possible. Intel's board of directors was informed early in 2001, and others who had to know were also told. There would, however, be no equivalent to the *Fortune* article of 1996 on prostate cancer. Grove's financial support for research into Parkinson's was managed through the Kinetics Foundation. Kinetics, established in 2002, was funded by the Grove Foundation. However, Kinetics itself, to state the obvious, does not have Grove's name attached to it. These pages are in fact the first public acknowledgment that Grove has Parkinson's disease.

In addition to all that comes with a major health problem such as Parkinson's disease, there were other important events in Grove's personal life that were shaping his days. His daughters both had children in 1997. By 2003, Andy and Eva had four grandchildren. Eva's friend Denise Amantea began to spend more time with both Andy and Eva.

Denise and Andy got off to a bit of a rocky start. She saw a lot of Eva, and when the two of them would go off to dine or to exercise, Andy found himself feeling left out. He wanted to be included in their activities, but Denise was not at all sure how much she wanted to be joined by "the grump," as she called him. Although having lived in the Valley for many years, Denise was not at all struck by Grove. She had not dealt with Intel in her legal career. To her, he was simply another big-shot CEO of the Valley. Not all such people are particularly pleasant to be around. With time, however, the relationship thawed, and the three of them have since forged quite a bond.

The years from 1998 down to 2006 saw their share of personal losses as well. Andy's mother died in 2002. He had supported her for years and been in touch with her daily. The relationship had contained its share of tension. Maria never stopped mourning her husband, who had died back in 1987.

She did not take to the United States the way her son did, and, however attentive they were, neither Andy nor Eva were able to provide Maria with the constancy of companionship that she needed.

The year before Maria Gróf died, Eva's mother passed away. Daughter and son-in-law had both been close to her. Her death was a painful blow.

26

"I Think That Experiment Has Been Run"

Asked to imagine Intel without Andy Grove, Steve Jobs said, "I think that experiment has been run." What he was referring to was the period between Andy's stepping down as CEO and February 14, 2005, when I asked him to use his imagination on this topic. "You have seen it [Intel] without Andy. I'm sure he has offered counsel, but I'm not so sure his counsel has been listened to. Every CEO wants to do their own thing. So I think we have seen an Intel without him. And we've seen the difference."[1]

A very different man from Jobs coming from a very different point of view arrived at the same conclusion. Craig Kinnie, even though he had at least a partial falling-out with Andy, cannot say enough good things about him. "He was my mentor, my hero at Intel." It was "a privilege to be part of his company as it grew up . . . being . . . part of what he created, and to have the freedom to be a renegade, and to have opposing ideas, and to have them heard."

Kinnie acknowledged Barrett's abilities but felt the special Intel culture did not survive the handoff from Grove to Barrett. "Craig was much more of a process guy." The door had been opened to politicization of decision-making. Kinnie left Intel, but "some of my old cronies are still there, and they are just totally frustrated."[2] These words were spoken in a calm, modulated tone. It is difficult to know how widely Kinnie's views are shared, but they are not unique to him.

How true was it that we had really seen an Intel without Andy during the Barrett years? Jobs overstated the case, at least for the first few years. Andy was still very present. He remained the face of Intel to the outside world. Highly telegenic, he was often on the air. A superbly accomplished public presenter, he gave scores of speeches in numerous settings. Always good copy because he refused to flatter the vanity of an interviewer, he was in the press all the time.

Grove had played the dual role of chairman of the board and CEO during 1997. It did not suit him because he was tired of being CEO. Furthermore, in addition to the many other factors at play that have already been discussed, David Yoffie, who had joined the board back in 1989, suggested to Andy that having one person serve as both CEO and chairman of the board was not a good idea. Grove agreed, as have his successors.

With Grove's monumental presence in the world, in the industry, and in the company, to what extent would Barrett's opportunity to put his own stamp on the company be rendered more difficult? Would it have been better for Barrett and for Intel if Grove had made a clean break in 1998? James Burke, the highly successful CEO of Johnson & Johnson from 1976 through 1989, spent one year in an advisory capacity after stepping down as CEO and then left the firm. He said he loved the place and would hang around until he was ninety if it made sense, but he "would not like me looking over his shoulder" if he was Ralph Larsen, Burke's successor.[3] This is an issue about which successful, reasonable people can disagree. Stay, and you are an ever-present reminder of the "good old days." Leave, and you deprive the company of decades of invaluable experience.

The weight of opinion in business schools today tends to be that it is better if the outgoing CEO cuts the cord with the company completely. This is especially true if the outgoing CEO was a founder. The thinking is that his or her (but almost always his) charismatic qualities can then be transferred to the successor and through the successor to the organization.[4] The weight of business school opinion about the offices of board chairman and CEO is that it is better that they be held by separate individuals. So if received wisdom is in fact wise, Intel got it half right in 1998.

Of one thing everyone could be certain. Andy was not going to be a potted palm as chairman. In whatever he did, he would be an impact player. If he was going to be chairman of the board of Intel, everyone had to have known that the chairmanship would become more important and the board more closely managed than had been the case previously. It was predictable that "corporate governance," rightly described by a *Fortune* magazine reporter as "an eye-glazing term if ever there was one," would get the kind of attention it received at few other companies.[5]

Where, precisely, did this leave Barrett? Could he chart a new course for the company if he wanted to? Might it happen that he would be blamed for any bumps in the road the company encountered, while Andy got the credit for what went right? Might people go around his back to complain to Andy about him? Would "Andy management" eat up Barrett's career as CEO?

Barrett is not a man who frightens easily. He had worked with Andy for a long time. He was not afraid to contradict him. He had Andy's respect. Nevertheless, Andy is rarely unconditional—perhaps unambiguous is a better word—in his human relationships.

Andy Grove is a suspicious man. Not suspicious about Barrett's ability, probity, or devotion to the company. He was suspicious about his own judgment. Succession is a complicated event. Had he really selected the right man?

The undeniable sterling qualities Barrett possesses have already been denominated. All his life, however, Grove had been concerned about the "Peter Principle." Barrett had clearly been a success as chief operating officer. But that had been in years past, and there was a world of difference between being COO and CEO of a company the size of Intel in the midst of an industry the wild gyrations of which were next to impossible to predict and to manage. When it came to execution, Barrett was second to none. But was he a strategic thinker?

As a figure in the business world, Barrett had more in common with Moore than with Grove. Grove had more in common with Noyce than with Moore or Barrett. All four had nothing to apologize for as technologists. Noyce and Grove by their nature grabbed the limelight. Moore and Barrett did not. Moore was not particularly noteworthy as a manager. His greatest stroke of genius in that realm was to recognize Grove's managerial abilities and give him free reign to exercise them.

To see Moore today is to be impressed by his seeming ordinariness. That very trait attracts attention. It is fair to say, and is often said, that Noyce, Moore, and Grove were the founders of Intel. But Intel's financier, Arthur Rock, only allowed Noyce and Moore—not Grove—to purchase founders' stock.[6] As a result of that decision, Moore is wealthier than Grove today.

Great wealth is always of interest in the United States, and Moore would be a subject of attention even if he had inherited that money rather than earned it. He recently donated $600 million to his alma mater, the California Institute of Technology ($300 million personally and $300 million from his foundation).[7] That kind of gift can change lives in a university.

Moore is also, of course, the source of Moore's law. To see the film clip in the Intel Museum of his discussing his discovery is to see an "aw-shucks" presentation of self. He made what to him was a simple observation, and he cringed when his friends began to describe it as his "law." When Moore is introduced at Intel's annual shareholders' meeting, spontaneous applause erupts.

There is to some degree an illusion about Moore. He is human like everyone else and capable of feeling unjustly treated if others are celebrated for achievements that are his, but this sentiment is virtually never expressed publicly. The fallible, human side of Moore is expressed more by what he does not say than what he does. He is a "withholding" man in issues relating to business. He is passionate, but the passion does not show. So seldom has he become angry in public that when such an "almost unheard-of" event takes place, those present are genuinely shocked.[8] He surely does not seek the limelight, but because of who he is, what he has, and what he has achieved, the limelight finds him.

The same cannot be said of Craig Barrett. He is not a charismatic man, and the limelight does not find him. He seems to believe that substance can carry the day unaccompanied by a painstaking management of the means by which news of substance reaches its audience. Although forthcoming, frank, and helpful when you meet with him one-on-one, those qualities are not, as one would say in Silicon Valley, scalable. In other words, Barrett is an uninspired public speaker.

These observations matter because these qualities are ones that Grove honed to perfection. He thought they were important. For years, he was Intel's public face and also the face top management showed to Intel's ever-growing cadre of employees. Grove was able to rally the troops in a way that Barrett was not.

Barrett had earned the top spot through years of outstanding performance in every assignment he had been given. He deserved it. But were those good reasons to promote him to it? It was the prevalence of this kind of thinking that has been cited as one reason for the decline of Sears, Roebuck, for decades the largest of American retailers.[9] Why did Grove settle on a successor who was so different on important dimensions from him? Succession is indeed a complicated phenomenon. This conundrum extends well beyond matters of style. Barrett had proven himself to be a superb director of operations. It was he, more than any other single individual, who turned Intel into a manufacturing powerhouse. Grove is passionate when he describes Barrett's unrivaled skill in whipping Intel's fabs into shape and making "copy exactly" a reality.[10] Barrett had not, however, proven himself as a strategist. This is a role a corporate CEO must play. Would Barrett thrive in this new role? No matter what doubts there might have been, in 1998 Grove became the nonexecutive chairman of the board and Barrett became president and CEO. No one was designated chief operating officer, as Barrett had been in the 1997 *Annual Report.*[11]

The first chairman of Intel's board was the founding financier, Arthur Rock. Rock was still on the board, which had almost doubled in size, from six to eleven, in 1997. Also still on the board was Gordon Moore. He was designated "chairman emeritus." Rock could have been called "chairman emeritus" as well, but he was not, perhaps because he was two incumbents away from the time he played that role. He had been succeeded by Noyce, who was succeeded by Moore.

Four of the eleven members of the board—Les Vadasz, in addition to Moore, Grove, and Rock—had been at Intel from the beginning. Investor and businessman D. James Guzy joined the board in 1969. Craig Barrett joined in 1993, after nineteen years with the company. Charles E. "Chuck" Young, chancellor of UCLA from 1968 to 1997 and of the University of Florida from 1999 to 2003, became a member in 1974, the same year that Grove did. Les Vadasz joined the board in 1988. The following year, Harvard Business School's David Yoffie joined. Winston H. Chen, former CEO of Solectron Corporation, an electronics firm, joined the board in 1993, as did Jane Shaw, CEO of the biotech firm AeroGen. John P. Browne, formally Lord Browne of Madingley, the chief executive officer of British Petroleum, joined in 1997.

Thus, when Grove became chairman in 1997, the eleven board members had a total of 235 years experience with Intel, or an average of almost twenty-two and a half years per person. Their service on the board added up to 151 years, or an average of almost fourteen years per person. Three board members—Grove, Barrett, and Vadasz—were executive directors, actively involved in running the company. A fourth, Moore, was not involved in day-to-day management but remained the senior member of the three-man office of the chief executive, Grove and Barrett being the other two, and his name was the first signature on the *Annual Report*.

Though only three board members had daily operating responsibilities, five, when we include Rock and Moore, can be considered part of the founding team. These five had been with Intel all twenty-nine years of its existence. Guzy was not as tightly connected, but he had been on the board for twenty-eight years and must have made a great deal of money as a result. The remaining members were relatively new to the company and the industry.

The following year, 1998, when Grove served Intel solely as chairman, a new member joined the board. David S. Pottruck was co–chief executive officer of the securities brokerage house Charles Schwab. A twelve-member board was a typical size for a company like Intel in 1998. The mix of corporate officers and outsiders was also probably typical.

What is the board of directors supposed to do? In theory, the board assures that the corporation is run for the benefit of the people who own it. The owners of a corporation are the people who hold its shares. They bought those shares in the expectation that the corporation would generate a more attractive return on their investment than other investment vehicles they could have purchased. The board works for the owners. Board members theoretically represent the owners in their oversight of the conduct of the corporation. This oversight includes, among other things, establishing the compensation of the CEO and other corporate officers, auditing the company's performance, evaluating major acquisitions or divestitures, reviewing strategic direction and new strategic initiatives, and selecting the next CEO as well as other top officers. Members of a board of directors have a "fiduciary duty" to shareholders. No other responsibility is greater than to see to it that the value of the property of the shareholders increases.

In the first half of the nineteenth century in the United States, the theoretical responsibilities of the board and its actual conduct and power were reasonably well matched. Firms were small by modern standards. The pace of business was slow. Most important, the directors of early American corporations were also usually their principal owners. When it is your money that a company's managers are allocating to various activities, you have a powerful incentive to keep a close watch on them. In the early years of America's business history, professional managers were a rarity. For the most part, owners and managers were one and the same. Owners managed. Managers owned.

In the 1840s, however, the railroad revolution got under way. Railroads demanded capital in theretofore undreamt-of amounts. By the 1850s, publicly traded railroad stock became a widespread business investment. The need of the railroads for capital created Wall Street. Not until the end of the century did an equity market for industrial corporations develop.[12] "Railroads," in the words of steel tycoon Henry Clay Frick, "are the Rembrandts of investment,"[13] and up until the early twentieth century that was true.

Along with the railroads came the telegraph. Indeed, without the telegraph, the growth of the railroads would not have been possible. Together, the railroad and the telegraph brought a speedy pace to American business that it had never known before. They created a national market. This speed, the far-flung nature of the new business world, and the intense demand for capital brought about what historian Alfred D. Chandler Jr. has called "the managerial revolution in American business."[14]

As corporations grew large, owners had to hire professional managers to run them. They were too complex and developments transpired too quickly for the owners to make all the major decisions themselves. A "professional" manager is an individual who is often located in a hierarchy of people who report up a chain of command to the CEO. These people, who make key decisions about a company, often own only a tiny percentage of that company's stock.

Today, for example, Intel has about six billion shares outstanding. A small fraction of these shares are held by the firm's managers and by its directors. Fund managers for firms like Fidelity, for state pensions, for union pensions, and other such entities own the bulk of Intel's shares. Yet these owners have precious little say over how the resources they have invested in Intel are allocated.

Theoretically, the owners elect the board, and the board appoints the executives who carry out the wishes of the owners. In actuality, the board is selected by the managers of almost every company that is not failing. In many companies, the outside members of the board, who should be freest to represent the interests of the owners, know very little about the company they are supposed to be supervising.

Think about it. What can an outside member of Intel's board really know? These are distinguished people, and most of them hold seats on boards of other companies in addition to Intel. Some of them run their own companies. They are, in other words, busy. They are not expert in the very difficult technological universe in which Intel operates. Moreover, most of the information they have about the corporation comes from the professional managers who run it.

What I am describing is a particular instance of a general problem called in the academic world "agency." Managers are supposed to be the "agents" of the owners. Members of the board are charged with seeing to it that they fulfill that obligation. Even supposing perfect honesty, which only a fool would take for granted after the myriad scandals of the past decade, and the best will in the world, board members can only play their role imperfectly.

To begin with, in a company the size of Intel, with so many shares outstanding and so many different shareholders, what is the definition of "owner"? Some owners, although from a percentage point of view very few, work for Intel. Most do not. Some owners are wealthy; others are not. Some owners want dividends to be high; others would rather see free cash flow reinvested in the company because they feel their investment will appreciate more quickly as a result.

The "owner" of Intel is thus a fiction. The board is charged with selecting CEOs to better serve the interests of a legal fiction. There are agency problems on the board itself. Each board member is pursuing his or her own interests and balancing those against his or her fiduciary responsibility. Or, put another way, each member sees his or her fiduciary responsibility through the lens of his or her own interests.

Thus, "corporate governance" boils down to about a dozen people theoretically selecting and compensating management in the service of a hypothetical owner. In practice, all the board can do is know the company as well as possible and try to evaluate how it is being managed in light of its goals. One professional board member told me that his job could be summarized as consisting of two tasks: to see to it that the CEO was neither a lunatic nor a thief.

The board of directors is not customarily a body that initiates action. Rather, it evaluates performance. Large companies are not run by boards. They are run by managers who, one is left to hope, have their interests sufficiently aligned with those of the owners who themselves, as we have seen, are a group mixed up beyond any hope of untangling so that they can manage the firm for the owners' benefit.

Pressure on boards to perform with greater effectiveness and in a more focused fashion only arose late in the twentieth century. From the growth of the large industrials prior to World War I and the accompanying dispersal of stock ownership, the top executives of America's biggest companies managed them relatively free of demands to increase shareholder value. The separation of ownership and management led to the control of corporate strategy and assets falling firmly into the hands of men (and they were almost all men) who were salaried employees in top executive positions in the business. It was becoming clear that although the modern corporation was private property, the owners of the property did not control it. They were left to hope that their property was managed in a way that benefited them.[15]

Perhaps no better example can be found of the relative unimportance of the owners as compared to the managers of the large corporation than the story of the change of leadership at IBM in the 1950s. Thomas J. Watson Sr., who became CEO of IBM in 1914, turned the company over to his oldest son, Tom Jr., in 1956. There was no question that the board of directors would acquiesce in this decision even though the Watson family never owned more than 5 percent of the company's stock. Soon after the retirement of Tom Watson Sr. in May and his death six weeks later in June 1956, Tom Jr. put his mother, Jeannette Kittredge Watson, on IBM's board. She retained her seat until her seventy-fifth birthday in 1959. Jeannette Watson was an admirable woman, but the fact that she had a seat on the IBM board of directors says a lot about the state of corporate governance in the late 1950s.[16]

Through the 1950s and 1960s, managerial prerogatives were almost never challenged in large, publicly held American corporations. The managers made the major decisions about strategy, finance, and succession planning. They were free to attend not only to shareholders but to others who had a stake in the conduct of the corporation. Seats on the board were essentially honorary positions that carried with them prestige and often considerable financial reward but not much in the way of power. As for shareholders, they were, speaking generally, quiescent.

This disposition of affairs began to change in the 1970s. A generation of managers had grown up in the aftermath of World War II, during which a large part of the global competitive infrastructure had been decimated. By the mid-1970s, however, in product category after product category, foreign competition became ever more aggressive. The apparel and textile industries were the first to feel the effects. During the 1970s, however, industries that had been created or long dominated by the United States began to experience the impact of foreign competition as well. European and Japanese firms made inroads into the electronics industries and the whole automobile value chain from parts such as tires to complete automobiles. America's profligacy with energy was manageable when oil cost a dollar and a half a barrel but not when prices skyrocketed after the oil shocks of 1973 and 1979.

The combined effects of inflation and economic stagnation, "stagflation" as it was called toward the end of the 1970s, gripped American businesses that for decades had as their primary concern the location of their next factory. The economic collapse of the Reagan recession in 1982 was accompanied by the accumulation of large blocks of stock in pension and investment funds. New ways of financing through, for example, the employment of "junk" debt, was another development that, in addition to what has just been mentioned, added up to greatly increased powers for stockholders. The hostile takeover, meaning the purchase of a company against the wishes of incumbent management, unthinkable in the mid-1950s, was on every manager's mind if he or she ran a publicly traded corporation in the mid-1980s. Recall Grove's concern that someone might, as the phrase went, "make a run" at Intel during its time of troubles in the mid-1980s. His worries were not unwarranted.[17] The founders might have risked losing control of that company had not friendly financing been arranged with IBM, which acted as a "white knight" before any corporate raider had the idea for a joust.

As late as 1990, the Business Roundtable, an association of CEOs of large firms that is often looked to as the spokesman for corporate America, could issue the following statement:

> Corporations are chartered to serve both their shareholders and society as a whole. The interests of the shareholders are primarily measured in terms of economic return over time. The interests of others in society (other stakeholders) are defined by their relationship to the corporation.
>
> The other stakeholders in the corporation are its employees, customers, suppliers, creditors, communities where the corporation does business, and society as a whole. The duties and responsibilities of the corporation to the stakeholders are expressed in various laws, regulations, contracts, customs, and practices.[18]

This may have been what the CEO members of the Business Roundtable wanted business to be—they, after all, were professional managers and this definition gave them the right to use other people's money to act like what might be thought of as junior varsity statesmen—but this description was outdated when it was published.

The corporation was an entity designed to make its investors rich. Even the conservative Business Roundtable came to terms with the reality that they were living in an era of investor capitalism in 1997, as the following statement, very different from the one above, illustrates:

> [T]he paramount duty of management and of boards of directors is to the corporation's stockholders; the interests of other stakeholders are relevant as a derivative of the duty to stockholders. The notion that the board must somehow balance the interests of stockholders against the interests of other stakeholders fundamentally misconstrues the role of directors. It is, moreover, an unworkable notion because it would leave the board with no criterion for resolving conflicts between interests of stockholders and of other stakeholders or among different groups of stakeholders.[19]

These two views stand in sharp contrast to one another. The first is backward-looking, a rather pathetic yearning among top professional managers for the good old days of the 1950s and 1960s. The second looks the facts in the face. It is not the job of the CEO to balance conflicting interests. Ultimately, he or she has one job and one job only—to get the price of the stock up. This was the reality of the day when Andy Grove became chairman of the board of directors of Intel.

27

Andy and the Board

Andy Grove's tenure as nonexecutive chairman of Intel's board coincided with developments that shook the business world to its foundations. The most important of these was the great boom of 1998 through 2000 and the equally great bust that followed. Fortunes were made and lost as a result of the volatility of the stock markets. The biggest bankruptcy in the history of American business took place. From the public in general, from investors, and from Congress, new demands were made on how corporations were to be governed. The board of directors took on a significance that it had never before possessed in modern times.

The world of high-technology companies was especially affected by the great bubble at the end of the twentieth century. Intel along with Microsoft and many other technology companies, including such stalwarts of the Valley as Apple, Cisco, Google, Oracle, Sun, and Yahoo!, are listed and traded not on the New York Stock Exchange, but on the NASDAQ. NASDAQ is an acronym for National Association of Securities Dealers Automated Quotations and was founded on February 8, 1971.[1] It describes itself as "the largest electronic screen-based equity securities market in the United States. With approximately 3,250 companies, it lists more companies and, on average, trades more shares per day than any other U.S. market."[2]

The great high-technology bubble is displayed in a line graph of the performance of Intel and of the NASDAQ composite index from 1998 to 2005.

FIGURE 13

NASDAQ Composite Index, 1997–2005

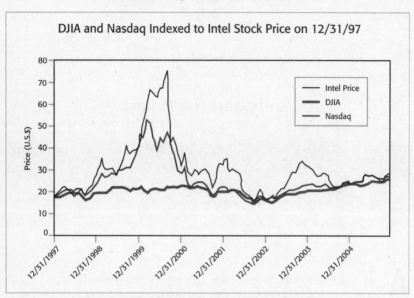

DJIA and Nasdaq Indexed to Intel Stock Price on 12/31/97

Source: Harvard Business School Business Information Analyst

The NASDAQ composite breached the 1000 mark in 1995, the year of the Netscape IPO. Between then and March 10, 2000, the apex of the dot-com boom, the NASDAQ soared by a factor of five to its peak at 5,048.62. The valuations that permitted this spectacular performance defied all traditional metrics. Not profits, but such measures as "share of eyeballs" became a way of analyzing the worth of businesses. This riot of speculative activity was a national phenomenon. Some students at, for example, the Harvard Business School were not completing their education, but were opting for dot-com start-up opportunity through which, because they could successfully "manage in the marketspace," they would supposedly make a fortune. Venture capitalists and other suppliers of funds were as swept up in this as the young people just out of business school at whom they were throwing money. The Internet, we were told, was the biggest thing to hit the world since the railroad. The locomotive for the Internet was the myriad dot-coms that promised to make their promoters rich instantaneously.

Though national in scope, this fever ran highest in Silicon Valley. It was the magnet for numberless business ideas. The restaurants on and near University Avenue in Palo Alto and the bars at places like the Stanford Park Hotel on El Camino Real in Menlo Park were packed with hopping people who either feverishly whispered tales of business magic to one another or drank too much and told the world they had struck the mother lode.

All this speculative activity did not seem like speculation at the time. These young entrepreneurs saw themselves as the vanguard of the "new economy." They had to move fast. The train was leaving the station, and if they didn't jump on, they would be left behind. This could be a missed opportunity that would haunt them for the rest of their lives. Better run fast to catch that train.

A lot of people did just that. They suspended their judgment about what makes a business profitable. They fell victim to the telltale phrase we have encountered before, "This time it's different."[3]

As the NASDAQ roared ever upward, Intel's stock did also. These developments were not independent of one another. Intel was a big company by the late 1990s and a major component of the NASDAQ.

If, as the Business Roundtable declared in 1997, the job of corporate management was to boost the stock price, no one could complain about Craig Barrett's performance for the two and a quarter years from the time he became CEO through August 2000. Barrett became the CEO in May 1998. The last trading day of that month, May 29, Intel stock closed at $18.53. Its market capitalization was $121.2 billion. On August 30, 2000, the stock hit the fantastic height of $74.88. Market capitalization was slightly over half a trillion dollars. The compound rate of growth of Intel's market capitalization for these twenty-seven months was 5.4 percent per month. The total dollar value of the company increased by more than a factor of four off a very high base.

Everyone was living a dream. Intel on August 30, 2000, was worth more than half a trillion dollars! The company was just thirty-two years old. It had lost money only a decade and a half previously. It had been a "slave" to IBM. In 1987, a great year for the company, the year that Andy became CEO, its market capitalization was $4.3 billion. Was this dream going to turn into the new reality of the new economy? Or was it a mere phantom that would disappear upon awakening?

When, after his two decades of wandering, Odysseus finally reached Ithaca and his one and true beloved Penelope, he was unrecognizable because he had been away so long. He had to convince her that he was indeed her husband. Penelope told Odysseus of a dream she had had. He interpreted her dream as proof that the greedy and evil suitors for her hand who had infested their palace would be destroyed.

The ever cautious Penelope responded:

> "Ah my friend," seasoned Penelope dissented,
> "dreams are hard to unravel, wayward drifting things—
> not all we glimpse in them will come to pass . . .
> Two gates there are for our evanescent dreams,
> one is made of ivory, the other made of horn.*
> Those that pass through the ivory cleanly carved
> are will-o'-the-wisps, their message bears no fruit.
> The dreams that pass through the gates of polished horn
> are fraught with truth, for the dreamer who can see them.
> But I can't believe my strange dream has come that way,
> much as my son and I would love to have it so."[4]

Did the dreams being dreamt by the American business world in general and by the technology sector in particular pass through the gates of "ivory cleanly carved" or of "polished horn"? Let's look at four Intel *Annual Reports* for the answer.

The 1998 *Annual Report* delivered a mixed message. Sales rose 5 percent to $26.3 billion. Profits, however, fell 13 percent from $6.945 billion in the previous year to $6.068 billion. The last time profits had dropped at Intel was in 1994, and that was the result of the $475 million write-off because of the uproar over the Pentium flaw. Even that year, profits dropped a mere three-tenths of a percent. Had it not been for the write-off, profits would have increased by more than one-fifth. The previous year in which Intel's profits had dropped was disastrous, money-losing 1986. When Grove took over as CEO in 1987, red ink turned to black. Barrett's debut as CEO in 1998 was not as auspicious.

What had gone wrong? Intel's leadership told its shareholders, "Competition in the value PC market segment, inventory corrections among some of our large customers in the first half of the year and an economic slowdown in some parts of the world took their toll."[5] The slowdown to which

---

*The distinction being drawn is that ivory is rare, valuable, and flashy; but horn, like the horn of a common animal such as a deer or a boar, is real and nothing more or less than it seems to be.

Moore, Grove, and Barrett were referring may have been the East Asian financial crisis of the late 1990s. No one knew how far the "Asian contagion," much talked about that year, would spread.

Intel had always been a company in which poor performance was not blamed solely or even primarily on impersonal "conditions." "With hindsight," the letter to the stockholders explained, "it's clear that we were caught off guard by the increase in demand for low-cost PCs. We were late in recognizing the emergence of this value PC market segment—and the competition took advantage of our delay." The result was a loss of market share in the United States. This is a blunt indictment of management's performance.

New initiatives were undertaken to correct these errors. Most important was the introduction of the Celeron microprocessor. This was Intel's entry into the "good enough" market segment. The "heart of our business" remained the Pentium II, the world's highest-selling microprocessor. The top Intel product offering was the "powerhouse" Pentium II Xeon aimed at mid- and high-range servers and workstations.[6] This new product policy was Intel's version of what Alfred P. Sloan Jr. had done for General Motors during the 1920s. Intel now marketed a microprocessor "for every purse and purpose."

Despite some disappointments in 1998, the company was optimistic about the future. "The Internet boom is transforming the world," the company announced. It also declared, "Our vision: getting to a billion connected computers worldwide." "[A] billion PCs connected around the world will require a whole lot of silicon." Therefore, Intel, with its mastery of silicon technology, "powers the Internet."[7] The PC had been "it" during the previous decade. The Internet was going to be "it" during the next. Intel was ideally positioned for this "exciting sea change." The company's "strategic intent" was "to be a major force behind the Internet revolution."[8]

Sounds good. Even though profits were down 13 percent, the capital markets bought into Intel's "vision," a word becoming more characteristic for this company to use than in the past. Intel's market capitalization jumped over 70 percent during the year, from $114.7 billion to $197.6 billion, a record.

Intel was dreaming big dreams, and in 1999 these dreams looked like they had passed through the gates of horn rather than of ivory. In their letter to Intel's stockholders, Moore, Grove, and Barrett wrote that "we worked to transform Intel: from being at the center of the PC industry to being at the center of the Internet economy."

What deeds backed up these words? The company launched fifteen new

Pentium III and Pentium III Xeon microprocessors, "the largest micro-processor product introduction in our history." It "ramped our new 0.18-micron manufacturing process" with unprecedented speed. It bought twelve companies for $6 billion, "augmenting our capabilities in a number of key product areas." Intel's venture capital arm had developed an $8 billion port-folio of investments in more than 350 companies related to the Internet. It produced samples of its "future powerhouse," the Itanium processor, "based on the revolutionary new IA-64 architecture designed to meet the needs of powerful Internet servers. We expect this architecture to be as important to the Internet infrastructure in the future as the current Intel architecture has been to PC computing for the last 15 to 20 years."[9]

In perhaps the most aggressively upbeat *Annual Report* in its history, In-tel announced that sales of $29.4 billion constituted an increase of 12 percent over the previous year. It was another record, and the thirteenth consecutive year of revenue growth. Profits soared 21 percent to $7.3 billion.[10]

As for Wall Street, there was a bull market for Intel stock.[11] Intel was listed for the first time as one of the thirty stocks in the Dow Jones Industrial Average (DJIA). This selection meant more than merely an endorsement of the company. Some funds purchase the DJIA automatically. Some individ-ual investors, impressed by reports that stock market analysts underperform the averages, buy the DJIA as well. Demand for the stock was thus generated automatically.

The stock performed terrifically. Intel's shares closed the year at $41.16, generating a market capitalization of slightly over $275 billion. This was an increase of almost 40 percent over the previous year's record high. For the decade ending in 1999, Intel's market capitalization rose at a compound an-nual rate of 48 percent.[12]

To be sure, there were some problems at Intel. There are always problems in any business. Nevertheless, the company's performance during the past decade, actually dating further back to 1987, had been spectacular. All the averages, including the NASDAQ, the New York Stock Exchange, and others, were moving upward too. Not quite at Intel's torrid pace, but certainly in the same direction.

Was it not, however, time to pause and ask how long this could go on? Was it a good idea to feature a 48 percent compound annual growth rate over a decade in your *Annual Report*? If that rate were to be maintained, In-tel's market capitalization in 2009 would be $13.9 trillion. Was that possible?

Alan Greenspan, the powerful, prestigious, ponderous, and self-important chairman of the Federal Reserve Board, issued a warning about "irrational exuberance." Greenspan did not have a reputation as a phrase-maker, and this particular phrase was buried in a question. "But how do we know," Greenspan rhetorically asked an audience, "when irrational exuberance has unduly escalated asset values, which then become subject to unexpected and prolonged contractions as they have in Japan over the past decade?"[13] "Irrational exuberance" was a phrase picked out of a lot of other phrases that crowded Greenspan's speech, and it was much discussed. But Greenspan made that speech in December 1996. Intel's market capitalization at the end of that month was $107 billion. It was not the time to sell.

28

The Bubble Bursts

Alan Greenspan spoke of irrational exuberance, but he was wrong in December 1996. And 1997. And 1998. And 1999. And, if you were an investor in Intel, until August 31, 2000.

The company's performance for 1999 was outstanding on almost every dimension. Sales of $33.7 billion marked the fourteenth straight year they had increased. This was becoming as predictable as anything ever is in life. Intel's annual sales rose as night follows day. The company ranked 39 on the Fortune 500. Profits increased at a rate far faster than sales, rising 44 percent to $10.4 billion. Profits in 1999 were far greater than sales as recently as 1993. They could easily have been higher. Intel spent $1.7 billion on costs related to acquisitions. These expenditures were discretionary. It also spent $3.9 billion on research and development, an enormous sum.

Head count was steadily rising. Intel employed 86,100 people at the end of 2000, an increase of almost 16,000 in a single year and of 61,500 from 1991. Well over 70 percent of the company's employees in 2000 had never known hard times. They had never seen sales go anywhere but up. At the end of 1994, the year of the floating point flaw, Intel employed 32,600 people, so we can be sure that over 60 percent of its employees had never seen a crisis at the company firsthand. The only blip on the screen of Intel's greatness a majority of them had experienced was the drop in profits in 1998, but that was nothing in the scheme of things. Market capitalization had risen that year, and profits continued what must have begun to seem like their foreordained onward march the following year.

What was on no one's agenda, especially given Intel's strong performance as far as business fundamentals were concerned, were hard and heavy tidings from Wall Street. On August 31, 2000, Intel's market capitalization stood at $501.512 billion, more than triple the $121.158 billion on May 29, 1998, the last trading day of the month in which Barrett became CEO. At that growth rate, by November 29, 2002, twenty-seven months later, Intel's market capitalization would have been $2.075 trillion. It wasn't.

The NASDAQ reached 4,696.69 on February 29. It stood at 4,206.53 when Intel peaked in August. In the month of September, as the NASDAQ dropped 13 percent to 3,672.82, Intel's market capitalization was almost cut in half to $278.286 billion. The price of a share of Intel stock varied more dramatically than in any other year of the preceding decade, from highs in the neighborhood of $75 to lows around $30.[1] Intel shares closed the year at $30.06, generating a market capitalization of $202.321 billion, down more than one-quarter from its close in 1999. From the end of August in 2000 to the end of the year, Intel's market capitalization declined by almost $300 billion. This loss in market value was greater than the company's market value at the end of 1999.

Gates of ivory or gates of horn?

Despite Wall Street's tempestuousness, the company did well in 2000, and the *Annual Report* was positive in tone. The letter to the stockholders explained that the first half of 2000 "was unexpectedly strong," but during the second half of the year "economic pressures affected the high-tech industry, including Intel."[2]

Nevertheless, Intel was well positioned to take advantage of a bright future. The 2000 *Annual Report* featured an interview with Grove and Barrett. Grove said that "in the midst of a transition to a pervasively digital world," Intel was "in the fortunate position to provide the essential technology building blocks that power many aspects of this evolving networked infrastructure."[3]

Intel saw itself at the center of the computing universe because at the center of the computing universe was silicon. "Intel silicon," announced the *Annual Report,* "is in PCs and laptops that deliver fast computing power and link users to the Internet . . . servers that are the processing plants and data warehouses of the Internet . . . networking and communications tools that link voice, data and the Internet."[4] The company conceived of itself as occupying the center of the high-technology world.

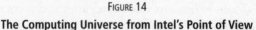

FIGURE 14

The Computing Universe from Intel's Point of View

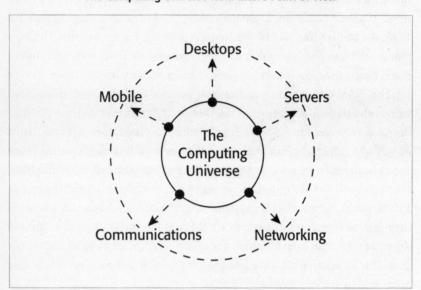

Source: *Intel Annual Report,* 2000, p. 5.

At the center of "The Computing Universe" was silicon. At the center of silicon technology was Intel. This led to a reassuring syllogism. The world was changing. In the *Annual Report,* Grove was asked to evaluate Intel's competitive environment. "[W]e do not have one single, overarching competitor," he said. No one at Intel could pass the "silver bullet" test anymore.

Barrett was asked whether the high-technology boom was over. "Absolutely not" was his response. "There's no question that the long-term opportunities for growth continue to be huge. There has been a shakeout of dot-com companies that perhaps weren't founded on solid business models. But for companies that have useful products to sell and make them well, the potential is vast."[5]

Could there be any doubt that Intel was among those special companies destined for great things? It had consistently invested heavily not only in R&D but also in its manufacturing facilities. It carried just over $15 billion on its books under "Net investment in property, plant and equipment."[6]

Thanks to Barrett and the team he had captained, Intel was able to produce astonishingly complex artifacts in massive quantities. Intel had far more property, plant, and equipment than any competitor. It had outstanding human talent. In addition to Grove, Moore, Barrett, and Vadasz, corporate officers in 2000 included CFO Andy Bryant; Sean Maloney running sales and marketing; Paul Otellini in charge of the Intel Architecture Group (both Maloney and Otellini, it will be recalled, had served as Grove's technical assistants); Mike Splinter running the Technology and Manufacturing Group; Mike Fister in charge of the Enterprise Platform Group (the "two Mikes" were among the most well-liked executives in the company); Sunlin Chou, working with Splinter at TMG; Tom Dunlap, chief counsel; Ron Smith running the wireless group; Albert Y. C. Yu, another top technologist, in charge of optoelectronics; Mike Aymar in charge of Intel Online Services; Doug Busch, responsible for IT; Pat Gelsinger, chief technology officer; Craig Kinnie at the Intel Architecture Lab in Oregon; Stephen Nachtsheim, director of Intel Capital; and numerous other top-flight executives.[7] Together, these executives constituted as capable a team of technologists and businesspeople as one was likely to find anywhere. Most of them had been at Intel for at least a decade, which meant that their stock options had made them very wealthy.

It is also notable, however, that a number of top executives with Intel in 1998 had left the company by the end of 2000. Dov Frohman, inventor of the EPROM and manager of Intel's large Israeli operations, a man thought by some very smart people to be technically a cut above, had left the firm. Dennis Carter, creator of Intel Inside, the man who taught Andy Grove marketing, had retired. Karen Alter, who had worked both with Carter and with Pam Pollace in public relations, was gone. So was Ron Whittier, the highly regarded head of the Content Group.[8] By the end of 2005, Mike Aymar, Tom Dunlap, Sunlin Chou, Craig Kinnie, and Stephen Nachtsheim were gone. Mike Splinter became the CEO of Applied Materials, which produces machines that manufacture semiconductors, in 2003. Thirteen months later, Mike Fister became the CEO of Cadence Design Systems, which is in the electronics design automation business. Would there be more defections in the years that followed? How would Intel do in the "war for talent" as Grove stepped further into the background?

Grove was busy writing *Swimming Across*, among other activities, in 2000 when he and C. Barr Taylor took that walk up Cow Hill, when Taylor told Grove he had to be evaluated for PD. When a well-known man or woman makes it public that he or she has an illness, there is an outpouring of anxiety, inquiry, and sympathy from people who know you and those who only know of you. Grove had experienced the "poster child" effect when he published his prostate cancer article in 1996. He is still much involved in its treatment, and he is still receiving questions from frightened people who have been newly diagnosed.

PD symptoms (such as "masked face," "Parkinsonian gait," and speaking softly) strike directly at some of the traits that Grove most prized in himself. He was a vigorous man who enjoyed skiing. Problems with balance would make that difficult. He is able to ski in 2006, thanks to l-dopa. He is a master of self-expression, but PD robbed him of the impact of his bass baritone voice. Interviews with the press could not extend too long because he would tire. Public speaking, in which he took great pleasure, was rendered far more difficult.

All these symptoms were much diminished after Grove began taking l-dopa in May 2005. Unlike two-fifths of Parkinson's patients, Grove was not clinically depressed. He learned a great deal about the illness, just as he did about prostate cancer. He almost seemed to believe that you could conquer PD medically if you could master it intellectually.[9] Grove used his knowledge of the disease as well as his personal wealth and his mastery of leverage, which he had been thinking about at least since the publication of *High Output Management* back in 1983, to speed progress toward mitigation of PD's symptoms and perhaps even toward a cure.

Andy is still attacking PD the way he has attacked all the other problems in his life. He refuses to be defeated before the battle is joined. He will give ground where he has no choice. If he has to modify his vanity in the face of symptoms that will not disappear, so be it. There are, he said recently, "simple answers" to the question of how he can maintain the aggressive optimism in his lifelong battle with his body. "I have an illness—and I am an engineer. I try to solve the problem at hand—and I get involved in the scientific/technical mystery."[10] Parkinson's disease thus took its place as another problem to solve as 2000 turned into 2001.

With 2001 we received our answer about business dreamers. The big dreams that were dreamt in the 1990s came through the gates of ivory. On its peak day, which it hit in March 2000, the NASDAQ closed at 5,049. At its nadir in September 2001, it sank to 1,423, a decline of over 70 percent.[11] It closed out 2001 at 1,950. Students at the Harvard Business School who had rocketed out of the place for the dot-com gold rush in 1999 were sending professors emails asking if were there openings for research assistants in 2001.

Oddly enough, Intel's market capitalization at the end of 2001 was $211.092 billion, which represented an increase of 4 percent over 2000. But that was the only dimension on which performance improved. Sales declined for the first time in a decade and a half. The decline was sharp, 21 percent to $26.5 billion. In a high-fixed-cost business, cratering like this devastates the bottom line. Profits plummeted a sickening 88 percent to $1.3 billion.

Barrett and Grove told investors that most technology companies "took a beating, and many investors wondered if technology was dead." They were undaunted. They referred to the history of the railroad and steel industries to support their view that the "history of technology revolutions is told in cycles of boom, bust, and build-out."[12] Barrett cited Intel's long-held approach to the "bust" phase of this progression. "Our core philosophy for these times is that you can't save your way out of a downturn. The only way you come out of a recession stronger than when you went into it is with new products and new technologies."[13]

That is why in 2001, Intel "did what may seem counter-intuitive: we accelerated our capital investments, spending $7.3 billion" compared to $10 billion in the previous two boom years combined.[14] Barrett did not quote the words of Andrew Carnegie: "[T]he man who has money during a panic is the wise and valuable citizen." But he could have. It was during the Panic of 1873 and the depression that followed that Carnegie put up his gigantic steel mills on the banks of the Allegheny and Monongahela.[15] Intel had plenty of cash on its balance sheet and no debt. As Carnegie also said, "[T]he real time to extend your operations was when nobody else was doing it."[16] That was what Intel under Barrett did, and it turned out to be wise policy. "Despite the turbulence of 2001," announced the *Annual Report,* "historical perspective supports our view that there's plenty of room for growth in the Internet revolution."[17]

This was correct. It was also on target to believe that Intel's products were vital for the Internet's growth. There was one question unanswered. It seems to have been unasked. Was Intel positioning itself to capture the value of the Internet if the prediction that 2001 was merely a temporary halt in its onward march came true?

At the top of the corporation, there were a number of moving parts. Chairman Emeritus Gordon Earle Moore stepped down from the board of directors at the annual stockholders' meeting in May. The *Annual Report* accurately described him as "a pioneer in the creation of Silicon Valley."[18] Though *in* the Valley for many, many years before anyone recognized it as a special place, though a protégé of Shockley at Shockley Semiconductor in 1955, though one of the "traitorous eight" who moved on in 1957 to found Fairchild Semiconductor, and founder along with Bob Noyce of Intel in 1968 as Intel employee number two, Moore was somehow never *of* the Valley. When one thinks of the great names of Silicon Valley in the past half century, somehow one feels these people all have more in common with one another than any of them do with Moore.

With Moore's retirement, the size of the board did not shrink. Rather, his seat was taken by Reed E. Hundt, who, in a rather surprising oversight, is not mentioned in the text of the *Annual Report* at all. He is listed in the corporate directory on page 38 of a forty-two-page *Annual Report,* where he is described as "Senior Advisor, McKinsey & Company."[19] That he was, but that is not the reason he was asked to join the board. Intel never had much use for management consulting firms, of which McKinsey is the best-known. Hundt, a former antitrust litigator for the law firm of Latham & Watkins, was the chairman of the Federal Communications Commission during Bill Clinton's first term as president. In that capacity, he learned a great deal about global telecommunications. Intel saw the convergence of computing and communications as the way of the future.

One important item that the annual letter to the shareholders did not fail to mention was the status of Paul Otellini. The board promoted him to the office of president and chief operating officer on January 16, 2002. Otellini, a twenty-seven-year Intel veteran, was now clearly in line to succeed Barrett as CEO. He had spent the previous four years running the Intel Architecture Group. Born in 1950, Otellini was eleven years younger than Barrett.

The rising tide of the booming 1990s had floated a lot of boats, not all of them in Silicon Valley or in the tech sector. General Electric, which is a century old and based in the East, had seen its stock skyrocket during the two-decade tenure of Jack Welch. So did the market capitalization of another conglomerate based in the East, Tyco, whose much-admired and much-quoted CEO, Leo Dennis Kozlowski, rose like Welch from a modest background. His father was a policeman in Newark, New Jersey. In the communications business, cable operator Adelphia had drawn a lot of attention. Under the leadership of the Rigas family, it had grown quickly, but not nearly as quickly as telephone giant WorldCom under the leadership of its seemingly unassuming CEO, Bernie Ebbers.

Located in an unlikely spot, Clinton, Mississippi, WorldCom grew by acquisition, and it grew fast. In 1996 it gobbled up MFS Communications for $12 billion. The next year it bought MCI for $40 billion, making it the second largest telephone company in the United States and leaving executives at AT&T puzzled over how it could price as low as it did and make so much money. In 1999, Ebbers tried to buy Sprint for $115 billion, but this purchase did not pass the scrutiny of antitrust authorities.

The headliner in the energy industry was Enron. In 1986, Kenneth Lay, born to the family of a poor Baptist preacher in Tyrone, Missouri, became CEO and chairman. He had always wanted to be rich. Enron was to be the vehicle to get him the money and power he craved.

His comrade-in-arms was Jeffrey K. Skilling. A graduate of Southern Methodist University and the Harvard Business School, Skilling was a McKinsey consultant before making his way to Enron. Together, he and Lay built a company that *Fortune* magazine called "America's most innovative" for six years in a row. The company was populated by hardworking, hard-living traders who liked to take chances. Its "asset light" model seemed the wave of the future.

Just as the rising tide of the stock markets floated all boats, when the tide went out, a lot of these boats ran aground. One after another, famous and much-praised companies turned out to be populated by thieves. Their lawyers, bankers, and auditors were revealed as compliant enablers. Their board members pocketed their fat fees but were derelict in their duties.

The first to fall was Enron.[20] The rise and collapse of this company caused the greatest public reaction during what became the era of the feet of clay, even though WorldCom's bankruptcy was larger in terms of market capitalization and assets destroyed.

The impact of Enron's collapse reverberated through corporate America, through the legal and accounting professions, through state and national politics, through the halls of Congress, and through the public at large. Its top executives had combined a preachy innocence, represented by Lay, with an unmatched arrogance represented by Skilling, and with an intricate scheme to defraud investors developed by Chief Financial Officer Andrew Fastow. Any challenge to the company's vision of its future greatness was dismissed.

The arbiters of corporate respectability jumped on the Enron bandwagon during the 1990s, especially toward the end of the decade. The company kept as high a profile as any in the United States. Both President Bushes had nothing but good things to say about it. When George W. Bush was elected in 2000, there was talk of Ken Lay becoming secretary of energy.[21] Enron's accountants, Arthur Andersen, blessed Fastow's intricate off-balance-sheet manipulations. So did its lawyers, Vinson & Elkins. So did its bankers, which included the fanciest names on Wall Street, such as Citigroup, JP Morgan Chase, Deutsche Bank, Credit Suisse First Boston, and Merrill Lynch. So did the bond rating agencies. Business "gurus" were uncritically enthusiastic as well. The business academy was not far behind.

With its gleaming tower gracing Houston's downtown business district, Enron became a monument to corporate greatness in the city that was its headquarters. Ken Lay established the "Enron Prize for Distinguished Public Service" in cooperation with Rice University in Houston. Award winners included Nelson Mandela, Colin Powell, and Mikhail Gorbachev. In 2001, the award went to Alan Greenspan.[22]

Enron was a contributor to many worthy civic causes. The world of sports got involved as well. "In 1996," Bethany McLean and Peter Elkind report, "when Lay read that the city's National League baseball team, the Houston Astros, might move unless it got a new stadium, he raced into action, working tirelessly to get a referendum passed authorizing construction of the stadium. In 1999, Enron agreed to pay $100 million over 30 years to have the stadium named Enron Field.... On the first day of the 2000 season, Lay was invited to throw out the first ball, while both generations of George Bushes and their wives cheered him on from their seats behind home plate."[23]

It was all a lie.

Enron was creating fictitious profits and hiding losses that grew in size during 2000 and 2001. All the mechanisms put in place to prevent fraud failed. The "professionals" at Arthur Andersen, Vinson & Elkins, the investment banks, Enron's own board of directors in this "model of corporate governance," and government regulatory agencies all turned out to be, in Lenin's famous phrase, "useful idiots."

Why had so many people gone along with this fraud as it grew ever more gigantic and as it became increasingly obvious that it would be impossible to hide forever the fact that Enron was a mirage? There are a number of reasons. A lot of people both within and outside the company were making a lot of money from its seeming success. To raise questions about how robust Enron's performance really was invited ridicule. The result was highly unconstructive confrontation. "Skilling, in particular, was infamous for dividing the world into those who 'got it' and those who didn't."[24] For those who didn't, he had nothing but scorn.

By March 2001, with the financial markets in free fall, cracks began to appear in Enron's façade. *Fortune* published an article that month asking in its title, "Is Enron Overpriced?"[25] We have encountered the author before. It was Bethany McLean, who had as her first assignment to fact-check Andy's prostate cancer article. She herself has said that her Enron article was not that hard-hitting. The title, after all, was a question, not a declaration.

As the financial indices continued to drop, Enron went into a nosedive. On August 13, Skilling told the board that he was resigning. He issued a press release the next day stating, "I am resigning for purely personal reasons." There were no accounting issues, Lay insisted.[26]

Things went downhill fast after that. At two o'clock on the morning of Sunday, December 2, 2001, Enron declared bankruptcy.[27] It was the biggest bankruptcy in American business history as $63.39 billion in assets were thrown into receivership. More than 20,000 people lost their jobs and saw more than $2 billion in their pension funds vaporize. Lay and Skilling were convicted of fraud on May 25, 2006. Lay died of heart disease on July 5.

It only took a month after Enron's bankruptcy in 2001 for the next bombshell. The telecommunications company Global Crossing, formally headquartered in Bermuda but essentially an American corporation, was once, according to the *Wall Street Journal*, "considered the strongest of the challengers taking on established telecom operators who were too slow to cater to New Economy demands for more bandwidth."[28] With the collapse of Global Crossing, over $30.19 billion in assets went into receivership in the fourth biggest bankruptcy in American business history.

Next in line was WorldCom. It too had cooked its books in an attempt to hide $3.8 billion in expenses. The size of the financial bomb it detonated became public late in June 2002, and "[c]onfidence in corporate America hit new lows."[29] "[C]rushed by its $41 billion debt load," WorldCom filed for bankruptcy late on Sunday, July 21, 2002. The company's $107 billion in assets meant that this was the biggest bankruptcy in American business history, "dwarfing that of Enron."[30] WorldCom had "loaned" Bernie Ebbers more than $400 million.

At Adelphia, the story was much the same. Accounting fraud resulted in bankruptcy on June 25, 2002.[31] Adelphia, named after the Greek word for "brotherhood," was founded by John Rigas in 1952 and run by him and his family.[32] They looted the company.

At Tyco, the story was similar yet again. L. Dennis Kozlowski was still being praised by *BusinessWeek* as late as January 2002. He was selected as one of their "Top 25 Managers of the Year" for 2001. Described as "perhaps the most aggressive dealmaker in Corporate America," his "ultimate goal" was said to be "inheriting the mantle once worn by Jack Welch."[33]

By June 2005, Kozlowski was being described as "epitomiz[ing] corporate greed." He and an associate were found guilty of stealing $600 million from Tyco "to finance lifestyles of kingly opulence." Kozlowski threw a $2 million "toga party" for his wife's fortieth birthday. Videotape made it look like something out of the movie *Animal House.* Tyco picked up half the cost. Kozlowski "became the object of ridicule" after it was revealed that the furnishings at his Manhattan apartment included a $6,000 shower curtain and other extravagances that brought the price of the place to more than $30 million.[34]

No recounting of greed in the era of feet of clay would be complete without mention of Jack Welch's compensation package. The benefits Welch received not only as perquisites while CEO but into retirement included use of GE aircraft (and we are not talking about some cheap Gulfstream jet; GE flew its top people on company-owned Boeing 737s); helicopters; the use of a lavish Manhattan apartment owned by the company, including wine, a cook, flowers, and newspaper subscriptions; courtside seats at Madison Square Garden for the basketball games of the New York Knicks and at Flushing Meadows for the U.S. Open; VIP seats at Wimbledon; a box at the Metropolitan Opera not far from his palatial apartment; a box at Fenway Park in Boston for Red Sox games and one at Yankee Stadium in the Bronx (apparently Welch did not follow the Mets); fees for four country clubs; and security devices for all four of his residences.

Welch caught a lot of flak when this compensation agreement became public knowledge. According to Jay W. Lorsch, an expert in corporate governance at the Harvard Business School, "The . . . question here is how many of these retirement expenses, such as the apartment in New York, are legitimate expenses that G.E. should even be willing to pay? Jack Welch got paid for doing a great job. Why should he get paid twice?"[35] Corporate compensation specialist Graef Crystal said, "This is an indictment of G.E.'s Board of Directors."[36]

No laws were broken. That is not the point. It was Welch's success as a manager that drew so much attention to the cozy arrangement for his retirement. "Because Mr. Welch has long been one of the most highly regarded chief executives," explained the *New York Times*, "his financial arrangements with G.E. are of interest not only to investors, but also to other chief executives."[37] Welch's eminence left people asking: "Is this what business really is?"

By mid-2002, it was clear that the era of the feet of clay was having repercussions in the form of "declining public and investor trust in companies, their leaders and America's capital markets." The Conference Board, which describes its mission as "[creating and disseminating] knowledge about management and the marketplace to help businesses strengthen their performance and better serve society," convened a twelve-member commission in June to study the situation and recommend remedies. The chairman was Peter G. Peterson, former secretary of commerce and chairman of the Blackstone Group (a financial organization whose CEO, Steve Schwartzman, had turned it into a fabulous success). Members included John W. Snow, CEO of transportation giant CSX at the time and later to become the secretary of the treasury; Ralph S. Larsen, former CEO of Johnson & Johnson; and Paul A. Volcker, former chairman of the Federal Reserve. Petersen persuaded a reluctant Grove to join. Andy did so on condition that he not have to fly to the East Coast for the meetings. He attended through teleconference, the son of ProShare.

The commission's findings were delivered in three parts.[38] The most notable aspect of Part 1 was that the commissioners could not agree on "Specific Best Practice" with regard to an issue of critical importance, executive compensation. Ten of the commissioners did agree that "To eliminate accounting bias in favor of one form of equity-based compensation, fixed-price stock options should be expensed on financial statements of public companies."[39] Paul Volcker did not feel that went far enough. "I believe," he wrote, "the use of such options should be strongly discouraged for public companies."[40]

Grove differed with the commission completely with regard to its stand on stock options, and he thought that Volker's view was beyond the pale. He published a four-column, two-page dissenting opinion in the commission's report.[41]

"My own views on stock options are well known," he wrote, and they were. Intel used them extensively, and Grove believed—he believed passionately although he did not use that word—that they should not be expensed. He conceded that stock options lead to the dilution of the holdings of people who already own shares of a company. To illustrate, say that there are a hundred shares of a company outstanding. Ten people own 10 shares apiece. However, an option to purchase an additional 10 shares has been granted to a manager. When the manager exercises that option, the original 10 shareholders who owned 10 percent of the company before the manager exercised his or her options now find themselves owning 9.1 percent of the company. They still have their 10 shares, but now there are 110 shares outstanding rather than 100.

Why grant options to managers? Because by doing so, the theory is that you will better align the incentives of the managers with the owners and attract better managers because they will have enhanced opportunities to make a lot of money. Better managers will build a more valuable company. Thus, although the percentage of the company owned by each of the original shareholders will decline from 10 percent to 9.1 percent, the value of that 9.1 percent will be greater than the 10 percent would have been because stock options led to better managers more aligned with shareholder interests who built a better company. Stock options were, as the Conference Board Commission itself acknowledged, "an appropriate and important tool for companies, particularly start-up companies and companies where an important part of the intellectual capital resides with employees, and . . . they have become a cultural way of life for high tech companies."[42]

The importance of stock options and the impact of expensing them were more than "cultural" matters. As the Conference Board recognized in a footnote, treating stock options as an expense on a company's income statement would, according to one study, lead to a decline of about 70 percent in earnings per share in the high-technology sector. Options were granted and not expensed in other industries as well. However, the difference in importance to high technology compared to the rest of the business world is illustrated by the fact that expensing stock options would result in declines of 12 percent in telecommunications, 9 percent in consumer products and "materials industries," between 2 and 7 percent in "other industries," and 10 percent in the Standard & Poor's 500.[43]

Grove conceded in his dissent to the Conference Board's view that expensing stock options "is a subject on which reasonable accountants differ."[44] For his part, however, he had no doubts about this issue. "Expensing options," he declared, "may or may not be good accounting, but as a practical matter it will not be an effective deterrent to abuse. It will create new and significant opportunities for managements to manipulate earnings."[45]

Expensing options, Grove complained, "has become an economic Rorschach test onto which people project their basic beliefs about American enterprise, their notions of how companies should be run, how management compensation should be controlled, and their preferences for investments." He was correct. He was also correct in asserting that "this does not encourage a rational discussion of accounting issues."[46]

Grove diagnosed the controversy about expensing stock options well. The issue was one about which reasonable people could disagree, and it was unrealistic to think that it could be discussed on its merits in the overheated atmosphere of 2002. Having grown up in a business environment in which he felt the spirit of risk-taking enterprise was heartily nourished by the opportunity to become very wealthy through options, he was loathe to see the incentives they provided compromised. He felt strongly—very strongly, perhaps too strongly—that expensing them would deal a serious blow to high technology in the United States.

Time may prove Grove's arguments correct. However, numerous major companies, including high-technology giants Microsoft and Dell, came to concede that this was a battle that could not be won, and they decided to expense their options. Grove, however, fought the inevitable as long as he could. It is hard to see how Intel benefited from a lonely stand that distracted the company from pursuing other matters in the cause of a fight that was predictably destined to prove fruitless. One feels that on the subject of stock options, one is dealing with the overinvolved Grove of the Pentium flaw rather than the above-the-battle Grove of the memory exit.

Not only were private groups such as the Conference Board involving themselves in corporate governance in 2002 as a result of the scandals just discussed, so also was the federal government. On July 30, 2002, President

George W. Bush signed into law "An Act to protect investors by improving the accuracy and reliability of corporate disclosures made pursuant to the securities laws, and for other purposes." The short title was the Sarbanes-Oxley Act of 2002. It passed both houses of Congress with ease, in one day. The vote in the House of Representatives was 423 to 3. In the Senate, it was 99 to 0.

The Sherman Antitrust Act of 1890, the most important piece of legislation dealing with business in American history, passed both houses of Congress with only one dissenting vote. That is because no one knew what it meant. No one knew what the implications of Sarbanes-Oxley were either. In the latter instance, there was a lot more not to know. The Sherman Act is two pages long. Sarbanes-Oxley is sixty-six pages.

Sarbanes-Oxley was an attempt to enforce greater integrity on the reporting of financial results by corporations. It was expensive to comply with it. The extra costs for audits in a company the size of Intel could run to between $10 million and $20 million. But it would be a lot more expensive not to comply if you were caught.

Judging from his public statements, Grove did not seem to be opposed to Sarbanes-Oxley. He did want to have some voice in shaping it. He called it "the most significant expansion of the federal securities and corporate law since World War II."[47] To Grove, Sarbanes-Oxley was all about corporate governance; and he could truthfully report, "We take corporate governance seriously."

In the 2002 *Annual Report*, Grove published a lengthy "Letter from your Chairman" about corporate governance at Intel. Eight of Intel's eleven directors were "not employees and do not have other business or consulting engagements with the company." The independent directors met regularly without the presence of corporate management, "led by an elected lead independent director who conducts and reports on the meetings." Intel's lead independent director was Harvard Business School professor David B. Yoffie. "Separating the roles of chairman and CEO is an important step toward better corporate governance," Grove wrote. Intel had taken that step back in 1998, in part at Yoffie's urging.

Intel's board was not only the tool for corporate governance at the company, the board itself was also governed. Each director filled out a form to assist in assessing how he or she was discharging assigned responsibilities. As chairman, "I preside," said Grove, "at board meetings . . . set board meeting agendas and ensure that the directors have sufficient time for discussion."

Grove was responsible along with Yoffie "for managing our board and CEO evaluation process." Everybody was evaluated. Everybody was charged with striving for "continuous improvement."

Structurally, "The board's Audit, Compensation, Corporate Governance, Finance and Nominating Committees consist solely of independent directors." This independence was designed to foster objectivity. "Our CEO is subject to the same '360' evaluation by which all Intel employees are evaluated."

Andy Grove, the most congenitally uncomfortable CEO in America, felt "very comfortable that the Board personifies our key Intel values." Board members were results-oriented problem solvers who engage in constructive confrontation. "Most importantly, the board demonstrates through its operations and values the key Intel value to conduct our business with uncompromising integrity and professionalism."[48]

Let it be said that before the scandals hit the front pages, glowing words were also written about Enron's board, which was populated by distinguished people who had not a clue about what was really going on in that company. Let it also be said that there was plenty of conflict on Intel's board during Grove's chairmanship and that not every board member would have written as complimentary a report as did the usually critical Grove. He criticized others. He criticized himself. Constant criticism was built into how Intel's board functioned. Nevertheless, when you take a step back, the fact is this was as honest a board as you will find. Intel emerged from the era of the feet of clay squeaky clean.

There was an interesting moment at Intel's 2002 stockholders' meeting in May of that year. After presentations by top executives for more than one hour, Grove as chairman presided over a question-and-answer session. Much of these proceedings were legally mandated. Much of the meeting was required boilerplate. But one moment was not.

When Andy began the question-and-answer session with management, he said that questioners would be limited to two minutes and that total discussion time was limited to ten minutes. You don't expect to encounter anything particularly interesting with such a format. The people who ask questions often own just a few shares of stock. For some of them, this is their moment in the sun, their chance to be the center of attention ever so briefly. They have a captive audience and get to hear themselves speak. You don't expect anything real to happen. A lot of this is ritual. A lot is pointless.

Twelve people asked unremarkable questions. Andy then said he would take one more question, and that would be the last. A man in a plaid shirt came to the microphone. His question touched reality. He wanted to hear from management that there was nothing going on at Intel similar to "the Enron/Andersen mess." He also wanted a firm commitment to financial transparency on the part of the company.

It is interesting to see this meeting on tape, because the feeling tone of the proceedings changed when this final question was asked. Andy asked Craig Barrett to respond first. In his typically direct way, Barrett said, "I know of nothing that we're doing that parallels Enron." Andy seconded the statement.

Then Grove called on Intel's chief financial officer, Andy Bryant, to address the question. Bryant, in a low-key tone, said that top management from Moore to Grove to Barrett always asked him what the right thing to do was. He had never been told even to skirt the edge of propriety. "No one," he said, "has ever asked me to do a single thing that I thought was wrong. And if they did, I wouldn't be here." Bryant wasn't playing to the crowd. He is not capable of doing that. His statement was met with applause.

The next speaker was Winston Chen, the head of the audit committee of the board. He spoke in notably accented English, but his meaning was clear. The audit committee had already studied Enron in great detail. There were no similarities between Enron and Intel. Intel had none of the "special purpose entities" that had existed at Enron. Intel did have some off-balance-sheet financing, but it was exceedingly minor and in no way comparable to the high-leverage off-balance-sheet casino Enron was running. Equally important, said Chen, was the tone set by top management. In his nine years on the board, he said, he had seen nothing but high integrity. There were "no aggressive accounting practices." The company was run in a manner that was ethical as well as legal. A spokesman for the outside auditors, Ernst & Young, then rose to state briefly (a little too briefly) that he agreed.[49] All told, Intel delivered an impressive response to an important question.

With the passage of time, Andy became progressively less involved with Intel. Nevertheless, during his tenure as chairman, he never missed a board meeting. And he was deeply committed to a new health care initiative at Intel. But between his PD, the growth of the Grove Foundation, and his other commitments, he spent less of his time on matters directly relating to Intel in 2004 than he did in 1998.

Two thousand and four was Andy's last full year as chairman of the board and Craig Barrett's final full year as CEO. It was a good year for the company by a number of measures. Record sales of $34.2 billion were up 13.5 percent from the previous year, and Intel placed at 50 on the Fortune 500. Profits jumped a third to $7.5 billion. This was well below the $10.4 billion for 1999, but profits were definitely moving in the right direction. The market capitalization story was not quite as happy. Intel closed out 2004 with a market capitalization of $147.859 billion. This was a decline of almost 30 percent from the close of $209.350 billion at the end of 2003.

The Intel *Annual Report* for 2004 was the last one in which Grove, who had joined the board in 1974, published a message. He wrote about succession planning as "one of the most important jobs of the Board because it ensures the continuity of the organization." Such planning was "not an event," it was "an ongoing process that takes years."

This is how Grove concluded: "I am asked sometimes what I would like to be remembered for. . . . I would like to be remembered for helping to build an organization that sustains itself long after my tenure. . . . Please join me in wishing the best to Paul and Craig in their new roles."[50]

29

---+---

Outside Intel

On May 18, 2005, Andrew Stephen Grove stepped down from full-time employment at Intel. Les Vadasz, whom Grove once described as an "engineer's engineer,"[1] retired in 2002. Andy was the last man associated with Intel's founding remaining. Now he was gone. Not completely gone, to be sure. He adopted the newly minted title of "senior advisor." His interest in Intel's health care initiative was, typical of him, vigorous and rigorous. As senior advisor, he meets with both CEO Paul Otellini and Chairman of the Board Craig Barrett regularly as well as exchanging frequent emails with them. Nevertheless, May 17, 2005, was Grove's last meeting as a member of the board. What were his parting observations?

Grove's final presentation to the board was brief. Three slides. Some members found it profoundly impressive. Others less so. On his first slide, Grove encouraged the board to "Trust the Business Judgment Rule," which, according to the American Law Institute, provides "broad protection to informed business judgments . . . in order to stimulate *risk-taking innovation*." The second slide encouraged the board to "Play the role of gravity for [the] governance pendulum. Lead as the swing starts, retard as the pendulum has swung to the . . . extreme."[2]

The final slide provided Grove with the opportunity to discuss Intel culture, a culture that he, more than any other single individual, had created.

Just as management should nourish and be guided by that culture, so should the board of directors. The board should "Conform to Intel Values." That meant:

Strive to:
— Encourage and reward informed risk-taking
— Be open and direct
— Constructively confront and solve problems
— Clearly communicate mutual intention and expectations
— Do the right things right.[3]

For Andy, these rules defined the job of the board. His tenure on the board had come to an end, but to describe him as retired would be quite mistaken. His attention turned both to health care and to the activities of the Grove Foundation and the Kinetics Foundation.

By force of circumstance, Grove had been involved in the health care delivery system since he was a four-year-old child in Hungary stricken with scarlet fever. His recent interest in health care was sparked by his prostate cancer in 1995 and by PD in 2000. Andy was approached by the University of California at San Francisco to head a capital campaign. His prostate condition was then and still is monitored by the urologists there. He holds Dr. Marc Shuman in the highest regard, and his view of Dr. Peter Carroll is probably unique. Often, if not usually, following quickly on the heels of praise from Grove is an amendment of some sort. "He's terrific at X but not so good at Y" is the sort of thing one gets used to hearing. There was no "yes, but" in Grove's view of Carroll. He is admirable on every dimension.[4]

Carroll is unquestionably a remarkable man. In addition to his skill at his profession, his openness to patients—his ability to listen—is all too rare in modern health care. Few surgeons are distinguished in this realm.

Grove chaired the UCSF capital campaign, working closely with Art Kern. Kern, cofounder and CEO of American Media, which owned radio stations and which Kern sold to Clear Channel Communications in October 1994, is a member of the board of Yahoo! and a philanthropist.

Ultimately responsible for the campaign was the chancellor of UCSF, Dr. J. Michael Bishop, holder of the Arthur Rock and Toni Rembe Rock Distinguished Professorship and winner of the Nobel Prize in Medicine in 1989. The goal of the capital campaign was to raise $1.4 billion. That goal was reached a year ahead of schedule.

Bishop was fully aware of Andy's "crucial relationship with some of our faculty." He also knew Andy's reputation, and, though obviously a self-confident man, Bishop found the idea of "entering into a partnership of this sort with him [Andy] a little intimidating."

Bishop credits Grove with at least two key contributions to the campaign's success. First, he could extend the reach of UCSF down into Silicon Valley. California is an amalgam of "micro-worlds." San Francisco forms the northern border of Silicon Valley. UCSF is the city's second largest employer, behind only the city itself, and it is a world-famous medical center. However, to penetrate the Valley, the community next door, it needed an ambassador. Andy could serve that role better than anyone else.

Andy's second contribution was his Andy-ness. Bishop says that he "would level with us and we could level with him. The impressive thing about him is that he is relentlessly analytical. He wants facts. He wants clear-headed thinking. No Pollyanna. And I appreciate that in an individual a great deal."[5]

Bishop is among what must be the small number of Nobel Prize winners in medicine who have read *Only the Paranoid Survive*. Its influence shows. "Andy is outspoken," he said, "doesn't mince words. I think he was known as the hammer, as I recall. I'm a scientist. I'm used to analysis, dispute over issues. Dispute's not the right word in the case with Andy, but Andy doesn't hesitate to ask tough questions, which I think was a big help for us. He was a constant reality tester . . . the ultimate Cassandra in certain ways."[6]

Grove also served on the board of CapCure. The first syllable stands for Cancer of the Prostate. The organization changed its name to the Prostate Cancer Foundation in 2002. The moving force behind this foundation is the brilliant financier Michael Milken. Milken, a man capable of creating a fanatical, almost cultlike loyalty, pleaded guilty in 1990 to six felonies related to his securities activities and served time in federal prison from 1990 to 1993. It was soon after his early release for good behavior that he was diagnosed with prostate cancer. He put his abilities and his fortune to work to fight the disease.

Directed by the highly informed Leslie D. Michelson, the Prostate Cancer Foundation has made a major impact on the management of the disease. Like anything connected with Milken, there are wheels within wheels in this organization. It is complex and can be frustrating. Nevertheless, in the fight against prostate cancer, the Prostate Cancer Foundation matters a great deal.

Barr Taylor was quoted earlier to the effect that Andy feels that learning about a disease intellectually can help you to master it physically. Grove has trained his analytical capabilities not only on prostate cancer, but on PD. Two wholly different illnesses. Both complex. Both menacing. Either one is enough to break your spirit.

Andy being Andy, that was never an issue. He created the Kinetics Foundation to combat PD and has partnered successfully with the Michael J. Fox Foundation in that effort. His approach toward PD is reminiscent of his business advice in *Only the Paranoid Survive:* "Let chaos reign" and then "Rein in chaos." PD is, literally, as complicated as the brain. The Kinetics Foundation is tapping resources around the nation and the world to come up with answers to PD. It is in the midst of developing a new device to measure the progress of the illness. Grove's enthusiasm and optimism in the face of PD are inspiring. His inspiration is contagious for those working with him and for organizations around the world partnering with Kinetics. Optimism in the face of PD—well, it does not comport with the image of himself that Grove has cultivated and projected to the world.

With regard to PD as well as prostate cancer, Grove brings what might be called a useful naiveté. Consistent with never allowing himself to be defeated before he starts, he will try anything. The United States was built by people who dared to attempt what more knowledgeable experts said could not be done.[7]

Let us take a step back from individual illnesses and consider the health care system as a whole both within Intel and as a national industry. Here Grove can claim considerable expertise. He has been teaching strategy at Stanford for almost two decades and is well informed of the main currents in academic thought with regard to strategy. In 2006, he published his sixth book, this one coauthored with his longtime Stanford collaborator, Robert A. Burgelman, and with the assistance of Philip E. Meza, entitled *Strategic Dynamics: Concepts and Cases.*[8]

Ask anyone who has spent time as an inpatient in a hospital, and there is a good chance you will hear a "hospital story" that is not a happy one. Why? Is the problem the doctors? Sometimes, but more often not. Is it the nurses?

No. Is it the staff? No. Is it the top administrators? No. Indeed, at most better hospitals in the United States, everybody from top to bottom is working very hard and trying very hard. The country is spending a fortune on health care. In 2006, health care costs will gobble up at least 12 percent of the gross domestic product.

If our health care providers are skilled, trying hard, and, speaking generally, people of great goodwill, and if we as a society are spending more money than anyone a generation ago was dreaming of, where, precisely is the problem? The answer is that the problem is the system. It is broken.

Grove's diagnosis is that from patient to provider to payer, the health care system is excessively fragmented. Only 7 percent of health care in the United States is delivered by a vertically integrated system. Without that vertical integration, there is too great a distance between the "R" and the "I." In other words, parties that had to make the investments (the "I") were not in a position to reap the rewards of returns (the "R") on that investment. This distance between the R and the I led to the "tragedy of the commons" which is America's health care system today. The "tragedy of the commons" refers to a situation in which the benefits of exploitation are enjoyed by individual participants in the system while the costs of exploitation are borne by all.

There is an irony here that was not lost on Grove. When Intel was born back in 1968, the computer business model was based on the vertical structure and accompanying strategy of IBM. The collapse of that model with the introduction of the PC, with its outsourced microprocessor and operating system, made possible the rise of Intel and Microsoft in the new sedimentary computer industry.

Health care, however, was a different industry with different problems operating in a heavily regulated environment. The only way to push through change was by way of united action. Grove felt certain that the digitization of health records, a key aspect of Intel's health care initiative, would save money and improve efficiency. Others were not so sure.[9] The technology existed. It was, however, devilishly difficult to sell it and deploy it to an environment as disorganized as the American health care system.

The heart of Grove's attention as he moved steadily further outside Intel was the Grove Foundation. The foundation was established at Eva Grove's urging back in 1986, and for many years it had no office space at all. As it grew in importance to the family, it established its comfortable and unassuming office, and the directors, Eva, Andy, and their two daughters, hired a general manager, Rebekah Saul Butler. Rebekah Butler came on board on July 7, 2004, and has made an important contribution to putting the foundation on a firm footing.

The foundation has no formal mission statement. Generally speaking, its goal is to help others realize the "American dream." This the family conceives of as, according to Butler, including "opportunities to learn, provide for yourself and your family, discover and contribute to science, to have civil liberties, and to have self-determination."[10] Andy and Eva wanted to give others the chance to enjoy what America had made possible for them.

Not surprisingly, the foundation was action-oriented. For all that has been written about strategy, Andy defined the word once again simply as "what we *do*." Strategy should change when "the external environment (the forces that affect us) and/or the internal environment (our capabilities and knowledge) change."[11]

Action was not the only essential. So was achievement. The old saying in retailing, "*in*spect what you *ex*pect," also prevailed at the Grove Foundation. It funded various initiatives, some of which were unorthodox. The family was interested in "orphan areas," charitable needs that might not have been met by others. Research would follow to determine whether the original hopes that inspired the philanthropy and the goals that had been established were being met. If they were, further funding might be in order. If not, easing off leading to an exit from a particular endeavor might ensue.

Therefore a list of principal recipients of Grove Foundation funding will change over the years. Some charities were, however, likely to remain constant. Foremost among these were probably those included in "Legacy." The goals of Legacy are, first of all, "Giving back." The family was in a position to provide financial support to institutions that had helped them when they had nothing or very little.

Contributions were made to the International Rescue Committee because it brought Andy to America and "Gave him the first rung." The Groves were concerned about that vital "first rung on the ladder" for immigrants. They thought it was being weakened but that the IRC effectively fought that trend. Andy himself served on the IRC's board of overseers. "I am extremely grateful to the International Rescue Committee for bringing me to the U.S.," he wrote in *Swimming Across*. "I have donated all of my royalties from this book to them so they can help today's refugees."[12]

Also an important part of Legacy were "Our Schools."[13] Andy's gratitude toward CCNY was expressed by his $26 million gift in 2005.[14] This donation came from his personal funds rather than the foundation.

Another area of the foundation's interest is "career training." The Groves feel that vocational education is an important and neglected aspect of education in the United States. The foundation's "School-to-Career" initiative was designed as a first stop in changing that situation. They also believe that junior colleges constitute an avenue on which students whose natural inclinations and talents might not lead to a four-year college directly out of high school could travel.

The Wilcox High School put it well. "The Grove Foundation started the 'School-to-Career scholarship' program in the 1998–1999 school year at the Wilcox High School in the Santa Clara Unified High School District. Andy and Eva Grove initiated the scholarship program to give students with a focused career goal who otherwise might not attend college the opportunity to achieve their potential." The Groves had in mind "computer technicians, automotive technicians, nurses, chefs, accountants and individuals pursuing technical or varied career paths that can be advanced through a community college or a technical training program."[15]

Another major area of concern for the foundation is "Reproductive Health." This is a cause that all four members of the family feel strongly about. Eva Grove has served as a volunteer in the local chapter of the Planned Parenthood Federation, and that organization has received contributions from the foundation regularly.

The Grove family also feels deeply about the separation of church and state. When the border between the two has become blurred, they have an eye for organizations that keep the line bright between them.

The foundation is opportunistic. When new challenges arise, the family has an open mind about new donations to make. "Is there a unifying theme?" they have asked themselves. They have answered in two bullet points:

- Defending/Reviving/Bolstering the American Dream
- GF [the Grove Foundation] fights for a secular government, the first rung, individual freedoms, and science unfettered by politics.[16]

30

Still Swimming

This book is the story of Andy Grove. The book is unfinished because his life is a work in progress.

To whom can we compare Grove in order to shed light on the mystery that he is? William Perry, former secretary of defense and former member of the Intel board of advisors, likened him to Benjamin Franklin.[1] There are some notable parallels. One is a devotion to technology. Another is the mastery of a variety of activities. Yet another is care and skill at image management. Both had outstanding senses of humor and of irony.

Both Franklin and Grove liked to write. Both were autobiographers. Grove's written output deserves note. In addition to scores of articles, he has written six books. He wrote them himself or, in one case, with collaborators. There was never a question about using a ghostwriter. No American CEO has ever generated a comparable output of published work.

Both Franklin and Grove remained active regardless of their ages. Both built their own worlds. In this regard lie the sharpest differences between the two. Franklin became a politician later in life. The world he contributed to building was the United States. Grove, though interested in politics, was always a business leader. The world for which he was primarily responsible was Intel.

Comparisons to Andrew Carnegie are obvious, and they extend well beyond sharing a first name. Both were immigrants. Both personified the ragsto-riches story. Both founded businesses based on high technology. Neither feared change. Both were profoundly devoted to America.

There are also differences. Carnegie himself was not a technologist. As he said, he had "no shadow of claim to rank as an inventor, chemist, investigator, or mechanician."[2] Grove had plenty to claim in that realm. Carnegie was better-known than Grove because he became the richest man in the world as a result of a company that, until he sold it in 1901 to J. P. Morgan, bore his name, the Carnegie Steel Corporation.

Is there a fictional character who can illumine Grove's life? I keep thinking of Odysseus.

If your first reaction to this suggestion is that it could not be more wrong, that would be understandable. After all, the whole point of *The Odyssey* is that Odysseus wants to get home to Ithaca. Nothing has ever persuaded Grove to return to Hungary, and nothing ever will. Homer has Nestor say of Odysseus, "More than all other men, that man was born for pain."[3] Nothing could be less true of Grove.

Where, then, are the similarities? The first line of *The Odyssey* describes Odysseus as "the man of twists and turns."[4] Like Odysseus, Grove has proven infinitely adaptable. Both, in fact, combined adaptability with focus. Both loved their wives. Both were born leaders. Neither would accept defeat. Both knew fear. Both had faced death.

Neither was ever done. When Odysseus finally reached Ithaca after two decades—it took Grove two decades to get out of Hungary and wind up in the country in which he should have been born—he was still charged by the gods to leave his palace and carry a "well-planed oar" far enough inland until "another traveler" didn't recognize the object as an oar but thought it to be "a fan to winnow grain."[5]

As for Grove, even though almost completely outside Intel, he still endeavors to make change where change needs to be made. He is still as smart as he ever was. He remains a force of nature.

The Odyssey is perhaps the greatest epic in the history of literature. Being an epic, it is about more than its subject.

"The Grove-iad" is about more than Andy Grove. It is about what Tennyson had Ulysses (the Latin form of "Odysseus") say at the end of his poem: "To strive, to seek, to find, and not to yield."

Not everybody loves Grove nor does everybody admire him. No one, however, denies that he is unique. We all are. But Andy Grove is uniquer than most. He never quits. He is pugnacious. He is tenacious.

And he deserves the last word. It is the sentence with which he concludes *Swimming Across.*

"I am still swimming."[6]

ACKNOWLEDGMENTS

Gratitude is due to innumerable people for making this book possible. The first person to thank is Andy Grove.

Andy permitted the massive intrusion of this project into his life between 2003, when it began, and its publication. The reader should know the conditions under which the book was written.

Andy saw not one word of this book until it was published, with one exception. This exception is direct quotation from him. Andy made himself available to me on many occasions, and we exchanged emails on a regular basis. We also saw a lot of each other and had many conversations.

The direct quotation exception was my idea, not his. The reason for my suggestion was that I wanted Andy to feel completely at ease in all his communications with me. He and I agreed this was the right thing to do.

Other than this exception, Andy, to repeat, read none of this book prior to publication. Nor is he financially involved in it.

I am a professional historian who has spent almost his entire career at an institution that has as its motto *"Veritas."* I have tried to provide an objective, truthful account of the extraordinary business life of a remarkable individual. If I have succeeded at least in part, I am pleased. I have tried to tell the truth as I see it. Nevertheless, for the sake of full disclosure, the reader should be aware that Andy Grove is a magnetic man. It is impossible, at least for me, to have spent as much time with him as I did and to have immersed myself as completely as I have in this project without developing feelings of admiration and affection that must have colored this account to some degree.

I learned much from Eva Grove, both in our formal interviews and in our many informal exchanges. She was kind to me in innumerable ways, most of which she is unaware. Generosity comes naturally to her.

The Groves' close friend, Denise Amantea, played a key role in this project. She is an astute woman who is a close and loyal friend of Andy and Eva. She interpreted Andy to me through a unique lens. Denise's friendship proved a valuable, unanticipated benefit of this work.

At Intel, where I had a cubicle during my stay in Silicon Valley from December 18, 2004, to February 10, 2006, Terri L. Murphy, Andy's administrative assistant, was unfailingly helpful. Intel is a complicated place. Terri helped me to decode it. Both she and her nephew, Alex Nomura, did a good deal of work on this book, including finding documents and especially, along with the Groves, preparing the pictures.

Present and former Intel employees were almost all cooperative, far more than I had any right to expect. I am, alas, not an engineer; and some highly gifted technologists like Craig Kinnie responded gracefully to questions that must have seemed, on a good day, sophomoric.

Special thanks are due to two of Andy's former technical assistants and to his current TA during the writing of this book. Dennis Carter, Sean Maloney, and Julie Coppernoll were not only vitally helpful, they were a joy to be around. I also want to acknowledge the valuable contributions of two former CEOs of Intel, Gordon E. Moore and Craig R. Barrett, and of Intel's present CEO, Paul S. Otellini.

To thank each present and former Intel employee would tax the reader's patience. But I must confess to a sense of unease when I think of how much I must have taxed theirs! Their names are listed in the bibliography.

Most of the people I interviewed are listed in the bibliography that follows. Some interviewees wished to remain anonymous. Everyone to whom I spoke contributed to my understanding of Andy Grove and his world. The reader should be aware of that, and so should the interviewees. Even if interviews are not directly cited in the footnotes, every one of them mattered. They shaped my thinking fundamentally, and I want to thank them all.

Many former students (and their spouses) were generous with their time and insight about that world unto itself that is Silicon Valley. I am especially grateful to John Bara, Michael Dearing, Sue Decker, Kim Malone, Cliff Reid (and his wife, Darlene Mann), and Sheryl Sandberg (and her husband, David Goldberg).

In the academic world, five names stand out: Andreas Acrivos, emeritus at Stanford; Leslie Berlin of Stanford; Robert Burgelman of Stanford; Istvàn Déàk, emeritus at Columbia; and Morris Kolodney, emeritus at CCNY.

In Budapest, my guide—and believe me I needed a good one—was Tamás Karman. He took me to Andy's schools and managed to get me inside the Kiraly Street apartment.

At the Harvard Business School, a full list of the people to whom gratitude is due would be lengthy indeed. The first name on it is Kim B. Clark, who retired as dean on June 30, 2005. In March 2005, I told Kim that I did not want to return to the East for my regular teaching assignments. I wanted to stay in Silicon Valley for as long as possible because I felt that now was the time to write this book.

This is not happy news for a dean. I offered to take an unpaid leave of absence. That still did not solve any of his problems. Kim, however, knows how important the Andy Grove story is. He told me to write the book. And he paid my salary.

On the faculty, the following people deserve my gratitude: Carliss Baldwin, Geoff Jones, Tom McCraw, Tom Nicholas, Julio Rotemberg, Bill Sahlman, and David Yoffie. Luckily for me, David Yoffie is an expert on Andy, having served on Intel's board since 1989. A visiting fellow, Michelle Craig McDonald, was also helpful.

On the staff, I benefited from the efforts of the best business librarians in the world: Sara Ericksen, Chris Allen, Jeff Cronin, Erika McCaffrey, and Kathleen Ryan. My research associate, David Ruben, was of inestimable assistance in preparing a complex manuscript for publication.

This manuscript did not type itself. Jacqueline Archer handled numerous versions of it. She worked harder on this project (including weekends) than anyone should. Aimée Hamel lent a hand. She has typed an awful lot of my writings over the years.

Friends matter in a project like this. My late wife's colleagues in the Department of Psychiatry at the Massachusetts General Hospital, Maurizio Fava, MD (and his wife, Stefania Lamon-Fava, MD, PhD), Jonathan Alpert, MD, PhD, Amy Farabaugh, PhD, and Andy Nierenberg, MD (and his wife, Karen Blumenfeld) were unfailingly kind.

I took one vacation during the writing of this book. Royce Yudkoff, CEO of ABRY Partners, a private equity firm in Boston, and his wife, Jody, took me on a cruise of the Mediterranean for thirteen days. Everything about that trip was a delight.

Reed E. Hundt is a special person, and he played a special role in providing both intellectual and emotional support for this task. Reed is a college classmate who is also a colleague of David Yoffie's on Intel's board.

My agent, Helen Rees, was staunchly supportive from start to finish. Little wonder that she is widely recognized as one of Greater Boston's Greater Bostonians. It was a pleasure once again to work with Adrian Zackheim and with his talented team at Penguin. Adrian always appreciated the potential of a book on Andy.

■   ■   ■

My greatest debt is to this book's dedicatee. My wife, Joyce, and I had the perfect marriage. It ended at 3:58 a.m. on October 2, 2003, when she died of ovarian cancer.

As Joyce was dying, we talked about how I could possibly survive without her. She knew I needed a project. But what should it be?

Joyce had met Andy and Eva Grove at a dinner arranged by David Yoffie in Newton, Massachusetts, in the mid-1990s. She was intrigued by Andy. It is impossible not to be. Early in 2003 she read *Swimming Across.* She said that its author was not your average CEO. There was a lot going on in this man. She suggested I write a book about him. On May 18, 2003, Joyce and I flew to California and talked about a biography with Andy and Eva. Joyce was a psychiatrist. She learned a great deal that weekend. On the flight home, she said that this is it.

Joyce died before the first word of this book was written. But her spirit suffuses the volume. The last words she spoke were a question to me: "Are you going to be okay?"

It was the only time in our marriage that I did not tell her the truth.

NOTES

Introduction

1. In January and February of 2004 alone, Grove was selected by a panel of professors at the Wharton School of the University of Pennsylvania for PBS's *Nightly Business Report* as the most influential businessperson in the United States during the preceding quarter century. He also received the Ernest C. Arbuckle Award sponsored by the Alumni Association of the Graduate School of Business at Stanford University to "[recognize] excellence in the field of management leadership.... Recipients demonstrate a commitment to both managerial excellence and to addressing the changing needs of society." The award was established in 1968. When Grove received it on February 11, the event was sold out, with more attendees than ever before.
2. "Refugee Heading Engineers' Class," *New York Times,* June 15, 1960.
3. Andrew S. Grove, *Swimming Across: A Memoir* (New York: Warner, 2001), p. 287. The resort was the Maplewood Hotel (which no longer exists). The interviewer who hired Grove was unpleasant. Grove was somewhat uneasy on his trip to the hotel. It was his first time away from New York and his relatives. But he adapted quickly. Author interview with Andrew S. Grove, April 13, 2005.
4. Author interview with Professor Andreas Acrivos, New York City, December 18, 2003. Grove and Acrivos coauthored (with others) four academic articles. They are F. H. Shair, A. S. Grove, E. E. Petersen, and A. Acrivos, "The Effect of Confining Walls on the Stability of the Steady Wake behind a Circular Cylinder," *J. of Fl. Mech.* 17, 546 (1963); A. S. Grove, E. E. Petersen, and Andreas Acrivos, "Velocity Distribution in the Laminar Wake of a Parallel Flat Plate," *Phys. of Fl.* 7, 7 (1964), A. S. Grove, F. H. Shair, E. E. Petersen, and Andreas Acrivos, "An Experimental Investigation of the Steady Separated Flow Past a Circular Cylinder," *J. of Fl. Mech.* 19, 60 (1964); Andreas Acrivos, D. D. Snowden, A. S. Grove, and E. E. Petersen, "The Steady Separated Flow Past a Circular Cylinder at Large Reynolds Numbers," *J. of*

Fl. Mech. 21, 737 (1965). The title of Grove's thesis is "An Investigation into the Nature of Steady Separated Flows at Large Reynolds Numbers."

5. Author interview with Andreas Acrivos, New York City, December 18, 2003.
6. For Grove at Stauffer, where he worked during the summer of 1960, see Linda Geppert, "Profile: Andy Grove," *IEEE Spectrum,* June 2000, p. 36. Also in conversation with author.
7. The letter of Professor Acrivos to Dr. T. Geballe recommending Grove for a position at Bell Labs has survived. The letter to Moore at Fairchild has not. However, Grove has informed me that the letter to Geballe "has text identical" to the letter Acrivos wrote to Moore. In the letter of recommendation, Acrivos wrote:

> From all points of view, he [Grove] is a top student, and although my conservative nature would normally prevent me from using superlatives to describe a person's technical competence, I will depart from past practice and provide him with the strongest possible recommendation.
>
> It is indeed most gratifying to see that only after a year on the project [which was "the experimental and theoretical investigation of a classical but difficult problem in fluid mechanics, the solution to which had eluded some of the very best fluid mechanicists"], he succeeded where others had failed. [Grove] is a truly outstanding technical person.

Acrivos to Grove, June 22, 1988, Acrivos to Geballe, November 14, 1962. Letters in author's possession. See also Gordon Moore's comment in Geppert, "Profile," p. 36.

8. This was down from eighth in 1985 and 1984. David B. Yoffie, "The Global Semiconductor Industry, 1987," Harvard Business School Case No. 9388-052, rev. March 22, 1993 (Boston: HBS Publishing, 1983), p. 19. For a critical assessment of Intel's prospects at this writing, see Adam S. Parker, "INTC and AMD—Management Decisions and What to Do Now," Bernstein Research, March 13, 2006.
9. This calculation was prompted by Robert A. Burgelman, *Strategy Is Destiny: How Strategy-Making Shapes a Company's Future* (New York: Free Press, 2002), p. 134. Professor Burgelman uses 1997 as his last year rather than 1998 and therefore comes up with different results, which are impressive nonetheless.
10. See the observations of Professor David B. Yoffie, lead independent director of the Intel board of directors, in Steve Hamm, "Former CEOs Should Just Fade Away," *BusinessWeek,* April 12, 2004.
11. Cliff Edwards, "Intel: Can CEO Craig Barrett Reverse the Slide?" *BusinessWeek,* October 15, 2001.
12. Michelle Kessler, "Intel Gets 2nd Chance to Build a Better Chip," *USA Today,* July 29, 2004.
13. Parker, "INTC and AMD."
14. This is a paraphrase of Emerson's famous observation: "An institution is the lengthened shadow of one man." Ralph Waldo Emerson, "Self Reliance," in Eduard C. Lindeman, ed. *Basic Selections from Emerson: Essays, Poems and Apothegms* (New York: Mentor, 1954), p. 60.

15. Andrew S. Grove, *Physics and Technology of Semiconductor Devices* (New York: Wiley, 1967).
16. Andrew S. Grove, *High Output Management* (New York: Vintage, 1983).
17. Andrew S. Grove, *One-on-One with Andy Grove: How to Manage Your Boss, Yourself, and Your Coworkers* (New York: Penguin, 1987).
18. Andrew S. Grove, *Only the Paranoid Survive: How to Manage the Crisis Points That Challenge Every Company* (New York: Doubleday, 1996).
19. Only one name can be mentioned in the same breath with Grove's in this regard. It is Alfred P. Sloan Jr., author of *My Years with General Motors* (Garden City: Doubleday, 1964). I believe this book is overrated. See my "Swimming Across: A Memoir in Historical Perspective," HBS Working Paper 04-050.
20. Andy Grove, "Taking on Prostate Cancer," *Fortune*, May 13, 1996.
21. Grove, *Swimming*, p. 7.
22. George was born on September 6, 1905; Maria on May 10, 1907. Thus he was twenty-seven and she was twenty-six on their wedding day.
23. Grove, *Swimming*, p. 7.
24. Grove, *Swimming*, p. 8.
25. Grove, *Swimming*, p. 11.
26. Grove, *Swimming*, p. 137. The distinguished Hungarian American historian István Deák, Seth Low Professor of History Emeritus at Columbia University, has commented, "[I]n this small country, everybody knew who was and who was not a Jew." István Deák, "A Fatal Compromise? The Debate over Collaboration and Resistance in Hungary," in István Deák, Jan T. Gross, and Tony Judt, eds., *The Politics of Retribution in Europe: World War II and Its Aftermath* (Princeton: Princeton University Press, 2000), p. 49.
27. Grove, *Swimming*, pp. 83, 227.
28. Joshua Cooper Ramo, "Man of the Year: A Survivor's Tale," *Time*, December 29, 1997. According to one source, it was not until the 1970s that surgery was able to restore Andy's hearing. Geppert, "Profile," p. 36. The last of the five operations he underwent was in the late 1980s.
29. See György Györffy, *King Saint Stephen of Hungary* (New York: Columbia University Press, 1994), pp. 88–98.
30. Technical University of Budapest, "Hungarian Home Page," http://www.fsz.bme.hu/hungary/history. Viewed on the Internet on February 28, 2004.
31. János Bak, "The Late Medieval Period, 1382–1526," in Peter F. Sugar, General Editor, Péter Hanák, Associate Editor, and Tibor Frank, Editorial Assistant, *A History of Hungary* (Bloomington: Indiana University Press, 1990), p. 82.
32. The use of the term "Budapest" in the year 1686 is an anachronism. Not until 1873 were the constituent parts of today's Budapest—Pest, Buda, and Obuda—unified as a single city; http://www.fsz.bme.hu/hungary/history.html, viewed on the Internet on February 28, 2004; Károly Vörös, "Birth of Budapest: Building a Metropolis, 1873–1918," in András Gerő and János Poor, eds., *Budapest: A History from Its Beginnings to 1998* (New York: Columbia University Press, 1997), pp. 103–138.

33. There are numerous translations. See, for example, "Magyar Nemzeti Himnusz," www.goo-bear.com/tree/magyar/anthem.cfm. Viewed on the Internet on March 12, 2004.

34. "The Nobel Prize in Literature 2002," http://nobelprize.org/literature/laureates/ 2002. Viewed on the Internet on February 21, 2004.

35. Imre Kertész, *Fatelessness*, trans. Tim Wilkinson (New York: Vintage, 2004). This book's title was originally translated less accurately as *Fateless* (Evanston, IL: Northwestern University Press, 1992). The novel has been made into a film that has retained the original translation of the title.

36. The quoted words are those of the physicist Otto Frisch paraphrasing Houtermans. Richard Rhodes, *The Making of the Atomic Bomb* (New York: Simon and Schuster, 1986), p. 106. What was not a joke was the remarkable concentration of scientific talent produced by "so remote and provincial a place." Included in this group are Theodor von Kármán, George de Hevesy, Michael Polanyi, Leo Szilard, Eugene Wigner, John von Neumann, and Edward Teller. All were products of "the prospering but vulnerable Hungarian Jewish middle class" of the late nineteenth and early twentieth century. All "made major contributions to science and technology." Two—de Hevesy and Wigner—won Nobel Prizes. Rhodes, *Atomic Bomb*, p. 106. See also the remark of the Nobel Prize–winning Italian American physicist Enrico Fermi that extraterrestrials do indeed exist and that they are among us now. They are called Hungarians. "Hungarian Home Page," http://www.fsz.bme.hu/ hungary/intro.html. Viewed on the Internet on January 17, 2006.

37. See, for example, George Marx, *The Voice of the Martians: Hungarian Scientists Who Shaped the 20th Century in the West* (Budapest: Akadémiai; Kiadó, 2001); Rhodes, *Atomic Bomb*, p. 106.

38. Thomas Sakmyster, *Hungary's Admiral on Horseback: Miklós Horthy, 1918–1944* (New York: Columbia University Press, 1994), pp. 91–121.

39. Miklós Horthy (1864–1953) was an admiral of the Austro-Hungarian Empire until its dissolution in 1918. "As Regent of Hungary," he wrote in his memoirs, "I was proud to wear my Admiral's uniform even after the Austro-Hungarian fleet had, to my undying grief, ceased to exist." *Admiral Nicholas Horthy: Memoirs*, annotated by Andrew L. Simon. Grove believes that every time Horthy appeared in public in his admiral's uniform, the implicit effect was to inflame Hungarian nationalism by reminding the nation that "Greater Hungary" stretched to the Adriatic Sea prior to the dismemberment mandated by the Treaty of Trianon. See http://www.hungarian history.hu/lib/horthy/horthy.pdf. Viewed on the Internet on February 21, 2004.

40. Ramo, "Tale," *Time*, December 29, 1997.

41. I am indebted to Reed E. Hundt for this observation.

42. I am not the only person who thinks so. See the remarks of Les Vadasz in Geppert, "Profile."

43. Andrew Grove's presentation on Intel's Strategy and History to Intel Employees, 1978. Tape in author's possession.

44. Author interview with Sean Maloney, Intel RNB, Santa Clara, CA, January 12, 2004.

45. Ramo, "Tale," *Time*, December 29, 1997.

46. Tim Jackson, *Inside Intel: Andy Grove and the Rise of the World's Most Powerful Chip Company* (New York: Penguin, 1997), p. 376. Jackson's narration of this interview differs in some respects from the transcript made available by the Video Monitoring Services of America, Inc. See *Fresh Air*, KQED-FM, San Francisco, November 19, 1996, 1:00–2:00 p.m. Transcript made available to me by Andy Grove. I have also heard a recording of this interview. See also Chris Gaither, "Andy Grove's Tale of His Boyhood in Wartime," *New York Times*, November 12, 2001.

47. Grove, *Swimming*, p. 285.

48. John William Ward, "Who Was Benjamin Franklin?" *American Scholar*, 32, 4 (Autumn 1963), p. 546. Franklin's classic statement of the creation of a public image can be found in Leonard W. Labaree et al., eds., *The Autobiography of Benjamin Franklin* (New Haven: Yale University Press, 1964). See especially pp. 125–126. See also John G. Cawelti, *Apostles of the Self-Made Man: Changing Concepts of Success in America* (Chicago: University of Chicago Press, 1968).

49. Grove, *Swimming*, p. 287. Despite this remark, Grove went to considerable lengths to keep in touch with his relatives who remained in Hungary.

1. Andy Grove Returns to Hungary

1. Speech before the Association for America's Holocaust Museum, Chicago, September 28, 2003. Tape in author's possession.

2. Sixteen nations that appear on a modern map of Europe were not then independent: Belarus, Bosnia and Herzegovina, the Czech Republic, Croatia, Estonia, Finland, Latvia, Lithuania, Macedonia, Moldova, Poland, Slovakia, Slovenia, and Ukraine add up to fourteen. The number becomes sixteen when you include the independent Austria and Hungary.

3. Tibor Hajdú and Zsuzsa L Nagy, "Revolution, Counterrevolution, Consolidation," in Sugar et al., eds., *Hungary*, p. 314. See also "The Treaty of Trianon," Peter N. Stearns, General Editor, *Encyclopedia of World History*, 6th ed., http://www.bartleby.com/67. Viewed on the Internet on March 2, 2004.

4. See, for example, "The Treaty of Trianon and the Dismemberment of Hungary," hipcat.hungary.org. Viewed on the Internet on March 1, 2004.

5. György Borsányi, *The Life of a Communist Revolutionary, Béla Kun* (New York: Columbia University Press, 1993), p. 1.

6. Borsányi, *Kun*, pp. 39–40.

7. Borsányi, *Kun*, pp. 57–77.

8. See "Red Terror in Hungary 1919," www.onwar.com. Viewed on the Internet on March 2, 2004.

9. "Béla Kun," www.nationmaster.com. Viewed on the Internet on March 2, 2004.

10. István Deák, "Survivor in a Sea of Barbarism," *New York Review of Books*, April 8, 1999.

11. Jerry Z. Muller, "Communism, Anti-Semitism & the Jews," *Commentary*, August 1988.

12. In France, the "Dreyfus Affair" polarized the nation and exposed the extent of the anti-Semitism in the French army and in conservative French society. Anti-

Semitism, historian István Deák has observed, "was more pronounced in pre-World War I France than in Germany." István Deák, "Holocaust Views: The Goldhagen Controversy in Retrospect," *Central European History,* 30, 2 (June, 1997), p. 302. Captain Alfred Dreyfus, a Jew, was convicted as a spy on the basis of forged documents in 1894. Not until 1906 was he exonerated. The uproar surrounding this scandal and the heroic role played by Emile Zola in freeing Dreyfus and saving his career have kept this episode alive in the French public mind down to the present day. As late as 1985, the French army refused to have a statue of Dreyfus, commissioned by the minister of culture, placed in the Ecole Militaire. Not until 1995 did General Jean-Louis Mourrut, head of the French army's historical service, publicly declare and accept the innocence of Dreyfus. Seventeen hundred people invited by France's Central Consistory of Jews attended Mourrut's presentation. Frederick Painton, "A Century Late, The Truth Arrives," *Time,* September 25, 1995. On January 13, 1998, the centennial of Zola's "*J'accuse . . . ,*" Jacques Chirac, president of France, publicly apologized to the Dreyfus and Zola families and described Dreyfus as a man "whose only crime was to be a Jew." "Chronology of the Dreyfus Affair," http://www.georgetown.edu/faculty/guieuj. Viewed on the Internet on March 12, 2004.

13. Thomas Sakmyster, *Hungary's Admiral on Horseback: Miklós Horthy, 1918–1944* (New York: Columbia University Press, 1994), p. 395.

14. A. J. P. Taylor, *The Habsburg Monarchy, 1809–1918* (London: Hamish Hamilton, 1948), p. 190.

15. Adolf Hitler, *Mein Kampf* (Boston: Houghton Mifflin, 1962. Originally published in 1925), p. 55.

16. "It is obvious that combating Jewry on such a basis could provide the Jews with small cause for concern. If the worst came to the worst, a splash of baptismal water could always save the business and the Jew at the same time . . . it was a sham anti-Semitism." Hitler, *Kampf,* pp. 120–121.

17. Taylor, *Habsburg,* p. 190. Anti-Semitism was rife in Russia prior to World War I. There we find the "pogroms." "Pogrom" is a Russian word that has entered the world's vocabulary. It means "riot" and refers specifically to the government-approved theft from and murder of Jews that took place in what seemed to be spontaneous eruptions. Pogroms broke out in 1881 and lasted until the Russian Revolution in 1917. Probably the best-known progroms took place in Kishinev in 1903 and 1905. Kishinev is today called Chisinau and is located in one of the new countries mentioned above, Moldova. Forty-five Jews were killed in 1903, and nineteen in 1905. Condemnations of these atrocities came from civilized countries around the world. The "Kishinev Massacres" stimulated the emigration of Jews from the Russia of the virulently anti-Semitic Tsar Nicholas II. On March 13, 1881, Tsar Alexander II was assassinated by a group calling itself "The People's Will." One member of this group (who was not among the assassins) was Jewish. That fact was sufficient pretext for the outbreak of anti-Semitism that ensued. Rhodes, *Atomic Bomb,* p. 180.

18. Muller, "Jews."

19. Muller, "Jews." Saturday is the Jewish Sabbath. Orthodox Jews do no work from sunset on Friday to sunset on Saturday.
20. Lucy S. Dawidowicz, *The War Against the Jews, 1933–1945* (New York: Bantam, 1986), p. 380.
21. A. J. P. Taylor, *The Second World War* (New York: Putnam, 1975), p. 218.
22. Hitler, *Kampf,* p. 121.
23. Hitler preached that a "final solution" was needed to what European anti-Semites had long referred to as the "Jewish Question." The very finality of that word "final" was, according to historian Lucy S. Dawidowicz, a special and cataclysmic addition of Hitler and his Nazis to the history of anti-Semitism:

> "Final" means definitive, completed, perfected, ultimate. "Final" reverberates with apocalyptic promise, bespeaking the Last Judgment, the End of Days, the last destruction before salvation, Armageddon. "The Final Solution of the Jewish Question" in the National Socialist [Nazi] conception was not just another anti-Semitic undertaking, but a metahistorical [more encompassing] program devised with an eschatological [concerned with the ultimate] perspective. It was a part of a salvational ideology that envisaged the attainment of Heaven by bringing Hell on earth. (Dawidowicz, *War,* p. xxxvi.)

24. Quoted in Stephen J. Whitfield, *Into the Dark: Hannah Arendt and Totalitarianism* (Philadelphia: Temple University Press, 1980), pp. 39–40.
25. Nevertheless, some did. Edward Teller's father warned him that anti-Semitism was a very real threat. Rhodes, *Atomic Bomb,* p. 109.
26. Dawidowicz, *War,* p. 380.
27. Email, Andy Grove to author, April 5, 2004.
28. Grove, *Swimming,* pp. 6–7.
29. György Ránki, "The Hungarian Economy in the Interwar Years," in Sugar et al., eds., *Hungary,* pp. 366–367.
30. Charles P. Kindleberger, *The World in Depression, 1929–1939* (Berkeley: University of California Press, 1986), pp. 144–151.
31. "Hungary: The Great Depression" in Stephen R. Burant, ed., *Hungary: A Country Study* (Washington D.C.: Federal Research Division, Library of Congress, 1990), http://lcweb2.loc.gov/frd/cs/hutoc.html. Viewed on the Internet on March 4, 2004.
32. Mária Ormos, "The Early Interwar Years, 1921–1938," in Sugar et al., eds., *Hungary,* p. 331; Ervin Pamlényi, ed., *A History of Hungary* (London: Collet's, 1975). pp. 486–487.
33. Hadjú and Nagy, "Revolution," in Sugar et al., eds., *Hungary,* p. 316, and Pamlényi, ed., *Hungary,* p. 488.
34. Burant, ed., *Hungary.* Viewed on the Internet on March 4, 2004.
35. Thus in Germany in 1933, Hitler rose to the position of chancellor because Franz von Papen persuaded an aging and reluctant Hindenburg as well as Papen's own right-wing, conservative friends that Hitler could be controlled. Papen convinced others and also himself that elevating Hitler to power meant acquiring his sup-

porters among the populace. Hitler himself would be nothing more than a puppet controlled by Papen. He posed "no danger at all," Papen reassured his friends, because "We've hired him for our act." In the words of Hitler's leading biographer, the late Lord Alan Bullock, Papen "had only himself to blame for one of the most egregious mistakes in twentieth-century history. Although Hitler constantly repeated his intention to observe 'legality,' he never made a secret of what he meant by it." For Hitler's rise to power, see Lord Alan Bullock, *Hitler and Stalin: Parallel Lives* (New York: Knopf, 1992), pp. 216–255, and *Hitler: A Study in Tyranny* (New York: Bantam, 1960), pp. 152–211.

36. Pamlényi, ed., *Hungary*, p. 488.
37. Pamlényi, ed., *Hungary*, p. 488.
38. Ormos, "Interwar," in Sugar et al., eds., *Hungary*, p. 332.
39. Radical Right in Power" in Burant, ed., *Hungary*, viewed on the Internet on March 4, 2004. In 1936, Hitler and Mussolini formed their alliance, which was called the "Axis Pact." Mussolini first used the term "axis" in a speech about the relations between Rome and Berlin that he delivered in Milan on November 1, 1936. The "Axis Pact" became the "Pact of Steel" when Italy and Germany concluded an alliance on May 22, 1939. The metaphor has apparently made a permanent entrance into the political lexicon. President George W. Bush used the phrase "Axis of Evil" to describe North Korea, Iran, and Iraq in his State of the Union address on January 29, 2002.
40. Burant, ed., *Hungary*, viewed on the Internet on March 4, 2004; Ormos, "Interwar," in Sugar et al., eds., *Hungary*, p. 335.
41. Ormos, "Interwar," in Sugar et al., eds., *Hungary*, p. 336; Burant, ed., *Hungary*, viewed on the Internet on March 4, 2004.
42. Pamlényi, ed., *Hungary*, p. 496.
43. Burant, ed., *Hungary*, viewed on the Internet on March 4, 2004.
44. Bullock, *Tyranny*, p. 380.
45. Bullock, *Tyranny*, pp. 5, 8, 381.
46. Hitler, *Kampf*, p. 52.
47. Hitler, *Kampf*, p. 57.
48. The words are those of Bullock, *Tyranny*, p. 229.
49. Bullock, *Hitler and Stalin*, pp. 567–568.
50. Bullock, *Hitler and Stalin*, p. 619. Poland was partitioned in 1772, 1793, and 1795 by Prussia, Austria, and Russia. It did not exist as an independent state again until after World War I.
51. A. J. P. Taylor, *The Second World War* (New York: Putnam, 1975), p. 35.

2. The Grove Family, Hungary, and the Early Years of World War II

1. Grove, *Swimming*, p. 5.
2. Grove, *Swimming*, p. 5.
3. Grove, *Swimming*, pp. 5–6.
4. Martin Gilbert, *A History of the Twentieth Century.* Vol. 2: *1933–1951* (New York: William Morrow, 1998), pp. 265–266.

5. Gilbert, *History*, p. 724; idem., *The Holocaust: A History of the Jews of Europe During the Second World War* (New York: Henry Holt, 1985), pp. 811–821.

6. George was born in Kiskoros, about two-thirds of the way from Budapest to Bacsalmas.

7. Grove, *Swimming*, p. 7.

8. Maiakovsky's "futurist verses rang the praises of the revolution and [his] 'Left March' [became] almost its unofficial poetic manifesto." Nicholas V. Riasanovsky, *A History of Russia* (New York: Oxford University Press, 1963), p. 631. Disillusioned by the revolution and disappointed in romance, Maiakovsky committed suicide in 1930.

9. Jörg K. Hoensch, *A History of Modern Hungary, 1867–1986* (New York: Longman, 1989), pp. 131–145.

10. Michael R. Wessels, "Streptococcal Infections," in Kurt J. Isselbacher et al., eds., *Harrison's Principles of Internal Medicine* (New York: McGraw-Hill, 1994), p. 619.

11. Grove, *Swimming*, pp. 16–17.

12. Grove, *Swimming*, p. 19.

13. Grove, *Swimming*, p. 19. The importance and meaning of this passage were explained to me by my late wife, Joyce R. Tedlow, MD. Joyce was a psychiatrist. She discussed this passage not only with me but with Andy Grove at a meeting the three of us had at his home on May 17, 2003.

14. Grove, *Swimming*, p.19.

15. Kertész, *Fatelessness*. See also István Deák, "Stranger in Hell," *New York Review of Books*, September 25, 2003.

16. Hoensch, *Hungary*, p. 153.

17. Hoensch, *Hungary*, p. 142–149.

18. Pamlényi, ed., *Hungary*, p. 627.

19. The official at the U.S. State Department to whom Hungary's *chargé d'affaires* delivered its declaration of war was perplexed.

> "Is Hungary a republic?" he asked. "No, it is a kingdom," was the reply.
> "Then you have a king?"
>   "No, we have an admiral." "Then you have a fleet?" "No, we do not have any sea." "Do you have any claims, then?" "Yes."
>   "Against America?" "No."
>   "Against England?" "No."
>   "Against Russia?" "No."
>   "But against whom do you have these claims?" "Against Romania."
>   "Then will you declare war on Romania?" "No sir. We're allies."

Krisztián Ungváry, *Battle for Budapest: One Hundred Days in World War II* (London: Tauris, 2003), pp. xiv–xv. President Franklin D. Roosevelt knew that Hungary did not have much choice about this declaration and did not take it seriously. Congress did not get around to declaring that a state of war existed between the United States and Hungary until July 18, 1942. John Flournoy Montgomery, *Hungary: The Unwilling Satellite*, chapter 11, p. 5, http://www.historicaltextarchive.com/books.php?op=viewbook&bookid=7&cid=11. Viewed on the Internet on April 18, 2004.

20. Loránd Tilkovszky, "The Late Interwar Years and World War II," in Sugar et al., eds., *Hungary,* p. 347.

21. Hoensch, *Hungary,* p. 154.

22. Pamlényi, ed., *Hungary,* pp. 525–526.

23. Why, one might ask, was there a large bronze statue of George Washington in the City Park in Budapest? It had been donated to the city by the Hungarian American Society in 1906. Why would such a statue have remained in place through two world wars in which the United States and Hungary were enemies? Who knows? These things happen. Neither Bismarck, North Dakota, nor Germantown, Pennsylvania, changed their names during those same wars. Moscow, Idaho, maintained its name throughout the cold war.

24. Grove, *Swimming,* pp. 29–30.

25. Telephone conversation with István Deák, Seth Low Professor of History Emeritus at Columbia University, April 5, 2004, and e-mail to author from István Deák, December 3, 2006.

26. Hoensch, *Hungary,* pp. 155–156.

27. Thomas Sakmyster, *Hungary's Admiral on Horseback,* p. 325.

28. Sakmyster, *Admiral,* p. 32

29. Sakmyster, *Admiral,* p. 36.

30. Sakmyster, *Admiral,* pp. 146–150.

31. Sakmyster, *Admiral,* p. 325

32. Deák, telephone conversation, April 5, 2004. See also István Deák "Survivor in a Sea of Barbarism," *New York Review of Books,* April 8, 1999.

33. Sakmyster, *Admiral,* p. 387.

34. Deák, "Compromise," in Deák et al., eds., *Retribution,* p. 41.

35. Pál Teleki (1920–1921); István Bethlen (1921–1931); Gyula Károlyi (1931–1932); Gyula Gömbös (1932–1936); Kálmán Darányi (1936–1938); Béla Imrédy (1938–1939); Pál Teleki (1939–1941); Lázló Bárdossy (1941–1942); and, Miklós Kállay (1942–1944).

36. István Deák, "A Fatal Compromise? The Debate over Collaboration and Resistance in Hungary," in István Deák, Jan T. Gross, and Tony Judt, eds., *The Politics of Retributation in Europe: World War II and Its Aftermath* (Princeton: Princeton University Press, 2000), p. 12.

37. Deák, "Fatal," pp. 218–219.

38. Randolph L. Braham, *Studies on the Holocaust: Selected Writings,* Vol. 1 (New York: Columbia University Press, 2000), pp. 1–11. The standard work on the murder of Hungary's Jews is Braham's comprehensive, detailed, and almost overwhelming treatise: *The Politics of Genocide: The Holocaust in Hungary,* 2 vols. (New York: Columbia University Press, 1981). Braham is the author or editor of numerous other books and essays. For a guide, see his *The Holocaust in Hungary: Selected and Annotated Bibliography* (New York: Columbia University Press, 2001). For a compilation of documents, see his *The Destruction of Hungarian Jewry: A Documentary Account,* 2 vols. (New York: Pro Arte, 1963). See also István Deák, "Could the Hungarian Jews Have Survived?" *New York Review of Books,* February 4, 1982.

39. For a statistical analysis, see Tamás Stark, *Hungarian Jews During the Holocaust and*

After the Second World War, 1939–1949: A Statistical Review (New York: Columbia University Press, 2000).

40. Randolph L. Braham, "The Holocaust in Hungary: A Retrospective Analysis," in David Cesarani, ed., *Genocide and Rescue: The Holocaust in Hungary, 1944* (New York: Berg, 1997), p. 38.

41. Braham "Retrospective," p. 41.

42. Eichmann joined the Nazi Party in 1932. In 1941 he became an SS lieutenant colonel, but it was not until he went to Budapest in March 1944 that the "desk-murderer [became] a public personality, working in the open and playing a leading role in the massacre of Hungarian Jewry." Eichmann became more famous after World War II than during it because, having escaped to Argentina, he was tracked down by Israeli agents, kidnapped, and brought to Israel to stand trial for crimes against humanity. He was convicted and hanged on May 31, 1962. "Adolf Eichmann (1906–1962)," http://www.jewishvirtuallibrary.org/jsource/Holocaust/eichmann. Viewed on the Internet on January 17, 2006.

43. Per Anger, *With Raoul Wallenberg in Budapest* (Washington, DC: Holocaust Library, 1996), p. 78.

44. John Bierman, *Righteous Gentile: The Story of Raoul Wallenberg, Missing Hero of the Holocaust* (New York: Viking, 1981), p. 116.

45. Grove, *Swimming*, p. 37.

46. Grove, *Swimming*, p. 38.

47. As early as June 8, 1944, if not earlier, Hungarian Jews were forced to wear the Star of David. See the photograph in "Hungary After the German Occupation," United States Holocaust Memorial Museum, Washington, D.C., http://www.ushmm.org/wlc/article.php?lang=en&ModuleId=10005458. Viewed on the Internet on March 22, 2004.

48. Grove, *Swimming*, p. 40.

49. László Karsai, "The People's Courts and Revolutionary Justice in Hungary, 1945–46," in István Deák, Jan T. Gross, and Tony Judt, eds., *The Politics of Retribution in Europe: World War II and Its Aftermath* (Princeton: Princeton University Press, 2000), p. 234.

50. Pamlényi, ed., *Hungary*, pp. 530–533; Deák, "Fatal," p. 231.

51. Grove, *Swimming*, p. 40.

52. "The Arrow Cross—Persecution of the Jews," http://www.osa.ceu.hu/. Viewed on the Internet on March 22, 2004.

53. "Ghettoization" was no simple matter. See Tim Cole, *Holocaust City: The Making of a Jewish Ghetto* (New York: Routledge, 2003), pp. 131–167 and passim.

54. Ungváry, *Battle*, p. 311. The battle took over a hundred days and cost about 160,000 lives, counting civilians, p. xi.

55. Grove, *Swimming*, pp. 53–54.

56. Grove, *Swimming*, p. 55. The fact that Andy knew this prayer indicates that he had at least some Jewish training.

57. Grove, *Swimming*, pp. 56–58.

58. Grove, *Swimming*, pp. 58–60.

59. Grove, *Swimming*, p. 61.

60. Grove, *Swimming*, p. 68.
61. Grove, *Swimming*, p. 72.
62. Grove, *Swimming*, pp. 73–74.
63. Grove, *Swimming*, p. 75.
64. Grove, *Swimming*, pp. 168–170.

3. Coming of Age in Stalinist Hungary

1. Imre Kertész, *Fatelessness* (New York: Vintage Books, 2004), p. 238. See also István Deák, "Stranger in Hell," *New York Review of Books*, September 25, 2003.
2. Deák, "Stranger," p. 67.
3. István Deák, "Survivor in a Sea of Barbarism," *New York Review of Books*, April 8, 1999, pp. 8–11.
4. László Karsai, "The People's Courts and Revolutionary Justice in Hungary, 1945–1946," in István Deák, Jan T. Gross, and Tony Judt, eds., *The Politics of Retribution in Europe: World War II and Its Aftermath* (Princeton: Princeton University Press, 2000), p. 233.
5. See Lord Alan Bullock's, *Hitler and Stalin: Parallel Lives* (New York: Knopf, 1991).
6. For some interesting speculation on the motives for Stalin's behavior, see Eric Roman, *Austria-Hungary & the Successor States* (New York: Facts on File, 2003), p. 246.
7. Roman, *Successor States*, p. 247.
8. The preceding account is based upon Roman, *Successor States*, pp. 246–247.
9. Roman, *Successor States*, pp. 246–247.
10. Jörg K. Hoensch, *A History of Modern Hungary, 1867–1986* (London: Longman, 1989), p. 161.
11. Observation of Tamás Kármán, Budapest, May 2004.
12. Hoensch, *Hungary*, p. 161.
13. Roman, *Successor States*, p. 248.
14. Grove, *Swimming*, p. 78.
15. Grove, *Swimming*, p. 77.
16. Grove, *Swimming*, p. 77.
17. Grove, *Swimming*, p. 81.
18. Grove, *Swimming*, p. 82.
19. Grove, *Swimming*, p. 76.
20. Grove, *Swimming*, p. 80.
21. The preceding is from Grove, *Swimming*, pp. 80–82.
22. Grove, *Swimming*, p. 83.
23. Roman, *Successor States*, p. 546.
24. Grove, *Swimming*, pp. 86–87.
25. There is a photograph on the Web of the entrance to the auditorium with these two busts. See "Budapesti Evangelikus Gimnazium," www.physics.umd.edu/robot/evangel.html. Viewed on the Internet on January 18, 2006.
26. Grove, *Swimming*, p. 93.
27. I was quite impressed that the school's administration was at a moment's notice able to produce grades recorded half a century ago.

28. Grove, *Swimming*, p. 92.
29. Grove, *Swimming*, p. 93.
30. Grove, *Swimming*, p. 93.
31. Grove, *Swimming*, p. 95.
32. Grove, *Swimming*, p. 95
33. See the photographs on pp. 90 and 164 of Grove, *Swimming*.
34. Hoensch, *Hungary*, p. 174.
35. Hoensch, *Hungary*, p. 166.
36. The preceding account is from Hoensch, *Hungary*, pp. 161–207.
37. Fyodor Dostoyevsky, *The Brothers Karamazov* (New York: Random House, 1950), pp. 922–930.
38. Eric Roman, *The Stalin Years in Hungary* (Lewiston, NY: Edwin Mellen Press, 1999), p. 24.
39. See William Sheridan Allen, *The Nazi Seizure of Power: The Experience of a Single German Town, 1930–1935* (Chicago: Quadrangle, 1965), pp. 207–26, for an enlightening discussion of the "atomization" of society following the Nazi takeover in Germany.
40. Grove, *Swimming*, p. 127.
41. Grove, *Swimming*, p. 127.
42. This point is well made in János Rainer, "The New Course in Hungary in 1953," Working Paper No. 38, Woodrow Wilson International Center for Scholars, Cold War International History Project (Washington, DC: 2002), p. 1.
43. Grove, *Swimming*, p. 98.
44. Grove, *Swimming*, p. 101.
45. Grove, *Swimming*, p. 115.
46. Grove, *Swimming*, p. 109. The Communist show trials are difficult for someone brought up in the United States to understand. The best guide is a novel: Arthur Koestler, *Darkness at Noon* (New York: Random House, 1941). Grove has told me that one must read this novel to understand his father.
47. Grove, *Swimming*, p. 128.
48. Grove, *Swimming*, pp. 128–129
49. "[I]f I had been a small boy in 1897 in the Southern part of the United States . . . I should then have known from my parents that history had happened to my people in my part of the world." Arnold J. Toynbee, *The Prospects of Western Civilization* (New York: Columbia University Press, 1949), as quoted in the epigraph of C. Vann Woodward, *Origins of the New South, 1877–1913* (Baton Rouge, LA: Louisiana State University Press, 1951).
50. Grove, *Swimming*, p. 130.
51. Grove, *Swimming*, pp. 142–143.
52. Grove, *Swimming*, p. 131.
53. Grove, *Swimming*, p. 141.
54. Grove, *Swimming*, p. 290.
55. Grove, *Swimming*, p. 152.
56. Grove, *Swimming*, p. 156.
57. Grove, *Swimming*, p. 161. Andy has translated this story from the Hungarian. An-

drás Gróf, "Despair," translated by Andrew S. Grove. I have read the story and find it quite surprising that a teenager who seemed to be as happy as Andy presents himself could so effectively capture genuine depression as he does in this piece. When I made this observation to him, he replied that being a teenager teaches one a lot about depression. Manuscript in author's possession.

58. Grove, *Swimming*, p. 162.

59. Grove, *Swimming*, p. 167.

60. Grove, *Swimming*, pp. 170–171. For a scholarly analysis of what Stalin's death meant in Hungary, see Rainer, "Hungary in 1953."

61. See Rainer's excellent discussion in "Hungary in 1953," passim.

62. Rainer, "Hungary in 1953," pp. 18–19.

63. Rainer, "Hungary in 1953," p. 46.

64. Grove, *Swimming*, p. 172.

65. Grove, *Swimming*, pp. 180–181.

66. Grove, *Swimming*, p. 202.

67. Grove, *Swimming*, p. 193.

68. Grove, *Swimming*, p. 204.

69. Estimates differ, but according to one source, 1.5 percent of 9,870,000 Hungarians were Jewish in 1956. This would mean there were just under 150,000 Jews in the country. Imre Kovács, ed., *Facts About Hungary* (New York: Hungarian Committee, 1959), pp. 272–275.

70. Grove, *Swimming*, p. 194.

71. In conversation with Eva Grove, Denise Amantea, Judith Estrin, and the author, February 10, 2006, Menlo Park, California.

72. "From Stettin in the Baltic to Trieste in the Adriatic, an iron curtain has descended across the Continent. Behind that line lie all the capitals of Central and Eastern Europe. Warsaw, Berlin, Prague, Vienna, Budapest, Belgrade, Bucharest and Sofia, all these famous cities and the populations around them lie in what I must call the Soviet sphere, and all are subject in one form or another, not only to Soviet influence but to a very high and, in many cases, increasing measure of control from Moscow." "The Sinews of Peace," address delivered by Winston Churchill on March 5, 1946, at Westminster College in Fulton, Missouri. http://www.hpol.org/. Viewed on the Internet on July 24, 2004.

73. Alexis de Tocqueville, *The Old Regime and the Revolution* (Chicago: University of Chicago Press, 1998), p. 222.

74. See "Modern History Sourcebook: Nikita S. Khrushchev: The Secret Speech—'On the Cult of Personality, 1956,'" http://www.fordham.edu/halsall/mod/1956krushchev-secret1.html. Viewed on the Internet on July 25, 2004.

75. "Poland: From Stalinism to the Polish October," http://www.country-data.com/cgi-bin/query/r10596.html. Viewed on the Internet on July 25, 2004.

76. "Poland: From Stalinism to the Polish October."

77. Grove, *Swimming*, p. 212.

78. Grove, *Swimming*, p. 213.

79. Grove, *Swimming*, p. 214.

80. Roman, *Austria-Hungary*, pp. 262–264.

81. For an enlightening discussion of Western propaganda during the revolt, see László Borhi, "Rollback, Liberation, Containment or Inaction? U.S. Policy and Eastern Europe in the 1950s," *Journal of Cold War Studies*, 1, 3 (Fall 1999), pp. 67–110.

82. See Borhi, "Rollback."

83. Roman, *Austria-Hungary*, p. 265.

84. Grove, *Swimming*, pp. 221-222.

85. Grove, *Swimming*, p. 227.

86. Grove, *Swimming*, pp. 226–227.

87. Grove, *Swimming*, p. 226.

88. Grove, *Swimming*, pp. 225–229.

89. Grove, *Swimming*, p. 229.

90. Grove, *Swimming*, pp. 225–230.

91. Grove, *Swimming*, p. 235.

92. Video Monitoring Services of America, *Fresh Air*, KQED-FM, November 19, 1996, 1:00–2:00 p.m.

93. They were Beethoven's *Fidelio*, Verdi's *Don Carlos*, and Mozart's *The Magic Flute*. For Verdi, "Verdiana," http://www.r-ds.com/verdiana.htm, viewed on the Internet on July 29, 2004, is a superb source. Verdi is not my favorite composer (with the exception of his *Requiem*). To voice such an opinion to Grove today is to invite an argument.

94. Grove, *Swimming*, p. 241.

95. Grove, *Swimming*, p. 233.

96. Author interview with Les Vadasz, May 24, 2004, Los Altos Hills, CA. "Interestingly," said Vadasz in 2006, "I could probably count on one hand the times when we have talked Hungarian since then." Email, Vadasz to author, June 7, 2006.

97. The man in question was Albert Szent-Györgyi, who won the Nobel Prize in medicine in 1937.

98. Grove, *Swimming*, p. 140.

99. Grove to his family, December 15, 1956. Letter in author's possession.

100. The International Rescue Committee still exists today. It was founded at the suggestion of Albert Einstein in 1933 to assist refugees from Hitler. http://www.theirc.org/about/index.cfm. Viewed on the Internet on January 20, 2005.

101. Grove, *Swimming*, p. 242.

102. Elie Abel, "Out of Hungary—Revolt of the Exiles," *New York Times*, November 25, 1956.

103. Abel, "Exiles."

104. Grove, *Swimming*, pp. 243–244.

105. Grove, *Swimming*, p. 245.

106. Grove, *Swimming*, p. 235.

107. Grove, *Swimming*, p. 245.

108. Grove, *Swimming*, p. 249.

109. Grove, *Swimming*, p. 253.

4. Andy Grove in America

1. "Man Born in Hungary Heads Jersey Aid Unit," *New York Times,* January 7, 1957. Carl T. Gossett Jr., "U.S. Presses Hungary," *New York Times,* January 8, 1957.
2. http://www.time.com/time/personoftheyear/archive/covers/1956.html. Viewed on the Internet on January 17, 2006.
3. Grove, *Swimming,* p. 255.
4. Grove, *Swimming,* p. 256.
5. The name Lajos is rendered Louis in English. Louis W. Kalman lived with his family at this address until moving at the end of the 1950s to 82–15 Britton Avenue in Elmhurst, Queens. Document provided to the author by Professor Emeritus Morris Kolodney of the City College of New York.
6. Grove, *Swimming,* p. 259.
7. Grove, *Swimming,* p. 262.
8. Grove, *Swimming,* p. 264.
9. John Kenneth Galbraith, *The Affluent Society* (Boston: Houghton Mifflin, 1998), p. 191.
10. Quoted in William E. Leuchtenburg, *A Troubled Feast: American Society Since 1945* (Boston: Little, Brown, 1979), p. 84.
11. William H. Whyte, *The Organization Man* (New York: Simon and Schuster, 1956).
12. The quoted phrase belongs to Ernest Braun and Stuart MacDonald, *Revolution in Miniature: The History and Impact of Semiconductor Electronics* (Cambridge, England: Cambridge University Press, 1978).
13. Sloan Wilson, *The Man in the Gray Flannel Suit* (New York: Simon and Schuster, 1955). The following year, this second-rate novel was made into a famous and perfectly dreadful motion picture, starring Gregory Peck and Jennifer Jones.
14. http://www.nobelprize.org. Viewed on the Internet on November 22, 2004.
15. Grove, *Swimming,* p. 270.
16. "Refugee Heading Engineers' Class," *New York Times,* June 15, 1960.
17. Grove, *Swimming,* p. 271.
18. Grove, *Swimming,* p. 275. In 1997, Professor Morris Kolodney, who became Andy's faculty advisor at CCNY in 1957, gave him a slide rule, that had a special sentimental meaning to him. Grove accepted the "trusteeship" of this slide rule observing that "I still have—and occasionally use—my original college slide rule." Kolodney to Grove, February 1, 1997; Grove to Kolodney, February 1997. Letters in author's possession.
19. Grove, *Swimming,* pp. 279–281.
20. Grove, *Swimming,* pp. 284–285.
21. Linda Geppert, "Profile: Andy Grove," *IEEE Spectrum,* June 2000, p. 35. The paper was a description of "heat transfer in fluidized beds." Grove explained that "Fluidized beds are like a bunch of ping-pong balls in a container. You start blowing air through them. The balls get lifted and separate from each other and start vibrating or bouncing around. You can tilt it, you can pour it, and because of all the motion of the particles, the rate of heat transfer skyrockets."
22. Interview with Professor Emeritus Morris Kolodney, April 24, 2004, Sarasota, Florida.

23. Kolodney to Grove, October 23, 1983. Letter in author's possession.

24. Grove, *Swimming*, p. 276.

25. "Refugee Heading Engineers' Class," *New York Times*, June 15, 1960.

26. "Intel Chair, Honored by City College, Reminisces About Grove of Academe," *CUNY Matters*, Fall 1998; "City College Gives Andrew Grove '60T a Hero's Welcome Home," *Alumnus*, Winter 1999, p. 15; Professor Robert A. Graff to Professor Morris Kolodney, February 19, 1998. Materials provided to author by Professor Morris Kolodney.

27. Kate Bonamici, "Grove of Academe," *Fortune*, December 12, 2005, p. 135.

28. Grove, *Swimming*, p. 282.

29. Dale Carnegie, *How to Win Friends and Influence People* (New York: Simon and Schuster, 1936), p. 84.

30. Grove, *Swimming*, p. 279.

31. Grove, *Swimming*, p. 285.

32. Grove, *Swimming*, pp. 284–285.

33. Geoff Lewis and Robert D. Hof, "The World According to Andy Grove," *Business-Week*, 1994 special issue: *The Information Revolution*, p. 76.

34. G. Grove, "Not the Cause," *New York Herald Tribune* (International Edition), February 23, 1962.

35. Author interview with Eva Grove, Anaheim, California, February 2, 2005.

36. Eva's father's sister became a devout Roman Catholic in the wake of World War I. When her father and her husband went off to fight, she swore she would convert to Catholicism if they returned safely. They did, so she did. Author interview with Eva Grove, Anaheim, CA, February 2, 2005. Neither Andy nor Eva remembers the name of the church. I have tried to find it. The church could not have been in Forest Hills. It may have been in Elmhurst.

37. Author interview with Andy Grove, November 11, 2005.

38. Andy Grove interview I with Arnold Thackray and David C. Brock, July 14, 2004.

39. Thackray interview I, p. 4.

40. Thackray interview I, p. 4.

41. Thackray interview I, p. 1.

42. Thackray interview I, p. 2.

43. Thackray interview I, p. 7.

44. Grove, to his family, December 15, 1956. Letter in author's possession.

45. Horace Greeley, *Hints Toward Reform* (New York: Harper and Brothers, 1850).

46. This point is made in Richard Hofstadter, *The Progressive Historians: Turner, Beard, Parrington* (New York: Knopf, 1968).

47. For Kennedy's acceptance speech, see http://www.jfklibrary.org. Viewed on the Internet on January 22, 2005.

48. President John F. Kennedy, "Special Message to the Congress on Urgent National Needs," www. jfklibrary.org. Viewed on the Internet on January 22, 2005.

49. Walter A. McDougall, . . . *The Heavens and the Earth: A Political History of the Space Age* (Baltimore: Johns Hopkins University Press, 1997), pp. xiv, 141–151.

50. Leslie Berlin, "Entrepreneurship and the Rise of Silicon Valley: The Career of Robert Noyce, 1956–1990." Unpublished dissertation (Stanford University, 2001), pp. 48–49.

51. Robert Noyce, "Integrated Circuits in Military Equipment," *IEEE Spectrum*, June 1964, p. 71, cited in Leslie Berlin, *The Man Behind the Microchip: Robert Noyce and the Invention of Silicon Valley* (New York: Oxford University Press, 2005), p. 112.

52. The Highway Act of 1956 was signed into law by President Eisenhower. It provided for building a 41,000-mile highway network at a cost in excess of $30 billion over a thirteen-year period.

53. Thackray interview I, p. 10.

54. Thackray interview I, p. 10.

55. Peter F. Drucker, *The Practice of Management* (New York: Harper, 1954).

56. Andrew Grove interview II with Arnold Thackray and David C. Brock, Sept. 1, 2004, pp. 12–13.

57. Thackray interview II, p. 12.

58. The man who made this observation was Samuel S. Marquis, dean of Detroit's largest Episcopal church and for a time the manager of the Sociological Department (which today would be called personnel or, more likely, human resources) of the Ford Motor Company. Marquis said this in 1923. Quoted in Richard S. Tedlow, *Giants of Enterprise: Seven Business Innovators and the Empires They Built* (New York: HarperBusiness, 2001), p. 139.

59. The preceding paragraphs are based upon Thackray interview II, pp. 15–16.

60. Mary Burt Baldwin interview with Andy Grove, 1981, available from Intel. Reference to Bill Lattin from author interview with Lattin, Hillsboro, Oregon, August 6, 2004.

61. Author interview with Andreas Acrivos, New York, New York, December 18, 2003.

62. Andreas Acrivos, "Curriculum Vitae," http://www-che.engr.ccny.cuny.edu/acrivos/acrivos_cv.html. Viewed on the Internet on December 1, 2003.

63. Thackray interview I, p. 16.

64. For the title of Grove's doctoral dissertation, see Preface note 4.

65. Thackray interview I, p. 17.

66. For the citations, see Preface note 4.

67. Thackray interview I, p. 17.

68. Thackray interview I, p. 18.

69. Thackray interview I, p. 32.

70. Acrivos interview with author, December 18, 2003.

71. Thackray interview I, p. 21.

72. Thackray interview I, pp. 20–23.

73. For this letter, see Preface note 7.

74. Thackray interview I, p. 36.

75. The preceding is based on Thackray interview I, pp. 21–28.

76. Author interview with Gordon E. Moore, Stanford Park Hotel, Menlo Park, California, May 24, 2004.

77. IEEE Virtual Museum, "Gordon E. Moore," www.ieee-virtual-museum.org, viewed on the Internet on January 28, 2005. According to this source, Moore took the postdoc at Johns Hopkins because at the time of his graduation from Cal Tech, high-technology jobs in northern California were scarce.

78. Shockley believed that everyone has a "mental temperature," with the brightest people having the highest temperatures. Berlin, *Man Behind the Microchip*, p. 58.

79. Berlin, *Man Behind the Microchip*, p. 62.

80. Berlin, *Man Behind the Microchip*, p. 61.

81. For the difference between the nature of invention and of inventors in the nineteenth and twentieth centuries in America, see Thomas P. Hughes, *American Genesis: A Century of Invention and Technological Enthusiasm, 1870–1970* (New York: Viking Penguin, 1989).

82. Tedlow, *Giants*, p. 371. Frederick Terman, engineering professor and Stanford provost, has also been called the father of Silicon Valley because of the way he strengthened Stanford's electrical engineering department. See Berlin's discussion in "Entrepreneurship," p. 22, n. 68. Terman introduced Hewlett and Packard to one another. Years later, they donated a building to the university in his name.

83. Tedlow, *Giants*, p. 384.

84. Tedlow, *Giants*, p. 385.

85. Berlin, *Man Behind the Microchip*, p. 68.

86. Tedlow, *Giants*, p. 385. Bardeen won the Nobel Prize in physics again in 1972, sharing it with L. N. Cooper and J. R. Schrieffer for the theory of superconductivity.

87. Berlin, *Man Behind the Microchip*, p. 60.

88. Tedlow, *Giants*, p. 387.

89. Berlin, "Entrepreneurship," p. 56.

90. Berlin, "Entrepreneurship," p. 58. See also, "8 Leave Shockley to Form Coast Semiconductor Firm," *Electronic News*, October 21, 1957. Shockley asserted in that article that the departure of these eight men "has no real effect on the Shockley lab." That, of course, could not have been further from the truth, and Shockley doubtless did not believe it himself.

91. Tedlow, *Giants*, p. 389. See, for example, Don Hoefler, "Semiconductor Family Tree," *Electronic News*, July 8, 1971.

92. In conversation with the author.

93. This phrase is borrowed from the title of a book: Dirk Hanson, *The New Alchemists: Silicon Valley and the Microelectronics Revolution* (Boston: Little, Brown, 1982).

94. Thackray interview I, p. 33.

95. Thackray interview I, p. 33.

96. Thackray interview I, p. 34.

97. Tedlow, *Giants*, pp. 36–38.

98. Thackray interview I, p. 35.

99. Author interview with Michael Dell, Dell, Inc. Headquarters, Austin, Texas, December 9, 2003.

100. Robert A. Burgelman, *Strategy Is Destiny: How Strategy-Making Shapes a Company's Future* (New York: Free Press, 2002), p. 154.

101. Thackray interview I, p. 34–35.

102. This thought was suggested to me by my colleague at Harvard Business School, Professor William Sahlman.

103. The original statement of Moore's law appeared in Gordon E. Moore, "Cramming

More Components onto Integrated Circuits," *Electronics,* 38, 8 (April 19, 1965). The editors of the journal described Moore as "one of the new breed of electronic engineers, schooled in the physical sciences rather than in electronics."

104. See, for example, Tim Jackson, *Inside Intel: Andy Grove and the Rise of the World's Most Powerful Chip Company* (New York: Penguin, 1997), pp. 24–25.

105. Tedlow, *Giants,* p. 404. Grove was not alone in this perception. See John Naughton, "Business Profile: Gordon E. Moore," *The Observer,* August 8, 1999. The article's first sentence is: "Gordon Moore looks like everyone's idea of a favorite uncle."

106. Author interview with Gordon Moore, Intel RNB, Santa Clara, California, 1999. Moore remembers this response. Unfortunately, the letter itself has not survived. Tedlow, *Giants,* p. 375.

107. This phrase is from Daniel J. Boorstin, *The Republic of Technology: Reflections on Our Future Community* (New York: Harper & Row, 1978).

108. Thackray interview I, p. 37.

109. Thackray interview II, p. 4.

110. Thackray interview I, p. 31.

111. Thackray interview II, p. 7.

112. Michael S. Malone, *The Big Score: The Billion-Dollar Story of Silicon Valley* (Garden City, NY: Doubleday, 1985), p. 75.

113. Quoted in Malone, *Score,* p. 74.

114. Tom Wolfe, "The Tinkerings at Robert Noyce: How the Sun Rose on the Silicon Valley," *Esquire,* December 1983.

115. Quoted in Tedlow, *Giants,* p. 378.

116. Ernest Braun and Stuart MacDonald, *Revolution in Miniature: The History and Impact of Semiconductor Electronics* (Cambridge, England: Cambridge University Press, 1978), p. 60.

117. The title of Noyce's thesis was "A Photoelectric Investigation of Surface States on Insulators." It was submitted and accepted for the PhD at MIT in 1953. Berlin, *Man Behind the Microchip,* pp. 39–42.

118. Tedlow, *Giants,* p. 382.

119. Malone, *Score,* pp. 78–82.

120. Quoted in Leslie R. Berlin, "Robert Noyce and the Rise and Fall of Fairchild Semiconductor, 1957–1968," *Business History Review,* 75, 1 (Spring 2001), p. 100.

121. Berlin, "Entrepreneurship," p. 61.

122. Noyce's titles at Fairchild were: director of research and development from 1957 to 1959, vice president and general manager from 1959 to 1965, and group vice president, Fairchild Camera and Instrument, from 1965 to 1968. Silicon Valley Engineering Council, "Silicon Valley Engineering Hall of Fame for 1993," http://www .svec.org/hof/1993.html#noyce, viewed on the Internet June 18, 2006, and email to author from Jodelle A. French, June 16, 2006.

123. Noyce to Grove, April 29, 1963. Document in author's possession.

124. Thackray interview II, p. 10.

125. Thackray interview II, p. 7.

126. Thackray interview II, pp. 11–12.

127. Thackray interview II, p. 15.

128. Thackray interview II, p. 16.
129. Thackray interview II, p. 12.
130. Thackray interview II, p. 11.
131. Author interview with Steven P. Jobs, Apple Headquarters, Cupertino, California, February 14, 2005; Tedlow, *Giants,* p. 418.
132. Author interview with Steven P. Jobs, Apple Headquarters, Cupertino, California; Tedlow, *Giants,* p. 418.
133. Berlin, *Man Behind the Microchip,* p. 98.
134. Thackray interview II, p. 12.
135. Grove to Moore, "Welcome Home—or—All the Reasons Why You Would Have Been Better Off Staying at the Great Barrier Reef . . . ," October 12, 1984. Grove notebooks. Author's possession.
136. Silicon Valley journalist Michael S. Malone has written of "the notorious 'reality distortion field' that emanated from Steve Jobs." *Infinite Loop: How the World's Most Insanely Great Computer Company Went Insane* (New York: Doubleday, 1999), p. 3.
137. Tedlow, *Giants,* p. 408.
138. Tedlow, *Giants,* pp. 408–409.
139. Berlin, *Man Behind the Microchip.* See especially pp. 214–218.
140. See Jackson, *Intel,* pp. 163–165.
141. Tedlow, *Giants,* p. 411.
142. Tedlow, *Giants,* pp. 411–418.
143. Author telephone interview with John Doerr, March 16, 2006.
144. Quoted in Tedlow, *Giants,* p. 405. Rock made this remark to me in an interview for a previous book.
145. Andrew S. Grove, *Physics and Technology of Semiconductor Devices* (New York: Wiley, 1967).
146. Andrew S. Grove, *High Output Management* (New York: Random House, 1983).
147. Quoted in Tedlow, *Giants,* p. 411.

5. "A Hotheaded 30-Year-Old Running Around Like a Drunken Rat," or Andy Grove Comes to the Valley of the Heart's Delight

1. Berlin, "Entrepreneurship," p. 18. Berlin writes movingly about the Valley prior to its development.
2. Author interview with Terri L. Murphy, Intel RNB, Santa Clara, California, January 9, 2006.
3. This information is courtesy of a Northwest Airlines pilot.
4. Leo Marx, *The Machine in the Garden: Technology and the Pastoral Ideal in America* (New York: Oxford University Press, 1964), pp. 34–72.
5. Quoted in Berlin, "Entrepreneurship," p. 18, n. 46.
6. Berlin, "Entrepreneurship," pp. 49–50.
7. Braun and MacDonald, *Revolution in Miniature,* p. 137.
8. A transistor is a semiconductor.
9. Richard N. Langlois and W. Edward Steinmueller, "The Evolution of Competitive

Advantage in the Worldwide Semiconductor Industry, 1947–1996," in David C. Mowery and Richard R. Nelson, eds., *Sources of Industrial Leadership: Studies of Seven Industries* (Cambridge, England: Cambridge University Press, 1999), p. 33.

10. Langlois and Steinmeuller, "Semiconductor Industry," p. 22.

11. Langlois and Steinmeuller, "Semiconductor Industry," p. 41.

12. Berlin, *Man Behind the Microchip,* p. 109. Berlin's discussion of these technical issues is authoritative and accessible. My account is much in debt to her work in this area.

13. Tedlow, *Giants,* pp. 393–394.

14. T. R. Reid, *The Chip: How Two Americans Invented the Microchip and Launched a Revolution* (New York: Simon and Schuster, 1984), p. 13.

15. Jack Kilby died on June 20, 2005.

16. Berlin, "Entrepreneurship," pp. 66–67.

17. Berlin, "Entrepreneurship," pp. 65–66.

18. AnnaLee Saxenian, *Regional Advantage: Culture and Competition in Silicon Valley and Route 128* (Cambridge, MA: Harvard University Press, 1994), p. 31. See also Berlin, "Entrepreneurship," pp. 109–110.

19. Wolfe, "Tinkerings."

20. Alfred D. Chandler Jr., "The Information Age in Historical Perspective," in Chandler and James W. Cortada, eds., *A Nation Transformed by Information: How Information Has Shaped the United States from Colonial Times to the Present* (New York: Oxford University Press, 2000), p. 31, quoted in Berlin, *Man Behind the Microchip,* p. 154.

21. Saxenian, *Advantage,* p. 31.

22. Saxenian, *Advantage,* p. 35.

23. Peter Drucker once used the phrase "company of companies in the industry of industries" to refer to General Motors after World War II. The phrase was appropriate to General Motors and automobiles in the mid-1940s, just as it was appropriate to IBM and information technology in the mid-1960s.

24. See above, p. 95

25. Thackray interview II, p. 2.

26. *Annual Report, 1963: Fairchild Camera and Instrument Corporation,* pp. 18–21.

27. A. S. Grove and C. T. Sah, "Simple Analytical Approximations to the Switching Times in Narrow Base Diodes," *Solid-State Electronics* 7, no. 1 (January 1964); A. S. Grove, O. Leistiko Jr., and C. T. Sah, "Diffusion of Gallium Through a Silicon Dioxide Layer," *Journal of Physics and Chemistry of Solids,* 25, no. 9 (September 1964); A. S. Grove, O. Leistiko Jr., and C. T. Sah, "Redistribution of Acceptor and Donor Impurities During Thermal Oxidation of Silicon," *Journal of Applied Physics,* 35, no. 9; A. S. Grove, A. Roder, and C. T. Sah, "Impurity Distribution in Epitaxial Growth," *Journal of Applied Physics,* 36, no. 3 (March 1965); A. S. Grove, E. H. Snow, Bruce E. Deal, and C. T. Sah, "Simple Physical Model for the Space-Charge Capacitance of Metal-Oxide-Semiconductor Structures," *Journal of Applied Physics,* 35, no. 8 (August 1964); A. S. Grove, Bruce E. Deal, E. H. Snow, and C. T. Sah, "Investigation of Thermally Oxidised Silicon Surfaces Using Metal-Oxide-Semiconductor Structures," *Solid-State Electronics,* 8, no. 2 (February 1965); Bruce

E. Deal, A. S. Grove, E. H. Snow, and C. T. Sah, "Observation of Impurity Redistribution During Thermal Oxidation of Silicon Using the MOS Structure," *Journal of The Electrochemical Society,* 112 (1965); Bruce E. Deal, A. S. Grove, E. H. Snow, and C. T. Sah, "Recent Advances in the Understanding of the Metal-Oxide-Silicon System," *American Institute of Mining, Metallurgical and Petroleum Engineers, Transactions,* 233 (1965); E. H. Snow, A. S. Grove, B. E. Deal, and C. T. Sah, "Ion Transport Phenomena in Insulating Films," *Journal of Applied Physics,* 36, no. 5 (May 1965); O. Leistiko Jr., A. S. Grove, and C. T. Sah, "Electron and Hole Mobilities in Inversion Layers on Thermally Oxidized Silicon Surfaces," *IEEE Transactions on Electron Devices,* 12, no. 5 (May 1965); A. S. Grove, P. Lamond, et al., "Stable MOS Transistors," *Electro-Technology* (December 1965); A. S. Grove and D. J. Fitzgerald, "The Origin of Channel Currents Associated with P+ Regions in Silicon," *IEEE Transactions on Electron Devices,* 12, no. 12 (December 1965); D. J. Fitzgerald and A. S. Grove, "Mechanisms of Channel Current Formation in Silicon P-N Junctions," *Physics of Failure in Electronics Symposium, vol. 4,* Rome Air Development Center, Rome, NY (1965); Bruce E. Deal and A. S. Grove, "General Relationship for the Thermal Oxidation of Silicon," *Journal of Applied Physics,* 36, no. 12 (December 1965); A. S. Grove and E. H. Snow, "A Model for Radiation Damage in Metal-Oxide-Semiconductor Structures," *Proceedings of the IEEE,* 54, no. 6 (June 1966); A. S. Grove and D. J. Fitzgerald, "Surface Effects on p-n Junctions: Characteristics of Surface SpaceCharge Regions under Non-Equilibrium Conditions," *Solid-State Electronics,* 9, no. 9 (September 1966); O. Leistiko Jr. and A. S. Grove, "Breakdown Voltage of Planar Silicon Junctions," *Sol.-St. Elec.* 9, 847 (1966); Andrew S. Grove, "Mass Transfer in Semiconductor Technology," *Industrial & Engineering Chemistry,* 48 (July 1966); D. J. Fitzgerald and A. S. Grove, "Radiation-Induced Increase in Surface Recombination Velocity of Thermally Oxidized Silicon Structures," *Proceedings of the IEEE,* 54, no. 11 (November 1966); Bruce. E. Deal, E. H. Snow, and A. S. Grove, "Properties of the Silicon Dioxide-Silicon System," *Semiconductor Products and Solid State Technology,* 9, no. 11 (1966); Les Vadasz and A. S. Grove, "Temperature Dependence of MOS Transistor Characteristics Below Saturation," *IEEE Transactions on Electronic Devices,* 13, no. 12 (December 1966); Bruce E. Deal, M. Sklar, A. S. Grove, and E. H. Snow, "Characteristics of the Surface-State Charge (Qss) of Thermally Oxidized Silicon," *Journal of Electrochemical Society,* 114, no. 3 (March 1967); A. S. Grove, O. Leistiko Jr., and W. W. Hooper, "Effect of Surface Fields on the Breakdown Voltage of Planar Silicon p-n Junctions," *IEEE Transactions on Electronic Devices,* 14, no. 3 (March 1967); E. H. Snow, A. S. Grove, and D. J. Fitzgerald, "Effects of Ionizing Radiation on Oxidized Silicon Surfaces and Planar Devices," *Proceedings of the IEEE,* 55, no. 7 (July 1967); D. J. Fitzgerald and A. S. Grove, "Surface Recombination in Semiconductors," *Surface Science* 9, 2, 347 (1968); S. T. Hsu, D. J. Fitzgerald, and A. S. Grove, "Surface-State Related 1/f noise in p-n Junctions and MOS Transistors," *Applied Physics Letters,* 12, no. 9 (May 1968).

The patents are: no. 3,463,977, *Optimized Double-Ring Semiconductor Device,* Andrew S. Grove, Otto Leistiko, and Ronald J. Whittier, filed April 21, 1966, issued

August 26, 1969; and no. 3,513,035, *Semiconductor Device Process for Reducing Surface Recombination Velocity,* Desmond J. Fitzgerald, Andrew S. Grove, and Edward H. Snow, filed November 1, 1967, issued May 19, 1970.

28. Thackray interview II, p. 5.

29. Andrew S. Grove, *Physics and Technology of Semiconductor Devices* (New York: Wiley, 1967), p. v.

30. Carver A. Mead to Donald C. Ford, January 3, 1967. Letter in author's possession. For Mead, see "Carver Mead," en.wikipedia.org/wiki/Carver_Mead. Viewed on the Internet on February 6, 2006. Mead, whom Gordon Moore says coined the phrase "Moore's law," is presently Gordon and Betty Moore Professor Emeritus at the California Institute of Technology, where he has taught for more than four decades.

31. Thackray interview II, p. 5.

32. Berlin, "Entrepreneurship," p. 134.

33. Berlin, *Man Behind the Microchip,* p. 150.

34. Thackray interview II, p. 6.

35. "National vs. Fairchild, 1967," April 24, 1967; Gordon E. Moore memorandum to All R&D Employees, "Bulletin #120: APPOINTMENT—A.S. Grove," April 26, 1967. Documents in author's possession.

36. Thackray interview II, p. 11.

37. Thackray interview II, p. 11.

38. Thackray interview II, p. 11.

39. The reader should note that this recollection of events, which Grove has repeated, does not square with Leslie Berlin's account in her dissertation on Noyce (see pp. 148–153). According to her, Noyce had been thinking about leaving Fairchild to found his own company at least since the beginning of 1968. He discussed the idea with Moore, who was unenthusiastic. "I was comfortable where I was," she quotes Moore as saying. "I was director of the laboratory. I thought we were the best one in the industry and was enjoying it pretty much most of the time." At length, for reasons described in the text following this note, Moore decided to leave Fairchild. He arrived at this final decision, according to Berlin, while on a brief vacation with his family in "a cabin in the Sierras," over the Fourth of July break.

Grove, writes Berlin, "appeared at the door of Moore's cabin one morning." Grove knew something was brewing, and he wanted to know what it was. According to Berlin, "Grove greatly admired Moore . . . and had told him that he wanted to be a part of whatever Moore and Noyce put together. The wait had become too much for the detail-oriented Grove, who had to know *right there,* at the cabin door, what Moore and Noyce were thinking of doing at the new company." Berlin cites as her source for the quotation above an interview with Moore on June 29, 1994, in the Intel archives.

Which account is correct—that in the text of this book, which is drawn from Grove's recollections, or Berlin's, at least part of which is drawn from an interview with Moore? We will never know. These are recollections of men no longer young, of events that took place decades previously, the historic nature of the details of which no one appreciated at the time. What we can say is that by both accounts, Grove was not asked to join Intel. He took the initiative before such an invitation was offered.

40. Berlin, "Entrepreneurship," pp. 141–144.

41. Berlin, "Entrepreneurship," p. 148.

42. Jackson, *Intel*, p. 22. As with so much about Intel's early days, there is no general agreement on this story. Executives at VenRock, first-round investors, say they saw a full-fledged business plan. VenRock bears no relation to Arthur Rock. VenRock is the venture capital arm of the Rockefeller family. Arthur Rock is an independent venture capitalist.

43. The other was the abortive Czechoslovakian democratic revolt. Rich Karlgaard, "What 1968 Really Meant," *Forbes*, September 1993.

44. Jackson, *Intel*, p. 23.

45. Moore interview with Harvard Business School professor Joseph L. Bower, Santa Clara, California, December 8, 1999. Transcript in author's possession.

46. Berlin, *Man Behind the Microchip*, p. 164.

47. Grove has made this remark in my presence.

6. "Off and Limping"

1. Andrew S. Grove, *Only the Paranoid Survive: How to Exploit the Crisis Points That Challenge Every Company* (New York: Doubleday, 1996), p. 17.

2. Berlin, "Entrepreneurship," p. 150.

3. Leslie Berlin made this observation at a seminar at the Harvard Business School, Boston, Massachusetts, November 7, 2005.

4. Peter Botticelli, David Collis, and Gary Pisano, "Intel Corporation: 1986–1997," Harvard Business School Publishing Case No. 9-797-137, rev. October 21, 1998 (Boston: HBS Publishing), p. 2.

5. Lauren R. Sklaroff, "Joe Louis and the Construction of a Black American Hero, 1935–1945," http://epsilon3.georgetown.edu/~coventrm/asa2000/panel1/sklaroff .html. Viewed on the Internet July 19, 2006.

6. Author interview with Eva Grove, Anaheim, California, February 2, 2005; email, Andy Grove to Denise Amantea, June 11, 2006; email, Denise Amantea to author, June 11, 2006; phone conversation, Andy Grove with author, June 12, 2006.

7. Author interview with Roger Borovoy, Los Altos, California, January 3, 2006.

8. Andrew S. Grove, *One-on-One with Andy Grove* (New York: Penguin, 1987), p. 25.

9. Tim Jackson, *Inside Intel: Andy Grove and the Rise of the World's Most Powerful Chip Company* (New York: Penguin, 1997).

10. Jackson, *Intel*, p. 31.

11. Author interview with Andy Grove, Intel RNB, Santa Clara, California, 1999.

12. Gordon E. Moore, "The Role of Fairchild in Silicon Technology in the Early Days of 'Silicon Valley,'" *Proceedings of the IEEE*, 86, 1 (January 1998), p. 56.

13. Margaret Grove Radford, "Technology Is Impossible to Hold Back," *Destiny*, Summer 1997.

14. Grove, *Paranoid*, p. 143.

15. Video Monitoring Services of America, *Fresh Air*, KQED-FM, San Francisco, November 19, 1996, 1:00–2:00 p.m.

16. Grove, *Paranoid*, p. 143.

17. Grove, *Paranoid*, p. 196.

18. Specifically, Grove suggested to Eric Schmidt, CEO of Google, that he teach a course at Stanford's Graduate School of Business. Schmidt took his advice and is doing it. Author interview with Eric Schmidt, Google headquarters, Mountain View, California, May 19, 2004. Grove would have been offered a seat on Google's board, but John Doerr, who provided venture backing for Google, knew he would decline the offer. Author telephone interview with John Doerr. The only for-profit corporate board on which Grove has ever served is Intel's.

19. www.libertystatepark.com/emma.htm. Viewed on the Internet on March 1, 2005.

20. We are not surprised to learn that the author of this observation, Tim Jackson, is himself a foreigner. He is English, a graduate of Oxford. Apparently he caught the entrepreneurial bug in Silicon Valley, because he returned to England to found an online auction house. See John Rossant, "The Stars of Europe—Innovators: Tim Jackson, Managing Director—Carlyle Internet Partners—Britain," *BusinessWeek International Edition*, June 12, 2000. For reviews of Jackson's book on Intel, see Regis McKenna, "Battle of the Chips," *Financial Times*, November 8, 1997; John Liscio, "The Steel Beneath the Silicon—A Revealing Look at How Andy Grove Willed Intel into a Powerhouse," *Barron's*, October 20, 1997; Andy Reinhardt, "Paranoia, Aggression, and Other Strengths," *BusinessWeek*, October 13, 1997; Stanley W. Angrist, "Business Book Shelf: Big Is Beautiful," *Wall Street Journal*, February 13, 1998; Luke Collins, "Intel Story Spotlights True Business Culture," *Electronics Times*, November 10, 1997, p. 28; Mike Magee, "Intel from the Inside," *Computing*, October 30, 1997.

21. For Grove's American citizenship, see above, p. 164. Wikipedia made an error in this regard. It states that "Only one of the last 10 Persons of the Year has been a non-American, that being the Hungarian Andy Grove." http://en.wikipedia.org/wiki/Person_of_the_Year. Viewed on the Internet on December 9, 2005. I corrected it by editing out the quoted sentence.

22. "A.S. Grove, Intel, 7/27/68–1972." Document in author's possession.

23. Conversation with author, March 2, 2005.

24. See, for example, "The Way to Wealth," which Franklin published on July 7, 1757. Available on the Internet at http://itech.fgcu.edu/faculty/wohlpart/alra/franklin.htm. Viewed on January 20, 2006. Also available in L. Jesse Lemisch, ed., *Benjamin Franklin: The Autobiography and Other Writings* (New York: New American Library, 2001), p. 189.

25. Wolfe, "Tinkerings."

26. Author interview with Karen Alter, Palo Alto, California, December 14, 2005.

27. Author interview with Sean Maloney, Intel RNB, Santa Clara, California, January 12, 2004.

28. Rick Tetzeli, "What Chief Executives Return to Shareholders Per Square Foot of Office Space," *Fortune*, April 19, 1993.

29. Grove, *Swimming*, pp. 186–187.

30. Grove, *Swimming*, p. 89.

31. Robert A. Burgelman, *Strategy Is Destiny: How Strategy-Making Shapes a Company's Future* (New York: Free Press, 2002), p. 134. Italics in original.

32. For Fermi and the birth of chain reaction, see Richard Rhodes, *The Making of the Atomic Bomb* (New York: Simon and Schuster, 1986), pp. 438–442.

33. Grove, *Swimming*, p. 76.

34. Richard S. Tedlow, *The Watson Dynasty: The Fiery Reign and Troubled Legacy of IBM's Founding Father and Son* (New York: HarperBusiness, 2003), p. 39.

35. In conversation with author, March 2, 2005.

36. Berlin, *Man Behind the Microchip*, pp. 173–174.

37. Burgelman, *Strategy*, p. 28.

38. "A.S. Grove, Intel, 7/27/68–1972."

39. Jackson, *Intel*, p. 27. Italics in original.

40. Jackson, *Intel*, p. 27.

41. Berlin, *Man Behind the Microchip*, pp. 181–182.

42. Gordon E. Moore, "The Role of Fairchild in Silicon Technology in the Early Days of 'Silicon Valley,'" *Proceedings of the IEEE*, 86, 1 (January 1998), pp. 62 and 53–62 passim.

43. Berlin, *Man Behind the Microchip*, p. 136.

44. Jack Robertson, "Study Impact of Microcircuit," *Electronic News*, April 1963, quoted in Berlin, "Entrepreneurship," p. 85.

45. Grove, *Paranoid*, p. 29.

46. Donald N. Sull, Richard S. Tedlow, and Richard S. Rosenbloom, "Managerial Commitments and Technological Change in the U.S. Tire Industry," *Industrial and Corporate Change*, 6, 2 (March 1997), pp. 461–501.

47. This phrase is Nietzsche's. Friedrich Nietzsche, *Human, All Too Human: A Book for Free Spirits* (Cambridge, England: Cambridge University Press, 1996).

48. "Intel Corp $2,500,000 Convertible Debentures," pp. 1–2. Document in author's possession. Interestingly, according to this document (p. 2), "The company expects to offer $2,500,000 of convertible debentures to a limited group of private investors, convertible at $5 per share." The figure $10 per share is not mentioned.

49. Burgelman, *Strategy*, p. 29.

50. Berlin, *Man Behind the Microchip*, p. 172.

51. Berlin, "Entrepreneurship," p. 186. See also Intel's first published *Annual Report*, that of 1971.

52. Brent Schlender, "Inside Andy Grove's Latest Crusade: Intel's Chairman Is Out to Change the Way Companies Are Governed. His First Job: Change Himself," *Fortune*, August 23, 2004.

53. Berlin, "Entrepreneurship," p. 186.

54. "A.S. Grove, Intel, 7/27/68–1972."

55. "A.S. Grove, Intel, 7/27/68–1972."

56. "A.S. Grove, Intel, 7/27/68–1972."

57. Quoted in Berlin, *Man Behind the Microchip*, p. 162. It took six years of offering before Borovoy himself decided to join Intel. Jackson, *Intel*, p. 124. Tim Jackson was a college friend of the daughter of Roger and Brenda Borovoy. He spent a lot of time with Borovoy while writing his book and those passages, at least, can be regarded as reliable.

58. Wolfe, "Tinkerings."

59. Berlin, "Entrepreneurship," p. 182.

60. Quoted in Berlin, *Man Behind the Microchip*, p. 182.

61. Burgelman, *Strategy*, p. 29.

62. "A.S. Grove, Intel, 7/27/68–1972."
63. 9/18/68 entry, "A.S. Grove, Intel, 7/27/68–1972."
64. Berlin, *Man Behind the Microchip*, p. 187.
65. This narrative relies on Berlin, "Entrepreneurship," p. 192.
66. "A.S. Grove, Intel, 7/27/68–1972."
67. The impact of this song is mentioned in Berlin, *Man Behind the Microchip*, p. 177.
68. Author interview with Andy Grove, March 18, 2005.
69. Berlin, "Entrepreneurship," p. 192, n. 7.
70. Quoted in Berlin, *Man Behind the Microchip*, p. 189.
71. Andy Grove speech at the Intel Manufacturing Excellence Conference, June 15, 2004, and email to author from Terri L. Murphy, May 30, 2006.
72. Berlin, "Entrepreneurship," pp. 194 and 194, n. 15.
73. Jackson, *Intel*, p. 40.
74. Burgelman, *Strategy*, p. 29.
75. Burgelman, *Strategy*, p. 404, n. 15.
76. No, Betty Crocker is not a real person. She was invented by General Mills in 1921 to put a human face on its products. At one time, she was the second most popular woman in the United Sates, behind only Eleanor Roosevelt. Susan Marks, *Finding Betty Crocker* (New York: Simon and Schuster, 2005), p. 4.
77. Berlin, "Entrepreneurship," pp. 197–198.
78. Interview with Gordon Moore and Andy Grove by Professor Joseph L. Bower of Harvard Business School, Intel RNB, Santa Clara, California, December 8, 1999.
79. Author interview with Andy Grove, March 18, 2005, and email to author from Terri L. Murphy, May 23, 2006.
80. Interview with Gordon Moore and Andy Grove by Professor Joseph L. Bower, December 8, 1999.
81. C. E. Unterberg, Towbin Co., "Intel Corporation," *Prospectus*, October 13, 1971, p. 12.
82. Moore's comments are in Burgelman, *Strategy*, pp. 29–30.
83. Intel *Annual Report*, 1972
84. Berlin, *Man Behind the Microchip*, p. 207.
85. Jackson, *Intel*, p. 49.
86. Author interview with Andy Grove, March 18, 2005, and email to author from Terri L. Murphy, May 23, 2006.
87. Burgelman, *Strategy*, p. 30.
88. Burgelman, *Strategy*, p. 30.
89. Jackson, *Intel*, p. 102.
90. The words are Jackson's, *Intel*, p. 102.
91. Burgelman, *Strategy*, p. 30.
92. T. R. Reid, *The Chip: How Two Americans Invented the Microchip and Launched a Revolution* (New York: Simon and Schuster, 1984), p. 141.
93. Jackson, *Intel*, pp. 70–73.
94. See "Intel's First Microprocessor—the Intel® 4004," *Intel Museum/Intel Corporate Archives*. http://www.intel.com/museum/archives/4004.htm. Viewed on the Internet April 2007. Like most inventions, the microprocessor has many fathers, and paternity is not clear cut. See William Aspray, "The Intel 4004 Microprocessor:

What Constituted Invention?" *IEEE Annals of the History of Computing*, 19, 3 (July – September 1997, pp. 4–15). The debate continues as of this writing. See John Flood, "Chipping in on History: Federico Faggin, Co-Inventor of the Microprocessor, Still Setting the Record Straight," *Los Altos Town Crier*, January 17, 2007, and John Flood, "Ted Hoff: Thinking Small Sparked a Worldwide Revolution," *Los Altos Town Crier*, April 4, 2007.

7. "Orchestrated Brilliance"

1. Burgelman, *Strategy*, p. 31.
2. Author interview with Andy Grove, March 18, 2005, and e-mail to author from Terri L. Murphy, May 23, 2006.
3. Intel *Annual Report*, 1972.
4. C. E. Unterberg, *Prospectus*.
5. Intel *Annual Report*, 1972.
6. Moore and Grove interview with Bower.
7. Christopher H. Schmitt, "At Work with the Valley's Toughest Boss: Andy Grove Keeps a Forceful Grip at Chip Giant Intel," *San Jose Mercury News*, May 26, 1986.
8. David McCullough, *Truman* (New York: Simon and Schuster, 1992), p. 481.
9. Moore and Grove interview with Bower.
10. Moore and Grove interview with Bower.
11. "A.S. Grove, Intel, 7/27/68–1972." Document in author's possession.
12. "A.S. Grove, Intel, 7/27/68–1972."
13. Author interview with Andy Grove, March 18, 2005.
14. "A.S. Grove, Intel, 7/27/68–1972."
15. Bruce LeBoss, "Frosch Raps Technological Substitutes," *Electronic News*, March 1969, clipping in "A.S. Grove, Intel, 7/27/68–1972."
16. "A.S. Grove, Intel, 7/27/68–1972." When Grove looked at the second sentence in this quotation recently, he said he still felt it was astute. Andy Grove interview with author, March 18, 2005. In "Despair," the story Grove wrote as a high school student, the "secret ambition" of the fictional protagonist "was to become a theatrical director. Theatrical director!—he savored the words." Manuscript in author's possession.
17. Laurence J. Peter and Raymond Hull, *The Peter Principle* (New York: William Morrow, 1969). See, for example, p. 25.
18. "A.S. Grove, Intel, 7/27/68–1972."
19. "A.S. Grove, Intel, 7/27/68–1972."
20. "A.S. Grove, Intel, 7/27/68–1972."
21. "A.S. Grove, Intel, 7/27/68–1972."
22. "A.S. Grove, Intel, 7/27/68–1972."
23. "A.S. Grove, Intel, 7/27/68–1972."
24. "A.S. Grove, Intel, 7/27/68–1972."
25. Author interview with Andy Grove, March 18, 2005.
26. http://silicongenesis.stanford.edu/transcripts/sporck.htm. Viewed on the Internet on March 24, 2005. See also Charles E. Sporck with Richard L. Molay, *Spinoff:*

A Personal History of the Industry That Changed the World (Saranac Lake, NY: Saranac Lake Publishing, 2001).

27. "A.S. Grove, Intel, 7/27/68–1972." Andy Grove interview with author, March 18, 2005.
28. "On the Organization of Operations," "A.S. Grove, Intel, 7/27/68–1972."
29. "A.S. Grove, Intel, 7/27/68–1972."
30. "A.S. Grove, Intel, 7/27/68–1972."
31. "Reorganization of Operations," "A.S. Grove, Intel, 7/27/68–1972."
32. Berlin, *Man Behind the Microchip*, pp. 157, 177, 198–99.
33. "A.S. Grove, Intel, 7/27/68–1972."
34. Berlin, "Entrepreneurship," p. 196, n. 28.
35. This discussion is based on the excellent treatment in Berlin, "Entrepreneurship," pp. 201–206.

8. The Long and Winding Road

1. Intel *Annual Report,* 1973.
2. Berlin, "Entrepreneurship," p. 207.
3. Berlin, "Entrepreneurship," p. 208.
4. "On Growth," November 10, 1973; "A.S. Grove, Intel, 11/1973–." Document in author's possession.
5. "A.S. Grove, Intel, 11/1973–."
6. "A.S. Grove, Intel, 11/1973–."
7. I am indebted to my colleague at the Harvard Business School, Professor Rakesh Khurana, for many of the ideas in this paragraph.
8. "Semiconductors Take a Sudden Plunge," *BusinessWeek,* November 16, 1974, pp. 64–65.
9. I am grateful to my former student, Cliff Reid, an entrepreneur in the Valley, for this observation.
10. Berlin, *Man Behind the Microchip,* p. 223.
11. "Non-growth," August 11, 1974; "A.S. Grove, Intel, 11/1973–."
12. Berlin, *Man Behind the Microchip,* p. 223.
13. Berlin, *Man Behind the Microchip,* p. 224.
14. Leslie Berlin, "Entrepreneurship and the Rise of Silicon Valley: The Career of Robert Noyce, 1956–1990," Unpublished dissertation (Stanford University, 2001), p. 232.
15. Berlin, *Man Behind the Microchip,* p. 224.
16. "Intel's Robert Noyce Kicks Himself Upstairs," *BusinessWeek,* December 14, 1974.
17. Oral history interview with Paul S. Otellini by Rachel Stewart, February 26, 2002, Santa Clara, California. Available at Intel.
18. Otellini oral history interview, February 26, 2002.
19. Intel *Annual Report,* 1974.
20. Intel *Annual Report,* 1975.
21. "Intel's Robert Noyce Kicks Himself Upstairs," *BusinessWeek,* December 14, 1974.
22. "Discussion with RNN/GEM on 12/14/73," "A.S. Grove, Intel, 11/1973–."

23. "My Worries . . . ," 11/10/74, "A.S. Grove, Intel, 11/1974–." Document in author's possession.

24. Intel *Annual Report,* 1974.

25. "After the first 3 [2½] weeks . . . ," 12/25/74. "A.S. Grove, Intel, 11/1973–."

26. Intel *Annual Report,* 1975.

27. Intel *Annual Report,* 1975.

28. Grove to Moore, June 6, 1975. Document in author's possession.

29. Grove to Moore, "WW47 'Happenings,'" November 21, 1975. Document in author's possession.

30. In 1974, for example, three design engineers at Intel (Federico Faggin, Ralph Ungermann, and Masatoshi Shima) decided to leave and create their own company. It was named Zilog, a name that meant to indicate that it was the "last word [z] in integrated [i] logic [log]." Jackson, *Intel,* pp. 130–131. Grove remarked that losing those three engineers cost Intel's microprocessor development up to a year. Robert A. Burgelman, Clayton M. Christensen, and Steven C. Wheelwright, *Strategic Management of Technology and Innovation* (New York: McGraw-Hill, 2004), p. 461, n. 6.

31. In 1975, a fire destroyed the Penang assembly facility. Two weeks later, the Penang group, in rented facilities, shipped 100,000 units. See Intel Fifteenth Anniversary Brochure, *A Revolution in Progress* (Intel Corporation, 1984), p. 42. http://www .intel.com/museum/archives/brochures/brochures.htm. Viewed on the Internet May 2006.

32. This is based upon Grove's memorandum to himself, dated May 16, 1975. Document in author's possession.

33. Intel *Annual Report,* 1976.

34. Intel *Annual Report,* 1976.

35. "Status as of 8/28/75," Grove memorandum to himself. Document in author's possession.

36. "To: GEM," 2/4/76. Document in author's possession.

37. "An Overview in Anticipation of Preparing 3rd Quarter Key Results," July 6, 1976. Document in author's possession.

38. Dick Boucher interview with author, Intel RNB, Santa Clara, California, April 19, 2005.

39. "Review," November 18, 1976. Document in author's possession.

40. "ESM," 11/2/76. Document in author's possession.

41. Gene Bylinsky, "How Intel Won Its Bet on Memory Chips," *Fortune,* November 1973.

42. The above statistics and quotations are from Intel *Annual Report,* 1977.

43. Intel *Annual Report,* 1977.

44. The above quotations are from *A Revolution in Progress,* pp. 38–39.

45. Burgelman, *Strategy,* p. 116.

46. Author interview with Dick Boucher, Intel RNB, Santa Clara, California, April 19, 2005.

47. Grove email to author, April 6, 2005.

48. Intel *Annual Report,* 1978.

49. Vadasz has discussed this with me on more than one occasion. He gets a kick out of it because this application was utterly unplanned. He does not know how the ba-

con packager happened upon the microprocessor as the solution to this particular problem.

50. Intel *Annual Report,* 1978.

51. Charles E. Sporck with Richard L. Molay, *Spinoff: A Personal History of the Industry That Changed the World* (Saranac Lake, NY: Saranac Lake Publishing, 2001), p. 199.

52. Michael S. Malone, *Infinite Loop: How the World's Most Insanely Great Computer Company Went Insane* (New York: Doubleday, 1999), p. 111.

53. Malone, *Loop,* p. 113.

54. Sporck, *Spinoff,* p. 199.

55. Malone, *Loop,* p. 170.

56. Sporck, *Spinoff,* p. 200.

57. A. S. Grove, "Key Points from Last Night's Dinner Meeting," February 23, 1978. Document in author's possession.

58. "Key Points from the Dinner Discussion of June 1, 1978," June 5, 1978. Document in author's possession.

59. Andy Grove, "The Ingredients Lacking to Make Us a Billion Dollar Company: 'Oomph' and Administration," July 7, 1978. Document in author's possession.

60. Grove to Moore, "Your Welcome Home Memo," August 25, 1978. Document in author's possession.

61. A. Grove, "Observations on Last Night's Dinner," October 4, 1978. Document in author's possession.

62. Intel *Annual Report,* 1979.

63. Jimmy Carter, "The Crisis of Confidence," http://www.pbs.org/wgbh/amex/carter/filmmore/ps_crisis.html. Viewed on the Internet on January 23, 2006.

64. http://www.pbs.org/wgbh/amex/carter/filmmore/pt_2.html. Viewed on the Internet on January 23, 2006.

65. Intel *Annual Report,* 1979.

66. Grove to Moore, "While You Were Away . . . ," July 3, 1979. Document in author's possession.

67. Intel *Annual Report,* 1972.

68. Intel *Annual Report,* 1979.

69. *A Revolution in Progress,* p. 31.

70. Ibid., pp. 30–41.

71. William H. Davidow, *Marketing High Technology: An Insider's View* (New York: Free Press, 1986), p. 2.

72. Davidow, *Technology,* p. 2.

73. Davidow, *Technology,* pp. 3–4.

74. *A Revolution in Progress,* pp. 14–15.

75. Davidow, *Technology,* p. 4.

76. Davidow, *Technology,* p. 6.

77. Davidow, *Technology,* p. 7.

78. Davidow, *Technology,* pp. 4–11; "A Revolution," p. 15.

79. Ed Gelbach, one of the key marketing managers at Intel at this time, insists that Paul Indigo deserves the credit for this sale. David House also believes that Paul Indigo's contribution has been overlooked. Author interview with David L. House,

February 15, 2005, Computer History Museum, Mountain View, California; author interview with Ed Gelbach, January 3, 2006, Palo Alto, California.

80. Burgelman, *Strategy,* p. 108.

81. Intel Twenty-fifth Anniversary Brochure, *Defining Intel: 25 Years/25 Events* (Intel Corporation, 1993), pp. 16–17. http://www.intel.com/museum/archives/brochures/ brochures.htm. Viewed on the Internet on July 20, 2005.

82. Malone, *Infinite Loop,* p. 218.

83. Burgelman, *Strategy,* p. 108.

84. Burgelman, *Strategy,* p. 113.

85. Intel Thirty-fifth Anniversary Brochure, *Intel: Thirty-five Years of Innovation* (Intel Corporation, 2003). http://www.intel.com/museum/archives/brochures/brochures .htm. Viewed on the Internet in May 2006.

86. See note 32.

87. Intel *Annual Report,* 1982.

88. Intel *Annual Report,* 1982.

89. Grove, "1982 was a terrible year . . . ," January 2, 1983. Document in author's possession.

90. Grove to Moore, "Welcome Home," February 19, 1982. Document in author's possession.

91. Intel *Annual Report,* 1982.

92. "Let's Make a Deal: IBM Buys 12% of Intel," *Fortune,* January 24, 1983.

93. Sabin Russell, "Intel to Get $250M Cash Infusion from IBM," *Electronic News,* December 27, 1982.

94. Russell, "Cash Infusion."

95. Grove in conversation with author.

96. Russell, "Cash Infusion." See also Michael Orme, "Why Intel Married for Money," *Management Today,* February 1985. For a good indication of how closely watched every financial move IBM made concerning Intel was and how complicated the relationship was between the two companies, see Loring Wirbel, "Is IBM Rethinking Its Fiscal Ties with Intel?" *Electronic News,* February 3, 1986.

97. Linda Sandler, "Intel's Detractors Say IBM Bond Sale Is Signal That Semiconductor Firm Has Poor Prospects," *Wall Street Journal,* February 12, 1986. See also Randall Smith, "IBM's $300 Million Sale of Eurobonds Is Seen as Move to Loosen Ties to Intel," *Wall Street Journal,* February 10, 1986; Hank Gilman, "IBM Cuts Intel Stake Further to 7.1% and Takes Profit Totaling $80 Million," *Wall Street Journal,* August 31, 1987; Ken Wells, "Intel Corp. Loosens Its Link with IBM in Repurchase of Large Block of Shares," *Wall Street Journal,* June 12, 1987; "IBM Is Planning to Shed the Rest of Its Intel Stock," *Wall Street Journal,* September 28, 1987.

98. Alfred D. Chandler Jr., *Inventing the Electronic Century: The Epic Story of the Consumer Electronics and Computer Industries* (New York: Free Press, 2001), p. 156.

99. "A.S. Grove, Intel, 11/1973–January 2, 1983." Document in author's possession.

100. Intel *Annual Report,* 1983.

101. Grove to Moore, "Welcome Home!" July 14, 1983. Document in author's possession.

102. Intel *Annual Report,* 1983.

103. Intel *Annual Report,* 1983.

104. Grove to Moore, "Welcome Home!" July 14, 1983. Document in author's possession.

105. Marilyn Chase, "Problem-Plagued Intel Bets on New Products, IBM's Financial Help," *Wall Street Journal,* February 4, 1983.

106. Grove to Moore, "Welcome Home!" July 14, 1983. Document in author's possession.

107. Grove to Moore, July 14, 1983.

108. A "Strategic Capability Segment" is defined as "A strategic business group within the Intel organization that creates a forum to present and gain consensus for development of a corporatewide strategy within a particular area." The Intel "Acronyms List" was kindly supplied to me by Andy Grove's administrative assistant, Terri L. Murphy. Intel has created its own language. There are 1,179 entries on this acronyms list. Most of these are TLAs. "TLA" is a three-letter acronym for "Three Letter Acronym." It is number 1,094 on the "Acronyms List."

109. Grove to Moore, July 14, 1983.

110. Grove to Moore, July 14, 1983.

111. "A.S. Grove, Intel, 11/1973–."

112. Chandler, *Electronic Century,* pp. 134–139.

113. Intel *Annual Report,* 1984.

114. William Pat Patterson, "Gloomy Days in Silicon Valley: It's Beginning to Look As If We Can't Beat The Japanese at Chipmaking. The Question Is: Will We Join Them?" *Industry Week,* November 25, 1985.

115. Intel *Annual Report,* 1985.

116. "Intel Lays Off 170 Employees After $35M Qtr. Opns. Loss," *Electronic News,* January 20, 1986. Intel reported its first quarterly operating loss of $23 million for the third quarter. No one else in "the battered semiconductor industry in Silicon Valley" was doing any better. AMD showed a $15.3 million operating loss for its second quarter. In its first quarter, National Semiconductor lost a record $53.5 million. Charles L. Howe, "Back to the Basics," *Datamation,* December 1, 1985.

117. Intel *Annual Report,* 1985.

118. Intel *Annual Report,* 1985.

119. Intel *Annual Report,* 1986.

120. Intel *Annual Report,* 1986.

121. Intel *Annual Report,* 1986.

122. John W. Wilson, "Andrew Grove," *BusinessWeek,* April 17, 1987, p. 252.

9. Andy Grove in 1986: At Work and at Home

1. Susan Ager, "Retirement Game: Knowing When to Quit," *San Jose Mercury,* November 22, 1982. This newspaper was later to be known by the name it has today, the *San Jose Mercury News.* Another clipping in the notebooks is Mortimer R. Feinberg and Aaron Levenstein, "Retirement as the Pinnacle of Your Career," *Wall Street Journal,* November 23, 1981. "A.S. Grove, Intel, 11/1973–." Document in author's possession.

2. " 'Succession' Strategy," December 27, 1983. "A.S. Grove, Intel, 11/1973–."

3. Sam Walton with John Huey, *Sam Walton: Made in America, My Story* (New York: Bantam, 1992), p. 203.

4. Burgelman, *Strategy,* p. 31.
5. Chase, "Problem-Plagued Intel," *Wall Street Journal,* February 4, 1983.
6. Steven Flax, "The Toughest Bosses in America," *Fortune,* August 6, 1984.
7. Jackson, *Intel,* pp. 114–115. The word quoted is Jackson's, not Faggin's.
8. Burgelman, *Strategy,* pp. 101–102.
9. For an interesting interview with Grove about this question, see Gail E. Schares, "'Connoisseur of Confrontation,'" *San Francisco Chronicle,* July 26, 1984.
10. Chase, "Problem-Plagued Intel." Grove refers to this note in his *One-on-One with Andy Grove: How to Manage Your Boss, Yourself, and Your Coworkers* (New York: Penguin, 1987), p. 95.
11. Burgelman, *Strategy,* pp. 280–281.
12. Author interview with Paul S. Otellini, Intel RNB, Santa Clara, California, January 23, 2006.
13. Andrew S. Grove, *High Output Management* (New York: Vintage, 1983), p. 53.
14. Grove, *Output,* p. 43–47.
15. Grove to Moore, "Welcome Home!" February 25, 1987. Document in author's possession.
16. I am indebted to my colleague at Harvard Business School, Professor Thomas K. McCraw, for this phrase.
17. Jackson, *Intel,* pp. 119–120.
18. "Silicon Genesis: An Oral History of Semiconductor Technology." Interview with Federico Faggin, Los Altos Hills, California, March 3, 1995. Hosted by Rob Walker, Cofounder, LSI Logic. There is still a firm called LSI Logic in Silicon Valley, in Milpitas. Walker, in his interview with Faggin, is exceptionally critical of Grove. Walker's view is in the minority. I report it because it is not absent from the Valley. Grove made his share of enemies on his climb to the top. http://silicon genesis.stanford.edu/ transcripts/faggin.htm. Viewed on the Internet on November 25, 2005.
19. Author interview with Eva Grove, February 2, 2005, and email from Eva Grove to author June 6, 2006.
20. Author interview with Eva Grove, February 2, 2005, and email from Eva Grove to author June 6, 2006.

10. "The Valley of Death"

1. See Intel Fifteenth Anniversary Brochure, "A Revolution in Progress" (Intel Corporation, 1984), p. 46, at http://www.Intel.com/museum/archives/brochures/brochures .htm, for a photograph of the plaque. E-mail, Jodelle A. French to author, May 5, 2006.
2. Intel *Annual Report,* 1987.
3. Martin Gilbert, *Churchill: A Life* (London: Heinemann, 1991), p. 645.
4. Carnegie Library of Pittsburgh, "The Point: William Pitt." http://www.clpgh.org/ exhibit/neighborhoods/point/point_n104.html. Viewed on the Internet on April 26, 2005.
5. See Abraham Zaleznik's classic, "Managers and Leaders: Are They Different?" *Harvard Business Review,* 55, 3 (May–June 1977), reprinted in Ralph Katz, ed., *Manag-*

ing Professionals in Innovative Organizations: A Collection of Readings (Cambridge, MA: Ballinger, 1988), pp. 170–182. See also Joel M. Podolny, Rakesh Khurana, and Marya Hill-Popper, "Revisiting the Meaning of Leadership," *Research in Organizational Behavior,* 26 (2005). I am grateful to my colleague at the Harvard Business School, Professor Rakesh Khurana for many of the thoughts in this paragraph.

6. Email, Grove to author, April 25, 2005.

7. "The Five Best-Managed Companies," *Dun's Review,* December 1980. The treatment therein of Intel is: "Intel: Master of Innovation." A photograph of this magazine is featured in Intel's Thirty-fifth Anniversary Brochure, *Intel: Thirty-five Years of Innovation* (Intel Corporation, 2003), http://www.intel.com/museum/archives/brochures/brochures.htm. Viewed on the Internet in May 2006.

8. Author telephone interview with John Doerr, March 16, 2006.

9. Andrew S. Grove, *High Output Management* (New York: Vintage, 1983).

10. Andrew S. Grove, *High Output Management* (New York: Vintage, 1983), pp. 13 and 3–36.

11. Burgelman, *Strategy,* p. 134.

12. Burgelman, *Strategy,* p. 31.

13. This metaphor was suggested to me by my colleague, Professor Rakesh Khurana.

14. "Intel," *Dun's Review.*

15. Burgelman, *Strategy,* p. 31.

16. Andrew S. Grove, *Only the Paranoid Survive: How to Exploit the Crisis Points That Challenge Every Company* (New York: Doubleday, 1996), p. 84.

17. Grove, *Paranoid,* p. 85.

18. Grove, *Paranoid,* pp. 85–87.

19. Richard Mackenzie, " 'The Industry Has Stopped Growing,' " *Insight,* October 7, 1985.

20. Grove, *Paranoid,* p. 86.

21. Burgelman, *Strategy,* pp. 35 and 63.

22. Grove, *Paranoid,* pp. 87–88.

23. Grove, *Paranoid,* pp. 88–89.

24. Grove, *Paranoid,* p. 89.

25. Grove, *Paranoid,* p. 91.

26. Grove, *Paranoid,* p. 89.

27. See above, pp. 28–29.

28. Richard S. Tedlow, "The Education of Andy Grove," *Fortune,* December 12, 2005.

29. Grove, *Paranoid,* p. 91.

30. Grove, *Paranoid,* p. 95.

31. Video Monitoring Services of America, *Technopolitics,* KCSM-TV San Francisco, September 22, 1996, 5:30 p.m.

32. Grove, *Paranoid,* p. 97.

33. Grove, quoted in Burgelman, *Strategy,* p. 82.

34. A brilliant example of how to keep top talent in a company after a fight is the story of Frederick P. Brooks Jr. and Bob O. Evans at IBM during the battles over the IBM 360 in the 1960s. In short, Evans favored the product; Brooks opposed it. Evans won and rewarded Brooks by asking him to contribute to "the juiciest part" of the work. Richard S. Tedlow, *The Watson Dynasty: The Fiery Reign and Troubled*

Legacy of IBM's Founding Father and Son (New York: HarperBusiness, 2003), pp. 235–236.

35. Burgelman, *Strategy*, p. 37.
36. Grove, *Paranoid*, pp. 93–94.

11. "The PC Is It"

1. Author interview with Andy Grove, Intel RNB, 1999.
2. Intel *Annual Report*, 1987.
3. Grove, *Paranoid*, pp. 39–40.
4. Grove, *Paranoid*, p. 40.
5. Glenn Rifkin and George Harrar, *The Ultimate Entrepreneur: The Story of Ken Olsen and Digital Equipment Corporation* (Rocklin, CA: Prima Publishing, 1990).
6. Grove, *Paranoid*, p. 150.
7. John W. Wilson, "Intel Wakes Up to a Whole New Marketplace in Chips," *Business-Week*, September 2, 1985.
8. J. I. Magid et al., "Intel—Company Report," New York Society of Security Analysis, February 13, 1986, p. 3.
9. See Aubrey Wilson and Bryan Atkin, "Exorcising the Ghosts in Marketing," *Harvard Business Review*, 54, 5 (Sept.–Oct. 1976).
10. John W. Wilson, "Can Andy Grove Practice What He Preaches?" *BusinessWeek*, March 16, 1987.
11. Intel *Annual Report*, 1985.
12. John W. Wilson, "Intel's Mad Dash to Keep Up with Japan," *BusinessWeek*, August 12, 1985.
13. Sir Isaiah Berlin, *Russian Thinkers*, Henry Hardy and Aileen Kelly, eds. (London: Penguin, 1978), pp. 22 and 22–81 passim.
14. Burgelman, *Strategy*, p. 133.
15. Leglise was referring to Hitachi, NEC, Fujitsu, Matsushita, and Toshiba. Otis Port and Richard Brandt, "Intel's New Chip May Light a Fire Under Computer Sales," *BusinessWeek*, October 28, 1985.
16. Definition courtesy of Dictionary.com. Viewed on the Internet on May 13, 2005.
17. Burgelman, *Strategy*, p. 137. The metaphor of marines and mercenaries is courtesy of my colleague, Professor Rakesh Khurana.
18. Burgelman, *Strategy*, p. 137.
19. Magid, "Intel," p. 6.
20. Magid, "Intel," p. 6.
21. Grove to Moore, "While You Were Away . . . ," June 27, 1980. Document in author's possession.
22. Dan C. Tenorio to Grove, April 12, 2005. Document in author's possession.
23. Grove to Moore, "Guess What—No Disasters This Week!" November 7, 1986. Grove notebooks. Document in author's possession.
24. Magid, "Intel," p. 6.
25. Magid, "Intel," p. 5.

26. Burgelman, *Strategy*, p. 135.

27. Author interview with Craig R. Barrett, Intel RNB, Santa Clara, California, January 14, 2004.

28. Author interview with F. Thomas Dunlap, Intel RNB, Santa Clara, California, February 24, 2004.

29. Magid, "Intel," p. 5.

30. Burgelman, *Strategy*, p. 138.

31. Author interview with Craig Barrett, Intel RNB, Santa Clara, California, January 14, 2004.

32. Grove, *Paranoid*, pp. 88–89.

33. Magid, "Intel," p. 3.

34. Grove to Moore, "Welcome Home!" October 6, 1986. Document in author's possession.

35. See p. 218.

36. Ken Siegmann, "An American Tale of Semi-Success: How American Chip Companies Regained Lead," *San Francisco Chronicle*, December 20, 1993. See also Ken Siegmann, "Improved Equipment Key to Chip Revival: U.S. Companies Learned to Cooperate," *San Francisco Chronicle*, December 21, 1993.

37. John Sweetman, *Balaclava 1854: The Charge of the Light Brigade* (Oxford, England: Osprey Publishing, 2002), p. 82. It is among the wonders of the Internet that you can actually hear Tennyson read "The Charge of the Light Brigade" on your computer through the reproduction of his voice on an ancient wax cylinder recording. "The Tennyson Page," http://charon.sfsu.edu/TENNYSON/poems/index.shtml. Viewed (and heard) on the Internet on May 16, 2005.

38. The quoted phrase is from Winston Churchill's speech "Their Finest Hour," delivered in the House of Commons on June 18, 1940: "Hitler knows that he will have to break us in this Island or lose the war. If we can stand up to him, all Europe may be free and the life of the world may move forward into broad, sunlit uplands. But if we fail, then the whole world, including the United States, including all that we have known and cared for, will sink into the abyss of a new Dark Age made more sinister . . . by the lights of perverted science." http://www.winstonchurchill.org. Viewed on the Internet on May 16, 2005.

39. E. C. White Jr., "Intel Corporation—Company Report," E. F. Hutton & Co., February 15, 1985, recommended "Aggressive Purchase" in both the short (upcoming half year) and long (beyond that) term, p. 1; V. J. Glinski et al., "Intel—Company Report," Drexel Burnham Lambert Inc., May 6, 1985, "We recommend purchase of Intel shares," p. 1; L. W. Borgman, "Intel Corporation—Company Report," Nomura Securities, September 23, 1985. This report is oddly unclear but appears to be recommending purchase, p. 1; V. J. Glinski, "Intel—Company Report," Drexel Burnham Lambert Inc., January 15, 1986, ". . . the stock remains on our BUY List," p. 1; A. J. Vitolo, "Intel Corporation—Company Report," C. J. Lawrence, Morgan Grenfell, October 16, 1986, "We recommend purchase of Intel's common stock, its warrants, and its outstanding convertible debentures," p. 2; E. C. White Jr., "Intel Corporation—Company Report," E. F. Hutton & Co., December 23, 1986, "We continue to advise accumulation of Intel's shares over both the near and long-term," p. 1.

40. Loring Wirbel, "New Intel 32-Bit MPU Runs MS-DOS Unix in Unison," *Electronic News*, October 21, 1985.

41. Burgelman, *Strategy*, p. 140.

42. Grove, *Paranoid*, p. 117. See also Steven Levy, "Intel Leader Says Fear a Healthy Thing," *Portland Oregonian*, September 8, 1996.

43. Grove, *Paranoid*, pp. 117–118.

44. Burgelman, *Strategy*, p. 139.

45. Author interview with Gordon Moore, Stanford Park Hotel, Menlo Park, California, May 24, 2004.

46. Author interview with Craig Barrett, Intel RNB, Santa Clara, California, February 6, 2006.

47. Paul Carroll, *Big Blues: The Unmaking of IBM* (New York: Crown, 1993), pp. 121–123.

48. Michael Dell, *Direct from Dell: Strategies That Revolutionized an Industry* (New York: HarperBusiness, 1999).

49. Author interview with Rod Canion, Houston, December 11, 2003.

50. Carroll, *Blues*, p. 120.

51. http://www.crn.com/sections/special/supplement/763/763p.25_hot.jhtml. Viewed on the Internet on May 17, 2005. According to Compustat, Compaq's sales in 1986 were $.625 billion. In 1987, they were $1.224 billion. Source: Business Information Analysts, Harvard Business School.

52. John Barnett, "$1 Billion in Sales: Compaq Milestone Takes Just Five Years," *Houston Chronicle*, February 2, 1988; "Compaq Sales Reach $1.2 Billion in Record Five Years; Sales Double, Net Income Triples in 1987," *PR Newswire*, February 1, 1988; Stuart Ganees, "America's Fastest Growing Companies," *Fortune*, May 23, 1988.

53. Grove, *Paranoid*, pp. 32–33.

12. "Awesome Intel"

1. A. J. Kessler, "Intel Corp.—Company Report," Paine Webber Inc., June 9, 1987, p. 1.

2. Kessler, "Intel," p. 3.

3. Observation of Kim B. Clark, at the time dean of the Harvard Business School, to author, Boston, June 2, 2005.

4. Burgelman, *Strategy*, p. 146. For intriguing observations about the changing structure of the computer industry that explicitly address Grove's view, see Timothy F. Bresnahan, "New Modes of Competition: Implications for the Future Structure of the Computer Industry," in *Competition, Innovation, and the Microsoft Monopoly: Antitrust in the Digital Marketplace*, Jeffrey A. Eisenach and Thomas M. Lenard, eds. (Norwell, MA: Kluwer Press, 1999), pp. 155–208.

5. Grove, *Paranoid*, p. 140.

6. Pat Gelsinger, *Balancing Your Family, Faith & Work* (Colorado Springs, CO: Life Journey Publishers, 2003). John H. Crawford and Patrick P. Gelsinger, *Programming the 80386* (San Francisco: Sybex, 1987). Author interview with Patrick P. Gelsinger, Anaheim, California, February 3, 2004.

7. Andy Reinhardt, "Bay Networks' Mr. House Finds His Fixer-Upper," *BusinessWeek*,

February 2, 1998. David Olive, "Newsmakers: Web Wizard," *National Post,* November 1, 1998. Author interview with David L. House, Mountain View, California, February 15, 2005.

8. Intel *Annual Report,* 1987.

9. Jackson, *Inside,* pp. 298–300. At this writing, Hootnick lives in Palo Alto and is a managing partner of Acuity Ventures, a venture capital firm.

10. Yu is the author of *Creating the Digital Future: The Secrets of Consistent Innovation at Intel* (New York: Free Press, 1998). This is a remarkably accessible book for the layperson, especially given that its author is a dyed-in-the-wool technologist. His *Insider's View of Intel* was published in his native language, Chinese, and became a bestseller. http://goldsea.com/Business/Corporate/corporate.html. Viewed on the Internet on May 20, 2005. At this writing, Yu sits on the boards of several high-tech companies in Silicon Valley. Interview with author, Santa Clara, California, January 16, 2004.

11. Author interview with Les Vadasz. In February 2005, Vadasz invited me to spend a weekend on his estate in Sonoma. He is exceptionally knowledgeable about wine. The house he and his wife have built there is a breathtakingly beautiful Tuscan-style villa, fully equipped with state-of-the-art electronics.

12. Author interview with Keith L. Thomson, Portland, Oregon, August 5, 2004.

13. See p. 162.

14. Author interview with Richard Boucher. Santa Clara, California, April 19, 2005.

15. Craig R. Barrett, William D. Nix, and Alan S. Tetelman, *The Principles of Engineering Materials* (Englewood Cliffs, NJ: Prentice Hall, 1973).

16. Author interview with Craig R. Barrett, Intel RNB, Santa Clara, California, January 14, 2004.

17. Author interview with Craig R. Barrett, Intel RNB, Santa Clara, California, January 14, 2004.

18. Evelyn Brodie, "The Master Mechanic Behind Intel's High-Tech Success," *Times* (London), February 11, 1993.

19. Author interview with Frank C. Gill, Heathman Hotel, Portland, Oregon, August 5, 2004.

20. Unless otherwise indicated, all the quotations above are from Intel *Annual Report,* 1987.

21. Michael Stroud, "Intel's Craig Barrett: Shortening Product Cycles So Rivals Struggle to Keep Up," *Investor's Business Daily,* January 28, 1993; Mary Hayes, "Craig Barrett: This 'Milquetoast' May Yet Be Tapped to Lead Intel Corp.," *San Jose Business Journal,* May 17, 1993.

22. Alden M. Hayashi, "The New Intel: Moore Mature, Moore Competitive," *Electronic Business,* November 15, 1987.

23. Andrew S. Grove, "The Age of Agile Giants," presentation to Montgomery Securities, January 27, 1987. Speech in author's possession.

24. Andrew S. Grove, *One-on-One with Andy Grove* (New York: Penguin, 1987).

25. Grove, *One-on-One,* p. 13. Email, Andy Grove to author, June 3, 2006.

26. Grove, *One-on-One,* p. 14.

27. Grove, *One-on-One,* p. 14.

28. Grove, *One-on-One,* pp. 234–235.

29. William Perry, entrepreneur, former secretary of defense, and a man equally at home in private enterprise and public life, said of Grove, "He's a genuine American hero," and compared him to Franklin. Author interview with William Perry, Stanford University, February 3, 2005.

30. Grove, *One-on-One*, p. 95.

31. Grove, *One-on-One*, p. 30.

32. Grove, *One-on-One*, p. 32.

33. Intel *Annual Report*, 1988.

34. Intel *Annual Report*, 1988.

35. Grove to Moore, "Welcome Home!" March 9, 1988. Document in author's possession.

36. Grove, *One-on-One*, p. 14 and elsewhere in the text.

37. Grove, *Output*, pp. 39–70.

38. Grove, *One-on-One*, p. 64.

39. Grove to Moore, "Welcome Home!" March 10, 1988. Document in author's possession.

40. Author interview with Tom Dunlap, Intel RNB, Santa Clara, California, February 24, 2004.

41. Grove to Moore, "Welcome Home!" March 10, 1988.

42. Grove to Moore, "Welcome Home!" March 10, 1988.

43. Victor K. McElheny, "Spotlight: High Technology Jelly Bean Ace," *New York Times*, June 5, 1977.

44. McElheny, "Jelly Bean."

45. Intel fifteenth anniversary brochure, "A Revolution in Progress." http:www.intel.com/museum/archives/brochures/brochures.htm. Viewed on the Internet in May 2006.

46. Andrew Pollack, "An 'Awesome' Intel Corners Its Market," *New York Times*, April 3, 1988.

47. At long last, after decades of bucking the trend in the industry, Steve Jobs, Apple's creator and CEO, announced in June 2005, that his company would make the transition to Intel microprocessors. John Markoff and Steve Lohr, "Apple Plans to Switch from I.B.M. to Intel for Chips," *New York Times*, June 6, 2005, p. 1.

48. Burgelman, *Strategy*.

49. Pollack, "Awesome."

50. Mary Hayes, "Craig Barrett: This 'Milquetoast' May Yet Be Tapped to Lead Intel Corp.," *San Jose Business Journal*, May 17, 1993. The characterization of Barrett as a "milquetoast" could not be further off the mark.

51. Intel *Annual Report*, 1989.

52. Burgelman, *Strategy*, pp. 142–144.

53. Jon Van, "Intel, Motorola Square Off in Capital Chip Rivalry: Newest Devices Promise More Capacity, Speed," *Washington Post*, April 11, 1989.

54. Louise Kehoe, "PC Chip That Packs a Mainframe Punch," *Financial Times* (London), April 12, 1989.

55. David Olmos, "Intel Introduces Computer Chip Twice as Fast as 80386," *Los Angeles Times*, April 11, 1989.

56. Author interview with Andy Grove, July 4, 2005.

57. John Markoff, "Intel Introduces High-Speed Computer Chip," *New York Times*, April 11, 1989.

58. Terry Costlow, "Users Chip In at Intel's 486 Launch: Standing Room Only at Comdex," *Electrical Engineering Times,* April 17, 1989.

59. Burgelman, *Strategy,* pp. 140–141. Estridge, a champion of the personal computer, died with his wife in the crash of a Delta Airlines flight trying to land during a thunderstorm in Dallas on August 2, 1985. Carroll, *Blues,* p. 80.

60. Author interview with Andy Grove, July 4, 2005.

61. Reports at Intel.

62. Mark Twain got such a kick out of this statement that he had Pudd'nhead Wilson make it in his novel by that name. Burgelman, *Strategy,* p. 159. Harold C. Livesay, *Andrew Carnegie and the Rise of Big Business* (New York: Longman, 2000)

63. Burgelman, *Strategy,* pp. 144–145. According to Webopedia, Cyrix was founded in 1988. It was acquired by National Semiconductor in 1997 and then by VIA in 1999. http://www.webopedia.com/TERM/C/Cyrix.html. Viewed on the Internet on June 11, 2005.

64. Burgelman, *Strategy,* p. 210.

65. Grove to Moore, "Guess What—No Disasters This Week!" November 7, 1986. Document in author's possession.

66. See Andrew Grove, "What Can Be Done, Will Be Done," *Forbes ASAP,* December 2, 1996.

67. "The future on schedule" is a phrase coined by historian Daniel J. Boorstin.

13. Intel Inside

1. Leslie Berlin, *The Man Behind the Microchip: Robert Noyce and the Invention of Silicon Valley* (New York: Oxford University Press, 2005), pp. 290–291.

2. Berlin, *Man Behind the Microchip,* p. 291. This not quite Berlin's interpretation of Grove's remark.

3. See David Needle, "Is Grove Behind Apple Chip Switch?" InternetNews.com, June 10, 2005. http://www.internetnews.com/bus-news/article.php/3512066. Viewed on the Internet on June 13, 2004.

4. Berlin, *Man Behind the Microchip,* pp. 305.

5. Intel *Annual Report,* 1990.

6. Kahn, CEO of the Borland software company, was thus quoted in 1992. Kathleen Wiegner, "The Empire Strikes Back," *Upside,* June, 1992.

7. Intel *Annual Report,* 1990.

8. Author interview with Dennis Carter, Mountain View, California, June 16, 2004.

9. Author interview with Dennis Carter, Mountain View, California, June 16, 2004.

10. Author interview with Dennis Carter, Mountain View, California, June 16, 2004.

11. Author interview with Dennis Carter, Mountain View, California, June 16, 2004.

12. Author interview with Dennis Carter, Mountain View, California, June 16, 2004.

13. Author interview with Andy Grove, July 4, 2005.

14. For these observations and for an excellent picture of the "Red X" advertisement, see Intel Twenty-fifth Anniversary Brochure, *Defining Intel: 25 Years/25 Events* (Intel Corporation, 1993) pp. 27–29, http://www.intel.com/museum/archives/brochures/brochures.htm. Viewed on the Internet on July 20, 2005.

15. Grove to Moore, "While You Were Gone (and having fun in glorious Japan)," June 9, 1989. Document in author's possession.

16. Burgelman, *Strategy,* p. 142.

17. Burgelman, *Strategy,* p. 142.

18. Don Clark, "Intel Lawyer Commands Chip War," *San Francisco Chronicle,* June 28, 1993.

19. I am indebted to my colleague Professor Al Silk for this observation.

20. Author interview with Dennis Carter; Mountain View, California, June 6, 2004.

21. For ingredient branding, see Donald G. Norris, "Ingredient Branding: A Strategy Option with Multiple Beneficiaries, *Journal of Consumer Marketing,* 9, 3 (Summer 1992); idem, " 'Intel Inside': Branding a Component in a Business Market," *Journal of Business & Industrial Marketing,* 8, 3 (1993); R. Venkatesh and Vijay Mahajan, "Products with Branded Components: An Approach for Premium Pricing and Partner Selection," *Marketing Science,* 16, 2 (1997); and Kalpesh Kaushik Desai and Kevin Lane Keller, "The Effects of Ingredient Branding Strategies on Host Brand Extendibility," *Journal of Marketing,* 66, 1 (January 2002).

22. For the Tylenol story, see Richard S. Tedlow with Wendy K. Smith, "James Burke: A Career in American Business" Harvard Business School Cases (A) (389-177) and (B) (390-030), rev. October 20, 2005, with the accompanying video (Boston: HBS Publishing).

23. Author interview with Dennis Carter, Mountain View, California, June 6, 2004.

24. For the technical differences between the 286 and the 386, see Crawford and Gelsinger, *80386,* passim, and especially pp. 683–684.

25. Michael Slater, "AMD Ends 386 Monopoly; AMD Shows—but Does Not 'Announce'—Fully Static Design," *Microprocessor Report,* November 28, 1990.

26. Slater, "386 Monopoly."

27. Burgelman, *Strategy,* p. 142.

28. See "Intel Sues AMD over 386 Trademark," *Microprocessor Report,* October 17, 1990, and Don Clark, "Intel Loses Chip Trademark Rights," *San Francisco Chronicle,* March 2, 1991.

29. A picture of an advertisement with this slogan can be found in Gary D. Fackler, ed., *Intel Leads Quarterly,* Q4, '96, p. 19.

30. Author interview with Dennis Carter, Mountain View, California, June 6, 2004.

31. Author interview with Craig R. Barrett, Intel RNB, Santa Clara, California, January 14, 2004.

32. Author interview with Dennis Carter, Mountain View, California, June 6, 2004.

33. Burgelman, *Strategy,* pp. 142–143.

34. Author interviews with various Intel executives—who will remain nameless in this note—and with Dennis Carter, Mountain View, California, June 6, 2004.

35. Intel *Annual Report,* 1991. Donald Norris, a marketing professor at Miami University of Ohio, published an article on ingredient branding in an academic journal in 1992 that did not even mention Intel Inside. Donald G. Norris, "Ingredient Branding: A Strategy with Multiple Beneficiaries," *Journal of Consumer Marketing,* 9, 3 (Summer 1992). The following year, he published another article on the same topic. This one featured Intel Inside, illustrating that the importance and unique-

ness of this campaign had penetrated the academy. Donald G. Norris, "'Intel Inside': Branding a Component in a Business Market," *Journal of Business & Industrial Marketing*, 8, 1 (1993).

36. D. L. Klesken, et al., "Intel Corp.—Company Report," Prudential-Bache Securities, January 28, 1991.
37. Klesken, "Intel."
38. Klesken, "Intel."
39. Intel *Annual Report*, 1991.
40. Klesken, "Intel."
41. Intel *Annual Report*, 1991.

14. "We Almost Killed the Company"

1. For the creation of NEC's V series, see John W. Wilson, "A Trial with More at Stake Than a Copyright," *BusinessWeek*, June 9, 1986.
2. Author interview with Grove, July 4, 2005, and email to author from Terri L. Murphy, May 23, 2006.
3. Burgelman, *Strategy*, pp. 156–157.
4. Wikipedia, "Instruction Set," http://en.wikipedia.org/wiki/Instruction_set. Viewed on the Internet on July 7, 2005.
5. Winn L. Rosch, "Calculated RISC," *PC/Computing*, December 1, 1988.
6. http://www.minuteclinic.com/. Viewed on the Internet on July 15, 2005. I am grateful to my colleague, Professor Clayton Christensen of the Harvard Business School, for bringing this company to my attention.
7. This quotation is courtesy of Dr. Mark Ellenbogen.
8. David A. Patterson and John L. Hennessy, *Computer Organization and Design: The Hardware/Software Interface* (San Mateo, CA: Morgan Kaufmann, 1998); http://www.stanford.edu/dept/president/biography/. Viewed on the Internet on July 8, 2005; Burgelman, *Strategy*, pp. 146–147.
9. Robert Ristelhueber, "Motorola, Intel Push Defensive Measures," *Electronic News*, February 5, 1990.
10. Bob Francis, "What's Taking the Risk out of RISC?" *Datamation*, January 15, 1990.
11. John C. Dvorak and Jim Seymour, "John C. Dvorak vs. Jim Seymour," *PC/Computing*, February 1, 1990.
12. Dvorak and Seymour, "Dvorak vs. Seymour."
13. See above, Chapter 12, note 46.
14. Dvorak and Seymour, "Dvorak vs. Seymour."
15. Dvorak and Seymour, "Dvorak vs. Seymour"; John Markoff, "Computer Chip Starts Angry Debate," *New York Times*, September 28, 1989.
16. See p. 245.
17. Markoff, "Debate."
18. Peter H. Lewis, "The Executive Computer; Can the Old Processing Technology Beat Back a Challenge?" *New York Times*, February 25, 1990.
19. Trotsky's famous description of the fate of the Mensheviks.

20. Burgelman, *Strategy*, p. 147.
21. Burgelman, *Strategy*, p. 147
22. Burgelman, *Strategy*, p. 147
23. Intel *Annual Report*, 1989.
24. Intel *Annual Report*, 1989
25. Burgelman, *Strategy*, p. 147
26. Quoted in Burgelman, *Strategy*, p. 148.
27. Burgelman, *Strategy*, p. 148.
28. Burgelman, *Strategy*, p. 148.
29. Burgelman, *Strategy*, p. 148.
30. Burgelman, *Strategy*, pp, 150–151.
31. "Robert Ristelhuber, "Motorola, Intel Push Defensive Measures," *Electronic News*, February 5, 1990.
32. Burgelman, *Strategy*, p. 151; author interview with Dennis Carter, Mountain View, California, July 7, 2005.
33. Burgelman, *Strategy*, p. 151.
34. Sean Maloney, executive vice president and general manager, Intel Mobility Group, used this phrase at the Harvard Business School Global Leadership Forum in London on June 22, 2005.
35. Lewis, "The Executive Computer."
36. The phrase is Dennis Carter's. Author interview with Dennis Carter, Mountain View, California, July 7, 2005.
37. Author interview with Dennis Carter, Mountain View, California, July 7, 2005. Author interview with D. Craig Kinnie, Hillsboro, Oregon, October 4, 2005.
38. Burgelman, *Strategy*, p. 153.
39. Burgelman, *Strategy*, p. 152.
40. Burgelman, *Strategy*, p. 153.
41. Author interview with Andy Grove, July 4, 2005.
42. See especially pp. 103–111.
43. Grove, *Paranoid*, p. 106.
44. Grove, *Paranoid*, p. 107.
45. Grove, *Paranoid*, pp. 107–108.
46. Grove, *Paranoid*, pp. 108–114.

15. Cultivating the Creosote Bush

1. A. J. Neff et al., "Intel Corporation—Company Report [Transcript]," Bear, Stearns & Co., July 22, 1991; author interview with Paul Otellini, Intel RNB, Santa Clara, California, July 14, 2005.
2. Grove, SLRP presentation, 1991. Document in author's possession.
3. Grove, SLRP presentation, 1992. Document in author's possession.
4. Burgelman, *Strategy*, p. 152.
5. Burgelman, *Strategy*, p. 152.
6. Grove, SLRP presentation, 1992.

7. Michael Slater, "Intel Loses 386 Trademark," *Microprocessor Report*, March 20, 1991.

8. Grove, SLRP presentation, 1991.

9. A. S. Grove, "Thoughts on the Marketing Inflection Point," July 13, 1992. Document in author's possession.

10. Email, Carter to author, November 21, 2005; email, Grove to author, November 22, 2005.

11. Author interview with Karen Alter, Palo Alto, California, December 14, 2005.

12. Email, Grove to author, July 16, 2005.

13. Grove, SLRP presentation, 1992.

14. Grove was the "father" of this particular TLA. It "was forgotten at birth," he told me, perhaps with a touch of wistfulness. Email, Grove to author, July 16, 2005.

15. Grove, SLRP presentation, 1992.

16. Burgelman, *Strategy*, p. 175.

17. Quoted in Burgelman, *Strategy*, p. 171.

18. Grove, SLRP presentation, 1992.

19. CRSP, Datastream, Moody's Industrial Manual, *Fortune*.

20. John Wharton, "Strategic Product Rescheduling: What's the Real Reason for Pentium's Late Release?" *Microprocessor Report*, March 29, 1993.

21. These are all taken from Grove's SLRP presentation, 1992. ACE stands for "Advanced Computing Environment." This is one TLA not invented at Intel.

22. Grove, SLRP presentation, 1992. Grove Papers.

23. Intel *Annual Report*, 1992.

24. Carsten left Intel in 1987 to join a venture capital firm. Don Clark, "Jack Carsten: Key Vice President Leaving Intel Corp.," *San Francisco Chronicle*, December 15, 1987.

25. Author interview with Andy Grove, July 4, 2005.

26. Burgelman, *Strategy*, p. 281. Gelbach has apparently come to dislike Grove, as I discovered in a rather unpleasant encounter. I have no idea why.

27. Burgelman, *Strategy*, p. 280–281; author interview with Andy Grove, July 4, 2005.

28. Author interview with Andy Grove, July 4, 2005.

29. Tim Flannery, *The Eternal Frontier: An Ecological History of North America and Its Peoples* (New York: Grove Press, 2001), p. 141.

30. Sir Isaiah Berlin, *Russian Thinkers*, Henry Hardy and Aileen Kelly, eds. (New York: Simon and Schuster, 1953). See above, p. 215.

16. That Championship Season

1. Intel Twenty-fifth Anniversary Brochure, *Defining Intel: 25 Years/25 Events* (Intel Corporation, 1993). http://www.intel.com/museum/archives/brochures/brochures .htm. Viewed on the Internet on July 20, 2005.

2. CRSP, Datastream, Moody's Industrial Manual, *Fortune*.

3. David Kirkpatrick, "Intel Goes for Broke," *Fortune*, May 16, 1994.

4. Kirkpatrick, "Intel."

5. Intel *Annual Report*, 1993. For a somewhat conspiratorial interpretation of the timing

of the Pentium release, see John Wharton, "Strategic Product Rescheduling: What's the Real Reason for Pentium's Late Release?" *Microprocessor Report*, March 29, 1993.

6. Jim Forbes, "Motorola Tries to Outmarket Pentium," *HTM News*, July 1993.

7. Jim Forbes, "Motorola Tries to Outmarket Pentium," *HTM News*, July 1993.

8. Robin McKie, *The Nasdaq Stock Market International Magazine*, n.d., 1993, clipping in Intel archives.

9. Kirkpatrick, "Intel."

10. For Sculley's account of how he migrated from Pepsi to Apple, see John Sculley, *Odyssey: Pepsi to Apple . . . A Journey of Adventure, Ideas, and the Future* (New York: Harper and Row, 1987). For Jobs's recruitment of Sculley, see pp. 56–91. For the firing of Jobs, see pp. 312–317.

11. Michael S. Malone, *Infinite Loop: How the Most Insanely Great Computer Company Went Insane* (New York: Doubleday, 1999), p. 455; Jeffrey S. Young and William L. Simon, *iCon: Steve Jobs, the Greatest Second Act in the History of Business* (New York: Wiley, 2005).

12. A graduation address is an impossible assignment which Jobs handled in an outstanding fashion. "'You've Got to Find What You Love,' Jobs Says," *Stanford Report*, June 14, 2005. http://news-service.stanford.edu/news/2005/june15/jobs-061505.html. Viewed on the Internet on August 26, 2005.

13. Frederic Golden, "Other Maestros of the Micro," *Time*, January 3, 1983.

14. Jay Cocks, "The Updated Book of Jobs," *Time*, January 3, 1983.

15. Carroll, *Blues*, p. 157.

16. Carroll, *Blues*, p. 153. The "central casting" remark is from Irving Shapiro, an IBM director who was formerly CEO of DuPont.

17. Carroll, *Blues*, p. 161.

18. Carroll, *Blues*, p. 339.

19. Carroll, *Blues*, p. 346.

20. Carroll, *Blues*, p. 355.

21. New York: Times Books, 1993.

22. Ferguson and Morris, *Wars*, p. xiii.

23. Carroll, *Blues*, p. 351.

24. Louis V. Gerstner Jr., *Who Says Elephants Can't Dance? Inside IBM's Historic Turnaround* (New York: HarperBusiness, 2002), p. 66.

25. Jim Carlton and Laurie Hays, "Power Play: New Computer Chip Hits Desktop Market with Intel in Its Sights—IBM, Apple, Motorola Stake Billions on the PowerPC; Fate Lies in the Software—a Secret Deal with Microsoft," *Wall Street Journal*, March 9, 1994.

26. Tim Clark in *Advertising Age*, February 7, 1994.

27. Lisa L. Spiegelman in *Investor's Business Daily*, April 28, 1994.

28. See Edgar H. Schein et al., *DEC Is Dead, Long Live DEC* (San Francisco: Berrett-Koehler, 2003).

29. Carlton and Hays, "Power Play."

30. Lee Gomes, "Setting Up a Challenge to Intel," *San Jose Mercury News*. For ACE, see p. 278 above.

31. *San Jose Mercury News*, April 10, 1991.

32. Peter Petre, "America's Most Successful Entrepreneur," *Fortune*, October 27, 1986.

33. Author interview with Sean Maloney, Intel RNB, Santa Clara, California, January 12, 2004.

34. Author interview with Dennis Carter, Mountain View, California, June 16, 2004.

35. Andy Grove to Craig R. Barrett (by way of Grove's administrative assistant, Karen Thorpe), June 4, 1993. Document in author's possession.

36. Gerstner, *Elephants*, p. 52.

37. Stratford Sherman, "Andy Grove: How Intel Makes Spending Pay Off," *Fortune*, February 22, 1993.

38. Carroll, *Blues*, p. 159.

39. Email, Gerstner to author, July 6, 2005.

40. Alan Rieper, "Intel (INTC): Still Undervalued," Morgan Stanley U.S. Investment Research, August 27, 1993.

41. These observations are taken from Sean Maloney's presentation at the Harvard Business School's Global Leadership Forum in London in June 2005.

42. Grove to Barrett, "Events of the Week," June 14, 1993. Document in author's possession.

43. Grove to Barrett, "Events of the Week," June 14, 1993.

44. Grove to Barrett, "Events of the Week," June 14, 1993.

17. The Buck Stopped There: Bill Gates and Andy Grove

1. Stephen Manes and Paul Andrews, *Gates: How Microsoft's Mogul Reinvented an Industry—And Made Himself the Richest Man in America* (New York: Simon and Schuster, 1994), p. 440.

2. Manes and Andrews, *Gates*, pp. 15–16.

3. Manes and Andrews, *Gates*, p. 51.

4. Manes and Andrews, *Gates*, p. 16.

5. Manes and Andrews, *Gates*, p. 34–35.

6. Manes and Andrews, *Gates*, p. 26.

7. Manes and Andrews, *Gates*, p. 29.

8. Manes and Andrews, *Gates*, p. 58.

9. Manes and Andrews, *Gates*, p. 78.

10. Manes and Andrews, *Gates*, p. 3.

11. Manes and Andrews, *Gates*, p. 3.

12. "The Forbes Four Hundred," *Forbes*, October 16, 1995; "The Forbes Four Hundred," *Forbes*, October 14, 1996.

13. Manes and Andrews, *Gates*, p. 361.

14. http://www.microsoft.com/presspass/exec/steve/default.mspx. Viewed on the Internet on September 1, 2005.

15. Manes and Andrews, *Gates*, p. 62.

16. This point was made to me by Sheryl Sandberg, vice president global online sales and operations, Google, Mountain View, California, August 31, 2005.

17. Manes and Andrews, *Gates*, p. 65.

18. Manes and Andrews, *Gates*, pp. 51–64.
19. Manes and Andrews, *Gates*, p. 66.
20. Manes and Andrews, *Gates*, p. 76.
21. Manes and Andrews, *Gates*, p. 84.
22. Manes and Andrews, *Gates*, p. 82.
23. Manes and Andrews, *Gates*, p. 103.
24. Manes and Andrews, *Gates*, p. 42.
25. Judge Thomas Penfield Jackson, "Findings of Fact," United States District Court for the District of Columbia, Civil Actions Nos. 98-1232 and 98-1233. http://www.analitica.com. Viewed on the Internet on August 30, 2005.
26. Manes and Andrews, *Gates*, p. 120.
27. Manes and Andrews, *Gates*, p. 93.
28. Manes and Andrews, *Gates*, pp. 164–165, 175–176.
29. Robert Watts, "Microsoft's Ballmer Vows to 'Kill' Google," *Sunday Telegraph* (London), September 4, 2005.
30. Brent Schlender, "A Conversation with the Lords of Wintel," *Fortune*, July 8, 1996.
31. Intel built a series of small computers called Intellec beginning in 1973, the purpose of which was to aid in the development of the company's microprocessors. The Intellec series of computers were not intended to be mass-marketed. The operating system for the Intellec was called ISIS. Microsoft sold a version of COBOL (Common Business-Oriented Language) to Intel for ISIS in 1978. http://www.old-computers.com. Viewed on the Internet on September 9, 2005. Manes and Andrews, *Gates*, p. 124.
32. Grove, *Paranoid*, p. 159.
33. Author interview with Andy Grove, September 7, 2005.
34. Author interview with Andy Grove, September 7, 2005.
35. Manes and Andrews, *Gates*, p. 196.
36. Schlender, "Wintel."
37. Journalist Paul Carroll has written that IBM was offered the opportunity to purchase only 10 percent of Microsoft, not 30 percent. Even at that, the magnitude of its error in not doing so runs into many billions of dollars. *Blues*, p. 119.
38. Manes and Andrews, *Gates*, p. 302.
39. Manes and Andrews, *Gates*, p. 306.
40. Manes and Andrews, *Gates*, pp. 301–307.
41. Carroll, *Blues*, p. 107.
42. Manes and Andrews, *Gates*, pp. 190–191.
43. Manes and Andrews, *Gates*, p. 191.
44. Carroll, *Blues*, pp. 90–91.

18. Wintel

1. Email, author to Grove and Grove to author, November 18, 2005. Author interview with Andy Grove, Los Altos Hills, California, September 7, 2005. Email to author from Terri L. Murphy, May 23, 2006.
2. David B. Yoffie, Ramon Casadesus-Masanell, and Sasha Mathu, "Wintel (A): Co-

operation or Conflict?" Harvard Business School Case No. 704-419, rev. March 16, 2004 (Boston: HBS Publishing), p. 8.

3. "Motorola, an Intel competitor, had recently developed the 68K microprocessor for servers running UNIX. Intel had the 286 processor that ran DOS and early versions of Windows, but lacked a UNIX offering. Intel decided to work with Microsoft to optimize XENIX, a UNIX-based operating system. A problem arose when Microsoft decided to pull out and wanted to reclaim the intellectual property it had contributed." Yoffie et al., "Wintel (A)," p. 8.

4. Author interview with Andy Grove, September 7, 2005.

5. Author interview with Andy Grove, September 7, 2005.

6. For Gibbons, see http://www.venture-concept.com. Viewed on the Internet on September 11, 2005.

7. Author interview with Andy Grove, September 7, 2005.

8. Author interview with Andy Grove, September 7, 2005.

9. That is the word used to describe the dinner by Yoffie et al. in the Wintel (A) case, p. 8. David B. Yoffie is the Max and Doris Starr Professor of International Business Administration at the Harvard Business School, where he is an expert on strategy and technology. He has been a member of Intel's board of directors since 1989 and is at this writing the lead independent director on Intel's board of directors. He has worked with Grove for a decade and a half.

10. Author interview with Andy Grove, September 7, 2005.

11. Author interview with Andy Grove, September 7, 2005.

12. Author interview with Andy Grove, September 7, 2005.

13. Schlender, "Wintel."

14. Schlender, "Wintel."

15. David B. Yoffie, "Microsoft in 2002," Harvard Business School Teaching Note, No. 702-459, February 19, 2002 (Boston: HBS Publishing), p. 7.

16. Michael G. Rukstad and David B. Yoffie, "Microsoft in 2002," Harvard Business School Case No. 702-411 (Boston: HBS Publishing), August 30, 2005, p. 1.

17. Yoffie, "Microsoft in 2002, p. 4.

18. Ken Auletta, *World War 3.0: Microsoft vs. the U.S. Government, and the Battle to Rule the Digital Age* (New York: Random House, 2001).

19. The estimate of $60 for the operating system is from Yoffie, "Microsoft in 2002," p. 4.

20. Richard S. Tedlow, *Giants of Enterprise: Seven Business Innovators and the Empires They Built* (New York: HarperBusiness, 2001), p. 57.

21. See above, pp. 278 and 287. Recall that ACE is an acronym for Advanced Computing Environment.

22. David B. Yoffie, "Wintel (A), (B), (C), (D), (E), (F)," Teaching Note, Harvard Business School Teaching Note No. 5-704-464, November 30, 2005 (Boston: HBS Publishing), p. 4.

23. Schlender, "Wintel."

24. http://www.perseus.tufts.edu/herakles/cerberus.html. Viewed on the Internet on September 12, 2005.

25. Yoffie, "Wintel," Teaching Note, p. 2.

26. See above, p. 307.

27. Yoffie, et al., "Wintel (A)," p. 3.

28. Yoffie et al., "Wintel (A)." p. 3.

29. Yoffie et al., "Wintel (A)," p. 11.

30. Yoffie et al., "Wintel (A)." p. 11.

31. Yoffie et al., "Wintel (A)," p. 12.

32. John Lettice, "Gates Memos Show How Microsoft Puts Screws on Intel," *The Register*, November 10, 1998. http://www.theregister.co.uk. Viewed on the Internet on September 15, 2005. See also John Lettice, "Intel Writes Lousy Software, Says Gates," *The Register*, November 9, 1998. Viewed on the Internet on September 16, 2005, and Louise Kehoe and Richard Wolffe, "Intel Testimony a 'Blip on the Screen of Our Relationship,'" *Financial Times*, November 13, 1998.

33. Schlender, "Wintel."

34. Schlender, "Wintel."

35. This conversation is reported in Schlender, "Wintel."

36. Steve McGeady, "The Lessons of Antitrust: A Case Study." Presentation to Stanford University Computer Systems Laboratory EE380 Colloquium, January 31, 2001. http://www.stanford.edu/class/ee380. Viewed on the Internet on September 17, 2005.

37. Grove, *Paranoid*, p. 18.

19. The Pentium Launch: Intel Meets the Internet

1. Intel *Annual Report*, 1994, p. 6.

2. Intel *Annual Report*, 1983, p. 2.

3. Intel *Annual Report*, 1993, n.p.

4. For a technical discussion of the Pentium, see "Advanced Computer Architecture," http://www.laynetworks.com. Viewed on the Internet on September 20, 2005.

5. Jon Stokes, "The Pentium: An Architectural History of the World's Most Famous Desktop Processor (Part I)," July 11, 2004. http://arstechnica.com/articles/paedia/cpu/pentium-1.ars/1. Viewed on the Internet on September 20, 2005.

6. Stratford Sherman, "The New Computer Revolution," *Fortune*, June 14, 1993.

7. See above, p. 255. This wisecrack resonated. David Kirkpatrick used it in his *Fortune* article on Intel, "Intel Goes for Broke," May 16, 1994.

8. See above, p. 259.

9. Mark L. Edelstone and Jay P. Deahna, "Intel Corp.: Company Update," Prudential Securities, July 29, 1994.

10. Kirkpatrick, "Intel."

11. Professor Nicely's email is reproduced verbatim in Jerry Useem and Joseph L. Badaracco, Jr., "comp.sys.intel: The Internet and the Pentium Chip Controversy (A)," Harvard Business School Case No. 395-246, rev. June 11, 1996 (Boston: HBS Publishing), pp. 5–6. For Professor Nicely's reflections on the flaw a decade after the event, see Thomas R. Nicely, "P*ntium FDIV flaw," http://www.trnicely.net/pentbug/pentbug.html. Viewed on the Internet on May 17, 2006.

12. Unseem and Badaracco, "comp.sys.intel (A)," p. 3.

13. Robert D. Hof, "The 'Lurking Time Bomb' of Silicon Valley," *BusinessWeek*, December 19, 1994.

14. Useem and Badaracco, "comp.sys.intel (A)," p. 2.

15. Useem and Badaracco, "comp.sys.intel (A)," p. 3.

16. Ray Weiss, "Megaprocessor Integrates 386 Elements, Exploits RISC Techniques," *Electronic Engineering Times*, April 17, 1989.

17. Useem and Badaracco, "comp.sys.intel (A)."

18. Useem and Badaracco, "comp.sys.intel (A)," p. 6

19. I am grateful to my colleague Professor Julio Rotemberg for this explanation.

20. http://www.trnicely.net/pentbug/pentbug.html. Viewed on the Internet on May 17, 2006.

21. The above material is from Useem and Badaracco, "comp.sys.intel (A)," p. 3.

22. Grove, *Paranoid*, p. 12.

23. See Robert H'obbes' Zakon, "Hobbes' Internet Timeline v8.1," http://www.zakon. org. Viewed on the Internet on September 21, 2005.

24. Richard S. Tedlow, *The Watson Dynasty: The Fiery Reign and Troubled Legacy of IBM's Founding Father and Son* (New York: HarperBusiness, 2003), p. 3. The television was demonstrated by RCA.

25. Useem and Badaracco, "comp.sys.intel (A)," pp. 5–6.

26. Jerry Useem and Joseph L. Badaracco, Jr., "comp.sys.intel: The Internet and the Pentium Chip Controversy (B)," Harvard Business School Case No. 395-247, rev. June 11, 1996 (Boston: HBS Publishing), p. 3.

27. Tony Thomas, Rudy Behlmer, and Clifford McCarty, *The Films of Errol Flynn* (New York: Citadel Press, 1969), p. 40.

28. Useem and Badaracco, "comp.sys.intel (A)," pp. 11–12.

29. Useem and Badaracco, "comp.sys.intel (A)," p. 13.

30. Andrew S. Grove, COMDEX presentation, November 16, 1994. Text in author's possession.

31. Brenda Borovoy, "Culture Clashes: The Role of Intel in the Pentium Flap," p. 9. Document in author's possession. This is an unpublished paper written by Brenda Borovoy for a course at Stanford on "Science and Technology in Silicon Valley," taught by Professor Timothy Lenoir, May 3, 1995. Mrs. Borovoy, wife of Intel's first chief counsel, Roger Borovoy, asked her friend Eva Grove whether it would be okay to interview Andy for this paper. Eva was skeptical. When Brenda went to see Andy at his home, he was at first rather frosty, to say the least.

32. Grove, *Paranoid*, pp. 12–13.

33. Grove, *Paranoid*, p. 11.

34. Grove, *Paranoid*, p. 13.

35. Useem and Badaracco, "comp.sys.intel (A)," pp. 13–14.

36. Useem and Badaracco, "comp.sys.intel (A)," pp. 13–14.

37. Grove, *Paranoid*, p. 13. For a timeline charting the rise in Internet discussion of the Pentium, see Useem and Badaracco, "comp.sys.intel (A)," p. 29.

38. Grove's posting is reproduced in part in Useem and Badaracco, "comp.sys.intel (A)," pp. 23–24.

39. Grove, *Paranoid*, p. 13.

40. Useem and Badaracco, "comp.sys.intel (B)," pp. 1–2.
41. Tim Clark, "IBM, Compaq Edging Away from Intel Chips: PowerPC Called Force Behind Big Blue's Move," *Advertising Age*, February 7, 1994.
42. T. R. Reid, "It's a Dangerous Precedence [*sic*] to Make the Pentium Promise," *Washington Post*, December 26, 1994.
43. Useem and Badaracco, "comp.sys.intel (B)," pp. 1–2.
44. Author interview with Karen Alter, Palo Alto, California, December 14, 2005.
45. Louis V. Gerstner Jr., *Who Says Elephants Can't Dance?: Inside IBM's Historic Turnaround* (New York: HarperBusiness, 2002).
46. Gerstner, *Elephants*, p. 236.
47. Grove, *Paranoid*, pp. 14–15.
48. See Grove, *Paranoid*, pp. 11–23.
49. Richard S. Tedlow, "The Education of Andy Grove," *Fortune*, December 12, 2005.
50. Useem and Badaracco, "comp.sys.Intel (B)," p. 3.
51. Grove, *Paranoid*, pp. 15–16.
52. Useem and Badaracco, "comp.sys.intel (B)," p. 14.
53. Reproduced in Useem and Badaracco, "comp.sys.intel (B)," p. 14.
54. Grove, *Paranoid*, p. 16.
55. Borovoy, "Culture Clashes," p. 15.
56. Useem and Badaracco, "comp.sys.intel (B)," p. 18.
57. Intel *Annual Report*, 1994, p. 1.
58. Intel *Annual Report*, 1994, p. 1, 14.
59. Author interview with Andy Grove, July 4, 2005.
60. Reid, "Pentium Promise."
61. T. R. Reid, "Doing Penance for Defending the Pentium Chip," *Washington Post*, February 6, 1995.
62. Grove, *Paranoid*, p. 17.
63. Grove, *Paranoid*, p. 19.
64. Grove, *Paranoid*, p. 19.
65. Grove, *Paranoid*, p. 19.
66. See above, p. 283.
67. Joel Brinkley and Steve Lohr, *U.S. v. Microsoft* (New York: McGraw-Hill, 2001), p. 6.
68. Brinkley and Lohr, *Microsoft*, p. 6.
69. Auletta, *World War 3.0*, p. 218.
70. Thomas K. Landauer, *The Trouble with Computers: Usefulness, Usability, and Productivity* (Cambridge, MA: MIT Press, 1995), p. 354.
71. This information was provided to me by a former student of mine, Michael Dearing, currently a consultant in Silicon Valley and formerly senior vice president and general merchandise manager, eBay. Email, September 23, 2005.
72. Jonathan Weber, "How 'Paranoia' Has Helped Intel Rise to the Top," *Los Angeles Times*, November 25, 1996.
73. Tedlow, "Education."
74. The identity of the executive in question is unclear. It may have been Jean-Claude Rivet (Andy Grove presentation to Intel Digital Health Summit, Marriott Hotel, Santa Clara, California, November 14, 2005, and e-mails to author from Terri L. Murphy,

May 30, 2006, and May 2, 2007), Jean-Claude Cornet (e-mail to author from Mike Richmond, January 20, 2007, or Bill Davidow (e-mail to author from Jodelle A. French, April 30, 2007).

75. Tedlow, "Education."

76. Author interview with Karen Alter, Palo Alto, California, December 14, 2005.

77. Author interview with Karen Alter, Palo Alto, California, December 14, 2005.

78. Author interview with Karen Alter, Palo Alto, California, December 14, 2005.

79. Useem and Badaracco, "comp.sys.intel (B)," p. 20.

80. Geoff Lewis and Robert D. Hof, "The World According to Andy Grove," *BusinessWeek*, 1994 special issue, *The Information Revolution*, p. 76. See also Grove's essay, "A High-Tech CEO Updates His Views on Managing and Careers," *Fortune*, September 18, 1995.

81. Grove, *Paranoid*, pp. 165–184.

82. For Intel's current view on the Pentium flaw, see "FDIV Replacement Program," http://support.intel.com/support/processors/Pentium/fdiv. Viewed on the Internet on November 18, 2005.

20. Life Is What Happens While You're Making Other Plans

1. Author interview with Karen Thorpe, Intel RNB, Santa Clara, California, June 17, 2004.

2. The workings of CompuServe were explained to me by Michael Dearing, September 21, 2005.

3. "CompuServe," Wikipedia, http://en.wikipedia.org/wiki/compuserve. Viewed on the Internet on September 29, 2005.

4. This observation was made to me by Martha McFadden, MD.

5. Author interview with Karen Thorpe, Intel RNB, Santa Clara, California, June 17, 2004.

6. Author interview with Leslie Michelson, Prostate Cancer Foundation, Santa Monica, California, January 12, 2006.

7. Author interview with Karen Thorpe, Intel RNB, Santa Clara, California, June 17, 2004.

8. My father, the late Samuel L. Tedlow, made this statement.

9. Author interview with Professor Robert Burgelman, Stanford Graduate School of Business, Stanford University, California, January 19, 2006.

10. Author interview with Andy Grove, September 7, 2005.

11. Andy Grove, "Taking On Prostate Cancer," *Fortune*, May 13, 1996.

12. John W. Huey Jr., "Our Reluctant Author Comes Forward," *Fortune*, May 13, 1996.

13. Author interview with Karen Thorpe, Intel RNB, Santa Clara, California, June 17, 2004.

14. Author interview with Karen Thorpe, Intel RNB, Santa Clara, California, June 17, 2004.

15. See p. 55.

16. Author interview with Karen Thorpe, Intel RNB, Santa Clara, California, June 17, 2004.

17. Author phone conversation with Andy Grove, October 2, 2004.
18. Author interview with Eva Grove, Anaheim, California, February 2, 2005.
19. Author interview with Dr. Peter R. Carroll, Mount Zion Medical Center, University of California at San Francisco, June 17, 2004.
20. Bethany McLean and Peter Elkind, *The Smartest Guys in the Room: The Amazing Rise and Scandalous Fall of Enron* (New York: Portfolio, 2003).
21. Email, Bethany McLean to author, November 2, 2005.
22. Email, Andy Grove to author, May 3, 2006.

21. The Darwinian Device

1. Address by President Nelson Mandela at the opening ceremony of TELECOM 95, the 7th World Telecommunications Forum and Exhibition, Geneva, Switzerland, October 3, 1995, http://www.anc.org.za/ancdocs/history/mandela/1995/sp951003.html. Viewed on the Internet on October 9, 2005. Among his many awards, Mandela in 2001 became the first living person to be made an honorary citizen of Canada. The first time that award was bestowed was posthumously to Raoul Wallenberg, the Swede who gave his life to rescue Hungarian Jews from the Nazis in 1944 and 1945. There is today a park dedicated to Wallenberg on the banks of the Danube on the Pest side of Budapest, not too far from Grove's childhood home in Kiraly Street. Also in 2001, Mandela was diagnosed with prostate cancer. Born in 1918, he is still alive at this writing.
2. "TELECOM 95 at a Glance," http://www.itu.int/TELECOM/wt95/fctsfigs.html. Viewed on the Internet on October 10, 1995.
3. DVD and text of this presentation in author's possession.
4. The computer as a Darwinian device by virtue of its adaptability was also a theme of Grove's keynote speech at the COMDEX trade show in 1994. Andrew S. Grove, COMDEX presentation, November 16, 1994. Text in author's possession.
5. Grove's comment from *Business Day,* CNN, September 24, 1996, 6:00–7:00 a.m.
6. "[R]each and richness" is a phrase used above on page 360. My use of the words "richness" and "reach" is suggested by Philip Evans and Thomas S. Wurster, *Blown to Bits: How the New Economics of Information Transforms Society* (Boston: Harvard Business School Press, 2000).
7. DVD of this presentation in author's possession.
8. Burgelman, *Strategy,* p. 264.
9. DVD of COMDEX '91 in author's possession.
10. Email, Grove to author, July 17, 2005.
11. Burgelman, *Strategy,* p. 264.
12. Burgelman, *Strategy,* p. 264.
13. Burgelman, *Strategy,* p. 266.
14. Burgelman, *Strategy,* p. 267.
15. Burgelman, *Strategy,* p. 268.
16. Burgelman, *Strategy,* p. 269.
17. Burgelman, *Strategy,* p. 269.
18. Burgelman, *Strategy,* p. 269.

19. Burgelman, *Strategy,* p. 266.
20. The phrase is Daniel J. Boorstin's from *The Americans: The Democratic Experience* (New York: Vintage, 1974), pp. 89–164.
21. Burgelman, *Strategy,* p. 280.
22. Intel *Annual Report,* 1996.
23. Burgelman, *Strategy,* p. 280.
24. Intel *Annual Report,* 1995, pp. 2–3.
25. David Wu and Christopher Garland, "Intel Corporation," The Chicago Corporation, October 2, 1995.
26. Intel *Annual Report,* 1995, p. 2.
27. Intel *Annual Report,* 1995, p. 13.
28. Intel *Annual Report,* 1995, pp. 3, 32.
29. See p. 189 above.
30. See especially AnnaLee Saxenian, *Advantage,* passim.

22. "What Are You Paranoid About These Days?"

1. Intel, *Annual Report,* 1996, p. 3.
2. Intel *Annual Report,* 1996, p. 1.
3. Intel *Annual Report,* 1996, p. 17.
4. Kirk Ladendorf, "The Book on Intel," *Austin American-Statesman,* September 23, 1996.
5. Krishna Shankar, "Intel Corp.," Donaldson, Lufkin & Jenrette, June 11, 1997, p. 2.
6. Alan Rieper, "Intel Corporation," Deutsche Morgan Grenfell, March 10, 1997, p. 20.
7. Intel *Annual Report,* 1996.
8. See p. 235.
9. Intel *Annual Report,* 1996.
10. Intel *Annual Report,* 1996.
11. Intel *Annual Report,* 1996.
12. Gregory L. Mischou, "Intel Corporation," Alex Brown, September 17, 1996, p. 18. Italics added.
13. Mischou, "Intel Corporation," p. 18.
14. Vincent J. Glenski, "Intel," Rodman & Renshaw, July 8, 1996, p. 14.
15. Author interview with Paul Otellini, Intel RNB, Santa Clara, California, February 2, 2004.
16. In addition to the Mischou and Glenski reports, see Krishna Shankar, "Intel Corp.," Donaldson, Lufkin & Jenrette, August 20, 1996.
17. See pp. 162–163 above.
18. Grove, *Paranoid,* p. xi.
19. Rubin left Currency/Doubleday on July 31, 1997, to become "a writer, consultant, and lecturer on leadership trends." http://www.fastcompany.com/events/realtime/sandiego/hrubin.html and http://www.inc.com/articles/1998/08/15616.html. Viewed on the Internet on November 26, 2005.
20. See above p. 121. See also Richard S. Tedlow, "The Education of Andy Grove," *Fortune,* December 12, 2005.

21. See pp. 224–229 and 270–271.

22. See p. 150.

23. Grove, *Paranoid*, p. 123.

24. Grove, *Paranoid*, p. 127.

25. Grove, *Paranoid*, p. 145.

26. Grove, *Paranoid*, pp. 35, 193.

27. In conversation with the author, August 5, 2005.

28. Grove, *Paranoid*, p. 22.

29. Grove, *Paranoid*, p. 132.

30. Grove, *Paranoid*, pp. 121–164.

31. Burgelman, *Strategy*, p. 208.

32. Grove, *Paranoid*, p. 130.

33. See above, pp. 340–349.

34. Andy Grove presentation to Intel Digital Health Summit, Marriott Hotel, Santa Clara, California, November 14, 2005, and email to author from Terri L. Murphy, May 30, 2006.

35. Tedlow, "Education." See also Burgelman, *Strategy*, p. 22: "This implies a first strategic leadership imperative: Leaders who want to maintain control of their company's destiny must embrace strategy and learn to think strategically while in action. They must learn to 'engage, then see.'" Following that last phrase, Burgelman refers us to a footnote in which he explains, "Discussing key aspects of his strategic approach to major battles, Napoleon supposedly said, '*On s'engage, et puis on voit*' (We engage, and then we see)," p. 402, n. 36.

36. Grove, *Paranoid*, p. 140.

37. Grove, *Paranoid*, p. 150.

38. Grove, "Prostate," p. 68.

39. Grove, *Paranoid*, p. 151.

40. Grove, *Paranoid*, p. 152.

41. Author interview with Andy Grove, November 18, 2005.

42. Author interview with Andy Grove, November 18, 2005.

43. Jackson, *Intel*, p. 129. Author interview with Roger S. Borovoy, Los Altos, California, January 3, 2006.

44. Burgelman, *Strategy*, p. 157.

45. Burgelman, *Strategy*, p. 157.

46. Burgelman, *Strategy*, p. 158.

47. See above, p. 249.

48. Grove, *Paranoid*, p. 145.

49. Video Monitoring Services of America, *Bloomberg Business News*, PBS, September 10, 1996.

50. Video Monitoring Services of America, WBBR-AM, Bloomberg News Radio, September 10, 1996, 6:12 a.m.

51. Richard Lacayo, "The *Time* 25: You've Read About Who's Influential, But Who Has the Power?" *Time*, June 17, 1996.

52. Video Monitoring Services of America, *Good Day Sacramento*, KPWB-TV, September 10, 1996, 8:00–9:00 a.m.

53. Grove, *Paranoid*, p. xi.

54. In conversation with the author.

55. Alistair Munro, *Delusional Disorder: Paranoia and Related Illnesses* (Cambridge: Cambridge University Press, 1999), p. xii.

56. Video Monitoring Services of America, *Fox Morning News*, WTTG-TV, Washington, DC, September 11, 1991, 6:30–9:00 a.m. The word "paranoid" was being used with regard to Intel as early as 1983. See above, p. 182. The word appeared again in *Fortune* combined with "greed" and "avarice" in 1994. See above, p. 320.

57. Video Monitoring Services of America, *Bloomberg Business News*, PBS, September 10, 1996, 6:30–7:00 a.m.

58. Alfred P. Sloan Jr., *My Years with General Motors* (Garden City, NY: Doubleday, 1964).

59. Tedlow, "Education." See also Robert J. Samuelson, "Ghosts That Still Haunt GM," *Washington Post*, November 30, 2005.

60. Video Monitoring Services of America, *Nightly Business Report*, PBS, September 10, 1996, 6:30–7:30 p.m.

61. Video Monitoring Services of America, *Good Day Sacramento*, KPWB-TV, September 10, 1996, 8:00–9:00 a.m.

62. James W. Michaels, "Only the Paranoid Survive," *Forbes*, October 7, 1996.

63. *InterNight*, MSNBC, September 24, 1996, 8:00–9:00 p.m.

64. Joshua Cooper Ramo, "Man of the Year: A Survivor's Tale," *Time*, December 29, 1997.

65. Adam M. Brandenburger and Barry J. Nalebuff, "Inside Intel," *Harvard Business Review*, November–December 1996.

66. Kirk Ladendorf, "The Book on Intel," *Austin American-Statesman*, September 23, 1996.

67. Video Monitoring Services of America, *Before Hours*, CNN, September 24, 1996, 7:00–8:00 a.m.

68. Video Monitoring Services of America, *Bloomberg Business News*, PBS, September 10, 1996, 6:30–7:00 a.m.

69. *InterNight*, MSNBC, September 24, 1996, 8:00–9:00 p.m.

70. Grove, *Paranoid*, p. 185.

71. Grove, *Paranoid*, pp. 193–194; email, Grove to author, December 3, 2005.

72. Grove, *Paranoid*, p. 191.

73. Grove, *Paranoid*, p. 194.

74. See above, p. 149.

75. Grove, *Paranoid*, p. 194.

76. Grove, *Paranoid*, p. 196–197.

77. Grove, *Paranoid*, pp. 197–198.

23. The Year of Decision

1. Video Monitoring Services of America, *Fresh Air*, KQED-FM, San Francisco, November 19, 1996, 1:00–2:00 p.m.

2. Krishna Shankar, "Intel Corp.," Donaldson, Lufkin & Jenrette, June 11, 1997.

3. John M. Geraghty, "Intel Corporation," Credit Suisse First Boston Corporation, July 29, 1997, pp. 4–5.

NOTES TO PAGES 388–396 / 525

4. Ken Pearlman, "Intel Corp.," CIBC Oppenheimer, November 10, 1997.
5. Alan Rieper, "Intel Corporation," Deutsche Morgan Grenfell, March 10, 1997, p. 18.
6. See pp. 211 and 379–380.
7. "ASG's Europe Trip, 1/25–2/9/97." Document in author's possession.
8. Confidential communication, December 12, 2005.
9. Berlin, *Man Behind the Microchip*, p. 225.
10. Leslie Berlin forcefully made this point at a session of the Business History Seminar at the Harvard Business School on November 7, 2005.
11. Email, Grove to Moore, December 5, 2005, and email to author from Terri L. Murphy, May 23, 2006.
12. Grove himself says of Moore, who was seven and a half years older than him: "He was a father figure." Ramo, "Tale."
13. Author interview with Andy Grove, Stanford University, July 4, 2005, and email to author from Terri L. Murphy, May 23, 2006.
14. Ramo, "Tale."
15. *InterNight*, MSNBC, September 24, 1996, 8:00–9:00 p.m.
16. Author interview with Denise Amantea, Menlo Park, California, December 26, 2005.
17. Wikipedia, "Person of the Year," http://en.wikipedia.org/wiki/Man_of_the_Year. Viewed on the Internet on December 9, 2005.
18. Tim Jackson, *Inside Intel: Andy Grove and the Rise of the World's Most Powerful Chip Company* (New York: Penguin, 1997).
19. See above, p. 61.
20. Walter Isaacson, "Man of the Year: The Microchip Is the Dynamo of a New Economy . . . Driven by the Passion of Intel's Andrew Grove," *Time*, December 29, 1997.
21. Email, Grove to author, December 3, 2005.
22. See above, pp. 370–371.
23. See Isaacson, "Dynamo."
24. Berlin, *Man Behind the Microchip*, p. 244. Author interview with Leslie Berlin, Palo Alto, California, January 26, 2006.
25. Berlin, *Man Behind the Microchip*, p. 245.
26. For Moore's one comment "indicating even the slightest resentment of Noyce's visibility," see Berlin, *Noyce*, p. 244. Eva Grove's remarks are from author interview with Eva Grove, Anaheim, California, February 2, 2005.
27. See above, pp. 240–241. Berlin, *Noyce*, p. 248. The article on Noyce that had appeared half a year earlier was Victor K. McElheny, "Dissatisfaction as a Spur to Career," *New York Times*, December 15, 1976.
28. Berlin, *Man Behind the Microchip*, p. 248.
29. Author interview with Andy Grove, December 26, 2005 and email to author from Terri L. Murphy, May 23, 2006.
30. Brent Schlender, "Inside Andy Grove's Latest Crusade: Intel's Chairman Is out to Change the Way Companies Are Governed. His First Job: Change Himself," *Fortune*, August 23, 2004.

24. "Frozen in Silicon"

1. Elizabeth Corcoran, "Intel CEO Andy Grove Steps Aside; A Founding Father of Silicon Valley," *Washington Post*, March 27, 1998.
2. Corcoran, "CEO."
3. See above, p. xiii.
4. Berlin, *Man Behind the Microchip*, p. 200.
5. Andrew Grove, "What Can Be Done, Will Be Done," *Forbes ASAP*, December 2, 1996.
6. Author interview with Craig R. Barrett, January 14, 2004, Intel RNB, Santa Clara, California.
7. Ramo, "Tale."
8. Berlin, *Man Behind the Microchip*, p. 283.
9. See above, p. 350.
10. I am indebted to Michael Dearing for this formulation.
11. Clayton Christensen, *The Innovator's Dilemma: When New Technologies Cause Great Firms to Fail* (Boston: Harvard Business School Press, 1997).
12. Corcoran, "CEO."
13. Ramo, "Tale."
14. "Silicon Genesis: An Oral History of Semiconductor Technology." Interview with Federico Faggin, Los Altos Hills, California, March 3, 1995. http://library.stanford.edu/depts./harsg/histsci/silicongenesis/faggin-htb.html. Viewed on the Internet on December 17, 2004. Rob Walker worked in both engineering and marketing at Fairchild and Intel. He was a founder of LSI Logic and presently runs a consulting firm in Menlo Park. http://silicongenesis.stanford.edu/transcripts/walker.htm. Viewed on the Internet on December 29, 2005.
15. Corcoran, "CEO."
16. See above, p. 190.
17. See above, p. 78.
18. Elizabeth Corcoran, "Intel's Blunt Edge: At 60, Andy Grove Is Still Learning, Looking Ahead and Speaking His Mind," *Washington Post*, September 8, 1996.
19. Corcoran, "Intel's Blunt Edge."
20. Burgelman, *Strategy*, pp. 262–270.
21. Ramo, "Tale."
22. Quoted in Corcoran, "CEO."
23. Anthony Ramirez, "New Doubts About the Pentium Chip Give Intel a Marketing Problem with Few Precedents," *New York Times*, December 14, 1994.
24. Author interview with Andy Grove, December 26, 2005.
25. Author interview with Karen Alter, December 14, 2005, Palo Alto, California.
26. Email, David Yoffie to author, June 3, 2006.
27. Vikas Kumar, "The Original Mr. Chip," *Economic Times* (India), June 2, 2005.
28. Kumar, "Mr. Chip."
29. See, for example, Kevin Maney, "Grove Sets New Course with Intel," *USA Today*, March 27, 1998. Some newspapers reported that the move surprised the computer industry, but they were clearly not well informed. The *Chicago Tribune* ran a story the headline of which was "Grove Steps Down as Chairman, CEO As Intel Stands at Critical Juncture," March 27, 1998. Grove was stepping down as CEO but not as chairman.

30. Maney, "New Course."
31. Kevin Maney, "Now's the Right Time for Change, Intel's Grove Says," *USA Today,* March 27, 1998.
32. Maney, "Right Time."
33. Maney, "New Course."
34. Kirk Ladendorf, "Intel Architect Andrew Grove to Step Down as CEO: Visionary Leader Will Take More Long-Term View as Chairman; President Will Take CEO Job," *Austin American-Statesman,* March 28, 1998.
35. Ladendorf, "Grove to Step Down."
36. Louise Kehoe, "Not a Grove in the Valley," *Financial Times* (London), March 28, 1998.
37. See above, p. 189.
38. Richard L. Brandt, "Attila the Hungarian," *UPSIDE Today,* March 27, 1998.
39. Sandy Plunkett, "Hello Mr. Chips," *Business Review Weekly,* March 30, 1998.
40. Jon Bigness, "Grove Steps Down as Chairman, CEO As Intel Stands at Critical Juncture," *Chicago Tribune,* March 27, 1998.
41. Steve Lohr, "Intel's Chief Steps Down After 11 Years," *New York Times,* March 27, 1998.
42. Tish Williams, "Boy the Media Were Happy to Take Intel Down a Few Notches Last Week . . . ," *UPSIDE Today,* April 6, 1998.
43. In conversation with author, and email from Terri L. Murphy, May 23, 2006.
44. Burgelman, *Strategy,* p. 280.
45. Burgelman, *Strategy,* p. 280.
46. Burgelman, *Strategy,* p. 280.
47. Burgelman, *Strategy,* p. 280.
48. Statement of Andy Grove in class at the Stanford Graduate School of Business, December 7, 2005, and email to author from Terri L. Murphy, May 30, 2006.
49. See above, p. 396.
50. Ken Auletta, *World War 3.0: Microsoft vs. the U.S. Government, and the Battle to Rule the Digital Age* (New York: Random House, 2001), p. 74.
51. http://www.oracle.com/corporate/about.html. Viewed on the Internet on December 24, 2005.

25. Andy Grove—Ex-CEO

1. Grove had received an honorary doctor of science degree from his alma mater, the City College of New York, in 1985, and an honorary doctor of engineering degree from the Worcester Polytechnic Institute in 1989.
2. "NINDS Parkinson's Disease Information Page," http://www.ninds.nih.gov/disorders/parkinsons_disease/parkinsons_disease.htm. Viewed on the Internet on December 31, 2005.
3. "NINDS Parkinson's Disease Information Page."
4. Amy Farabaugh, PhD, Massachusetts General Hospital Depression Clinical and Research Program, Boston, Massachusetts, brought the following reference to my attention: J. R. Slaughter, K. A. Slaughter, D. Nichols, S. E. Holmes, and M. P. Martens, "Prevalence, Clinical Manifestations, Etiology, and Treatment of Depression in Parkinson's Disease," *J Neuropsy Clin Neurosc* 13, 2 (2001), pp. 187–196.

5. Email, Andy Grove to author, June 5, 2006.

6. Cliff Edwards, "Inside Intel: Paul Otellini's Plan Will Send the Chipmaker into Uncharted Territory. And Founder Andy Grove Applauds the Shift," *BusinessWeek*, January 9, 2006.

26. "I Think That Experiment Has Been Run"

1. Author interview with Steven P. Jobs, Apple Computer Headquarters, Cupertino, California, February 14, 2005.

2. Author interview with Craig Kinnie, Hillsboro, Oregon, October 4, 2005.

3. Author interview with James E. Burke, New Brunswick, New Jersey, April 1, 1989.

4. I am indebted to my colleague at the Harvard Business School, Professor Rakesh Khurana, for these observations. The "institutionalization of charisma" is, according to Professor Khurana, a concept developed by the German sociologist Max Weber.

5. Brent Schlender, "Inside Andy Grove's Latest Crusade: Intel's Chairman Is Out to Change the Way Companies Are Governed. His First Job: Change Himself," *Fortune*, August 23, 2004.

6. Author interview with Roger S. Borovoy, Los Altos, California, January 3, 2006.

7. "Caltech Receives $600 Million in Two Gifts: Largest Academic Donation in History," http://pr.caltech.edu/events/moore/. Viewed on the Internet on May 3, 2006.

8. See, for example, Berlin, *The Man Behind the Microchip: Robert Noyce and the Invention of Silicon Valley* (New York: Oxford University Press, 2005), p. 227.

9. See, for example, Carol J. Loomis, "Dinosaurs?" *Fortune*, May 3, 1993.

10. Author discussion with Andy Grove, Flea Street Café, Menlo Park, California, February 10, 2006.

11. Intel *Annual Report*, 1997, p. 26.

12. Thomas R. Navin and Marion V. Sears, "The Rise of a Market for Industrial Securities, 1887–1902" *Business History Review*, 29, 2 (June 1955).

13. Quoted in Matthew Josephson, *The Robber Barons: The Great American Capitalists, 1861–1901* (New York: Harcourt, Brace & World, 1934), p. 343.

14. Alfred D. Chandler Jr., *The Visible Hand: The Managerial Revolution in American Business* (Cambridge, MA: Harvard University Press, 1977).

15. For the classic statement of the separation of ownership from management leading to ambiguity in the control of the corporation, see Adolf A. Berle and Gardiner C. Means, *The Modern Corporation and Private Property* (New York: MacMillan, 1932). See also Thomas K. McCraw, "In Retrospect: Berle and Means," *Reviews in American History*, 18, 4 (December 1990), pp. 578–596. For the demographic makeup (including gender) of top executives of the large corporation in the United States, see Walter A. Friedman and Richard S. Tedlow, "Statistical Portraits of American Business Elites: A Review Essay," *Business History*, 45, 4 (October 2003), pp. 89–113; Richard S. Tedlow, Kim Eric Bettcher, and Courtney A. Purrington, "The Chief Executive Officer of the Large American Industrial Corporation in 1917," *Business History Review*, 77, 4 (Winter 2003), pp. 687–701; and Richard S.

Tedlow, "The Chief Executive Officer of the Large American Industrial Corporation." Manuscript in author's possession.

16. Tedlow, *Dynasty*, pp. 196–197, 230.

17. See above, p. 181.

18. The Business Roundtable, *Statement on Corporate Governance and American Competitiveness*, March 1990.

19. The Business Roundtable, *Statement on Corporate Governance*, September 1997. http://www.businessroundtable.org/pdf/11.pdf. Viewed on the Internet in May 2006. These two statements were brought too my attention by my colleague at the Harvard Business School, Professor Rakesh Khurana.

27. Andy and the Board

1. "NASDAQ," http://en.wikipedia.org/wiki/NASDAQ. Viewed on the Internet on February 15, 2006.

2. http://www.nasdaq.com/newsroom/news/pr2005/ne_section05_044.stm. Viewed on the Internet on February 15, 2006.

3. See above, pp. 214–215.

4. Homer, *The Odyssey*, translated by Robert Fagles (New York: Viking, 1996), p. 408. This passage was brought to my attention by Sheldon Roth, MD.

5. Intel *Annual Report*, 1998, p. 1.

6. Intel *Annual Report*, 1998, p. 1

7. Intel *Annual Report*, 1998, pp. 3, 9–11.

8. Intel *Annual Report*, 1998, p. 3.

9. Intel *Annual Report*, 1999, p. 1.

10. Intel *Annual Report*, 1999, p. 1.

11. See, for example, Stephen C. Dube, "Intel Corp.," Wasserstein Perella Securities, January 20, 1999; Andrew J. Neff, "Intel Corporation," Bear, Stearns & Co., May 3, 1999; and Charlie Glavin, "Intel Corporation," Credit Suisse First Boston, November 22, 1999.

12. Intel *Annual Report*, 1999, n.p.

13. "The Challenge of Central Banking in a Democratic Society." Remarks by Chairman Alan Greenspan at the Annual Dinner and Francis Boyer Lecture of the American Enterprise Institute for Public Policy Research, Washington, D.C., December 5, 1996, http://www.federalreserve.gov/boarddocs/speeches/1996/19961205.htm. Viewed on the Internet on February 18, 2006.

28. The Bubble Bursts

1. Intel *Annual Report*, 2000, n.p.

2. Intel *Annual Report*, 2000, p. 1.

3. Intel *Annual Report*, 2000, pp. 3–4.

4. Intel *Annual Report*, 2000, pp. 7–13.

5. Intel *Annual Report,* 2000, p. 6.
6. Intel *Annual Report,* 2000, p. 17.
7. Intel *Annual Report,* 2000, p. 42.
8. Intel *Annual Report,* 1998, p. 38.
9. Author interview with C. Barr Taylor, MD, Stanford University Medical School, Palo Alto, California, January 24, 2006.
10. Email, Grove to author, February 9, 2006.
11. Intel *Annual Report,* 2001, p. 6.
12. Intel *Annual Report,* 2001, pp. 1, 3–8.
13. Intel *Annual Report,* 2001, p. 1.
14. Intel *Annual Report,* 2001, p. 1.
15. Tedlow, *Giants,* pp. 52–56.
16. Tedlow, *Giants,* p. 52.
17. Intel *Annual Report,* 2001, p. 8.
18. Intel *Annual Report,* 2001, p. 2.
19. Intel *Annual Report,* 2001, p. 38.
20. Of the books on the subject, the best is Bethany McLean and Peter Elkind, *The Smartest Guys in the Room: The Amazing Rise and Scandalous Fall of Enron* (New York: Portfolio, 2003).
21. Ken Lay raised a lot of money for George W. Bush, but he did not manage the relationship without error. McLean and Elkind, *Enron,* pp. 86–89.
22. McLean and Elkind, *Enron,* p. 240.
23. McLean and Elkind, *Enron,* p. 86.
24. McLean and Elkind, *Enron,* p. 233.
25. Bethany McLean, "Is Enron Overpriced?" *Fortune,* March 5, 2001.
26. McLean and Elkind, *Enron,* p. 345.
27. McLean and Elkind, *Enron,* p. 405.
28. Dennis K. Beman, Phillip Day, and Henry Sender, "Global Crossing Ltd. Files for Bankruptcy—Telecom-Industry Casualty Hinges Recovery Plan on Lifeline from Asia," *Wall Street Journal,* January 29, 2002.
29. Jake Ulick, "WorldCom's Financial Bomb: From the President On Down, Officials Worried About Investor Confidence Weigh In," *CNN/Money,* June 25, 2002, http://money.cnn.com/2002/06/25/news/worldcom/. Viewed on the Internet on February 23, 2006.
30. Luisa Beltran, "WorldCom Files Largest Bankruptcy Ever: Nation's No. 2 Long-Distance Company in Chapter 11—Largest with $107 Billion in Assets," *CNN/Money,* July 22, 2002, http://money.cnn.com/2002/07/19/news/worldcom_bankruptcy. Viewed on the Internet on February 23, 2006.
31. Derek Caney, "Adelphia Files for Chapter 11 Bankruptcy," *Reuters,* June 25, 2002.
32. "Adelphia," Wikipedia, http://en.Wikipedia.org/wiki/Adelphia. Viewed on the Internet on February 26, 2006.
33. "The Top 25 Managers: L. Dennis Kozlowski," *BusinessWeek,* January 14, 2002.
34. Samuel Maull, "Kozlowski Faces up to 30 Years in Prison," *Associated Press Newswires,* June 18, 2005.

35. Geraldine Fabrikant and David Cay Johnston, "G.E. Perks Raise Issues About Taxes," *New York Times*, September 9, 2002.
36. Geraldine Fabrikant, "G.E. Expenses for Ex-Chief Cited in Filing," *New York Times*, September 6, 2002.
37. Geraldine Fabrikant, "Ex-G.E. Chief Challenges His Wife's Report of Lavish Perks," *New York Times*, September 13, 2002.
38. See the Conference Board Commission on Public Trust and Private Enterprise, *Findings and Recommendations* ("Part 1: Executive Compensation" [September 17, 2002], "Part 2: Corporate Governance" [January 9, 2003], and "Part 3: Audit and Accounting" [January 9, 2003]). In addition to Grove, Petersen, Snow, Larsen, and Volcker, other members included John H. Biggs, former CEO of TIAA-CREF (Teachers Insurance and Annuity Association—College Retirement Equities Fund); John C. Bogle, founder and former chairman of Vanguard Group; Peter M. Gilbert, chief investment officer of Pennsylvania's State Employees' Retirement System; Arthur Levitt Jr., former chairman of the Securities and Exchange Commission; Professor Lynn Sharp Paine of the Harvard Business School; and former senator Warren B. Rudman. It was a blue-ribbon group.
39. Conference Board, Part 1, p. 12.
40. Conference Board, Part 1, p. 13.
41. Conference Board, Part 1, pp. 13–14.
42. Conference Board, Part 1, p. 7.
43. Conference Board, Part 1, p. 7, n. 5.
44. Conference Board, Part 1, p. 14. You can follow the debate in the *Harvard Business Review*. Opposed to expensing stock options is Professor William A. Sahlman, an expert in entrepreneurial finance. See his "Expensing Options Solves Nothing," *Harvard Business Review*, 80, 12 (December 2002). In favor of expensing options are economists Zvi Bodie and Robert C. Merton and an expert in accounting and control, Robert S. Kaplan. See their "For the Last Time: Stock Options Are an Expense," *Harvard Business Review*, 81, 3 (March 2003). Sahlman, Merton, and Kaplan are professors at the Harvard Business School. Brodie is a professor at the Boston University School of Management.
45. Conference Board, Part 1, p. 13.
46. Grove also believed that the Conference Board Commission, because it "is not an accounting body," should not be pronouncing conclusions on this issue. Conference Board, Part 1, p. 14.
47. Intel *Annual Report*, 2002, n.p.
48. Intel *Annual Report*, 2002, n.p.
49. DVD of May 2002 Intel stockholders' meeting. Author's possession.
50. Intel *Annual Report*, 2004, n.p.

29. Outside Intel

1. DVD of May 2002 Intel annual stockholders' meeting. Author's possession.
2. Slides in author's possession.

3. Slide in author's possession.
4. Numerous conversations between author and Grove.
5. Author interview with Dr. J. Michael Bishop, Mount Zion Medical Center, University of California at San Francisco, February 8, 2006.
6. Author interview with Dr. J. Michael Bishop, Mount Zion Medical Center, University of California at San Francisco, February 8, 2006.
7. This is the message of Daniel Boorstin's Pulitzer Prize–winning trilogy *The Americans.*
8. Robert A. Burgelman and Andrew S. Grove with Philip E. Meza, *Strategic Dynamics: Concepts and Cases* (Boston: McGraw-Hill/Irwin, 2006).
9. Dr. J. Michael Bishop at UCSF felt that digitization was inevitable but the costs and the failures of digitization that were being reported by first-class hospitals were matters of major concern to him. Author interview with Dr. J. Michael Bishop, Mount Zion Medical Center, University of California at San Francisco, February 8, 2006.
10. Author interview with Rebekah Saul Butler, January 31, 2006.
11. Grove Foundation, "Board of Directors Meeting: Strategic and Long-Range Planning," August 30, 2005. Document in author's possession.
12. Grove, *Swimming,* p. 290.
13. CCNY (Andy); Hunter (Eva); Berkeley (Andy and Karen); the University of Puget Sound (Robie); and the University of Seattle Law School (Robie).
14. See above, pp. 58–60.
15. Wilcox High School, "Grove Scholars," http://wilcox.ca.compusgrid.net/home/students+in+the+spotlight/2004+-+2005/ Grove+scholars, viewed on the Internet on March 4, 2006; the Grove Foundation School-to-Career Scholarship Program, http://www.grovescholars.org. Viewed on the Internet July 19, 2006. See also Robert A. Burgelman and Philip E. Meza, "Grove Scholars Program: Putting Rungs Back on the Ladder," Stanford Graduate School of Business Case no. SM-144, July 29, 2005.
16. Grove Foundation, "Board of Directors Meeting."

30. Still Swimming

1. Author interview with William Perry, Stanford University, February 3, 2005.
2. Tedlow, *Giants,* p. 57.
3. Homer, *The Odyssey,* trans. Robert Fagles (New York: Viking, 1996), p. 110.
4. Homer, *The Odyssey,* p. 77.
5. Homer, *The Odyssey,* p. 464.
6. Grove, *Swimming,* p. 290.

BIBLIOGRAPHY

In addition to the books, articles, cases, and interviews cited below, this book is based on innumerable private, unpublished, and miscellaneous sources that are too voluminous to list. These include:

- Internal memoranda, private diaries, emails, and other documents that are now in my possession;
- Speeches that I either attended or of which I have recordings;
- Annual reports;
- Reports by securities analysts;
- Business databases, such as Compustat, Investext, Factiva, etc.;
- Numerous Web sites—particularly Intel's, which extensively documents the company's history;
- Many conversations with principals and observers in Silicon Valley, Budapest, and points in between.

Specific information provided by these sources is documented in the endnotes. But those notes, extensive as they are, do not begin to capture the cumulative impact that these sources had on my understanding of Andy Grove, the company he built, and the industry he shaped. The truth is, I lived and breathed this book for three years. A complete bibliography would require a day-by-day listing of my calendar from October 2003 through September 2006.

—RST

Books

Allen, William Sheridan. *The Nazi Seizure of Power: The Experience of a Single German Town, 1930–1935.* Chicago: Quadrangle, 1965.

Anger, Per. *With Raoul Wallenberg in Budapest.* Washington, D.C.: Holocaust Library, 1996.

Arendt, Hannah. *Eichmann in Jerusalem: A Report on the Banality of Evil.* New York: Penguin, 1963.

Aspray, William, ed. *Technological Competitiveness: Contemporary and Historical Perspectives on the Electrical, Electronics, and Computer Industries.* Piscataway, NJ: IEEE Press, 1993.

Auletta, Ken. *World War 3.0: Microsoft vs. the U.S. Government, and the Battle to Rule the Digital Age.* New York: Random House, 2001.

Barrett, Craig R., William D. Nix, and Alan S. Tetelman. *The Principles of Engineering Materials.* Englewood Cliffs, NJ: Prentice Hall, 1973.

Bassett, Ross Knox. *To the Digital Age: Research Labs, Start-Up Companies, and the Rise of MOS Technology.* Baltimore: Johns Hopkins University Press, 2002.

Berle, Adolf A., and Gardiner C. Means. *The Modern Corporation and Private Property.* New York: Macmillan, 1932.

Berlin, Isaiah. *The Hedgehog and the Fox.* New York: Simon & Schuster, 1953.

———. *Russian Thinkers,* edited by Henry Hardy and Aileen Kelly. London: Penguin, 1978.

Berlin, Leslie. *The Man Behind the Microchip: Robert Noyce and the Invention of Silicon Valley.* New York: Oxford University Press, 2005.

Bierman, John. *Righteous Gentile: The Story of Raoul Wallenberg, Missing Hero of the Holocaust.* New York: Viking, 1981.

Boorstin, Daniel J. *The Americans: The Democratic Experience.* New York: Vintage, 1974.

———. *The Republic of Technology: Reflections on Our Future Community.* New York: Harper & Row, 1978.

Borsányi, György. *The Life of a Communist Revolutionary, Béla Kun.* New York: Columbia University Press, 1993.

Braham, Randolph L. *The Destruction of Hungarian Jewry: A Documentary Account.* Vols. 1 and 2. New York: Pro Arte, 1963.

———. *The Holocaust in Hungary: Selected and Annotated Bibliography.* New York: Columbia University Press, 2001.

———. *The Politics of Genocide: The Holocaust in Hungary.* Vols. 1 and 2. New York: Columbia University Press, 1981.

———. *Studies on the Holocaust: Selected Writings.* Vol. 1. New York: Columbia University Press, 2000.

Braun, Ernest, and Stuart Macdonald. *Revolution in Miniature: The History and Impact of Semiconductor Electronics.* Cambridge, England: Cambridge University Press, 1978.

Brinkley, Alan. *American History: A Survey. (Vol. II: Since 1865).* New York: McGraw-Hill, 2003.

Brinkley, Joel, and Steve Lohr. *U.S. v. Microsoft.* New York: McGraw-Hill, 2001.

Browning, Larry D., and Judy C. Shetler. *SEMATECH: Saving the U.S. Semiconductor Industry.* College Station, TX: Texas A&M University Press, 2000.

Bullock, Lord Alan. *Hitler and Stalin: Parallel Lives.* New York: Knopf, 1992.

———. *Hitler: A Study in Tyranny.* New York: Bantam, 1960.

Burant, Stephen R., ed. *Hungary: A Country Study.* Washington, D.C.: Federal Research Division, Library of Congress, 1990. http:lcweb2.loc.gov/frd/cs/hutoc.html (accessed March 4, 2004).

Burgelman, Robert A. *Strategy Is Destiny: How Strategy-Making Shapes a Company's Future.* New York: Free Press, 2002.

———, and Andrew S. Grove, with Philip E. Meza. *Strategic Dynamics: Concepts and Cases.* Boston: McGraw-Hill/Irwin, 2006.

———, Clayton M. Christensen, and Steven C. Wheelwright. *Strategic Management of Technology and Innovation.* New York: McGraw-Hill, 2004.

Caddes, Carolyn. *Portraits of Success: Impressions of Silicon Valley Pioneers.* Palo Alto: Tioga Publishing, 1986.

Carnegie, Dale. *How to Win Friends and Influence People.* New York: Simon & Schuster, 1936.

Carroll, Paul. *Big Blues: The Unmaking of IBM.* New York: Crown, 1993.

Cawelti, John G. *Apostles of the Self-Made Man: Changing Concepts of Success in America.* Chicago: University of Chicago Press, 1969.

Cesarani, David, ed. *Genocide and Rescue: The Holocaust in Hungary, 1944.* New York: Berg, 1997.

Chandler Jr., Alfred D. *Inventing the Electronic Century: The Epic Story of the Consumer Electronics and Computer Industries.* New York: Free Press, 2001.

———. *The Visible Hand: The Managerial Revolution in American Business.* Cambridge, MA: Belknap Press, 1977.

Chandler, Jr., Alfred D., and James W. Cortada. *A Nation Transformed by Information: How Information Has Shaped the United States from Colonial Times to the Present.* New York: Oxford University Press, 2000.

Christensen, Clayton M. *The Innovator's Dilemma: When New Technologies Cause Great Firms to Fail.* Boston: Harvard Business School Press, 1997.

Cole, Tim. *Holocaust City: The Making of a Jewish Ghetto.* New York: Routledge, 2003.

Crawford, John H., and Patrick P. Gelsinger. *Programming the 80386.* San Francisco: Sybex, 1987.

Cusumano, Michael A., and David B. Yoffie. *Competing on Internet Time: Lessons from Netscape and Its Battle with Microsoft.* New York: Free Press, 1998.

———, and Richard W. Selby. *Microsoft Secrets: How the World's Most Powerful Software Company Creates Technology, Shapes Markets, and Manages People.* New York: Simon & Schuster, 1998.

Davidow, William H. *Marketing High Technology: An Insider's View.* New York: Free Press, 1986.

Dawidowicz, Lucy S. *The War Against the Jews, 1933–1945.* New York: Bantam, 1986.

Deák, István, Jan T. Gross, and Tony Judt, eds. *The Politics of Retribution in Europe: World War II and Its Aftermath.* Princeton: Princeton University Press, 2000.

Dell, Michael. *Direct from Dell: Strategies that Revolutionized an Industry.* New York: HarperBusiness, 1999.

Dostoyevsky, Fyodor. *The Brothers Karamazov.* New York: Random House, 1950. (Originally published in 1880.)

Drucker, Peter F. *The Practice of Management.* New York: Harper, 1954.

Eisenach, Jeffrey A., and Thomas M. Lenard, eds. *Competition, Innovation, and the Microsoft Monopoly: Antitrust in the Digital Marketplace.* Boston, MA: Kluwer Press, 1999.

Evans, Philip, and Thomas S. Wurster. *Blown to Bits: How the New Economics of Information Transforms Society.* Boston: Harvard Business School Press, 2000.

Ferguson, Charles H., and Charles R. Morris. *Computer Wars: How the West Can Win in a Post-IBM World.* New York: Times Books, 1993.

Flannery, Tim. *The Eternal Frontier: An Ecological History of North America and Its Peoples.* New York: Grove Press, 2001.

Forester, Tom, ed. *The Microelectronics Revolution: The Complete Guide to the New Technology and Its Impact on Society.* Cambridge, MA: The MIT Press, 1981.

Friedman, Walter A. *Birth of a Salesman: The Transformation of Selling in America.* Cambridge: Harvard University Press, 2004.

Galbraith, John Kenneth. *The Affluent Society.* Boston: Houghton Mifflin, 1998.

Gates, Bill. *Business @ the Speed of Thought: Succeeding in the Digital Economy.* New York: Warner Books, 1999.

———. *The Road Ahead.* New York: Viking Penguin, 1995.

Gawer, Annabelle, and Michael A. Cusumano. *Platform Leadership: How Intel, Microsoft, and Cisco Drive Industry Innovation.* Boston: Harvard Business School Press, 2002.

Gelsinger, Pat. *Balancing Your Family, Faith & Work.* Colorado Springs, CO: Life Journey Publishers, 2003.

Gero, András, and János Poór, eds. *Budapest: A History from Its Beginnings to 1998.* New York: Columbia University Press, 1997.

Gerstner, Louis V., Jr. *Who Says Elephants Can't Dance? Inside IBM's Historic Turnaround.* New York: HarperBusiness, 2002.

Gilbert, Martin. *Churchill: A Life.* London: Heinemann, 1991.

———. *A History of the Twentieth Century, Volume 2: 1933–1951.* New York: William Morrow, 1998.

———. *The Holocaust: A History of the Jews of Europe During the Second World War.* New York: Henry Holt, 1985.

———. *The Righteous: The Unsung Heroes of the Holocaust.* New York: Henry Holt, 2004.

Gilder, George. *Microcosm: The Quantum Revolution in Economics and Technology.* New York: Simon & Schuster, 1989.

Greeley, Horace. *Hints Towards Reform.* New York: Harper and Brothers, 1850.

Grove, Andrew S. *High Output Management.* New York: Vintage, 1995.

———. *One-on-One with Andy Grove: How to Manage Your Boss, Yourself and Your Coworkers.* New York: Penguin, 1987.

———. *Only the Paranoid Survive: How to Exploit the Crisis Points That Challenge Every Company.* New York: Doubleday, 1996.

———. *Physics and Technology of Semiconductor Devices.* New York: Wiley, 1967.

———. *Swimming Across: A Memoir.* New York: Warner, 2001.

Györffy, György. *King Saint Stephen of Hungary.* New York: Columbia University Press, 1994.

Hanson, Dirk. *The New Alchemists: Silicon Valley and the Microelectronics Revolution.* Boston: Little, Brown, 1982.

Hiltzik, Michael A. *Dealers of Lightning: Xerox PARC and the Dawn of the Computer Age.* New York: Harper Business, 1999.

Hitler, Adolf. *Mein Kampf.* Boston: Houghton Mifflin, 1962. (Originally published in 1925.)

Hoensch, Jörg K. *A History of Modern Hungary, 1867–1986.* New York: Longman, 1989.

Hofstadter, Richard. *The Progressive Historians: Turner, Beard, Parrington.* New York: Knopf, 1968.

Homer. *The Odyssey.* Translated by Robert Fagles. New York: Viking, 1996.

Hughes, Thomas P. *American Genesis: A Century of Invention and Technological Enthusiasm, 1870–1970.* New York: Viking Penguin, 1989.

Isselbacher, Kurt J., ed. *Harrison's Principles of Internal Medicine.* New York: McGraw-Hill, 1994.

Jackson, Tim. *Inside Intel: Andy Grove and the Rise of the World's Most Powerful Chip Company.* New York: Penguin, 1997.

Josephson, Matthew. *The Robber Barons: The Great American Capitalists, 1861–1901.* New York: Harcourt, Brace & World, 1934.

Katz, Ralph, ed. *Managing Professionals in Innovative Organizations: A Collection of Readings.* Cambridge, MA: Ballinger, 1988.

Kertész, Imre. *Fatelessness.* Translated by Tim Wilkinson. New York: Vintage, 2004.

Kindleberger, Charles P. *The World in Depression, 1929–1939.* Berkeley: University of California Press, 1986.

Koestler, Arthur. *Darkness at Noon.* New York: Random House, 1941.

Kovács, Imre, ed. *Facts About Hungary.* New York: Hungarian Committee, 1959.

Labaree, Leonard W., Ralph L. Ketcham, Helen C. Boatfield, and Helene H. Fineman, eds. *The Autobiography of Benjamin Franklin.* New Haven: Yale University Press, 1964.

Landauer, Thomas K. *The Trouble with Computers: Usefulness, Usability, and Productivity.* Cambridge, MA: MIT Press, 1995.

Lee, Chong-Moon, William F. Miller, Marguerite Gong Hancock, and Henry S. Rowen, eds. *The Silicon Valley Edge: A Habitat for Innovation and Entrepreneurship.* Stanford, CA: Stanford University Press, 2000.

Lemisch, L. Jesse, ed. *Benjamin Franklin: The Autobiography and Other Writings.* New York: New American Library, 2001.

Leuchtenburg, William E. *A Troubled Feast: American Society Since 1945.* Boston: Little, Brown, 1979.

Levitt, Theodore. *The Marketing Imagination.* New York: Free Press, 1983.

Lindeman, Eduard C., ed. *Basic Selections from Emerson: Essays, Poems and Apothegms.* New York: Mentor, 1954.

Livesay, Harold C. *Andrew Carnegie and the Rise of Big Business.* New York: Longman, 2000.

McCullough, David. *Truman.* New York: Simon & Schuster, 1992.

McCraw, Thomas K. *American Business, 1920–2000: How It Worked.* Wheeling, Illinois: Harlan Davidson, 2000.

————, ed. *Creating Modern Capitalism: How Entrepreneurs, Companies, and Countries Triumphed in Three Industrial Revolutions.* Cambridge, MA: Harvard University Press, 2000.

McDougall, Walter A. *The Heavens and the Earth: A Political History of the Space Age.* Baltimore: Johns Hopkins University Press, 1997.

McLean, Bethany, and Peter Elkind. *The Smartest Guys in the Room: The Amazing Rise and Scandalous Fall of Enron.* New York: Portfolio, 2003.

Mair, George. *The Barry Diller Story: The Life and Times of America's Greatest Entertainment Mogul.* New York: Wiley, 1997.

Malone, Michael S. *The Big Score: The Billion Dollar Story of Silicon Valley.* Garden City, New York: Doubleday, 1985.

————, *Infinite Loop: How the World's Most Insanely Great Computer Company Went Insane.* New York: Doubleday, 1999.

————, *The Microprocessor: A Biography.* New York: Springer-Vellag, 1995.

Manes, Stephen, and Paul Andrews. *Gates: How Microsoft's Mogul Reinvented an Industry—and Made Himself the Richest Man in America.* New York: Simon & Schuster, 1994.

Marks, Susan. *Finding Betty Crocker.* New York: Simon & Schuster, 2005.

Marx, George. *The Voice of the Martians: Hungarian Scientists Who Shaped the 20th Century in the West.* Budapest: Akadémiai Kiadó, 2001.

Marx, Leo. *The Machine in the Garden: Technology and the Pastoral Ideal in America.* New York: Oxford University Press, 1964.

Mnookin, Seth. *Hard News: The Scandals at* The New York Times *and Their Meaning for American Media.* New York: Random House, 2004.

Montgomery, John Flournoy. *Hungary: The Unwilling Satellite.* New York: Devin-Adair Company, 1947. Historical Text Archive, 1996. http://historicaltextarchive.com/books.php?op=viewbook&bookid=7 (accessed April 18, 2004).

Mowery, David C., and Richard R. Nelson, eds. *Sources of Industrial Leadership: Studies of Seven Industries.* Cambridge, England: Cambridge University Press, 1999.

Munro, Alistair. *Delusional Disorder: Paranoia and Related Illnesses.* Cambridge, England: Cambridge University Press, 1999.

Negroponte, Nicholas. *Being Digital.* New York: Vintage Books, 1996.

Nietzsche, Friedrich. *Human, All Too Human: A Book for Free Spirits.* Cambridge, England: Cambridge University Press, 1996.

Packard, David. *The HP Way: How Bill Hewlett and I Built Our Company.* New York: HarperBusiness, 1995.

Pamlényi, Ervin, ed. *A History of Hungary.* London: Collet's, 1975.

Patterson, David A., and John L. Hennessy. *Computer Organization and Design: The Hardware/Software Interface.* San Mateo, CA: Morgan Kaufmann, 1998.

Peter, Laurence J., and Raymond Hull. *The Peter Principle.* New York: William Morrow, 1969.

Porter, Michael E. *Competitive Advantage: Creating and Sustaining Superior Performance.* New York: Free Press, 1985.

Pugh, Emerson W. *Building IBM: Shaping an Industry and Its Technology.* Cambridge, MA: The MIT Press, 1996.

————, *Memories That Shaped an Industry: Decisions Leading to IBM System/360.* Cambridge, MA: The MIT Press, 1986.

Reid, T. R. *The Chip: How Two Americans Invented the Microchip and Launched a Revolution.* New York: Simon & Schuster, 1984.

Rhodes, Richard. *The Making of the Atomic Bomb.* New York: Simon & Schuster, 1986.

Riasanovsky, Nicholas V. *A History of Russia.* New York: Oxford University Press, 1963.

Rifkin, Glenn, and George Harrar. *The Ultimate Entrepreneur: The Story of Ken Olsen and Digital Equipment Corporation.* Rocklin, CA: Prima Publishing, 1990.

Roman, Eric. *The Stalin Years in Hungary.* Lewiston, NY: Edwin Mellen Press, 1999.

————. *Austria-Hungary: The Successor States.* New York: Facts on File, 2003.

Rosenbloom, Richard S., and William J. Spencer, eds. *Engines of Innovation: U.S. Industrial Research at the End of an Era.* Boston: Harvard Business School Press, 1996.

Sakmyster, Thomas. *Hungary's Admiral on Horseback: Miklós Horthy, 1918–1944.* New York: Columbia University Press, 1994.

Saxenian, AnnaLee. *Regional Advantage: Culture and Competition in Silicon Valley and Route 128.* Cambridge, MA: Harvard University Press, 1994.

Schein, Edgar H., Peter S. DeLisi, Paul J. Kampas, and Michael M. Sonduck. *DEC Is Dead, Long Live DEC.* San Francisco: Berrett-Koehler, 2003.

Sculley, John. *Odyssey: Pepsi to Apple . . . A Journey of Adventure, Ideas, and the Future.* New York: Harper & Row, 1987.

Simon, Andrew L., ed. *Admiral Nicholas Horthy, Memoirs.* Safety Harbor, FL: Simon Publications, 2000. http://www.hungarian-history.hu/lib/horthy/horthy.pdf (accessed February 21, 2004).

Sloan, Alfred P., Jr. *My Years with General Motors.* Garden City, NY: Doubleday, 1964.

Smith, Merritt Roe, and Leo Marx. *Does Technology Drive History? The Dilemma of Technological Determinism.* Cambridge, MA: The MIT Press, 1995.

Smolan, Rick, and Jennifer Erwitt. *One Digital Day: How the Microchip Is Changing Our World.* New York: Times Books, 1998.

Snow, C. P. *Variety of Men.* New York: Charles Scribner's Sons, 1967.

Sporck, Charles E., and Richard L. Molay. *Spinoff: A Personal History of the Industry That Changed the World.* Saranac Lake, NY: Saranac Lake Publishing, 2001.

Stark, Tamás. *Hungarian Jews During the Holocaust and After the Second World War, 1939–1949: A Statistical Review.* New York: Columbia University Press, 2000.

Starr, Kevin. *Americans and the California Dream, 1850–1915.* New York: Oxford University Press, 1986.

Stearns, Peter N., ed. *The Encyclopedia of World History.* 6th ed. New York: Houghton Mifflin, 2001.

Sugar, Peter, Péter Hanák, and Tibor Frank, eds. *A History of Hungary.* Bloomington: Indiana University Press, 1990.

Suleiman, Susan Rubin. *Budapest Diary: In Search of the Motherbook.* Lincoln, Nebraska: University of Nebraska Press, 1996.

Sweetman, John. *Balaclava 1854: The Charge of the Light Brigade.* Oxford, England: Osprey Publishing, 2002.

Taylor, A. J. P. *The Habsburg Monarchy, 1809–1918.* London: Hamish Hamilton, 1948.

———. *The Second World War.* New York: Putnam, 1975.

Tedlow, Richard S. *Giants of Enterprise: Seven Business Innovators and the Empires They Built.* New York: HarperBusiness, 2001.

———. *The Watson Dynasty: The Fiery Reign and Troubled Legacy of IBM's Founding Father and Son.* New York: HarperBusiness, 2003.

Thomas, Tony, Rudy Behlmer, and Clifford McCarty. *The Films of Errol Flynn.* New York: Citadel Press, 1969.

Tocqueville, Alexis de. *The Old Regime and the Revolution.* Chicago: University of Chicago Press, 1998.

Toynbee, Arnold J. *The Prospects of Western Civilization.* New York: Columbia University Press, 1949.

Ungváry, Kristián. *Battle for Budapest: One Hundred Days in World War II.* London: Tauris, 2003.

Walton, Sam, with John Huey. *Sam Walton: Made in America, My Story.* New York: Bantam, 1992.

Whitfield, Stephen J. *Into the Dark: Hannah Arendt and Totalitarianism.* Philadelphia: Temple University Press, 1980.

Whyte, William H. *The Organization Man.* New York: Simon & Schuster, 1956.

Wilson, Sloan. *The Man in the Gray Flannel Suit.* New York: Simon & Schuster, 1955.

Woodward, C. Vann. *Origins of the New South, 1877–1913.* Baton Rouge, LA: Louisiana State University Press, 1951.

Yoffie, David B., ed. *Competing in the Age of Digital Convergence.* Boston: Harvard Business School Press, 1997.

———, and Mary Kwak. *Judo Strategy: Turning Your Competitors' Strength to Your Advantage.* Boston: Harvard Business School Press, 2001.

Young, Jeffrey S., and William L. Simon. *iCon: Steve Jobs, the Greatest Second Act in the History of Business.* New York: Wiley, 2005.

Yu, Albert Y. C. *Creating the Digital Future: The Secrets of Consistent Innovation at Intel.* New York: Free Press, 1998.

Doctoral Dissertations

Berlin, Leslie. "Entrepreneurship and the Rise of Silicon Valley: The Career of Robert Noyce, 1956–1990." PhD diss., Stanford University, 2001.

Grove, Andrew S. "An Investigation into the Nature of Steady Separated Flows at Large Reynolds Numbers." PhD diss., University of California, Berkeley, 1963.

Lécuyer, Christophe. "Making Silicon Valley: Engineering, Culture, Innovation, and Industrial Growth, 1930–1970." PhD diss., Stanford University, 1999.

Noyce, Robert. "A Photo-electric Investigation of Surface States on Insulators." PhD diss., Massachusetts Institute of Technology, 1953.

Articles

Abel, Elie. "Out of Hungary—Revolt of the Exiles." *New York Times,* November 25, 1956.

Acrivos, Andreas, D. D. Snowden, A. S. Grove, and E. E. Petersen. "The Steady Separated Flow Past a Circular Cylinder at Large Reynolds Numbers." *Journal of Fluid Mechanics* 21, no. 4 (April 1965).

"Advocates Raise $12 Million for Prostate Cancer Research." *University of California San Francisco Department of Urology Newsletter,* Fall 2001. http://www.ucsfhealth.org/adult/pubs/urology/UCSF_Urology_Fall_2001.pdf (accessed May 23, 2006).

Ager, Susan. "Retirement Game: Knowing When to Quit." *San Jose Mercury News,* November 22, 1982.

Akera, Atsushi. "IBM's Early Adaptation to Cold War Markets: Cuthbert Hurd and His Applied Science Field Men." *Business History Review* 76 (Winter 2002).

Angrist, Stanley W. "Business Book Shelf: Big Is Beautiful." *Wall Street Journal,* February 13, 1998.

Aspray, William. "The Intel 4004 Microprocessor: What Constituted Invention." *IEEE Annals of the History of Computing* 19, no. 3 (July–September 1997).

Bak, János. "The Late Medieval Period, 1382–1526." In *A History of Hungary,* edited by Peter F. Sugar, Péter Hanák, and Tibor Frank. Bloomington: Indiana University Press, 1990.

Barnett, John. "$1 Billion in Sales: Compaq Milestone Takes Just Five Years." *Houston Chronicle,* February 2, 1998.

Beltran, Luisa. "WorldCom Files Largest Bankruptcy Ever: Nation's No. 2 Long-Distance Company in Chapter 11—Largest With $107 Billion in Assets." *CNN/Money,* July 22, 2002. http://money.cnn.com/2002/07/19/news/worldcom_bankruptcy/ (accessed February 23, 2006).

Berlin, Leslie R. "Robert Noyce and the Rise and Fall of Fairchild Semiconductor, 1957–1968." *Business History Review* 75, no. 1 (Spring 2001).

Berman, Dennis K., Phillip Day, and Henny Sender. "Global Crossing Ltd. Files for Bankruptcy—Telecom-Industry Casualty Hinges Recovery Plan on Lifeline from Asia." *Wall Street Journal,* January 29, 2002.

Bigness, Jon. "Grove Steps Down as Chairman, CEO as Intel Stands at Critical Juncture." *Chicago Tribune,* March 27, 1998.

Bodie, Zvi, Robert C. Merton, and Robert S. Kaplan. "For the Last Time: Stock Options Are an Expense." *Harvard Business Review* 81, no. 3 (March 2003).

Bonamici, Kate. "Grove of Academe." *Fortune,* December 12, 2005.

Borhi, László. "Rollback, Liberation, Containment or Inaction? U.S. Policy and Eastern Europe in the 1950s." *Journal of Cold War Studies* 1, no. 3 (Fall 1999).

Braham, Randolph L. "The Holocaust in Hungary: A Retrospective Analysis." *Genocide and Rescue: The Holocaust in Hungary, 1944,* edited by David Cesarani. New York: Berg, 1997.

Brandenburger, Adam M., and Barry J. Nalebuff. "Inside Intel." *Harvard Business Review* 74, no. 6 (November–December 1996).

Brandt, Richard L. "Attila the Hungarian." *UPSIDE Today,* March 27, 1998.

Bresnahan, Timothy F. "New Modes of Competition: Implications for the Future Structure of the Computer Industry." *Competition, Innovation, and the Microsoft Monopoly: Antitrust in the Digital Marketplace,* edited by Jeffrey A. Eisenach and Thomas M. Lenard. Boston: Kluwer Press, 1999.

Brodie, Evelyn. "The Master Mechanic Behind Intel's High-Tech Success." *Times* (London), February 11, 1993.

Brown, Hannah. "Intel CEO Resigns." *New York Post,* March 27, 1998.

Bylinsky, Gene. "How Intel Won Its Bet on Memory Chips." *Fortune,* November 1973.

Caney, Derek. "Adelphia Files for Chapter 11 Bankruptcy." *Reuters,* June 25, 2002.

Carlton, Jim, and Laurie Hays. "Power Play: New Computer Chip Hits Desktop Market With Intel in Its Sights—IBM, Apple, Motorola Stake Billions on the PowerPC; Fate Lies in the Software—A Secret Deal with Microsoft." *Wall Street Journal,* March 9, 1994.

Chandler, Alfred D., Jr. "The Information Age in Historical Perspective." *A Nation Transformed by Information: How Information Has Shaped the United States from Colonial Times to the Present,* edited by Alfred D. Chandler Jr. and James W. Cortada. New York: Oxford University Press, 2000.

Chase, Marilyn. "Problem-Plagued Intel Bets on New Products, IBM's Financial Help." *Wall Street Journal,* February 4, 1983.

"City College Gives Andrew Grove '60T a Hero's Welcome Home." *Alumnus* (CCNY), Winter 1999.

Clark, Don. "Intel Lawyer Commands Chip War." *San Francisco Chronicle,* June 29, 1993.

———. "Intel Loses Chip Trademark Rights." *San Francisco Chronicle,* March 2, 1991.

———. "Jack Carsten: Key Vice President Leaving Intel Corp." *San Francisco Chronicle,* December 15, 1987.

Clark, Tim. "IBM, Compaq Edging Away from Intel Chips; PowerPC Called Force Behind Big Blue's Move." *Advertising Age,* February 7, 1994.

Cocks, Jay. "The Updated Book of Jobs." *Time,* January 3, 1983.

Collins, Luke. "Intel Story Spotlights True Business Culture." *Electronics Times,* November 10, 1997.

"Compaq Sales Reach $1.2 Billion in Record Five Years; Sales Double, Net Income Triples in 1987." *PR Newswire,* February 1, 1988.

Corcoran, Elizabeth. "Intel CEO Andy Grove Steps Aside; A Founding Father of Silicon Valley." *Washington Post,* March 27, 1998.

———. "Intel's Blunt Edge; At 60, Andy Grove Is Still Learning, Looking Ahead and Speaking His Mind." *Washington Post,* September 8, 1996.

Costlow, Terry. "Users Chip in at Intel's 486 Launch: Standing Room Only at Comdex." *Electrical Engineering Times,* April 17, 1989.

Deák, István. "Could the Hungarian Jews Have Survived?" *New York Review of Books* 29, no. 1, February 4, 1982.

———. "A Fatal Compromise? The Debate Over Collaboration and Resistance in Hungary." *The Politics of Retribution in Europe: World War II and Its Aftermath,* edited by István Deák, Jan T. Gross, and Tony Judt. Princeton: Princeton University Press, 2000.

———. "Holocaust Views: The Goldhagen Controversy in Retrospect." *Central European History* 30 (June 1997): 295–307.

———. "Stranger in Hell." *New York Review of Books,* September 25, 2003.

———. "Survivor in a Sea of Barbarism." *New York Review of Books,* April 8, 1999.

Deal, Bruce E. and A. S. Grove. "General Relationship for the Thermal Oxidation of Silicon." *Journal of Applied Physics* 36, no. 12 (December 1965).

————, E. H. Snow, and C. T. Sah. "Observation of Impurity Redistribution During Thermal Oxidation of Silicon Using the MOS Structure." *Journal of the Electrochemical Society* vol. 112 (1965).

————. "Recent Advances in the Understanding of the Metal-Oxide-Silicon System." *American Institute of Mining, Metallurgical and Petroleum Engineers, Transactions* 233 (1965).

Deal, Bruce E., M. Sklar, A. S. Grove, and E. H. Snow. "Characteristics of the Surface-State Charge (Qss) of Thermally Oxidized Silicon." *Journal of the Electrochemical Society* 114, no. 3 (March 1967).

————, E. H. Snow, and A. S. Grove. "Properties of the Silicon Dioxide-Silicon System." *Semiconductor Products and Solid State Technology* 9, no. 11 (1966).

Desai, Kalpesh Kaushik, and Kevin Lane Keller. "The Effects of Ingredient Branding Strategies on Host Brand Extendibility." *Journal of Marketing* 66, no. 1 (January 2002).

Dvorak, John C., and Jim Seymour. "John C. Dvorak vs. Jim Seymour." *PC/Computing*, February 1, 1990.

Edwards, Cliff. "Can CEO Craig Barrett Reverse the Slide?" *BusinessWeek*, October 15, 2001.

————. "Inside Intel: Paul Otellini's Plan Will Send the Chipmaker into Uncharted Territory. And Founder Andy Grove Applauds the Shift." *BusinessWeek*, January 9, 2006.

"8 Leave Shockley to Form Coast Semiconductor Firm." *Electronic News*, October 21, 1957.

Emerson, Ralph Waldo. "Self Reliance." *Basic Selections from Emerson: Essays, Poems and Apothegms*, edited by Eduard C. Lindeman. New York: Mentor, 1954.

Fabrikant, Geraldine. "Ex-G.E. Chief Challenges His Wife's Report of Lavish Perks." *New York Times*, September 13, 2002.

————. "G.E. Expenses for Ex-Chief Cited in Filing." *New York Times*, September 6, 2002.

————, and David Cay Johnston. "G.E. Perks Raise Issues About Taxes." *New York Times*, September 9, 2002.

Feinberg, Mortimer R., and Aaron Levenstein. "Retirement as the Pinnacle of Your Career." *Wall Street Journal*, November 23, 1981.

Fitzgerald, D. J., and A. S. Grove. "Mechanisms of Channel Current Formation in Silicon p-n Junctions." *Physics of Failure in Electronics Symposium*, Vol. 4, *Rome Air Development Center, Rome, NY* (1965).

————. "Radiation-Induced Increase in Surface Recombination Velocity of Thermally Oxidized Silicon Structures." *Proceedings of the IEEE* 54, no. 11 (November 1966).

————. "Surface Recombination in Semiconductors." *Surface Science* 9, no. 2 (1968).

"The Five Best-Managed Companies." *Dun's Review*, December 1980.

Flax, Steven. "The Toughest Bosses in America." *Fortune*, August 6, 1984.

Flood, John. "Chipping in on History: Frederico Faggin, Co-Inventor of the Microprocessor, Still Setting the Record Straight." *Los Altos Town Crier*, January 17, 2007.

Flood, John. "Ted Hoff: Thinking Small Sparked a Worldwide Revolution." *Los Altos Town Crier*, April 4, 2007.

"The Forbes Four Hundred." *Forbes*, October 14, 1996.

"The Forbes Four Hundred." *Forbes*, October 16, 1995.

Forbes, Jim. "Motorola Tries To Outmarket Pentium." *HTM News*, July 1993.

Francis, Bob. "What's Taking the Risk out of RISC?" *Datamation,* January 15, 1990.

Friedman, Walter A., and Richard S. Tedlow. "Statistical Portraits of American Business Elites: A Review Essay." *Business History* 45, no. 4 (October 2003).

Friedrich, Otto. "Machine of the Year: The Computer Moves In." *Time,* January 3, 1983.

Gaither, Chris. "Andy Grove's Tale of His Boyhood in Wartime." *New York Times,* November 12, 2001.

Ganees, Stuart. "America's Fastest Growing Companies." *Fortune,* May 23, 1988.

Geppert, Linda. "Profile: Andy Grove." *IEEE Spectrum,* June 2000.

Gilman, Hank. "IBM Cuts Intel Stake Further to 7.1% And Takes Profit Totaling $80 Million." *Wall Street Journal,* August 31, 1987.

Golden, Frederic. "Other Maestros of the Micro." *Time,* January 3, 1983.

Gomes, Lee. "Setting Up a Challenge to Intel." *San Jose Mercury News.* April 10, 1991.

"Gordon E. Moore." *IEEE Virtual Museum.* http//:www.ieee-virtual-museum.org (accessed January 28, 2005).

Gossett Jr., Carl T. "U.S. Presses Hungary." *New York Times,* January 8, 1957.

Grove, Andrew. "What Can Be Done, Will Be Done." *Forbes ASAP,* December 2, 1996.

———. "A High-Tech CEO Updates His Views on Managing and Careers." *Fortune,* September 18, 1995.

———. "Mass Transfer in Semiconductor Technology." *Industrial & Engineering Chemistry* 48, July 1966.

Grove, A. S., Bruce E. Deal, E. H. Snow, and C. T. Sah. "Investigation of Thermally Oxidised Silicon Surfaces Using Metal-Oxide-Semiconductor Structures." *Solid-State Electronics* 8, no. 2 (February 1965).

———, and D. J. Fitzgerald. "The Origin of Channel Currents Associated with P+ Regions in Silicon." *IEEE Transactions on Electron Devices* 12, no. 12 (December 1965).

———. "Surface Effects on *p-n* Junctions: Characteristics of Surface Space-Charge Regions Under Non-Equilibrium Conditions." *Solid-State Electronics* 9, no. 8 (August 1966).

———, P. Lamond, et al. "Stable MOS Transistors." *Electro-Technology,* December 1965.

———, O. Leistiko Jr., and W. W. Hooper. "Effect of Surface Fields on the Breakdown Voltage of Planar Silicon p-n Junctions." *IEEE Transactions on Electron Devices* 14, no. 3 (March 1967).

———, O. Leistiko Jr., and C. T. Sah. "Diffusion of Gallium Through a Silicon Dioxide Layer." *Journal of Physics and Chemistry of Solids* 25, no. 9 (September 1964).

———. "Redistribution of Acceptor and Donor Impurities During Thermal Oxidation of Silicon." *Journal of Applied Physics* 35, no. 9 (1964).

———, E. E. Petersen, and Andreas Acrivos. "Velocity Distribution in the Laminar Wake of a Parallel Flat Plate." *Physics of Fluids* 7, no. 7 (July 1964).

———, A. Roder, and C. T. Sah. "Impurity Distribution in Epitaxial Growth." *Journal of Applied Physics* 36, no. 3 (March 1965).

———, and C. T. Sah. "Simple Analytical Approximations to the Switching Times in Narrow Base Diodes." *Solid-State Electronics* 7, no. 1 (January 1964).

———, F. H. Shair, E. E. Petersen, and Andreas Acrivos. "An Experimental Investigation of the Steady Separated Flow Past a Circular Cylinder." *Journal of Fluid Mechanics* 19, no. 1 (May 1964).

————, and E. H. Snow. "A Model for Radiation Damage in Metal-Oxide-Semiconductor Structures." *Proceedings of the IEEE* 54, no. 6 (June 1966).

————, Bruce E. Deal, and C. T. Sah. "Simple Physical Model for the Space-Charge Capacitance of Metal-Oxide-Semiconductor Structures." *Journal of Applied Physics* 35, no. 8 (August 1964).

Grove, Andy, with Bethany McLean. "Taking on Prostate Cancer." *Fortune*, May 13, 1996.

Grove, G. "Not the Cause." *New York Herald Tribune* (International Edition), February 23, 1962.

Hajdú, Tibor, and Zsuzsa L. Nagy. "Revolution, Counterrevolution, Consolidation." *A History of Hungary*, edited by Peter F. Sugar, Péter Hanák, and Tibor Frank. Bloomington: Indiana University Press, 1990.

Hamm, Steve. "Former CEOs Should Just Fade Away." *BusinessWeek*, April 12, 2004.

Hayashi, Alden M. "The New Intel: Moore Mature, Moore Competitive." *Electronic Business*, November 15, 1987.

Hayes, Mary. "Craig Barrett: This 'Milquetoast' May Yet Be Tapped to Lead Intel Corp." *San Jose Business Journal*, May 17, 1993.

Hoefler, Don. "Semiconductor Family Tree." *Electronic News*, July 8, 1971.

Hof, Robert D. "The 'Lurking Time Bomb' of Silicon Valley." *BusinessWeek*, December 19, 1994.

Howe, Charles L. "Back to the Basics." *Datamation*, December 1, 1985.

Hsu, S. T., D. J. Fitzgerald, and A. S. Grove. "Surface-State Related $1/f$ noise in p-n Junctions and MOS Transistors." *Applied Physics Letters* 12, no. 9 (May 1968).

Huey Jr., John W. "Our Reluctant Author Comes Forward." *Fortune*, May 13, 1996.

Isaacson, Walter. "Man of the Year: The Microchip Is the Dynamo of the New Economy . . . Driven by the Passion of Intel's Andy Grove." *Time*, December 29, 1997.

"IBM Is Planning to Shed the Rest of Its Intel Stock." *Wall Street Journal*, September 28, 1987.

"Intel Chair, Honored by City College, Reminisces About Grove of Academe." *CUNY Matters*, Fall 1998.

"Intel Lays Off 170 Employees After $35M Qtr. Opns. Loss." *Electronic News*, January 20, 1986.

"Intel's Robert Noyce Kicks Himself Upstairs." *BusinessWeek*, December 14, 1974.

"Intel Sues AMD Over 386 Trademark." *Microprocessor Report*, October 17, 1990.

Karlgaard, Rich. "What 1968 Really Meant." *Forbes*, September 1993.

Karsai, Lázló. "The People's Courts and Revolutionary Justice in Hungary, 1945–46." *The Politics of Retribution in Europe: World War II and Its Aftermath*, edited by István Deák, Jan T. Gross, and Tony Judt. Princeton: Princeton University Press, 2000.

Kehoe, Louise. "Not a Grove in the Valley." *Financial Times* (London), March 28, 1998.

————. "PC Chip that Packs a Mainframe Punch." *Financial Times* (London), April 12, 1989.

————, and Richard Wolffe. "Intel Testimony a 'Blip on the Screen of Our Relationship.'" *Financial Times* (London), November 13, 1998.

Kessler, Michelle. "Intel Gets 2nd Chance to Build a Better Chip." *USA Today*, July 29, 2004.

Kirkpatrick, David. "Intel Goes for Broke." *Fortune*, May 16, 1994.

Kumar, Vikas. "The Original Mr. Chip." *The Economic Times* (India), June 2, 2005.

Lacayo, Richard. "The Time 25: You've Read About Who's Influential, but Who Has the Power?" *Time,* June 17, 1996.

Ladendorf, Kirk. "The Book on Intel." *Austin American-Statesman,* September 23, 1996.

————. "Intel Architect Andrew Grove to Step Down as CEO: Visionary Leader Will Take More Long-Term View as Chairman; President Will Take CEO Job." *Austin American-Statesman,* March 28, 1998.

Langlois, Richard N., and W. Edward Steinmueller. "The Evolution of Competitive Advantage in the Worldwide Semiconductor Industry, 1947–1996." *Sources of Industrial Leadership: Studies of Seven Industries,* edited by David C. Mowery and Richard R. Nelson. Cambridge, England: Cambridge University Press, 1999.

LeBoss, Bruce. "Frosch Raps Technological Substitutes." *Electronic News,* March 1969.

Leistiko, O., Jr., and A. S. Grove. "Breakdown Voltage of Planar Silicon Junctions." *Solid-State Electronics* 9, no. 9 (September 1966).

————, and C. T. Sah. "Electron and Hole Mobilities in Inversion Layers on Thermally Oxidized Silicon Surfaces." *IEEE Transactions on Electron Devices* 12, no. 5 (May 1965).

Lettice, John. "Gates Memos Show How Microsoft Puts Screws on Intel." *The Register,* November 10, 1998, http://www.theregister.co.uk (accessed September 15, 2005).

————. "Intel Writes Lousy Software, Says Gates." *The Register,* November 9, 1998. http://www.theregister.co.uk (accessed September 16, 2005).

"Let's Make A Deal: IBM Buys 12% of Intel." *Fortune,* January 24, 1983.

Levy, Steven. "Intel Leader Says Fear a Healthy Thing." *Portland Oregonian,* September 8, 1996.

Lewis, Geoff, and Robert D. Hof. "The World According to Andy Grove." Special issue, The Information Revolution, *BusinessWeek,* 1994.

Lewis, Peter H. "The Executive Computer; Can the Old Processing Technology Beat Back a Challenge?" *New York Times,* February 25, 1990.

Liscio, John. "The Steel Beneath the Silicon—A Revealing Look at How Andy Grove Willed Intel into a Powerhouse." *Barron's,* October 20, 1997.

Lohr, Steve. "Intel's Chief Steps Down After 11 Years." *New York Times,* March 27, 1998.

Loomis, Carol J. "Dinosaurs?" *Fortune,* May 3, 1993.

McCraw, Thomas K. "In Retrospect: Berle and Means." *Reviews in American History* 18, no. 4 (December, 1990).

McElheny, Victor K. "Dissatisfaction as a Spur to Career." *New York Times,* December 15, 1976.

————. "Spotlight: High Technology Jelly Bean Ace." *New York Times,* June 5, 1977.

McKenna, Regis. "Battle of the Chips." *Financial Times,* November 8, 1997.

Mackenzie, Richard. "'The Industry Has Stopped Growing.'" *Insight,* October 7, 1985.

McKie, Robin. *The Nasdaq Stock Market International Magazine,* 1993. Document in author's possession.

McLean, Bethany. "Is Enron Overpriced?" *Fortune,* March 5, 2001.

Magee, Mike. "Intel from the Inside." *Computing,* October 30, 1997.

"Man Born in Hungary Heads Jersey Aid Unit." *New York Times,* January 7, 1957.

Maney, Kevin. "Grove Sets New Course with Intel." *USA Today,* March 27, 1998.

————. "Now's the Right Time for Change, Intel's Grove Says." *USA Today,* March 27, 1998.

Markoff, John. "Computer Chip Starts Angry Debate." *New York Times*, September 28, 1989.

————. "Intel Introduces High-Speed Computer Chip." *New York Times*, April 11, 1989.

————, and Steve Lohr. "Apple Plans to Switch from I.B.M. to Intel for Chips." *New York Times*, June 6, 2005.

Maull, Samuel. "Kozlowski Faces Up to 30 Years in Prison." *Associated Press Newswires*, June 18, 2005.

Michaels, James W. "Only the Paranoid Survive." *Forbes*, October 7, 1996.

Moore, Gordon E. "Cramming More Components onto Integrated Circuits." *Electronics* 38, no. 8 (April 19, 1965).

————. "The Role of Fairchild in Silicon Technology in the Early Days of 'Silicon Valley.'" *Proceedings of the IEEE* 86, no. 1 (January 1998).

Moser, Petra, and Tom Nicholas. "Was Electricity a General Purpose Technology? Evidence from Historical Patent Citations." *American Economic Review* 94, no. 2 (May 2004).

Muller, Jerry Z. "Communism, Anti-Semitism & the Jews." *Commentary*, August, 1988.

Naughton, John. "Business Profile: Gordon E. Moore." *The Observer*, August 8, 1999.

Navin, Thomas R., and Marion V. Sears. "The Rise of a Market for Industrial Securities, 1887–1902." *Business History Review* 29, no. 2 (June 1955).

Needle, David. "Is Grove Behind Apple Chip Switch?" *InternetNews.com*, June 10, 2005. http://www.internetnews.com/bus-news/article.php/3512066 (accessed June 13, 2005).

Norris, Donald G. "Ingredient Branding: A Strategy Option with Multiple Beneficiaries." *Journal of Consumer Marketing* 9, no. 3 (Summer 1992).

————. "'Intel Inside': Branding a Component in a Business Market." *Journal of Business & Industrial Marketing* 8, no. 1 (1993).

Olegario, Rowena. "IBM and the Two Thomas J. Watsons." *Creating Modern Capitalism: How Entrepreneurs, Companies, and Countries Triumphed in Three Industrial Revolutions,* edited by Thomas K. McCraw. Cambridge, MA: Harvard University Press, 2000.

Olive, David. "Newsmakers: Web Wizard." *National Post*, November 1, 1998.

Olmos, David. "Intel Introduces Computer Chip Twice as Fast as 80386." *Los Angeles Times*, April 11, 1989.

Orme, Michael. "Why Intel Married for Money." *Management Today*, February 1985.

Ormos, Mária. "The Early Interwar Years, 1921–1938." *A History of Hungary,* edited by Peter F. Sugar, Péter Hanák, and Tibor Frank. Bloomington: Indiana University Press, 1990.

Painton, Frederick. "A Century Late, The Truth Arrives." *Time*, September 25, 1995.

Patterson, William Pat. "Gloomy Days in Silicon Valley: It's Beginning to Look as if We Can't Beat the Japanese at Chipmaking. The Question Is: Will We Join Them?" *Industry Week*, November 25, 1985.

Petre, Peter. "America's Most Successful Entrepreneur." *Fortune*, October 27, 1986.

Plunkett, Sandy. "Hello Mr. Chips." *Business Review Weekly*, March 30, 1998.

Podolny, Joel M., Rakesh Khurana, and Marya Hill-Popper. "Revisiting the Meaning of Leadership." *Research in Organizational Behavior* 26 (2005).

Pollack, Andrew. "An 'Awesome' Intel Corners Its Market." *New York Times*, April 3, 1988.

Port, Otis, and Richard Brandt. "Intel's New Chip May Light a Fire Under Computer Sales." *BusinessWeek*, October 28, 1985.

Radford, Margaret Grove. "Technology Is Impossible to Hold Back." *Destiny*, Summer, 1997.

Rainer, János. "The New Course in Hungary in 1953." Working Paper no. 38, Woodrow Wilson International Center for Scholars, Cold War International History Project. Washington, D.C., 2002.

Ramirez, Anthony. "New Doubts about the Pentium Chip Give Intel a Marketing Problem with Few Precedents." *New York Times*, December 14, 1994.

Ramo, Joshua Cooper. "Man of the Year: A Survivor's Tale." *Time*, December 29, 1997.

Ránki, György. "The Hungarian Economy in the Interwar Years." *A History of Hungary*, edited by Peter F. Sugar, Péter Hanák, and Tibor Frank. Bloomington: Indiana University Press, 1990.

"Refugee Heading Engineers' Class." *New York Times*, June 15, 1960.

Reid, T. R. "Doing Penance for Defending the Pentium Chip." *Washington Post*, February 6, 1995.

———. "It's a Dangerous Precedence [*sic*] to Make the Pentium Promise." *Washington Post*, December 26, 1994.

Reinhardt, Andy. "Bay Networks' Mr. House Finds His Fixer-Upper." *BusinessWeek*, February 2, 1998.

———. "Intel: Paranoia, Aggression, and Other Strengths." *BusinessWeek*, October 13, 1997.

Ristelhuber, Robert. "Motorola, Intel Push Defensive Measures." *Electronic News*, February 5, 1990.

Robertson, Jack. "Study Impact of Microcircuits." *Electronic News*, April 1963.

Rosch, Winn L. "Calculated RISC." *PC/Computing*, December 1, 1988.

Rossant, John. "The Stars of Europe—Innovators: Tim Jackson, Managing Director—Carlyle Internet Partners—Britain." *BusinessWeek International Edition*, June 12, 2000.

Russell, Sabin. "Intel to Get $250M Cash Infusion from IBM." *Electronic News*, December 27, 1982.

Sahlman, William A. "Expensing Options Solves Nothing." *Harvard Business Review* 80, no. 12 (December 2002).

Samuelson, Robert J. "Ghosts That Still Haunt GM." *Washington Post*, November 30, 2005.

Sandler, Linda. "Intel's Detractors Say IBM Bond Sale Is Signal That Semiconductor Firm Has Poor Prospects." *Wall Street Journal*, February 12, 1986.

Schares, Gail E. " 'Connoisseur of Confrontation.' " *San Francisco Chronicle*, July 26, 1984.

Schlender, Brent. "A Conversation with the Lords of Wintel." *Fortune*, July 8, 1996.

———. "Inside Andy Grove's Latest Crusade: Intel's Chairman Is Out to Change the Way Companies Are Governed. His First Job: Change Himself." *Fortune*, August 23, 2004.

Schmitt, Christopher H. "At Work With the Valley's Toughest Boss: Andy Grove Keeps a Forceful Grip at Chip Giant Intel." *San Jose Mercury News*, May 26, 1986.

"Semiconductors Take a Sudden Plunge." *BusinessWeek,* November 16, 1974.

Shair, F. H., A. S. Grove, E. E. Petersen, and Andreas Acrivos. "The Effect of Confining Walls on the Stability of the Steady Wake Behind a Circular Cylinder." *Journal of Fluid Mechanics* 17, no. 4 (December 1963).

Sherman, Stratford. "Andy Grove: How Intel Makes Spending Pay Off." *Fortune,* February 22, 1993.

———. "The New Computer Revolution." *Fortune,* June 14, 1993.

Siegmann, Ken. "An American Tale of Semi-Success: How American Chip Companies Regained Lead." *San Francisco Chronicle,* December 20, 1993.

———. "Improved Equipment Key to Chip Revival: U.S. Companies Learned to Cooperate." *San Francisco Chronicle,* December 21, 1993.

Slater, Michael. "AMD Ends 386 Monopoly; AMD Shows—but Does Not 'Announce'—Fully Static Design." *Microprocessor Report,* November 28, 1990.

———. "Intel Loses 386 Trademark." *Microprocessor Report,* March 20, 1991.

Slaughter, J. R., K. A. Slaughter, D. Nichols, S. E. Holmes, and M. P. Martens. "Prevalence, Clinical Manifestations, Etiology, and Treatment of Depression in Parkinson's Disease." *Journal of Neuropsychiatry and Clinical Neurosciences* 13, no. 2 (May 2001).

Smith, Randall. "IBM's $300 Million Sale of Eurobonds Is Seen as Move to Loosen Ties to Intel." *Wall Street Journal,* February 10, 1986.

Snow, E. H., A. S. Grove, and D. J. Fitzgerald. "Effects of Ionizing Radiation on Oxidized Silicon Surfaces and Planar Devices." *Proceedings of the IEEE* 55, no. 7 (July 1967).

———, B. E. Deal and C. T. Sah. "Ion Transport Phenomena in Insulating Films." *Journal of Applied Physics* 36, no. 5 (May 1965).

Spiegelman, Lisa L. "PowerPC Consortium Challenges Intel with the Fastest PC Chip Yet." *Investor's Business Daily,* April 28, 1994.

Stearns, Peter N., ed. "The Treaty of Trianon." *The Encyclopedia of World History.* 6th ed. New York: Houghton Mifflin, 2001.

Stokes, Jon. "The Pentium: An Architectural History of the World's Most Famous Desktop Processor (Part I)." July 11, 2004. http://arstechnica.com/articles/paedia/cpu/pentium-1.ars/1 (accessed September 20, 2005).

Stroud, Michael. "Intel's Craig Barrett: Shortening Product Cycles so Rivals Struggle to Keep Up." *Investor's Business Daily,* January 28, 1993.

Sull, Donald N., Richard S. Tedlow, and Richard S. Rosenbloom. "Managerial Commitments and Technological Change in the U.S. Tire Industry." *Industrial and Corporate Change* 6, no. 2 (March 1997).

"Talking Business with Grove of Intel: New Approach to Hierarchy." *New York Times,* December 23, 1980.

Tedlow, Richard S. "The Chief Executive Officer of the Large American Industrial Corporation." Unpublished manuscript.

———. "The Education of Andy Grove." *Fortune,* December 12, 2005.

———. "Swimming Across: A Memoir in Historical Perspective." HBS Working Paper no. 4-050, 2006.

———, Kim Eric Bettcher, and Courtney A. Purrington. "The Chief Executive Officer of the Large American Industrial Corporation in 1917." *Business History Review* 77, no. 4 (Winter 2003).

Tetzeli, Rick. "What Chief Executives Return to Shareholders Per Square Foot of Office Space." *Fortune*, April 19, 1993.

Tilkovszky, Loránd. "The Late Interwar Years and World War II." *A History of Hungary*, edited by Peter F. Sugar, Péter Hanák, and Tibor Frank. Bloomington: Indiana University Press, 1990.

"The Top 25 Managers of the Year: L. Dennis Kozlowski." *BusinessWeek*, January 14, 2002.

Ulick, Jake. "WorldCom's Financial Bomb: From the President on Down, Officials Worried About Investor Confidence Weigh in." *CNN/Money*, June 25, 2002. money.cnn.com/2002/06/25/news/worldcom/index.htm (accessed February 23, 2006).

Vadasz, Les, and A. S. Grove. "Temperature Dependence of MOS Transistor Characteristics Below Saturation." *IEEE Transactions on Electron Devices* 13, no. 12 (December 1966).

Van, Jon. "Intel, Motorola Square Off in Capital Chip Rivalry: Newest Devices Promise More Capacity, Speed." *Washington Post*, April 11, 1989.

Venkatesh, R., and Vijay Mahajan. "Products with Branded Components: An Approach for Premium Pricing and Partner Selection." *Marketing Science* 16, no. 2 (1997).

Vörös, Károly. "Birth of Budapest: Building a Metropolis, 1873–1918." *Budapest: A History from Its Beginnings to 1998*, edited by András Gero and János Poór. New York: Columbia University Press, 1997.

Ward, John William. "Who Was Benjamin Franklin?" *The American Scholar* 32, no. 4 (Autumn 1963).

Watts, Robert. "Microsoft's Ballmer Vows to 'Kill' Google." *Sunday Telegraph* (London), September 4, 2005.

Weber, Jonathan. "How 'Paranoia' Has Helped Intel Rise to the Top." *Los Angeles Times*, November 25, 1996.

Weiss, Ray. "Megaprocessor Integrates 386 Elements, Exploits RISC Techniques." *Electronic Engineering Times*, April 17, 1989.

Wells, Ken. "Intel Corp. Loosens Its Link with IBM in Repurchase of Large Block of Shares." *Wall Street Journal*, June 12, 1987.

Wessels, Michael R. "Streptococcal Infections." *Harrison's Principles of Internal Medicine*, edited by Kurt J. Isselbacher. New York: McGraw-Hill, 1994.

Wharton, John. "Strategic Product Rescheduling: What's the Real Reason for Pentium's Late Release?" *Microprocessor Report*, March 29, 1993.

Wiegner, Kathleen. "The Empire Strikes Back." *Upside*, June, 1992.

Williams, Tish. "Boy the Media Were Happy to Take Intel Down a Few Notches Last Week," *UPSIDE Today*, April 6, 1998.

Wilson, Aubrey, and Bryan Atkin. "Exorcising the Ghosts in Marketing." *Harvard Business Review* 54, no. 5 (Sept.–Oct. 1976).

Wilson, John W. "Andrew Grove." *BusinessWeek*, April 17, 1987.

———. "Can Andy Grove Practice What He Preaches?" *BusinessWeek*, March 16, 1987.

———. "Intel's Mad Dash to Keep Up with Japan." *BusinessWeek*, August 12, 1985.

———. "Intel Wakes Up to a Whole New Marketplace in Chips." *BusinessWeek*, September 2, 1985.

————. "A Trial With More at Stake than a Copyright." *BusinessWeek,* June 9, 1986.

Wirbel, Loring. "Is IBM Rethinking Its Fiscal Ties With Intel?" *Electronic News,* February 3, 1986.

————. "New Intel 32-Bit MPU Runs MS-DOS Unix in Unison." *Electronic News,* October 21, 1985.

Wolfe, Tom. "The Tinkerings of Robert Noyce: How the Sun Rose on the Silicon Valley." *Esquire,* December, 1983.

"'You've Got to Find What You Love,' Jobs Says." *Stanford Report,* June 14, 2005. http//:news-service.sanford.edu/news/2005/june15/jobs-061505.html (accessed August 26, 2005).

Zaleznik, Abraham. "Managers and Leaders: Are They Different?" *Harvard Business Review* 55, no. 3 (May–June 1977). Reprinted in *Managing Professionals in Innovative Organizations: A Collection of Readings,* edited by Ralph Katz. Cambridge, MA: Ballinger, 1988.

Cases and Teaching Notes

Botticelli, Peter, David Collis, and Gary Pisano. "Intel Corporation: 1968–1997." Harvard Business School Case no. 9-797-137; rev. October 21, 1998. Boston: HBS Publishing.

Burgelman, Robert A., and Philip E. Meza. "Grove Scholars Program: Putting Rungs Back on the Ladder." Stanford Graduate School of Business Case no. SM-144, July 29, 2005.

Rukstad, Michael G., and David B. Yoffie. "Microsoft in 2002." Harvard Business School Case no. 702-411; rev. August 30, 2005. Boston: HBS Publishing.

Tedlow, Richard S., with Wendy K. Smith. "James Burke: A Career in American Business." Harvard Business School Case (A) no. 389-177 and (B) no. 390-030 with the accompanying videotape; rev. October 20, 2005. Boston: HBS Publishing.

Useem, Jerry, and Joseph L. Badaracco Jr. "comp.sys.intel: The Internet and the Pentium Chip Controversy." Harvard Business School Case (A) no. 395-246 and (B) no. 395-247; rev. June 11, 1996. Boston: HBS Publishing.

Yoffie, David B. "The Global Semiconductor Industry, 1987." Harvard Business School Case no. 388-052; rev. March 22, 1993. Boston: HBS Publishing.

————. "Microsoft in 2002." Harvard Business School Teaching Note no. 702-459, February 19, 2002. Boston: HBS Publishing.

————, "Wintel" (B) no. 704-420, (C) no. 704-421, (D) no. 704-422, (E) no. 704-423, (F) no. 705-413; rev. March 16, 2004. Boston: HBS Publishing.

————, and Ramon Casadesus-Masanell. "Wintel (A), (B), (C), (D), (E), and (F) (TN)." Harvard Business School Teaching Note no. 706-495, November 30, 2005. Boston: HBS Publishing.

————, and Sasha Mathu. "Wintel (A): Cooperation or Conflict." Harvard Business School Case no. 704-419; rev. March 16, 2004. Boston: HBS Publishing.

Patents

Grove, Andrew S., Otto Leistiko, and Ronald J. Whittier. *Optimized Double-Ring Semiconductor Device.* US Patent 3,463,977, filed April 21, 1966, and issued August 26, 1969.

Fitzgerald, Desmond J., Andrew S. Grove, and Edward H. Snow. *Semiconductor Device Process for Reducing Surface Recombination Velocity.* US Patent 3,513,035, filed November 1, 1967, and issued May 19, 1970.

Author Interviews

Acrivos, Andreas. December 18, 2003.
Alter, Karen. December 14, 2005.
Amantea, Denise. January 2, 2006.
Aufmuth, Larry. January 3, 2006.
Aymar, Mike. January 9, 2006.
Banks, Andrew. August 5, 2005.
Bara, John. February 11, 2005.
Barrett, Craig R. January 14, 2004.
———. February 6, 2006.
Berlin, Leslie. January 26, 2006.
Bishop, J. Michael. February 8, 2006.
Borovoy, Roger S. January 3, 2006.
Boucher, Dick. April 19, 2005.
Bryant, Andy. June 17, 2004.
Burgelman, Robert. February 11, 2004.
———. July 18, 2005.
———. January 19, 2006.
Burke, James E. 1999.
Butler, Rebekah Saul. January 31, 2006.
Canion, Rod. December 11, 2003.
Carroll, Peter R. June 17, 2004.
Carter, Dennis. June 16, 2004.
———. August 3, 2004.
———. July 7, 2005.
Casto, Maryles. August 2, 2004.
Deák, István. December 5, 2004.
Deal, Bruce. June 16, 2004.
Dearing, Michael. September 6, 2005.
Dell, Michael. December 9, 2003.
Diller, Barry. April 29, 2004.
Doerr, John. March 16, 2006.
Dunlap, F. Thomas, Jr. February 24, 2004.
Fister, Michael. August 4, 2004.

Gelbach, Ed. January 3, 2006.
Gelsinger, Patrick P. February 3, 2004.
Gill, Frank C. August 5, 2004.
Grove, Andrew S. 1999.
———. February 7, 2004.
———. May 21, 2004.
———. October 2, 2004.
———. March 2, 2005.
———. March 18, 2005.
———. April 13, 2005.
———. July 4, 2005.
———. September 1, 2005.
———. September 7, 2005.
———. November 11, 2005.
———. November 18, 2005.
———. December 6, 2005.
———. December 26, 2005.
———. January 10, 2006.
———. January 27, 2006.
———. February 10, 2006.
Grove, Eva. February 2, 2005.
———. January 27, 2006.
Grove, Karen. January 31, 2006.
Hoefflinger, Michael. June 17, 2004.
Hoff, Marcian (Ted). June 15, 2004.
House, David L. February 15, 2005.
Hundt, Reed. March 23, 2005.
James, Renee. August 5, 2004.
Jarrett, James. January 16, 2004.
Jobs, Steven P. February 14, 2005.
Kern, Arthur H. June 18, 2004.
Kinnie, D. Craig. October 4, 2005.
Klafter, Cary. August 3, 2004.
Kolodney, Morris. April 24, 2004.
Kubota, Ken. January 24, 2006.

Kuehler, Jack. January 25, 2005.
Lattin, Bill. August 6, 2004.
McGeady, Steven. October 4, 2005.
Maloney, Sean. January 12, 2004.
Meza, Philip. October 11, 2005.
Michelson, Leslie. January 12, 2006.
Moore, Gordon. 1999.
———. May 24, 2004.
Murphy, Terri L. January 9, 2006.
Nachtscheim, Stephen. June 18, 2004.
Nichols, Elizabeth. November 20, 2003.
Nichols, Joe. November 20, 2003.
Opdendyk, Terry. April 20, 2005.
Otellini, Paul S. February 2, 2004.
———. July 14, 2005
———. January 23, 2006.
Perry, William. February 3, 2005.
Pitofsky, Robert. November 25, 2003.

Pollace, Pam. February 11, 2004.
Roach, Mack. December 28, 2005.
Rock, Arthur. 2000.
Schlender, Brent. August 4, 2004.
Schmidt, Eric. May 19, 2004.
Shuman, Marc. January 13, 2006.
Taylor, Barr. January 24, 2006.
———. March 10, 2005.
Thomson, Keith L. August 5, 2004.
Thorpe, Karen. June 17, 2004.
Vadasz, Les. May 24, 2004.
———. January 24, 2005.
———. September 26, 2005.
Yoffie, David. 1999.
———. June 29, 2004.
Young, Chuck. June 15, 2006.
Yu, Albert Y.C. January 16, 2004.
Yudkoff, Royce. August 5, 2005.

Interviews by Others

(Except where otherwise noted, all transcripts are in author's possession.)
Faggin, Federico. "Silicon Genesis: Oral Histories of Semiconductor Industry Pioneers." By Rob Walker (March 3, 1995). http:silicongenesis.stanford.edu/transcripts/faggin.htm (accessed November 25, 2005).
Grove, Andrew S. By Mary Burt Baldwin (1981).
Grove, Andrew S. By Arnold Thackray and David C. Brock (July 14, 2004). (Thackray I.)
Grove, Andrew S. By Arnold Thackray and David C. Brock (September 1, 2004). (Thackray II.) For further information, see the Oral History Collection at the Chemical Heritage Foundation, http://www.chemheritage.org.
Grove, Andrew S. "Before Hours." CNNfN (September 24, 1996).
Grove, Andrew S. "Bloomberg Business News, PBS" (September 10, 1996).
Grove, Andrew S. "Bloomberg News Radio." WBBR-AM, New York, NY (September 10, 1996).
Grove, Andrew S. "Fox Morning News." WTTG-TV, Washington, D.C. (September 11, 1991).
Grove, Andrew S. "Fresh Air." KQED-FM, San Francisco (November 19, 1996).
Grove, Andrew S. "Good Day Sacramento." KPWB-TV, Sacramento, CA (September 10, 1996).
Grove, Andrew S. "InterNight." MSNBC-TV (September 24, 1996).
Grove, Andrew S. "Nightly Business Report." PBS-TV (September 10, 1996).
Grove, Andrew S. "Technopolitics." KCSM-TV, San Francisco (September 22, 1996).
Grove, Andrew S., and Gordon Moore. By Harvard Business School Professor Joseph L. Bower (December 8, 1999).
Otellini, Paul. Oral history interview by Rachel Stewart (February 26, 2002).

INDEX

Page numbers in *italics* refer to figures.

ABC (American Broadcasting Company), 363

Abel, Elie, 58–59

ABRY Partners, 373

Academy of Fine Arts (Vienna), 9

ACE (Advanced Computing Environment), 287

Acer, 227

Acrivos, Andreas "Andy," xiv, 76–77, 80, 88, 90

Adelphia, 441, 444

AeroGen, 420

AF of L (American Federation of Labor), 380

Aiken Computation Laboratory, 296

Akers, John Fellows, 284–85, 286, 290–91

Allen, Herb, 388

Allen, Paul, 295, 296, 298–99, 301, 302, 309, 395

Altair, 298–99

Alter, Karen, 124–25, 276–77, 338, 399–400, 437

Amantea, Denise, 389, 393, 414

AMD (Advanced Micro Devices), 115, 142, 150, 159, 203, 226, 236–37, 240, 246, 255, 256–57, 261, 274, 320, 369, 404

American Express, 286

American Institute of Chemical Engineers, 65

American Law Institute, 452

American Media, 453

American Physical Society, 83

Andrei (Russian soldier), 27–28

Andrews, Paul, 297, 298, 301

Andrew S. Grove School of Engineering, 66
    see also City College of New York (CCNY)

anti-Semitism, 3–6, 8, 9, 19, 20, 21, 22–25, 30, 32, 50, 60

Antonescu, Ion, 24

AOL, 359

Apple Computer, xvi, 98, 146, 168, 169–70, 177, 242, 250, 282, 283, 286–87, 301, 309, 358, 361, 365, 409, 427

Apple I, 169–70

Applied Materials, 437

Architecture and Applications Group (Intel), 254

Architecture Development Lab. *See* Intel Architecture Lab

Army Terminal (Brooklyn), 61

ARPANET, 296

Arrow Cross Party, xviii, 16, 24–25

Arthur Andersen, 442, 450

ASIC (Applications Specific Integrated Circuit) Components Group (Intel), 231, 234

AT&T, 103, 441

Audit Committee (Intel), 449, 450

Audrey (Grove's girlfriend), 69

Auschwitz, 21, 22, 25, 31, 33, 55, 119, 221

Austrian Empire, 35

Austro-Hungarian Empire, xix, 2

"'Awesome' Intel Corners Its Market, An" (Pollack), 242, 243, 264–65

Aymar, Mike, 437

Balancing Your Family, Faith & Work (Gelsinger), 232
Ballmer, Steve, 297–98, 302, 309
Bardeen, John, 63, 83, 93–94
Barrett, Craig, xv–xvi, 159, 160, 164, 211, 219, 220, 226, 227, 233, 234–35, 242, 243, 259, 279–80, 289, 293, 337, 338, 369–70, 388, 393, 394, 395, 397–98, 400, 402–5, 407, 410, 413, 416–17, 418, 419–21, 429, 430, 431, 435, 436–37, 439, 450, 451, 452
Bay Networks, 233
Bear, Stearns & Co., 273
Beckman Instruments, 63
   see also Shockley Semiconductor Laboratory
Beirut, Boleslaw, 52
Belarus, 212
Bell Canada, 138, 141, 150
Bell Laboratories, xiv, 63, 78, 80–81, 85, 94, 103
   Transistor Physics Department at, 63
Bem, Jozef, 53
Beria, Lavrenty, 47
Berlin, Isaiah, 215
Berlin, Leslie, 85, 98, 104, 112, 118, 129, 140, 142, 391, 392, 395
Berlin Wall, 211–12
Betty Crocker, 139
BF Goodrich, 131
Bishop, J. Michael, 453–54
Blackstone Group, 445
Blank, Julius, 83, 84
Blitzkrieg, 17
Bloomberg Business News, 377
Bookends (Simon & Garfunkel), 137
Borland, 307
Borovoy, Roger S., 134, 376
Boucher, Richard D., 162, 165, 167
Bowers, Ann S., 98, 249
Bozak, Len, 406
Brattain, Walter H., 63, 83, 93–94
Brezhnev, Leonid, 113
Brin, Sergey, 408
British Petroleum, 420
Brokaw, Tom, 382, 383, 389
Brooklyn College, 62, 64
Brooklyn Polytech Institute, 64
Brothers Karamazov, The (Dostoyevsky), 40
Browne, John P., 420
Broz, Josip "Tito," 51–52, 54
Bryant, Andy, 437, 450
Buchenwald, 31
Buckhout, Don, 178–79
Budapest, Battle of, 26, 42
Budapest, University of, 48, 49, 50, 51, 154
Budapesti Evangelikus Gimnazium (Budapest Lutheran High School), 36–37, 41–42, 44

Bulganin, Nicolay, 47
Burgelman, Robert A., 127, 129, 143, 168, *205, 207,* 216, *216,* 224, 231, 255, 266–67, 268, 269, 270, 274, 277, 325, 349, 360, 362, 365, 373, 376, 406, 407, 455
Burke, James E., 256, 285, 286, 417
Busch, Doug, 437
Bush, George H.W., 388, 442
Bush, George W., 442, 447–48
Busicom, 144
Business Insiders, 362
Business Roundtable, 425–26, 429
BusinessWeek, xv, xvi, 158, 159, 160, 214, 321, 391, 444
Butler, Rebekah Saul, 457

Cadence Design Systems, 437
California, University of:
   at Berkeley, xiv, xx, xxi, 71, 73, 74, 75–78, 79, 82, 89, 108–9, 119, 121, 159, 196–97, 235, 308
   at Davis, 235
   at San Francisco (UCSF), 355, 410, 453, 454
California Institute of Technology (Cal Tech), 82, 233, 419
California Landmarks Commission, 82–83
Cambridge, Godfrey, 300
Camp Kilmer, 61–62, 64, 68
Canion, Rod, 228, 245, 246, 264, 287
Cannavino, Jim, 245, 246, 264
Canopus, 323, 324, 336
CapCure, 414, 454–55
Carnegie, Andrew, 86–87, 122, 246, 311, 439, 459–60
Carnegie, Dale, 66
Carnegie-Mellon University, 296
Carnegie Steel Corporation, 460
Carroll, Paul, 227, 228, 284, 285, 286
Carroll, Peter R., 355, 453
Carsten, Jack, 169, 279
Carter, Dennis Lee, 190, 220, 251–58, 268–69, 272, 276, 399, 400, 437
Carter, Jimmy, 172–73
Cary, Frank T., 284
Casadesus-Masanell, Ramon, *314*
Casali, Clovis, 359
Catholic Church, 39
Celeron microprocessor, 431
Chandler, Alfred D., Jr., 106, 181, 422
"Charge of the Light Brigade, The" (Tennyson), 222–23
Charles Schwab, 421
Chase, 442
Chen, Winston H., 420, 450
Chevron laboratory, xiv, 70

Chez Yvonne, 135
China, 212
Chips & Technologies, 261, 278
Chiu, George, 281
Chou, Sunlin, 210, 437
Christensen, Clayton, 396
Christianity, 4
Christian Socialist Party, 4, 5, 10
Churchill, Winston, 46, 51, 199
CIBC Oppenheimer, 386
CIO (Congress of Industrial Organizations), 380, 381
Cisco Systems, 365, 404, 406, 409, 427
Citigroup, 442
City College of New York (CCNY), xiii, xx, 64–67, 70–71, 75–76, 77, 79, 89, 119, 458
Civil War, U.S., 47, 114
Clark, Nobuko, 281
Clear Channel Communications, 453
Clevite, 103
Clinton, Bill, 377, 440
CNBC, 362
CNN, 276, 326, 336, 362, 382
Coca-Cola, 255, 332, 333
Cold War, 51–52
Columbia University, 70, 113
COMDEX (Computer Dealer Exposition), 244, 264, 325, 360–62
Communist Party, 7, 33, 36, 48, 53–55, 55, 67, 221, 237
Compaq, 228–29, 231, 233, 245, 246, 278, 286, 292, 293, 358, 374–75
Compaq Deskpro, 228, 229, 243, 274, 375, 386
Compensation Committee (Intel), 449
Components Group, 231
Components Technology and Manufacturing Group (Intel), 231, 234–35
comp.sys.intel, 323–24, 326–27, 331, 335, 336
CompuServe, 323, 324, 341, 344, 359
Computer Center Corporation (C-Cubed), 295
computer industry, 212–16
    business models in, 213
    defined standards in, 309–10
    IBM failure to recognize PC potential in, 229
    IBM PC clones in, 227–29
    as industrial democracy, 290
    rise of PC in, 213–14
    shift from vertical to horizontal structure in, 231, 245, 373
Computer Organization and Design: The Hardware/Software Interface (Hennessy), 264
Computer Wars: How the West Can Win in a Post-IBM World (Ferguson and Morris), 285

Conference Board Commission, 445–47
Congress, U.S., 72, 388, 427, 441, 448
Conner Peripherals, 290
Content Group (Intel), 437
Coppernoll, Julie, 413
Corcoran, Elizabeth, 394, 397
Cornell University, 152
Cornet, Jean-Claude, 337
Corporate Governance Committee (Intel), 449
Corporate Marketing Group (Intel), 258
corporate scandals, 440–50
    see also Adelphia; Enron; Global Crossing; WorldCom
Creative Artists Agency, 370
Credit Suisse First Boston, 386, 442
Crimean War, 222
Cromwell, Oliver, 391
Crystal, Graef, 445
CSX, 445
CTMG GOR ("Corporate Technology and Manufacturing Group" "General Operations Review"), 221
Cultural Revolution (China), 113
Currency Books, 372
Currie, Gerard, 133
Curtis, Tony, 300
Cypress Semiconductor, 246–47, 278
Cyrix Semiconductor, 246–47, 261, 369

Darányi, Kalman, 9
Dartmouth College, 286
Data General, 153
Data Technology, 133
Davidoff, Monte, 299
Davidow, William H., 164, 175–76, 178, 337
Dawidowicz, Lucy, 6
Deák, István, 20
DEC (Digital Equipment Corporation), 213, 245, 275, 287
Defense Department, U.S., 296
Defiant Ones, The, 300
de Gaulle, Charles, 113
Dell, 227–28, 292, 293, 300–301, 311, 447
Dell, Michael, 88, 125, 227–28, 249, 358
Deming, W. Edwards, 224
Democratic National Convention (1968), 114
Democratic Party, 113
Deskpro 386, 228, 229, 243, 274, 375
"Despair" (Grove), 162
Deutsche Bank, 442
Deutsche Morgan Grenfell, 386
Dinah's Shack, 83
Disney, 283, 377
Dobbs, Lou, 276

Dob Street School, 41–42, 44
Doerr, John, 99, 200, 396, 397, 401, 407
Donaldson, Lufkin & Jenrette, 246, 386
Dostoyevsky, Fyodor, 40
dot-com bubble, xv, 117, 404, 427–40
    rise of boom before, 214–15, 428–38
Doubleday, 371, 372
Dow Jones Industrial Average (DJIA), 172,
    244, 250, 259, 278, 404, 432
Drucker, Peter F., 74
Dubcek, Alexander, 113
Dunlap, Tom, 219–20, 232, 240, 437
Dun's Review, 200, 202

Eastman, George, 248
Eastman Kodak, 248
eBay, xvi, 301, 365, 408
Ebbers, Bernie, 441, 444
Edison, Thomas, 82
EDS, 292
Eichmann, Adolf, 24
Eisenhower, Dwight D., 63, 72
Eisner, Michael, 377
Electronic Engineering Times, 324, 336
Electronic News, 180–81
electronics industry
    see also Silicon Valley; specific companies
Elephant Furniture Store (Elefánt
    Bútoráruház), 14
Elkind, Peter, 442
Ellis, Carlene, 366–67
Ellison, Larry, 125, 307, 409
email, growing importance of, 333–36
ENIAC, 166, 321
Enron, 284, 355, 356, 441–43, 444, 449, 450
Enterprise Platform Group (Intel), 437
Epson, 227
Ernst & Young, 450
Esquire, 93
Europe:
    anti-Semitism in, 3–4, 32
    postwar retribution throughout, 32, 34
Europe Online, 359
Evans, Daniel, 299
Excel, 310, 397
ExxonMobil, 130

Fab 1, 146, 154, 174, 242
Fab 2, 146, 154, 174, 242, 244
Fab 3, 146, 154, 174, 242, 244
Fab 4, 174–75
Fab 5, 174–75
Fab 7, 218
Fab 12, 369
Faggin, Federico, 144, 156, 189, 195, 397
Fairchild, George Winthrop, 106
Fairchild, Sherman, 106, 112

Fairchild Camera and Instrument Corpora-
    tion, 85, 108, 110, 111
Fairchild Semiconductor, xiv, xx, 57–58, 78,
    80, 81, 84, 85–86, 87–89, 91, 94, 95, 96,
    99, 102–3, 104–8, 109–13, 114, 115–16,
    118, 119, 121, 124, 128, 129–31, 134,
    137, 140, 142, 147–48, 152, 154, 156,
    159, 165, 169, 174, 187, 200, 210, 233,
    235, 238, 376, 387–88, 440
"Fakin' It" (Simon), 137, 154
Fasori Jewish boys' orphanage, 33
Fastow, Andrew, 441–42
Fatelessness (Kertész), xx, 16, 31, 48
Federal Communications Commission, 440
Federal Reserve, 433, 445
Ferdinand, Franz, Archduke of Austria-
    Hungary, xix
Ferguson, Charles H., 285
Fidelity Investments, 422
Filo, David, 408
Finance Committee (Intel), 449
Firestone, 131
Fister, Mike, 437
Flath, Gene, 133, 154, 174
Flynn, Errol, 325
Forbes, 114, 297, 352, 381–82
Ford, Henry, 74–75, 236
Forester, C.S., 44
Fore Technologies, 406–7
Fortran, 86, 87, 88
Fortune, xvii, 125, 133, 166, 180, 183, 184, 225,
    250, 282, 287, 302, 319, 320, 351–52,
    355–56, 371, 372, 403, 414, 418, 441, 443
Fortune 500, 172, 184, 186, 198, 238, 259,
    278, 282, 331, 365, 385, 434, 451
Franklin, Benjamin, xxii, 123, 238, 459
Franz Josef, Emperor of Austria-Hungary,
    xix, 4
"Free Speech Movement," 76
Fresh Air, xxi-xxii, 392
Frick, Henry Clay, 422
Frohman, Dov, 143–44, 168, 437
Fujitsu, 175, 183

Galbraith, John Kenneth, 62
Gale, Grant O., 93–94
Gates, Bill, 125, 202, 244–45, 258, 264, 282,
    287, 293, 294–304, 306–9, 311–12,
    315–17, 361, 395, 401
Gates, Kristianne, 294, 299
Gates, Libby, 294
Gates, Mary, 294
Gates, Melinda, 317
Gateway, 293
Gaudette, Frank, 304
GE (General Electric), 78, 94, 103, 152, 295,
    440, 444–45

Gelbach, Ed, 138, 155–56, 255, 279
Gelsinger, Pat, 232, 362, 363, 437
General Assembly of the Church of Scotland, 391
General Mills, 139
General Motors, 130, 248, 285, 380–81, 431
General William G. Haan, 61
Geraghty, John M., 386
Germany, 9, 11
    Hungary occupied by, 20, 21–26
    Poland invaded by, 12–13
    after World War I, 5
    World War II and, 16–18, 19
Gerstner, Louis V., Jr., 286, 287–91, 327, 328, 358
Gibbons, Fred, 307
Gill, Frank C., 190, 235, 279
Gizi (Gróf family maid), 14, 23–24, 29, 30, 43
Global Crossing, 443
Goizueta, Roberto, 255
Goldman Sachs, 304
Gömbös, Gyula, 7–8
Gomulka, Wladyslaw, 52–53
Good Morning America, 363
Google, xvi, 301, 302, 333, 365, 406, 408, 427
Gorbachev, Mikhail, 442
Graham, Bob, 152–53, 169
Great Depression, 5, 8, 92, 118, 180, 380
Greeley, Horace, 71
Greenspan, Alan, 433, 434, 442
Grinich, Victor, 83, 84
Grinnell College, 93, 94
Gróf, George "Gyurka," xvii–xviii, 6–7, 10, 12–14, 15–16, 17, 18, 27, 29–31, 34–35, 39, 41, 42–43, 45, 48–49, 54, 55, 56, 62, 64, 65, 66, 67–68, 71, 78, 79, 101, 119, 126, 127, 188, 189, 211, 215, 414
Gróf, Maria, xvii–xviii, 6–7, 10, 12–14, 15, 18–19, 20, 21, 22–31, 34–35, 37, 39, 41, 43, 44, 55, 56, 62, 64, 65, 66, 67–68, 71, 78, 79, 101, 126, 188, 189, 196, 208, 353, 414–15
Gross, Terry, xxi–xxii, 392
Grove, Andy:
    as adaptable, 120–21, 187, 208
    Americanization of, 62, 64, 66–68, 121–22
    arrival as refugee in America of, xiii, 61–62
    the arts as interest of, 43–44, 49, 57
    athletic interests of, 37, 38, 438
    books written by, xvi–xvii, xxii, 107–8, 181, 183, 191, 200–201, 237–38, 270–71, 402; *see also specific titles*
    career development of, 99–100, 114–15, 120–21, 147, 148, 154
    "Cassandras" cultivated by, 271–72, 373
    as CEO, xiv–xv, 186–87, 191, 211, 212–13, 214, 216, 261, 277–78, 376, 387, 399–403, 449

    as chairman of Intel board, 191, 211, 387, 402, 417–18, 426–27, 448–51
    chemistry as interest of, 45
    childhood and adolescence of, xvii–xix, xviii–xix, xxi–xxii, 1–2, 10, 12–16, 18–20, 19–51, 21–31, 33–39, 54–55, 200, 299
    childhood illnesses of, xviii–xix, 15–16, 19, 37
    communism as viewed by, 40–42, 46–47
    on Conference Board commission, 445–48
    coping mechanisms of, 15–16, 28–29, 35, 37, 119, 128, 196, 352–54, 438, 460
    cult of personality around, 401–2
    curiosity about, xiii, xvi, xxii
    in departure from Intel board, 452–53
    dreams of, 122–24, 125–26, 127–28
    as early Apple investor, 170
    education of, xiii, xx, 19, 33, 35, 36–37, 42, 43–44, 48–51, 64–65, 70–71, 75–78, 79
    1103 deal opposed by, 141, 153
    in escape from Hungary, xviii, xxii, 55–60
    on failure of Fairchild, 129, 148
    at Fairchild, xiv, 81, 86, 87–89, 91–92, 95, 99, 102–3, 104, 106, 107–8, 110–11, 128
    fame of, 248, 403–4, 410
    fear as motivator for, 224–26
    finances of, 160–61, 418
    first U.S. impressions of, 61–64, 66
    and formation of Intel, xiv, 111, 114–15, 118, 119–20, 123–24, 146–47
    Gates's relationship with, 293, 302, 306–8, 315–17
    graduate thesis of, 77–78, 79–80, 81
    health care interests of, 410–12, 453–56
    hearing loss of, xix, 15, 19, 37, 49, 58, 90
    hiring philosophy of, 156, 170–71
    home life of, 188–89, 196–97, 341, 389, 393, 414
    Intel culture established by, 125, 189–90, 452–53
    Intel as proxy in Hungarian return of, 2
    as Intel senior advisor, xv, 191, 402, 452
    interpersonal style of, 70–71, 74–75, 78, 90, 95–98, 150–51, 189, 190, 195, 237–38, 343, 390–91, 392–93, 397–99, 414, 418, 449–50
    Jewish identity of, xviii, 1–2, 31, 49–50, 69, 122
    on leadership vs. management, 199–200, 249
    management and leadership style of, 74, 89, 92, 97, 98, 99–100, 106–61, 127, 156–57, 163–66, 170–71, 189–96, 199–201, 202, 205–6, 234, 239–41, 270–72, 288–90, 293, 383–84, 399–403, 419–20, 449–50
    marriage of. *See* Grove, Eva Kastan

Grove, Andy: (*cont.*)
media management by, 241, 351, 376, 438
name change of, 66–67, *67*, 68
named to Intel's board of directors, 159, 162
named as Intel's president and COO, 174
named as Intel's VP of operations, 159, 160
notebooks kept by, 133–34, 135–37, 148–50, 151, 160–61, 170, 179, 180, 183–84, 186, 231, 329, 384
as parental caretaker, 67–68, 71, 78, 188–89, 414–15
Parkinson's disease of, 411–14, 437–38
person vs. persona of, xxi–xxii
philanthropy of, 65–66, 453–58; *see also* Grove Foundation
philosophy of change of, 372–77
and ProShare failure, 362–64
prostate cancer of, 340–56, 362, 374, 388–89, 414
PR skills of, 241–42
public speaking and appearances by, 357–58, 360–63, 377–83, 412–13, 414, 438
as public spokesperson for Intel, 376–77, 387–88
reading of, 44
retirement considered by, 188–91, 243
and RISC/CISC decision, 261–62, 264, 266–70, 349
sabbaticals of, 191
scarlet fever of, xviii–xix, 15–16, 37, 221
as self-identified with Intel, 165–66, 337–38, 354, 380
as showman, 45, 49, 89, 97–98
structural shift in computer industry as seen by, 213, 215, 224, 227–29, 373
summer jobs of, 68–69, 73
as teacher, 76, 107–8, 121, 376
as *Time* Man of the Year, 61, 100, 225, 389–93
U.S. as dream destination for, 55, 58, 59
Valley life of, 101–2
verbal style and skills of, xx–xxii, 35, 57–58, 59, 65, 74, 361, 397–98, 413–14, 438
weight problems of, 37–39, 48
work ethic of, 63–64, 73–74, 99, 107–8, 188–90, 195, 343, 356, 385
World War II experiences of, xxi–xxii, 15–16, 18–20, 21–30
writings of, 44, 45–46, 77–78, 80, 88, 99, 107–8, 162–63, 225, 237, 351–52, 355–56, 414, 437, 459
see also Intel
Grove, Eva Kastan, xiii–xiv, xx, 69–70, 72, 80, 96, 101, 102, 119, 188–89, 196–97, 211, 308, 343, 354, 387, 389, 391–92, 393, 412, 413, 414–15, 456, 457, 458

Grove, Karen, 102, 189, 196–97, 340–41, 392–93, 399, 414, 456
Grove, Robie, 102, 189, 197, 340, 392–93, 399, 414, 456
Grove Foundation, 197, 414, 450, 453, 456–58
Guzy, D. James, 420, 421

Habsburg monarchy, xix, xx, 9
Hadden, Briton, 389
Haie (Russian sergeant), 27–28
Hambrecht & Quist, 180
Harris, Jim, 228, 308
Harsanyi, János, 36
Harvard Business School, 209, 251–52, *253*, 276, 286, 287, 322, 338, 396, 399, 420, 428, 438–39, 441, 444, 448
Harvard University, 248, 296, 297, 298, 408, 410
    Aiken Computation Laboratory at, 296
Hennessy, John L., 264
Herzl, Theodor, 50
Hewlett, William, 82
Hewlett-Packard, 82–83, 164, 265, 287
High Output Management (Grove), xvii, 99, 191–95, 200–201, 239–40, 288–89, 438
Hill, Bert, 179
Hindenberg und Beneckendorff, Paul Ludwig Hans Anton von, 8
Hitachi, 175, 185
Hitler, Adolf, xviii, 3, 4, 5–6, 7–8, 9–10, 11, 16, 17–18, 21, 32, 40, 50, 60, 212, 390
HMOS (High-speed Metal-Oxide-Semiconductor), 168
Hoerni, Jean, 83, 84, 85, 104, 105, 106
Hoff, Marcian E. "Ted," 135, 144, 169
Hofstadter, Richard, 162
Holocaust, 3, 5–6, 22, 25, 31, 50, 128
Holocaust Museum, 1
Honeywell, 156, 298
Hootnick, Lawrence R., 233, 243, 279
Hoover, Helen, 162
Horthy de Nagybánya, Miklos, xx, 4, 7, 8, 9, 17–18, 20–21, 24, 32, 189
House, David L., 232, 233, 243, 254, 279, 375
House of Representatives, U.S., 448
Houtermans, Fritz, xx
How to Win Friends and Influence People (Carnegie), 66
Huey, John, 351, 352
Hughes, 103
Hundt, Reed E., 440
Hungarian Communist Party, 3, 39–43, 47
Hungary:
    anti-German sentiment in, 16
    anti-Jewish legislation in, 9
    anti-Semitism in, 3–6, 8, 9, 19, 20, 21, 22–25, 30, 32, 50

assimilation of Jews in, xviii, 6–7
Communist control of, 32, 33, 39–42, 46,
    47, 48, 53–55
deportation of Jews from, 21, 22–23, 25,
    26, 29
expulsion of Communists from, 4
German occupation of, 20, 21–26
interwar economy of, 7–8
interwar German links to, 15
as interwar haven for Jews, 21, 49–50
Jews in, xviii, 1–7, 15–16, 19, 20–30
political prisoners in, 43, 44, 46, 47–48
postwar economy of, 32–33, 40
postwar retribution in, 32, 34
rise of fascism in, 7–9, 20–21
Soviet invasion of, 24, 25, 26, 28
Stalinist period in, 31–60
World War II and, 16–30

IBM (International Business Machines
    Corporation), 36, 103, 105–6, 107, 127,
    132, 176–82, 184, 185, 187, 212–13, 214,
    215, 216, 219, 224, 226–29, 230–31, 239,
    242, 243, 245–47, 252, 263, 265, 275,
    278, 281, 282, 283–93, 295, 300–301,
    303–5, 306, 309, 310, 323, 327–29, 330,
    332, 336, 337–38, 358, 361, 367, 375,
    395, 401, 424, 425, 429, 456
    Entry Systems Division of, 245
IEEE (Institute of Electrical and Electronics
    Engineers), 149
If Japan Can, Why Can't We?, 218
IIT, 261
Imrédy, Béla, 9
Incredible Universe, 292
Independent Smallholders' Party, 33
India, 212
Indigo, Paul, 177
Industry Week, 184
Innes, Tom, 281
Innovator's Dilemma, The: When New Tech-
    nologies Cause Great Firms to Fail
    (Christensen), 396
Inside Intel: Andy Grove and the Rise of the
    World's Most Powerful Chip Company
    (Jackson), 120, 121–22, 195, 390
instruction set architecture (ISA), 262–63
Intel, xii, xiv–xvi, xix, xxi, xxii, 2, 57, 73, 74,
    75, 81, 86, 89, 97, 98–99, 101, 122–23,
    128, 129, 286, 287–93, 298, 300, 301,
    302–8, 310, 311–33, 343, 348, 350, 351,
    354, 356, 358, 361, 362–71, 372–80, 381,
    382, 392–407, 405, 410, 414, 427,
    429–37, 438–40, 446, 447, 455, 456
    Annual Reports of, 142, 160, 161, 166, 169,
    173, 174, 179, 180, 182, 184, 186–87,
    233, 238–39, 244, 250, 260, 265, 266,

275, 279, 319, 331, 366, 368, 369, 371,
    416–23, 430, 432, 435–36, 436, 439, 440,
    451
architectural leadership of, 218–19,
    242–43, 250–51, 261–72, 313, 365
Atlantic Region of, 175
backward compatibility and, 245–46, 265
board of directors of, 159, 162, 191, 211,
    387, 402, 420–26, 440, 448–53
capacity constraints at, 179–80, 182
competitive threats to, 175–76, 185–86,
    187, 203–4, 206, 212, 215, 216–17, 218
corporate culture of, 124–25, 134–35,
    148–51, 167, 170, 189–90, 202, 217, 371,
    452–53
corporate governance and, 448–50
creosote bush metaphor at, 279–80
cyclical business strategy of, xv–xvi
Device Development Lab of, 91
direct to consumer branding at, 251,
    252–58, 269, 274–79, 312–13, 332–33,
    373, 374
and dot-com bubble, xv, 117
early product failures of, 137–38
elimination of second sourcing sought by,
    219–21, 224–25, 226–27
in exit from memory market, 205–10, 215,
    216, 236, 246, 247, 266, 270, 329, 362,
    394–95
facing bad news at, xvi, 98, 137, 178–79,
    185, 431
fame of, 248, 251, 302
first profits of, 138–39
as flexible and adaptable, 121, 124, 150,
    187, 205–10, 236, 370
formation and start-up days of, xiv, 96,
    111, 114–15, 118, 119–20, 123–24,
    146–47
future ramifications of Internet on, 407–9
"good enough" as threat to, 396–97, 431
Grove's early management of, 120–30,
    133–34, 135–38, 141, 145, 146–51
Grove on growth management of, 156–57,
    162, 163–64, 165–66, 170–71
Grove's management of 1103 process at,
    145
Grove's shift in business model for, 214–15
growth and sales at, 156–60, 162, 163,
    165–66, 168–69, 170–72, 173, 179,
    181–86, 198, 230–31, 239, 243–44, 250,
    259–60, 278–79, 291–92, 316, 329,
    365–66, 368–69, 385–87, 401, 403,
    432–36
hierarchy changes at, 279–80, 437, 440
hostility toward, 320, 325–33, 336–37
IBM relationship with. See IBM
as increasingly complex, 231–32

Intel (*cont.*)
  as industry innovator, 161–62, 166,
    168–69, 236
  internal vs. acquisition-based growth at,
    406–7
  internal dogmas of, 208
  IPO and stock shares of, 138, 146, 368–69
  Japanese competition and, 203–4, 206,
    212, 215, 216–17, 218, 394
  Japanese SCS (Strategic Capability
    Segment) of, 183
  layoffs from, 158–59
  licensing of products by, 138–39, 141–42,
    153, 220–21
  losses sustained by, 198, 204–6, 209–10,
    214–15
  manufacturing processes and sites of, 140,
    142–43, 145, 146, 148, 174–75, 179–80,
    217–18, 226, 241, 369
  marketing at, 146, 155–56, 167, 169, 175,
    178, 208, 218, 220, 251, 253–58, 268,
    399–400, 412–13
  microprocessor-related lawsuits of, 274,
    292
  Microsoft relationship with. *See* Microsoft
  middle management at, 170–71, 173, 209,
    270
  Mobility Group of, 125
  Operation CRUSH at. *See* Operation
    CRUSH
  PC-driven success of, 215–16, 226–27, 231,
    236, 238–39, 243, 277, 321–22, 365–66,
    431–32
  Pentium branding at, 276–77
  Pentium flaw crisis and, 320–33, 336–39,
    362, 379–80, 399–401
  pricing strategy of, 243
  product line expansion of, 145–46, 161–62,
    164, 166, 167–68, 185, 244–45
  ProShare initiative of, 360–64, 399
  RISC/CISC decision and, 246, 261–75, 280,
    312, 349, 370, 372
  Sales and Marketing Conferences of, 202,
    396, 412–13
  second sourcing of microprocessors from,
    139–40, 219–20
  seen as Grove's company, xvi, 99–100, 115,
    165–66, 392, 401, 419
  senior executives under Grove at, 232–36,
    252, 267–69
  sole sourcing policy of, 226–27, 230,
    236–37, 240, 246, 266, 337, 374–76,
    399–401
  start-up management problems at, 115–16
  strategic objectives of, 277, 436–37, 439
  succession at, 369–70, 402–3, 404, 416–20
  takeover concerns at, 180, 181
  transition to branded product company of,
    274–79
  transition from memory to microproces-
    sors at, 205–10
  twenty-fifth anniversary of, 281–82
  see also Grove, Andy; Pentium; *specific
    departments and groups of Intel; specific
    operating groups; specific products*
Intel Architecture, xv, 274, 315
Intel Architecture Group, 437, 440
Intel Architecture Lab, 269, 437
Intel Capital, 437
Intel inside campaign, 251, 256–58, 332, 374,
  395
Intel Museum, 419
Intel Online Services, 437
Intel Sales and Marketing Conference (2000),
  202
Intel Video Phone, 369
Interexchange Carriers, 362
Internet, 85, 323, 326, 327, 333–36, 338–39,
  341, 344, 359–60, 366, 382, 390, 397,
  400, 406, 407–8, 428–29, 431, 436, 439
  future of Silicon Valley and, 408–9
  as vehicle for Pentium flaw story, 333–39
Iowa Conference of Congregational
  Churches, 93
iPod, 168, 409
Iraq war, 405
IRC (International Rescue Committee),
  58–59, 457
Isaacson, Walter, 390–91
Itanium processor, 432
ITT, 162

Jackson, Tim, 120, 121–22, 189, 195, 390, 397
Jani (George Gróf's friend), 22
Japan, 203–4, 206, 212, 215, 216–17, 218, 222,
  247
Japanese SCS (Strategic Capability Segment),
  183
Jenkins, Ted, 281
Jews, Judaism:
  Grove and, xviii, 1–2, 31, 49–50, 69, 122
  killed in Poland, 13, 16
  see also Hungary
Jobs, Steve, 96, 97, 98, 168, 169–70, 202, 250,
  282, 283, 284, 294, 297, 365, 395, 409,
  416, 417
Johannesburg General Hospital, 358
Johns Hopkins University, 82
Johnson & Johnson, 256, 285, 400, 417, 445
Jones, Jean, 281
Journal of Fluid Mechanics, 77
Jozef (George Gróf's business partner), 25
Jozsi (Grove's uncle), 12–13, 14–15, 119,
  127–28

JP Morgan, 442, 460
Justice Department, U.S., 334
Jutka (Grove's classmate), 33

Kadar, Janos, 63
Kahn, Philippe, 251, 307
Kállay, Miklós, 24
Karman, Tamás, 58
Kennedy, John F., 72, 75
Kennedy, Robert F., 113–14
Kern, Art, 453
Kertész, Imre, xx, 16, 31, 48
Khrushchev, Nikita, 47, 52–53, 54, 63
Kilby, Jack, 83, 105, 143
Kinetics Foundation, 414, 453, 455
King, Martin Luther, Jr., 113
Kinnie, Craig, 269, 272, 416, 437
Kissinger, Henry, 289
Kleiner, Eugene, 83, 84
Kleiner, Perkins, 396, 399
Kohn, Les, 267–68, 270, 274
Kolodney, Morris, 65, 66, 70
Korean War, 42, 43
Kozlowski, Leo Dennis, 440, 444
Kozmetsky, George, 106
Kramer, Stanley, 300
Kreditanstalt Bankverein, 7
Kremlin, 47
Kuehler, Jack, 292
Kun, Béla, 3, 4, 36

Lajos (Grove's uncle), 56, 61–62, 64, 66, 68
Lakeside private day school, 295, 298
Larsen, Ralph S., 417, 445
Last, Jay, 83, 84, 106
"Late List," 189, 200
Lattin, Bill, 76, 308
Laurence, Calar Louise, 102
Lay, Kenneth, 441–43
League of Nations, 16
Leglise, Claude M., 216–17, 274
Lemkin, Raphael, 5
Lenin, Vladimir Ilyich Ulyanov, 3, 46, 442
Lenke (Grove's relative), 56, 62, 64, 66, 68
Lennon, John, 155
Lerner, Sandy, 406
Levitt, Theodore, 287
Lewi, Israel, 13, 16
Lewi, Liebe, 13, 127
Life, 389
Lincoln, Abraham, 47
Lincoln Technical Institute, 232
Linux operating system, 287
List, Harvey, 70
L. M. Ericsson, 236
Lockheed, xiv, 78
Lorsch, Jay W., 444–45

Lotus, 307
Louis, Joe, 119
Lovgren, Rich, 255
Lowe, Bill, 185, 239
Luce, Henry, 389
Lueger, Karl, 4, 10
Lynchburg College, 321

McDonald's, 174, 241, 242
McGeady, Steve, 315, 316
McGill University, 115
Macintosh, 297
MacKay, Bruce, 150–51, 152
McKenna, Regis, 391, 392
McKinsey & Company, 171, 286, 440, 441
McLean, Bethany, 355–56, 442, 443
McNealy, Scott, 264
Madach Gymnasium, 44, 45, 48, 49, 58
Magda (Grove's schoolteacher), 19
Magyars, xix, 2, 16, 17, 53
Mahendroo, Vinod, 252
Maiakovsky, Vladimir Vladimirovich, 14
Maitland, Frederick W., 5
Malenkov, Georgy, 47
Malone, Michael, 94, 99–100, 177, 283
Maloney, Sean, 125, 288–89, 437
Manci (George Gróf's cousin), 35, 36, 55, 56, 62, 119, 221, 353
Mandela, Nelson, 357, 358, 359, 442
Manes, Stephen, 297, 298, 301
Maney, Kevin, 402
Manzi, Jim, 307
Markkula, Armas Clifford "Mike," 169–70, 188
Marquardt, David, 302
Marx, Leo, 102
Maryland, University of, 233
Massachusetts General Hospital, 263
Mattu, Sasha, *314*
Mazor, Stan, 144
MCI, 441
Mead, Carver, 109
Mein Kampf (Hitler), 4, 9–10
Merrill Lynch, 246, 442
Meza, Philip E., 455
MFS Communications, 441
Michael J. Fox Foundation, 455
Michelin, 131
Michels, Doug, 287
Michels, Larry, 287
Michelson, Leslie D., 454
Michigan Technological University, 232
Microcomputer Components Group (Intel), 231, 232, 233, 254
Microma, 146, 160–61, 162, 165, 167–68, 210, 234, 254, 364, 373
Microprocessor Products Group (Intel), 273
Microprocessor Report, 256–57

Microsoft, 127, 130–31, 227, 258, 282, 288, 290, 293, 297, 298, 299, 300, 301–5, 306–17, 329, 333–34, 396, 404, 427, 447, 456
Microsoft Internet Explorer, 333
Microsoft Office, 310
Microsystems International, Ltd., 138–39, 141–42, 143, 219
Miklos (Grove's uncle), 15
Milken, Michael, 414, 454, 455
Miller, Bob, 287
MinuteClinic, 263
MIPS Technologies, 261, 274, 278, 287
MIT (Massachusetts Institute of Technology), 94, 233
MITS (Micro Instrumentation and Telemetry Systems), 298–99
Mitsubishi, 183
Mobility Group, 288
Molotov, Vyacheslav, 47
Moneyline, 276, 326, 362
Mongolian Tatars, xix
Moore, Betty, 96
Moore, Gordon, xiv, 74, 81–82, 83, 84–85, 86, 89–92, 93, 95–96, 97, 98, 99, 100, 110–14, 116–23, 128, 129, 131–34, 138–40, 141–44, 146–47, 151, 153, 154, 158–59, 160, 162, 165, 166, 171, 173, 174, 177, 178, 180, 182, 183, 186–87, 191, 195, 197, 198, 199, 202, 208, 211, 214, 217, 218, 220, 221, 225, 226–27, 232, 236, 238, 239, 240, 243, 244, 246, 247, 254–55, 259, 264, 279, 281, 308, 318, 328–29, 354, 369–71, 372, 387–88, 391, 392, 395, 403, 418–19, 420–21, 431, 437, 440, 450
Moore's Law, 89, 99, 217, 220, 231, 255, 273, 370, 371, 391, 419
Morgan Stanley, 291–92
Morris, Charles R., 285
Morse code, 87
MOS (metal oxide semiconductor) technology, 128–29, 131–32, 135, 137, 146, 181
Mossberg, Walter, 338
Motorola, 103, 175, 176–77, 180, 203, 219, 242, 247, 259, 261, 278, 282–83, 286, 401
MS-DOS (Microsoft Disk Operating System), 303, 309
MSNBC, 382
Munich Pact, 10
Murphy, Terri L., 101
Mussolini, 8, 9
Mutro, Bill, 228
My Years with General Motors (Sloan), 380

Nachtsheim, Stephen, 437
Nagy, Imre, 47, 54

NASA (National Aeronautics and Space Administration), 73, 295
    Jet Propulsion Laboratory of, 326
NASDAQ, 327, 404, 427–29, 428, 432, 435, 438
National Cash Register Company, 128
National Institute of Neurological Disorders and Stroke, 411
National Institutes of Health, U.S., 411
National Public Radio, xxi–xxii
National Semiconductor, 110, 142, 174, 175, 247, 267
Nazis, Nazism, xviii, 9, 10, 21, 24, 32, 49, 69, 119, 128
NBC, 218
NEC, 175, 219, 261
Netscape, 310, 333, 407–8, 428
Neukom, William H., 334
Neumann, János (John von), 36
Newsweek, 352
New York Herald Tribune, 68
New York Society of Security Analysts, 214, 217, 218, 221
New York Stock Exchange, 427, 432
New York Times, 152, 241, 242, 243, 245, 264–65, 334, 391, 392, 400, 445
New York World's Fair (1939), 222, 323
NexGen, 261
Nicely, Thomas, 321, 322–23, 324, 329, 333, 336
Nike, 332, 333
Nippon Electric Corporation. See NEC
Nixon, Richard, 72, 161
Nobel Prize, xx, 36, 83, 84, 105, 388, 454
Nominating Committee (Intel), 449
Nortel, 233
Northeastern University, 233
Noyce, Elizabeth Bottomley "Betty," 98
Noyce, Harriet, 92
Noyce, Ralph, 92, 93
Noyce, Robert Norton, xiv, 57, 73, 74, 83, 84, 85, 86, 89, 91, 92–100, 104–6, 110, 111–13, 114, 116, 117–19, 122, 123, 124, 128, 133, 134–35, 141, 142, 143, 152–54, 158–59, 160, 165, 173–74, 199, 200, 218, 225, 232, 238, 249–50, 366, 377, 391–92, 395, 397, 403, 412–13, 418, 420, 440
NSP (Native Signal Processing), 312, 313–16, 313
Nutrasweet, 256

Odyssey, The (Homer), 429–430, 460
Olsen, Ken, 213, 287
One-on-One with Andy Grove: How to Manage Your Boss, Yourself and Your Coworkers (Grove), xvii, 237–38, 239

Only the Paranoid Survive: How to Exploit the Crisis Points That Challenge Every Company (Grove), xvii, xxi, 12, *204*, 221, 224, 225, 228, 270–71, 358, 371–74, 376–80, 381–84, 385, 454, 455
Opel, John R., 182, 284, 290
Operation CRUSH, 176–79, 203
Oracle, 125, 307, 409, 427
Osborne, 227
Otellini, Paul S., 159, 164, 191, 233, 245, 252, 257, 258, 273–74, 275, 276, 413, 437, 440, 451, 452
"Out of Hungary-Revolt of the Exiles" (Abel), 58–59

Packard, David, 82, 250
Page, Lawrence E., 408
Palo Alto Times, 114
Palevsky, Max, 133
PALEXPO, 357
Panic of 1873, 439
Parkinson's disease (PD), 411–14, 437–38, 450, 453, 455
Parliament, British, 199
Patterson, John Henry, 128
Paul (Grove's cousin), 62
PC Expo, 289
Pearlman, Ken, 386
Peck, Gregory, 400
Pennsylvania Railroad, 86–87
Pentium, 248, 276, 282, 292, 318–33, *319*, 321, 336–39, 341, 354, 362, 366, 370–71, 379–80, 381, 395, 399–401, 430, 447
Pentium flaw crisis, 320–33, 336–39, 362, 379–80, 395, 399–401
Pentium Pro, 362, 366
Pentium III, 432
Pentium III Xeon, 432
Pentium II, 431
Pentium II Xeon, 431
PeopleSoft, 409
PepsiCo, 283
Perry, William, 459
"Personality Cult and Its Consequences, The" (Khrushchev), 52
"Peter Principle," 150, 271, 372, 418
Peterson, Peter G., 445
Petőfi, Sandor, 35, 53, 388
Pfeiffer, Eckhard, 358
Philadelphia Semiconductor Index, 404
Philco, 83, 94, 103
Philips, 175
Physics and Technology of Semiconductor Devices (Grove), xvi-xvii, 99, 109
Picasso, Pablo, 297

Pitt, William, the Elder, First Earl of Chatham, 199
Pixar, 283
Planned Parenthood Federation, 458
Poitier, Sidney, 300
Poland, 52–53
    Germany invasion of, 12–13
    Jews killed in, 13, 16
Polish Communist Party, 53
Pollace, Pam, 399, 437
Pollack, Andrew, 242, 264–65
Popular Electronics, 298
Pottruck, David S., 421
Powell, Colin, 442
PowerPC microprocessor, 282–83, 286–87, 290, 322, 327, 333
PowerPoint, 310
Practice of Management, The (Drucker), 74
Procter & Gamble, 275, 297
ProShare, 358–60, 362–64, 369, 398, 445
Prostate Cancer Foundation, 414, 454–55
Prudential-Bache Securities, 246, 259, 320
Puget Sound, University of, 197
Purdue University, 251

Queen Elizabeth II, 213

Radio Free Europe, 54
Radio Shack, 301
Rajk, László, 40, 42
Rákosi, Mátyás, 4, 36, 39, 40, 41, 47, 53, 388
Ramo, Josh, 392–93, 397
Raytheon, 233
RBOCs (Regional Bell Operating Companies), 362
RCA, 94, 103, 222
Reagan, Ronald, 173, 180, 425
Red Army, 18, 25, 26, 212
"Red X" campaign, 255, 275, 373–74
Reed, Robert W., 235
Regitz, Bill, 156
Reid, T.R., 332
Reiling, Henry, 251–52
Reliance Insurance Company, 335
Rice University, 442
Rickey's, 107, 135
Rieper, Alan, 386
Rigas, John, 444
Rigas family, 441, 444
RISC/CISC debate, 248, 262–72, 273–75, 279, 280, 312, 349, 370, 372
Rivet, Jean-Claude, 337
RJR Nabisco, 286
Robert Noyce Building (RNB), xxi, 124, 250, 269, 328, 371
Roberts, Ed, 298, 299

Roberts, Sheldon, 83, 84, 106
Rock, Arthur, 84, 98, 99, 111, 114, 117, 119,
    132, 133, 134, 154, 158–59, 160, 199,
    250, 382, 402, 418, 420, 421, 453
Rockefeller family, 133
Rockwell International, 251
Rodgers, T.J., 246–47
Roman Catholic Church, 4, 52, 69
Romancz (George Gróf's friend), 23
Rose Hulman Institute of Technology, 251
Roundhouse, 135
Rubin, Harriet, 372, 378
Rubin, Robert, 388
Russian Revolution, 46

Sah, Tom, 91
Sales and Marketing Group, 231, 235
Salomon Brothers, 246
Samsung, 247
Sanders, Jerry, 142, 150, 151
Sanford C. Bernstein, xvi
San Francisco, University of, 159
San Francisco Chronicle, 222
San Jose Mercury News, xvii, 188, 237, 287
San Jose State University, 82
Santa Clara University, 232, 240
Santa Cruz Operation (SCO), 287
Sanyi (Grove's uncle), 25, 43, 44, 45, 48
Sarbanes-Oxley Act of 2002, 448
Sarnoff, David, 222
Savio, Mario, 76
Schmidt, Alois X., 65, 66, 70–71
Schmidt, Eric, 302
Schwartzman, Steve, 445
Scientific Data Systems, 133
Scott, Thomas A., 86–87, 89
Sculley, John, 283
Sears, Roebuck, 419
Seattle World's Fair of 1962, 294–95
Second Hungarian Army, 17
second sourcing, 139–40, 219–20
Seipel, Ignaz, 4, 10
Seitz, Frederick, 85
SEMATECH, 99, 249–50, 377
semiconductor industry, xiv–xvi
    as cyclical, xv–xvi
    discipline brought by Grove to, 189, 200
    growth of, 103–4
    Japanese competition of, 218
    second sourcing in, 139–40, 219–20
    space race and, 73
    see also Silicon Valley; specific companies
Senate, U.S., 448
September 11, 2001 terrorist attacks, 405
Sequoia High School, 82
Seven Years War, 199
Shakespeare, William, 102

Shankar, Krishna, 386
Sharp, 290
Shaw, Jane, 420
Shearson Lehman Hutton, 246
Sherman Antitrust Act of 1890, 448
Shockley, William Bradford, 63, 82, 83–85,
    93–94
Shockley Semiconductor Laboratory, 63, 82,
    83–85, 105, 113, 118, 387, 440
Shuman, Marc, 453
Siemens, 175, 219
Silicon Gate Research, 135
Silicon Graphics, 274, 278
Silicon Valley, 101–3
    bad management as characteristic of, 107,
        115, 200
    birth of, 82–83
    fame of, 248
    Grove's impact on, 397–98
    growth as preoccupation of, 258–59
    Internet's impact on future of, 408–9
    job mobility within, 115, 118
    microeconomy of, 106–7
    Microsoft as evil empire in, 302
    open culture of, 135
    retirement age in, 188
    start-up failures in, 118
    stock options as compensation in, 259,
        446–47
    see also dot-com bubble; semiconductor
        industry; specific companies
Simon, Paul, 137
Singleton, Henry, 106
Sinko (Gizi's husband), 14, 29, 43
Skilling, Jeffrey K., 441, 443
Sloan, Alfred P., Jr., 248, 380–81, 431
SLRP ("Strategic Long Range Planning"),
    231, 274, 277, 278–79, 287
"Smart Connections of the World," 357–59
Smartest Guys in the Room, The (McLean and
    Elkind), 355
Smith, Charles B., 133
Smith, Ron, 437
Smith, Stephen, 326
Smith Barney, 246
Snow, John W., 445
Solectron Corporation, 420
Sonoma State Mental Hospital, 70
Soviet Union, 16–18, 19, 30, 72–73, 212
    control of satellites by, 32, 33, 39–42, 46,
        47, 48, 51–54
    Hungary invaded by, 24, 25, 26, 28
space race, 72–73
Sperry Univac, 213
Spindler, Michael, 358
Splinter, Mike, 437
Sporck, Charlie E., 110, 112, 142, 151–52, 174

Sprint, 441
Sputnik, 72–73
SS Death's Head Formations, 10
Stalin, Josef, 11, 32, 33, 36, 39, 40, 46–47, 51, 52, 54
Standard & Poor's 500, 278, 387, 447
Stanford University, xxi, 74, 77, 144, 159, 197, 224, 233, 234, 235, 264, 279, 283, 341, 406, 407, 408, 455
    Graduate School of Business, 127, 266, 297, 325, 363, 364
"Star House," 25
Statue of Liberty, 122
Stauffer Chemical Company, xiv, 73
Stephen, king of Hungary, xix, 53
stock options:
    as compensation, 259, 446–47
    expensing of, 445–47
Strategic Dynamics: Concepts and Cases (Burgelman and Grove with Meza), 455
Strategy Is Destiny: How Strategy-Making Shapes a Company's Future (Burgelman), 205, 207, 216
Sun Microsystems, 261, 263–64, 274, 291, 427
Swimming Across: A Memoir (Grove), xvii, xxii, 2, 14, 15–16, 44, 162, 237, 410, 437, 457, 461
Sylvania, 103
Sylvester II, Pope, xix
Systems Group (Intel), 231, 233–34
Szálasi, Ferenc, 16, 24–25
Sztójay, Döme, 24

Tandy, 227
Taylor, C. Barr, 410–11, 412, 437–38, 455
Technology and Manufacturing Group (Intel), 437
Technology Venture Investors, 302
TELECOM 95, 357–60, 366
Teledyne, 106
Telegdi, Mr. (Grove's teacher), 44, 45
Teleki, Pál, 9
Tempest, The (Shakespeare), 102
Tennyson, Alfred, Lord, 222
Tet offensive, 113
Texas, University of, at Austin, 228
Texas Instruments, 78, 83, 103, 105, 143, 150, 155, 175, 180, 228, 246, 247, 404
Thomson, Keith L., 234, 242
Thorpe, Karen, 101, 340, 342, 343, 351–52
Time, xxi, 61, 100, 149, 225, 248, 284, 377, 389–91, 392–93, 397
"Tinkerings of Robert Noyce, The: How the Sun Rose on the Silicon Valley" (Wolfe), 93, 106, 108, 134–35, 366
Tintswalo Community Hospital, 358
Tiso, Jozef, 10

Tocqueville, Alexis de, 52
Toshiba, 290
Traf-o-Data, 298
Transitron, 103, 115
Trianon, Treaty of, 2–3, 7, 11, 18, 72
Tripartite Pact of Germany, 16
Truman, Harry S., 147
Tufts University, 98
Turks, xix, 17
Twelve O'Clock High, 400
Twentieth All-Union Party Conference, 52
Tyco, 440, 444
Tylenol, 256, 324, 400

UAW (United Automobile Workers), 380, 381
Ukraine, 212
Ultimate Entrepreneur, The, 213
Union Carbide, 124, 242
United States, 47
    as dream destination for Grove, 55, 58, 59
    economy of, 62–63, 221–22
    entry into World War II of, 17
    and Korean War, 42
    as New Frontier, 71–72
Univac, 162, 321
USA Today, 402

Vadasz, Judy, 234
Vadasz, Les, xix, 57–58, 85, 115–16, 117, 123, 137, 151, 156, 169, 233–34, 243, 279, 281, 420, 437, 452
Valentine, Don, 169
Vasarhelyi, Edith (Grove's teacher), 58
Verne, Jules, 44
Versailles, Treaty of, 2
Vicki (Grove's classmate), 54
Vienna State Opera, 57
Vietcong, 113
Vietnam War, 113, 405
Vinson & Elkins, 442
Voice of America, 54
Volcker, Paul A., 445–46
Volenski, Mr. (Grove's teacher), 44

Wagon Wheel, 107, 135
Walker, Rob, 397
Wallenberg, Raoul, 22
Wall Street Journal, 181, 285, 286, 287, 338, 443
Wal-Mart, 189
Walton, Sam, 189
Wang, 213
Warsaw Pact, 212
Washington, University of, 197
Washington Post, 332, 394, 397
Washington State University, 298
Watergate scandal, 161, 338

Watson, Jeannette Kittredge, 424
Watson, Tom, Jr., 286, 424
Watson, Thomas J., Sr., 286, 424
"Way to Wealth, The" (Franklin), 238
Welch, Jack, 440, 444–45
Whetstone, Earl, 176–77
White, John, 256, 257
"White Terrorists," 3
Whittier, Ronald J., 235, 437
Who Says Elephants Can't Dance?: Inside IBM's
    Historic Turnaround (Gerstner), 328
Wigner, Jeno (Eugene), 36
Wilcox High School, 458
Williams, Gregory H., 66
Williams College, 355
Windows, 287, 305, 306, 307, 309–10, 312
Windows 3.0, 305, 396
Windows 3.1, 293, 314
Windows 95, 314, 315, 316
Wintel, 287, 305, 306–17
"Wintel (A): Cooperation or Conflict?"
    (Yoffie, Casadesus-Masanell, and
    Mattu), 314
Wisconsin, University of, 93–94
Wolfe, Alexander, 324–25
Wolfe, Tom, 93, 106, 108, 134–35, 366
Word, 310
WorldCom, 441, 443–44

World Economic Forum, 387
World University Service, 64, 65
World War I, xx, 2, 3, 4, 7, 16, 21, 49, 50, 424
World War II, xx, xxi-xxii, 8, 12–32, 33, 48,
    51, 55, 60, 63, 119, 212, 221, 424
    end of, 31–32
    and Hungary, 16–30
Wozniak, Steve, 170

Xerox, 133

Yahoo!, xvi, 301, 408, 427, 453
Yale University, 284
Yang, Jerry, 408
Yates, William, 298
Yoffie, David B., 312, 313, 314, 364, 400–401,
    417, 420, 448, 449
Yom Kippur War (1973), 161
Young, Charles "Chuck," 420
Young, Steve, 326
Yu, Albert Y.C., 233, 437
Yudkoff, Royce, 373
Yugoslavia, 51–52

Zenith, 227
Zilog, 175
Zionist League, 20
Zoltan (Grove's classmate), 50–51